BRITISH ACADEMY CENTENARY
1902-2002

The Organisation of Knowledge in Victorian Britain

edited by
Martin Daunton

Published for THE BRITISH ACADEMY
by OXFORD UNIVERSITY PRESS

Oxford University Press, Great Clarendon Street, Oxford OX2 6DP

Oxford New York
Auckland Bangkok Buenos Aires Cape Town Chennai
Dar es Salaam Delhi Hong Kong Istanbul Karachi Kolkata
Kuala Lumpur Madrid Melbourne Mexico City Mumbai Nairobi
São Paulo Shanghai Singapore Taipei Tokyo Toronto

First published 2005

British Library Cataloguing in Publication Data
Data available

ISBN 0-19-726326-7

Typeset in Times by
Alden Bookset, Osney Mead
Printed in Great Britain
on acid-free paper by
Antony Rowe Limited,
Chippenham, Wiltshire

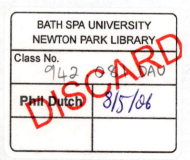

Contents

Notes on Contributors

Samuel J. M. M. Alberti researches the history of museums, the history of science and medicine, and Victorian civic culture. He is Lecturer in Art Gallery and Museum Studies at the University of Manchester and Research Fellow at the Manchester Museum.

Carol Atherton teaches English at Bourne Grammar School, Lincolnshire. She completed her Ph.D. at the University of Nottingham in 2003 and has published essays on the history of English Studies and the reform of English at A-level.

Mary Beard is Professor of Classics at the University of Cambridge and a Fellow of Newnham College; her books include *The Invention of Jane Harrison* (2000).

Michael Bentley is Professor of Modern History in the University of St Andrews. He has written several books about the political history of modern Britain, most recently *Lord Salisbury's World* (2001) and is the editor of the *Companion to Historiography* (1997). He is currently organising a project on the historical audience across time and space.

Daniel J. Cohen is an Assistant Professor in the Department of History and Art History and a Fellow at the Center for History and New Media at George Mason University. In addition to research interests in Victorian intellectual history and the history of science, he is the co-author of *Making Online History*.

Martin Daunton is Professor of Economic History at the University of Cambridge, Master of Trinity Hall and President of the Royal Historical Society. His most recent publications are *Trusting Leviathan: The Politics of Taxation in Britain, 1799–1914* (2001) and *Just Taxes: The Politics of Taxation in Britain, 1914–1979* (2002).

Richard Drayton is University Senior Lecturer in History at the University of Cambridge and a Fellow of Corpus Christi College. His book *Nature's Government*, awarded the Morris Forkosch Prize by the American Historical

Association in 2001, is mainly a study of the organisation and application of scientific knowledge in the Victorian Empire.

Jim Endersby is a Research Fellow in the History of Science at Darwin College, Cambridge. He was a contributor to the *Cambridge Companion to Darwin* (2003) and is currently writing two books: a popular history of biology and an account of Hooker and Darwin's friendship.

John R. Gibbins is a Principal Lecturer in the School of Social Sciences and Law at the University of Teesside and a Senior Member of Wolfson College, Cambridge. He has published extensively on the Moral Sciences in Cambridge, as well as teaching, learning and curriculum.

Lawrence Goldman is Fellow and Tutor in Modern History at St Peter's College, Oxford, where he teaches modern British and American history. He is the author of *Science, Reform and Politics in Victorian Britain: the Social Science Association, 1857–1886* (2002). He was appointed Editor of the *Oxford Dictionary of National Biography* in 2004.

Josephine M. Guy is Professor of Modern Literature at the University of Nottingham. She has published a number of monographs on late nineteenth-century literary history and culture, and has co-written a book on the discipline of English with Ian Small. She is currently editing Oscar Wilde's critical writings for the Oxford English Texts edition of *The Complete Works of Oscar Wilde*.

Max Jones is a Lecturer and Programme Director of the MA in Modern British History at the University of Manchester. His first book, *The Last Great Quest: Captain Scott's Antarctic Sacrifice*, was published in 2003.

W. C. Lubenow is Professor of History at the Richard Stockton College of New Jersey. He is the author of *Parliamentary Politics and the Home Rule Crisis* (1988) and *The Cambridge Apostles, 1820–1914*. He is President-elect of the North American Conference on British Studies.

David McKitterick is Fellow and Librarian of Trinity College, Cambridge. His books include *Cambridge University Library: the Eighteenth and Nineteenth Centuries* (1986) a three-volume *History of Cambridge University Press* (1992–2004), and *Print, Manuscript and the Search for Order, 1450–1830* (2003).

John Pickstone trained in physiology before turning to history and philosophy of science. Since 1974 he has worked in Manchester where he established the Centre for the History of Science, Technology and Medicine, in which he is now Wellcome Research Professor. He has published widely on the history of biomedical sciences, especially for France, on the social history of medicine, especially for Britain, and on ways of reframing the history of science, technology and medicine.

James Raven is Professor of Modern History at the University of Essex and has written extensively on the history of printing, publishing, and reading in Britain, Europe and the colonies since the fifteenth century. His most recent books include *The English Novel 1770–1799* (2000) and *London Booksellers and American Customers* (2002). An edited volume, *Lost Libraries: The Destruction of Great Book Collections since Antiquity*, was published in 2004.

Christopher Stray is Honorary Research Fellow in the Department of Classics, University of Wales Swansea. His publications include *Grinders and Grammars* (1995) and *Classics Transformed: Schools, Universities, and Society in England 1830–1960* (1998).

Keith Tribe retired from his post as Reader in Economics at Keele University in 2002 in order to pursue his scholarly interests in the history of economics and the work of Max Weber. He is the author of *Governing Economy: the Reformation of German Economic Discourse, 1750–1840* (1988) and *Strategies of Economic Order: German Economic Discourse 1750–1950* (1995); he edited, with Alon Kadish, *The Market for Political Economy: the Advent of Economics in British University Culture 1850–1905* (1993). He is currently working on the history of early 'neoclassical' economics as it emerged in Continental Europe, North America and Britain in the later nineteenth and early twentieth centuries.

Frank M. Turner is Director of the Beinecke Rare Book and Manuscript Library at Yale University. He is the author of *The Greek Heritage in Victorian Britain* (1981), *Contesting Cultural Authority: Essays in Victorian Intellectual Life* (1993) and *John Henry Newman: The Challenge of Evangelical Religion* (2002).

Acknowledgements

This collection of papers is a product of the distinctive organisation of knowledge in the early twenty-first century, and a reflection of lively discussion across the disciplinary lines so effectively established in the Victorian period. Its origins date from the conference on 'Locating the Victorians' organised by the Science Museum in 2001 to mark the one hundred and fiftieth anniversary of that quintessentially Victorian phenomenon, the Great Exhibition, as well as the centenary of the death of Queen Victoria. The conference was, aptly, held in South Kensington in the institutions constructed on the estate of the Commissioners of the 1851 exhibition, where Victorian knowledge was organised in a plethora of museums and colleges. Robert Bud of the Science Museum was the prime mover of the conference, endlessly enthusiastic in facilitating intellectual exchanges. The British Academy contributed to funding the conference, and the modern history section of the Academy supported my suggestion of developing the theme of organising knowledge in Victorian Britain as part of its centenary celebrations. I am grateful to the section, to the Publications Committee and to the officers of the Academy. The process of converting the conference into a book was facilitated by the Centre for Research in the Arts, Humanities and Social Sciences at Cambridge, whose first director, Ian Donaldson, made the organisation of knowledge a theme for its initial two years. A highly enjoyable and productive workshop was held at Cambridge in May 2002, where early versions of the papers for this volume were read and discussed. I am grateful to everyone who attended and in particular to Peter Burke for his perceptive and challenging overview of the entire event. In the final stages of publication, the task was eased by Vicky Aldred who provided assistance in preparing the typescript; by Auriol Griffith-Jones who produced an excellent index; and by Colin Baldwin who saw the book through the press with great efficiency.

Martin Daunton
Trinity Hall, Cambridge
December 2004

CHAPTER ONE
Introduction

MARTIN DAUNTON

'I am the Master of this College/And what I don't know isn't knowledge.' The gibe against Benjamin Jowett, the Master of Balliol College, expressed one simple, highly personalised definition of knowledge and what it meant to be knowledgeable. In reality, the term 'knowledge' has a multiplicity of meanings with troubling relationships. Indeed, we should really use the plural 'knowledges' and follow Michael Bentley's definition: 'paradigms of what was and what was not to count as worth knowing'.[1] These paradigms were contested at any one time and changed over the Victorian period, with shifts in who did the defining, by what means, and with what criteria. The claim to have knowledge is an assertion of authority, a way of dealing with the questions: 'What do you know and how do you know it?' It also involves the questions: 'Why do you want to know it, and what do you wish to do with it?' Knowledge may be instrumental, a credential designed to secure a post, whether as an Anglican clergyman with a basic grasp of the classics or as a senior civil servant able to pass the competitive examinations for entry which effectively excluded anyone without a highly specific form of education. Equally, knowledge could be a means of understanding God's will; of securing a commercial advantage; or imposing imperial power.

Knowledge may be arcane and esoteric: the ability to comprehend quantum mechanics, the finer points of legal reasoning, the abstruse methods of macroeconomics or, for that matter, the niceties of social precedence and ceremonial ritual. Such esoteric knowledge is closed to the uninitiated by its technical complexities, the need for long study and aptitude, but also by

[1] Below, pp. 174 n7, 175. For an interesting overview of the early modern period which establishes an agenda for the nineteenth century, see P. Burke, *A Social History of Knowledge from Gutenberg to Diderot* (Cambridge, 2000). He considers how knowledge was professed, established, located, controlled, sold, acquired and trusted or distrusted. I am grateful to Peter Burke for his comments at the conference in Cambridge in 2002 which have helped to shape my thinking.

social boundaries established by knowledge communities. Jowett, as the Master of Balliol, had the status of his degree and position to establish his authority as a man of learning and knowledge. But it was a particular type of authority, authenticated in a highly specific manner: his knowledge rested on a narrow corpus of classical texts, studied in a distinctive way that was challenged in the later nineteenth century by a new approach to antiquity.[2] His reputation did not rest on what would come to be called 'research', a social practice alien to many fellows of Oxbridge colleges in the Victorian period, which came to be authenticated by new forms of authority with the emergence of doctoral theses and professional refereed journals.

The relationship between esoteric knowledge and its popularisation is also a major theme in the social and intellectual history of the nineteenth century. Few people have the time or ability to understand evolutionary biology or wave theory, but the assumptions and language of these esoteric disciplines may move from a particular knowledge community so as to enter into the wider discourse of society. Scientific language was used in imaginative literature, from the science fiction of popular novelists to the more arcane use of new theories of light by Gerard Manley Hopkins. The process was not one way: scientists drew on myth and poetry for metaphors and symbols to express findings and theories which strained comprehension.[3]

The mechanisms of diffusion and understanding are of considerable interest, and the relationship between esoteric and popular knowledge was mediated in a variety of ways. Amateur naturalists might meet in their local pub and make field trips; or aspiring artisans might attend classes at the mechanics institutes.[4] Lectures were delivered in regular series to a well-to-do

[2] F. M. Turner, *Contesting Cultural Authority: Essays in Victorian Intellectual Life* (Cambridge, 1993), ch. 12 on Jowett's Platonism and his chapter in this volume.

[3] On the impact of wave theory and evolution, see G. Beer, *Open Fields: Science in Cultural Encounter* (Oxford, 1996) ch. 11 and *Darwin's Plots: Evolution Narrative in Darwin, George Eliot and Nineteenth-Century Fiction* (Cambridge, 2nd edn., 2000). On the use of Lucretius in scientific discourse, see Turner, *Contesting Cultural Authority*, ch. 10.

[4] See A. Secord, 'Science in the pub: amateur botanists in early nineteenth-century Lancashire', *History of Science*, 32 (1994); on popular natural history, see D. E. Allen, *The Naturalists in Britain: A Social History* (London, 1976). On the continued interaction between professional biologists and local field clubs, see S. J. M. M. Alberti, 'Amateurs and professionals in one county: biology and natural history in late Victorian Yorkshire', *Journal of the History of Biology*, 34 (2001). See also H. Gay, 'East End, West End: science education, culture and class in mid-Victorian London', *Canadian Journal of History*, 32 (1997) on the trade interests of the East End and the elite of the West End, and the creation of a new cultural hybrid. On mechanics institutes, see M. Tylecote, *The Mechanics Institutes of Lancashire and Yorkshire before 1851* (Manchester, 1957); J. F. C. Harrison, *Learning and Living 1790–1960: A Study in the History of the English Adult Education Movement* (London, 1961); I. Inkster, 'The social context of an educational movement: a revisionist approach to the English mechanics' institutes, 1820–50', *Oxford Review of Education*, 2 (1976), 277–307.

audience at the Royal Institution by major figures such as Michael Faraday, at the annual peripatetic meetings of the British Association for the Advancement of Science from 1831, or in one-off performances in provincial lecture halls.[5] These lectures might shade into entertainment. The leading scientists were themselves showmen, using dramatic presentations to win an audience and hold their attention. Equally, showmen used the marvels of science and nature to attract paying customers. *The Origins of Species* sold many copies for a serious work of science; even so, its major themes were popularised by less cerebral means, such as touring shows of gorillas and *Punch* cartoons about the 'missing link'.[6]

New ideas were presented in the magazines, quarterlies and reviews which were such a feature of Victorian publication. The work of Geoffrey Cantor and Sally Shuttleworth shows how the latest thinking on science was interspersed with serialised novels, travellers tales, or political discussions in the pages of reviews, from the most serious *Quarterly*, *Edinburgh* and *Westminster Reviews* to more popular and entertaining magazines such as Dickens's *Household Words*, the *Illustrated London News*, or the *Literary Gazette* which was a leading populariser of science.[7] Until the 1870s or 1880s, the serious quarterly reviews provided a common context for writing about all aspects of knowledge, mediating between specialists in different disciplines, let alone between specialists and the laity. But the common context could not survive. By the second quarter of the nineteenth century, there was already a need to explain advances in one discipline to specialists

[5] M. Berman, *Social Change and Scientific Organization: The Royal Institution, 1799–1844* (London, 1978), pp. 124–7, 186: the Institution was established by the Royal Society in 1799 and offered annual subscription lectures held in the afternoon, which combined popular as well as scientific subjects; private morning lectures, mainly for medical students; and Friday evening discourses which mixed entertainment and technical subjects. The Royal Institution also had the best laboratory in the early nineteenth century and undertook research and testing for the government and commercial firms. The Royal Institution lost its standing after the middle of the century. Lectures were also offered at the London Institution which broke away to develop closer links with industry and commerce. On the British Association, see J. Morrell and A. Thackeray, *Gentlemen of Science: The Early Years of the British Association for the Advancement of Science* (Oxford, 1981). For a discussion of lectures in London, see J. N. Hays, 'The London lecturing empire, 1800–50', in I. Inkster and J. B. Morrell (eds.), *Metropolis and Province: Science in British Culture* (London, 1983).

[6] The point is made in the current work of Jim Secord, as explained in his inaugural lecture at Cambridge in 2003.

[7] <www.sciper.leeds.ac.uk> for 'Science in the nineteenth-century periodical', last accessed on 24 Feb. 2004; publications arising from the project are L. Henson, G. Cantor, G. Dawson, R. Noakes, S. Shuttleworth and J. R. Topham (eds.), *Culture and Science in the Nineteenth-Century Media* (Aldershot, 2004) and *Science Serialised: Representations of the Sciences in Nineteenth-Century Periodicals* (Cambridge, 2004). I am grateful to Professors Cantor and Shuttleworth for demonstrating the SciPer database in 2001.

in other areas, which led to the publication of journals and magazines such as the *Athenaeum*, *Saturday Review* and the *Philosophical Magazine* to report on the latest discoveries. Leading scientists such as T. H. Huxley and John Tyndall and the X-Club wished to establish a more authoritative forum for the dissemination of knowledge between specialists, and the commercial publishing firm of Macmillan filled the gap in 1869, with the publication of the weekly magazine *Nature*. The pattern of publication was changing. Scientists now learned about the discoveries of colleagues in other disciplines from *Nature*, or published in their own specialist academic journals. Non-specialists could turn to the *Nineteenth Century*, the most popular review in the last quarter of the nineteenth century, which brought together politics, literature and science at a somewhat less complex level of analysis. What was now less apparent was the extended essay written for an educated audience by the leading specialists in the field.[8]

The process of popularisation was troubling. As Max Jones shows, the Royal Geographic Society was concerned by the relationship between specialised and popular publications, a common theme at the close of the nineteenth century. Some senior scientists such as Tyndall in *Fragments of Science* and Huxley in his *Lay Sermons* themselves engaged in popularisation as a self-conscious activity, and the latest views on science and the humanities were encapsulated in authoritative essays in the *Encyclopaedia Britannica.* But in many cases the task was left to commercial firms and more-or-less competent amateurs. They included somewhat unsystematic writers such as William Graham whose book *The Creed of Science, Religious, Moral and Social* (1881) offered a muddled reassurance that there were no deep divisions; he also wrote books on the economic and social aspects of social problems, on political philosophy from Hobbes to Maine, on socialism, and free trade. The study of socialism appeared in the popular International Scientific Series published by H. S King and subsequently Kegan, Paul and Trench, which attempted to bring together science with ethics, politics and history for a wider audience. The second volume in the series was Walter Bagehot's *Physics and Politics, or Thoughts on the Application of the Principles of 'Natural Selection' and 'Inheritance' to Political Society* (1872). Other volumes with a similar desire to link science and society or

[8] R. Young, 'Natural theology, Victorian periodicals and the fragmentation of a common context', in his *Darwin's Metaphors: Nature's Place in Victorian Culture* (Cambridge, 1985), pp. 126–63 and pp. 265–71; R. MacLeod, 'The genesis of *Nature*', *Nature*, 224 (1969) and 'The social framework of *Nature* in the first 50 years', *Nature*, 224 (1969), both reprinted in his *The 'Creed of Science' in Victorian England* (Aldershot, 2000).

psychology included books by major figures such as Alexander Bain's *Mind and Body: The Theories of Their Relations* (volume 4, 1873) and George Romanes's *Animal Intelligence* (volume 41, 1882). Commercial firms published popular magazines, often linked with flourishing 'hobbies' or with the growing needs of secondary schools. For example, *The Historical Course for Schools* was not widely different from the specialist *English Historical Review* and the gap between popular and professional, commercial and learned, remained blurred at the end of the nineteenth century.[9]

Of course, the diffusion of esoteric knowledge through these various channels raised the vexed question of how competing claims and conflicting interpretations could be assessed by the uninitiated. Indeed, the transmission of esoteric into popular knowledge raises another issue: the transmission of ignorance. How was knowledge validated in the process of popularisation, and how could outdated information and interpretations no longer accepted by the dominant voices in the knowledge community be excluded from the realms of legitimate knowledge? Who was a fraud and who was making a genuine contribution to understanding? Formal academic qualifications, membership of elite bodies such as the Royal Society—and later the British Academy—provided some assurance. So did incorporation into authoritative encyclopaedia and inclusion in the formal curricula of schools and universities.[10]

The emergence of a formal curriculum offered a means of legitimating knowledge, incorporating new ideas and theories into the teaching of schools and colleges. What was expected to be known by those who claimed to be knowledgeable, and how was mastery of the curriculum to be tested? The nature of knowledge shaped, and was shaped by, the methods of assessment and testing. As John Gibbins argues, the curriculum was set by those with legitimacy to determine what constituted knowledge. It was intimately connected with the growth of universities and academics as the key sites and authorities for validating knowledge, with increasing influence over the schools. Authority ceased to rest on the social status of disinterested amateur gentlemen scholars or on the reputation of 'sages'. Rather, authority rested on the provision of systematic guidance, a course of reading, and instruction.

[9] Young, 'Natural theology', pp. 157, 269; on the International Scientific Series, see D. Fleming, *John William Draper and the Religion of Science* (Philadelphia, 1950). On 'hobbies', see R. McKibbin, *The Ideologies of Class: Social Relations in Britain, 1880–1950* (Oxford, 1990).

[10] On the changing nature of the Royal Society, see M. B. Hall, *All Scientists Now: The Royal Society in the Nineteenth Century* (Cambridge, 1984); on encylopaedia see A. Rauch, *Useful Knowledge: The Victorians, Morality and "The March of Intellect"* (Durham, NC, and London, 2001); his current work on subscription libraries continues his interest in 'information sites'.

And authority was acquired by passing competitive tests. The universities devised more systematic and formalised curricula, and also new means of testing knowledge.

At the start of the nineteenth century, most examinations were oral, a public disputation between student and examiner with the participation of other students and graduates who had the right to intervene. Success depended on the ability of the other participants and on the calibre of those bested in debate. The shift from oral to written examinations started in Cambridge, with its heavy reliance on Newtonian mathematics as the basis for education: the mathematical tripos was introduced in 1747 and formed the basis of the education of students seeking an honours degree for the next hundred years. Mathematics could less easily be tested in disputations, and by 1858 oral examinations had ended in all disciplines in Cambridge. The change was linked with another trend: the emergence of formal boards of examiners who defined a curriculum and minimised the risk of sudden changes according to the whim of an individual examiner. New triposes—courses of study and examinations in a specific subject—were established, starting with classics in 1822, and moral and natural sciences in 1848. As MacLeod and Moseley remark, the triposes moved Victorian Cambridge 'from the traditional ideology of *universitas* and the conception of a liberal education ... to an ideology of specialised knowledge'.[11] In Oxford, oral examinations survived to the end of the century, reflecting a greater stress on logic and divinity. Different methods of examination reflected different forms of knowledge and varying social or moral assumptions. Written examinations were better at testing analysis, but oral examinations could more easily catch those who 'crammed' or merely memorised fact. Oral examinations, their defenders believed, offered a better way of testing the permanent knowledge of eternal truths than did written examinations driven by research-based knowledge. Oral examinations implied a socio-moral assessment of candidates by examiners who could be trusted to be fair in their cross-examination; written examinations entailed a cognitive assessment of individuals with a standard set of questions set by specialised examiners.[12]

[11] On the creation of moral sciences, see D. Palfrey, 'The moral sciences tripos at Cambridge University, 1848–60', Ph.D. thesis, University of Cambridge, 2002; on natural sciences, R. MacLeod and R. Moseley, 'Breaking the circle of science: the natural sciences tripos and the "examination revolution"', in R. MacLeod (ed.), *Days of Judgement: Examination and the Organization of Knowledge in Late Victorian England* (Driffield, 1982), reprinted in R. MacLeod, *The 'Creed of Science' in Victorian England* (Aldershot, 2000); the quotation is from p. 190.

[12] C. Stray, 'The shift from oral to written examination: Cambridge and Oxford, 1700–1900', *Assessment in Education*, 8 (2001).

Increasingly, examinations tested specialised epistemologies, not simply measuring what was known but how it was known and why it was knowable. In the natural sciences, teaching and examining also moved to practical experiments and exercises in the laboratory. The proposition of Isaac Todhunter no longer seemed defensible: ‘experimentation is unnecessary for the student. The student should be prepared to accept whatever the master told him.’ In 1869, a Cambridge university committee recommended the construction of a physics laboratory. The new Cavendish laboratory opened in 1873, financed by the Chancellor of the university, the seventh duke of Devonshire who had been the senior wrangler (top mathematician) of his year. Its first head—James Clerk Maxwell—took a different view from Todhunter. Students attended lectures and demonstrations, and were asked to undertake practical examinations such as finding the focal length of a lens or the time of vibration of a magnet. The natural sciences examination in the 1870s was spread over eight days, with two days of practicals in the middle.[13]

As well as popularising and legitimating knowledge, the reverse might also apply: knowledge might be made esoteric and separated from the commonplace. Enjoyment of novels and poetry, and reading of history, were accessible to anyone with a decent level of literacy. How could English and history claim to be esoteric academic disciplines, on a par with classics or mathematics with their need for intensive study? To claim that reading English literature needed special critical skills would devalue the moral claims of reading emphasised by Matthew Arnold; to stress aesthetic judgement (as did Walter Pater) would undervalue professionalism and give priority to personal feeling. One solution was to base the discipline of English on philology, drawing on German academics for inspiration. Another was to turn to editing texts or to literary history. F. J. Furnivall combined philology, as the leading figure in the Philological Society and its *New English Dictionary*, with his central role in the Early English Texts Society (1864), Chaucer Society (1868), Ballad Society (1869), New Shakespere Society (1873) and Wyclif Society (1881). He was also committed to popular education through the workingmen’s college.[14] The question of how to define English as a field of study was contested, as Josephine Guy and Carol Atherton show—and

[13] D. Moralle, ‘The first ten years’, in Cambridge University Physics Society, *A Hundred Years and More of Cambridge Physics* (3rd edn., 1995), pp. 8, 16; MacLeod and Moseley, ‘Breaking the circle of science’, p. 198.

[14] See K. M. E. Murray, *Caught in the Web of Words: James A. H. Murray and the Oxford English Dictionary* (New Haven and London, 1977), pp. 87–9; obituary of Furnivall in *Proceedings of the British Academy* 4, pp. 375–8.

the uncertainty of the status of English meant that literary scholarship was excluded from the Academy and could only be admitted as philology, literary history and editing of texts—as in the election of Furnivall to the fellowship in 1903, and of James Murray, his associate on the *New English Dictionary*, as a founding fellow in 1902. Hermeneutics—the process of deriving meaning—had relatively little space in the hierarchy of knowledge in Victorian Britain.

The issue was not simply esoteric versus popular knowledge, or even knowledge versus ignorance. There were also competing, alternative, unofficial or subordinate forms of knowledge. Radical or socialist systems of economics countered orthodox economics. Ayurvedic medicine from India offered a different approach to western medicine. Practical knowledge of industrial processes and economic life accumulated by merchants and traders countered more formal theory or information collected by the state. Such knowledge could be used to challenge the interpretations of state officials or could be incorporated into the understanding of the state. The question of who generates and possesses knowledge is vital to understanding the growth of the state. Was information on social conditions held by trade unions with information on unemployment rates, by industrialists with statistics on output, or gathered by a government agency? Would these different sources of information result in conflict over policies; or could the state 'capture' and utilise knowledge?[15] The issue was particularly pressing in the colonial state, where British officials often relied on information derived from indigenous forms of governance.[16] In addition, there is tacit knowledge—things we know through observation and experience, which are simply taken for granted without being formalised. Tacit knowledge is usually held in low esteem, lacking the formal authentication that provides status and authority.

These differing forms of knowledge are far from straightforward, both internally and in their relationships with each other. Tacit knowledge might be protected and policed by guilds which laid down apprenticeship regulations and craft practices—a formalisation of experience to exclude outsiders and maintain profits. In some societies, the guilds held considerable power and might block change. Elsewhere, knowledge might be shared within a

[15] For the role of the state in generating knowledge, see M. O. Furner and B. E. Supple (eds.), *The State and Economic Knowledge: The American and British Experiences* (Cambridge, 1990); also J. C. Scott, *Seeing Like a State: How Certain Schemes to Improve the Human Condition Have Failed* (New Haven and London, 1998).

[16] C. A. Bayly, *Empire and Information: Intelligence Gathering and Social Communication in India, 1780–1870* (Cambridge, 1996).

craft community such as the scientific instrument makers of Clerkenwell or the specialist steel trades of Sheffield. The possession of tacit knowledge could entail conflict between capital and labour. A workman at an iron furnace might have tacit knowledge of the consistency and temperature of the metal by observing the colour of the flame, allowing him to judge when to add more materials or draw off the product. However, employers feared that leaving the brains under the workman's cap gave them power over production, and led them to systematise practical knowledge in the hands of engineers and chemists.[17] And how should engineers be trained? Men such as George Stephenson were trained 'on the job', through apprenticeship and practical experience, and civil engineers continued this tradition throughout the nineteenth century, unlike the French or German pattern of formal education at *Écoles,* polytechnics, or technical schools. In the case of sophisticated products such as the crucible steel of Sheffield, laboratories were increasingly important by the later nineteenth century, both within firms and in Firth College which formed the basis of the university.[18] Equally, the shift from tacit to formalised knowledge could have a gender dimension, as with the medicalisation (and at the same time masculinisation) of child-birth in the later nineteenth century. The tacit knowledge possessed by indigenous peoples of terrain and animal and plant species might be highly valuable to western 'explorers' who were 'discovering' a new world and formalising this knowledge. Of course, the knowledge systems of the colonised peoples were often themselves highly developed and esoteric, such as Chinese or Indian medicine. From the sixteenth to eighteenth centuries, western practitioners were willing to learn from these alternative systems; in the early nineteenth century, they were downgraded as subordinate or even illegitimate knowledge before returning in the twentieth century as an alternative, oppositional system to the dominance of western scientific medicine. Imperial powers and their scholars might seek to understand and even incorporate elements of these alternative, unofficial, or subordinate knowledge systems—or exclude and marginalise them.

Although the relationships between esoteric and popular, official and alternative knowledge, are vitally important, the main concern in this collection of essays is with academic, official and legitimate knowledge, reflecting both the intention of marking the centenary of the British Academy and

[17] For some examples, see W. Lazonick, *Competitive Advantage on the Shop Floor* (Cambridge, MA, 1990).

[18] G. Tweedale, *Steel City: Entrepreneurship, Strategy and Technology in Sheffield, 1743–1993* (Oxford, 1995).

pragmatic realisation of what is practical in one volume. It is also the best starting place, for only when we have a clear understanding of official, legitimate and academic knowledge can we move to the wider questions of its relationships with alternative, unofficial, subordinate or popular forms of knowledge. The process of shaping official knowledge often implies separating a defined core of esoteric expertise from contamination by other forms of knowledge: popularisation can only be safely undertaken when the bounds of legitimate knowledge have been determined; alternative and competing knowledge systems can only be marginalised and subordinated when official knowledge has been properly validated and methods established to police the boundaries. Indeed, understanding the nature of academic, official and legitimate knowledge in the Victorian period is in itself an ambitious project, and many gaps remain.

Knowledge is a complicated term. What about organisation? It involves a combination of the social and institutional foundations of knowledge, the processes of obtaining cultural authority in order to speak as a knowledgeable person. The relationship between what is known and how it is organised is by no means simple. What is organised and how it is organised might change together or vary independently of each other; they might influence one another in a process of mutual interaction; or they might be in tension as an expansion of what is known collides with a rigid system of organisation. The prime aim of this collection is to consider the epistemological sites of Victorian Britain and how they were ordered. These sites included loose social networks; clubs or societies such as provincial literary and philosophical societies and archaeological societies, and national bodies such as the Royal Geographical Society, open to anyone (or at least any man) who cared to join and could afford the subscription; and the most exclusive, closed bodies of the elect, such as the Royal Society and the British Academy. They might include state institutions such as the Royal Botanic Gardens at Kew, the Royal Observatory, Admiralty or British Museum.

Each of these bodies had their own distinctive structures of power and authority. The gardens at Kew emerged from a royal initiative of the 1750s whose future shape was contested in the 1830s, between those who wished to convert it into a place of scientific botany against a more entrepreneurial form of horticulture. The botanists' victory was not entirely secure, for the gardens became part of the Board of Woods and Forests with the prospect of control by officials. One response by the scientific directors was to appeal to their imperial role as a justification for professional botany. By contrast, the British Museum was insulated from official interference by trustees drawn from the principal officers of state—the Lord Chancellor, archbishop of Canterbury,

Speaker of the House of Commons, and government ministers—complemented by elected trustees who were responsible for the detailed work. The nature of the trustees was debated in the 1830s, with the principal librarian arguing that scientists and scholars were not needed, for 'science and literature would be possessed by a well-educated gentleman in sufficient quantity to make him a Trustee'. He lost the argument, and trustees were selected for their 'eminence in literature, science and art'. They were able to secure more money from the government: the grant rose from £17,796 in 1835/6 to £100,850 in 1860/1. In other words, the precise constitutional or organisational form of institutions affected the strategy and success of bodies.[19]

At the start of the period, universities played a relatively small role, especially in England; they assumed ever larger authority as the Victorian period drew to a close, developing major research laboratories that were often connected to the needs of the state and industry, as well as sites of 'pure' research.[20] As William Lubenow points out, some sites (such as the Synthetic Society) could destabilise knowledge, creating an intimate space where value and meaning could be negotiated, and the line between amateur and professional, political and academic worlds could be blurred. The Synthetic Society dealt with issues of belief and religion, allowing free exchange of opinions; it was more limited in its membership than the earlier Metaphysical Society (1869–80) which tried to bring leading scientists into a common context of discussion of the large themes of existential meaning. Although the Metaphysical Society failed, and its remaining funds were passed to the specialist philosophical journal *Mind*, scientists themselves felt the need for informal, sociable bodies such as the Red Lion Club or B-Club where they

[19] On Kew, see R. Drayton, *Nature's Government: Science, Imperial Britain and the 'Improvement' of the World* (New Haven and London, 2000), ch. 5; on the British Museum, D. M. Wilson, *The British Museum: A History* (London, 2002), pp. 21, 50, 86, 88, 138–9, 196–7.

[20] There is now a large literature on sites in the strict sense of physical spaces as places of knowing. David Livingstone argues that knowledge was conducted in sites other than the privileged spaces of laboratories, observatories and museums, such as the rectory, garden, ship and tent: '*Where* witnesses were located, both socially and spatially, counted in warranting the records they delivered'. D. Livingstone, 'Reading the heavens, planting the earth: culture of British science', *History Workshop Journal*, 54 (2002), 241, and *Putting Science in its Place: Geographies of Scientific Knowledge* (Chicago, 2003). See also S. Forgan, 'The architecture of display: museums, universities and objects in nineteenth-century Britain', *History of Science*, 32 (1994); ' "But indifferently lodged": perception and place in building for science in Victorian London', in C. Smith and J. Agar (eds.), *Making Space for Science: Territorial Themes in the Making of Knowledge* (Basingstoke, 1998); 'Bricks and bones: architecture and science in Victorian Britain', in P. Galison and E. Thompson (eds.), *The Architecture of Science* (Cambridge, MA, 1999); with G. Gooday, ' "A fungoid assemblage of buildings": diversity and adversity in the development of college architecture and scientific education in nineteenth-century South Kensington', *History of Universities*, 13 (1994).

could exchange ideas and express emotions in a way that was not possible in formal learned societies. Further, the members might be younger men setting themselves against established institutions which they dare not challenge in a more confrontational manner.[21] Other sites, such as the Royal Society and British Academy, were designed to stabilise knowledge and the status of those claiming knowledge. Membership of these sites overlapped: Arthur Balfour, James Bryce, Albert Dicey and Richard Jebb were all members of the Synthetic Society, as well as founding fellows of the Academy and active participants in public life.

How are disciplinary boundaries constituted and how was a hierarchy of status defined? During the period, disciplines emerged and became well established with societies, professorships and journals. There was nothing preordained about where these disciplinary lines would be drawn, and differences emerged between England and Scotland, London and the provinces, Oxbridge and the rest, as well as more generally between Britain and Continental Europe. In other cases, such as classics, the definition of the discipline changed fundamentally over the period. As chapters in this book show, disciplines formed a hierarchy, determined by the status of their practitioners, the social cachet provided by different forms of knowledge, and the intellectual standing of their epistemology. Natural history, for example, was often carried out by gentlemen and above all Anglican clergy in search of God's order in the universe. In the eighteenth and early nineteenth century, it had considerable social esteem, and practitioners such as Joseph Banks were at the peak of the Royal Society and closely involved with the imperial state—somewhat to the dismay of mathematicians.[22] But from the second quarter of the nineteenth century, it was held in lower intellectual esteem, for it rested on description, collection and classification. Natural history might be infected by its amateur status, allowing uneducated men and superficial women to engage in plant classification. Botanists with a desire to establish their scientific reputation needed to raise its intellectual standing as well as preserving its social status, by moving to a more analytical approach. The result was a battle between forms of classification with the Linnean Society adhering to an older system which was accessible to local, colonial and even female-naturalists, while 'philosophical' botanists developed their own system of

[21] H. and J. Gay, 'Brothers in science: science and fraternal culture in nineteenth-century Britain', *History of Science*, 35 (1997) and Young, 'Natural theology'.

[22] J. Gascoigne, *Joseph Banks and the English Enlightenment: Useful Knowledge and Polite Culture* (Cambridge, 1994) shows how Banks marked a shift from the wide and unsystematic interests of gentlemen collectors to specialism—a change he did not entirely welcome, fearing a threat to the polite culture of the Royal Society by more specialist scientific societies in the early nineteenth century.

classification. Issues of social status and scientific standing were intertwined: the authority of the system of classification depended on who was doing the classifying. The contest between professionals and amateurs was not clear cut, with the amateurs marginalised by the advance of laboratories and academic status; the amateurs could play a role in the emergence of the professional discipline, and themselves respond through what has been called 'amateurisation'. In the emerging civic colleges of Yorkshire, for example, there was an overlap with members of the field clubs which grouped together in the Yorkshire Naturalists Union in 1861. As its president remarked in 1898, the Union was 'an integrating machine' complementing the universities.[23]

Increasingly, the intellectual and social status of a discipline depended on the adoption of analytical procedures which emerged from the 1820s. Until the emergence of experimental science from the 1860s, classification and analysis were in the ascendant. In the words of Jim Secord, 'Zoologists and botanists classified living beings; astronomers studied the distribution and order of the heavens; chemists analyzed new compounds; geologists mapped strata and their fossils; philologists compared different languages. Not surprisingly, the museum—not the laboratory—was the central institution of Victorian science.'[24] In Britain, much of this work was carried out in museums and other sites outside the universities, such as the government's Geological Survey (created in 1832) or the Natural History Museum. The emergence of analysis also meant that mathematics achieved high standing, with an attempt to insert its approach into other disciplines such as economics. Mathematicians wished to use terms precisely in order to facilitate harmony and agreement—an ambition reflected in the London Mathematical Society's use of Christian, Jewish and Muslim symbols in its insignia on its formation in 1865. Not all mathematicians believed their discipline could have transcendental significance, but it could at least provide a practical tool of precise reasoning. Mathematicians were sceptical of John Stuart Mill's system of logic which was taught in the universities; they were equally sceptical of the Idealism of many philosophers who linked a particular view

[23] In addition to the chapter by Jim Endersby, see A. Desmond, 'Redefining the X axis: "professional", "amateurs" and the making of mid-Victorian biology: a progress report', *Journal of the History of Biology*, 34 (2001) on the process of professionalisation; R. Bellon, 'Joseph Hooker's ideals of a professional man', *Journal of the History of Biology*, 34 (2001); and for a somewhat different provincial perspective, Alberti, 'Amateurs and professionals', pp. 136, 142.

[24] J. V. Pickstone, 'Museological science? The place of the analytical/comparative in nineteenth-century science, technology and medicine', *History of Science*, 32 (1994), 114; J. A. Secord, 'Introduction', to R. Chambers, *Vestiges of the Natural History of Creation and other Evolutionary Writings* (Chicago, 1994), p. xii.

of Plato with Hegel. The mathematical philosophy of Bertrand Russell and Alfred Whitehead contrasted with the Idealism of T. H. Green which was such an important strand in social thinking in the late nineteenth and early twentieth centuries.[25] By the end of the nineteenth century, analysis started to give way to experimentation in an attempt to control the world, with the emergence of new laboratories at Cambridge and other research universities.

Unlike in France and Germany, analysis and experimentation were defined as 'science' in a way which excluded the humanities. In Germany, Wissenschaft was inclusive; in Britain, science was exclusive. The difference was not simply semantic: the humanities were excluded from the Royal Society which rejected two options at the close of the century: to open itself to the humanities or to support the creation of a new body. Hermeneutics as a form of knowledge was distinct from science, and the practitioners of the humanities were in any case slow to accept this methodology. We have noted the difficulties for English in asserting its disciplinary claim: could it rise above moral teaching or mere listing of authors to achieve the form of analysis found in the sciences? The issue also troubled classicists. Of course, the classics had a great advantage that a basic grasp of Greek and Latin marked out the elite: knowledge entailed social status, a means of socialising the ruling class and marking its boundaries. It was, in other words, a system of credentialising. University teachers usually left after a few years for other careers in the church or law: they did not see themselves as researchers seeking to extend knowledge but rather as teachers passing on what was already known. Research was inappropriate and unmanly: as William Whewell pointed out in 1845, English universities educated laymen who did not enter into a profession, so that the model of a German professoriate was not applicable. Indeed, in the words of Kemble, 'the Germans have become the most learned men in the world, but the least manly, the least capable of being members of free and independent communities'.[26] The beginning of a change towards a more professional and research-based approach may be found in the emergence of classical archaeology in the 1860s and 1870s, with its concern for ancient religion and social structures, so widening the remit of the classics from ahistorical translation exercises. Plaster casts and excavations offered classicists the same analytical approach as geologists and

[25] J. Harris, 'Political thought and the welfare state, 1870–1940: an intellectual framework for British social policy', *Past and Present*, 135 (1992).

[26] Kemble cited in Palfrey, 'Moral sciences', p. 220; on Whewell, see R. Yeo, *Defining Science: William Whewell, Natural Knowledge, and Public Debate in Early Victorian Britain* (Cambridge, 1993).

chemists. Meanwhile, the approach to texts changed at the end of the nineteenth century, when A. E. Housman criticised his predecessors in much the same way as the naturalists of the mid-century attacked clerical natural theologians. His approach, as many in the new discipline of English, was to create secure texts by technical precision.

In the early years of Victoria's reign, few men (and we are essentially talking of men) could claim to be polymaths or even to possess mastery over more than a few adjacent fields. There was a knowledge explosion in the nineteenth century, generated by an increase in the supply of information and its rapid diffusion through cheap printing, and by an increase in demand for knowledge with an expansion in education and income. Technological change in printing meant a fall in the price of books, as James Raven shows. Equally, an expansion of the market allowed publishers to sell more books at a smaller margin. There were two distinct but overlapping processes: the generation of new knowledge and dissemination by new media.

The publication of knowledge entailed 'gate keepers' who controlled access to journals or publishers' lists. Learned societies offered opportunities to read papers with some assurance of quality or legitimacy, but the selection of lecturers was a matter of internal politics, of professional rivalries, ideological conflicts or a simple desire to attract an audience. Such societies were exclusive, limiting the ability of outsiders or the heterodox to secure a stage; and the process of publication was slow, with readers largely confined to fellow specialists. By the end of the century, specialised scholarly journals were becoming more common. Specialist journals such as *Mind* (1876), the *English Historical Review* (1886) or the *Economic Journal* (1891) were somewhat more open, uncoupling publication from an invitation to read a paper at a society's meeting—but there was still the hurdle of editors and readers' reports to act as gatekeepers and validators of legitimate knowledge. Many ventures were still undertaken by commercial publishers and major university presses were not as dominant as they were to become in the twentieth century. As Raven shows, publication of books at the beginning of the period might depend on the willingness of authors to cover some of the costs; at the end of the period publishers were more likely to bear the financial risk. Publishers needed to consider the market for their books, not simply from individuals but from circulating libraries, the new public libraries and, at the end of the century, a more academic market. Commercial companies could sponsor major research undertakings which would later become the responsibility of state funding. The publication of the *Dictionary of National Biography* is a case in point, a venture of Smith, Elder before it migrated to Oxford University Press in 1917, joining the *Oxford English Dictionary* which had started as a voluntary venture under the auspices of the Philological Society before moving to the Press in 1879.[27] Who decided what to publish or to translate, on what criteria; and how were books then selected for purchase by libraries or individuals? Was the content of libraries and museums determined by expert librarians and curators, or democratically by the town councillor and lay trustees? Initially, literary and philosophical societies made their libraries available to the new civic colleges, such as the Royal Institution at Liverpool and the Statistical Society at Manchester; over time, the balance changed and the universities took over the collections, perhaps limiting access to a distinct academic community and purchasing books for a specialised disciplinary curriculum.

Knowledge could be devalued by the sheer amount of information made available. Both lay readers and specialists were perplexed by the sheer quantity of information. Although individuals might keep pace with new thinking within their own specialism, through the transactions of a learned society and its regular meetings of the knowledgeable, sifting other publications was more difficult. How could this mass of information be reduced to some order? How could existing knowledge be archived and reproduced? How were books to be classified, an issue of taxonomy which troubled librarians; how could relevant material be located and the most important items identified? Libraries, archives and catalogues were important epistemological sites. Catalogues were crucial, but only part of the process: they did not measure quality. The mechanisms for validating what was published changed over the period, and so did the use of book reviews to sift quality and significance. Until the 1870s, the *Edinburgh* and *Quarterly Reviews* published extended essays, making recent publications accessible to an educated audience. By the end of the century, new scholarly journals assessed recent work for a specialist audience. In 1902, the *Times Literary Supplement* offered the educated literary public a guide to the most important and interesting books on a range of topics.[28] For most readers, information on what to read relied on reviews in the press or word of mouth.

The accumulation of information might itself generate specialisation and professionalisation. In other words, intellectual change might drive social change with the emergence of a new social cadre of academic experts. Conversely, social and economic change might impel intellectual change: the development of trade and industry led to more information and the

[27] N. Annan, *Leslie Stephen: The Godless Victorian* (2nd edn., London, 1984); Murray, *Caught in the Web of Words.*

[28] M. Derwent, *Critical Times: The History of the Times Literary Supplement* (2002), fails to ask how books were selected, or to probe the relations with publishers.

commercialisation of knowledge resulted in a 'knowledge industry' of teachers, booksellers, and journalists. The social position and intellectual standing of men of letters—in their highest incarnation 'sages' or 'prophets'—came under pressure: individuals such as John Ruskin or John Stuart Mill or Thomas Babington Macaulay who combined a literary and public role, speaking to a general public as men of intellectual authority.[29] Early fellows of the British Academy included some survivors of these 'sages', such as W. H. Lecky whose authority did not rest upon academic training and distinctions, or upon publication in professional journals. Leading politicians might themselves engage in scholarship in the humanities, drawing on their own private libraries such as Gladstone at Hawarden. Similarly, gentlemanly *savants* engaged in scientific work, using private means and private laboratories. By mid-century, gentlemen of science in the Royal Society were challenged by a demand for publicly supported science, led by men such as T. H. Huxley.[30] But up to the end of the century, gentlemen scientists and scholars were still able to make major contributions, both inside and outside the universities. The boundary between private scholars and the universities was permeable. Lord Rayleigh, the brother-in-law of Balfour and Maxwell's successor as the head of the Cavendish, was a major landowner with private means and laboratories in addition to his university post. Indeed, country houses could be major research centres, such as Charles Darwin's Down House, William Armstrong's Cragside, and even Lord Salisbury's Hatfield House.[31] Lord Acton brought German historical scholarship to Cambridge as a result of his own European aristocratic background and education, supported by his own impressive library.[32] However, sages were in decline by the end of the nineteenth century, largely replaced by 'public intellectuals' who derived authority from one sphere of intellectual life and generalised it to others, often from a secure base in academic life.[33]

The German model of the research university had a rival: the French model of the *grandes écoles* and museums, which was perhaps more applicable to Britain in the mid-nineteenth century. One of the main sites of knowledge was South Kensington, the location of the Great Exhibition and the

[29] T. W. Heyck, *The Transformation of Intellectual Life in Victorian England* (London, 1982).

[30] A. Desmond, *Huxley: The Devil's Disciple* (London, 1994) and *Huxley: Evolution's High Priest* (London, 1997).

[31] S. Schaffer, 'Physics laboratories and the Victorian country house', in Smith and Agar (eds.), *Making Space for Science*.

[32] R. Hill, *Lord Acton* (New Haven and London, 2000).

[33] S. Collini, *Public Moralists: Political Thought and Intellectual Life in Britain, 1850–1930* (Oxford, 1991).

cultural institutions which it fostered: the museums and schools were more akin to the French model. The exhibition left a surplus of between £150,000 and £200,000 which Prince Albert suggested should be used to purchase land in South Kensington where the work of the exhibition could continue in a more permanent way through a series of exhibitions and a cluster of museums and colleges. The Commissioners remained in existence, developing 'Albertopolis' as one of the greatest collections of museums and colleges in the world. Their origins and status varied. The Royal College of Chemistry was a private body which sought to link science and industry; the Royal School of Mines was a state-financed body, exploring the mineral resources of Britain and its empire; the Normal School of Science was inspired by the French *École Normale*, and became the Royal College of Science.[34]

Comparison with the organisation of knowledge in Paris and Berlin may lead to the conclusion that London was lagging behind both, and miss the distinctive pattern of British institutions that fitted into neither of the Continental models. In common with other aspects of British society in the nineteenth century, the organisation of knowledge rested on a 'mixed economy' of provision and funding, with a preference for voluntarism and the market over the state whose role was to facilitate or support much more than to provide on its own initiative.[35] The market, voluntary societies, and the state each had their own institutional structures and sources of funding, with different implications for the role of those who claimed expertise. The balance within the 'mixed economy' of knowledge changed over the nineteenth century, as it did in other aspects of economic and social life. Richard Drayton is puzzled by the late formation of the British Academy, which was provoked by the first meeting of the International Association of Academies in 1900 to mark the bicentenary of the Berlin Academy. The *Academie Française* had an even longer history from its foundation in 1635. He explains the lag by the willingness of Victorian intellectuals to accept that propertied independence was preferable to dependence on the state. Further, he argues that the British state was hostile to funding research in general, and to the humanities in particular. His case has some support from the low level of spending on libraries compared with many Continental European states (McKitterick); the limited state support for British universities which was equivalent to the grant just to the Zurich Polytechnic (Alberti); the earlier

[34] H. Hobhouse, *The Crystal Palace and the Great Exhibition: Art, Science and Productive Industry: A History of the Royal Commission for the Exhibition of 1851* (London, 2002).

[35] For this approach to welfare, see G. B. M. Finlayson, *Citizen, State and Social Welfare in Britain, 1830–1990* (Oxford, 1994).

creation of German or French schools in Rome and Athens (Stray and Beard); and the absence of historical projects on the scale of the *Monumenta* (Bentley). A number of contemporaries did complain of the parsimony of British state support of museums and libraries.[36] But does Drayton's proposition rest on a particular assumption about the role of the state which many contemporaries would not have accepted? A different conclusion might be drawn from an analysis of the values of the period.

A reduction in state funding and a preference for voluntarism were general phenomena in the second and third quarters of the nineteenth century as the 'fiscal military state' of the long eighteenth century was dismantled. Of course, state involvement was not entirely absent. The state did invest in the Public Record Office (PRO) and British Museum, as it did in the Royal Observatory at Greenwich from 1675, in the scientific work of the Admiralty, and in the mapping of the geology of Britain and its empire.[37] In an age of retrenchment, public science survived through its utility. If there was a lower level of spending on scholarly projects in the humanities, it was in part because—as Bentley points out—professional scholarship in Britain post-dated the consolidation of the state. In societies undergoing invasion, revolution and unification, the state sponsored historical knowledge in a way it need not do in Britain, where history could be left to amateurs and research had a low status. Most historical and archaeological writing was local, amateur or literary in the mid-Victorian period, reflecting the polite and gentlemanly culture of the Society of Antiquaries established in the 1580s, and the growing body of local record and archaeological societies. In Ranke's Prussia, historians became *Beamte*; in Britain, Macaulay was paid a £20,000 advance for volumes three and four of his history. Although the PRO and Royal Commission on Historical Manuscripts published calendars and catalogues,[38] historical research had low status until European standards of scholarship

[36] For example, G. W. Norman, *An Examination of Some Prevailing Opinions as to the Pressure of Taxation in This and Other Countries* (4th edn., London, 1864), pp. 10, 116–21.

[37] On one highly significant career, see R. A. Stafford, *Scientist of Empire: Sir Roderick Murchison, Scientific Exploration and Victorian Imperialism* (Cambridge, 1989). Murchison was similar to Banks in combining an official post, as Director-General of the Geological Survey, with positions in leading societies such as the Royal Geographical, so providing 'a crucial connection between the decentralised structure of British science and the imperial government. . . . Murchison manoeuvred to institutionalise natural science as an integral component of both imperial administration and foreign policy' (p. 1). On the role of John Barrow at the Admiralty, see F. Fleming, *Barrow's Boys* (London, 1998); and on the mapping of India by the Great Trigonometric Survey, M. H. Edney, *Mapping an Empire: The Geographical Construction of British India, 1765–1843* (Chicago, 1997).

[38] P. Levine, *The Amateur and the Professional: Antiquarians, Historians and Archaeologists in Victorian England, 1838–86* (Cambridge, 1986).

made an impact from the 1880s. But in the mid-Victorian period, it was widely believed that cultural provision, as with welfare and economic enterprise, should be left to voluntary impulse: the state delegated to subsidiary bodies, whether in local government, professional bodies, or charities, and supplied the legal framework within which they could operate. In this way, science and the arts were part of a wider process rather than being singled out for harsh treatment.

Here was a general trend, a decision on the structure of the state rather than hostility to science and the arts. As George Biddle Airy, the head of the Greenwich observatory, remarked in 1851, 'in Science, as well as in almost everything else, our national genius inclines us to prefer voluntary associations of private persons to organisation of any kind dependent on the state'.[39] He was writing at the time of the Great Exhibition, a mixture of initiatives so typical of the British polity in the mid-nineteenth century: it connected the Royal Society of Arts, private enterprise, local committees, the Crown and a Royal Commission of the great and good, without direct state involvement.[40] The approach was entirely normal in mid-nineteenth century Britain, with its aversion to direct state action and its positive commitment to individual initiative. Henry Cole, one of the key figures in the exhibition and in Victorian cultural life, celebrated the British way of doing things without compulsory taxes. 'No public works are ever executed by any foreign government which can vie for magnificence, completeness or perfection with those that our countrymen execute for themselves [hear, hear].' Similarly, Richard Jebb did not expect state support for the British schools in Athens and Rome in order to catch up with the earlier French and German institutes. Rather, he looked to a British Herodes Atticus for assistance. His approach was akin to Gladstone's assumption that state action in other countries was a sign of lack of philanthropic spirit compared with Britain, where the greatest endowments existed.[41] The lag between the formation of the *Academie Française* and the British Academy was not necessarily a sign of philistinism or lack of concern for the humanities. The *Academie* was more concerned with canonising the 'immortals' than anything more effective. Rather than complaining of the absence of an Academy and of state support, we might consider the widespread activities of bodies such as the Manchester Literary and Philosophical Society which was formed in 1781, and had close links with other bodies such as the Portico Library (1806), Royal

[39] Turner, *Contesting Cultural Authority*, p. 203.
[40] J. A. Auerbach, *The Great Exhibition of 1851: A Nation on Display* (New Haven and London, 1999).
[41] Hobhouse, *Crystal Palace Exhibition*, pp. 13–14; see below, pp. 376–8.

Manchester Institution (1823) and Manchester Statistical Society (1833). The phenomenon was not confined to aspiring provincial cities: in the counties, archaeological, naturalists and record societies proliferated. The result was a pluralistic and inclusive sense of English culture compared with Continental Europe, where there was more effort to create an 'official' canon of authors and a sense of the past.[42]

State involvement in cultural projects in Germany and France was much more easily implemented than in Britain. The careful vetting of public expenditure by the British parliament meant that every single item of spending had to be scrutinised.[43] In France and Germany, spending was more a matter of the will of the crown or executive. In Britain, crown involvement was part of this wider philanthropic endeavour: it assisted the Hellenic Society, a characteristic form of 'welfare monarchy' designed to encourage voluntarism and contain state action.[44] Both locally and nationally, private gifts could lever state action, as with the gifts of the Wills family that secured support from the city council for an art gallery in Bristol, or Henry Tate's support of a national gallery of British art.[45] As Alberti indicates, British cities had an active civic culture, expressed in learned societies, the creation of museums and art galleries to establish the status of urban elites and to stabilise class relations. By the late nineteenth century, the agents of a voluntaristic civic culture formed an alliance with local government in the creation of new civic colleges and the expansion of cultural institutions in most major cities.[46] Although many historians of Victorian Britain have argued that the urban elite distanced itself from the cities and fell into the embrace of the countryside,[47] the civic colleges provide a strong counter case. Their growth depended on a

[42] On literary and philosophical societies, see M. Neve, 'Science in a commercial city' and D. Orange, 'Rational dissent and provincial science: William Turner and the Newcastle Literary and Philosophical Society', in Inkster and Morrell (eds.), *Metropolis and Province*; on the inclusive and pluralistic nature of culture, see Collini, *Public Moralists.*

[43] M. Daunton, *Trusting Leviathan: The Politics of Taxation in Britain, 1799–1914* (Cambridge, 2001), ch. 3.

[44] F. Prochaska, *Royal Bounty: The Making of a Welfare Monarchy* (New Haven and London, 1995).

[45] H. E. Meller, *Leisure and the Changing City, 1870–1914* (London, 1976); F. Spalding, *The Tate: A History* (London, 1998).

[46] See also R. Morris, 'Structure, culture and society in British towns' in M. Daunton (ed.), *Cambridge Urban History of Britain, III, 1840–1950* (Cambridge, 2000); and R. Fox and A. Guagini (eds.), *Laboratories, Workshops and Sites: Concepts and Practice of Research in Industrial Europe, 1800–1914* (Berkeley, CA, 1999).

[47] F. M. L. Thompson, *The Rise of Respectable Society* (London, 1988), pp. 166, 173, 360; 'Town and city', in Thompson (ed.), *Cambridge Social History of Britain, 1750–1950, III, Regions and Communities* (Cambridge, 1990), pp. 47–8, 67, 72.

well-developed institutional culture and the consolidation of a provincial middle-class identity.

Such an approach also connects with the arguments of Lawrence Goldman who suggests that the apparent 'failure' of sociology as a discipline in Britain, the lack of new concepts and theories, should be read less as a sign of the limited mental world of Victorian Britain than a measure of the general diffusion of social thinking. The Social Science Association (SSA) offered another way of organising knowledge, not in a learned society or university discipline, but as a public body stimulating debate through empirical, synthetic and statistical analysis, an attempt to find regularities in social and moral behaviour akin to the shift of the natural sciences towards analysis. As in the case of history, limited concern for national identity, nationalism and questions of revolution and social structure affected the social sciences. The SSA focused on solvable, immediate issues of legislation and the compilation of data to show the regularities of social life. The wider cultural effects of the emergence of a market society were left to the literary-cultural sages—Carlyle and Ruskin—and to novelists and poets. As Goldman argues, Victorian society was intensely self-critical; social science was not an academic discipline but a matter of public engagement. The earlier emergence of academic disciplines in the social sciences in other countries may be seen as a defensive retreat into the cloister rather than a sign of maturity compared with Britain.

Economics did make a shift to formal academic status, moving from a more generalist and widely diffused political economy to a more exact and technical economics. Even so, the development was slow. In 1890, when the British Economic Association was formed, there were only two full-time professors of economics, in Cambridge and Liverpool; and the *Economic Journal* was not linked with a university as in the case of the *Quarterly Journal of Economics* (Harvard) and the *Journal of Political Economy* (Chicago). Only 86 of the British Economic Association's 501 members in 1891 came from universities, compared with 113 from business, 51 lawyers and 48 bankers (Tribe). The economics tripos at Cambridge was only created in 1903 when it broke away from the moral sciences tripos.

The retreat of the state from direct involvement in cultural institutions may be seen as a strategy of removing the state from issues which were deeply contentious and divisive. So long as there was a tussle for cultural authority between clergy and scientists, government grants were not feasible. The relationship between science, the arts and culture and the state started to change in the later nineteenth and early twentieth centuries. The success of the SSA was in providing a venue for discussion absent in the formal structures of the state. In the second quarter of the nineteenth century, the official machinery of government still lacked expertise and politicians turned to knowledge generated outside the state. In the final quarter of the nineteenth century, the emergence of an expert civil service meant that more knowledge was generated within the state, and there was greater confidence in the ability of officials to understand social processes. The result was to shift the balance of advantage away from bodies such as the SSA and the medical profession to the state and parliament.[48]

Similarly, scientific rhetoric shifted in the later nineteenth century, away from the role of science in free trade and peace to a concern for security and military preparedness. Scientists criticised politicians and short-sighted electors who did not supply enough money and so threatened national security and economic efficiency: science was seen as the victim of democracy.[49] For example, Rayleigh campaigned for the creation of a state-funded National Physical Laboratory which was founded in 1900 by his brother-in-law's government to make links between science and industry. When it opened in 1902, the same year as the creation of the Academy, the Prince of Wales remarked that it was 'the first instance of the State taking part in scientific research... Does it not show in a very practical way that the nation is beginning to realise that if its commercial supremacy is to be maintained, greater facilities must be given for furthering the application of science to commerce and industry?'[50] Of course, some historians take the scientists' account at face value in order to indicate the state's failure to invest in science, a neglect they often link with an assumption that the educational system and cultural values were skewed towards the classics, English, and history. More plausibly, the scientists' rhetoric should be read as a cultural account by one professional group, and moreover one which succeeded in securing state support.[51] At the time, it seemed to classicists that they were on the defensive, and they needed to devise their own forms of protection.

[48] L. Goldman, *Science, Reform and Politics in Victorian Britain: The Social Science Association, 1857–1886* (Cambridge 2002), pp. 298, 301, 319, 339–45, 345–63; F. Mort, *Dangerous Sexualities: Medico-Moral Politics in England since 1830* (London, 1987).

[49] Turner, *Contesting Cultural Authority*, ch. 8; see also R. MacLeod, *Public Science and Public Policy in Victorian England* (Aldershot, 1996), chs. 7–9 on government support for science and the campaign for the 'endowment' of science which succeeded from 1900: research was defined as a resource to be cultivated like labour and capital. Scientists argued that their promise should be financed and that they be left to their own devices. They needed to create a sense of urgency and of value in investment in science, against the competing claims that the state should use its resources to reduce poverty or improve urban conditions.

[50] <www.npl.co.uk/about/historical_events/1902.html> last accessed on 24 Feb. 2004.

[51] D. Edgerton, *Warfare State: Militarism, Expertise and Twentieth-Century Britain*, forthcoming.

The role of the universities as centres of research became much greater towards the end of the nineteenth century. Unlike in Germany, the professoriate had fewer claims to status and intellectual authority. In Oxford and Cambridge, the dons—teaching fellows of colleges—had more power over the syllabus than the professors. By the end of the century, professors were gaining more power and status, and shifting the universities towards research in terms of an advancement of knowledge, on the lines of Germany. In classics, for example, the approach of Housman at Cambridge was very different from Jowett at Oxford a generation earlier. Medicine also moved into the universities with the merger of medical colleges with the civic universities and university of London, shifting to laboratory-based training. Local businessmen were concerned about industrial competition and invested in new laboratories. The Royal Geographical Society turned to Oxbridge to promote education and research in response to its own institutional dynamic as it turned from costly expeditions, seeking a new function with the completion of mapping and attempting to resolve the tensions over the admission of women to membership.[52] By the end of Victoria's reign, universities were moving to the centre of the organisation of knowledge, in a way that had not been true at the start of the period when they were both few in number and somewhat marginal in their engagement in research. In the later nineteenth century, the university of Cambridge successfully redefined itself as a major research university on the German model, and the provincial colleges of England followed a similar trajectory. Of course, the Scottish universities had their own distinctive identity.[53]

How important was imperialism in the changing role of the universities? At Cambridge, both the King Edward VII Professorship of English Literature and the Professorship of Imperial and Naval History were financed by Harold Harmsworth, later Lord Rothermere, owner of the *Daily Mail* and *The Times*, and advocate of imperialism. The reformation of the colleges of South Kensington into Imperial College suggests that servicing the needs of the Edwardian empire was at least one impulse. At Oxford, the diploma in anthropology was created in 1905 to train colonial officials, and the emergence of archaeology, Egyptology and oriental languages also had clear connections with imperialism. But the relationship between academic disciplines

[52] On the history of geography, see D. N. Livingstone, *The Geographical Tradition: Episodes in the History of a Contested Enterprise* (Oxford, 1992), especially chs. 6 and 7.

[53] For example, R. D. Anderson, *Education and Opportunity in Victorian Scotland* (1983) and M. Moss, J. F. Munro and R. H. Trainor, *University, City and State: The University of Glasgow since 1870* (Edinburgh, 2000).

and the empire was not simply one of complacent orientalism. Sanskritists such as Max Muller (the Professor of Sanskrit at Oxford) and George Grierson (Indian civil servant, superintendent of the Linguistic Survey of India, and fellow of the Academy from 1917) argued against the idea of Indian inferiority propounded by 'scientific' racialism. The Sanskritists argued that Aryans in India and Europe were joined by language and race rather than divided—a view expressed by the Indian Institute at Oxford. It opened in 1889, with an inscription in Sanskrit announcing that 'This building, dedicated to Eastern sciences, was founded for the use of Aryas (Indians and Englishmen) by excellent and benevolent men desirous of encouraging knowledge. May the mutual friendship of India and England constantly increase!'[54] As Max Jones suggests, imperialism was only one factor at work in the turn of geography towards the universities, and much the same applies to Imperial College.

At the time of the creation of the British Academy, the interests of state, industry, empire and science were intersecting in new, highly complicated ways. The formation of Imperial College from the science colleges in South Kensington reflected a shift in perspectives on Britain's economic problems.[55] At the Great Exhibition, the concern was taste: how to ensure that British goods could compete with those of France in style and elegance, a task to be fulfilled by training artists at the Government Schools of Design and National Art Training School, and exhibiting good design at the South Kensington (Victoria and Albert) Museum. By 1902, the emphasis had shifted from taste to science, from France to Germany, both in economic competition and state rivalry. The dominance of British industry was now threatened by Germany, not least because of its 'quite exceptional wealth of scientific knowledge and training'. Cole's confidence in the superiority of private initiatives now seemed suspect, not least to scientists. At the Great Exhibition, science was enrolled in the cause of peace. At the end of the nineteenth century, science moved towards nationalism and militarism, and scientists claimed that the state should provide them with more money as a measure of national security. In 1902, in the aftermath of the Boer War, the eighth duke of Devonshire (whose father created the Cavendish laboratory), Lord Rosebery (the former prime minister and leading Liberal Imperialist)

[54] G. W. Stocking, *Victorian Anthropology* (New York, 1987); and *After Tylor: British Social Anthropology, 1888–1951* (Madison, 1995); T. R. Trautmann, *Aryans and British India* (Berkeley, 1997).

[55] On similar trends in the provinces see Fox and Guagini (eds.), *Laboratories, Workshops and Sites*, and Alberti in this volume.

and A. J. Balfour (the Conservative prime minister) proposed the formation of Imperial College in response to the great research centres of the German Reich at Charlottenberg and the university of Berlin. The initiative came to fruition in 1907.[56]

At the end of the period, the relationship between the state, civil society, universities, and knowledge was changing in many ways. Although many historians have argued that the British state and the governing elite at the end of the nineteenth century were dominated by classicists who were hostile to science and technology, in reality the state was militant and technological, turning to scientists in the reformed universities and within its own agencies to create effective machinery for war and to sustain a strong economy. The British Academy was created at around the same time as the reformation of Imperial College and the establishment of the National Physical Laboratory, so that it could be seen as a defensive reaction against a threat to the old cultural authority of the classics and humanities. Nevertheless, a simple story of tension between 'two cultures' is misplaced. As we have seen, Balfour was himself a philosopher and founding fellow of the Academy who served as president from 1921 to 1928; as prime minister, he linked the humanities with the world of politics, science and imperial strategy. Similarly, Rosebery was involved with the creation of Imperial College; he was also a historian of Pitt and Napoleon, and was another founding fellow. In 1908, George Nathaniel Curzon was elected to the fellowship, reflecting his work as a historian and commentator on the politics of the Middle East as well as his involvement with the archaeology of India during his time as viceroy. The humanities were deeply involved with public concerns, alongside science and technology rather than in opposition to them. The year 1902 was also important for the passage of the education act and the expansion of secondary education, with its demand for more teachers in the expanding grammar schools. The Academy marked not just a culmination of trends in the Victorian period, but the beginning of a new era of professionalised disciplines, the ascendancy of universities as research institutions, and the development of clear curricula from the grammar schools to higher education.

The chapters in this book place the establishment of the Academy in the context of the Victorian organisation of knowledge; another volume would be needed to look forward from 1902 to the present, and the Academy's publication of its report on the 'knowledge economy'—an attempt to convince the Treasury that the humanities and social sciences are as valuable to

[56] Hobhouse, *Crystal Palace and the Great Exhibition*, pp. 258–64. I am grateful to Hannah Gay for providing insights from her forthcoming book on Imperial College.

society as science and technology.[57] State funding has become ever more important, with all that entails in the way of audit and control. In his concluding essay, Richard Drayton complains of the British state's low level of support for humanities in the past, and he criticises the rhetoric of the independent propertied scholar which limited action. Others might now look back with nostalgia to a lost world of independence, and hope that Herodes Atticus might again appear to endow universities and scholarship.[58] Victorians looked to the museums and schools of Paris and the reformed universities of Germany; their successors are more inclined to look across the Atlantic to the great private universities and galleries of the United States. The experience of the past century since the creation of the British Academy is another, complex, story of changing definitions of knowledge, processes of legitimation, flows of funding, and mechanisms of popularisation.

[57] British Academy, *'That Full Complement of Riches': The Contributions of the Arts, Humanities and Social Sciences to the Nation's Wealth* (London, 2004).
[58] See below, p. 376.

CHAPTER TWO

Science in Nineteenth-Century England: Plural Configurations and Singular Politics

JOHN PICKSTONE

There can be few locales for which the history of science, technology and medicine is better known than for Victorian England. Most of Britain's historians of science over the last thirty years have contributed something to this area, and so have many historians in North America. Good studies abound—for science, ideology and religion; for politics, class relations and gender; for research schools, laboratories and museums; for knowledge and practice; for field-work and the business of publication; and for metropolis, provinces and empire.[1] True, the history of technology is relatively underdeveloped, including military and agricultural technologies, but all disciplines have areas of relative weakness. It is perhaps more challenging to ask about absences in the heartlands, as it were—about the questions still to be advanced where the scholarship is densest and the information seems most available.

Some of these concern the relations between cognitive and social structures. There is wonderful and expansive work on the British Association of the

I owe thanks to Jack Morrell, Sam Alberti, Andrew Cunningham and David Edgerton for comments on earlier outlines and drafts, and to the Wellcome Trust for support.

[1] Recent reviews of nineteenth-century science include David Cahan (ed.), *From Natural Philosophy to the Sciences. Writing the History of Nineteenth-Century Science* (Chicago, 2003), which is international, arranged largely by disciplines, contains a large, consolidated bibliography, and has a chapter by Cahan on social organisation. Four volumes of *The Cambridge History of Science,* series editors David C. Lindberg and Ronald L. Numbers, include articles on the nineteenth century: vol. 5, Mary Jo Nye (ed.), *The Modern Physical and Mathematical Sciences* (Cambridge, 2002); vol. 7, Theodore M. Porter and Dorothy Ross (eds.), *The Modern Social Sciences* (Cambridge, 2003); vol. 6, Peter Bowler and John V. Pickstone (eds.), *The Modern Earth and Biological Sciences* (forthcoming); and vol. 8, David N. Livingstone and Ronald L. Numbers (eds.), *Modern Science in National and International Contexts* (forthcoming), in which the article on Britain 1750–2000 is by David Edgerton and John V. Pickstone.

Advancement of Science (BAAS), the politics of science, Darwin and Huxley, on geology and evolution, and on mathematics and energy,[2] but overall, the literature, by its very virtues, might be seen as begging *general* questions on the relations between scientific content and institutions. For example, to summarise as questions the concerns of this chapter—how might we problematise, for British sciences, the emergence of new disciplines, their different institutional niches, and their federation into the British version of Science as an apparently unitary enterprise?[3] In recent work I have tried to address related framework questions for modern science, technology and medicine generally;[4] in this essay I use some of these tools to try to characterise the sciences and their politics in nineteenth-century Britain.

Framework-thinking has been unpopular in recent decades, because of the cohabitation of micro-empiricist practices with a postmodern suspicion of grand narratives. But if we do not get new frameworks, we shall continue to use old ones against which most of the case studies were directed. Or we diminish the intellectual standards and utility of our enterprise by tacitly using concepts that are not set out for criticism. To give but one example, many historians of science seem now to accept that there was a 'second scientific revolution' around 1800; they know that the meaning of 'science' then changed considerably, at least in Britain; indeed, some would claim that many disciplines, even Science itself, were products of this period. But the general literature on this complex issue remains miniscule in comparison with that on the seventeenth-century scientific revolution—a topic of debate that we inherit from the 1950s. To caricature but slightly: scarcely anyone now 'believes' in the first scientific

[2] For example, Jack Morrell and Arnold Thackray, *Gentlemen of Science. Early Years of the British Association for the Advancement of Science* (Oxford, 1981); Roy Macleod's two collections of essays: *Public Science and Public Policy in Victorian England* (Aldershot, 1996) and *The 'Creed of Science' in Victorian England* (Aldershot, 2000); Janet Browne, *Darwin*, vol. 1, *Voyaging*, vol. 2, *The Power of Place* (London, 1995, 2002); Adrian Desmond and James Moore, *Darwin* (London, 1992); Adrian Desmond, *Huxley* (London, 1998); Martin Rudwick, *The Great Devonian Controversy: The Shaping of Scientific Knowledge Among Gentlemanly Specialists* (Chicago, 1985); James A. Secord, *Controversy in Victorian Geology: The Cambrian–Silurian Dispute* (Princeton, 1986), and *Victorian Sensation* (Chicago, 2001); Crosbie Smith and Norton Wise, *Energy and Empire: A Biographical Study of Lord Kelvin* (Cambridge, 1989); Crosbie Smith, *The Science of Energy: A Cultural History of Energy Physics in Victorian Britain* (London, 1998).

[3] I will capitalise Science when referring to this claimed unity; science without a capital will be used for knowledge in general. I have begun to explore some of the later consequences of the British construction in my 'Innovation, diverse knowledges, and the presumed singularity of Science', in Helga Nowotny (ed.), *Cultures of Innovation* (Oxford, 2005).

[4] John V. Pickstone, *Ways of Knowing. A New History of Science, Technology and Medicine* (Manchester, 2000 and Chicago, 2001).

revolution, but good general studies continue to appear; for the second scientific revolution, quite the reverse seems to be the case.[5]

If we do not focus, sometimes, on large issues for recent centuries, then we will scarcely be able to answer the most obvious questions about Victorian science—such as 'what was nineteenth-century about it?' And if we cannot characterise and periodise nineteenth-century science transnationally, we will be seriously handicapped in answering a second obvious question about Victorian science—'what was British about it?' Such questions seem to me significant, whether for linking with political and social histories of Britain and other nations, for the better contextualisation of micro studies, or simply for understanding the diversity of natural knowledges over time. To give adequate accounts of sciences in one country and century, we need better analytical frames in which to conduct comparisons across time and space.

We might then go further. The better we can characterise Victorian science, technology and medicine analytically, in contrast with other times and places, the better placed we will be to highlight the various standpoints and perspectives adopted by the historical actors. Specifically, if we can see the *variety* of their sciences, we might better understand their construction of 'Science' as an apparently single enterprise, under which banner they could all call for support and funds. As historians we may need to see the *unity* of such political constructions against the *diversity* of practices and interests in the social worlds of the sciences.

This essay covers and, it is hoped, connects, three aspects of nineteenth-century Science—the diversity of conceptual structures, the relations of various sciences with state and professional institutions, and the meanings of Science as a claimed unity. For the first, I begin by suggesting a model for the configurations of natural knowledge in the late eighteenth century. I then argue for the emergence of a series of parallel analytical disciplines in the decades around 1800. My model of nineteenth-century science—after the 'second scientific revolution'—is of parallel 'sciences', each with its own elements, and each related to aspects of natural history and natural philosophy. In the second section—on sciences and 'institutions'—I suggest that these disciplines owed much to French museums and professional schools, and then to German universities. For those countries and for Britain, I briefly ask how the analytical disciplines continued to relate to state institutions and to scientific professions such as medicine and engineering. But these relations were not just about the sciences in their diversity. Perhaps especially for

[5] James A. Secord, 'Introduction' (to 'The Big Picture' special issue), *The British Journal for the History of Science*, 26 (1993), 387–90.

Britain, they were about Science in the singular, here meaning the physical and biological sciences taken together and presented in terms of common methods and understandings. That claim to unity, as made and remade in a class-divided society, is the focus of my third section.

My discussion of Science arises in part from the recent writings of Andrew Cunningham and his colleagues, who maintained, correctly, that natural philosophy prior to about 1800, and Science thereafter, were different activities which need to be analytically separated, rather than being run together in a continuous, perhaps transcendent, history of natural knowledge. In Wittgensteinian terms, Science in the nineteenth-century sense was a game with rules that were radically different from those of natural philosophy, which for Cunningham was the previous 'game' concerned with natural knowledge. I want to push this discussion further, in part by dissenting from the view that general labels such as natural philosophy and Science can be taken as defining 'the game' for particular periods. In outlining a model for the later century, I will suggest that natural philosophy was then but one of the relevant games. But more importantly for this essay, I want to further problematise 'Science' by suggesting that the word did not define a game such as chess, with well-specified rules; it was a collective. If we may continue the game game, I am suggesting that 'Science' might have worked more like 'athletics'—a (variable) set of games with organisation in common; or perhaps more like 'sport'—a number of games, with their own organisations, which were variously seen as similar and were sometimes judged or promoted together. Neither of these sporting choices seems adequate alone—but together they may help us define a useful set of organisational questions, directing us to the historical politics of unity and diversity, and preventing us from taking Science as a given.[6]

In this essay I use the excellent secondary literature on the politics of Science to develop the hypothesis that Science, as a supposedly unitary body of knowledge, was invented in an England that was newly disparate, cognitively as well as geographically; that claims for the unity of Science served to hold together the emergent analytical disciplines for purposes that were variously political. In the third section of this essay, I explore this theme by considering three generations of 'scientists': first, the Anglican gentlemen of the BAAS in the 1830s; secondly, T. H. Huxley and his metropolitan,

[6] Andrew Cunningham and Perry Williams, 'De-centring the big picture: *The Origins of Modern Science* and the modern origins of science', *British Journal for the History of Science*, 26 (1991), 407–32; Andrew Cunningham, 'Getting the game right: some plain words on the identity and invention of science', *Studies in the History and Philosophy of Science*, 19 (1988), 365–89.

educationist friends from the 1850s; and thirdly, a few professors who developed research laboratories from the 1870s. In each case, I ask what they understood by Science and how the claims to unity may have been related to the social and political projects variously characteristic of each generation. I will argue that the meaning of Science, over the century, changed markedly, reflecting shifts of class and geography.

But to understand the formations of the nineteenth century, we must first understand what came before them.

The Changing Structures of Knowledge

Before the second scientific revolution

No one in 1750, say, used the word 'science' in the sense that became common in the nineteenth century; the word still referred to knowledge in general. The science of medicine, say, was such knowledge as attached to the reflective, reasoned, liberal art of medicine. Words such as 'biology' or 'geology' or 'physics' did not exist or did not denote disciplinary entities that the Victorians would recognise. So what was the structure of eighteenth-century knowings in the areas later encompassed as Science? Where can we start to discuss the formation of nineteenth-century configurations?

I suggest that we model this eighteenth-century knowledge as made up of three ways of knowing. First, descriptive and classificatory studies; secondly, mathematical analysis of natural phenomena and artefacts; and thirdly, general theories about nature, God and man. In actor's terms, these respectively become natural history, mixed mathematics, and natural philosophy. Natural history described what was in the world—from rocks to angels.[7] Mixed mathematics analysed patterns—not what moved, or why, but how?[8] Natural philosophy explained the world qualitatively—from first principles of which there were several varieties.[9] Matter and motion were universal

[7] N. Jardine, J. A. Secord and E. C. Spary (eds.), *Cultures of Natural History* (Cambridge, 1996).

[8] On mixed mathematics see John Heilbron, 'A mathematicians' mutiny, with morals', in Paul Horwich (ed.), *World Changes. Thomas Kuhn and the Nature of Science* (Boston, 1993), pp. 81–129, esp. pp. 81–2; and his 'Experimental natural philosophy', in G. S. Rousseau and Roy Porter (eds.), *The Ferment of Knowledge. Studies in the Historiography of Eighteenth-Century Science* (Cambridge, 1980).

[9] Simon Schaffer, 'Natural philosophy' in Rousseau and Porter (eds.), *Ferment*; Lawrence Brockliss, 'Science, the universities, and other public spaces: teaching science in Europe and the Americas', in Roy Porter (ed.), *Eighteenth-Century Science*, vol. 4 of the *The Cambridge History of Science* (Cambridge, 2003), pp. 44–86.

elements for some savants, but it was hard to dispense with the Greek four-elements in chemistry and parts of medicine.

Natural history here has to be understood widely, as encompassing accounts of artefacts and indeed of certain experiments; but this wider-than-ours usage in fact accords with that of the eighteenth century. The 'scientific revolution' of the seventeenth century, by which accounts of the forms of plants, say, had been detached from considerations of botanical mythology, etymology, emblematics etc., had also enlarged the scope of natural knowledge to include the works of man as well as those of God. And this same 'Baconian' tradition also included the effects of men on natural objects; the results of 'torturing nature' were recorded as 'experimental histories'.[10]

From the same period, the success of mixed mathematics had allowed the partial replacement of the qualitative, earth-centred natural philosophy of Aristotle by the quantitative, universalistic aspirations of Newtonianism; but success was limited, and for most of the world, and especially for qualitative change, savants operated at the level of natural history and natural philosophy—description and classification plus hypothetical, general explanations.

But additionally, especially towards the end of the century, they looked to limited operational regularities which sat between specifics and first-principles, to pragmatic concepts which seemed to work in particular fields of study—to the membranes which interested some doctors as components of many different organs, to the recombinations of salts, acids and alkalis with which chemists worked, or to the recurrent superpositions of rocks which surveyors were beginning to describe.[11] Experimental philosophy, where it went beyond experimental histories, sought regularities of this sort, especially for heat, magnetism and electricity;[12] but non-experimental studies, such as anatomy, also sought their elements.

When considering the antecedents of nineteenth-century Science, Theodore Porter recently concluded that 'Up to date Anglophone historians of early modern science, eschewing anachronism, are left with no encompassing label to designate their object of study but only a multitude of antique names: natural philosophy, natural history, experimental physics, mixed mathematics'. This seems to me correct in fact but wrong in tone. To my

[10] Pickstone, *Ways of Knowing*, pp. 137–9.

[11] Heilbron, 'Experimental natural philosophy'; for chemistry, see Ursula Klein, 'Origin of the concept of chemical compound', *Science in Context*, 7 (1994), 163–204; for geology, Martin Rudwick, 'The emergence of a visual language for geological science, 1760–1840', *History of Science* (1976), 149–95.

[12] Heilbron, 'Experimental natural philosophy', esp. p. 374.

mind, Porter's is a hopeful conclusion. The forms of knowledge so named are not irredeemably antique, and these terms may continue to point us to persistent components of natural knowledge—to general explanations of the world, to description and classification, to the search for pragmatic regularities, and to mathematical reductions. Such terms help us realise the *range* of methods and concerns which were operative in the eighteenth century, and which continued to be relevant, albeit developed in radically different configurations under the newly constructed umbrella of Science.[13]

The social structure of natural knowledge in Britain was congruent with its intellectual configuration. Natural history was socially prestigious, not least for its connections with landed estates and imperial expansion. Much of the *Proceedings of the Royal Society of London* was taken up with reports of singular occurrences, and the President, Sir Joseph Banks, was involved with royal promotions of agricultural improvement and of voyages of exploration and appropriation. The particular subject areas of natural history were but weakly delimited, and many enthusiasts collected plants and rocks, birds and antiquities. Though specialist societies were appearing in London which encouraged members to focus, say on plants, many naturalists were interested in a range of objects, especially those collected in their particular locality.[14]

Natural history, even in specialist societies, was accessible to men (and women) without special education; but mixed mathematics was more demanding. As John Heilbron and others have shown, the relations between mathematicians and natural historians could be fraught. When Banks was elected President, the mathematicians in the Royal Society feared its degeneration into a 'cabinet of trifling curiosities'. Their fears were confirmed when Banks blocked the election of two mathematicians; but the consequent rebellion of 1784 against Banks failed. A majority felt the Society needed its royal and aristocratic connections, and especially its 'men of general literature' who had little difficulty forming 'a right opinion concerning the general value of philosophical observations and experiments which are produced at the Society's meetings'.[15] Newton's fame, it was said, rested on his contributions to natural philosophy, appreciation of which did not demand high mathematical proficiency.

At much the same time, other expert groupings were beginning to emerge. The Royal Society of Medicine provided a meeting point for reformist physicians, many of whom were interested in chemistry and natural philosophy as well as medical science. There was no special society of chemists, but the

13 Theodore S. Porter, 'The social sciences', in Cahan (ed.), *From Natural Philosophy*, p. 257.
14 On provincial and London scientific societies see Morrell and Thackray, *Gentlemen*, pp. 12–19.
15 Heilbron, 'Mathematicians' mutiny', p. 88.

Royal Institution—founded in 1799 as part of efforts to better the condition of the poor—came to support a laboratory which was largely used for chemical and electrical studies.[16] The Animal Chemistry Club, which brought together doctors and chemists, was founded as an informal affiliate of the Royal Society; and the new general scientific societies of the provinces contained much chemistry. The Manchester Literary and Philosophical Society, founded in 1781 from a doctor's dining club, supported a laboratory for John Dalton, who made his living as a teacher of mathematics and natural philosophy but contributed chiefly to chemistry.

One can see here some emergent specialist groupings of savants, but the major knowledge formations remained general and extensive; indeed Banks did all he could to prevent specialisation. Physiology remained the theory of medicine (part of natural philosophy), and chemistry stretched across natural philosophy, medicine and the chemical crafts. In the spaces where the biomedical and earth disciplines later emerged, the major formations remained natural-historical: this natural history included the heavens, and it articulated closely with the natural theology.[17]

To early Victorian configurations

When by the 1820s, Britain emerged victorious from the French wars and the subsequent depression, its scientific landscape had changed and continued to do so rapidly. I do not wish to argue that the evident specialisation depended solely on new intellectual formations or on Continental models. New natural history societies in the provinces around 1830, for example, might well be seen as part of the differentiation of an expanding urban middle class, alongside the proliferation of chapels and of medical charities; but that is only part of the story. Whereas the majority of the amateurs who followed the sciences continued to do so at the level of natural history, many of the new activists were proponents of analytical approaches which they had learned directly or indirectly from the Continent, or which had been developed in parallel from British roots. To an extent which needs researching, the institutional differentiation of science depended on new paradigms and research programmes that were discipline specific, and perhaps on the awareness of British researchers that they were competing with men for whom research was a part of their professional duties.

[16] Morris Berman, *Social Change and Scientific Organisation: The Royal Institution, 1799–1844* (London, 1978).

[17] On this and later forms of organisation, see the useful narrative history by Colin A. Russell, *Science and Social Change, 1700–1900* (London, 1983).

I tried in *Ways of Knowing* to show how and why one may characterise the new disciplines as analytical. They each involved elements, such as chemical elements, tissues or strata, that were peculiar to that discipline, and in terms of which the objects and phenomena of the discipline could be analysed. The elements were no longer matter and motion, which served in most of mixed mathematics and which were potentially universal; rather they were discipline-specific and pragmatic. Chemistry analysed substances into chemical elements—into substances which had not (yet) been themselves split; the new mineralogy relied on new ideas of unit crystals to go beyond mere taxonomy; geology explained landscapes and earth history in terms of newly conceptualised strata, and puzzled over the relations of strata in different sites or countries; phrenology analysed human character into faculties, the development of which could be assessed from the shape of an individual's skull; pathological anatomy used tissues, the lesions of which were the true basis of diseases; comparative anatomy, zoology and botany operated chiefly in terms of organs, to analyse form and function. Political economy reduced complex social phenomena to mathematical relations between population and resource growth, or agricultural fertility and land rents; and languages found in philology their new elements and laws. The physical sciences dealt with elements such as 'heat', mechanical action, magnetism or light—some of which were created from regularities in the Baconian experimental sciences of the eighteenth century, some of which could be measured and treated mathematically, thus linking with the mixed mathematical formations of the previous century.[18]

On the basis of such analyses, I then argued, *experimentation* could achieve a new meaning. By experiments one could try-out the *interactions* of elements, whether in chemistry, physical sciences or physiology; not just to confirm the analysis (though this was important), but to 'synthesise', to explore new possible 'combinations' and 'effects'. I suggested that Faraday, for instance, was primarily concerned with the mutual reactions of physical elements, and that such approaches became more common at the end of the nineteenth century, as outlined below. I certainly do not wish to deny the experimentalist possibilities in early nineteenth-century sciences, but to my mind, the key to understanding the sciences of the early century *and* to seeing the shifts in the later century, is to recognise the centrality of analysis in the decades around 1800—in sciences of dynamic systems as well as those of static configurations. We should not be misled by claims about Scientific

[18] Pickstone, *Ways of Knowing*, chs. 4 and 5.

Method, as if they were more or less stable from the seventeenth century, and as if experimentation had a constant meaning that was always central; rather, we need to focus on the historical question of what happened to eighteenth-century formations after about 1800.

I am suggesting here that sections of natural historical studies, and of mixed mathematics, along with the emergent components of experimental philosophy, became bound into analytical disciplines which focused on pragmatic elements for particular domains of nature. I am further suggesting that this process is not to be seen simply as a differentiation of previous natural knowledge, but as a radically new configuration in which questions of the unity of natural knowledge were deeply problematical. Natural philosophy, one might suggest, did not continue as an old stock or trunk, dividing into branches; rather, at least in England, a new unity of Science was proclaimed in the face of a new diversity of analytical sciences.

Sciences and Institutions

France and England: museums and the scientific professions

Many of the new analytical disciplines were in large measure the creation of the professional schools and state collections set up (or reformed) in France after the Revolution. It was at the Museum of Natural History in Paris that nineteenth-century zoology and botany and mineralogy took shape; the same institution was important for stratigraphy, as was the German school of mines at Freiburg. The museum also had links with the medical schools (and the private medical classes) in which the anatomy and physiology of tissues was developed, along with the routines of clinical examination and autopsy which constituted the new hospital medicine. For chemistry, the French workers were attached to the Academy of Sciences, the Museum, or to government projects such as for gunpowder. For the physical sciences, the teachers and products of the Ecole Polytechnique were crucial. Though I do not wish to claim any simple and comprehensive causal connection, I do believe that the demands of these new organisations, especially for pedagogical organisation and textbooks, provided both incentives and resources for the creation of analytical programmes deliberately situated between the specificities of natural history and the generalities of natural philosophy.[19]

[19] For references on the analytical sciences in France, see Pickstone, *Ways of Knowing*, chs. 4 and 5.

The French institutional pattern seems to have been little explored as a template for Britain, and, indeed, Britain did not develop engineering schools or medical schools after the French model. Its engineering was mostly civil, at least to the 1890s, and most of the training was by apprenticeship till late in the century, when it was in universities or new, lower technical colleges rather than in separate polytechnics on the Continental pattern. Until the same period, English medical education (though not Scottish) was dominated by medical schools which were run as adjuncts to charity hospitals, and the predominant mode of practice was the natural historical method of elite physicians. Only at the end of the century were the London schools incorporated into London University, following a pattern which was already succeeding in the provinces. In as much as the emphasis in British medical and engineering education was on the techniques of professional practice, there was relatively little space for the autonomy and advance of pre-professional, analytical disciplines, perhaps even when incorporated into universities. In London and the English provinces *circa* 1900, the medical schools remained dominated by clinicians; and though the teachers of analytical anatomy and physiology were by then career academics, they were rarely able to propagate their discipline by research; they were chiefly educators and/or administrators.[20]

If we focus on the biological sciences, however, for all that they were much smaller in student numbers, then mid-century London looks a little more Parisian. By 1860, London boasted the Geological Survey, the Museum of Economic Geology, the School of Mines, and the Royal College of Chemistry—all supported directly by the state. The disciplinary base had been enlarged from geology to include chemistry, botany, zoology and physical science—all sciences which could be presented as required for the analysis of specimens. This whole complex, together with Kew Gardens, somewhat resembled the Museum of Natural History (and School of Mines) in Paris, albeit with less funding and less teaching. Museums were crucial to this London activity. The expansion of state science to include science education for schoolteachers (here drawing on the French Normal schools), and technical education for the workers, benefited from the 1851 exhibition and the funding for the South Kensington site. The natural history collections of the British Museum moved there in 1883, alongside the museums for geology and for manufactures.[21]

[20] Christopher Lawrence, *Medicine in the Making of Modern Britain, 1700–1920* (London, 1994); Stella Butler, 'A transformation of training: the formation of university medical faculties in Manchester, Leeds and Liverpool, 1870–1884', *Medical History*, 30 (1986), 115–31.

[21] Sophie Forgan, 'The architecture of display: museums, universities and objects in nineteenth-century Britain', *History of Science*, 32 (1994), 139–62.

We shall return to this institutional complex below when we discuss the work of T. H. Huxley and his friends, but first we turn to the other major Continental model—the German universities and especially their research schools; for it was in such research schools that academic scientists found a role which was not dependent on professions outside the university, nor on large hospitals or state museums. Of course, universities could carry many of the functions of higher professional education—but with a potential difference of crucial importance for the future of the sciences. Universities were largely run by academics, and in defining academic life around the creation of new knowledge and of new researchers, German universities pioneered a form of social and intellectual growth and reproduction which proved immensely powerful. Whereas a chemist in a medical school helped educate practitioners, a chemist in a research university made more chemists through making more chemistry—reproduction of the institution was central to (some parts of some) universities, whilst it remained a secondary function of professional schools.[22]

Germany and England: universities and research

Where France boasted national museums and high-level professional schools for doctors, engineers and teachers, the key German institutional type was the reformed, neo-humanist university with its stress on the creation of new knowledge in a wide range of disciplines. Analytical research programmes in Germany were developed first for philology and mathematics, based on seminars and specialist libraries; they spread to the natural sciences, especially chemistry and physiology. Some emergent German methods were seen as opposed to Gallic analyses that seemed too reductive and thus in danger of losing the essence of phenomena. The morphological, romantic approach to minerals, plants and animals stressed the derivation of complex patterns from basic archetypes—perhaps involving bilateral symmetry or polarity. The same approaches were applied in physical sciences, not least electricity. It is plausibly argued that such approaches were important for embryology, histology, and for the emergence in physical sciences of concepts of energy and field.

I have suggested that we think of such morphological approaches as an alternative form of analysis, stressing derivation rather than composition.

[22] On German universities, see R. S. Turner, 'The growth of professorial research in Prussia, 1818–48: causes and contexts', *Historical Studies in the Physical Sciences*, 3 (1971), 137–82; and the very useful survey of science in German Europe by Kathryn Olesko to appear in vol. 8 of *The Cambridge History of Science*.

But at the start of the nineteenth century, they were presented as rooted in the claims of nature philosophy, rather than in the operations of particular professions or the need to classify the specimens of the world. In as much as they stressed the features of the knowing mind, they claimed a unity for all knowledge (which contrasted both with the French separation of analytical disciplines, and with the British delineation of Science). That unity of knowledege was seen as fundamental to particular sciences and particular professional practices. Medical doctors mattered, to be sure, but German professors had status way beyond that accorded in England.[23]

One should be careful not to overstate the difference—German universities were concerned with professional education as well as knowledge creation. In the case of chemistry, it is clear that professional education, for example of pharmacists, was crucial to the success of laboratories. Without large numbers of medical students, the history of chemistry and the medical sciences would doubtless have been different. And yet, for the most part, the reputation of the professors in these pre-professional subjects rested more on their contributions to research than to the profession of medicine; they were not waiting to be appointed to clinical chairs, or to succeed in private practice as common in England. As we noted, chemistry, by the early nineteenth century was in the Philosophical Faculty, alongside physics and mathematics, and physiology might be seen as in some ways following on towards independence—as later also pathology, and such daughter disciplines of physiology as biochemistry and hygiene. They were seen as the knowledge on which rational practice could be developed.[24]

Of course, universities were not all thus—mostly they were liberal arts colleges plus training schools for professionals. That, more or less, was the model in Scotland, and for the colleges of the University of London from the 1830s. Of the university-level colleges after mid-century, some were primarily science schools (Birmingham, Sheffield), and some were initially aimed chiefly at the liberal arts (Manchester). Medicine was important to many, especially after about 1870, but as we noted, much English medical training remained external to the universities. Science—chiefly chemistry—was but part of the dynamic; and research, in any subject, was not a preoccupation of university leaders until the 1890s.[25] Medical, technical, and liberal education

[23] Pickstone, *Ways of Knowing*, pp. 117–19; Andrew Cunningham and Nicholas Jardine (eds.), *Romanticism and the Sciences* (Cambridge, 1990).

[24] W. H. Brock, *Justus von Liebig: The Chemical Gatekeeper* (Cambridge, 1997), and the special number of *Ambix*, 50 (2003).

[25] See Chapter 15 in this book by my colleague Sam Alberti.

could have been supplied separately, after the French model—and to some extent they were, as we have seen. It is not hard to imagine an England educated in medical schools (London hospitals), technical schools (such as South Kensington or Sheffield), and liberal arts colleges (for example Oxford). We shall see that T. H. Huxley and his friends were keen to insert sciences into all such colleges. They were not especially focused on universities, though some of their campaigns—such as for more scientific education as a preliminary to medicine, served in fact to strengthen university medical schools at the expense of proprietary or hospital schools.

But for these reasons and others that would merit closer scrutiny, universities which encompassed all three kinds of education had become dominant by 1910. And in some of these universities, research schools were developed in England on the German model, from about 1870 where individuals led, and from the 1890s when universities made promotion of research into a matter of policy. Though substantial research programmes remained for decades the prerogative of a few key universities, they substantially changed the relations of the sciences to the scientific professions and to major collections.[26] To the extent that teachers of 'pre-professional' subjects became recognised as the chief national suppliers of new knowledge, they achieved significant independence from the associated professions. This was relatively easy in chemistry, which was effectively a new scientific profession, loosely articulated with pharmacy, medicine, industry and agriculture; universities were major suppliers of chemists, and university research came to be seen as part of higher professional training. But in medicine, pre-clinical specialists attained substantial power only where the clinical schools were weak compared to the organised sciences.

It was also in such places, notably Cambridge, that experimentalist programmes were created. Through laboratory experimentation, preclinical specialists gained their own (animal) equivalents of clinical material, and they could use research methods from which clinicians were debarred. The equivalent in chemistry or physics may have been *synthesis* or the invention of devices for new effects; in both spheres, experimentalism went beyond the analysis on which it was built; it could directly change the world. Meanwhile, however, the majority of university scientists, even in Cambridge, would teach analytical methods which could refine the existing-world practices of scientific professionals (and scientific teachers).[27]

[26] Mark Pendleton, ' "A place of teaching and research": University College London and the origins of the research university in Britain, 1890–1914' (Ph.D. thesis, University of London, 2001).
[27] Pickstone, *Ways of Knowing*, ch. 6.

Towards the end of this essay, I shall enquire about the relations of research schools to the public meanings of Science. But that is the third of our brief explorations on the changing constitutions of Science-as-one. If we want to understand how claims for Science helped the insertion of the analytical and experimentalist sciences into museums, professional education and universities, then we must first return to the early nineteenth century and discuss two earlier (and continuing) cultures—the world of scientific societies, and the mid-century educational world which I dubbed as French.

Diverse Claims for the Unity of Science

In the previous sections I have tried to highlight the diversity of analytical disciplines created in the decades around 1800. I have then tried to relate them to the different institutions in which they were taught and developed. But none of these relations were peculiar to the natural sciences, as opposed to other disciplines; the natural sciences did not obviously share essential characters that separated them clearly from other subjects. The separation would indeed have seemed odd in Germany, where it was apparently not common to focus on the natural sciences independently of the rest of scholarship, except perhaps towards the end of the century in debates over the relationship of universities to polytechnics and to industry. But in Britain we have come to accept the limits of Science as basic or tacit when we attempt to explain the intellectual and educational worlds of the Victorians and their successors. History can put that acceptance into question

First we may suggest that it was the relative absence of research universities and major state scientific institutions in England that led to our peculiar view of Science. Characteristically, the English definition of Science was forged in the age of reform, and in that classically liberal arena—the public space of voluntary associations; it was created around the British Association, and under that typical tension of the age—between provincial dissent and metropolitan establishments. The English definition was not primarily about existing professional institutions, though that minor theme became major by mid-century; rather, it was about the relations of the new sciences to older hegemonies of natural philosophy and theology. For that purpose, sciences closely associated with radical politics were marginalised; those best controlled by metropolitan elites were promoted—including mathematics.

In the following sections, I shall draw on the earlier parts of this essay, as I try to show how and why this 'exclusive-unity' of Science was created and maintained. We may see it as a banner passed on by advocates who maintained the unity and the limits of Science, though their positions, purposes and understandings varied markedly over three generations. As noted above, I begin with the British Association gentlemen of the 1830s, and then shift to the professional-scientist 'players' from the 1850s. Lastly, I consider some of the professors of 1870, and the ways in which successful research schools in the German manner came to establish new meanings and hierarchies in Science.

I try to relate the histories of Science to those of education, to the shifts in the character of particular disciplines, and to the changing social relations of the communities around science, technology and medicine. To do so, my three mini-studies follow a sequence of themes—from the coordination of widely dispersed voluntary associations, to the promotion of state (and usually metropolitan) institutions for teaching and display, to the advancement of key research schools in new or reformed universities. In terms of geography, this is a story of the industrial provinces, London and Cambridge (I apologise here for the lack of attention to Scotland, Ireland, and Wales).

Cambridge and the provinces in the 1830s

Much of the scholarship on Science as public concern has focused on the BAAS, which was founded in 1831 and remained an important forum and campaigning agency throughout the century. Historical analysis has concentrated on the relationships between the emergent scientific societies of the provinces, and the metropolitan elite groupings which dominated the specialist societies based in London.[28] Morrell and Thackray have greatly illuminated the inner workings of the BAAS, including its committee structures; I use their findings to consider the relations of Science to the emergent analytical disciplines and to the older formation of natural philosophy.

The BAAS was arranged in York as a get-together for the leaders of provincial societies. Many such societies were engaged in rational recreation, but members often claimed utility for the sciences—for example through the new Mechanics' Institutes. In a few places, notably Manchester, societies acted as meeting points for experts who could claim national authority in chemical and engineering analysis. Most of the leadership of the provincial societies was liberal in politics and reformist over the government of municipalities and the organisation of professions.

[28] My account of the BAAS relies on Morrell and Thackray, *Gentlemen*, and Susan F. Cannon, *Science in Culture: The Early Victorian Period* (New York, 1978), esp. pp. 1–72.

In many respects, the BAAS resembled other middle-class campaigns—for medical reform, or indeed for free trade. It drew together activities in different cities and different sciences, and much of the strength of the BAAS came from northern middle-class dissenters opposed to the state church. But the BAAS was less radical than the leaders of its provincial components; and science was presented as a way of overcoming sectarian divisions. That the BAAS was founded at York, the chief northern outpost of the Anglican church, symbolised the alliance of dissent and establishment in a time of conflict. But the alliance proved unequal: the provincials had the numbers but metropolitan gentlemen had 'position'. Within a few years, the BAAS was dominated by the Cambridge graduates and by their ideas of the hierarchy and limits of Science.

For the most part, Cambridge around 1830 still fitted the general model we suggested for eighteenth-century savant knowledge: mathematics stood for rigour, whether in the minds of students or in God's Newtonian universe, whilst studies of animals, plants and their physical surroundings showed how nicely God had made the earth as a habitation for man. This image of our world as both ordered and designed seemed crucial to the science-minded Anglicans who were worried about French materialism and the spiritual condition of Britain's new industrial workers. As Cannon showed, the Cambridge reformers were much concerned to protect this 'truth complex',[29] in part by ensuring that it was technically defensible and apparently progressive—that it was up to date with the new sciences under creation in Paris, in German universities, and in mercantile and industrial Britain. Given the professionalism of the Continental centres, Cambridge mathematics had to catch up with French modes of analysis; and botany and geology had to keep in touch with the Paris Museum of Natural History. It no longer seemed appropriate that the Royal Society of London, the premier institution for natural knowledge, should be headed by aristocratic amateurs and devoted chiefly to old-fashioned natural history. Like the Geological Society or the Cambridge Philosophical Society, it ought to be run by experts—but preferably by gentlemanly experts whose independence was guaranteed by their lack of salaries.[30]

Most of the young men who headed these campaigns in the 1820s and 1830s were moderate reformers connected by their education at Cambridge,

[29] Cannon, *Science*, ch. 9.

[30] Roy Macleod, 'Whigs and savants: reflections on the reform movement in the Royal Society, 1830–48', in Jack Morrell and Ian Inkster (eds.), *Metropolis and Province: Science in British Culture, 1780–1850* (Philadelphia, 1983), pp. 55–90.

especially in mathematics. They succeeded in the modernisation of Cambridge mathematics, failed in a bid to elect a reformer as President of the Royal Society of London, and got involved with the BAAS. Thereby, these metropolitan natural philosophers gained a national following, whilst the provincials gained a certain cachet. In this alliance, we may argue, Science in Britain took its form for a purpose—to gradually reform the ancient regime, retaining the state church and its universities as centres of authority at a time when some radicals thought them so past repair as to be no longer deserving of privilege.

But by the 1830s, as we noted, the country already had specialist societies for many of the new sciences; so if the BAAS was to act as a national federation for all these interests, it had to recognise the distinctiveness of these sciences and the claims of the different supporters. It managed this by establishing a series of committees, each covering a group of disciplines—but they were all seen as components of Science. The sciences were to be presented as a single hierarchy with common methods, and Science was the new name for this edifice.[31] We know that John Herschel, a crucial figure in all these movements, was worried about the possibility of 'Science' being read as 'the sciences'. He was well aware of the structure of the new disciplines and their pragmatic separations in so far as they each had their own elements,[32] but he stressed the supremacy of mathematical sciences, and he wrote a book which underlined the commonality of experimental method. It was from concern with the unity of Science that Vernon Harcourt ensured that the first BAAS meeting would not have sections.[33]

Unity mattered because Science for the gentlemen was not just a federation of parts; it was a hierarchy. Pride of place was given to mathematical and physical sciences, especially physical astronomy. Then came chemistry with mineralogy, electricity and magnetism; geology and geography; and zoology, botany, physiology, and anatomy. Each of the committees was led by 'professionals' and functioned as a national organisation for a particular group of sciences, including the relevant specialist societies in London.[34] Thus the BAAS tied provincials into a hierarchy of London-based societies for particular disciplines, and hence into a common understanding of what mattered in Science.

[31] Morrell and Thackray, *Gentlemen*, ch. 8.
[32] John Herschel, *Preliminary Discourse on the Study of Natural Philosophy* (London, 1835).
[33] Cannon, *Science*, p. 46; Morrell and Thackray, *Gentlemen*, p. 452.
[34] Morell and Thackray, *Gentlemen*, pp. 21–9, 267–76, 481–4.

Medicine and engineering were marginal, except in as much as practitioners saw themselves as devoted to natural philosophy rather than professional knowledges. The new social sciences were also marginal. When pushed by one of its radicals, Charles Babbage, the BAAS allowed a section for Statistics, but it was meant to confine itself to facts about social conditions, not the deductions and generalisations which were the pride and the prerogative of the savants in other sciences. As Morrell and Thackray pointed out in their important study, the managers of the BAAS, unlike the provincial advocates of Statistics, regarded political economy as dangerously political. Anthropology was also marginal, and there was little or no room for archaeology or philology, still less for moral philosophy or biblical studies. Phrenology, though then popular and well-organised in many towns, was kept out.[35] As Theodore Porter has noted, one of the major functions of nineteenth-century discussion of scientific method was to exclude or include various social or human would-be sciences.[36]

The BAAS seems to have represented the old order of natural philosophy, so developed that it could be imposed on the potentially divergent interests of new disciplines and new towns. No question now of being able to prevent the formation of new disciplinary societies, as Banks had tried to do. But no question, either, of surgeons, provincial chemists, or geological surveyors simply going their own ways, or establishing the likes of John Hunter, John Dalton or William Smith as the peaks of British science.

In some ways, as we shall see, this story of the 1830s links with the history of university science at the end of the century, when Cambridge elites would again attain national importance. But the story is not continuous; the old elite did not directly create the conditions for the new. Between these two Cam-centred generations there worked a very different group of reformers, few of whom had university degrees—and those mostly from Germany. Science for them was not about natural philosophy, and still less about theology.

Science and the liberal order

The mid-century activists grouped around T. H. Huxley were mostly employed in London, and mostly from relatively humble backgrounds, often provincial. Several had first trained as surveyors, some as surgeons or apothecaries; they occupied a variety of positions in the museums, University

[35] Morrell and Thackray, *Gentlemen*, pp. 276–97.
[36] T. Porter, 'Social sciences', p. 258.

College London or the Royal Institution. Not all had come up the hard way—Joseph Hooker followed his father as Director of the Royal Botanic Garden of Kew, and Lubbock was a metropolitan banker. Such connections surely helped the rest, but compared to the early Cambridge group, Huxley's associates were mostly outsiders—members of the new middle classes, intent on making careers for themselves and ensuring that their own protégés would find careers more easily.[37]

The claims were simple and powerful (and as worrying to conservatives then, as surprising for institutionalised academics now). The continued progress of society depended on new knowledge, so scientific research could be counted a 'public good'. Researchers thereby merited public support—at least as much as the (Anglican) clergymen who lived off endowments. But the moral authority of Science did not rest solely on its results: scientific research was the very model of free enquiry. It questioned traditional authority; it was the secure path to a new future. (They did not make those claims for history, or even for political economy.)

It followed that the state should support competent scientific researchers by payment for work; and that it should maintain public laboratories and expand its museums, gardens and surveys, ensuring that they were open to competent investigators. It should also ensure that education for the professions which involved Science, especially medicine, contained a thorough and practical grounding in the sciences concerned. As a basis for medical study, and because all children needed to understand health and disease, the new science of biology was to be taught in schools and universities. The country needed lots more science teachers as well as science graduates.[38]

Most members of this metropolitan pressure group were at some stage associated with the complex of institutions maintained in London by the Department of Science and Arts, and discussed previously in connection with Parisian models. The initial impetus for Huxley's X-Club was to bring together aspirant *naturalists*. Chemists and physicists were then added, as was the mathematician Thomas Hirst—but there was no presumption in favour of mathematical sciences, still less for long-established science such as Whewell had favoured in Cambridge. Indeed, in a group so oriented to change and the future, any such preference was unthinkable.

[37] Adrian Desmond, *Huxley: The Devil's Disciple* (London, 1994); Roy Macleod, 'The X-Club: a social network of science in late Victorian England', reprinted with much other excellent material in MacLeod, *The Creed of Science.* Also the first section of the essay by Frank Turner, 'Public science in Britain, 1880–1919', *Isis*, 71 (1980), 589–608.

[38] Turner, 'Public science'; H. E. Roscoe, 'Original research as a means of education', in *Essays and Addresses by the Professors and Lecturers of Owen's College Manchester* (London, 1874).

Huxley's associates pushed for professional opportunities across a wide range of institutions including surveys, collections and laboratories; and across many kinds of education—whether for professionals, soldiers, technicians, schoolteachers and working men. Several of the group were involved with the University of London, then a large examining body which covered University College and King's College, but which also examined candidates from many other colleges across much of the country (and Empire). And here we may note that London University established a Faculty of Science in the 1850s to award science degrees. Though we take such things for granted in Britain, Science faculties were not customary in Germany, where the natural sciences sat in faculties of Philosophy or the professional faculties such as Medicine. American universities were to follow the German model, in usually having a College of Arts and Sciences, from which students might go on to professional faculties (or graduate school). The English framing, that seems to have been extended to Scotland in the 1890s[39] and to the new Northern universities in the early twentieth century, would seem to fit with the unitary and exclusive promotion of Science.

More especially, it may have fitted with a growing standardisation of science education in ways that loosely corresponded to the Comtean view of the sciences. For mid-century reformers, the sciences all had their own methods (in my terms, their own forms of analysis)—but they were to be studied 'in series'. First mathematics, then physics, and chemistry, and biology (and then, maybe—for Comte, if not for British education—sociology).[40] That the disciplines were to be thus ontogenetically related, may help explain the mutual support of their proponents, and the grouping of teachers into faculties of Science which could deliver the required programmes, both to would-be chemists, engineers and doctors, and to students who might graduate in maths or the sciences and then go into teaching. Such curricular matters would repay more serious historical attention. I suspect we need to problematise the teaching arrangements that were still familiar after the Second World War. We need to see what was required for graduate chemists going into practice, or the range of disciplines expected for intending teachers of science, or the ways in which Huxley's conception of biology as a unified

[39] See for example, Robert Young Thomson (ed.), *A Faculty for Science. A Unified Diversity. A Century of Science in the University of Glasgow* (Glasgow, 1993), pp. 7–12; and for a major figure in Manchester re-arrangements, Peter Davies, 'Sir Arthur Schuster, 1851–1934' (Ph.D. thesis, UMIST, Manchester, 1983).

[40] On Comte and the sciences see Annie Petit 'Le systeme positiviste. La philosophie des sciences d'A. Comte et de ses premiers disciples, 1820–1900', to be published by Vrin, Paris.

analytical science was meant to articulate with physical sciences (and likewise for new versions of geology). Discussions of 'the relations of the sciences' have often been rather abstract; curricular studies may help us root such theories in the educational practices of British colleges.

Some of Huxley's friends, however, had been to German universities—not for B.Sc.s, but to learn to research in chemistry or physical sciences. The group's chemist, Edward Frankland, had tried to spread research training to Manchester, but had become discouraged in the 1850s (Roscoe took over his post at Owens College). But by 1870 support for provincial colleges was increasing, partly from the local communities;[41] partly also because Huxley and his friends had succeeded in pushing more sciences into medical education, a move approved by the profession as likely to reduce its recruitment and raise its status, and by Government, whose chief medical advisor was keen to raise the standards of the increasing number of medical officers who worked for the state in public health.[42]

University research laboratories from the seventies

From this point we divert somewhat from the public presentations of Science which have been well analysed by MacLeod and Turner through to the Great War. These historians have stressed the increasing importance of technocratic appeals to the national interest as Britain felt itself increasingly threatened by the industrial growth of Germany and the USA and by the military strength of the former. They pointed to the campaigns for technical education, and the considerable expansion of government funding from the 1890s,[43] but MacLeod also noted the public difficulties which Huxley's friends had raised by aligning Science with anticlericalism.

Turner suggested that until the 1890s the public campaigns had largely failed, but here I want to stress a different aspect: the extent to which the 1870s saw the institutionalisation of disciplinary research schools in a few universities, with considerable consequences for the subsequent configurations of elite science in Britain, especially by the Edwardian period when indeed more money became available.

[41] On the relations of the provincial university colleges to the existent scientific cultures of the cities, see the chapter in this volume by Alberti.

[42] Butler, 'Transformation'.

[43] MacLeod, 'The support of Victorian science: the endowment of research movement in Great Britain, 1868–1900', *Minerva*, 4 (1971), 197–230, esp. 220–6, reprinted in MacLeod, *Public Science*; Turner, 'Public science'.

As a marker, 1870 was the beginning of the Devonshire Commission, a remarkably comprehensive state survey of provision and desiderata for the sciences. The enquiry was suggested by a military astronomer, promoted by the BAAS, and chaired by the Duke of Devonshire—an intellectual aristocrat who had shone at Cambridge in mathematics and classics and had since made a fortune from iron mining in the north of England. The Duke's commission, on which Huxley sat, provided a mountainous survey of what had been done for Science, and what should be done. Its consequences, however, were minor; the expected funds were not forthcoming, and so it came to be seen as but one of a long series of reports which then continued, especially for technical education, up to and after the First World War. That is the negative side. But Devonshire was personally related to two university developments which made the early 1870s crucial. He was Chancellor of Cambridge University and also of Owens College, Manchester.

At Cambridge, as we shall see, the founding of new laboratories for physics and physiology proved critical for national elites in twentieth-century Britain. At Manchester, a new chemistry laboratory was built, followed by laboratories for other physical sciences—a pattern which became common in the civic universities where faculties of Science were dominated by chemistry and physics and linked with industry, but were not so closely tied to the faculties of Medicine still dominated by clinicians.

Manchester, chemistry and other sciences

When Owens College moved in 1873 from its initial, city-centre site in Richard Cobden's old town-house to suburban premises designed by Alfred Waterhouse, about half of the new building was essentially an institute for chemistry. It had been planned and funded by Henry Roscoe who had studied chemistry at Heidelberg with Bunsen, and was well connected with local industrialists and politicians; he had been a driving force in the 'extension movement' for Owens College. His chemistry institute boasted two large teaching laboratories, one for quantitative analysis and one for qualitative, plus smaller rooms for special equipment, private research and offices. It was as good as anything in Germany—maybe better in terms of student laboratory space. It was, moreover, intended to house not just a 'practical school' but a 'research school'.[44]

[44] H. E. Roscoe, *Description of the Chemistry Laboratory at Owens College, Manchester* (Manchester, 1881).

At the opening ceremony for the new buildings, Roscoe invented a history of nineteenth-century science. Back at the start of the century, he maintained, potential discoveries had been lying around, and an intelligent interest in science was sufficient to secure success. But the easy pickings were long gone, and successful research now required thorough professional training. This could only be gained in a research school, such as were found in German universities, where you could work with a master to gain the necessary knowledge and skills, and then attempt a research project of your own. Such research was full of setbacks and difficulties, but from it you would emerge as a competent contributor to knowledge—or indeed to any other task which required intellect, judgement, practical skills and perseverance.[45]

Roscoe's institute was linked with local chemical manufacturers, though not in the ways which became notable for the German synthetic dyestuffs. It seems to have seen its task as providing chemists capable of solving industrial problems and aiding industrial development—but the best of Roscoe's men went on to be professors. By the end of the century, most of the provincial colleges which were jostling for university status had substantial departments of chemistry. The expansion of technical education, especially after 1890, plus the steady expansion of school science, added to the market for chemical graduates. By 1900 too, the main London colleges had their own research schools. The geography of chemistry was that of commerce and industry, dominated by London and the Northern cities. To be sure, Oxford and Cambridge had chairs, but little more.

One might begin a sketch of the history of the physical sciences in civic universities by noting that the next big laboratory added at Manchester was for engineering, and that an institute was opened for physics and electrotechnics at the end of the century. All three departments taught students the routines of analysis and measurements which were crucial to the sciences and to their future professions.[46] By the end of the century, with the rapid spread of mains electricity, physics had acquired an industry (at least until the territory was ceded to electrical engineering). By then, the advance of synthetic chemistry and of new electrical devices meant that university laboratories might collaborate with industry in the experimental creation of new products, not just through analysis.

By then too, Manchester had a Faculty of Science comprising chemistry, physics, engineering and mathematics, plus the small departments of geology,

[45] Roscoe, 'Original research', pp. 31–8.

[46] Graham Gooday, 'Precision measurements and the genesis of physics teaching laboratories in Victorian Britain', *British Journal for the History of Science*, 23 (1990), 25–51.

botany and zoology which had differentiated from the initial chair in natural history. That, more or less, was the standard formation of Science for most of the twentieth century, especially in the provincial universities and London. It was related to industry—through research but especially through consultancies and the education of graduates in useful analytical methods. That formation was also the basis for school science, especially for senior students—the 'sixth-form Science' of the Grammar Schools, to which chemistry and then physics were central.

When Roscoe spoke at the opening of the new chemistry laboratory, he had hoped for similar developments in physiology, in which Manchester had funded a chair, appointed a new professor and established a studentship to help build research. A medical school had been built behind the new college, including laboratories, to supersede the proprietary school in the city centre. When the new physiology professor, Arthur Gamgee, spoke on how medicine might become a science, he looked to the extension of laboratory physiology and pathology until they were capable of clinical application. Here was an experimentalist vision, perhaps derived from Claude Bernard's then recent book on 'Experimental Medicine', but not to the taste of the medical profession.[47]

Gamgee was a Scottish medical graduate who had researched on physiological chemistry; he had been recommended by Huxley and was expected to link the Owens medics to the scientists, especially the chemists. But like most of his physiological confrères appointed later to similar positions in provincial and London schools, he did little research and failed to develop a school. Generally, the professors so appointed, like those in anatomy, served as teachers and administrators rather than researchers.[48] The medical schools remained dominated by clinicians; provincial medical scientists did not generally achieve the independence of the chemists, nor did they build research schools. Instructively, the medical scientists who fitted best were bacteriologists, who, like chemists, taught new and useful analytical methods; indeed, university bacteriology departments in the northern provinces came to rely heavily on fees for analytical services.

We need more mapping of the different configurations of Science across the various universities and colleges, but it is clear that there was another pattern, one not led by chemistry. The exceptional university was Cambridge, which proved crucial both for experimental physics and for biological disciplines, especially for those which analysed the processes of life by laboratory

[47] Arthur Gamgee, 'Science and medicine', in *Essays and Addresses* (1874).

[48] Butler, ' Transformation', and her 'Centres and peripheries; the development of British physiology, 1870–1914', *Journal of the History of Biology*, 21 (1988), 473–500.

experiment. In Cambridge, unlike provincial universities, natural sciences developed as a binary formation, led by physics and physiology;[49] the Royal Society came to have much the same shape.

Physiology and Physics in Cambridge

Cambridge had established a Natural Sciences degree in 1853, at much the same time as London University had established science degrees and a Faculty of Science. But numbers were small and little attention was attracted to medical sciences until *circa* 1870, when a physiology laboratory was built and a lecturer appointed chiefly to teach the students who intended to go on to study medicine (mostly in the hospitals of London). The appointment was comparable to that at Owens, but the appointee was better prepared and the structural features were substantially different. The man was Michael Foster, a protégé of William Sharpey, the full-time medical science teacher at University College London who had supported many of the young medics who were interested in the French and German medical sciences that remained marginal to most of the London medical schools.[50]

Foster was also a member of the group of young biologists who had helped to run Huxley's South Kensington summer schools for schoolteachers. The stress there was on practical classes, on experiencing science, on seeing for yourself. The work was often called experimental, but experiential would be more accurate in our terms; there was little or no experimenting on animals or plants, but much analysis of structures and development. But teachers who had worked with Huxley and Foster at South Kensington were crucial to new schools of botany and zoology in Cambridge, London, Glasgow and some provincial colleges; their protégés in turn dominated most of Britain's university colleges. They combined anatomical analysis with physiological experimentation, and they created the 'new' biology which remained standard through the mid-twentieth century, not least as a preparation for medicine.[51]

[49] There is very useful material, especially on the separation of physics and chemistry from biology and geology, in Roy MacLeod and Russell Moseley, 'Breaking the circle of science; the natural science tripos and the 'examination revolution' in R. M. MacLeod (ed.), *Days of Judgement: Science, Examination, and the Organisation of Knowledge in Late Victorian England* (Driffield, 1982), pp. 189–212, reprinted in MacLeod, *Creed.*

[50] Gerald Geison, *Michael Foster and the Cambridge School of Physiology* (Princeton, 1978); Mark Weatherall, *Gentlemen, Scientists and Doctors: Medicine at Cambridge, 1800–1914* (Cambridge, 2000).

[51] Bernard Thomason, 'The new botany in Britain, 1870–1914' (Ph.D. thesis, UMIST, Manchester, 1987).

At Cambridge, Foster developed teaching programmes in biology, but especially in experimental physiology, for which some students stayed on to do research. Cambridge rapidly became Britain's first major research school for physiology, and it proved politically powerful. Foster was Biological Secretary of the Royal Society for twenty years, served on Royal Commissions, and sat as the Liberal MP for London University from 1900 to 1906. The school gave rise to the country's main school of biochemistry, and also extended into experimental pathology.

Physiologists, especially in Cambridge, made intellectual space for themselves by creating a laboratory world of normal and abnormal animals, where they could find and demonstrate causal linkages. They could show by experiment how nerves caused glands to secrete, or muscles to contract. In Cambridge, especially, they linked physiology to the new biology rather than to clinical medicine. And it seems that sustained research from this environment had a cachet in scientific circles denied to discoveries in the field or in practice. For example, by 1900, whilst provincial and London bacteriologists sold their services to hospitals and local authorities, they lacked the distinctiveness and distance cultivated by physiologists. Diagnostic bacteriologists refined medicine, one might say; experimentalist physiologists intended to rebuild it.

By the interwar years, Cambridge research on vitamins and hormones was undeniably important to clinical practice and public health. By then too, the Cambridge physiology school and its branches dominated the politics of the new Medical Research Council, set up under the National Health Insurance legislation of 1911. Bacteriologists had expected it to concentrate on near-practice problems; but it defined its mission largely in terms of basic medical science. Many clinicians felt they had been marginalised, and they were right. One might reasonably say that nationally through the MRC, as earlier at Cambridge, the scientific fledgling in the nest of medicine had proved something of a cuckoo.

In most London and provincial medical schools, where physiology remained overshadowed by clinicians, or where the funding for young researchers was much less generous than at Cambridge, it continued to function as an ancillary to medicine. In Cambridge, with the support of Trinity College, and in a university where clinical medicine was weak, it had become established as a fundamental science of great power and promise. It depended heavily on the substantial numbers of medical students, but in as much as they mostly went to London for their clinical studies, Cambridge worked like a new American university—would-be doctors were included as science students. The inclusion of medical sciences in the Natural Sciences Tripos was important.

When, around 1930, a separate Medical Science Tripos was proposed, the physiologists reacted vigorously, fearing that their subject would come under the influence of clinicians, as elsewhere, thus undermining Cambridge's special contribution to British medicine.[52] Cambridge physiology was lined up with physics and the other sciences rather than with medicine.

This alliance as Science, to coin a phrase, operated through mutual support in the Natural Sciences Tripos, where about half the students were intending medical careers. They provided lots of business for physics, chemistry and biology teachers, and hence support for those programmes. Foster's own links, and those of his research school, seem to have been chiefly with biology. Geison's splendid study says scarcely anything about links with physics, except that the Cavendish laboratory (a gift of the Duke of Devonshire) thrived in parallel with the physiology laboratory. These common roots and situation proved crucial to the shape of British Science, but their direct linkages are not obvious. The Cambridge physics–physiology binary needs researching, at various levels, including the Royal Society.

The Cavendish Museum, as it was sometimes called, was meant to provide for physics students the practical experience that geology or botany students gained in the museums, field trips or the botanical garden. It became famous under its first director Clerk Maxwell, but the research school developed especially when the second director, Lord Rayleigh, set up group work on electrical standards, long promoted by the BAAS. At the end of the century, the new National Physical Laboratory took over these functions, but by then the Cavendish was becoming known for experimental work which was far from industry.[53] The new work on radioactivity was not analysis by measurement, nor was it mathematical theory, it was an experimentalist programme uncovering new kinds of reactions. But these were not any old reactions, or chosen for potential 'application', these were experiments about 'fundamentals'.

It would be wrong to see Cambridge physics as generally divorced from industry or practical concerns—clearly the electrical work was useful, indeed some of it was testing for fees, rather like Kelvin at Glasgow.[54] In Cambridge, as elsewhere, physics from about 1870 was boosted by the growth of the

[52] Weatherall, *Gentlemen,* p. 265.

[53] R. Sviedrys, 'The rise of physical science at Victorian Cambridge', *Historical Studies in the Physical Sciences,* 2 (1976), 127–51; Roy MacLeod and Russell Moseley, 'The 'naturals' and Victorian Cambridge: reflections on the anatomy of an elite, 1851–1914', *Oxford Review of Education*, 6 (1982), 177–96, reprinted in MacLeod, *Creed,* esp. p. 182; the essays by MacLeod and Moseley reprinted in MacLeod, *Creed.*

[54] Smith and Wise, *Energy.*

electrical industry, for which it was the obvious university preparation until separate programmes in electrical engineering were developed at the end of the century, around the time when J. J. Thomson was establishing his new research field. But Cambridge research was also rooted in electromagnetic field theory and the mathematical tradition for which Cambridge was famous. In some sense, the competitive rigour of the maths tripos, and perhaps the tradition of group working with a coach, was extended to experimental studies in physics.[55]

That such groups of outstanding students could be created—both in physics and in physiology—owed much to the considerable material and social resources available there for staff and students alike. Once the barriers to Dissenters had been removed, Cambridge became attractive to the modernising classes. There, from the 1870s, they could find a new combination of scientific prowess, elaborate teaching, social prestige and hallowed amenities—contrasting markedly with the sooty turbulence of London and the industrial cities. Cambridge, like Oxford, was the natural university for public schoolboys whose parents had the funds to support them through undergraduate studies and perhaps for some years afterwards.

In an age which had accepted industrial relevance and scientific education, where technical colleges were sprouting across industrial England and the sciences were growing in relation with old and new professions, elite Cambridge science was neither industrial nor professional; it was the closest British approximation to the German ideal of research. In as much as the university attracted bright and privileged scholars, it perpetuated research and its own intellectual reputation. There students found experimentalist laboratories which were in some ways collegiate—new places of shared work, where seniors led juniors, and juniors emulated each other. They could be model communities, and not just in their social relations. The laboratories were not at the beck and call of industrialists or clinicians; researchers pursued their own programmes, modelling the messy world in controlled ways to produce (relatively) clear results. In many cases, the relationships formed between researchers were maintained throughout their careers.[56] In as much as younger researchers moved to found their own research programmes, and graduates of the laboratories taught in good colleges and schools, so too, at various levels,

[55] Andrew Warwick, *Masters of Theory: Cambridge and the Rise of Mathematical Physics* (Chicago, 2003).

[56] On Cambridge and Oxford physiology, see Abigail O'Sullivan, 'Networks of creativity: a study of scientific achievement in British physiology, *c.*1881–1945', (Ph.D. thesis, University of Oxford, 2002).

the net was extended. The catchment and sphere of influence was England and its Empire, when most of the newer universities were but regional.[57]

By the early twentieth century, it was mostly the leaders of such research schools who represented science to the statesmen and administrators of the national and imperial government, most of whom had been educated at Oxford or Cambridge. In many areas of high British culture, as at Oxford, Science remained odd; but in the more technical areas of government, as in Cambridge, Science was a secure presence.

Politics, Geography and Science

By 1900, then, our 'third phase' of nineteenth-century British Science was well-established. The first, from 1830, had been led by natural philosophers, by gentlemen of London and Cambridge who sought to federate, and thus control, the centrifugal tendencies doubly evident in the new analytical disciplines and the great towns of the North. I have argued that the issues here were not about the 'specialisation' of science, for the new disciplines were not branches of some common stock; they were new formations each with their own characteristics, and Science was invented to link them under the hegemony of mathematics, so extending the old prestige of natural philosophy and marginalising the disciplines which were closest to medicine and to engineering. The provinces and the professions were interested in utility and local or professional ornament; the gentlemen wanted national truth consonant with established religion—and so they focused on unity, method and mathematics.

Huxley and his mid-century friends were different. They were exponents of the new analytical sciences, and they wanted jobs for themselves and others, especially as teachers. Because they wished the world to appreciate scientific knowledge and free enquiry, they argued for new educational institutions, at all social levels. They wanted professional scientists to be responsible for the pre-practical instruction of doctors and engineers, and for developing and explaining the national museum collections. In some ways, chemistry was their model—as a new university-based profession serving several professions and arts, but not beholden to any.

We have seen a little of how science came to be organised in Manchester and other civics, and that engineering and (electrical) physics came to share

[57] On students from the Empire, see Roy M. MacLeod and E. Kay Andrews, 'Scientific careers of 1851 Exhibition scholars' *Nature*, 224 (1969), 1–28, reprinted in MacLeod, *Creed.*

some of the attributes pioneered by professors of chemistry. Electricity was important here because, like chemistry, it was a new scientific profession, shaped as much by teachers as by practitioners. We might see Huxley's campaigns as effectively establishing science teachers throughout the expanding institutions of professional and liberal higher education. And these campaigns for Science continued, for higher education and especially for technical education. The sciences involved were mostly physical and analytical, with strong emphasis on procedures, instruments and measurements that were useful for industry and the technical professions. From about 1870, the London and provincial colleges established research schools, especially for chemistry, and physics and engineering followed; but in these sites, as in the BAAS, medical sciences were usually marginal.

It would not have surprised Huxley that the Science he advocated would thrive in London and the provinces—in the universities of the busy, as the civics were called in Edwardian England. But that was not the whole story, especially for physics and the biological sciences. By 1900 the influence of Cambridge University on the great cities of England was clear in this most modern of enterprises. Whereas the Huxleyites had operated largely through state-institutions which were as close to the French model as England ever got, Cambridge professors demonstrated, as nowhere else in Britain, the potential of the university research school for creating disciplinary elites. They were helped by the supply of students who intended to go on to scientific professions, especially medicine, and by the relative weakness in Cambridge of the professionals themselves. Cambridge built on mathematics and the fame of Darwinian biology, but above all on the university's social and material resources, as directed by a handful of inspirational figures, mostly at Trinity College.

What then was the ideology of physics and physiology around 1900, and how did that relate to Science as a cause? We have seen that polemics for Science continued in connection with national efficiency and the need for expertise. Cambridge professors could offer expertise—if not on the details of pressing clinical or industrial issues, then perhaps as subject leaders who were judicious, well-connected and decently removed from practicalities. They seem not to have demanded new structures, perhaps because they had most of what they wanted. They were good at getting funds, from the universities and from the government; and the elite of science ensured, especially around the Great War, that government research money came in ways which were distanced from particular ministries, and largely controlled by professional scientists. Scientists could appear not just as educators or adjuncts to the technical professions, but as a caste of professional researchers who commanded new realms that might eventually change the world. Government, like the scientific professions and industry, were to cough-up and keep their distance.[58]

In some ways, the application of Cambridge resources through the mutiplier of research schools had re-established a metropolitan ascendancy by attracting provincial and colonial talent. In Cambridge, between 1830 and 1880, thanks chiefly to London reformers, experimental physics had replaced mathematical physics as discipline of the day, and experimental physiology in some ways had replaced stratigraphy.[59] The new Cambridge binary was reflected in the two sections of the Royal Society—one for physical science and one for biological. In the first half of the twentieth century, the officerships of both halves were dominated by Cambridge professors.

'Science is one and the university is its teacher.'[60] Here was the old claim with a new twist, but again it was a unity which was shaped and exclusive. At its pinnacle were the mostly pure, mostly experimentalist sciences incarnate in the Fens, then came the more analytical and practical disciplines such as chemistry that flourished in London and the universities of industrial England. And beyond them the realms of technical education, industrial practice and clinical medicine.

The scientific disciplines had changed much since 1830: analytical disciplines were now well-established, Science was neither clerical nor anticlerical, and experimentalist programmes promised new futures. Many new sites had been produced—in state museums, university colleges, technical colleges and in the preliminary training for scientific professionals. Yet 'Science' still served as a means to connect those spaces and to advance the common interests of their inhabitants—whether for equipment, room on curricula, charitable research-funds, or the ears and the purses of government. And through the development of Cambridge laboratories, elite Science had been reconnected with the institutions of the Establishment. Through the new experimentalism of physics and physiology, as through the BAAS a life-time before, the meritocrats of an ancient university had managed to retain a substantial hold on British Science.

[58] Joan Austoker and Linda Bryder (eds.), *Historical Perspectives on the Role of the MRC* (Oxford, 1989).

[59] On the new geology see Roy Porter, 'The natural science tripos and the "Cambridge school of geology", 1850–1914,' *History of Universities*, 2 (1982), 193–216.

[60] See MacLeod, 'Support', 228.

CHAPTER THREE

Classifying Sciences: Systematics and Status in mid-Victorian Natural History

JIM ENDERSBY

The mid-Victorian natural history sciences were pre-eminently concerned with collecting and classifying, activities that some practitioners of the physical sciences regarded with disdain. As a result, natural history tended to be held in low esteem both by some leading members of the British Association for the Advancement of Science (BAAS) and by influential writers in the non-specialist periodical press. Many naturalists worried that their status problems were being exacerbated by fractious debates over classification within both the zoological and botanical communities. Zoologists argued over the merits of William Macleay's quinary system (which claimed that all organisms could be classified in groups of five), while career-minded botanists disagreed as to what should replace the eighteenth-century Linnaean (or Sexual) system, which they regarded as a hindrance to the progress of their science, despite (or, perhaps, because of) its continuing popularity. These debates, and in particular the strategies that were adopted to try and end them, illuminate the often complex relationships between social and scientific status during this period.

The difference in status between the prestigious mathematical sciences, such as astronomy, and their collecting and classifying cousins was also reflected in the material rewards available to their practitioners. There were few paid positions in natural history, and they were badly paid, facts that added urgency to the desire of some naturalists, such as the botanists John Lindley and Joseph Hooker, to use their personal prestige and institutional position to foreclose classification debates that they saw as damaging to both the reputation of their science and their career prospects. However, during the 1840s and 1850s it was still not clear whether earning a living from science added to one's status or diminished it; many still regarded the disinterested, gentlemanly pursuit of knowledge as more prestigious than any activity that smacked of commercialism. Examining these debates highlights difficulties with prevailing accounts of the 'professionalisation' of the Victorian sciences, which have tended to assume that men of science strove for paid, professional status because they saw it as both inevitable and desirable. By contrast, I will argue that men like Lindley and Hooker, struggling to maintain a delicate balance between commercial and scientific considerations, avoided describing themselves as 'professionals', preferring to be known as 'professed' or 'philosophical' naturalists, terms that were intended to confer both social and intellectual prestige. Examining the relationship between classification *as a* science and the classification *of* sciences (into a hierarchy or more and less perfect ones) clarifies some of the key issues for those who sought to reorganise Victorian scientific knowledge.

Scientific hierarchies

The BAAS received only one major report on botany in its early years. In 1834, John Lindley, professor of botany at University College London, gave a brief summary of the state and progress of botany, in which he said that he had:

> presumed that the object of the British Association will be attained if the present Report is confined to the most interesting only of those subjects upon which botanists have been recently occupied.[1]

The 'most interesting' subject was plant physiology, despite the fact that, as Lindley acknowledged, it was one in which British botanists were not competing with their colleagues in France and Germany. Even more surprising was his statement that 'I have also excluded everything that relates to mere systematic botany', since this was the field the British dominated and in which Lindley himself was a leading expert.

Lindley's report encapsulates the dilemma that faced British botanists at the time. Their science was primarily concerned with classification, and was therefore scarcely a science at all in the eyes of some. Yet the more prestigious matters of physiology and anatomy, which sought the underlying causes of phenomena, were not widely studied in Britain. The other natural history sciences, most notably zoology, shared this problem to a degree;

[1] J. Lindley, 'On the Principal Questions at present debated in the Philosophy of Botany', *Report of the British Association for the Advancement of Science* (London, 1834), pp. 27–57 at 27.

although zoologists were more involved in understanding the structure and function of organisms, the great theorists were all foreigners. The greatest accolade that could be offered Richard Owen was to describe him as 'the British Cuvier'.[2]

These dilemmas were one cause in the implicit hierarchy of disciplines that was embodied in the British Association's specialist sections: the Mathematical and Physical Sciences formed Section A; close behind came Chemistry & Mineralogy, Section B; Section C was Geology & Geography; while the naturalists met as Section D. Furthest down the table came Medicine (E), Statistics (F) and the Mechanical Sciences (G).

The pre-eminence of the mathematical sciences was widely accepted by practitioners of the lower ones. In 1836, Charles Daubeny, despite being the Professor of Botany at Oxford University, used his British Association presidential address to proclaim that 'all the physical sciences aspire to become in time mathematical: the summit of their ambition, and the ultimate aim of the efforts of their votaries, is to obtain their recognition as worthy sisters of the noblest of these sciences—Physical Astronomy'. He added that 'their reception into this privileged and exalted order is not a point to be lightly conceded'.[3] Despite the acknowledged importance of fact-gathering, no amount of facts would make botany a worthy sister to astronomy in the absence of mathematical laws. The Cambridge philosopher William Whewell argued that 'the mere gathering of raw facts may be compared to the gatherings of the cotton from the tree. The separate filaments must be drawn into a connected thread, and the threads woven into an ample web, before it can form the drapery of science.'[4] Botanists in his audience would probably have noticed that he had chosen a botanical analogy to describe mere fact-gathering.

The low opinion that the Association's leaders had of natural history, and of botany in particular, was reflected in the general committee's expenditure on the various sciences. In 1838, for example, Section A got £2,263. 10*s*. while Section D got a princely £6 (Table 1). While 1838 was a bad year for natural history, it was not much worse than other years (Table 2): natural history did not get much money, botany got even less than zoology.

The BAAS's published reports on the state of various sciences partly served to define which disciplines were (or were not) to be considered properly

[2] N. Rupke, *Richard Owen: Victorian Naturalist* (New Haven, 1994), pp. 117–37.

[3] C. Daubeny, 'Address to the British Association for the Advancement of Science', *Report of the British Association for the Advancement of Science* (London, 1836), p. xxiii.

[4] Quoted in J. Morrell and A. Thackray, *Gentlemen of Science: Early Years of the British Association for the Advancement of Science* (Oxford, 1981), p. 273.

Table 1. British Association expenditure, 1838

Total	£3,742.10*s.*
Mathematical and physical sciences (Section A)	£2,263.10*s.*
Natural history (Section D)	£6.00*s.*

Table 2. British Association expenditure, 1835–56

Section	% of total
Mathematical and physical sciences (Section A)	38.5
Geology and geography (Section C)	8.0
Natural history (Section D)	6.5
— of which, botany got:	2.0

scientific (Table 3). Although Section D was well-represented, its reports were almost all zoological: for example, in the 1839 BAAS *Report* there were two zoological reports in the main section (Richard Owen wrote 94 pages on British fossil reptiles and Edward Forbes 22 pages on molluscs), there were none on botany. In 1840, there was a 58 page report on Ireland's fauna and a two page report on methods for preserving both animal and vegetable substances, with no other botanical reports. In 1841, a committee on preserving the vegetative power of seeds got two pages to report its findings, while Owen got another 145 pages on fossil British reptiles. In 1843, zoology got 64 pages, botany five; in 1844, zoology won again (163 pages to five); and again in 1845 (146 pages to nine); and once more in 1845 (142 pages to 11). The pattern is too strong to ignore—natural history as a whole was respected (if poorly funded), but botany was clearly zoology's poor relation.[5]

Although the mathematical sciences were the most prestigious and best-rewarded, numbers alone did not bring status, as we shall see below. It was more important that a discipline be considered 'philosophical'. I will consider some of the meanings of this term in this paper, but the geologist Roderick Murchison gave a brief definition when he presided over the Association's 1846 meeting, and acknowledged that 'British naturalists have annually

[5] Summaries are compiled from the official reports of the BAAS (John Murray, London, 1839–46). The brief reports of the Association's specialised sections show a similar bias, with Section A receiving the most space and the reports of Section D being dominated by zoology. A similar pattern can be discerned in the Royal Society's priorities, which showed a strong bias towards the experimental sciences: R. MacLeod, 'The Royal Society and the Government Grant: Notes on the Administration of Scientific Research, 1849–1914', *Historical Journal*, 14 (1971), 323–58 at 329–30.

Table 3. BAAS, published reports by Section, 1835–44

Section	'35	'36	'37	'38	'39	'40	'41	'42	'43	'44	Total	%
A (maths and physical science)	7	6	6	4	7	6	8	2	4	8	58	40
B (chemistry and mineralogy)	1	1	2	0	0	1	0	1	0	1	7	5
C (geology and geography)	0	0	0	0	1	1	2	4	4	5	17	12
D (natural history)	**1**	**3**	**1**	**0**	**1**	**2**	**2**	**5**	**5**	**6**	**26**	**18**
E (statistics)	4	4	3	0	0	2	1	0	1	0	15	10
F (medicine)	1	0	1	0	0	0	0	1	0	0	3	2
G (mechanical sciences)	1	0	3	2	0	1	3	3	3	2	18	13
Annual totals	15	14	16	6	9	13	16	16	17	22	144	

become more philosophical, and have given to their inquiries a more physiological character, and have more and more studied the higher questions of structure, laws and distribution'. Murchison's triad—'structure, laws and distribution'—can serve as a loose definition of what the Association saw as philosophical. 'Laws', of course, were the highest goal, and 'Structure' and 'Distribution' were two ways to reach them. However, as the BAAS reports make clear, when Murchison praised 'naturalists', he meant zoologists. In Britain, it was the latter who mainly studied 'Structure' (anatomy and physiology). For the botanists, 'Distribution' was more promising: studying why plants grew in particular places meant looking at potential causal factors that explained the relationship between characteristic plant communities and their climates, altitudes and soil types, thus discovering the laws of the vegetable kingdom.

Distribution studies, or 'botanical geography', preoccupied British botanists during the middle decades of the century, partly because it was an area where they dominated both the zoologists and their foreign rivals. Distribution also offered a chance to raise the status of their studies, by uncovering natural laws. As the *Edinburgh Review* observed:

> The investigation of these facts, of the presumed origin and subsequent migrations of plants, and of the causes which influence the phenomena observed, constitute those sciences in which the labours of the botanist are connected with those of the geographer and geologist.[6]

Remember that the 'geographer and geologist' belonged to section C, a rung up from their fellow naturalists.

[6] [G. Bentham], 'Review of De Candolle's *Geographical Botany* and other works', *Edinburgh Review or Critical Journal*, 104 (1856), 490–518 at 491.

Botanical geography also provided a chance for botanists to demonstrate their usefulness to a nation with a vast maritime trading empire, many of whose commodities were derived from plants.[7] However, 'mere systematic botany' could not be ignored; the chief technique of British distribution studies was 'botanical arithmetic', the calculation of the ratios between species and genera in different countries in order to give precision to widely accepted generalisations, such as that islands were dominated by small genera (i.e. those with few species).[8] However, as the *Edinburgh Review* noted, 'these numerical calculations, founded upon no fixed principles, [were] seldom even comparative', because the botanists who classified the plants held a 'great diversity of views entertained as to what constitutes a species'. Given these disagreements, the ratios were meaningless since some systematists lumped together numerous varieties that others classified as separate species or even genera. Hence the *Edinburgh Review*'s conclusion that botanical arithmetic 'cannot even now lead to any useful or satisfactory conclusions, unless accompanied by a research into cause and effect'.[9]

Mere systematics

Before botanists could study the causes of plant distribution and thus discover the laws of vegetation, they had to rescue botany from the rancorous debates between competing classificatory systems that were going on in the metropolis. Botany's status as a properly philosophical discipline largely rested on settling these disputes, which centred on the Linnaean or sexual system of classification, which, despite claims to the contrary, remained in use in Britain well into the second half of the century. Its survival, long after the rest of Europe had abandoned it, contributed to the perception that British botany was backward and unfit to take its place alongside the physical sciences. However, those attacking the Linnaean classification were divided over what should replace it: the most widely used of its rivals was known as the natural

[7] P. J. Cain, 'Economics and Empire: The Metropolitan Context', in A. Porter (ed.), *The Oxford History of the British Empire. Vol. III: The Nineteenth Century* (Oxford, 1999), pp. 31–52; R. Drayton, *Nature's Government: Science, Imperial Britain and the 'Improvement' of the World* (New Haven, 2000).

[8] For more on botanical arithmetic, see J. Browne, 'C.R. Darwin and J.D. Hooker: Episodes in the History of Plant Geography, 1840–1860', *History of Science and Technology* (1979), 299; J. Browne, 'Darwin's Botanical Arithmetic and the "Principle of Divergence", 1854–1858', *Journal of the History of Biology*, 13 (1980), 53–89; J. Browne, *The Secular Ark: Studies in the History of Biogeography* (New Haven, 1983).

[9] [Bentham], 'Geographical Botany', 491.

system, founded by Antoine-Laurent de Jussieu in 1789 and refined by Augustin-Pyramus de Candolle and others. The naturalists who subsequently developed this system found themselves disagreeing over its definitions and principles, thus fragmenting it, yet only a single, settled natural system could vanquish the Linnaean one. The prominence of these destabilising debates was exacerbated by the existence of numerous other classificatory systems (including the binary or dichotomous system, the quinary and septenary systems, and others), all based on completely different principles from those of de Jussieu, yet which all claimed to be 'natural'. Both the debates within the natural system and the chaos of rival systems contributed to perceptions that botany was an unphilosophical study which lacked guiding principles.[10]

The irony for those trying to stabilise classification was that a few decades earlier, there had been a single, settled, universally used classification—the Linnaean or sexual system.[11] The British took it up with particular enthusiasm; its simple names and even simpler methods made it easy to learn and use and it played a large role in making botany popular both in Britain and its colonies.[12]

Britain's Linnaean enthusiasm partly resulted from Sir James E. Smith's purchase of Linnaeus' private collections: he brought them to London, founded the Linnean Society, and devoted the rest of his life to preserving Linnaeus' intellectual and physical legacy.[13] In 1833, the *Edinburgh Review* assessed Smith's *Memoirs and Correspondence* and the reviewer was 'impressed with the great progress in systematic botany which has been made in England during the last fifty years'. Behind this compliment, however, was a barely concealed attack on Smith, since the *Edinburgh Review* noted a point that 'is less flattering to our national vanity': during this same period, 'British botanists

[10] Peter Stevens has argued that the instability of the natural system was a major reason for botany's low status: P. Stevens, *The Development of Biological Systematics: Antoine-Laurent de Jussieu, Nature, and the Natural System* (New York, 1994), p. 212. And Harriet Ritvo also argues that classification was an unglamorous, low-prestige activity in the Victorian period, in part because of disputes between classifiers, H. Ritvo, 'Zoological Nomenclature and the Empire of Victorian Science', in B. Lightman (ed.), *Victorian Science in Context* (Chicago, 1997) pp. 336–9.

[11] For a discussion of the system and its British popularity, see: D. Allen, *The Naturalist in Britain: a Social History* (Princeton, NJ, 1994), pp. 36–7, 39, 43; Schiebinger, 'Gender and natural history', in N. Jardine, J. Secord and E. Spary (eds.), *Cultures of Natural History* (Cambridge, 1996), pp. 163–77: 172–4; L. Koerner, 'Carl Linnaeus in his time and place', in Jardine, Secord and Spary (eds.), *Cultures of Natural History,* pp. 145–62 at 149–50; L. Koerner, *Linnaeus: Nature and Nation* (Cambridge, Mass., 1999), pp. 33–55; Drayton, *Nature's Government*, pp. 18–19.

[12] P. Bowler, *The Fontana History of the Environmental Sciences* (London, 1992), p. 164.

[13] P. White, 'The Purchase of Knowledge: James Edward Smith and the Linnean Collections', *Endeavour,* 23 (1999), 126–9; Allen, *Naturalist in Britain*, p. 40; Drayton, *Nature's Government*, pp. 141–2.

have been comparatively inactive in examining the structure of vegetable bodies,—in explaining their hidden functions'.[14] Many of the *Edinburgh Review*'s readers would have understood the implication: Smith and the Linnean Society bore considerable responsibility for the British neglect of physiology in favour of lowly systematics.

By the 1830s, the perception that Britain was falling behind in botany's more philosophical branches led many botanists to question the usefulness of the Linnaean system. Lindley described the Linnean Society as a 'positive incubus upon science' that was holding back British botany by promoting a system that had been largely abandoned elsewhere in Europe.[15] And in its comments on Smith, the *Edinburgh Review* noted that 'Botany has hitherto been chiefly a science of observation', since it was dominated by the kind of 'botanist who knows a plant only by its parts of fructification'. It compared these Linnean botanists to the kind of mineralogist who classified a rock 'by throwing its lustre upon his eye, and by shaking it knowingly in his hand'. Nevertheless, botanists need not despair, since mineralogy had now progressed to be one of science's 'most interesting branches'. The reviewer concluded that 'Botany will, we doubt not, soon rise to the same dignity'.[16]

Although de Jussieu's system had been introduced into Britain by Robert Brown in 1810, it took many years to become established.[17] Some historians have argued that it had largely triumphed by the 1830s, but there are good reasons to doubt this claim, not least because men like Lindley felt the need continually to stress the natural system's superiority.[18] In 1833, he had reviewed an introductory volume whose author claimed he was going to describe 'the present state of Systematic Botany,' but had in fact outlined the

[14] [Brewster], 'Memoir and Correspondence of the late Sir James Edward Smith', *Edinburgh Review or Critical Journal,* 57 (1833), 39–69 at 69.

[15] J. Lindley, *A Synopsis of the British Flora* (London, 1835), p. vi; see also Stevens, *Biological Systematics*, p. 210.

[16] [Brewster], 'Memoir of J. E. Smith', 68–9.

[17] R. Brown, *Prodromus Florae Novae Hollandiae et Insulae Van Diemen* (New York, 1830 (1960)); D. Mabberley, *Jupiter Botanicus: Robert Brown of the British Museum* (Braunschweig, 1985); P. Stevens, *Biological Systematics*, p. 100.

[18] The claim that the Linnaean system was disused by the 1830s or 1840s has been made by many historians, including: A. Morton, *History of Botanical Science: An Account of the Development of Botany from Ancient Times to the Present Day* (London, 1981), pp. 364–75; D. Allen, *The Botanists: A History of the Botanical Society of the British Isles through a hundred and fifty years* (Winchester, 1986), pp. 4–5; M. Foucault, *The Order of Things: an Archaeology of the Human Sciences* (London, 1989), pp. 125–65; Bowler, *History of Environmental Sciences*, pp. 258–60; A. Larsen, 'Not Since Noah: The English Scientific Zoologists and the Craft of Collecting, 1800–1840', *History of Science* (1993), 167; A. Shteir, 'Gender and "Modern" Botany in Victorian England', *Osiris,* 12 (1997), 29–38 at 31; W. Stearn (ed.), *John Lindley, 1799–1865: Gardener–Botanist and Pioneer Orchidologist* (Woodbridge, Suffolk, 1999), p. 34.

Linnaean system, which—Lindley claimed 'has been disused these forty years'.[19] This claim was, as he knew, disingenuous to say the least—the Linnaean system was discussed repeatedly in general periodicals throughout the 1830s, 1840s and 1850s. Long after those who called themselves 'professed' botanists had largely agreed on the superiority of the natural system, the Linnaean one continued to be used in both medical textbooks and the general works aimed at gardeners, flower-painters, part-time enthusiasts and the myriad others with an interest in plants. As Lindley's income partly depended on selling books to these audiences, he could not surrender them to the Linneans. Hence his decision to write *Ladies' Botany* which, as a reviewer noted, was 'intended for the instruction of ladies in one of the most delightful of all the sciences'.[20] Written using a popular genre of the period (as letters 'addressed to a lady on the botanical education of her children'), it was nevertheless, as its subtitle proclaimed a 'Familiar Introduction to the study of the Natural System of Botany'. Lindley's preface noted that 'no one has, as yet, attempted to render the unscientific reader familiar with, what is called, the Natural System, to which the method of Linnæus has universally given way among Botanists'. He observed that few women managed to master it, because 'on all hands they are told of its difficulties; books, instead of removing those difficulties, only perplex the reader by multitudes of unknown words'.[21] While many introductions to the natural system had been written (including his own), 'for those who would become acquainted with Botany as an amusement and a relaxation, they are far too difficult'.[22]

The need to capture the popular and medical audiences was one reason why Lindley used both his own books and anonymous reviews in reforming journals like the *Athenaeum* to attack the Linnaean system. In 1834, the *Monthly Review* commented that 'for a great number of years,' Lindley had 'unceasingly, not merely disparaged, but actually persecuted unto death the ancient Linnean system'.[23] Almost twenty years later, the Tory *Quarterly Review* still defended the Linnaean method from Lindley's persecutions by claiming that its simplicity made it an ideal starting point for learning botany—even if the serious student must eventually graduate to the natural system. The reviewer quoted Lindley's claim that the sexual system was 'well

[19] [Lindley], 'Review of Thomas Castle *A Synopsis of Systematic Botany*', *Athenaeum* (1833), 870.

[20] Anon., 'Review of Lindley *Ladies' Botany*', *Monthly Review or Literary Journal*, 2 (1834), 342–53 at 342.

[21] J. Lindley, *Ladies' Botany: Or a Familiar Introduction to the Study of the Natural System of Botany (volume 1)* (London, 1834), p. iii.

[22] Lindley, *Ladies Botany, vol. 1*, p. iv.

[23] Anon., 'Lindley's Ladies' Botany', p. 342.

adapted indeed to captivate the superficial inquirer, but exercising so baneful an influence on botany, as to have rendered it doubtful whether it ever deserved a place among the sciences'.[24] The *Quarterly Review* responded:

> With all deference to the Doctor, we might rejoin that, if the Natural System were permitted entirely to extinguish the Linnæan, botany would soon deserve a place among the *mysteries* instead of the sciences. The 'superficial inquirer' is the very person who wants a clear and frank-minded guide that *will* show him what he wants, instead of letting him lose himself in a boggy maze where he can find no firm footing.[25]

The reviewer claimed the natural system was only suitable for the 'practiced adept,' having apparently been designed as 'an excellent contrivance for fencing off the profane vulgar'. By contrast, J. E. Smith's *English Botany* (which, of course, used the Linnaean system) would allow the novice to identify a plant 'in five minutes'. The *Quarterly Review* therefore suggested that 'the English student is advised to begin with Sir James Smith's works and end with Dr. Lindley's. The Knight should preside over the catalogue, the Professor over the herbarium.'[26] Ease of use was seen as more important than dubious philosophical claims made with the help of foreign (particularly French) classificatory systems. The *Quarterly Review*'s comments on Lindley appeared sandwiched between practical gardening tips and a discussion of salad vegetables and their dressings, the implication being that botany should remain a genteel and improving pastime.

Nevertheless, one might wonder why Lindley and others did not simply follow the *Quarterly Review*'s advice by retaining the Linnaean system in their popular books while using the natural one to 'fence off the profane vulgar' from their more technical works. Instead of making de Jussieu's system accessible to ladies, why not use it to differentiate those of properly philosophical status? To some extent, that was what happened: William Hooker used both the Linnaean and natural systems in his books, using the former as an introductory key to the latter, and his son Joseph Hooker did the same in the *Flora Novae-Zelandiae* (1853) when he added a key 'arranged according to the artificial or Linnaean system,' in order to 'facilitate the reference to many of the obscure genera to their proper places', while stressing that its use did not 'obviate the necessity' for, nor 'supersede the use of a sound elementary acquaintance with the Natural Orders'.[27] Even Lindley—despite supposedly

[24] J. Lindley, *An Introduction to the Natural System of Botany* (1st edn., 1830). Quoted in [Dixon], 'Gardening: reviews of *Transactions of the Horticultural Society of London*, and other titles', *Quarterly Review*, 89 (1851), 1–32.

[25] [Dixon], 'Gardening', 10.

[26] [Dixon], 'Gardening', 12.

[27] J. Hooker, *Flora Novae-Zelandiae (Botany of the Antarctic voyage: volume 2)* (London, 1851–3), p. 312.

having 'persecuted unto death the ancient Linnean system' gave a brief synopsis of its features in his books, conceding that 'although now disused by men of science ... many books have been arranged on its plan'.[28] Far from erecting barriers to the 'vulgar', the use of both systems was intended to provide a bridge to the natural system, across which the widest possible audience could be guided.

However, while the Linnaean system might be permitted a subordinate role in introducing readers to botany, there were several reasons why philosophical botanists preferred the natural one. Perhaps the most important was that the sexual system perpetuated the separation between botanical classification and its more prestigious branches, such as distribution and physiology. The Linnaean system used only the plant's reproductive organs; the natural one required the use of all the plant's characters, so that its users therefore needed a comprehensive knowledge of plant anatomy. As Joseph Hooker noted in his introductory essay to the *Flora Novae-Zelandiae*, the botanist would find that even 'an elementary acquaintance with the Natural Orders and Species of plants' required him to

> commence with the knife and the microscope, tracing the development of important organs, however minute; and if he desire to obtain that knowledge of the affinities of plants which alone will enable him to prosecute other branches of the science, he can only do so by first making himself thoroughly acquainted with their comparative anatomy.[29]

The natural system made 'the knife and the microscope' essential, and Hooker made it clear that he saw this marriage of anatomy and physiology with classification as the key to the 'other branches of the science,' such as distribution studies. For a systematic botanist like Hooker, the great attraction of the natural system was not that it made classification *one* of the philosophical studies; it turned it into the key to the whole of botany, the central practice that connected the others. He was not alone in this view; the *Edinburgh Review*'s review of Smith's memoirs included the hope that 'the botanists of the next age will apply themselves to these important objects'

> and follow the example which has been set them by our countryman, Mr Brown (whom Humboldt has justly characterised as the *Botanicorum facile Princeps*) in making the microscope and the dissecting knife indispensable instruments of their science.[30]

28 J. Lindley, *The Elements of Botany: Structural and Physiological* (London, 1847), p. 124.
29 Hooker, *Flora Novae-Zelandiae*, p. i.
30 [Brewster], 'Memoir of J. E. Smith', 68–9.

Robert Brown was Britain's foremost exponent of physiological plant studies, whose work raised botany above the mere counting of stamens; the reviewer explicitly linked Brownian physiology with the higher status sciences, noting that 'the botanist has the same occasion for powerful microscopes that the astronomer has for telescopes of great penetrating and magnifying power'. The Linnaean system prevented botany from reaching to the status of astronomy, and the *Edinburgh Review* explicitly recommended that 'the young and aspiring student' should 'consider systematic botany only as the means by which he is to attain higher objects', as the necessary preliminary to physiology and distribution studies. He should 'pursue those objects assiduously and ardently, with the Microscope in one hand, and the torch of Chemistry and Physics in the other'.[31]

By contrast with Lindley, whose work focused on British plants, Joseph Hooker was primarily interested in the plants of Britain's colonies, and he relied on an informal network of largely unpaid collectors to provide him with specimens. Eradicating the Linnaean system thus had an additional significance for Hooker: by persuading colonial plant collectors to learn and use the natural system, he hoped to inculcate his philosophy of classification, especially his definition of a species. The natural system was the key to his attempt to promulgate both standardised collecting practices and species definitions.

From the perspective of practitioners like Hooker, there were many reasons why the Linnaean system had to go, yet it cast a long shadow over British botany and played a major role in establishing its low status. The final date of its death can, for symbolic purposes at least, be set as 1863, when the third edition of the *English Botany* appeared. Although the original plates had been retained, Smith's text—and with it the Linnaean classification—was finally gone, to be replaced by a natural classification. The *Athenaeum* welcomed this, commenting that since the 1840s, 'no general account of our native plants *written by men of note* has appeared which did not reject the Linnean classification'.[32] The author of a flora that used the Linnaean system was, by definition, not 'a man of note', whereas one who used the natural system was; Lindley had effectively made the same move when he declared that the Linnaean system was 'disused by men of science'. The natural system, and its attendant philosophical practices of anatomy and distribution, helped to define a clearer science of botany, and as a consequence, a botanist

[31] [Brewster], 'Memoir of J. E. Smith', 68–9.

[32] [Seemann], 'Review of John T. Boswell-Syme (ed.), *English Botany*', *Athenaeum* (1863), 327–8 at 327, emphasis added.

was no longer defined as someone 'fond of flowers', but as a man of science; the shifting gender identity of the botanist being, as Ann Shteir and others have noted, an important side effect of the broader issues of status and of career formation.[33]

Stabilising the natural system

However, while the persistence of the Linnaean system was an obstacle to capturing a wider audience, the instability of its natural rival was a more pressing problem for those botanists who wanted to avoid writing popular books. The *Athenaeum*'s review of Lindley's *Vegetable Kingdom* (1846) compared it to his earlier works on the natural system and observed that 'the present arrangement differs materially from that in his former books':

> This will, undoubtedly, be urged by many not only as an objection to the author's views on the ground of unsettledness, but, perhaps, amongst the remnants of the Linnean systematists left in this country, as an objection to the natural system itself.[34]

The *Athenaeum* attempted to refute this objection by noting that just as 'every observation on the heavenly bodies influences the calculations of the astronomer, so does every observation on the tissues of plants, the discovery of every new form, tend to modify the views of the botanist'. Yet such corrections do not alter 'the fundamental principles on which that system has been constructed'.[35]

The continuing need to shore up the unsettled natural system explains why, in 1850, the *Westminster Review* felt compelled to devote much of a review on 'Natural Systems of Botany' to attacking the Linnaean system once again.[36] The reviewer claimed that the natural system was so widely accepted that 'the appearance of a book whose professed object it is to depreciate the more rational principles of arrangement, and to advocate an unconditional return to the professedly artificial system of Linnæus, could hardly have been anticipated at the present day'. Nevertheless, that was what James L. Drummond,

[33] Shteir, 'Gender and "Modern" Botany'; A. Shteir, *Cultivating Women, Cultivating Science: Flora's Daughters and Botany in England, 1760 to 1860* (Baltimore, 1996); A. Shteir, 'Elegant Recreations? Configuring Science Writing for Women', in Lightman (ed.), *Victorian Science in Context*, pp. 236–55.

[34] [Lankester], 'Review of Lindley's *Vegetable Kingdom*', *Athenaeum* (1846), 573–4 at 573.

[35] [Lankester], 'Lindley's Vegetable Kingdom', 573.

[36] [Luxford], 'Natural Systems of Botany: review of Lindley's *Vegetable Kingdom* and other works', *Westminster Review*, 54 (1850), 38–65.

an Irish professor of anatomy and leading promoter of the Belfast botanic garden, had produced in his *Observations on Natural Systems of Botany*. 'It must be confessed,' the reviewer wrote, 'that Dr. Drummond's "Observations" display far more ingenuity than could have been expected in the defence of a cause so hopeless and so ungrateful'—hence the need to devote eight pages to slaying a system that was supposed to be dead and buried.[37]

Like the Linnaean system's other advocates, Drummond defended its ease of use; he claimed that 'the greatest possible recommendation of any system is the facility with which a person previously ignorant of all, save its merest rudiments, can master it and ascertain the name of the first plant he picks up'.[38] The *Westminster Review*'s reviewer demurred, commenting that 'we are no advocates for such a very superficial knowledge', but fortunately 'a recurrence to the Linnæan system is impossible at the present day'. Nevertheless, the reviewer felt obliged to condemn this impossible quest in case, he explained, Drummond's book deterred beginners from studying botany.[39]

The real problem facing the promoters of the natural system was that it did not exist; there was no one 'natural system', instead there were several incompatible ones, all of which claimed to be natural.[40] This was cited by Drummond as a reason for retaining the Linnaean system, and the *Westminster Review* had to admit that the advocates of the natural system 'are far from being [unanimous] with regard to the grouping of the orders into cohorts, alliances, or whatever they may be called':

> This circumstance is put forth by Dr. Drummond, as a proof of the want of agreement on first principles amongst modern botanists; and he has copied into his book a great part of the view, prefixed to Professor Lindley's 'Vegetable Kingdom,' of the various natural classifications, in order to show that his system 'is one chaotic mass of confusion and uncertainty.'[41]

The natural system's apparent 'confusion and uncertainty' was problematic to the philosophical botanists for two reasons: it encouraged provincial and colonial botanists to speculate; and it led many to remain loyal to the undeniably stable Linnaean system.

[37] [Luxford], 'Natural Systems', 38; R. Desmond, *Dictionary of British and Irish Botanists and Horticulturalists: including Plant Collectors, Flower Painters and Garden Designers* (London, 1994), p. 218; *Dictionary of National Biography*.

[38] Quoted in [Luxford], 'Natural Systems', 41.

[39] [Luxford], 'Natural Systems', 41, 58.

[40] Stevens, *Biological Systematics*, p. 212.

[41] [Luxford], 'Natural Systems', 46.

The *Westminster Review* disputed Drummond's claims, asserting that the disagreements were 'far less than is generally supposed' and in any case were 'of very secondary importance in practice, since the orders still remain, altogether, or for the most part, intact'.[42] Yet, the *Westminster Review* then went on (presumably inadvertently) to provide good evidence for Drummond's argument, since its reviewer, George Luxford, devoted much of the rest of the review to explaining and defending a radical alternative to the natural system—the septenary system of classification.

'A predilection for favorite numbers'

The septenary system had been devised by the Quaker naturalist, printer and publisher, Edward Newman, who tried to show that all living things could be classified in groups of seven, with affinities joining the members of the groups and analogies connecting the groups to one another.[43] His friend George Luxford, who edited the *Phytologist* under Newman's direction, had introduced this obscure system into his review because he regarded it as having been 'unintentionally confirmed by Professor Lindley', the latter having classified plants into seven main natural classes.[44]

Despite its unusual numerological basis, Luxford—like Newman—argued that the septenary system was a natural one:

> most systematists have laboured hard to *invent* what they call a natural system, instead of contenting themselves with the endeavour to *discover* the system already existing in nature; and many of them, besides perversely following some certain track which they had previously marked out, have frequently encumbered themselves with a predilection for favorite numbers or cabalistic figures in which, as they imagined, lay the key to the mysteries of nature.[45]

According to Newman, the pattern based on the number seven was not a 'predilection for favorite numbers', but simply emerged from a study of nature. In this, and in other regards, his system was similar to the quinarian one developed by William Sharp Macleay in his *Horae Entomologicae*, 1819–21, which used groups of five, rather than seven (with groups of three

[42] [Luxford], 'Natural Systems', 46.

[43] At various times Newman published and/or edited *The Field*, *The Phytologist*, *The Entomological Magazine* and *The Zoologist*, and was a founder of the Entomological Society. The Septenary system was first outlined in Newman's *Sphinx Vespiformis* (1832) and further developed in his *System of Nature* (1843). See J. Endersby, 'Edward Newman', in B. Lightman (ed.), *Dictionary of Nineteenth-Century British Scientists* (Bristol, 2004)

[44] [Luxford], 'Natural Systems', 61.

[45] [Luxford], 'Natural Systems', 62.

serving a subsidiary role).[46] Macleay had an a priori belief in God's designing power, but also mentioned a range of independent facts to support the supposed naturalness of the system. Just as Luxford felt that septenary classification had been confirmed by Lindley, Macleay believed quinarianism was confirmed because 'different persons have respectively stumbled upon it in totally distinct departments of the creation'.[47]

Although numerological classifications seem strange to modern eyes, they were widely discussed in the early decades of the century and quinarianism in particular attracted many adherents. During his first voyage, Joseph Hooker wrote to his father about his preliminary attempts to classify the Antarctic mosses, telling him 'there are five groups I consider quite natural, and the three first of them abnormal; these are what McLeay's quinary system acknowledges'. Hooker met Macleay in Sydney and discussed classification with him, but told his father that 'you must not think that I am led away by any system, for I formed this system before I saw McLeay's and before I understood his views'.[48] Nevertheless, Hooker recorded that

> I cannot, however, forget a remark he made, saying 'he was glad I had paid so much attention to the minute Orders and to Cryptogamic Botany, *for in them would be found the foundation of a truly natural system.*' Now, though I do not put any faith in the quinary arrangement, I believe that 5 *happens to be* the number of groups into which mosses most naturally divide themselves, and I am convinced of the truth of the circular system.[49]

[46] There has, as yet, been no detailed study of quinarianism and its impacts; however discussions of the system can be found in M. Winsor, *Starfish, Jellyfish, and the Order of Life: Issues in Nineteenth-Century Science* (New Haven, 1976); Browne, 'Plant Geography'; M. di Gregorio, 'In Search of the Natural System: Problems of zoological classification in Victorian Britain', *History and Philosophy of the Life Sciences*, 4 (1982), 225–54; Browne, *Secular Ark;* P. F. Rehbock, *The Philosophical Naturalists: Themes in Early Nineteenth-Century British Biology* (Madison, Wisconsin, 1983); A. Desmond, 'The Making of Institutional Zoology in London, 1822–1836', *History of Science*, 23 (1985), 153–85, 224–50; R. O'Hara, 'Representations of the Natural System in the Nineteenth Century', *Biology and Philosophy*, 6 (1991), 255–74; D. Ospovat, *The Development of Darwin's Theory: Natural History, Natural Theology and Natural Selection, 1838–1859* (Cambridge, 1995), p. 101; G. McOuat, 'Species, Rules and Meaning: The Politics of Language and the Ends of Definitions in Nineteenth-Century Natural History', *Studies in the History and Philosophy of Science*, 27 (1996), 473–519; H. Ritvo, *The Platypus and the Mermaid: and Other Figments of the Victorian Classifying Imagination* (Cambridge, Mass., 1997); G. McOuat, 'Cataloguing power: delineating "competent naturalists" and the meaning of species in the British Museum', *British Journal of the History of Science*, 34 (2001), 1–28.

[47] W. S. Macleay, 'Remarks on the Identity of certain general Laws which have been lately observed to regulate the natural distribution of Insects and Fungi', *Transactions of the Linnean Society of London*, 14 (1825), 46–68: 63; Ospovat, *Development of Darwin's Theory*, p. 107.

[48] J. D. Hooker to W. J. Hooker, 7 March 1843: L. Huxley, *Life and Letters of Joseph Dalton Hooker (Volume I)* (London, 1918), p. 84. The Macleay family name was commonly spelt 'McLeay' in the nineteenth century.

[49] J. D. Hooker to W. J. Hooker, 7 March 1843: Huxley, *Hooker Letters (I)*, p. 84.

Hooker quoted the work of several other botanists to support his opinion, mentioning in particular the Swedish botanist Elias Fries, director of the botanic gardens at Uppsala, who had classified the fungi into groups of five quite independently of Macleay's work. After receiving a copy of Lindley's latest book, Hooker told his father that 'Lindley's Elements seems a most valuable work to me and the very one I wanted, for I have a very high opinion of him as a Nat. Order man'. Although he thought Lindley recognised too many orders, Hooker was impressed with his attempt to arrange them into a coherent plan:

> A linear arrangement will never do, and Fries's Motto 'omnis ord. nat. circulum per se clausum exhibet' is daily gaining proof, Lindley's groups and alliances of plants ... must be invaluable. I am no judge of the goodness of this arrangement of the groups, but it is the throwing the Nat. Orders into groups and showing the dependence of one group on another which impresses me.[50]

Fries' motto that all the natural orders exhibited circularity was precisely the point that Macleay had seized on when he claimed that the Swede's independent discovery of circular groups proved that his system was indeed natural.[51] These apparent confirmations of the numerical systems by other naturalists led to a surge of interest in them, and both Hooker and Darwin were briefly interested in quinary classification, as were (at different times) Richard Owen, J. E. Gray, William B. Carpenter, Robert Chambers (anonymous author of the *Vestiges*) and Thomas Huxley (who also met Macleay in Sydney, during the *Rattlesnake*'s voyage).[52] Quinarianism also gained acceptance in Britain because it was promoted by Nicholas Aylward Vigors and others as uniquely British (despite its roots in German *Naturphilosophie*), and as an alternative to the work of European systematists.[53]

Vigors, like Macleay, was one of the young reformers in the Linnean Society's Zoological Club who sought to replace the existing Linnaean classification with a radical alternative, but were unable to agree among themselves as to what the new scheme might be.[54] Adrian Haworth, another

[50] J. D. Hooker to W. J. Hooker, 25 Nov. 1842: Huxley, *Hooker Letters (I)*, p. 132. Fries motto translates as 'every natural order exhibits a self-enclosed circle'. My thanks to Dr Sachiko Kusukawa for the translation.

[51] Macleay, 'Remarks on the Identity of certain general Laws which have been lately observed to regulate the natural distribution of Insects and Fungi', 48–9.

[52] Ospovat, *Development of Darwin's Theory*, pp. 107–8.

[53] McOuat, 'Species, Rules and Meaning', 482–5.

[54] Desmond, 'Institutional Zoology', 158–62; McOuat, 'Species, Rules and Meaning', 482; McOuat, 'Cataloguing power', 16–17.

member of the Zoological Club, argued for a 'binary' or dichotomous classification, beginning with 'Mind' and 'Matter' and then proceeding by divisions of two until it encompassed all of nature—a system that had ancient precedents, but whose immediate inspiration was the philosopher Jeremy Bentham (uncle of the botanist, George).[55] Even within the narrow confines of the Linnean Society's Zoological Club, there were several different post-Linnaean systems in use, while outside it were Newman, Luxford and the septenary system. There were also specifically botanical systems in circulation, of which the most unusual may have been Thomas Baskerville's 'Arrangement of the System of Vegetable Affinities, on the principle of a Sphere'. Yet Baskerville, like the other naturalists discussed, claimed to have worked out a natural system; the preface to his book explained that the new system had grown out of his wish to 'express upon paper the connexions of some of the more intricate portions of the vegetable kingdom, and the intention was by constructing circles of affinity to be able to concentrate attention on any required group of Plants'. Although Baskerville's aims were similar to those of the quinary and septenary systems, he mentioned neither in his book, but instead dedicated it to Lindley, with the latter's permission.[56] Like other would-be systematic reformers, Baskerville stressed the superiority of a natural system to the Linnaean one, because only a natural system allowed 'the study of Affinities', which he hailed as 'a new department of botanical science' since it was 'by its aid alone that science has any claim to be philosophical'.[57]

The intensity of the feelings aroused by these debates is illustrated by an 1841 letter from the entomologist William Edward Shuckard to the editor of the *Annals and Magazine of Natural History* complaining about Edward Newman's review of the entomological article in *Lardner's Cabinet Cyclopaedia*. The article was by Shuckard and William Swainson, Macleay's most devoted supporter, but the quinarian classification of insects was, as the article made clear, by Swainson alone. However, Newman had implied the two authors were jointly responsible, sarcastically writing that 'If the views of Messrs. Swainson and Shuckard display the slightest approach to nature, then are those of Mr. Macleay the most distorted, wild and unnatural: there is

[55] See [Adrian Haworth] 'A few observations on the Natural Distribution of Animated Nature. By a Fellow of the Linnean Society', *Philosophical Magazine*, 62 (1825), 200–2. Also A. Haworth, 'A New Binary arrangement of the Brachyurous Crustacea', *Philosophical Magazine*, 65 (1825), 105–6, 183–4; McOuat, 'Species, Rules and Meaning', 482–5.

[56] T. Baskerville, *Affinities of Plants: with some Observations upon Progressive Development* (London, 1839): Thomas Baskerville was a Canterbury doctor, Desmond, *Dictionary of Botanists.*

[57] Baskerville, *Affinities of Plants*, pp. v–vii, 1.

no point of similarity between the systems, except the frequent recurrence of the number Five.'[58] Not only was quinarianism a fantasy in Newman's view, it was unstable because Swainson's version of the system diverged markedly from his mentor's.

Shuckard was anxious to distance himself from quinarianism, stating that 'I had no participation whatever in Mr. Swainson's system of classification', adding that his own views were such as 'ought to secure me from the suspicion of being wedded to any of these dictatorial systems'. Yet Shuckard's description of his approach of classification once again illustrates the difficulty facing those who wanted a stable system:

> I conceive that when all the created species are fully ascertained, the true system will be found to be neither circular, square, nor oval, neither dichotomous, quinary, nor septenary, but a uniform meshwork of organization spread like a net over the universe. But what gaps remain to be filled! We are truly as yet upon the threshold of the great temple, and consequently still remote from the adytum where the veiled statue reposes. We have not yet learned our alphabet, for species are the letters whereby the book of nature may be read.[59]

Shuckard's 'uniform meshwork' implies yet another approach to classification, and also suggests that much more work would be needed before the true natural system could be uncovered.

The range of rival classifications was positively dizzying and in several cases, their unique classificatory principles brought an equally novel nomenclature. This cacophony of competing classifications threatened natural history's claims to be a mature science; especially when it was contrasted with geology, mineralogy or chemistry, all of which were rapidly converging on internationally agreed, stable naming systems. Several metropolitan naturalists felt the need to bring stability by settling these arguments; Hugh Strickland was the most prominent zoological stabiliser, an opponent of quinarianism and other forms of classificatory radicalism.[60] He argued that 'the natural system is an accumulation of facts which are to be arrived at only by a slow inductive process', while numerical systems attempted to avoid the necessary hard work by making a priori assumptions and then trying to force organisms into them: 'these arrangements are based on an assumption that

[58] Newman's comment is quoted by Shuckard in his letter, W. E. Shuckard, 'On his falsely alleged participation in Mr Swainson's views of Natural Arrangement', *The Annals and Magazine of Natural History*, 7 (1841), 41–3 at 41. Newman's original review had appeared in the *Entomologist*, a journal he edited and published, which was presumably why Shuckard's complaint did not appear there, but had to be sent to the *Annals and Magazine of Natural History*.

[59] Shuckard, 'Mr Swainson's views', 42.

[60] McOuat, 'Species, Rules and Meaning', 494–5.

organic beings have been created on a regular and symmetrical plan, to which all true classifications must conform'.[61] He noted that there were many such a priori systems; they included linear scales, 'from man to a monad', 'a series of circles', 'the reticulations of a network', or 'the prevalence throughout of a constant number, such as 2, 3, 4, 5, or 7', but in each case the scheme necessitated 'applying a Procrustean process' to fit nature into its strictures.[62]

As Gordon McOuat has shown, these competing systems prompted Strickland to try and establish the world's first formal rules of zoological nomenclature and he attempted to use the authority of the British Association to impose them on naturalists.[63] It was an appropriate forum to use, since in 1836 Daubeny had used his presidential address to comment on the disputes between rival systems, especially the numerical ones, and had noted that however much the natural history sciences aspired to join the 'privileged and exalted order' of astronomy, they were not to be 'admitted into this august circle, merely because their admirers have chosen to cast over them a garb, oftentimes ill-fitting and inappropriate, of mathematical symbols'. Numbers could not make a science philosophical in the absence of agreement over first principles.[64] A committee headed by Strickland was set up in February 1842—Shuckard was one of its members—to report on a new system, and although its proposed zoological rules were never formally adopted, Strickland succeeded in giving them quasi-official status by ensuring they were published in the Association's *Report*.[65] He built on this by publicising them widely, thus turning them into a de facto standard.[66]

Strickland's committee came up with an ingenious solution to the problems created by the competing systems; the rules they framed deliberately avoided the contentious issue of defining a species, especially since that might have led them into the explosive issue of transmutation.[67] Instead a pragmatic definition was used: species were whatever competent naturalists

[61] H. Strickland, 'On the true method of discovering the Natural System in Zoology and Botany', *The Annals and Magazine of Natural History,* 6 (1841), 184–94 at 185–6.

[62] Strickland, 'On the true method of discovering the Natural System in Zoology and Botany', 186.

[63] McOuat, 'Species, Rules and Meaning', 476. Strickland's rules are also discussed in Ritvo, 'Zoological Nomenclature', 340–3.

[64] Daubeny, 'Address', xxiii.

[65] The zoological committee—whose members were Strickland, J. Philipps, J. Richardson, R. Owen, L. Jenyns, W. J. Broderip, J. S. Henslow, W. E. Shuckard, G. R. Waterhouse, W. Yarrell, C. Darwin and J. O. Westwood—was granted £10 for its work while, in yet another example of the BAAS's priorities, a rival committee on the nomenclature of stars, led by Herschel and Whewell, got a grant of £32: McOuat, 'Species, Rules and Meaning', 506.

[66] McOuat, 'Species, Rules and Meaning', 508–10.

[67] McOuat, 'Species, Rules and Meaning', 511.

said they were. As Strickland proclaimed, 'Nature affords us no other test of the just limits of a genus (or indeed of any other group) than the estimate of its value which a competent and judicious naturalist may form'. Competent naturalists were of course, gentlemanly ones who exhibited their competence by joining metropolitan societies and publishing in their journals. By tacitly defining who was entitled to pronounce rather than defining the basis on which pronouncements were to be made, Strickland's rules limited the range of speculators and speculations by disbarring local naturalists from the classificatory process.[68] Parallel tactics were adopted by other metropolitan specialists; Hooker's solution to the problem of instability in botanical systematics had some similarities with Strickland's approach.[69]

Thanks in part to the efforts of Strickland and his allies, metropolitan interest in quinarianism gradually faded; by 1845, Hooker was writing to Harvey that 'as to McLeay's theory, I fairly worked myself out of that error by the mosses, which I first arranged to please McLeay himself'.[70] However, the debates—and the instability they created—were far from over.

'A classification of changeful pattern'

Lindley, the Hookers, George Bentham and many other leading British botanists argued that 'the' natural system was the only acceptable alternative to either the Linnaean system or its various numerological and other rivals. They were all referring to the version of de Jussieu's system that had been refined by A-P de Candolle, yet this system still required considerable individual expertise to decide whether to create a new systematic group or abolish an existing one.[71] As a result, while all systematists agreed that there could only be one natural system, in practice they all had slightly different versions of it; as fast as some botanists split species and published new names, some of their contemporaries were busy lumping them and abolishing names.

[68] Strickland quoted in McOuat, 'Species, Rules and Meaning', 512. For Strickland, the local naturalists were mainly those in Britain's provinces, who had many features in common with the colonial naturalists.

[69] Hooker regarded Strickland's rules as useful but limited since they were devised for zoological rather than botanical purposes. As he would later write: 'With every wish to bind ourselves by the canons (most of which are excellent) laid down by the British Association for nomenclature in Natural History, we have, in common with every botanist who has tried to do so, been obliged to set them aside in many instances', J. D. Hooker and T. Thomson, *Introductory Essay to the Flora Indica* (London, 1855), p. 43.

[70] J. D. Hooker to Harvey, 8 June 1845: Huxley, *Hooker Letters (I)*, p. 123.

[71] Bowler, *History of Environmental Sciences*, p. 260.

In 1865, the *Edinburgh Review* noted that such disputes between classifiers had created 'the fashion of late years' for systematic botany to be held 'in so much contempt'. This was an urgent problem since classification was 'the groundwork upon which the correctness of the speculation of the physiologist and geographical botanist must mainly depend'.[72] The anonymous reviewer was Bentham, who admitted that the 'contempt' in which his discipline was held was perhaps understandable, given that botanists could not even agree on how a species was to be defined, or even whether they existed. The definition of basic categories, especially of species, was the most divisive issue for systematics (which was precisely why Strickland's committee had tried to avoid explicit definitions). Bentham asked 'What is a genus?', noting that this was 'a question which has led to as much controversy and difference of opinion as any other of the fundamental principles of botanical arrangement'. Such differences over basic concepts meant that 'Many naturalists of the present day consider [a genus] to have no existence in nature, but to be a mere creature of the imagination, a kind of instrument to enable man to classify the infinity of forms exhibited by nature', while others believed that genera were not only real but 'more natural than species themselves'. Bentham asserted that 'the truth probably lies between these two extremes', in that 'all species may be arranged into groups indicated by nature', but it had to be accepted that 'the precise limits and extent of each group,—call it class, order, family, tribe, genus, or section,—are purely arbitrary'.[73]

Debates between experts over defining systematic categories were complicated by the need to regulate the speculations of provincial and colonial naturalists. Describing the precise limits of taxa as 'purely arbitrary' was a dangerous admission; if they were merely the whims of individual botanists, why should a local botanist accept the judgement of a so-called expert who might never have seen the plants he purported to describe?

Squabbles between rival experts were equally confusing for the wider botanical public. What, for example, would a botanical enthusiast who bought Hewett Cottrell Watson's *Cybele Britannica* in 1860 to learn about 'British Plants and their Geographical Relations' have made of its distinguished author's attack on botanical classification in general, and on Lindley in particular? Watson argued that 'classification is sometimes erroneously supposed to require much ratiocinative capacity. It requires this in a very

72 [Bentham], 'Geographical Botany', 518.
73 [Bentham], 'Geographical Botany', 517.

small degree only, as presently executed,' adding that Lindley was 'only a describer, very feebly a reasoner':

> After labouring on it during many years, *he has utterly failed to reason out a system*, properly so designated; and he has latterly even abandoned the word 'system' as a book title. Through many changes, during which the natural system has become a natural system, and a natural system has sunk into no natural system, the learned Lindley has at last achieved a sort of mosaic classification of changeful pattern;—one much resembling Mrs Fanny Ficklemind's patchwork counterpanes.[74]

If the natural system was perceived by some as a 'changeful pattern' rather than a stable classification, it is no wonder that displacing the Linnaean system and its would-be successors proved so difficult. Such heated controversies also undermined botany's claims to scientific status; after all, individual physicists did not have their own versions of Newton's laws. Faced with such instability, it was hard for men like Hooker to claim that theirs was a genuinely philosophical science, and even harder to establish their authority over the unpaid collectors.

Watson's description of Lindley as 'very feebly a reasoner' and comparing his system to a 'patchwork counterpane' implies it was feminine in its lack of rigour and precision; whoever 'Mrs Fanny Ficklemind' might be, she was clearly no Newton.[75] Watson observed that 'men who are gifted with an observing intellect considerably in excess over their endowment of reasoning intellect, are those who now chiefly hold the lead in botanical reputation in this country' and that such men were 'not those on whose judgement it is wise or safe to rely, in regard to matters of causal reasoning, philosophical inference, or logical definition'. He described this view as 'a sort of truism in the eyes of the phrenological psychologist'.[76] As a phrenologist, Watson regarded men who lacked 'reasoning intellect' (like Lindley) as feminine (akin to Mrs Fanny Ficklemind), since phrenology held that women were generally deficient in the higher faculties required for mathematical and logical reasoning. This phrenological rationale was becoming an unorthodox

74 H. C. Watson, *Part First of a Supplement to the Cybele Britannica: to be Continued Occasionally as a Record of Progressive Knowledge Concerning the Distribution of Plants in Britain* (London, 1860), p. 24.

75 As far as I have been able to discover, 'Fanny Ficklemind' was invented by Watson, presumably in a reference to the mid-century fashion for 'crazy patchwork' ('crazy' meaning cracked as in 'crazy paving'). The name suggests a gentlewoman who constantly changed her mind and became distracted during the many months it took to stitch a large piece of work, such as a counterpane. I am grateful to Linda Cluckie for this suggestion.

76 Watson, *Cybele, Supplement*, pp. 24, 19–20. Watson had first observed that women and systematic botanists shared these intellectual deficiencies in 1833, see Stevens, *Biological Systematics*, p. 211.

one among men of science, but his views coincided well with the widespread belief that botany was peculiarly suitable for women.[77] Yet, while botany's feminine identity undoubtedly contributed to its low status in the masculine world of British science, Watson's attack on Lindley suggests that the natural system's instability was the deeper reason for botany's low prestige.

Conclusion

In conclusion, I want to ask why the main term of approval for Hooker and his contemporaries was 'philosophical', rather than 'professional'? After all, the careers of men like Hooker are often discussed in the context of the professionalisation of the sciences and Hooker was undoubtedly preoccupied with earning a living from his science, which is one way we might define 'professional'.

But I think we can understand why Hooker never uses the term 'professional' to describe himself by considering his relationship with his collectors. I mentioned earlier that—in general—he could not afford to pay them to collect. But it is clear from many of their letters that they would have refused payment even if it had been offered. For example, after his main Tasmanian collector, Ronald Campbell Gunn, had sent specimens to Lindley, and initially got no response, he told Hooker that he had a 'slight feeling of annoyance', especially 'when I compare your Conduct to his'. Gunn explained that his motive for collecting 'was purely taste, and a mind bent upon some pursuit, and not necessity or for a livelihood & I was afraid Mr. Lindley whom I only knew from his public name, might forget those points'. That is, Lindley might think Gunn was trying to sell specimens.

Gunn's stress on his 'taste' for botany and his description of it as a 'pursuit' fit with his description of himself and Hooker as 'enthusiasts like ourselves';[78] he was anxious to be seen as botanising in a gentlemanly way and gentlemen did not work for a living. One of botany's attractions for Gunn was precisely that it was a genteel pastime, something—as he said in another letter—that he pursued 'con amore' (for love). Similar sentiments were expressed by Hooker's main collector in New Zealand, the Reverend William Colenso; after his ordination, he told Hooker 'I think you know my mind—to

[77] Stevens, *Biological Systematics*, p. 199, 210–11; Huxley, *Hooker Letters (I)*, pp. 5–30.

[78] Gunn to J. D. Hooker, 26 Sept. 1844, *Kew Director's Correspondence, 1865–1900*. Vol. 218, Archives, Royal Botanic Gardens, Kew.

be devoted to the welfare of the poor Natives. *As a recreation*, however, Botany is, and will be, my darling pursuit.'[79]

But of course, Hooker could not pursue botany purely 'con amore'; he did need 'a livelihood'. In a letter to Bentham, he explained his fury against those he called 'splitters', who confused the nomenclature of botany by constantly creating new species. Hooker wrote: 'I am a *rara avis,* a man who makes his bread by specific Botany, and I feel the obstacles to my progress as obstacles on my way to the butcher's and baker's.'[80] But that need to make his bread from botany had the potential to make him seem socially inferior to his collectors, a distinctly awkward position for a man who was trying to assert his intellectual authority over them, to prevent them from naming new species. Given these circumstances, 'philosophical' was a very useful term: it was used to describe ideas, practices *and* people, but—unlike the term 'professional'—it did not define people in relation to how they earned their income. The early nineteenth century was a transitional period, in which the earlier ideal of the disinterested natural philosopher was in decline, but the idea of science as a full-time profession had not quite taken hold. Only a gentleman could be philosophical, and so anyone who wanted to be philosophical had to become a gentleman. But that required knowing what a gentleman was; in earlier times, he was defined by his pedigree, but in the early nineteenth century such clear distinctions were being replaced by the less certain ones of manners, wealth and education. Negotiating who and what was philosophical relates to a larger debate over the nature of gentility.

[79] Colenso to J. D. Hooker, 17 May 1843, *Letters to J. D. Hooker, 1843–1902*. Vol. 4, Archives, Royal Botanic Gardens, Kew. For more on Gunn and Colenso, see J. Endersby, '"From Having No Herbarium". Local Knowledge vs. Metropolitan Expertise: Joseph Hooker's Australasian Correspondence with William Colenso and Ronald Gunn', *Pacific Science*, 55 (2001), 343–58.
[80] J. D. Hooker to G Bentham, [1853], quoted in Huxley, *Hooker Letters (I)*, p. 473.

CHAPTER FOUR

Victorian Social Science: From Singular to Plural*

LAWRENCE GOLDMAN

The history of social science in nineteenth-century Britain has laboured for too long under a handicap. Its first historians presented it as an example of intellectual and institutional failure, rather than the vibrant and complex intellectual culture that will be presented here, and so deterred further systematic research. In a rather too-familiar argument, it was contended that the Victorians failed to develop systematic social theories. The sociological imagination was stunted, its impulse redirected towards the routine tasks of social investigation and social administration.[1] The British conceived of a policy-science at best; they had no taste and aptitude for theory because they had no experience of the social dislocations that prompted the more ambitious intellectual projects undertaken elsewhere. Native empiricism was explicitly and implicitly contrasted with the expansive aims and achievements of socologists elsewhere in Europe and the United States.[2] The relatively slow development of the subject in British universities was, in this view, evidence of intellectual torpor and perhaps also of academic prejudice. The plethora of types and styles of social analysis was taken as proof of a lacuna at the heart of late-Victorian intellectual life, the absence of 'an intellectually vital conceptual core'.[3] As will be argued here, such judgements depend upon false views of the development of sociology both at home and abroad. The expectation that the Victorians should have constructed a single and coherent

* This chapter draws upon material from Lawrence Goldman, *Science, Reform and Politics in Victorian Britain: The Social Science Association, 1857–1886* (Cambridge University Press, 2002), and is reproduced here with permission.

[1] Philip Abrams, *The Origins of British Sociology, 1834–1914* (Chicago, 1968), pp. 4–5, 148–9.

[2] Perry Anderson, 'Components of the National Culture', *New Left Review*, 50 (1968), 1–57.

[3] Reba Soffer, 'Why do Disciplines Fail? The Strange Case of British Sociology', *English Historical Review*, 97 (1982), 802.

discipline of sociology misinterprets the history of the subject wherever it has been professed, and requires that the remarkable public interest in a social science, and intense intellectual debate over its nature, be ignored. The aim of this essay is to write about what was, rather than what should have been.

I

'La Science Sociale' emerged in public discourse in late eighteenth-century France among the liberal intelligentsia of the Revolution gathered around Condorcet in the 'Society of 1789'. The term had developed from the earlier Physiocratic conception of 'l'art social' with which it was synonymous, and carried practical and reformist connotations as a guide to public policy and social reconstruction.[4] It was used by Comte and the Saint-Simonians in the 1820s, and it was probably from these sources that it entered discourse in Britain in the following decade,[5] though Bentham had used it in correspondence as early as 1812.[6] J. S. Mill was one obvious conduit given his French contacts: he used the term in a letter to Gustave d'Eichtal in 1829,[7] and in an important article 'On the Definition of Political Economy' written in 1831 and first published in 1836.[8] John Bowring had also used the term in his introduction to Bentham's *Deontology* published in 1834.[9] But it was not the sole property of the utilitarians. Robert Owen wrote of a 'science of society' in 1830, and of a 'social science' in the *Book of the New Moral World* in 1836, and the Ricardian Socialist, John Gray, used the term in 1831[10]—usages suggesting that 'social science' had radical connotations, as well. In 1838 and 1839 the term was employed by the Statistical Society of London

[4] K. M. Baker, 'The Early History of the Term "Social Science"', *Annals of Science*, 20 (1964), 211–26; Brian W. Head, 'The Origins of "La Science Sociale" in France', *Australian Journal of French Studies*, 19 (1982), 115–32.

[5] Peter R. Senn, 'The Earliest Use of the Term "Social Science"', *Journal of the History of Ideas*, 19 (1958), 568–70; J. H. Burns, 'J. S. Mill and the term "Social Science"', ibid., 20 (1959), 431–2; Georg G. Iggers, 'Further Remarks about the Early Uses of the Term "Social Science"', ibid., 433–6.

[6] Baker, 'The Early History of the term "Social Science"', 225; J. H. Burns, *Jeremy Bentham and University College* (London, 1962), pp. 7–8.

[7] Burns, 'J. S. Mill and the Term "Social Science"', 432.

[8] [J. S. Mill], 'On the Definition of Political Economy; and on the Method of Philosophical Investigation in that Science', *London and Westminster Review*, iv and xxvi (Oct. 1836), 11, 19.

[9] Jeremy Bentham, *Deontology: or the Science of Morality* (ed. J. Bowring) (London, 1834), 'Introduction', pp. ii, 1.

[10] Robert Owen, *Outline of a Rational System of Society* (London, 1830), p. 6, and *Book of the New Moral World* (1836), p. 61; John Gray, *The Social System. A Treatise on the Principles of Exchange*, vol. i (Edinburgh, 1831), p. 2.

to describe its own enterprise, the collection of social data.[11] By the 1850s its use was unexceptional and it had begun to be used as a general term for the full range of social, economic and historical disciplines.[12]

If we begin by sampling some of the institutions and networks that might be plotted on the map of social science we note immediately how prolific and varied they were. The statistical societies of the 1830s and 1840s, the National Association for the Promotion of Social Science, or Social Science Association as it was known, from the 1850s to the 1880s, and later the Sociological Society at the end of the Victorian era, staked a claim to the term; while a variety of institutions were founded to appropriate parts of the whole, including the Political Economy Club, the Ethnological Society of London and the Anthropological Society among many others.[13] Beyond institutions, there were groups of different types with a claim on social science. Some were recognisably academic such as the Cambridge inductivists of the 1830s including the natural scientist, William Whewell; the mathematician, Charles Babbage; and the political economists, Malthus and Richard Jones, who together sought to establish a statistical social science in reaction against deductive political economy.[14] Others were intrinsically political, such as the philosophical radicals of the 1820s and 1830s who followed Bentham. There were movements, part social and also quasi-religious, like the Owenites and the English Positivists, whose followers looked to Robert Owen and Auguste Comte respectively, both of whom claimed to have discovered the laws of social science. Later, Darwinian ideas and their corruption inspired attempts to demonstrate the identity of the social and natural worlds premised on the concept of 'social evolution'. There were also lone scholars who laboured to show the system within society: Henry Thomas Buckle was one such, whose most famous work, *History of Civilization in England*, was published in 1857 at a moment when social science inspired its greatest interest among the Victorians.

[11] 'Fourth Annual Report of the Statistical Society of London', *Journal of the Statistical Society of London* (May 1838), 8; 'Fifth Annual Report of the Statistical Society of London', ibid (April 1839), 133.

[12] See for example [David Masson] 'The Social Science: its History and Prospects', *The North British Review*, 15, xxx (Aug. 1851), 291–330.

[13] M. J. Cullen, *The Statistical Movement in Early Victorian Britain: The Foundation of Empirical Social Research* (Hassocks, 1975); R. J. Halliday, 'The Sociological Movement, the Sociological Society and the Genesis of Academic Sociology in Britain', *Sociological Review*, NS, 16 (1968), 377–98.

[14] Lawrence Goldman, 'The Origins of British "Social Science": Political Economy, Natural Science and Statistics, 1830–1835', *The Historical Journal*, 26 (1983), 587–616; Mary Poovey, *A History of the Modern Fact. Problems of Knowledge in the Sciences of Wealth and Society* (Chicago and London, 1998), pp. 307–17.

Nineteenth-century social science was the product of three great changes, intellectual, material, and spiritual. The European Enlightenment of the seventeenth and eighteenth centuries had stimulated the development and institutionalisation of the natural sciences and had created a new 'map of knowledge' and taxonomy of subjects—a new 'order of things' in Foucault's phrase—which is with us to this day.[15] This map included social science as one of the departments of human speculation. The very success of Enlightenment natural science in explaining the principles of a Newtonian universe provided a model for the study of human societies. Indeed, social science would be the culmination of Enlightenment science, applying the new philosophy to that most recalcitrant subject, man himself. As Buckle wrote,

> It is this deep conviction, that changing phenomena have unchanging laws and that there are principles of order to which all apparent disorder may be referred,—it is this, which, in the seventeenth century, guided in a limited field Bacon, Descartes, and Newton; which in the eighteenth century was applied to every part of the material universe; and which it is the business of the nineteenth century to extend to the history of the human intellect.[16]

The material changes of an industrial age were a second reason for taking up the subject. Nineteenth-century social science was held together by a common agenda of objects of analysis: the expansion of population and the growth of industries and manufacturing which were of interest to members of the provincial statistical movement in the early Victorian period; the development of mass culture and democracy, which were central themes in the work of Tocqueville and Mill a generation later; and, in the late-nineteenth century, the growing awareness of complexity, interdependence and specialisation within mature industrial societies which encouraged, even before publication of *The Origin of Species*, an evolutionary framework of thought in which human societies, like biological organisms, were seen to develop from simple to complex structures.[17]

Together, rationalism and industrialisation caused the third change, the decline of conventional Christian belief and worship. Sociology emerged 'out of the collapse or revaluation of older theories, philosophical and religious'.[18] New social authorities were required, based not upon divine sanction, but on

[15] Michel Foucault, *The Order of Things: An Archaeology of the Human Sciences* (London, English edn., 1974), xix–xxii; Poovey, *History of the Modern Fact*, esp. pp. 16–18.
[16] Henry Thomas Buckle, *History of Civilization in England*, 2 vols. (London, 1857, 1861), i, p. 807.
[17] See, for example, [Herbert Spencer], 'Progress: Its Law and Cause', *Westminster Review*, NS, xi (April 1857), 445–85.
[18] J. W. Burrow, *Evolution and Society. A Study in Victorian Social Theory* (Cambridge, 1966), p. 264.

what could be known by men and women themselves from the study of society, and then applied by them in its reform. Beatrice Webb defined 'the mid-Victorian time-spirit' as 'the union of faith in the scientific method with the transference of the emotion of self-sacrificing service from God to man'.[19] She thus captured both aspects of the contemporary meaning of the term 'positivism' as derived from the assimilation of Comte's ideas into British intellectual culture in the 1850s and 1860s.[20] On the one hand positivism denoted a commitment to natural science as a model for all disciplines because, it was argued, natural science was the only type of knowledge that could be tested and proven. On the other, it denoted the attempt to establish a new basis for ethical action in reason and humanity rather than supernatural inspiration.[21] If we can map social science according to the nature of the institutions which investigated it, we can also represent it in terms of the distinctive intellectual and material changes that gave rise to it, and the particular social questions on which different generations focused.

However, these *objects* of analysis did not throw up new *concepts* of analysis. Nineteenth-century social science, at least before the classical era of Weber and Durkheim, was synthetic, modelling itself on other sciences, and employing ideas drawn from them. Even here there was no agreement as to the most appropriate model: mathematics, physics or biology? Bentham wrote of a 'social calculus'.[22] Comte in France, and Quetelet, the Belgian statistician, both of whom had powerful influence over British contemporaries, imagined a 'social physics'.[23] Meanwhile, the language of social science had always and instinctively employed biological analogies. One member came before the Social Science Association in 1858 to outline a 'comparative sociology' modelled on 'the principle of comparative anatomy, that of proceeding from the simplest type to the most complicated and highly developed condition'.[24] George Eliot went further still, comparing

[19] Beatrice Webb, *My Apprenticeship* (London, 1926), p. 221.

[20] T. R. Wright, *The Religion of Humanity: The Impact of Comtean Positivism on Victorian Britain* (Cambridge, 1986); Christopher Kent, *Brains and Numbers: Elitism, Comtism and Democracy in Mid-Victorian Britain* (Toronto, 1978); Royden Harrison, *Before the Socialists. Studies in Labour and Politics, 1861–1881* (Pt. 6, 'The Positivists. A Study of Labour's Intellectuals') (London, 1965).

[21] Charles D. Cashdollar, *The Transformation of Theology, 1830–1890. Positivism and Protestant Thought in Britain and America* (Princeton, NJ, 1989), pp. 16–18.

[22] Mary P. Mack, *Jeremy Bentham: An Odyssey of Ideas* (London, 1962) pp. 18, 243–53, 269–70.

[23] Adolphe Quetelet, *Sur l'Homme et le Développement de ses Facultés: Physique Sociale* (Brussels, 1835).

[24] Revd W. N. Molesworth, 'Suggestions for the Institution of a new Social Science, under the name of Comparative Sociology', *Transactions of the National Association for the Promotion of Social Science, 1858* (London, 1859), 697.

different facets of social science with the full range of natural scientific disciplines:

> So Social Science, while it has departments which in their fundamental generality correspond to mathematics and physics, namely those grand and simple generalizations which trace out the inevitable march of the human race as a whole, and as a ramification of these, the laws of economical science, has also, in the departments of government and jurisprudence, which embrace the conditions of social life in all their complexity, what may be called its Biology, carrying us on to innumerable special phenomena which outlie the sphere of science, and belong to Natural History.[25]

In many different projects, human society was compared to an organism, subject to periods of disorder, and hence requiring remedial intervention whether by the state or some voluntary agency. Such language also encouraged the wholesale integration of social with organic paradigms in the form known as 'Social Darwinism', in which a version of evolutionary theory was held to apply to human society and to mandate social ethics and organisation founded upon it.

To add to this pluralism among those who professed to be developing social science, there were competitors in the field. In Britain social science had to contend with the claims of political economy in particular. The original Enlightenment project of a social science, as developed in the Scotland of Smith and Hume, had encouraged the study of economic life as a component of the science of morals and legislation. But economic transformation led minds of great insight to focus on a limited set of economic interactions and to explain them in a deductive system of beguiling clarity. Ricardian economics was the greatest triumph of Enlightenment science applied to the study of man.[26] But its exactitude entailed a weakness: the neglect of non-economic aspects of human behaviour and non-economic institutions. To achieve the form of a deductive science, political economy made assumptions about human nature which were vigorously contested; ignored the diversity of economic practices across different societies and periods; and disregarded empirical data which might confute its deductions. To its critics it had so limited its scope and method as to be of little value in the explanation of real economic interactions. Among many others George Eliot judged it mistaken 'to believe that all social questions are merged in economical science, and that the relations of men to their neighbours may be settled by algebraic

[25] George Eliot, 'The Natural History of German Life', *Westminster Review* (July 1856), in George Eliot, *Selected Essays, Poems and Other Writings* (Harmondsworth, 1990), p. 130. I am grateful to Eric Southworth for this reference.

[26] David Ricardo, *On the Principles of Political Economy, and Taxation* (London, 1817); Mark Blaug, *Ricardian Economics: A Historical Study* (New Haven, 1958).

equations'.[27] Nevertheless, political economy achieved pre-eminence in Victorian life, filling the intellectual space that devotees of social science believed was rightfully theirs. Many of the social-scientific projects of the age, including the inductivism of Jones and Whewell, the Positivism of Frederic Harrison, and the institutionalism of Beatrice Webb, were designed to analyse social and economic interactions as they actually occurred, and to demonstrate the limitations of classical and neo-classical political economy.[28] Marxism—developing in mid-Victorian Britain along an axis often seen as independent from Victorian social science, but still coinciding with it at several points—was also 'a contribution to the critique of political economy' as Marx's text of 1859 was entitled. It sought to vindicate its claim to be a 'science' by demonstrating that political economy was but a bourgeois ideology.

The historian of Victorian social science faces the problem of definition. Are all these competing projects to be included, and, if so, what unites them? The problem has sometimes been 'solved' by ignoring the need for definition entirely, or by presenting only a limited spectrum of projects which are definable because conformable. The latter approach usually entails narrowing social science to the work of social theorists and the analysis of their texts at the expense of projects that did not take this form, and of any wider consideration of social science as an aspect of general culture. Invariably, it has meant the neglect of what has become known as 'empirical sociology'—the investigation of society through the collection of social data. It is agreed that this neglect results in a very inaccurate account of the development of the discipline but correcting the imbalance is notoriously difficult.[29] And it has had adverse effects on an estimation of specifically British social science given the national tradition of empirical social investigation. The standard division in the literature between social theory and social research does little justice to the intellectual aspirations of the Victorian age. The statistical movement in Britain was more than an exercise in the collection of useful information: William Farr and other pioneers aspired to collect data to demonstrate the regularities in human behaviour and social organisation, and hence establish statistics as a predictive social science in itself.[30]

[27] Eliot, 'The Natural History of German Life', 111–12.

[28] Goldman, 'The Origins of British "Social Science"', 615–16.

[29] Raymond Aron, *Main Currents in Sociological Thought* (2 vols., Harmondsworth, 1967 edn.), vol. ii, p. 8; E. Shils, 'Tradition, Ecology and Institution in the History of Sociology', *Daedalus*, 99 (1970), 766; P. F. Lazarsfeld, 'Toward a History of Empirical Sociology' in E. Privat (ed.), *Mèlanges en l'Honneur de Fernand Braudel: Methodologie de l'Histoire et des Sciences Humaines* (Toulouse, 1973), p. 290.

[30] John M. Eyler, *Victorian Social Medicine. The Ideas and Methods of William Farr* (London, 1979); Lawrence Goldman, 'Statistics and the Science of Society in Early Victorian Britain: An Intellectual Context for the General Register Office', *Social History of Medicine*, 4 (1991) 415–34.

If certain types of social science have been ignored, therefore, so also have certain ways in which knowledge was institutionalised in the nineteenth century. For example, a cursory glance through the voluminous *Transactions* of the Social Science Association will show very quickly that it was not a learned society and that it sponsored relatively little social investigation itself. It attracted the occasional participation of social theorists—Mill, Spencer and Le Play attended—but only in discussions on matters eminently practical. It represents a different way of organising and applying social knowledge that is not easily classifiable in our contemporary terms. Very few of its members were employed in social research, and none at all in social speculation; and no one among its membership of over a thousand people derived their professional identity from social science, though this is not unusual in our story: the professionalisation of the social sciences in Britain was a slow process over many decades, and many of the most important social-scientific contributions before the mid-twentieth century were made by members of other professional groups, such as lawyers, doctors, businessmen and gentlemen-scholars. In similar fashion, we can acknowledge the contributions of public servants to the development of Victorian social science, and trace back the state's competence in social research to the age of Chadwick, Farr and Simon. But we must be aware that these men worked in a relatively unformed state structure in which the boundaries between government and civil society were unmarked. Thus they appeared to their contemporaries to be members of scientific and learned communities, and also of activist pressure groups, as well as members of the central bureaucracy simultaneously. Again, a contemporary sense of the boundaries between different types of institution and different social and intellectual practices does not fit the past.

The difficulty of appreciating the ways in which social science was institutionalised in the nineteenth century only increases when considering movements like Owenism and Positivism, which claimed to be based on the principles of social science, and which spread knowledge of those principles in Owenite Halls of Science and the Positivist Church rather than lecture rooms and learned periodicals. Social science was, for both movements, the foundation of a secular faith. As Christianity ebbed and the Bible lost its social authority, so other systems of knowledge were devised to instruct and direct society. For members of 'secular religions' like Positivism and Owenism, science would promote reason, reason would promote brotherhood, and in brotherhood society would be reformed to comply with the principles of social science. Yet these movements do not fit into the familiar categories of historical and sociological analysis: the combination of science and religion (and non-Christian religion at that) is as much a challenge to our sense of academic proprieties as it was to Victorian religious sensibilities.

A comprehensive history of social science must also grasp the existence of a 'sociological imagination' that was never institutionalised at all, and never recognised its affinities with formal academic projects in social science. The American sociologist, C. Wright Mills, once observed that in comparison with other industrial societies, England was late to recognise the educational claims of sociology and institutionalise it in universities. Yet the culture was remarkably self-analytical: 'In England... sociology as an academic discipline is still somewhat marginal', he wrote, 'yet in much English journalism, fiction, and above all history, the sociological imagination is very well developed indeed.'[31] Dickens, Carlyle, Thackeray, Macaulay and Mayhew gave mid-Victorians an acute sense of themselves, and of the depths to which their compatriots could sink or be pushed, without claiming the authority of science. As Hawthorn concluded in his history of sociology published in the mid-1970s, at the turn of the twentieth century 'sociology was virtually absent in England as an intellectually and academically distinctive pursuit because it was virtually everywhere present as part of the general liberal and liberal-socialist consciousness'.[32]

These observations throw up a further 'problem of genre' in writing the history of nineteenth-century social science. A discipline lacking agreed procedures and aims encouraged a plethora of analytical styles: the learned periodical article; the communication to a provincial statistical society; the formal public address and informal intervention at the Social Science Association; the grand, theoretical treatise. To define social science in terms of a limited number of theoretical texts has scholarly advantages. But it was also part of popular culture, capturing the imagination and participation of thousands of non-specialists attracted to the fashionable and modish science of the day. Sir James Stephen, the great colonial civil servant, expecting to address a scientific society, learnt this to his cost at the Liverpool congress of the Social Science Association in 1858 where he delivered a learned essay on colonial emigration which was ill-judged for such an organisation. As he explained to his son, 'I had quite misunderstood what sort of discourses were to be delivered, & when I heard them one after another, & perceived how completely out of concert pitch my own meditated sayings would be, I should, I think, have bolted by the first express train, if, as good luck would have it, I had not

[31] C. Wright Mills, *The Sociological Imagination* (1959; Harmondsworth, 1970 edn.), p. 26 n.

[32] G. Hawthorn, *Enlightenment and Despair. A History of Sociology* (Cambridge, 1976), p. 170.

been absolved from speaking on the same day.'[33] He noted 'the strange contrast between my lecturing and other people's exhortations': undoubtedly it was the latter style that commanded the podium at the Social Science Association. As such, 'social science' must be approached in ways more sensitive to the popularisation of Victorian knowledge and to cultural history in general. In the mid-nineteenth century, 'social science' drew new groups into civic reform and political life, and promised social improvement and consensus based on reasoned solutions to practical problems of the age. These are aspects of the history of social science which a conventional history of texts must overlook.

A final difficulty concerns the different national contexts from which social science emerged. Its exponents sought a universal account of human communities, but were rooted in different societies, and, for that reason, either concentrated on different issues, or reached different answers to similar questions. Nineteenth-century Britain had, by common consent, the most ordered polity and most plural civil society of any nation in Europe. Little wonder that its social science eschewed great questions of national identity, class conflict and social structure, which did not need to be answered because they were not being posed, and concentrated instead on the refinements of civic order—on the investigation and remedy of small-scale social ills. Conversely, in societies that had experienced national disunity, like the United States; or lacked political stability, like France; or could not achieve social and political consensus, like Germany after unification, the questions asked were of a different order, and called forth answers of much greater ambition and scope.[34] And when there *was* a convergence on similar questions, different national cultures provided answers in different genres. As Raymond Williams suggested, though there are similarities linking the subjects of British social debate in the nineteenth century with the developing discipline of sociology on the continent, the two traditions took root in different institutional settings and generated dissimilar styles of discourse. The British tradition of 'culture and society'—the literary-critical tradition of Carlyle, Ruskin and Arnold—which was concerned with the cultural effects of the development of an industrial, market society, was addressing 'the main

[33] James Stephen to James Fitzjames Stephen, 20 Oct. 1858, James Fitzjames Stephen Papers, Cambridge University Library, Add. 7349, Box 1, f. 80. *The Times*, 18 Oct. 1858, 6. Perhaps Stephen need not have worried: the earl of Carlisle (Morpeth) who also attended the 1858 congress thought the address 'very striking and most interesting' — though praise from such an earnest, industrious and dutiful Whig administrator may actually confirm Stephen's impression. Diaries of the 7th earl of Carlisle, 13 Oct. 1857, Castle Howard MSS, J 19/8/36, 1857–8.

[34] J. D. Y. Peel, *Herbert Spencer. The Evolution of a Sociologist* (London, 1971), p. 240.

theme of European Sociology from its founding moment onwards', according to Williams, but made no effort to develop its critique in a scientific discourse.[35]

II

The analysis of two influential and representative projects may assist in the characterisation of Victorian social science. The first, the 'statistical movement' so-called, established a dominant genre of social science in the generation up to 1860; the second, the discipline of social evolution, provided the leading—though never dominant—paradigm for sociological thinking from the mid-century.

The proliferation and analysis of social statistics seemed to offer the early Victorians a means to self-knowledge of a new type and on a new scale.[36] In most accounts, the collection of social data has been understood as the product of a now mature industrial society seeking information on which to base new social policies. The investigative Royal Commissions of the 1830s and 1840s, especially the Poor Law Commission that preceded the New Poor Law of 1834; the foundation of the General Register Office in 1836; and the improvement of the decennial census from 1841, seem to fit an expected pattern linking the gathering of information to new social legislation, enhanced and more expert social administration, and the growth of government. This was the age that witnessed the first systematic social policies, and social information was crucial to the process. But if statistical enquiry had obvious relevance for social reform and improvement, it also had its place in intellectual life and the attempt to develop a new science of society. The complex history of the movement's origins in the late 1820s and early 1830s illustrates the several opportunities made possible by the generation and collection of statistics.

The statistical movement had different and not always compatible outposts in the courts and alleys of Manchester; the colleges of Cambridge; Burlington House in Piccadilly where scientific societies convened; the streets of Clerkenwell and the shipyards of the Thames. The Manchester Statistical Society, the model of several such societies formed in provincial cities in Britain in the 1830s, was called into being in response to the local house-to-house medical surveys undertaken during the 1832 cholera

[35] Raymond Williams, *Politics and Letters* (London, 1979), pp. 113–14.

[36] Cullen, *The Statistical Movement in Early Victorian Britain*, *passim*.

epidemic in the city.[37] Its membership was largely drawn from the urban business and professional elite; its focus was on civic reform; its politics were as we might expect—hostile to state regulation of enterprise and labour, but much more accommodating to legislation on matters of public health, for cholera was no respecter of persons. The collection of data on economic and social life was the motive and cue for local improvements but demonstrates also the profound interest by the 1830s in charting, analysing and explaining the remarkable changes through which urban Britain was passing. Sheer curiosity, civic pride and the imperatives of social regulation explain this particular form of social science. As the society's first annual report put it, 'The Manchester Statistical Society owes its origins to a strong desire felt by its projectors to assist in promoting the progress of social improvement in the manufacturing population by which they are surrounded.'[38]

In Cambridge, however, the statistical project was very different. There, under the aegis of William Whewell, fellow and later Master of Trinity College, the collection of social statistics was intimately bound up with a particular type of natural science and with an attempt to develop a new political economy.[39] Humboldtian Science, so-called by Cannon, and named after the German naturalist Alexander von Humboldt, was championed by Whewell as a method by which the regularities of nature could be demonstrated and assessed.[40] By measuring and counting, be it in astronomy, tidology or economics, it would be possible to demonstrate the laws and relationships which governed the behaviour of different natural and also social phenomena. In opposition to the deductivism of Ricardian political economy, Whewell and his closest collaborator, the Revd Richard Jones, later Professor of Political Economy at King's College, London, hoped also to establish a more accurate, sensitive and useful inductive economics, that did not depend on a priori reasoning and generalisations about human behaviour, but which explained—on the basis of history, actuality and statistics—how and why

[37] T. S. Ashton, *Economic and Social Investigation in Manchester, 1833–1933: A Centenary History of the Manchester Statistical Society* (London, 1934); T. R. Wilkinson, 'On the Origin and History of the Manchester Statistical Society', *Transactions of the Manchester Statistical Society'*, 1875–6, pp. 9–17; David Elesh, 'The Manchester Statistical Society: A Case Study of Discontinuity in the History of Empirical Social Research' in Anthony Oberschall (ed.), *The Establishment of Empirical Sociology: Studies in Continuity, Discontinuity and Institutionalization* (New York, 1972), pp. 31–70.

[38] Ashton, *Economic and Social Investigation*, p. 14.

[39] Goldman, 'The Origins of British "*Social Science*"', *passim*.

[40] Susan Faye Cannon, *Science in Culture: The Early Victorian Period* (New York, 1978), pp. 104–5. See also pp. 240–4.

economic interactions took place.[41] Interestingly, Jones and Whewell were among the first in Britain to read and be influenced by the Saint-Simonians and Auguste Comte, designated 'founders' of sociology. Assisted by John Herschel, Charles Babbage and Robert Malthus, they made a remarkable group, sometimes referred to as the Cambridge Inductivists. When the British Association for the Advancement of Science held its third meeting in Cambridge in 1833 they were instrumental in establishing within the organisation, despite opposition, a department devoted to 'statistical science', Section F, which quickly became a key Victorian platform for the many variants of social science. For Jones and Whewell the multiple measurements which had unlocked the pattern of the natural world offered the same key to the social realm. Statistics were the raw material and the methodology of an inductive science of society.

The creation of Section F was the precursor to the construction of the Statistical Society of London (now the Royal Statistical Society) in the following year.[42] And here a further constituency was added to the statistical movement, a group of the political class, largely Whig in affiliation, who rubbed shoulders with the civic reformers, physicians and savants at meetings of the society, and looked to social statistics to provide the information for the legislation concerning pauperism, elementary education and the regulation of factory hours, which was to be a defining feature of the administrations of the 1830s. There was a national political interest in statistics as the 'raw material of social legislation' as one newspaper was to put it,[43] and throughout the nineteenth century leading parliamentarians and civil servants attended the Society's meetings to learn about the state of the nation and assimilate information as a basis for reform, or, in some cases, as confirmation of the social achievements of the age. Thus Gladstone took great solace from the 1883 presidential address to the Statistical Society by Robert Giffen, head of the Statistical Department of the Board of Trade, on 'The Progress of the Working Class in the Last Half Century', which seemed to demonstrate to the prime minister the unambiguous improvement, by various measurements, of the living standards of the people. It was, he wrote, 'a masterly paper', and 'probably in form and in substance the best answer to [Henry] George',

[41] Richard Jones, *An Essay on the Distribution of Wealth and on the Sources of Taxation. Part I. Rent* (London, 1831); W. L. Miller, 'Richard Jones: A Case Study in Methodology', *History of Political Economy*, 3 (1971), 198–207.

[42] V. L. Hilts, '*Aliis Exterendum*, or the Origins of the Statistical Society of London', *Isis* (1978), 21–43; J. Bonar and H. W. Macrosty, *Annals of the Royal Statistical Society, 1834–1934* (London, 1934).

[43] *Daily Telegraph*, 6 Oct. 1871, 4.

whose *Progress and Poverty*, published in 1879, had so revitalised socialism in Victorian Britain.[44]

But the Statistical Society of London was founded some years after another body, the elusive London Statistical Society, a creation of the mid-1820s. And the first of the capital's statistical societies was very different in composition and aim from its more illustrious successor. It was formed by artisans apparently close to John Gast, the shipwright and leading London trades unionist.[45] Among them, the clockmaker, John Powell of Clerkenwell, who wrote on political economy, stands out.[46] It was claimed that a network of co-workers and sympathisers across the nation had worked to funnel information to them, and the product was a volume entitled *Statistical Illustrations... of the British Empire*, ('every line a moral: every page a history') published in 1825.[47] But there could be no satisfaction for the political elite in the statistical tables and compilations in its pages: for the purpose of these artisan statisticians was to prove the immiseration of the working classes and the deterioration of social conditions over a period of a generation or so. They were the original pessimists, we might say, in the famous 'standard of living debate' of the 1960s and 1970s, compiling data on rising levels of pauperism, prices and crime, and declining wages to illustrate the privations of working people. Their researches remind us of similar forms of working-class protest against social injustice, particularly that critical and often satirical genre represented by John Wade's *Extraordinary Black Book* of 1831, which sought to detail the unmerited privileges of the rich and the institutionalised larceny—'Old Corruption', in fact—of the servants and placemen of state, often in statistical form.[48]

All these groups sought to compile and make use of the newly available statistical data. Among them were some who believed that statistics would

[44] Robert Giffen, 'The Progress of the Working Classes in the Last Half-Century', *Journal of the Statistical Society of London*, xlvi (1883), 593–622. For Gladstone's response, see ibid., xlvii (1884), 174. See also *The Gladstone Diaries* (ed. H. C. G. Matthew), XI (Oxford, 1990), 26–7 Dec. 1883, pp. 83–4.

[45] Iorwerth Prothero, *Artisans and Politics in Early Nineteenth-Century London. John Gast and his Times* (1979; London, 1981 edn.), pp. 224–5.

[46] See, for example, John Powell, *An Analytical Exposition of the Erroneous Principles and Ruinous Consequences of the Financial and Commercial Systems of Great Britain. Illustrative of Their Influence on the Physical, Social and Moral Condition of the People* (London, 1826).

[47] *Statistical Illustrations of the Territorial Extent and Population, Commerce, Taxation, Consumption, Insolvency, Pauperism and Crime of the British Empire* (London, 1825).

[48] John Wade, *The Extraordinary Black Book: An Exposition of the United Church of England and Ireland; Civil List and Crown Revenues; Incomes, Privileges, and Power of the Aristocracy...* (London, 1831). *The Black Book* was originally serialised between 1820 and 1823. The 1831 edition was much amended and updated.

form the basis of a new social science, more accurate and faithful to human actions than anything which had gone before. Insofar as this social science was modelled on natural science and was to provide the basis for local reform and national statescraft, it fulfilled both of the defining criteria for what has become known as 'positivism'. But it is also clear that statistics had multiple meanings and functions, and were collected and used by mutually antagonistic groups: workers, employers and whig social reformers among them. We might better speak of 'statistical movements' in the plural than a single statistical movement. And we should be aware that these movements demonstrate very effectively that nineteenth-century social science was a 'contest' in which different groups strove to develop and control social science in their own interests, be they intellectual or purely political, and to dignify those interests by claiming higher, 'scientific' sanction for them.[49]

From this complex point of origin the statistical movements spread their influence through many different sectors of society.[50] In the shape of the Statistical Department of the Board of Trade statistics entered the heart of government and provided the data on which the mid-Victorian policy of free trade was founded.[51] In provincial statistical societies and the press, criminal statistics and their interpretation became a subject of public controversy.[52] In the absence of microbiological understanding of the origin and propagation of disease the medical profession looked to statistical analysis of the pattern of distribution of cases, the relationship of disease to specific environmental and locational factors and so forth, to provide a new basis for a science of health. The celebrated Dr William Farr, 'compiler of abstracts' in the General Register Office and the designer of the mid-Victorian censuses, and colleagues like William Guy, Professor of Medicine at King's College, London and a founder of the Health of Towns Association, and Dr John Simon, Medical Officer at the Privy Council between 1858 and 1871, linked statistics to medicine in heroic efforts to explain and control mid-Victorian epidemics and to force successive administrations to do something to assist the public's health.[53] For Florence Nightingale also, statistical science was the most important key to the laws of health and the reform of medical care.

[49] Eileen Yeo, *The Contest for Social Science. Relations and Representations of Gender and Class* (London, 1996).

[50] Lawrence Goldman, 'Statistics and the Science of Society in Early Victorian Britain: An Intellectual Context for the General Register Office', *Social History of Medicine,* 4 (1991), 415–34.

[51] Lucy Brown, *The Board of Trade and the Free Trade Movement, 1830–42* (London, 1958), pp. 76–93.

[52] Cullen, *The Statistical Movement*, pp. 139–44.

[53] Eyler, *Victorian Social Medicine, passim*; Royston Lambert, *Sir John Simon, 1816–1904, and English Social Administration* (London, 1963).

It was 'the one Science essential to all Political and Social Administration' as she described it in a letter to William Farr, and she is seen more accurately as an avid reader of Blue Books than the mythical 'lady with the lamp'.[54] Meanwhile the pre-eminent intellectual influence on the British statistical movements, the Belgian astronomer and mathematician Adolphe Quetelet, sometime tutor to Prince Albert, had used the measurement of man himself—his height and weight, his features and physical capacity—to found the new science of anthropometry as set out in his classic study of 1835, *Sur L'Homme et le Développement de ses Facultés: Physique Sociale*, one of the founding texts in any version of the history of sociology, and a book that points forward to the development of eugenics by Galton and Pearson later in the century.[55]

III

The promise of statistics, and intense public expectation that a social science of reform would provide a guide to social practice, led to that juncture when, it may be argued, Victorian social science reached its apogee, its moment, its brief period of cultural centrality. This came in the late 1850s and early 1860s and was evident at two grand public events, the International Statistical Congress in London in 1860, which secured the patronage and participation of Prince Albert and the prime minister, Palmerston,[56] and the London congress of the Social Science Association two years later when its members took over the capital and were allowed the rare privileges of a service at Westminster Abbey, a soirée in the Palace of Westminster, and a banquet at the Crystal Palace.[57] Public interest was matched by intellectual endeavour for at this point also some of the most compelling and influential social-scientific projects were conceived and launched by many of the intellectual leaders of the age including Buckle, Spencer, Darwin, and Ruskin.

[54] Florence Nightingale to William Farr, 23 Feb. 1874, quoted in Marion Diamond and Mervyn Stone, 'Nightingale on Quetelet', *Journal of the Royal Statistical Society*, series A, vol. 144 (1981), 66–79 and 176–213 (quote at 73); F. B. Smith, *Florence Nightingale: Reputation and Power* (London, 1982).

[55] We lack a recent study of Quetelet's work and influence. See F. H. Hankins, 'Adolphe Quetelet as Statistician', *Columbia University Studies in History, Economics and Public Law*, 31 (New York, 1908).

[56] [William Farr (ed.)], *Report of the Proceedings of the Fourth Section of the International Statistical Congress, Held in London, July 16, 1860 and the Five Following Days* (London, 1861).

[57] *Transactions of the National Association for the Promotion of Social Science 1862* (vol. vi, London, 1863); Goldman, *Science, Reform, and Politics*, pp. 74–6.

To start with the first of these figures, in June 1857 Buckle published his *History of Civilization in England* which was acclaimed, in Mark Pattison's words, as 'the most important work of the season'[58] and welcomed as 'the *Novum Organum* of historical and social science'.[59] In his famous introductory chapter Buckle noted the 'extensive information, not only respecting the material interests of men, but also respecting their moral peculiarities' which society now possessed. Yet no one had attempted to combine the 'separate parts' of the 'history of man' now available 'into a whole, and ascertain the way in which they are connected with each other'.[60] Hence arose the central question of his inquiry, indeed the central issue of nineteenth-century social science: 'Are the actions of men, and therefore of societies, governed by fixed laws, or are they the result either of chance or of superfluous influence?'[61] Buckle noted 'proofs of the existence of a uniformity in human affairs which statisticians had been the first to bring forward'.[62] The incidence of murder, suicide and crime, as well as more benign aspects of human social behaviour were established as predictable and calculable.[63] On the basis of perceived statistical regularities in human actions when considered in the aggregate, *en masse*, he claimed in 1857 that a scientific history was possible. The chapter concluded with the prediction that 'before another century has elapsed the chain of evidence will be complete, and it will be as rare to find an historian who denies the undeviating regularity of the moral world, as it now is to find a philospher who denies the regularity of the material world'.[64] Buckle was wrong—one imagines that no one now would agree—but there was no more characteristically optimistic mid-Victorian prediction of the potential of social science.

It is conceivable that public interest in Buckle's work during the summer of 1857 influenced the founders of the Social Science Association, which first convened in October of that year, in their choice of 'social science' as a description of their organisation and aims.[65] It can be asserted with greater confidence that Buckle's faith in the statistical demonstrability of social regularities analogous to the 'fixed and universal laws' of the natural world, and

[58] [Mark Pattison], 'History of Civilization in England', *The Westminster Review*, NS, xii (Oct. 1857), 375.

[59] [W. Frederick Pollock], 'Buckle's History of Civilization in England', *Quarterly Review*, civ, no. 207 (July 1858), 38.

[60] Buckle, *History of Civilization in England*, i, pp. 2–3.

[61] Ibid., p. 8.

[62] Ibid., p. 20

[63] Ibid., pp. 23, 25.

[64] Ibid., p. 31.

[65] Goldman, *Science, Reform, and Politics*, pp. 304–5, 309.

his attempts to encompass all aspects of human behaviour within a single system captured the imagination of mid-Victorians, and demonstrate to us that science and synthesis were in the air in the later 1850s. As Lord Acton observed, Buckle's *History*, 'must have powerfully appealed to something or other in the public mind... in order to have won so rapid a popularity'.[66]

The point may be reinforced with evidence that Herbert Spencer's 'crucial moment of intellectual enlightenment' occurred a few months after publication of Buckle's volume (and a matter of weeks after the inauguration of the Social Science Association) in January 1858.[67] At this point Spencer came to realise that his various ideas 'have suddenly crystallized into a complete whole'. As he wrote then to his father, 'Many things which were before lying separate have fallen into their places as harmonious parts of a system that admits of logical development from the simplest general principles.'[68] To Mill he explained that 'the various special ideas which I had decided hereafter to publish on certain divisions of Biology, Psychology and Sociology, have fallen into their places as parts of the general body of doctrine thus originating'. To Hooker he explained that his chief aim was 'to treat Psychology and Sociology after the spirit and methods of physical science'.[69] Spencer's fundamental principle was the identity of organic, inorganic and social evolution from simple to complex forms: as he was to express it later, 'the transformations passed through during the growth, maturity and decay of a society, conform to the same principles as do transformations passed through by aggregates of all orders, inorganic and organic'.[70] He recognised that this was the maturing product of his essays and speculations through the preceding decade. In *Social Statics* (1850) he had promoted the essential comparability of social and organic forms: 'Instead of civilization being artificial, it is a part of nature; all of a piece with the development of the embryo or the unfolding of a flower.'[71] In 'The Development Hypothesis' (1852) he rejected the doctrine of a special creation and attached himself to Lamarckian evolution.[72] In his essay on the 'Theory of Population' (1852)

[66] Giles St Aubyn, *A Victorian Eminence. The Life and Works of Henry Thomas Buckle* (London, 1958), p. 184; Charles D. Cashdollar, *The Transformation of Theology, 1830–1890. Positivism and Protestant Thought in Britain and America* (Princeton, NJ, 1989), pp. 74–80.

[67] W. H. Greenleaf, *The British Political Tradition. Vol. 2. The Ideological Heritage* (London, 1983), p. 53.

[68] Herbert Spencer, *An Autobiography* (2 vols., London, 1904), ii, p. 17.

[69] Spencer to J. S. Mill, 29 July 1858, *Autobiography*, ii, p. 23. Spencer to J. D. Hooker, 13 Dec. 1858, in David Duncan, *The Life and Letters of Herbert Spencer* (London, 1908), p. 89.

[70] Herbert Spencer, *The Study of Sociology* (London, 1873), p. 329.

[71] Herbert Spencer, *Social Statics* (London, 1850) (1954 edn., New York), p. 60.

[72] Herbert Spencer, 'The Development Hypothesis', *The Leader* (1852), repr. in Spencer, *Essays: Scientific, Political, and Speculative* (1863; 1868 edn., London), pp. 377–83.

he turned Malthusianism on its head in an argument that population pressure was the mainspring of social progress.[73] In 'Progress: its Law and Cause' (1857) he provided a general description, if not an explanation, of the evolutionary process—'the advance from the simple to the complex'—at work in all contexts.[74] By 1858 Spencer's life-project stretched before him: the synthesis of biology, psychology, sociology and morality in an evolutionary framework.[75] His 'programme of the synthetic philosophy', which was to detain him for the rest of his long career and fill many volumes as the *System of Synthetic Philosophy* and the *Descriptive Sociology*, was outlined in 1860 in a prospectus requesting subscribers.[76]

There is no direct link to be made between Buckle, Spencer and the Social Science Association. But this simultaneous focus towards the end of the 1850s on synthesising a social science modelled on natural science from hitherto separate disciplines, is suggestive of a common cultural trend. We have become aware that even the most important and influential natural-scientific ideas may be influenced by external social and intellectual conditions. Recent work on Darwin has shown how much the theory of natural selection depended on the influence of contemporary political economy and demography.[77] We should not be surprised if common intellectual currents were thus acting independently on different minds and institutions over the same period, guiding them towards the construction of unitary social theories. Indeed, we might go further and suggest the methodological identity of the projects of this period: if Spencer and Buckle were uniting hitherto separate branches of knowledge in great schemes in 1857 and 1858, Darwin was doing the same in the synthesis of biology, geology, political economy and demography that he called 'natural selection' in 1859—though we recognise, of course, that the Darwinian synthesis had been in gestation since the late 1830s. To turn to another writer who is usually thought to have followed a lone and idiosyncratic intellectual route at this historical moment, but whose intellectual transformation was conformable with

[73] Herbert Spencer, 'A Theory of Population Deduced from the General Law of Animal Fertility', *Westminster Review*, 57 OS, 1 NS (April 1852), 468–501.

[74] Herbert Spencer, 'Progress: Its Law and Cause', *Westminster Review*, 11 NS (April 1857), 445–85. On Spencer's intellectual development in the 1850s see Burrow, *Evolution and Society*, pp. 187–90.

[75] 'On glancing over these stages it is, indeed, observable that the advance towards a complete conception of evolution was itself a process of evolution.' Spencer, *Autobiography*, ii, p. 12.

[76] Spencer, *Autobiography*, ii, pp. 479–84; Cashdollar, *The Transformation of Theology*, p. 146; Herbert Spencer, *System of Synthetic Philosophy* (10 vols., 1862–96) and *Descriptive Sociology* (17 vols., 1873–1933). Eight volumes of the *Descriptive Sociology* appeared between 1873 and 1891; after Spencer's death a further nine volumes were published.

[77] Robert Young, 'Malthus and the Evolutionists: the Common Context of Biological and Social Theory' in id., *Darwin's Metaphor. Nature's Place in Victorian Culture* (Cambridge, 1985), pp. 23–55. Adrian Desmond and James Moore, *Darwin* (London, 1991).

this wider pattern, through the 1850s John Ruskin had been working out *his* distinctive and controversial synthesis of aesthetics, morality and political economy. Intimations of this are clear in his work from the *The Stones of Venice* onwards, and its most influential formulation was *Unto this Last*, written between 1860 and 1862 as a critical attempt to shape a new *social* economy in harmony with Christian ethics and human sympathies, and in opposition to the rigidity, amorality and licensed greed of orthodox economics. As he wrote to his friend, the physician Henry Acland, in 1856, 'I am forced by precisely the same instinct to the consideration of political questions that urges me to examine the laws of architectural or mountain forms. I cannot help doing so: the questions suggest themselves to me, and I am *compelled* to work them out.'[78] One of Ruskin's biographers has written of his 'need to see unity not division' and of his 'search for rhetorical ways in which to communicate the wholeness' at this time.[79] The parallel determination of the Social Science Association to provide 'an opportunity for considering social economics as a great whole', as proclaimed in the first sentence of its *Transactions*, hence drew on intellectual models of the moment.[80] As Spencer was to put it in retrospect, 'the time was one at which certain all-embracing scientific truths of a simple order were being revealed'.[81] Synthesis was the compelling trend and intellectual project of the late-1850s and out of it came various attempts to systematise social knowledge.

One of these was the development of the concept of social evolution, already immanent in the thinking of the mid-Victorians, but given a tremendous impetus by Darwin's theory of natural selection and Spencer's rapid assimilation of that theory in his own work as it poured from the presses in the 1860s and 1870s. At the moment when one version of social science, based on the collection and manipulation of useful knowledge in the service of reform, reached its widest audience, so another and quite different version was launched which would influence public social and political attitudes, and fire intellectual controversy, until the end of the century.

IV

The idea of social evolution can be traced back to the Enlightenment in France (in the work of Turgot and Condorcet) and Scotland (Adam Ferguson

[78] John Dixon Hunt, *The Wider Sea. A Life of John Ruskin* (New York, 1982), p. 253.

[79] Ibid., p. 302.

[80] *Transactions* (1857), p. xxi.

[81] Spencer, *Autobiography*, ii, p. 13.

among others). Stimulated by the accumulation of ethnographical information in the first half of the nineteenth century, it was established at the core of the sociological tradition in Comte's law of the three stages by which human society and the human intellect 'pass successively through three different theoretical conditions: the theological, or fictitious; the metaphysical, or abstract; and the scientific, or positive'.[82] When linked to the concept of biological evolution after 1859, Comtism and variants of it (such as Spencerian sociology) became increasingly influential. In the varied work of Bagehot on politics, Maine on the development of the law, Galton and Pearson in eugenics, the Fabians on collectivism, and Hobhouse on the development of mind and ethics, a developmental account of institutional and intellectual 'progress' was enshrined at the heart of British sociology.[83] Thus as late as 1908 Hobhouse, in his editorial introduction to the *Sociological Review*, understood that the central tasks of 'sociological science' were 'to form by a philosophic analysis a just conception of human progress, and trace this progress in its manifold complexity in the course of history, to test its reality by careful classification and searching comparisons, to ascertain its conditions, and if possible to forecast its future'.[84]

Half a century before, Spencer's social thought in the 1850s was unquestionably evolutionary in its attempt to fit all organic and inorganic development into a pattern that led from simple to complex forms, 'from an indefinite, incoherent homogeneity to a definite, coherent heterogeneity'.[85] But this was just a descriptive generalisation: what he then lacked, and what Darwin provided in natural selection, was a more convincing explanation than that provided by Lamarck of the mechanism by which changes in nature occurred. For social evolutionists, the concept of struggle within natural selection, which Darwin had himself absorbed from a reading of Malthus in October 1838, was taken to be the crucial motor of progress.[86] However, they added a moral dimension which was absent from Darwinism. Natural selection is an amoral and random process, which is one of several reasons why many Victorians, holding to the belief that they lived in a universe in which justice was assured, found the doctrine so shocking. But vulgar Social Darwinism (though there were certainly more sophisticated variants)

[82] Auguste Comte, 'The Positive Philosophy', in *Auguste Comte and Positivism: The Essential Writings* (Chicago, 1983), p. 71.
[83] Sandra M. Den Otter, *British Idealism and Social Explanation. A Study in Late Victorian Thought* (Oxford, 1996), p. 89.
[84] *The Sociological Review*, 1 (1908), quoted in Abrams, *Origins of British Sociology*, p. 259.
[85] Herbert Spencer, *First Principles* (1862) (New York, 1888 edn.), p. 396.
[86] Charles Darwin, *Autobiography* (1887; Nora Barlow (ed.) 1958 edn., London), p. 120.

rationalised and legitimated the victory in the struggle that was won by those individuals, classes, nations, races, or species with supposedly superior features and abilities. In this way the 'fittest' survived and deserved their biological or societal success.

Given the centrality of evolution to natural scientific discourse it was impossible for aspiring social scientists to ignore the idea. And in applying natural selection and uniformitarianism—the concept of long-run change as a consequence of constant causes—to human society, social evolution was appropriating and adapting the most potent and successful scientific ideas of the age in the explanation of social development.[87] Social evolution posited that natural and social phenomena were both subject to the developmental process, and might both be investigated by the same methods. Development was understood to be regular and uniform; only a few social evolutionists accepted that different societies might develop at different rates. For most, if not all, social development was identified with progress.[88]

But an evolutionary sociology was not only fashionable. It provided an account of social development rooted in history and the evidence of other cultures that could be used to challenge the deliberate ahistoricism of utilitarianism and political economy, the hitherto dominant forms of social explanation.[89] It might serve as a guide in the construction of social policies: according to Beatrice Webb, '[o]nly by watching *the processes* of growth and decay during a period of time, can we understand even the contemporary facts at whatever may be their stage of development'.[90] By reaffirming the unity of mankind—for according to social evolution all cultures must tread the same path to the present and future, though at different rates—it sought to establish the constancy of human nature—a sociological equivalent of the political economists' 'homo economicus'—and thus made social-scientific generalisation possible. And social evolution was an especially persuasive idea for the mid-Victorians: they lived in a society which had recently gone through rapid and unexampled transformations and in a culture which celebrated technological change and social adaptation to it. It was a way of explaining the Victorians to themselves.[91]

But social evolutionists discovered that their manner of understanding social development was alarmingly malleable, and attractive to quite divergent movements and creeds. As is well known, Spencer laboured to ensure

[87] Burrow, *Evolution and Society*, p. 111.
[88] Jerzy Szacki, *History of Sociological Thought* (London, 1979) pp. 209–15.
[89] Burrow, *Evolution and Society*, pp. 97–8.
[90] Webb, *My Apprenticeship*, p. 246.
[91] Peel, *Herbert Spencer*, p. 257.

that social evolution should buttress his pre-existing commitment to laissez-faire and the minimal state even when, as many contemporaries recognised, his organicism seemed to point to a quite contrary social outlook. A later evolutionist like Benjamin Kidd could argue that its true political corrolary was a form of ethical state socialism.[92] And a new liberal like Hobhouse contended that the most effective evolutionary strategy for ensuring progress in the context of the interdependence of late-Victorian society was a cooperative rather than a competitive one.[93] As Sandra Den Otter has so deftly shown, philosophical idealism mounted a comprehensive critique of social evolutionism at the end of the century. Idealists like D. G. Ritchie and Bernard Bosanquet sought to extract man from nature and from a crude biological determinism, arguing that something other (and more) than scientific naturalism was required for a full understanding of individual and social development: the ethical and biological spheres should be treated as distinct. They were centrally concerned with human consciousness and the degree to which it could influence the evolutionary process itself: they rejected materialist accounts of human behaviour as inadequate in general, and inappropriate when applied to particular aspects of that behaviour.[94] In mounting this critique they were developing arguments made by John Stuart Mill half a century before in the sixth book of the *System of Logic*, concerning the logic of the moral sciences, which formed his blueprint for the philosophy and methodology of social science. Here Mill had questioned whether the type of exact and predictive laws that defined the form of the physical sciences could be applied to the complexity and diversity of human behaviour. Instead, social science must start from generalisations founded on the study of human psychology, which would form the basis for a science of human character, ethology, in which discipline different and less rigorous standards of proof must, in the nature of things, apply.[95]

This divergence and contradiction, and the related contestation, help explain why social evolutionism was losing its hold on the British sociological imagination at the end of the nineteenth century. But there were other reasons as well. The assumptions that human social development is unilinear and that all societies move through similar stages of development were not supported by the new and more copious anthropological evidence. The failure

[92] Benjamin Kidd, *Social Evolution* (London, 1894).

[93] Stefan Collini, *Liberalism and Sociology. L. T. Hobhouse and Political Argument in England 1880–1914* (Cambridge, 1979).

[94] Den Otter, *British Idealism and Social Explanation*, pp. 88–148.

[95] J. S. Mill, *A System of Logic Ratiocinative and Inductive (1843), Collected Works of John Stuart Mill* (ed. J. M. Robson) (33 vols., Toronto, 1963–91), viii, pp. 831–952.

to explain how human communities move through the different stages, or to specify the characteristics of each stage, led to justifiable criticism of an idea which lacked clarity and rigour.[96] As for Spencer, to many of his readers he seemed rather *too* rigorous in his attempts to assimilate convenient illustrations of social evolution into his predetermined scheme while excluding those inconvenient facts that pointed to other conclusions. In 1884 Beatrice Webb pictured him 'sitting alone in the centre of his theoretical web, catching facts, and weaving them again into theory'. According to his friend Huxley, three years later, Spencer 'merely picks up what will help him to illustrate his theories'.[97] In the face of all the late-Victorian evidence that poverty, destitution and want were still constant aspects of the lives of millions, the tide was running against a specifically laissez-faire liberalism. Indeed, with liberalism beyond Britain weakening and sickening during the *fin de siècle*, the faith in progress which had underpinned social evolutionism and was so central a feature of the mid-Victorian age, was dissipating.[98]

V

The foundation of the Sociological Society in London in June 1904 was a reaction to the breakdown of the evolutionary paradigm and an attempt to bring renewed definition and coherence to sociology. In actuality it demonstrated the divisions among those professing social science who variously represented competing conceptualisations of the discipline, including civics, eugenics, social psychology, empirical social investigation and the formation of social policy, as well as social evolution. Compromised in this manner, the Sociological Society never found its purpose, and balanced uneasily between an academic forum, debating society, and policy institute.[99] Faced with this lack of agreement, one historian described turn-of-the-century sociology as 'a desperate piecing together of intellectual interests whose real tendency was to fly off in a dozen different directions'.[100] Another has claimed that Edwardian sociology was theoretically barren, lacking a distinctive theory to explain social events.[101] They may be answered in three different ways: first, by reference to

[96] Szacki, *History of Sociological Thought*, pp. 234–39.
[97] Webb, *My Apprenticeship*, pp. 28, 30.
[98] Peel, *Herbert Spencer*, pp. 240–5.
[99] Den Otter, *British Idealism and Social Explanation*, pp. 133–41; Halliday, 'The Sociological Movement, the Sociological Society and the Genesis of Academic Sociology in Britain', *passim*.
[100] Abrams, *The Origins of British Sociology, 1834–1914*, p. 101.
[101] Soffer, 'Why do Disciplines Fail?', 781.

the fragmented nature of social science in Britain at any time from the 1830s to the present; second, by reference to the wider history of specialisation in the late-Victorian period, for in this context the divisions between competing sociologies appear consonant with a much broader pattern of cultural development; and third, with reference to the unacknowledged assumptions about the nature of social science that these scholars have brought with them to this history.

If even the statistical movement turns out, on closer inspection, to be a series of movements with different objectives and personnel, it should be evident that at no time in its history has there ever been a consensus on the definition and purpose of social science in Britain. Rather, there has always been (as there still is) a vigorous debate on these matters. And the debate itself is part of the evidence that a rich and complex social-scientific culture existed in nineteenth-century Britain—though historians looking for assured and accepted definitions of the subject have been blind to this. As Sandra Den Otter has observed: 'The arguments which idealists raised in the charged and intense context of late nineteenth century debate about social explanation deny that the apparent failure of sociology can be attributed to the poverty of ideas.'[102] If we borrow the terms made famous by Thomas Kuhn, there never was something that could be called 'normal science' among the social scientists of Victorian Britain, nor accepted paradigms by which their discipline was to develop, nor any 'scientific revolutions' that remade the intellectual landscape and claimed the support and approbation of all practitioners.[103] Rather, there was constant and often enlivening (rather than disabling) competition between different projects. Had Spencer not been so monomaniacal, he might have smiled to observe a process not unlike natural selection at work among the various species of social scientist who roamed and struggled across the 'darkling plain' of intellectual life in Victorian Britain.[104]

Secondly, we must appreciate how the process of specialisation worked in several ways from the 1870s to undermine the project of a unitary social science and of a single Social Science Association. In one aspect, it was characterised by the proliferation of new professional societies and voluntary welfare agencies in late-Victorian Britain. Deepening knowledge and broader experience of specific problems encouraged a more limited focus, and led practitioners to band together and maximise their impact and professional status. In a second aspect, specialisation destroyed the Liberal political

[102] Den Otter, *British Idealism and Social Explanation*, p. 148.

[103] Thomas Kuhn, *The Structure of Scientific Revolutions* (Chicago, 1962).

[104] The reference is to Matthew Arnold's famous evocation of Victorian doubt in his poem of 1851, 'On Dover Beach'.

synthesis of the mid-century, as the coalition briefly held together by the prospect of Gladstonian reform fractured into splinter groups agitating for specific causes and gave rise to the faddism and crotchets which disrupted both the unifying project of the Social Science Association and the Liberal Party itself in the 1870s and 1880s.[105] Thirdly, specialisation changed the map of knowledge, as new social disciplines—economics, economic history, political science, sociology, anthropology—were developed that made a unifying social science antiquated, if not also impossible.

'Why have a monster association?' That was the question posed by *The Times* when the Social Science Association was inaugurated. Why could not separate groups 'each collect its own facts and publish them at its own annual meeting?'[106] Contemporaries replied that there was then a need for cross-fertilisation; something would be gained by uniting independent action and disparate bodies in one forum. In the mid-Victorian years there was a predisposition for synthesis. In politics the Liberal party emerged from the synthesis of different parliamentary groups with extra-parliamentary opinion. In intellectual life, as we have seen, the tendency in the work of Buckle, Spencer and Darwin, was towards composite general theories. In culture, 'monster associations' like the Social Science Association and the British Association for the Advancement of Science were characteristic expressions of the 'unity of science', to which all deferred, and symbols of renewed social cohesion. If the grand congress was the preferred mode of mid-Victorian association, the divisions within Liberalism laid bare in the 1870s and 1880s, the impossibility of constraining knowledge and expertise in any single forum, and the restlessness of provincial Britain and Ireland, encouraged separation, specialisation and 'faddism'. After 1870 the centre did not hold. As Robert Young argued in his seminal article on late-Victorian periodicals, the 1870s and 1880s in Britain mark the end of a 'common context'. A unitary culture, bound together by the great reviews and quarterlies which maintained a broad readership among educated Victorians, fell apart in the last quarter of the century and was fissured into discrete specialisms.[107]

In the written history of social science in Britain two issues have generally been to the fore: why was the subject's academic institutionalisation so relatively late as compared with Germany, France and the United States,

[105] Goldman, *Science, Reform, and Politics*, pp. 349–67.
[106] *The Times*, 15 Oct. 1857, 6.
[107] Robert Young, 'Natural Theology, Victorian Periodicals and the Fragmentation of a Common Context', in C. Chant and J. Fauvel (eds.), *Darwin to Einstein. Historical Studies on Science and Belief* (Harlow, Essex, 1980), pp. 69–107.

and why did social science give rise to so much diversity and so many dissimilar styles of analysis? As the material in this paper may suggest, both questions misunderstand the nature of Victorian social science. Conceived as a type of policy science and as a guide to legislation and 'improvement', it was not understood as an academic discipline pure and simple, but as a type of public practice whose practitioners—civil servants, statisticians, doctors, educationists, intellectuals, professionals and reformers—inhabited the realm of public affairs. Indeed, the argument has been advanced that, paradoxically, it was in national cultures where this form of public engagement with the problems of social administration was less common or a political impossibility that social science took to the haven of the academy.[108] In Britain, by contrast, in a culture rather more open to the influence of expertise, the focus of social science was on government and institutional reform. Academic social science came so late because bodies like the Royal Statistical Society and the Social Science Association could point to their successes in shaping policy according to 'science'. And in any case, 'the idea of the university' in Victorian Britain was not so elastic as in the United States or Germany and largely resisted the institutionalisation of the social disciplines until the twentieth century.

In thinking about the heterogeneity of Victorian social science, meanwhile, we must be aware of another paradox: that the diversity of styles of social science contradicted the established nineteenth-century model of disciplinary formation and progress we know as 'positivism'. The Victorians expected to witness the development of a science of society as rigorous in form, cumulative in construction, and unilinear in direction as natural science had by then become. In actuality no single social-scientific system was able to command intellectual authority, define the discipline, and take it forward. From observing the plethora of styles of social science in the academic and quasi-academic institutions of our own age, we know that social science has not developed in this hoped-for manner since the 1830s and that it still displays enormous and sometimes disabling diversity. We appreciate that models of its form and development borrowed from the natural sciences are simply inapplicable to bodies of knowledge which are, by their very nature, contestable and contested. If we tolerate intellectual diversity and competition in our own academic and public institutions and procedures, we should respect it among the Victorians as well. The time has come to reject an approach to nineteenth-century social science based on the idea that this

[108] Lawrence Goldman 'A Peculiarity of the English? The Social Science Association and the Absence of Sociology in Nineteenth-Century Britain', *Past and Present*, 114 (1987), 133–71.

diversity is evidence of the discipline's failure to establish itself—which has been the dominant theme in the literature since the 1960s—and simply write the history as it occurred, devoid of preconceptions of 'how it should have been'. Let us draw on the map what we see, rather than lament a terrain rather different from and rather more complex than the one we—and the Victorians themselves—had hoped for.

CHAPTER FIVE

Political Economy and the Science of Economics in Victorian Britain

KEITH TRIBE

> Political economy is an older science than chemistry, and is far older than the science of electricity and several other most prolific branches of physical science. Yet so difficult is the subject that we have not yet advanced safely beyond the lowest and simplest generalisations. Political economy is not yet an exact science. But the difficulty of this subject is not the worst difficulty in the way of the political economist. The worst difficulty is the obstinacy, prejudice, and incredulity of those he has to convince.[1]

Throughout the nineteenth century Political Economy was broadly understood as the study of the 'nature and causes of the wealth of nations', so formulated by Adam Smith in the title of what was widely recognised as its canonical text.[2] Criticised, revised, 'improved', excerpted and popularised, Smith's work, together with Fawcett's *Manual of Political Economy*,[3] was still being assigned to Oxford Pass men in the 1880s.[4] William Stanley Jevons

[1] William Stanley Jevons, *An Introductory Lecture on the Importance of Diffusing a Knowledge of Political Economy* (Manchester, 1866), p. 16.

[2] Adam Smith, *An Inquiry into the Nature and Causes of the Wealth of Nations*, 2 vols. (London, 1776).

[3] Henry Fawcett, *Manual of Political Economy* (London, 1863). In his Preface Fawcett noted: 'Adam Smith wrote the first systematic treatise on the subject, and his work will long continue to be read as a masterpiece of clear exposition. Mr. John Stuart Mill's treatise on "The Principles of Political Economy" [1848] is perhaps the most remarkable work of that great author, and the book will be remembered as amongst the most enduring literary productions of the nineteenth century.' Fawcett presented his own *Manual* as a shorter, more accessible, version of Mill.

[4] See Wolseley P. Emerton, *An Analysis of Adam Smith's Inquiry into the Nature and Causes of the Wealth of Nations Pt. I* (Oxford, 1877); this text was itself an updated version of Jeremiah Joyce's 1797 précis of Smith—see items 199, 208 in Keith Tribe (ed.), *A Critical Bibliography of Adam Smith* (London, 2002), pp. 267–8.

had published in 1871 his own *Theory of Political Economy* that took a different point of departure: the calculus of pleasure and pain, shifting attention from general questions of national welfare to the motivation of human conduct in a move which was soon recognised to be a decisive revision of the subject matter of political economy. Jevons still held the work of Smith in high regard—in the late 1870s he had begun work on his own edition of *Wealth of Nations*.[5] But in the 'Preface' to the second edition of his *Theory*, Jevons expressed his doubt concerning the suitability of the term 'political economy' for the field of inquiry he had in mind:

> Among minor alterations [with respect to the first edition, K.T.], I may mention the substitution for the name Political Economy of the single convenient term *Economics*. I cannot help thinking that it would be well to discard, as quickly as possible, the old troublesome double-worded name of our Science. Several authors have tried to introduce totally new names, such as Plutology, Chrematistics, Catallactics, &c. But why do we need anything better than Economics?[6]

Alfred Marshall, he noted, had likewise mooted the same substitution;[7] and it was Marshall who in 1890 formalised this development with the publication of his *Principles of Economics, Vol. I*, a work that, during the first half of the twentieth century, became the founding textbook in the development of economics as a university discipline in the English-speaking world.

The change of name signified a break with a 'classical' economics preoccupied with the role of capital and labour in the production of value and the distribution of national wealth, and relaunched economics as a science of exchange and price formation. In place of a theory of production and distribution centred on rent, profit and wages with their corresponding agents of production—landlords, capitalists and labourers—the new science of economics became a theory in which the allocation of scarce resources was effected by the calculations of an abstract economic agent. A new theory of value turned on the interactions of these self-interested agents, whose drive to satisfy their own wants led them in turn to satisfy the needs of others and hence create

[5] Jevons broke up two early (1790s) octavo copies of *Wealth of Nations*, pasted the first 182 pages on to foolscap and added editorial notes—'Political Economy. A. Smith—Wealth of Nations', Jevons Papers, John Rylands Library, Manchester JA6/6/7.

[6] William Stanley Jevons, *Theory of Political Economy*, 2nd edn. (London, 1879), p. xiv.

[7] 'The nation used to be called "the Body Politic." So long as this phrase was in common use, men thought of the interests of the whole nation when they use the word "Political"; and then "Political Economy" served well enough as a name for this science. But now "political interests" generally mean the interests of some part or parts of the nation; so that it seems best to drop the name "Political Economy," and to speak simply of **Economic Science**, or more shortly, **Economics**.' Alfred and Mary Paley Marshall, *The Economics of Industry* (London, 1879), p. 2.

market prices. Historians have long thought of this transition period as one of revolutionary change in economic thinking, laying new foundations for the development of a neoclassical economics later elaborated in the course of the twentieth century. Henceforth economic agents were buyers and sellers of commodities with diminishing marginal utility: and this shift in perspective has become known as the 'Marginal Revolution' of the 1870s. Jevons in Britain, Carl Menger in Vienna, and Léon Walras in Lausanne more or less simultaneously, and entirely independently, published books embodying this basic idea. The story is of course a great deal more complicated than this: first Walras, then Jevons, both keen to assert priority claims, found that an essential part of what each had thought original in their own work had been anticipated in a book published by a German writer, Hermann-Heinrich Gossen, in 1854.[8] Furthermore, each had difficulty in gaining due recognition for the significance of their insights. Walras is today regarded as the originator of the mathematical system of general equilibrium, but his lasting reputation was secured chiefly by his successor in the Lausanne chair, Vilfredo Pareto. Jevons for his part 'mathematised' exchange relationships with respect to the diminishing utility derived from additional amounts of any good or service, formalised in a calculus of 'pleasure and pain' borrowed from Jeremy Bentham; but this approach never became popular, and was in any case quickly displaced by Marshall's more accessible geometry of the demand curve.[9]

Priority disputes are a common phenomenon, and in the history of the sciences it is now usual to employ a cultural and sociological framework in explaining the course and outcome of such disputes, treating them as part of a struggle over resources and careers as much as 'ideas'. Historians of economics have largely resisted this trend, persisting with a model of economics as a science elaborated over the years in a progressive, cumulative and rational manner that has culminated in the achievements of the modern discipline. Mainstream history of economics consequently mirrors the

[8] Léon Walras, 'Un économiste inconnu: Hermann-Henri Gossen', first published in *Journal des Économistes* 4e serié, t. XXX, n. 4 (April–May 1885), 68–90 and 260–1; reprinted in Walras, *Études d'économie sociale (théorie de la répartition de la richesse sociale)*, Auguste et Léon Walras Oeuvres Économiques Complètes IX, ed. Pierre Dockès *et al.* (Paris, 1990), pp. 311–30. For a recent account of the response of Walras and Jevons to their discovery of Gossen, see my '"The Price Is Right": Léon Walras and Economic Justice', *Schweizerische Zeitschrift für Geschichte,* 50 (2000), 388–402. The best general treatment of this period is still R. S. Howey, *The Rise of the Marginal Utility School, 1870–1889* (Lawrence, Kansas, 1960). The papers by Blaug and Stigler in particular in Robert D. Collison Black, A. W. Coats, Crawford Goodwin (eds.), *The Marginal Revolution in Economics. Interpretation and Evaluation* (Durham, NC, 1973) touch on issues developed in the discussion below.

[9] Alfred Marshall, *Principles of Economics, Vol. I* (London, 1890) 157.

self-understanding of mainstream academic economists. However, the corollary to this latter self-understanding is either that academic economists have no need to know about 'obsolete economics'; or, if for some reason they do take an interest, then the appropriate analytical tools are those that they already possess as trained economists. Seen from the latter perspective, the marginal revolution is a necessary turning point that provided an adequate platform for progressive theoretical development in a way that the classical model did not.[10] Political economy, as classical economics, is hence more or less the 'pre-history' of modern economic science; the change of name symbolises the change from old to new. And this change itself is driven first and foremost by scientific advance, the elaboration of concepts, arguments, reason and intellectual progress.

'Scientific Progress' is however often inexplicably delayed; new insights are successfully disputed, or even entirely ignored for long periods of time. The market for knowledge is an imperfect one, and the chronology of 'progress' is neither as unilinear nor as uniform as the dictate of pure reason might presume. So long as we adhere to rationalist historiographical models of scientific development, such 'delays' and 'deviations' seem merely irrational. Jevons can be forgiven for talking of the prevailing 'obstinacy, prejudice, and incredulity' of the audience a political economist had to convince, and suggesting that the chief barrier to the diffusion of economic knowledge was sheer ignorance—this is a natural intellectual reflex. But the opposition of truth to ignorance in this way makes for poor history. There are 'rational' explanations for delay in the acceptance of a new idea, not least in determining what counts as 'new'. Originality and purpose are not self-evident, and a new insight might even appear quite absurd. Introducing (yet another) new edition of *Wealth of Nations* in 1887, Ernest Belfort Bax wrote:

> The late Professor Jevons ... expresses [value] in terms of what he calls the 'final utility' of a commodity, that is the degree of need for it, at the moment, on the part of the consumer. This degree of utility is determined by the supply, and the supply in turn is dependent on the cost of production or the labour expended on it. This, it will be seen, does not absolutely differ from the labour theory of Adam Smith, and still less from Ricardo's; but the mathematical language in which this writer

[10] It might be added that as a consequence of this second perspective many of the received ideas about the history of economics are apocryphal, such as the idea that there is a Walrasian auctioneer, that the invisible hand is a metaphor for price formation, that Ricardo is the originator of the conception of comparative advantage, that there is such a thing as a 'Giffin Good', that Joan Robinson's account of imperfect competition is comparable to Chamberlin's account of monopolistic competition, or that in water and diamonds there is a 'paradox of value'.

> exhibits much of his reasoning is pedantic, and often meaningless. ... He is, consequently, often credited with the obviously absurd theory that the ultimate criterion of value is the current estimation of a commodity, or, to use the ill-chosen Jevonian expression, 'the final degree of utility.' Such a theory, like many others of a similar kind, would confound the essence or substance of a thing with its mere phenomenal expression or manifestation.[11]

Bax therefore briskly garbles Jevons' basic proposition so that he does indeed look a bit like Smith or Ricardo—only then to dismiss as 'obviously absurd' a conception that is, today, simply taken for granted by academic economist and estate agent alike.

Bax, sometime editor with William Morris of *The Commonweal*, socialist journalist and barrister, would not have been thought even by his contemporaries to command specialist knowledge of economics. Nonetheless, the misunderstandings and misconceptions he so forthrightly expressed are suggestive in reconstructing the background to what might appear to be a simple terminological change: the simple substitution of 'economics' for 'political economy' during the last two decades of the nineteenth century. Several things stand in need of explanation. Why should an underlying theoretical shift prompt this change of name? Only from the perspective of an established twentieth-century science does this seem to be a rational and necessary development. But this is to confuse cause with consequence. Why did this shift happen then? Why, in the 1870s, do we have a clear case of a simultaneous and independent 'discovery' of a new approach to economic analysis?[12] Why finally, was the process of diffusion so slow, if the idea was so good? We are not here directly concerned with the 'truth' of the relative merits of the economic writings of Walras or Jevons, or the degree to which Marshall built upon the work of the latter. We are here concerned solely with the issue of the substitution of 'economics' for 'political economy', and the associated redefinition of the field of study. The new term could only gain currency if an existing readership could be persuaded, or alternatively a new readership created. We need therefore to look beyond the texts themselves to the contexts in which they were used.

At issue then is not so much the intellectual substance of the shift from classical to neoclassical economics, if only out of consideration of length

[11] Ernest Belfort Bax, 'Introductory Sketch of the History of Political Economy' in Adam Smith, *An Inquiry into the Nature and Causes of the Wealth of Nations*, 2 vols. (London, 1887), p. xxxvi.

[12] Blaug disputes that there is a case of simultaneous discovery, distinguishing a marginal utility revolution in Britain and America, a subjectivist revolution in Austria, and a general equilibrium revolution in Switzerland and Italy. See his 'Was there a Marginal Revolution?' in Collison Black, Coats, Goodwin, *The Marginal Revolution in Economics*, p. 14.

and accessibility.[13] Rather, we seek to account for the timing and duration of this shift. Explanation of these factors means that we have to look beyond the 'ideas' to their context, and it is this context that lends them meaning. A preliminary indicator can be found in the problem with which Jevons and Walras found themselves confronted. The bald sequence of events runs as follows. Jevons presented the elements of his 'new theory' in a paper sent to the meeting of the British Association held at Cambridge in 1862. Subsequently a longer version was published in the *Journal of the Statistical Society of London* in 1866.[14] That year Jevons was appointed Professor of Logic, Mental and Moral Philosophy, and Political Economy at Owen's College, Manchester; so far as the Political Economy component went, he 'followed somewhat the order of subjects in Mill's Political Economy in perfect independence, however, of his views and methods where desirable.'[15] Jevons went on in 1875 to a chair at University College London, but as in Manchester the audience here for Political Economy was a largely unspecialised one; if they were reading for a degree, it was for the University of London BA in which Political Economy was a subsidiary subject. There is no evidence that Jevons made any special or specific use of his *Theory of Political Economy* in his teaching.[16] Walras by contrast had a rather more specialised (or perhaps more captive) student audience in Lausanne, teaching two hours of 'pure political economy' to the first year, and three of applied to the second and third. From 1874 he used his *Éléments d'économie politique pure* as a textbook for the first year, the Department of Public Instruction

[13] An attempt to sketch a non-teleological account of political economy in the nineteenth century can be found in my 'Continental Political Economy from the Physiocrats to the Marginal Revolution', in T. Porter and D. Ross (eds.), *The Cambridge History of Science Vol. 7* (Cambridge, 2003), pp. 154–70.

[14] Howey, *Rise of the Marginal Utility School*, pp. 16–18.

[15] Quoted in Robert D. Collison Black, 'Jevons's Contribution to the Teaching of Political Economy in Manchester and London', in Alon Kadish and Keith Tribe (eds.), *The Market for Political Economy* (London, 1993), p. 176.

[16] Jevons gave two courses of twenty lectures during 1876–7, announced in the *Calendar* as follows: 'The first Course will commence on Thursday, 12th October, and will treat of the general principles of Political Economy, the Nature of Utility, the Laws of Consumption, Production and Distribution, Population, &c. It will also include a critical review of the principal doctrines concerning the nature of Value, with especial reference to the opinions, of Say, Malthus, Ricardo, Senior, Mill, Cairnes, and the Mathematical Theory of Value. The second Course will commence on Monday, January 15th, and will be devoted (during the present Session) to the subjects of Money, metallic and representative; Credit; the rate of Interest, the history of Prices; the variations in the value of Gold and Silver; Commercial Fluctuations—seasonal, periodic, or irregular; Speculative Manias; Crises and Panics; the Money Market; the Bank Charter Act; and the present constitution of the English Monetary and Banking System.' University College London, *Calendar 1876–1877,* p. 38. By 1880 the course had been updated, but cut to twenty lectures in total.

eventually supplying around 100 copies for the purpose.[17] Neither Jevons nor Walras had any students who continued their study of economics—but their position as university teachers of political economy was not in any doubt. Walras only came across Jevons' *Theory of Political Economy* in May 1874 when drafting the preface for his *Éléments*, and from the subsequent exchange Jevons naturally considered that he had priority. But then in 1878 he was shown a copy of Gossen's book, and realised that both he and Walras had been in large part anticipated.[18]

This delay in appreciating the importance of Gossen's work, and his enduring obscurity, were largely due to the fact that Gossen never was an academic, but spent most of his working life as a reluctant civil servant; a keen supporter of the 1848 Revolution, he was subsequently involved in an unsuccessful life assurance scheme, and died in 1858. Jevons, Walras, Pareto and Marshall by contrast lived chiefly from their teaching, and through the institutions in which they taught participated in the development of academic networks which effected an increasingly international diffusion of knowledge. So long as individuals contributed to contemporary economic discourse through writing books, pamphlets and articles, as was chiefly the case in Britain up until the 1870s, the diffusion of 'economic knowledge' was individualised. The principles of political economy were not thought to be especially esoteric, and might be absorbed by reading Mill, or even Smith, whose *Wealth of Nations* was reprinted more or less annually in Britain from the early 1860s to the end of the century. Despite this, the evidence is that Smith's actual arguments were poorly understood. Nobody could account for the structure of the book, and such casual discussion as there was related to the first two of five books only. McCulloch's 1828 edition of *Wealth of Nations* incorporated extensive notes on the relation of Smith to the political economy of the 1820s, views dutifully reiterated through several editions until 1889. Most of the editorial apparatus was severely dated by the 1840s, but this did not seem to deter publishers, nor those who continued to buy the book. And the obsolescence of the edition suggests that buyers were not necessarily assiduous readers.[19] Individuals such as Gossen might publish new

[17] General introduction to Léon Walras, *Cours*, Auguste et Léon Walras Oeuvres Économiques Complètes XII, ed. Pierre Dockès *et al.* (Paris, 1996), pp. 18, 21.

[18] See for detail on this John K. Whitaker, 'Jevons and Gossen', in Antoin E. Murphy and Renée Prendergast (eds.), *Contributions to the History of Economic Thought. Essays in Honour of R. D. C. Black* (London, 2000), pp. 154–68.

[19] Sidgwick complained of the bankers who attended meetings of the Political Economy Club that it would be '... an exaggeration to say that they know no Political Economy; I think they read Mill some time ago and look at him from time to time on Sundays'—excerpt from *The Life of Henry*

works incorporating novel approaches to economic phenomena, as did Auguste Walras, Léon's father, but if Smith attracted few serious readers, there was little chance that anything more arcane would.

Books became significantly cheaper in the course of the nineteenth century, and available to an increasing share of the population, but greater access to works adumbrating the principles of political economy did not translate straightforwardly into ongoing critical elaboration of these principles. Political economy might well have carried on like this in a public domain dominated by the works of Smith and Mill had not its entry into formal and informal educational institutions created a vehicle in which theoretical elaboration and revision were increasingly the norm. The transformation of political economy into economics certainly signified a change of concepts and arguments in studying the production and distribution of wealth, but it was this institutional change that facilitated the increasingly rapid diffusion of new ideas, and in turn created a context where new ideas were in demand.

This shift can be registered in the nature of the periodicals in which economists most commonly published their work. Starting with the *Edinburgh Review* in 1802, there followed the *Quarterly Review*, the *London and Westminster Review*,[20] and later the *Nineteenth Century* and the *Fortnightly Review*. These were publications for an emergent intelligentsia, widely read but whose contents did not demand of the reader specialist capacities beyond the general educational standards of the day. Consequently they did not lend themselves to, or facilitate, the systematic development of knowledge that we today associate with the sciences. None of these publications was linked institutionally or editorially to university institutions.

By the last third of the century this had begun to change—an international trend to create specialist journals edited by academics developed, in Britain headed by the foundation of *Mind* in 1876 and the *English Historical Review* in 1886. The new academic economic journals—in France the *Revue d'économie politique*, founded in 1887; the *Jahrbuch für Gesetzgebung, Verwaltung und Volkswirtschaft im Deutschen Reich* refounded under Schmoller's editorship in 1877; the *Political Science Quarterly* edited from 1886 by the Faculty of Political Science of Columbia College; and the Harvard

Sidgwick (1906), diary entry dated 11 April 1885, reprinted in Political Economy Club, *Minutes of Proceedings, 1899–1920. Roll of Members and Questions Discussed, 1821–1920. With Documents Bearing on the History of the Club*, Vol. VI (London, 1921), p. 315.

[20] John Stuart Mill's seminal article 'On the Definition of Political Economy; and on the Method of Investigation Proper to It' was first published in the *London and Westminster Review* in 1836, and reprinted in *Essays on some Unsettled Questions of Political Economy* (London, 1844).

Quarterly Journal of Economics founded in 1887—all of these were linked to academic institutions, and designed to diffuse specialist knowledge, printing extensive notes on foreign publications, together with summaries of academic developments elsewhere.

Alfred Marshall, Professor of Political Economy in Cambridge from 1885, was alert to these developments. In 1890 he was President of Section F (Economic Science and Statistics) of the British Association, and he used the opportunity to circulate a paper to members of its committee proposing the establishment of an economic association and a journal. Marshall could point to the foundation of the American Economic Association (AEA) in 1885, but the purpose he had in mind was rather different from any existing body. The *American Economic Review*, the journal of the AEA, did not begin publication until 1911; the *Quarterly Journal of Economics* was published from Harvard, and the *Journal of Political Economy*, which was to begin publication in 1892, came from the University of Chicago. And in fact the first British economic periodical, the *Economic Review*,[21] was to begin publication in Oxford in early 1891,[22] pre-empting the first issue of the *Economic Journal* that was part of Marshall's strategy for British economics. Marshall sought a truly independent journal, and the sole purpose of the national economic association that he proposed was to provide institutional backing for such a journal. The British Economic Association that was formed in November 1890 was 'open to all schools and parties'[23]—in fact of the 501 members one year later 113 were businessmen, 51 lawyers, 48 bankers, and only 86 university teachers.[24] *The Times* of 21 November 1890 reported Marshall's address to the inaugural meeting as follows:

> A strong and widespread feeling that English economists, and especially the younger men among them, are thus placed at a great disadvantage through the want of an easy means of communication with one another, has led to the holding of many private meetings and discussions on the subject in Oxford, Cambridge, London, and possibly elsewhere; and lately the matter has come under consideration of the committee of Section F (Economics and Statistics) of the British Association.

[21] Discounting of course *The Economist*, which reported weekly on current economic affairs—see Ruth D. Edwards, *The Pursuit of Reason. The Economist, 1843–1993* (London, 1993).

[22] The *Economic Review* was published by the Oxford University branch of the Christian Social Union and its pages were dominated by Oxford contributors. It ceased publication in 1914.

[23] 'The British Economic Association', *Economic Journal,* 1 (1891), 1. In 1902 the Association was chartered as the Royal Economic Society.

[24] Of which in turn only a handful were teachers of economics—see my essay 'Economic Societies in Great Britain and Ireland' in Massimo M. Augello and Marco E. L. Guidi (eds.), *The Spread of Political Economy and the Professionalisation of Economists* (London, 2001), esp. pp. 45–8.

> It was also felt 'that some security should be afforded that the journal should always represent all shares of economic opinion, and be the organ not of one school of English economists, but of all schools; and it is thought that this end will be best attained by the publication of the journal under the authority of an economic association.'

The *Economic Journal* began publication in March 1891, edited by Francis Ysidro Edgeworth, then Tooke Professor of Political Economy at King's College London. It was a journal quite different from the general literary periodicals hitherto open to contributions in political economy. But although recognisably academic in focus, it did reflect the diversity of subject matter then thought relevant to 'economics'. Each issue was divided into Articles, Book Reviews, Notes and Memoranda, Current Topics and Recent Periodicals and New Books,[25] and this allowed scope for a wide range of contributions. The very first article was by John Rae on the eight-hour day in Victoria, Australia; and this was followed by articles on the recent American census and French peasant proprietorship. The Notes and Memoranda section was similarly heterogeneous—the German Social Democratic Party's Erfurt Programme appeared here within a contribution simply entitled 'The German Socialist Party',[26] and many of Edgeworth's own contributions were included in the 'Notes' section, rather than as articles in their own right. The kind of contribution with which a reader today might be familiar—a dozen terse pages on a specific technical topic[27]—first regularly appeared in the pages of the *Economic Journal* from the pen of Arthur Pigou, Marshall's successor in the Cambridge chair.

It was clear from the first issue that the editorial standards of the *Economic Journal* were academic standards; the church might have been broad, but there was little room for dissenters such as Henry George, John Hobson, Major Douglas or Frederick Soddy.[28] At the time there were in fact

[25] Other sections developed and were then abolished or absorbed into Current Topics or Notes over the years, such as reports from foreign correspondents, City Notes, Recent Legislation, and Official Papers.

[26] Vol. 1 (1891), pp. 531–3.

[27] For example, 'Producers' and Consumers' Surplus', *Economic Journal,* 20 (1910), 358–70. This piece was followed by Lujo Brentano, 'The Doctrine of Malthus and the Increase of Population during the Last Decades', *Economic Journal,* 20 (1910), 371–93. Pigou's next contribution to the journal was in December, when 'A Method of Determining the Numerical Value of Elasticities of Demand' appeared in the 'Notes and Memoranda' section, pp. 536–40. Edgeworth also contributed technical pieces, but these would not strike the present-day reader as so 'modern' in format as those by Pigou—see for example 'The Incidence of Urban Rates', *Economic Journal,* 10 (1900), 172–93, followed by Part II, pp. 340–8 and Part III, pp. 487–517 of the same volume.

[28] Henry George, *Progress and Poverty: an Inquiry into the Cause of Industrial Depressions and of Increase of Want with Increase of Wealth: the Remedy* (London, 1882); John A. Hobson and A. F. Mummery, *The Physiology of Industry: Being an Exposure of Certain Fallacies in Existing Theories*

only two full-time Professors of Political Economy in England: Marshall in Cambridge, and E. C. K. Gonner as Brunner Professor of Economic Science in Liverpool. In the autumn of 1891 Edgeworth became Drummond Professor at Oxford, but the duties associated with the post were at this time minimal. H. S. Foxwell also held the chair at University College London as a successor to Jevons, but this continued as a part-time appointment requiring on average only two lectures a week. Teaching in the subject at Manchester only began to increase with the appointment of Alfred Flux in 1893; but by the early 1900s economics was being regularly taught by William Ashley in Birmingham, John Clapham in Leeds, Stanley Chapman in Manchester, Joseph Shield Nicholson in Edinburgh, and William Smart in Glasgow. The rapid expansion of university teaching in economics towards the end of the century created cadres of students whose training increasingly turned upon the absorption of the Marshallian *organon*, the standardised 'toolbox' of economic principles.

The new academic understanding of economics which the *Economic Journal* promoted had therefore barely taken institutional root in the early 1890s, but the size and occupational variety of the British Economic Association's membership is suggestive of broad support for the idea that sound instruction in the principles of economics was the business of a university education, not of self-education. In this it was distinct from those associations generally thought of as its predecessors. First of these was the Political Economy Club, a London private dining club formed in 1821. The impetus came from a dinner party in January 1820 where Thomas Tooke observed that, while all those attending supported free trade, the list of exempt goods grew longer as the evening wore on. He concluded from this that London men of affairs required a forum through which they could deepen their understanding of the principles of free trade, and the inaugural meeting was held in April 1821, its draft constitution being presented by James Mill.[29] Membership was to be limited to thirty, it was to meet on the first Monday of each month December to June, and at each meeting questions tabled by members would be debated. Mill's suggestion that the Society's members should be encouraged to read widely and propagate the principles of political economy was voted down. 'Political economists' whose names might today be recognised were always in a minority, but most of the questions tabled came

of Economics (London, 1889); Clifford H. Douglas, *Social Credit* (London, 1924); Frederick Soddy, *Cartesian Economics: the Bearing of Physical Science upon State Stewardship* (London, 1922).

[29] Tribe, 'Economic Societies in Great Britain and Ireland', 38–40.

from this quarter; from which it might be assumed that they also guided discussion at the monthly meetings.

At this time open discussion of Political Economy was still thought potentially subversive. Ricardo might expound its principles in Parliament, and London diners could discuss the merits of free trade behind closed doors, but public discussion was commonly ruled out—for example in the regulations of the new Mechanics' Institutes and Literary Societies that flourished from the later 1820s as vehicles of popular education. A contributor to *Blackwood's Magazine* wrote that

> We believe to a certain extent in political economy, for it comprehends a number of stale old truths which were familiar to all men before the name was ever heard of; but we may say that it combines with these truths many falsehoods . . . Its doctrines bring into question a very large portion of our political system; they strike at some of the main pillars of British Society; they seek the destruction of many sentiments and regulations which, in our judgement, are essential for binding man to man and class to class—for cementing together and governing the community... This is sufficient to convince us that a large part of political economy is yet anything but knowledge, and that it is therefore unfit to be taught to the working classes.[30]

This Tory view of Political Economy as an instrument of class struggle was not without foundation, even if today social historians have moderated the once commonly accepted view that radical political economy was an important medium for the enlightenment of the working class. There was of course a clear connection between Political Economy and socialism, for it provided the means of making systematic arguments concerning the relation of the worker to manufacturer and landlord. But we cannot simply infer from the existence of texts embodying such arguments that their principles were widely accepted. Understanding how readers read and comprehended what they read has to begin with the reader, not the text; and we should not impute our understanding of the principles of political economy to an historical individual who happens to have come across a book on the subject. As with the diffusion of Smith's *Wealth of Nations*, the fact that the work was constantly reprinted testifies to a general recognition that political economy was an important matter, but we should not assume that all those who confidently referred to the principles in Smith's book had actually read it. Indeed, most readers of Smith seem to have read a very different book from the work with which we are today familiar. Acknowledging this problem is, however, merely the first step in seeking historical understanding of political economy, and is certainly not a basis for the 'correction' of past misreadings.

[30] Quoted in Mark Blaug, *Ricardian Economics* (New Haven, 1958), p. 145. n. 15.

Marx and Engels' early understanding of English political economy highlights this problem. Friedrich Engels' *Condition of the Working Class in England in 1844* was written following his first stay in Manchester, and in 1843 he had drafted an 'Outline of a Critique of Political Economy' which showed a surer grasp of the principles of English political economy than Marx's own contemporary critique of James Mill's *Elements of Political Economy*.[31] Engels has always been assigned a role subordinate to Marx in the development of their critique of political economy, despite his great efforts in editing Marx's voluminous unfinished drafts into the second and third volumes of *Capital*. Engels' 1843 'Outline' seems therefore to show that it was he, not Marx, who first grasped the revolutionary implications of English political economy. But it can be shown that most of Engels' early ideas about political economy were not taken directly from his reading of Smith, Ricardo and Malthus, but from John Watts, an Owenite writer whose lectures he had regularly attended while in Manchester.[32] Engels' account seemed novel to Marx because he was unfamiliar with the language of Owenite socialism; commentators later drew attention to its apparent novelty for the same reason.

Marx's political economy was constructed from the mid-1840s onward upon the foundations of post-Smithian English political economy; he remained generally ignorant of contemporary Continental European political economy. That of which he was aware, such as that of the popular writers Friedrich List or Frédéric Bastiat, was summarily dismissed. The Marxian political economy over whose principles socialists and communists later argued so dogmatically derived almost entirely from English writings of the first third of the century, projecting these debates on production and distribution forward into the twentieth century where they appeared to present a possible alternative to the academic economics that had, by then, become the new conventional wisdom. But Marxian political economy was only ever popular with controversialists and dogmatists. It was no accident that Ernest Bax associated with William Morris, or that John Hobson wrote a book on John Ruskin. Morris and Ruskin belong to a cultural critical canon which has

[31] (London, 1826). The book was written up from notes a young John Stuart Mill made of his father's impromptu lectures on political economy, its object being to summarise its principles in plain language. Marx's essay is notable chiefly for the risible consequences of a collision between his dense post-Hegelian language and a simple textbook exposition of political economy. Guy Debord did this kind of thing better than Karl Marx.

[32] Gregory Claeys, *Machinery, Money and the Millennium. From Moral Economy to Socialism, 1815–1860* (Cambridge, 1987), pp. 167–8.

developed almost entirely independently of the Marxian version of political economy. Nineteenth-century working-class autodidacts would instead typically gain their understanding of political economy from Ruskin's *Unto this Last*,[33] or from Henry George's *Progress and Poverty*, works since reviled by Marxists and academic economists alike.[34]

By the 1830s the idea that public discussion of political economy was dangerous because it was potentially seditious had faded, its association with free trade and social reform having blunted its radical edge. This followed on from the expansion of the public for social reform, a process marked by the formation of the British Association in 1831 as an annual, independent peripatetic conference committed to the diffusion of scientific knowledge. At the 1833 Cambridge meeting the 'Statistical Section' was added following a meeting in Cambridge between Adolphe Quetelet, Richard Jones and T. R. Malthus, and it was of course in this forum that Jevons first presented his new mathematical theory of political economy in 1862. Shortly following the Cambridge meeting the Statistical Society of Manchester was formed with the objective of improving the condition of Manchester people by collecting information and demanding practical reforms.[35] Problems of poverty, health, housing and education were regarded as 'social questions'—while this was never generally articulated in Britain as 'the Social Question' as became common later in Continental Europe, the linkage of political economy to social issues was clear—and an 1838 guide for local societies listed economic statistics as 'relating to the Social Condition of Man'.[36] Alongside the British Association and other major statistical societies there emerged the National Association for Moral and Social Improvement in 1857, its name being changed to the Social Science Association shortly before the first meeting in Birmingham. Its fifth section was 'Social Economy', the range of topics that it dealt with until its dissolution in 1886 lent focus by its emphasis on

[33] See for a recent assessment Jane Garnett, 'Political and Domestic Economy in Victorian Social Thought: Ruskin and Xenophon', in Stefan Collini, Richard Whatmore and Brian Young (eds.), *Economy, Polity, and Society. British Intellectual History, 1750–1950* (Cambridge, 2000), pp. 205–23.

[34] Jonathan Rose's important study of the reading habits of the British working class shows that along with Bunyan's *Pilgrim's Progress*, Ruskin's *Unto this Last* was widely read and popular. A survey of the reading habits of the first Labour MPs to sit in Parliament (1906) showed that Ruskin was the author whose formative influence was most frequently mentioned—*The Intellectual History of the British Working Classes* (New Haven, 2001), pp. 405-6.

[35] Alon Kadish, 'Free Trade and High Wages. The Economics of the Anti-Corn Law League', in A. Marrison (ed.), *Free Trade and its Reception, 1815–1960. Freedom and Trade Vol. I* (London, 1998), p. 15.

[36] S. Hare, 'Outline of Abstract of Subjects for Statistical Enquiries', *Journal of the Statistical Society of London*, 1 (1838), 427.

pressure for reform, rather than the diffusion of knowledge as with the British Association.[37]

Knowledge of political economy was therefore firmly linked in mid-century to issues of social reform, either with respect to pressure on municipal and national authorities as with the Social Science Association, or as part of a radical critique of popular conceptions of wealth and welfare. But this concern with social issues, while it drew much of its framework from the categories and arguments of political economists, did not presuppose or demand any intricate or detailed familiarity with the principles of the science. Knowledge of political economy was widely, but shallowly, diffused. Both of these altered with the new science of economics. Knowledge of its principles could be gained only through systematic training, preferably in a university. It became a higher-status knowledge separate from everyday argument; its principles were perhaps better understood, but by far fewer people. This development did not however initially eliminate the manifest concern for social justice that formed the impulse to economic learning. Later, during the first half of the twentieth century, English economists commonly shared a deep concern with social issues such as unemployment and poverty that marked their interest in the subject. Writing in the new edition of his earlier work *Wealth and Welfare*, Pigou chose to reiterate the ethical stance that Marshall had espoused in his 1885 inaugural address:[38]

> The complicated analyses which economists endeavour to carry through are not mere gymnastic. They are instruments for the bettering of human life. The misery and squalor that surrounds us, the dying fire of hope in many millions of European homes, the injurious luxury of some wealthy families, the terrible uncertainty overshadowing many families of the poor—these evils are too plain to be ignored. By the knowledge that our science seeks it is possible that they may be restrained. Out of the darkness light! To search for it is the task, to find it, perhaps, the

[37] Lawrence Goldman, 'The Social Sciences Association, 1857–1886: A Context for mid-Victorian Liberalism' *English Historical Review,* 101 (1986), 95–134.

[38] Criticising the excessive abstraction of Ricardo and other English political economists, Marshall suggested that: 'It led them to regard labour simply as a commodity without throwing themselves into the point of view of the workman; without allowing for his human passions, his instincts and habits, his sympathies and antipathies, his class jealousies and his class adhesiveness, his want of knowledge and of the opportunities for free and vigorous action. They therefore attributed to the forces of supply and demand a much more mechanical and regular action than they actually have; and laid down laws with regard to profits and wages that did not really hold even for England in their own time. But their most vital fault was that they did not see how liable to change are the habits and institutions of industry. In particular they did not see that the poverty of the poor is the chief cause of that weakness and which are the cause of their poverty: they had not the faith, that modern economists have, in the possibility of a vast improvement in the condition of the working classes.' A. Marshall, *The Present Position of Economics. An Inaugural Lecture* (London, 1885), pp. 16–17.

> prize, which the 'dismal science of Political Economy' offers to those who face its discipline.[39]

In 1928 Keynes gave a talk to the Cambridge Political Economy Club which looked forward one hundred years to a time when this 'economic problem' might be solved, a time when man will be confronted with his real problem: how 'to live wisely and agreeably and well'.[40] The economic problem was, he suggested, a transitional issue, best left to 'humble, competent people', specialists of the new science of economics. And in this vision of the future there is a clear echo of Ruskin:

> I see us free, therefore, to return to some of the most sure and certain principles of religion and traditional virtue—that avarice is a vice, that the exaction of usury is a misdemeanour, and love of money is detestable, that those walk most truly in the paths of virtue and sane wisdom who take least thought for the morrow. We shall once more value ends above means and prefer the good to the useful.[41]

Jevons, Marshall, Pigou and Keynes clearly thought the Political Economy of the early nineteenth century a truly 'dismal science', and sought to create a new science capable of transforming the world. The transition from Political Economy to Economics is therefore, in this reading, not one in which an abstract, formal 'hard' science displaces a broader, more ethical body of knowledge. The abstract, formal science created by Ricardo, McCulloch and their associates was, from the standpoint of the later nineteenth and early twentieth centuries, widely accepted to have been an unfortunate deviation. This was no basis for the construction of a positive science of social reform, and it is this understanding that drove teachers and students alike into the new science of economics. It was the new educational structures of the later nineteenth century that made it possible to elaborate a new alternative.

Nominally, university teaching in political economy goes back to the early part of the century: the Cambridge Chair for Political Economy was founded in 1828, the same year that J. R. McCulloch was appointed Professor of Political Economy to the newly opened University of London.[42] Cambridge could plausibly make some claim of precedence since their appointee, George Pryme, had been lecturing on the subject to interested

[39] A. C. Pigou, *The Economics of Welfare* (London, 1920), p. vi.

[40] John Maynard Keynes, 'Economic Possibilities for our Grandchildren', *Collected Writings of John Maynard Keynes,* IX (London, 1972), p. 328.

[41] Keynes, 'Economic Possibilities', 331.

[42] i.e. what we today know as University College London. See J. Maloney, 'The Teaching of Political Economy in the University of London', in Kadish and Tribe (eds.), *The Market for Political Economy,* p. 23.

fellows and students since 1816; London on the other hand could argue that their man was a prominent exponent of the new science. The point is, however, moot, since McCulloch's initial audience of thirty-three students quickly dwindled, he resigned in 1835, and the post remained vacant until 1854. Pryme remained as the Cambridge incumbent until 1863, but this was neither an eminent nor a demanding appointment, for it was unpaid and required only that the course last for a term; and by the 1840s these were being delivered every second year. The audience for these lectures was composed chiefly of pass men, students not reading for the Classical or Mathematical Triposes, and who were required to attend a minimum number of lectures before being allowed to graduate with an Ordinary BA. No examination in the subject was required. The creation of the Moral Sciences Tripos in 1848 created another constituency for the Chair, but moral sciences was widely regarded as an easy option and few students sat its examinations. Even as late as the 1860s the teaching of political economy in Cambridge amounted to basic principles according to Mill plus observations based upon contemporary social and political issues.[43] Pryme was succeeded by Fawcett in 1863, and Fawcett by Marshall in 1885, at which point teaching in the subject began to develop. The story is rather different in Oxford, but with a similar outcome. The Drummond Chair of Political Economy was founded in 1825, but its incumbent, appointed for five years only, was merely obliged to give a short course of lectures annually. The Drummond Professor was consequently more like a guest lecturer than a member of the university. Not until 1871 with the formation of the School of Modern History did political economy have a certain place in the programme of study,[44] and with the development of the Extension Movement Oxford was during the 1880s the centre of academic economics in Britain. Edgeworth, appointed to the Drummond

[43] Phyllis Deane, 'Henry Fawcett: The Plain Man's Political Economist', in L. Goldman (ed.), *The Blind Victorian. Henry Fawcett and British Liberalism* (Cambridge, 1989), p. 97. She sums up Fawcett's work thus: 'His *Manual* expounded orthodox classical political economy in the hallowed tradition of Adam Smith, as sharpened by Ricardo and broadened and updated by J. S. Mill. He wrote in the spirit of a determinedly non-doctrinaire political economist, pragmatically applying the agreed principles of a well-established discipline to the practical economic and social issues confronting government in the second half of the nineteenth century. . . . His chosen role was that of a teacher, a populariser of political economy. Accepting Mill's *Principles* as constituting the accredited theory of the subject, he set out to analyse current economic trends and policy problems in the light of that orthodoxy. The *Manual* was designed to provide a clear, relevant and uncomplicated introduction to the current state of economic knowledge and illuminate its applicability to a changing real world' (pp. 108–9).

[44] A. Kadish, 'Oxford Economics in the Later Nineteenth Century', in Kadish and Tribe (eds.), *The Market for Political Economy*, pp. 42–3.

Chair in 1891, never had any institutional ambition for the new science of economics, and when the PPE degree was created in 1920, at last providing a sure base for teaching and research in economics, the impulse came from elsewhere.

Strictly speaking, Malthus held the first chair in Political Economy in Britain at the East India College, first at Hertford Castle and then at the new building at Haileybury, where he taught around five hours a week from 1806 to his death in 1834. Although not formally a university, it had been established by the East India Company to provide for cadets selected for service in India some practical training lasting four terms, covering law, languages, mathematics, history and political economy. The cadets were formally examined, but since they were selected through a system of patronage, it was virtually impossible to fail any of them. Examination papers have survived which suggest that, into the 1830s, the main text of reference was Smith's *Wealth of Nations*—not, then, Malthus's more recent *Principles of Political Economy* published in 1820, nor the equivalent works of Ricardo, Mill, or McCulloch.[45] This does strongly suggest that Malthus' teaching at Haileybury was not only based upon *Wealth of Nations*, but remained essentially unaltered from the foundation of the college until shortly before his death. Richard Jones, whose tenure of the chair ran from 1834 to his death in 1855, moved from a position at King's College, London where he had received three-quarters of the fees paid by his students. The salary of £500, house, candles and coals that went with the Haileybury post meant that, from the mid-1830s, Jones was the only fully paid teacher of political economy in Britain.[46]

Haileybury is important to our story because the manner of its dissolution was linked to the development of a public examination system for the British civil service, in the case of the Indian Civil Service political economy playing a small but significant part. This also coincided with the transformation of the University of London into a body administering a national system of higher academic qualifications, complemented in the early 1860s by the creation of a national system of school-level examination run from Cambridge. These developments in turn encouraged some teaching in political economy either as part of the University Extension Movement[47] or in local colleges.

[45] One of the students, Inverarity, copied questions that Malthus set in 1830 into an interleaved copy of Smith's *Wealth of Nations*: see John M. Pullen, 'Notes from Malthus: the Inverarity Manuscript', *History of Political Economy*, 13 (1981), 794–811.

[46] See my essay 'Professors Malthus and Jones: Political Economy at the East India College 1806–1858', *European Journal for the History of Economic Thought,* 2 (1995), 327–54.

[47] Courses of lectures and classes in provincial centres run by peripatetic tutors and administered from the universities of Oxford, Cambridge and London.

The diffusion of political economy was therefore part of wider educational and cultural developments, where individuals sought in a modern curriculum a preparation for a career in commerce, public and municipal administration, and the expanding system of public education.

The assumption of direct Crown control of India ended the existing system through which Indian Civil Servants had been recruited. The substitution of selection by examination rather than patronage left the function of Haileybury formally intact; but in the process of committee discussion the college lost its status as qualifying institution, and thus its *raison d'être*. The college was closed at the end of January 1858.[48] Political economy continued as a small part of the preparation for the Indian Civil Service examination, but the associated development of examinations for entry into higher clerkships of the Civil Service was of little significance, either for political economy or for the Civil Service. During the second half of the nineteenth century there were rarely more than ten places available per year in the higher Civil Service, in 1876 for example thirty-eight candidates competing for four places.[49] With such a small annual intake there was little incentive for any individual institution to develop an independent 'modern' programme of study that might have included political economy. And without such a programme of study there would be no academic appointments to teach political economy.

More significant in (eventually) promoting more systematic discussion of political economy was the reorganisation of the University of London in the same year that East India College closed. A new two-part BA was introduced which, in its second year, included logic, moral and mental philosophy—roughly the domain of the moral sciences within which political economy

[48] Discussion over the future of the college played a major role in the development of arguments in the early 1850s concerning recruitment for public service and the function of written examinations in the selection of candidates and the assessment of qualification. Sir Charles Trevelyan was asked the following question in June 1853 by a Select Committee: 'From your knowledge of our general university courses here, do you think that it would be possible to carry on at Oxford or at Cambridge those extended and practically applied courses of jurisprudence, law, and political economy, which are introduced at Haileybury, and which, possibly, under a freer system, might be carried advantageously further?' His reply expressed strong support for the educational provision of Haileybury, which he saw as unique. *Second Report from the Select Committee of the House of Lords, appointed to inquire into the Operation of the Act 3 & 4 Will.4,c.85, for the better Government of Her Majesty's Indian Territories*, BPP 1852–3, Vol. XXXII, Q.6910, p. 217. John Stuart Mill on the contrary questioned the utility of continuing Haileybury as a separate institution, and it was this argument which prevailed—see *Report from the Select Committee of the House of Lords appointed to inquire into the Operation of the Act 3 & 4 Will.4, c.85, for the better Government of Her Majesty's Indian Territories,* BPP 1852–3, Vol. XXX, 22 June 1853, Q.3169, p. 331.

[49] William J. Reader, *Professional Men* (London, 1966), p. 96.

was at this time formally included. In 1859 pressure on examination space was so great in London that two provincial examination centres were established, at Owens College in Manchester, and Queen's College in Liverpool.[50] The prime immediate significance of this was that, when new provincial colleges began to be founded—Yorkshire College of Science, Leeds (1874), University College, Bristol (1876), Mason College, Birmingham (1880), Firth College, Sheffield (1879), University College, Nottingham (1881) and University College, Liverpool (1881)—they could immediately teach to the London BA syllabus and offer its degree. Although the teaching of political economy in such institutions was peripheral to the curriculum, provincial interest in the subject was supported by peripatetic lecturers of the Oxford and Cambridge University extension movement, offering classes in political economy during the winter months in towns and cities throughout the north and the Midlands.

The shift from political economy as a general understanding of the creation of wealth and its distribution to a new science of economics, taught in an academic setting to students willing to spend several years on the subject, is therefore closely linked in Britain for the development of new foundations and a relevant examination structure. The movement for wider access to higher education in the second half of the century—extending university education offering secular tuition for both sexes to provincial cities—was associated with the formation of new university subjects in the humanities—languages, English, and geography. Among these modern subjects commerce and economics were prominent as new disciplines of study relevant to the modern world. By the early 1900s most of the institutions listed above, together with others like Cardiff, Reading and Newcastle, were transforming themselves into independent universities teaching all subjects in the humanities and natural sciences. A new generation of economists was entering full-time academic employment, and these individuals would quickly assume the prerogative of ultimate authority over new knowledge.

The timing of this transition from political economy to economics can therefore be plausibly linked to the development of British university education in the later nineteenth century, the reorganisation of university life around teaching and research in modern subjects. But, considering our point of departure, how precisely might this institutional development illuminate the intellectual development that has come to be known as the 'Marginal Revolution'? To return to the questions posed above: why should this

[50] Negley Harte, *The University of London, 1836–1986* (London, 1986), p. 106.

transition involve a change of name? Why should it have begun in the 1870s? And why did it take so long for the 'neoclassical revolution' to be recognised, let alone named, as such?

The first point is perhaps the easiest to deal with. 'Political economy' as classically understood concerned the self-organisation of the body politic, 'economy' being used not so much in the sense of 'parsimony' as in that of internal order. In the tripartite division of production, distribution and consumption introduced by Jean-Baptiste Say in the early 1800s the economic agents on which the system rested were workers or entrepreneurs, rentiers or landlords—perhaps, when analysing specific issues, identifiable as farmers or manufacturers, bankers or merchants, peasants or factory workers. But the fate of worker or peasant, merchant or manufacturer, was inscribed upon their location in the system of production and distribution. Prices were mainly thought to rise and fall according to fluctuations in supply rather than changes in demand, a conception of market functioning closely tied to the priority of agricultural production in societies hitherto dependent upon an annual harvest. The economics that Jevons had in mind broke with this and was relaunched as a system of mutual exchange between consumers and producers, prices arising out of fluctuations in the urgency of aggregated need and the constraints of supply at the market prices. Menger and Walras did not approach the problem in exactly this way, but each sought to demarcate the new core theory from 'applied economics' and economic policy.

As for the timing of the 'Revolution', political economy had in Britain long been associated with social and political reform. The educational reforms of the last third of the century were closely related to a general democratisation of society built upon the partial realisation of demands for reform, opening the prospect of social mobility through the acquisition of intellectual skills and qualities hitherto the almost exclusive property of a strict class monopoly. The 'sciences' gained recognition as master discourses; Jevons' knowledge of chemistry and logic led him to a perspective on a possible 'science of human conduct' very different from that of John Stuart Mill. Mirowski has observed that 'more than half of Jevons's published work concerns the logic and philosophy of science' and that physical science was the unifying principle of his work.[51] From that perspective the introduction of a calculus of pleasure and pain does indeed look more like social physics than the simple application of an earlier Benthamite idea.

[51] Philip Mirowski, *More Heat than Light. Economics as Social Physics, Physics and Nature's Economics* (Cambridge, 1990), p. 219.

Jevons' lack of familiarity with the sheer ordinariness of Continental discussions of utility sets him apart from Menger and Walras. But in the Continental context it is not so very hard to account for the timing of their works. Throughout Europe the teaching of political economy was linked to the teaching of law, and unlike England, Faculties of Law in European universities were the sole route to private legal practice or higher public administration. Political economy had a secure, if small, part in the curriculum for legal training, and this in turn provided regular academic positions for the teaching of political economy. The conditions therefore existed for the limited elaboration of its principles. French was the international language of Continental Europe and the writings of Jean-Baptiste Say were highly influential. His emphasis on the creation and destruction of utility as the point of departure for political economy quickly became the mainstream view. By the 1860s Hans von Mangoldt had presented the idea of diminishing utility in graphical representations of supply and demand curves. In some respects Menger simply spelled out the implications of propositions to be found in German literature since mid-century, a qualification he would have been the first to acknowledge. His direct and indirect influence upon students and colleagues led to a body of economic writing known today as 'Austrian economics'. Similarly with Walras: although his appointment in Lausanne resulted from his participation in a local essay competition in 1861 where his essay on taxation, advocating the nationalisation of land, was commended alongside a contribution from Proudhon, he quickly elaborated a scheme of teaching that underpinned his publishing plans. Changes in university routine related to advances in scholarship and science took the established teaching of political economy with it. Across Europe 'scientific scholarship' became the prerogative of the university rather than the private scholar or autodidact.

Making a science of economics was, however, uphill work. Menger's own propositions for the development of economics as a science quickly ran into controversy when Gustav Schmoller denounced his abstract and deductive approach in an episode today known as the *Methodenstreit*, a debate over analytical versus historical method.[52] German economics was a flourishing and self-confident enterprise dominated by the 'Historical School', a pragmatic synthesis of theory, institutional description and policy that lived on in American Institutionalism. Menger was rather more fortunate than either Jevons or Walras in that he created a local 'school' of his own

[52] See for an outline of this controversy my article 'Historical Schools of Economics: German and English' in W. J. Samuels, J. E. Biddle and J. B. Davis (eds.), *A Companion to the History of Economic Thought* (Oxford, 2003), p. 224.

which eventually became recognised internationally, and his basic theses have been recycled by the American 'neo-Austrian' school of economics. But in contemporary Germany his new economics found at first no ready place in the established teaching of university professors and the journals for which they wrote. Walras spent a small fortune propagating his work, to little avail in his working lifetime. That he eventually gained wide recognition as the intellectual founder of the general equilibrium core of modern neoclassicism is due to his successor, Vilfredo Pareto, and a small group of Italian economists.

In Britain it was Marshall, not Jevons, who made the decisive intellectual and institutional moves, using his secure position as Professor of Political Economy in Cambridge to create a lasting framework—the British Economic Association, the *Economic Journal*, and the new Cambridge Economics Tripos, which when it began in 1903 was the first honours economics undergraduate course in the world.[53] It was more than fifty years before it began to produce the quality and numbers of graduates that Marshall envisaged.[54] Marshall thought that it took at least three years for a bright student to become proficient in the basic skills of economic analysis; and as such proficiency became the touchstone of what it meant to be an economist it is easy to see how Jevons' frustration with the 'ignorance' of the general public has survived into the present century. By the 1920s to be an 'economist' meant that a person had completed a systematic university training in the subject, and very likely was a university teacher. Not until the 1960s did the government formally employ more than a handful of economists,[55] the picture being very similar in banking, commerce and industry. This low level of demand for economists outside universities itself hindered the propagation of the new science. Economics quickly became an esoteric, academic subject and as such poorly understood by those lacking the appropriate training.

[53] An 'ordinary' degree was not specialised in the manner of an 'honours' degree, so that for example degrees in commerce offered at many English universities in the early twentieth century were 'ordinary' by virtue of the wide range of subjects included, among them of course economics. Likewise, as noted above, 'political economy' was in the later nineteenth century a small part of the (ordinary) London BA which certified its graduates in 'arts' rather than 'sciences'. The Cambridge Economics Tripos was indeed preceded by the London B.Sc. (Econ.) but this was not an 'economics' degree in the way that the Cambridge one was, and is more properly thought of as a social sciences degree with opportunities for later specialisation. See *London University Gazette*, Vol. I, No. 3 (21 Dec. 1901), 23.

[54] See for an account of this my essay 'The Cambridge Economics Tripos, 1903–55 and the Training of Economists', *Manchester School*, 68 (2000), 222–48.

[55] The significant number of economists who entered government service during the Second World War and made such a great contribution to social, economic and military planning nearly all went back to their academic careers at the end of the war.

CHAPTER SIX
Reasoning and Belief in Victorian Mathematics

DANIEL J. COHEN

Given the great vitality and immense progress of mathematics in the nineteenth century, even a purely technical history of the discipline stripped of its larger intellectual and social context would not soon run out of material. Existing mathematical fields diversified and new fields arose in response to significant breakthroughs. The eastern European mathematicians János Bolyai and Nikolai Ivanovich Lobachevsky formulated non-Euclidean geometry in the Victorian period, a set of principles counterintuitive to normal human experience that led to a complete redefinition of this most ancient of mathematical pursuits. Mathematics and its associated methodologies also expanded into realms of knowledge other than the natural sciences (where they had been especially at home in physics and astronomy), often through pioneering work by theorists who began their careers as mathematicians but who branched out later in life. At the same time that this move outward occurred, there was a move inward in nineteenth-century mathematics. Concerns about the foundations of the discipline—an interest in the fundamental nature of mathematical knowledge and the process whereby mathematicians come to conclusions—occupied a significant portion of the research agenda. In Great Britain the adoption of Gottfried Leibniz's more suggestive form of the calculus over Isaac Newton's method, although far from rapid and unchallenged, eventually led to an acceleration of mathematical discovery in the British isles, and it signalled a greater integration with Continental mathematics that would ultimately result in the first major international conferences toward the end of the century.

British interest in the formal aspects of mathematics was particularly apparent in the growing interest in mathematical, or symbolic, logic. As George Boole (1815–64) summarised the nature of this critical field of pure mathematics, it was 'not of the mathematics of number and quantity alone, but of mathematics in its larger ... truer sense, as universal reasoning expressed in symbolical forms, and conducted by laws, which have their ultimate abode in the human mind'.[1] Alfred North Whitehead (1861–1947), following decades of British work on Boole's project, would provide an even stronger statement about mathematics at the end of the Victorian period:

> Mathematics in its widest signification is the development of all types of formal, necessary, deductive reasoning. The reasoning is formal in the sense that the meaning of propositions forms no part of the investigation. The sole concern of mathematics is the inference of proposition from proposition ... The ideal of mathematics should be to erect a calculus to facilitate reasoning in connection with every providence of thought, or external experience, in which the succession of thoughts, or of events can be definitely ascertained and precisely stated. So that all serious thought which is not philosophy, or inductive reasoning, or imaginative literature, shall be mathematics developed by means of a calculus.[2]

Whitehead thus envisioned mathematics in 1898 as a discipline that applied to a much larger region of human thought than it did before the nineteenth century. No longer was mathematics simply about familiar elements such as the numbers with which we count or the arc of comets through the solar system. Mathematics could be responsible for sound reasoning and conclusions regardless of the topic, and thus encroached on, or even assumed territory once commanded by philosophy.

While research fields abounded and British mathematicians of this era studied and contributed to many of them, they showed a special interest in this abstract field of symbolic logic, and they pursued it with special intensity. Many of the pioneers in this field were British, a remarkable three generations that furthered the association between British thought and logic while creating a new mathematical field in concert with European counterparts: Boole and Augustus De Morgan (1806–71), William Stanley Jevons (1832–85) and John Venn (1834–1923), Bertrand Russell (1872–1970) and Whitehead. The 1840s and 1850s saw the ground-breaking publication of Boole's *The Mathematical Analysis of Logic, being an Essay towards a Calculus of Deductive Reasoning* (1847) and *An Investigation of the Laws of Thought on which are Founded the Mathematical Theories of Logic and Probabilities* (1854), as well as De Morgan's *Formal Logic* (1847). Jevons, a student of De Morgan's at University College London, began his career by formulating his own symbolic logic (*Pure Logic*, 1864), which led to his landmark treatise *The Principles of Science* (1874), and he continued to work

[1] G. Boole, *Studies in Logic and Probability* (La Salle, 1952), p. 195.

[2] A. N. Whitehead, *A Treatise on Universal Algebra* (New York, 1960), pp. vi, viii.

in the field as he carried its methods into economics and the social sciences in general. Venn expanded upon Boole's theories in two critical texts in the 1880s, *Symbolic Logic* (1881) and *The Principles of Empirical Logic* (1889), in the process inventing the diagrams of overlapping shapes that would come to bear his name. *Principia Mathematica* (1910–13), in which Russell and Whitehead equated logic and mathematics at the deepest level possible, was a culmination of the innovative mathematical research of the Victorian age. Before this seminal collaboration, Russell and Whitehead had independently penned monographs exploring mathematical logic (Russell's *The Principles of Mathematics*, 1903; Whitehead's *A Treatise on Universal Algebra*, 1898). Though far from the totality of British mathematics in the nineteenth century, these were among the most highly influential figures in Victorian mathematical circles due to their wide-ranging thought (e.g., Boole penned an important treatise on differential equations in addition to his logical work) and institutional positions (especially true for Augustus De Morgan and John Venn).

While intellectual historians have given a great deal of attention to Russell and Whitehead, the embryonic theories and methods of their predecessors provide useful insights into the state of mathematical knowledge in the Victorian age and its relationship to other disciplines and other elements of Victorian culture in general. Exploring such relationships demands a wider view than that of a purely technical history, of course; questions about mathematical research agendas naturally lead to broader questions about the goals and motivations of Boole, De Morgan, Jevons, and Venn. Why did mathematical logic flourish in the British isles in the second half of the nineteenth century, and why did British mathematicians pursue this particular region of their discipline with such passion? What motivated the founders of mathematical logic, Boole and De Morgan, and why were promising young British mathematicians eager to embrace and extend their work? More specifically, why did these mathematicians criticise words and common methods of reasoning as notoriously unreliable and seek to replace them with what they believed were far more exact symbolic replacements and logical processes? In a larger sense, what did these processes say about mathematical reasoning and knowledge? How widely applicable was mathematics? Was mathematical knowledge unlimited or limited? Objective or subjective? Perfect or merely approximate?

While the Victorians Boole, De Morgan, Jevons, and Venn had their differences, they shared a great curiosity about such questions and their broader significance. Tellingly, they also shared important experiences and concerns that had a clear impact on the way they thought about these questions. By tackling logic these thinkers set mathematics on a collision course with schools of philosophy both ancient and modern, and they had to struggle against the calcification of logic in educational curricula. This was not unusual in the history of Victorian mathematics; Victorian geometers faced an uphill battle against the long-standing dominance of Euclid in mathematical education at Cambridge.[3] In addition to these institutional difficulties, the mathematical logicians addressed theological and sectarian debates both indirectly and directly. The reader of works of Victorian symbolic logic is struck by the high frequency and extra-mathematical overtones of words such as 'clarity', 'conviction', 'certainty', 'fallibility', and 'belief', and cannot help but notice how certain mathematical investigations functioned as proxies for religious inquiries. It is also notable that without exception the mathematical logicians drifted away from the Church of England and toward what they saw as more ecumenical expressions of spirituality, and had social agendas marked by liberalism, cosmopolitan internationalism, and pacifism. Unsurprisingly, much of their pioneering mathematical work took place outside of the traditional English stronghold of mathematics (and until 1871 an institution that mandated orthodoxy), Cambridge University. De Morgan taught at University College London; Boole at Queen's College, Cork; Jevons split his time between the University of Manchester and University College London. Only John Venn, from a prominent line of Cantabrigians, taught at Cambridge and took holy orders, though he later resigned those orders.

Given the contentiousness and upheaval of early Victorian religious, social, and political life, Augustus De Morgan's quest for a 'logic of relations' took on much larger connotations, and a mathematical logic presented to George Boole a possible way out of the 'idle disputation' and 'wordy wrangling' that he saw as the unfortunate hallmark of his day.[4] Theological factions, as well as political and social ones (often intertwined with the religious sects), and their frequently heated, turbulent relationships made a cool, calm system of logic based on mathematics exceedingly attractive to these figures. Although Boole and De Morgan had disparate views of the fundamental nature of mathematical knowledge, both saw their creation of a symbolic logic as a social act as well as a technical achievement. A precise understanding of terms and the relationships between them would allow for a more nuanced and thus less contentious dialogue between opposing groups,

[3] See J. Richards, *Mathematical Visions: the Pursuit of Geometry in Victorian England* (San Diego, 1989).

[4] G. Boole, 'Lines written in the autumn of 1846', Dublin, Royal Irish Academy, MS 12.K.45, f. vii (hereafter referred to as RIA).

they believed. Support for every conclusion would have to come through logical methods accepted even by those who were disinclined to the position in question. Boole and De Morgan saw mathematics as particularly well suited to this task. After all, it was an international language that transcended so many human-drawn lines. De Morgan's insignia for the London Mathematical Society, founded in 1865, neatly encapsulated this idea. Based on a triangular symbol from Euclid's *Elements*, it displayed the Christian, Jewish, and Muslim years on its three sides—a symbol of the unity of peoples across religious faiths.

De Morgan expressed in words as well as symbols the ecumenism that often characterised researchers in mathematical logic, and that was particularly important in the genesis of this field in Great Britain. Born in India, and after adolescence disdainful toward his parents' evangelicalism, De Morgan called himself a 'Briton unattached' and a 'Christian unattached'.[5] He was unable to take his master's degree at Trinity College, Cambridge because of an unwillingness to subscribe to the thirty-nine articles of the Church of England,[6] and later referred to subscriptions as 'deadly poison' which 'foster[ed] every kind of dishonesty' because in the realm of private conscience many of the faithful did not agree with the doctrines of their church.[7] De Morgan's favourite quip about the Bible summarised his contempt for doctrinaire sectarians: 'One day at least in every week/The sects of every kind/Their doctrines here are sure to seek/And just as sure to find.'[8] Less flippant and more heartfelt was his declaration of religious heterodoxy to his mother. In early adulthood he wrote her a letter distancing himself from Church of England orthodoxy 'because I see in all that is orthodox a lack of that charity which Paul considers as more essential than everything else, coupled with what virtually amounts to a claim of infallibility'.[9] Instead of pursuing a career at Cambridge or Oxford, he instead signed on as the first professor of mathematics at the new University College London in 1828, cherishing its novel non-denominational status. He hoped for the realisation of Lord Brougham's prediction that the new university would 'do more to crush bigotry and intolerance than all the Bills [we] will ever see carried, at

[5] De Morgan to W. R. Hamilton, 2 Feb. 1852, Dublin, Trinity College Library, Hamilton papers, 1493/541; Sophia Elizabeth De Morgan, *Memoir of Augustus De Morgan* (London, 1882), p. 86.

[6] A. De Morgan, autobiographical sketch written in the third person, London, British Library, MS 28509, f. 421.

[7] De Morgan to Hamilton, 27 July 1852, in R. Graves, *Life of Sir William Rowan Hamilton* (3 vols., Dublin, 1885), iii, p. 395.

[8] De Morgan to Hamilton, 1 Sept. 1852, in Graves, *Hamilton*, iii, p. 410.

[9] S. De Morgan, *Memoir*, p. 142.

least until a Reform happens'.[10] De Morgan was an early supporter of the Catholic Emancipation Bill and an eager mentor of dissenting Christian as well as Jewish students.

De Morgan's friend George Boole found himself in a more unsettling non-denominational educational experiment during the time he was developing mathematical logic. Indeed, as a shy, distressed young faculty member in Cork, Ireland, the 'father of pure mathematics' (as Russell called Boole[11]) is perhaps a more interesting case study for understanding the relationship between work on the foundations of mathematical reasoning in the Victorian age and the ideologies and experiences of its creators. Throughout his life Boole was fond of talking about the unity of all human beings on a higher plane, above the lines drawn by culture, politics, and religion. As one of his poems declared in 1848, a year after his publication of *The Mathematical Analysis of Logic*, 'Oh, too long sever'd in the thought and speech/Of mortal men, too oft as rivals set/Who kindred are, and in firm union met/One consummation in the Heavens shall reach.'[12] Desperately concerned with forging interdenominational agreement, he was drawn to the idea of a highly abstract form of mathematics that might have some very real implications for the world outside his study.

While others argued over the nature of the Holy Trinity or the eucharist, or engaged in charged debates about the meaning of single lines or words from the Bible, George Boole developed an increasing distaste for the state of religious affairs in Great Britain. Although he was raised in a family that subscribed to Low Church Anglican principles, he fell away from the Church of England in his early adulthood, eventually settling on a faith that came closest to Unitarianism, closely informed by philosophical idealism. (There are also hints that he had an affinity toward Judaism, since to him it represented a pure, 'pre-sectarian' religiosity.[13]) Boole's mature faith was difficult to define because he found such religious definitions to be based, more often than not, on theological conjectures and nebulous terms. Instead, the best indicator of this faith came from his actions rather than his adherence to specific tenets or formulations. He enjoyed reading all kinds of religious works, including the lives of saints (Roman Catholic as well as Protestant), eastern

[10] Quoted. in A. Desmond, *The Politics of Evolution: Morphology, Medicine, and Reform in Radical London* (Chicago, 1989), p. 25.

[11] B. Russell, n.d., RIA, untitled tribute to G. Boole.

[12] G. Boole, 'Sonnet XIII', 3 July 1849, RIA, MS 12.K.45, f. vi.

[13] Boole to J. Hill, 30 May 1837, Cork, University College Library, Boole papers, 1/221(6) (hereafter referred to as UCC). Boole to De Morgan, 4 Nov. 1861, London, University College Library, De Morgan papers, MS Add. 97.

and western mystic philosophy, the Hebrew and Christian Bibles, writings by puritan divines and church fathers, and Christian and Jewish Prayer Books. He could be found on any given Sunday in services at a Society of Friends house, a Roman Catholic or Church of England cathedral, or a Unitarian communion—as long as the liturgy included music. 'Once a man thinks himself bound to a settled creed, it seems as if truth, faith, and charity become impossible to him, except in so far as he evades his creed', Boole told his wife.[14] In short, he was a spiritual omnivore who resisted and deplored the notion of religious sects.

Unfortunately, as a teacher in England and then a professor in Ireland Boole found himself perpetually in the middle of sectarian firestorms. In his first teaching job in the 1830s, at a Methodist school in his home town of Lincoln, the young mathematician became the centre of attention when the Methodist community discovered that he was not a Methodist himself. As the Methodists began to pray publicly for his conversion, a highly uncomfortable Boole decided he would be better off somewhere else.[15] He sought an environment that would downplay partisanship and promote unity across sectarian boundaries, and he believed that he had found it in the late 1840s when he was appointed the first professor of mathematics at the recently created Queen's College in Cork, Ireland (now known as University College, Cork). With characteristic idealism he thought that a new institution of higher education in a city roughly split between Roman Catholics and Protestants would show his nation and the world that sectarian coexistence—and even friendship—was a real and desirable possibility. Boole told a Lincoln audience before setting off for his new position that a primary mission of QCC was 'the bringing together and associating of the Catholic and the Protestant youth', and that it 'would contribute to the harmony of Ireland, and that [the Queen's colleges] would in their internal management prove models of that peace and harmony which they recommended'.[16]

The experiment did not turn out, however, as Boole had hoped. Catholic/Protestant and Irish/British tensions actually intensified during Boole's tenure in Cork from the late 1840s until his death in 1864, only reinforcing his sense that the greatest trouble of his age was a tremendous factionalism that threatened to swamp civil society and destroy Christian brotherhood. In response to the founding of the Queen's colleges in Ireland,

[14] M. E. Boole, 'Home-side of a scientific mind', in *Collected Works,* 4 vols. (London, 1931), i, p. 3.
[15] J. Dyson to M. Boole, undated letter, UCC, 1/256.
[16] Lincoln, Lincolnshire Central Library, Local history collection, MS UP 9663, undated newspaper clipping, probably from *The Stamford Record* (hereafter referred to as LCL).

Pope Pius IX began to consider funding a countervailing system of Roman Catholic colleges. Following the summer 1850 session at the Synod of Thurles, where the primate of Ireland, Dr Cullen, warned of the 'godlessness' of the Queen's colleges,[17] local priests began advising their flocks to turn away from the schools. As he returned to campus for his second year at QCC, Boole discovered that his Catholic students were extremely apprehensive and increasingly absent. He wrote to Augustus De Morgan in October 1850 describing in horror 'the storm of religious bigotry which is at this moment raging around us here'.[18] Adding fuel to the fire was the publication in 1850 of a work by one of Boole's Protestant housemates that seemed to undermine the authority of the pope by exploring the misty circumstances of pontifical succession in the early Christian era.[19] With a president, Sir Robert Kane, who was impolitic and unable to maintain a sense of fairness and balance at QCC, and with the famine heightening the sense of injustice among the Roman Catholic populace, the taciturn Boole frequently and painfully found himself at the wrong end of coarse diatribes at formal dinner parties.[20] The mathematician's early concern that the new college would fail in its noble mission 'if that charity which was the essence of true religion was lost amid the turmoil of theological disputation' quickly became a reality.[21]

Sadly for Boole, it did not seem possible to escape from this sectarian strife by returning to England. The autumn of 1850 saw the rise of strong anti-Catholic and anti-papist sentiments across England in response to Pius's attempt to re-establish the Roman Catholic hierarchy there. Lord Russell questioned the intent of the pope and attacked the tractarians for complicity. A wave of popular anti-Catholicism crested on Guy Fawkes Day, 5 November, with 'No Popery' riots and physical assaults on Roman Catholic priests. In that same month George Boole received an offer to teach in Manchester, but he politely declined, worrying in a letter to his sister about 'the ill feeling which is springing up between Protestant and Catholic in England'.[22] Later in the 1850s Boole received an offer to teach mathematics at Oxford University, yet despite the tense situation in Cork he feared worse back in England because of the Oxford Movement and its vocal antagonists.

[17] Quoted. in W. Ralls, 'The papal aggression of 1850: a study in Victorian anti-Catholicism', in G. Parsons (ed.), *Religion in Victorian Britain* (Manchester, 1988), p. 127.

[18] Boole to De Morgan, 17 Oct. 1850, in G. C. Smith (ed.), *The Boole–De Morgan Correspondence* (Oxford, 1982), p. 38.

[19] L. R. de Vericour, *An Historical Analysis of Christian Civilisation* (London, 1850), p. 18.

[20] G. Boole to M. E. Boole, 20–5 Mar. 1850, UCC, 1/150.

[21] LCL, undated newspaper clipping (probably from *The Stamford Record*).

[22] G. Boole to M. Boole, 18 Nov. 1850, UCC, 1/46.

'He would be expected to take one side or the other in [the] theological controversy' between High and Low Churchmen, his wife later explained, 'the life of a man who would be a partisan of neither side might be made very uncomfortable'.[23] Boole nervously delayed his response and ultimately put in a half-hearted application that was rejected.

In retrospect Boole might have been better off taking either position in England as factionalism increasingly disrupted QCC. When Boole tried to admonish Kane in the mid-1850s to instill a more harmonious, non-denominational spirit, he was rebuffed with a disturbing counter-accusation of being sectarian himself. 'When the most reasonable and temperate efforts to bring about a better state of things expose a man to the charge of faction and subject them to the frown of power, I do not see what but ruin can be expected', Boole lamented to a friend.[24] Ultimately, the Roman Catholic unease with the Queen's colleges led to a final papal condemnation of them in the spring of 1857 and the establishment of a rival university system. Catholic students at QCC were confronted with the option of leaving the school or facing the possibility of excommunication, a terrible and tragic dilemma in Boole's mind.[25] Near the end of his life, while still at work in Cork, Boole complained bitterly that 'the Roman Catholic Priesthood seem to have been doing all they can to preach disloyalty. Between them and a bigoted Calvinistic Protestant population this is a country which does not on the whole present the most favourable picture of Christianity.'[26] The Cork experiment had failed; far from diminishing sectarian feelings, the new college had actually magnified them.

Unsuccessful in his mostly timid public entreaties, George Boole more productively channelled his drive to forge common ground between factions by developing a logic based on mathematical principles. Mathematics, Boole believed, was a divine language that transcended human differences and vagaries, and thus was perfectly suited to be the basis of a new, dispassionate system of arbitration. A mathematical logic might ease tensions by undermining the excessive verbiage and fatuous arguments that had flourished in the sectarian atmosphere of the nineteenth century. In doing so, Boole modestly proposed, this symbolic method could 'render service in the investigation of social problems'.[27] In *The Laws of Thought* (1854) Boole emphasised

[23] M. E. Boole, 'Home-side,' p. 2.

[24] G. Boole to W. Brooke, 18 June 1855, UCC, 1/161(a).

[25] G. Boole to M. Boole, 25 May 1857, UCC, 1/125.

[26] G. Boole to A. T. Taylor, 26 Jan. 1860, UCC, 1/232.

[27] G. Boole, *An Investigation of the Laws of Thought on which are Founded the Mathematical Theories of Logic and Probabilities* (London, 1854), pp. 20–1.

the inherent neutrality of his mathematical system, which could be established without regard for intent or content—it involved objects and processes that were completely independent of all viewpoints, tenets, debaters, or interest groups. 'In employing the method of this treatise, the order in which premises are arranged, the mode of connexion which they exhibit, with every similar circumstance, may be esteemed a matter of indifference, and the process of inference is conducted with a precision which might almost be termed mechanical,' he proudly explained.[28] By replacing tenuous arguments and nebulous terms with more exact mathematical representations, and by analysing the relationships between such representations, mathematical logic could directly challenge the 'wordy wrangling' and 'idle disputation' that Boole loathed.

Published and unpublished sources show that Boole thought that his mathematical logic would be particularly useful in deflating overreaching theological declarations and exposing the often tautological or vague meanings of tightly held or exclusionary religious dogmas. 'I do think that when we know all the scientific laws of the mind we shall be in a better position for a judgment on its metaphysical questions', Boole wrote to Augustus De Morgan as he worked on his system.[29] To prove his point, in chapters of *The Laws of Thought* Boole analysed the much debated theological doctrines of Spinoza and Samuel Clarke, ultimately finding them empty and unworthy of serious discussion or controversy. Boole's notebooks contain attempts to deconstruct passages from John Henry Newman, Plato, the Hebrew and Christian Bibles, and contemporary writings on theodicy using his symbolic method.[30] For those who felt this dissection of theological arguments was unwarranted or unnecessary, Boole responded that 'the necessity of a rigorous determination of the real premises of a demonstration ought not to be regarded as an evil; especially as, when that task is accomplished, every source of doubt or ambiguity is removed'.[31] The carefully marshaled Xs and Ys of a mathematical system could replace the unclear and unhelpful terms, and the often suspect logic, that only served to draw lines between human beings, particularly in religion. 'Theology always has been, and always will and must be, reformed from the outside, and very much from the side of science', Mary Everest Boole wrote about her husband's motivation.[32]

[28] Boole, *Laws of Thought*, pp. 185–6.
[29] Boole to De Morgan, 8 Oct. 1852, in Smith, *Boole–De Morgan Correspondence*, p. 62.
[30] G. Boole, London, Royal Society of London, Boole papers, C1.6, C.35–7.
[31] Boole, *Laws of Thought*, pp. 185–6.
[32] M. E. Boole, 'Home-side', p. 7.

George Boole thought that a mathematical logic might provide salvation from the sectarian strife of the Victorian age.

Despite the technical benefits of the symbolic logic of George Boole and Augustus De Morgan, as well as the passionate ecumenical motivation behind it, their new method was hidden for a long time in the shadow of a prominent non-mathematician. While Boole and De Morgan published their initial research on the mathematical principles of logic in 1847, this was just four years after the publication of John Stuart Mill's landmark *System of Logic* (1843), which swiftly became one of the most important texts on the subject and a standard treatise in classes on logic, moral science, and philosophy. Mill, like Boole and De Morgan, had realised that it was high time for the ancient science of logic to undergo a major revision—Aristotle was still a major touchstone at the beginning of the Victorian period—yet from there, their methodologies diverged enormously. Extending and evolving an optimistic strain of British scientific philosophy from the early modern period and the thought of Francis Bacon, Isaac Newton, and John Locke, Mill was confident in the ability of the human mind to reach certain conclusions through the use of experience and the process of induction. This process would not replace the ancient logic based on the syllogism, but supplement it by providing a logical framework for sciences both natural and human.

Mill's reputation and his imposing *Logic* clouded the arrival of mathematical logic and its associated advances. 'I have often deplored the fact that though these works [of Boole] were published in the years 1847 and 1854, the current handbooks, and even the most extensive treatises on logic, have remained wholly unaffected thereby', Stanley Jevons lamented to the Royal Society in 1870.[33] That John Stuart Mill should eclipse George Boole and mathematical logic infuriated Jevons, the greatest proponent of Boole's system. Finding Mill's mind to be 'essentially illogical', Jevons wrote a series of articles and books in the 1870s and 1880s that tried to debunk Mill's logic and promote the ideas of the mathematicians instead.[34] He was outraged that he had to teach Mill's *Logic* in his courses on moral science while the works of his mentor Augustus De Morgan and his intellectual forerunner Boole languished. 'I will no longer consent to live silently under the incubus of bad logic and bad philosophy which Mill's Works have laid upon us', Jevons bemoaned in 1864, 'He has expressed unhesitating opinions, and his sayings are quoted by his admirers as if they were the oracles of a perfectly wise and

[33] W. S. Jevons, *Pure Logic and Other Minor Works* (London, 1890), p. 171.
[34] Ibid., p. 201.

logical mind.'[35] Like others interested in the new mathematical methods, Jevons was captive to the standard curriculum, which enshrined certain works and ruthlessly excluded others. With clear anger Jevons did not mince words regarding the role of Mill in the curriculum: 'For the last fourteen years I have been compelled, by the traditional requirements of the University of London, to make [the] works [of Mill] at least partially my text-books in lecturing ... Nothing surely can do so much intellectual harm as a body of thoroughly illogical writings, which are forced upon students and teachers by the weight of Mill's reputation, and the hold which his school has obtained upon the universities.'[36] Jevons ultimately quit teaching in 1880 so that he did not have to lecture any more on topics that seemed dated and utterly inferior to the newer subjects he admired.[37]

What Mill had failed to account for in the eyes of most of the Victorian mathematical logicians was the confusion of the very words we use to describe experience in the process of induction, as well as the often faulty methods we use to make connections and conclusions. Augustus De Morgan spent a great deal of his life deconstructing flawed reasoning and the inadequate language that almost always went along with it. 'The growth of inaccurate expression' that has arisen from a poor understanding of language and logic, De Morgan proclaimed in his groundbreaking work *Formal Logic* (1847), 'gives us swarms of legislators, preachers, and teachers of all kinds, who can only deal with their own meaning as bad spellers deal with a hard word, put together letters which give a certain resemblance, more or less as the case may be'.[38] As De Morgan cautioned the audience at the first meeting of the London Mathematical Society in 1865, 'If we do not attend to extension of language, we are shut in and confined by it.'[39] Mathematical logic, on the other hand, had clearer terms and the benefit of rigorous mathematical processes. Much of *Formal Logic* recounts the problems of human reasoning, which De Morgan felt had reached a low point in his age, with the vague application of language greatly intensifying partisanship. A reasonable, moderate disposition is quite rare, De Morgan observed: 'Many minds, and almost all uneducated ones, can hardly retain an intermediate state' regarding their beliefs. He thought that any query would do to prove this point: 'Put it to the first comer, what he thinks on the question whether there be volcanoes

[35] Jevons, *Pure Logic*, p.171.
[36] Ibid., p. 202.
[37] R. Harley, *Obituary Notices of the Royal Society*, no. 226 (Sept. 1883), p. xi.
[38] A. De Morgan, *Formal Logic* (London, 1847), p. 241.
[39] A. De Morgan, *Address to the London Mathematical Society* (London, 1865), p. 8.

on the unseen side of the moon larger than those on our side. The odds are, that though he has never thought of the question, he has a pretty stiff opinion in three seconds.'[40] De Morgan's *A Budget of Paradoxes* (1872) compiled cases of such mental shortcomings into an encyclopedic criticism of common modes of human thought.[41]

In his 1876 primer on logic Stanley Jevons spoke about the critical importance of removing the ambiguity endemic to so many of the words we use, often casually and without consideration, in both our everyday life and in the realms of speculative thought. 'Nothing indeed can be of more importance to the attainment of correct habits of thinking and reasoning than a thorough acquaintance with the great imperfections of language,' Jevons intoned at the beginning of the primer. 'Comparatively few terms have one single clear meaning and one meaning only, and whenever two or more meanings are unconsciously confused together, we inevitably commit a logical fallacy.'[42] What was needed, he believed, was greater attention to 'univocal' terms—words with just a single, well-defined meaning—rather than the far more common 'equivocal' terms—words that have more than one meaning and are thus inherently ambiguous. 'Equivocal terms are astonishingly common,' Jevons noted, 'They include most of the nouns and adjectives which are in habitual use in the ordinary intercourse of life.'[43] With this sort of ambiguity, how could it be possible to engage in Mill's 'loose kind of inference from particulars to particulars' with complete confidence?[44] It seemed to Jevons that human beings also needed a 'universal reasoning', such as the rigorous logic of the mathematicians Boole and De Morgan, which had been constructed without reference to particulars and in which all of the terms were definitively univocal.[45]

Jevons' concern about the frailty of human reasoning and its inferiority compared to symbolic logic went so far that he proposed replacing the actions of the human mind with a logical machine. In a paper celebrated in the annals of the history of computing, Jevons told a Royal Society of London audience in January 1870 about a new machine for the computation of logical conclusions. After a series of more prosaic terms he arrived at the evocative name 'logical piano' for his new machine, which he actually had built and which now sits in the Museum of the History of Science in Oxford. Jevons could

[40] De Morgan, *Formal Logic*, pp. 182–3.
[41] A. De Morgan, *A Budget of Paradoxes* (London, 1872).
[42] W. S. Jevons, *Elementary Lessons in Logic* (new edn., London and New York, 1895), pp. 27–8.
[43] Ibid., pp. 29–30.
[44] Jevons, *Pure Logic*, p. 203.
[45] Ibid.

scarcely contain his glee at the prospect that with the logical piano the faulty connections made by the human mind would be replaced by unmatched mechanical accuracy and sure conclusions. 'We have but to press a succession of keys in the order corresponding to the terms, conjunctions, and other parts of the propositions, in order to effect a complete analysis of the argument,' he happily told his audience, for 'the parts of the machine embody the conditions of correct thinking.'[46] Jevons's machine had an early 'enter' key—more artfully titled the '*finis* key'—that the operator pressed when he had completed entering the arguments and wished to explore the conclusions these arguments justified.

Like Jevons and De Morgan, John Venn similarly drew a contrast between conventional language, including the ordinary language of traditional logic, and a more scientific formulation that reduced the possibility for error. 'In ordinary life it is notorious that very many of the propositions to which the logician insists upon prefixing his bare "some", had really presented themselves with the more quantitative prefixes of "many" or "most" ', Venn cautioned. To sharpen and improve thought, language would have to be clarified with an eye on 'the universal and the definite'.[47] 'The intimate connexion between Language and Thought', he declared in his seminal book *The Principles of Empirical or Inductive Logic* (1889), 'is an abundantly sufficient ground for looking to some reform in the former as likely to afford powerful help towards advance in the latter.'[48] Venn's diagrammatical system of overlapping ellipses, a graphical version of Boole's mathematical system for encapsulating language and thus thought in a more precise, scientific way, was his attempt at such a reform. Methods for replacing language with clearer symbolic equivalents, like his own scheme or those of Boole or De Morgan, were not 'a mere system of shorthand', Venn emphasised; they were a means 'of improving at the fountain head both the ideas themselves and the methods of combining and analysing them'.[49] Moreover, like the contemporaneous introduction of 'universal' languages like Esperanto, he saw symbolic logic as part of a critical modern quest for improved communications across boundaries—a mission of great social importance. The diversity of the spoken word may not be as problematic as the inequality of wealth, he observed in *The Principles of Empirical or Inductive Logic*, but it is surely an 'evil' that must be addressed.[50]

[46] Jevons, *Pure Logic*, p. 170.
[47] J. Venn, *Symbolic Logic* (2nd edn., New York, 1894), p. 131.
[48] J. Venn, *The Principles of Empirical or Inductive Logic* (2nd edn., New York, 1907), p. 515.
[49] Ibid., p. 519.
[50] Ibid., p. 532.

Despite this emotional appeal that matched the early to mid-Victorian ecumenism and activism of Jevons, De Morgan, and Boole, Venn nevertheless felt more upbeat about the prospects for clarity and economy in language. Ambiguity of terms and its associated problems of weak reasoning and logical fallacies were giving way to a better age, he increasingly felt toward the turn of the century (notably well beyond the tragically shortened lifetimes of Boole and Jevons). It was an 'irresistible course of events', Venn believed, that human speech and thus thought would become clearer. 'As concerns subordinate departments of life, one class of communications after another is tending to the adoption of abbreviated symbols or conventional and artificially framed words for conveying widely recognized conceptions ... as was long ago noticed by Leibnitz in the parallel case of mathematical notation,' Venn concluded in *The Principles of Empirical or Inductive Logic*.[51] Given this optimism, Venn unsurprisingly felt much more charitable toward John Stuart Mill's notions of induction and even the traditional logic of the syllogism. If language was steadily improving, such linguistic methods might not have to be thrown out in favour of a purely mathematical system after all.

Beyond such concerns about human language and reasoning, the mathematical logicians, including Venn, had a darker worry about the implications of Mill's *Logic*, and indeed a broader worry about the knowledge of their age, mathematics included: that it might become so materialistic as to remove God from the universe. In this sense it is often difficult to separate discussions of mathematical knowledge in this period from more familiar discussions relating to the Victorian crisis of faith. It is noteworthy how often religious questions crept into Victorian mathematical works. Boole's seminal *Laws of Thought* (1854) had a critical chapter on the theology of Spinoza and Samuel Clarke; Venn's *Logic of Chance* (1866) delved extensively into questions of how we believe and concluded with a chapter on the credibility of miracle testimony; Jevons similarly ended his most important work, *The Principles of Science* (1874), with a heartfelt psalm on the place of the divine in an increasingly scientific world. With regard to mathematical logic and the foundations of mathematics in general, these Victorians had to come to an understanding of whether their symbolical containers and methods and the science they underwrote were exhaustive, or instead limited in applicability and thus accommodating of other, perhaps more transcendental, knowledge.

George Boole's lecture on the 'The Claims of Science', which inaugurated the difficult school year of 1851 at Queen's College, Cork, was typical of the relationship between faith and concerns about the nature of modern

[51] Ibid., p. 534.

scientific knowledge. Boole explored the worrisome prospect that science—broadly construed as formal human knowledge based on experience—might lead to scepticism or even atheism. 'If, before the time of Bacon, the external sources of human knowledge were too little regarded,' Boole declared, 'we may, in the strong reaction of a subsequent age against this form of error, discern perhaps too much of the contrary tendency.'[52] For Boole, a disciple of Kant and Plato with an affinity for philosophical idealism, it seemed improper for Mill's mode of induction to take excessive precedence over deduction from higher principles found in the mind. What his age needed, the mathematician conceived, was a healthy combination of induction and deduction—'the material and the mental'—in order for science to progress and serve humanity properly.[53] The laws of thought that Boole believed he had found using mathematical techniques were of the same universal nature and necessity as the path of a heavenly body, and he believed that both showed the guiding hand and design of God. 'Does the dominion of science terminate with the world of matter, or is there held out to us the promise of something like exact acquaintance, however less in extent, with the interior and nobler province of the mind?' Boole rhetorically asked his diverse audience.[54] He concluded his lecture by drawing a parallel between natural theology and the theology that he felt naturally evolved out of his mathematical laws of thought. 'With instances of mechanical adaptation in the works of the Divine Architect, we are all familiar. But to the reflective mind, there are few adaptations more manifest, there is none more complete, than that which exists between the intellectual faculties of man, and their scenes and occasions of exercise. Shall we not then confess that here also design is manifest?' Boole exclaimed.[55] Such a Kantian faith in the correspondence between the human mind and a divinely planned universe allowed Boole to ward off the spectre of sceptical materialism.

Boole's followers adopted both his symbolic logic and his interest in preserving a role for religious knowledge and belief, though they diverged somewhat from his divine conception of mathematical knowledge. Stanley Jevons made smaller claims about mathematics that he felt would reserve space for religion apart from science. As Jevons bluntly asserted in *The Principles of Science*, 'Even mathematicians make statements which are not true with absolute generality.'[56] Rather, Jevons believed, mathematical and

[52] Boole, *Studies in Logic*, p. 191.
[53] Ibid.
[54] Ibid., p. 194.
[55] Ibid., p. 199.
[56] Jevons, *The Principles of Science* (reprint of 1877 edn., London, 1924), p. 43.

scientific knowledge—even knowledge aided by the clear terms and rigour of symbolic logic—could only address a limited realm and generally did so with mere probability rather than certainty. Continuing a line of argument he began in his analysis of Mill's thought, Jevons impugned the workings of scientific induction, which supposedly used a series of observations to come to a 'certain' law:

> In the majority of cases it is impossible to collect together, or in any way to investigate, the properties of all portions of a substance or of all the individuals of a race. The number of objects would often be practically infinite, and the greater part of them might be beyond our reach, in the interior of the earth, or in the most distant parts of the Universe. In all such cases induction is *imperfect*, and is affected by more or less uncertainty... The powers of the human mind are so limited that multiplicity of detail is alone sufficient to prevent its progress in many directions.[57]

Jevons hoped that pure mathematics would show the way toward a more perfect form of induction, but the road would be difficult and the destination a realm where probability supplanted certainty. 'The whole question now becomes one of probability and improbability', Jevons remarked about this new realm of knowledge, 'We do not really leave the region of logic; we only leave that where certainty, affirmative or negative, is the result, and the agreement or disagreement of qualities the means of inference.'[58] As faith in scientific certainty waned, so would insidious materialism, Jevons believed, since it fed off arrogant and expansive theories of scientific knowledge.

Furthermore, the Unitarian Jevons maintained God's ultimate role in human knowledge, and even held out the possibility of His activity in the material world. 'We hang ever upon the will of the Creator: and it is only so far as He has created two things alike, or maintains the framework of the world unchanged from moment to moment, that our most careful inferences can be fulfilled,' Jevons declared in *The Principles of Science*.[59] We rely on God for the certainty that is by nature missing from the human mind's process of induction. At the conclusion of *The Principles of Science*, Jevons reiterated that scientific knowledge is limited, and thus unable to destroy transcendental beliefs. 'The conclusions of scientific inference appear to be always of a hypothetical and provisional nature,' he repeated emphatically, 'the best calculated results which it can give are never absolute probabilities; they are purely relative to the extent of our information.'[60] One can sense the genesis

[57] Ibid., pp. 146–8. Emphasis in the original.
[58] Ibid., p. 151.
[59] Ibid., p. 149.
[60] Ibid., p. 765.

of a familiar modern compromise here: science is impressive and powerful but ultimately limited in its purview and certainly not invalidating of religion, which functions in another sphere entirely. Thus the larger intent of Jevons's theoretical work became clear:

> My purpose … is the purely negative one of showing that atheism and materialism are no necessary results of scientific method. From the preceding reviews of the value of our scientific knowledge, I draw one distinct conclusion, that we cannot disprove the possibility of Divine interference in the course of nature … From science, modestly pursued, with a due consciousness of the extreme finitude of our intellectual powers, there can arise only nobler and wider notions of the purpose of Creation.[61]

Mathematics and symbolic logic had clearly helped Jevons come to this conclusion that science and materialism were not inextricably linked. As he noted, pure mathematics allows the mind to conceive and explore the infinite as well as entities that do not conform to the normal laws of space and time.[62] Such investigations inform the mind that the material realm might not be all that there is.

John Venn also used pure mathematics and probability theory in his attempt to understand certainty and belief, both in everyday life as well as in religion. He found it hard to conceive of pinpointing belief, however, on some kind of a mathematical spectrum. In day-to-day existence we are constantly swayed by hope and fear regarding the supposition to be believed, as well as a vast array of other emotions, Venn thought. Moreover, like Stanley Jevons he highlighted our imperfect knowledge of the world and our exceedingly limited experience.[63] 'The substructure of our convictions is not so much to be compared to the solid foundations of an ordinary building,' Venn strikingly wrote in *The Logic of Chance*, 'as to the piles of the houses of Rotterdam which rest somehow in a deep bed of soft mud.' With shades of David Hume's characterisation of personal identity in his *Treatise of Human Nature*, Venn continued, 'We are like a person listening to the confused hubbub of a crowd, where there is always something arbitrary in the particular sound we choose to listen to.'[64] The world is thus a bewildering realm of probability and fallibility.

[61] Jevons, *Principles of Science*, pp. 766–8.

[62] Ibid., pp. 767–8. Jevons noted on pp. 768, 'The study of logical and mathematical forms has convinced me that even space itself is no requisite condition of conceivable existence. Everything, we are told by materialists, must be here or there, nearer or further, before or after. I deny this, and point to logical relations as my proof.'

[63] Venn, *The Logic of Chance* (3rd edn., London, 1888), pp. 125–7.

[64] Ibid., p. 127.

Venn, who like many Victorian intellectuals was the product of an evangelical Church of England upbringing followed by periods of doubt (in part brought on by his reading of Mill's *Logic*), and who resigned from the clergy under the Clerical Disabilities Act in 1883 while maintaining an idiosyncratic faith, spent much of his life trying to comprehend how a heavenly realm could make itself known in the midst of such perplexity. His remarkable chapter 'On the Credibility of Extraordinary Stories' in *The Logic of Chance* shows Venn's questioning mind at its most nimble, as he retraced Hume's footsteps in analysing revealed religion using probability theory. On the one hand, Venn noted, people may be more careful when describing miracles since they are so unusual, and congruent descriptions of such experiences among many different people mathematically should have a higher probability of being true. On the other hand, he argued, how could one really measure the veracity of testimony and the character of witnesses? The pure mathematics of probability theory, with its parochial examples of coin tosses and lottery numbers, surely was hopelessly inadequate to the task of confirming or even assessing evidence of the divine.[65]

Such commonsensical conclusions slowly distanced John Venn philosophically from the mathematician he most wished to emulate, George Boole. By the late Victorian era, as Venn was writing his own *Symbolic Logic* (1881), it seemed naïve to believe that mathematical logic would have any serious affect on British society or perennial (and frequently predictable) religious disputes. Too often there is not enough common ground between antagonists on which to base moderating logical analysis, Venn realised. As early as his 1865 discussion of miracles in *The Logic of Chance*, Venn appreciated the radically different assumptions held by those on each side of the debate. Those who battled over the veracity of 'extraordinary stories' were separated by a 'chasm', where regardless of the format of the arguments—couched in mathematical terms or not—there was little chance for resolution. 'What is to be complained of in so many popular discussions on the subject is the entire absence of any recognition of the different ground on which the attackers and defenders of miracles are so often really standing,' he concluded.[66] Materialists and others who scorn revealed religion simply have an irreconcilable viewpoint from those who have faith in miracles, Venn thought: 'How therefore can miraculous stories be ... taken account of, when the disputants, on one side at least, are not prepared to admit their actual occurrence anywhere or at any time? How can any arrangement of bags and balls, or other

[65] Ibid., pp. 406–34, *passim*, esp. pp. 427–8.
[66] Ibid., p. 434.

mechanical or numerical illustrations of unlikely events, be admitted as fairly illustrative of miraculous occurrences?'[67] To Boole's ideal 'laws of thought,' universally found in every human mind, Venn therefore added a realist's understanding of human nature. We are stubborn, dogmatic, and indelibly coloured by our assumptions and limited experiences; no amount of mathematical reasoning appears capable of closing the gap between those with starkly different beliefs. For Venn, mathematical logic was thus more of a practical tool, albeit a powerful one, than a tool of social and transcendental significance.[68]

A year before the founding of the British Academy, Bertrand Russell extended and further refined Venn's understanding of symbolic logic with a sense of mathematics stridently devoid of extra-mathematical meanings. 'Mathematics may be defined as the subject in which we never know what we are talking about, nor whether what we are saying is true,' Russell informed the lay readership of *The International Monthly* in 1901.[69] He meant this as a compliment, of course, not a criticism: mathematical processes derive their power solely from the clarity of their terms and the rigour of their logic, with no external referents; mathematicians can develop methods that are internally consistent and divorced from any specific content, goal, application, or agenda. In its most pure form mathematics simply involved the containers into which we could place a variety of things, and the ways we can manipulate those containers, while setting aside an interest in the things themselves. From this perspective a purely technical history of mathematics in the Victorian age is perhaps all that is needed.

[67] Venn, *Logic of Chance*, p. 424.

[68] Venn, *Symbolic Logic*, pp. xviii–xxvii.

[69] B. Russell, 'Recent work on the principles of mathematics', *The International Monthly*, 4 (1901), pp. 83–101, at p. 84.

CHAPTER SEVEN

Victorian Classics: Sustaining the Study of the Ancient World

FRANK M. TURNER

The history of the organisation of Victorian classical studies is the story of how a long established, broadly honoured, and culturally privileged mode of intellectual activity survived the slings and arrows of modern, utilitarian social and intellectual forces, and how against all odds and often better arguments, it survived and even prospered. In that respect, classical study and education represented still one more conservative British institution that successfully rode the waves and avoided wreckage on the shoals of cultural change during the Victorian era. This achievement was the result of British classicists maximising their existing privileged situation, reluctantly accommodating themselves to new mid-century intellectual currents, opportunistically claiming new relevance for the ancient world in the late-century imperial climate, and eventually wrapping themselves in the garb of academic professionalism.

The situation of classical study occupying a securely recognised place in the culture explains why the Victorian proponents of the classics behaved so differently from contemporary scientists, social scientists, or national historians. The classicists basically needed to continue to hold the position that past centuries had bequeathed to them rather than to make claims for new attention and resources. Those who studied the classics had to protect already existing cultural space, expand it where possible, continue to hold the socially, if not necessarily, scholarly high ground, and demonstrate that whatever the claims of other forms of knowledge the classics could deliver the same as well or better.

Indeed, if one looked at British classical studies in 1900, it had survived a century of critical challenges, social, intellectual, and educational, and against many odds achieved a position actually stronger than it had enjoyed in 1800. The teaching and knowledge of the classics in Britain had expanded throughout the Victorian era as the number of educational institutions grew and as the numbers of people with the aspiration for social mobility through education had similarly expanded. More people wanted some kind of knowledge of the classical languages and the classical world because of the social benefits that such knowledge conveyed. During the high Victorian age a few progressively minded classicists had drawn modern methods of philology, textual criticism, and comparative religion into classical studies, had studied the ancient world in light of both modern rationalism and philosophic idealism, and had thus provided classics with a new conceptual framework that conveyed modern relevance. Moreover, by the turn of the century a few Greek and Roman scholars had begun to accommodate themselves to the relatively novel research demands of universities, thus demonstrating that the classics could function in a research environment as much as science or other modern subjects. Although toward the end of the nineteenth century, other areas of new study had entered the university curriculums, none had achieved the general prestige attached to the classics. Consequently, in 1904 J. W. MacKail could confidently assure the Classical Association that even if classics suffered 'temporary eclipses of fashion, we may await the revolution of the wheel with confidence'.[1]

The fundamental building block for the organisation and preservation of the classics in Victorian England was the requirement of classical training in secondary schools for admission to the universities. The entire system of elite education consequently assumed education in Greek and Latin. The preparatory schools educated for the secondary schools, which in turn educated for the universities. There were also requirements in the classics for admission to the military academies. Critics complained about this system throughout the century, but virtually nothing was done to change it. This inertia was an essential factor in the long lasting cultural authority of the classics throughout British education.

Moreover, the number of secondary schools so training students grew in the course of the century as more and more middle-class parents sought to provide their sons with the classical education that would admit them to the universities or that would mark them as educated persons of the upper social strata. In a very real sense the more numerous and vociferous the calls for useful education in modern languages, modern history, and the mechanical arts, the more obvious was the social value of a non-utilitarian education in the classics. Furthermore, the early women's colleges, determined to prove they were every bit as vigorous as their male predecessors, also organised themselves around the classics.

[1] *Classical Association of England & Wales, Proceedings, 1904*, pp. 21–2.

The study of the classics in this fashion pervaded Victorian intellectual life more completely than that of any other academic subject. Thousands of students, overwhelmingly male, studied Greek and Latin. There existed a substantial body of teachers of the ancient languages. Knowledge and work in the classics, not always at a particularly high level to be sure, provided avenues for advancement in secondary schools, the universities, the church, the military, the professions, and the Civil Service. As Christopher Stray and others have so clearly argued, a knowledge of classical languages and the experience of a classical education, if not necessarily any powerful knowledge of the classics, constituted one of the chief defining factors in the education of gentlemen who could in one way or another claim to belong to the social and political elite throughout Great Britain.[2] Education in the classics was thus an avenue for social advancement, even if often modestly so.

Why did this frequently criticised system, if indeed it actually may be called a system, continue to exist so long? First, it was quite simply there and throughout the century the forces sustaining it were stronger than those attacking it. A significant body of teachers at various levels had an interest in its perpetuation and little incentive for its reform. The teaching of the classics required the acquisition of a modest body of knowledge and language skills, which thereafter did not require additional training or research. The very factors of instruction that led so many people to complain about the dullness and inadequacy of classical language teaching and training ironically kept it in place. Such instruction could be accommodated to the high rates of turnover among the various persons teaching languages in the universities. Moreover, the turnover rate discouraged practitioners from trying to change the system in which they normally saw themselves working for only a relatively brief time. The same texts could be taught and examined year after year. Mark Pattison once remarked that one reason for the teaching of Aristotle's *Ethics* at Oxford was the ease with which it could be examined.[3]

Second, the teaching of the classics because it was already in place was cheaper for schools and universities to maintain than to undertake new alternative studies. Classics as pursued in Victorian Britain did not even require any ongoing substantial library investments. Mathematics was equally cheap, but never achieved the standing of classics. Serious science education required new capital investment and the training of new teachers. Even the investment by publishers in science textbooks was more uncertain than providing

[2] Christopher Stray, *Classics Transformed: School, Universities, and Society in England, 1830–1960* (Oxford, 1998), pp. 7–82.
[3] Mark Pattison, 'Philosophy at Oxford', *Mind*, 1 (1876), 90.

textbooks to the already well-established classics market. Before the investment of significant state funds in education, these issues of costs were very real considerations and would remain so. Such was particularly true in the last quarter of the century when the income from land held by Oxford and Cambridge colleges as well as some secondary schools declined. With very little money available for new educational initiatives, it was far cheaper to underwrite subjects that could thrive primarily upon teaching a set body of knowledge than subjects that required research for their proper instruction.

Third, passage through training of some kind in the classics provided the veneer of social respectability associated with genteel and elite education. In his *Idea of a University* John Henry Newman prominently separated the liberal education from useful knowledge.[4] The social function of those lectures, both when delivered in 1852 and throughout their later, more widely influential literary career, has often been overlooked. Newman was addressing the Irish Catholic elite of Dublin and attempting to persuade them to send their sons to his Catholic University, then in the process of being founded. One of his arguments was that a liberal education in this Irish Catholic setting would mimic the education of the English gentleman at Oxford and Cambridge—an educational experience then closed to Roman Catholics. For Newman the Roman Catholic Christian, education in the classics alone was a morally and religiously incomplete education, but it was the education that would produce the Gentleman.

Although advocates of classical education in the universities generally spurned the ideal of utility, their argument was profoundly disingenuous. Receiving a classical education proved enormously beneficial and constituted a genuine socially 'useful' education. Such was also true in Continental Europe, where for example German engineers demanded some classical education so they could mix socially with those who had received classical university training. If one wanted a university education in Victorian Britain and all that such an education implied socially and politically, one had to embrace the classics. The military academies until after the turn of the century required Latin for admission. The Civil Service and India Service examinations provided disproportionate numbers of points for Greek and Latin over all modern languages. Consequently, to the extent that higher education served as either a vehicle for social mobility or a device for confirming the existing social elite, education in the classics proved to be a highly instrumental path

[4] A. Dwight Culler, *Imperial Intellect: A Study of Newman's Educational Ideal* (New Haven, 1955); Martha McMackin Garland, 'Newman in His Own Day', in *John Henry Newman, The Idea of a University,* ed. Frank M. Turner (New Haven, 1996), pp. 265–81.

of learning. Moreover, its advocates clearly assumed that classical study served as a credentialing system and not as preparation for ongoing academic research or knowledge creation.

It is not insignificant that until the very end of the century the organisation of British education virtually ensured the exclusion of women from both serious classical training and the benefits accruing thereto. Whereas most of the existing literature on the subject of classical education has emphasised its role in securing ongoing class division, the role of classical education in sustaining ongoing gender roles is no less important and one that deserves fuller consideration.[5] Only with the creation of women's colleges could women receive serious training in the classics. The establishment of Newnham College opened the way for Jane Harrison's career as a classicist,[6] but she was the great exception.

A passage in George Eliot's *Middlemarch* illustrates the situation for the early- and mid-Victorian woman. Dorothea, the heroine of this novel is a young woman who marries an elderly scholar named Casaubon, who is writing *The Key to All Mythologies*. The young Dorothea still not yet married seeks to please her fiancé by aiding him in this apparently important work by reading to him passages of Greek, *which she does not understand*. In the key passage of the novel on this subject, Mr Casaubon says,

> 'I expect you to be all an exquisite young lady can be in every possible relation of life. Certainly it might be a great advantage if you were able to copy the Greek character, and to that end it were well to begin with a little reading.'
>
> Dorothea seized this as a precious permission ... but it was not entirely out of devotion to her future husband that she wished to know Latin and Greek. Those provinces of masculine knowledge seemed to her a standing-ground from which all truth could be seen more truly. As it was, she constantly doubted her own conclusions, because she felt her own ignorance: ...
>
> However, Mr. Casaubon consented to listen and teach for an hour together ... But Dorothea herself was a little shocked and discouraged at her own stupidity, and the answers she got to some timid questions about the value of the Greek accents gave her a painful suspicion that here indeed there might be secrets not capable of explanation to a woman's reason.
>
> Mr. Brooke [Dorothea's father] had no doubt on that point, and expressed himself with his usual strength upon it one day that he came into the library while the reading was going forward.
>
> 'Well, but now, Casaubon, such deep studies, classics, mathematics, that kind of thing, are too taxing for a woman—too taxing, you know.'

[5] Simon Goldhill, *Who Needs Greek? Contests in the Cultural History of Hellenism* (Cambridge, 2002), pp. 178–245.
[6] Mary Beard, *The Invention of Jane Harrison* (Cambridge, MA, 2000).

> 'Dorothea is learning to read the characters simply,' said Mr. Casaubon, evading the question. 'She had the very considerate thought of saving my eyes.'
>
> 'Ah, well, without understanding, you know—that may not be so bad.' [said Mr Brooke].[7]

This passage captures the world in which no matter what a woman's intelligence both the structures of education and the prejudices of the day prevented access to the wider world of classical learning and the personal improvement and social mobility thereby opened.

To sketch out, however, the core relationship between the schools and universities as the basis for the organisation of classical knowledge and training is to suggest the presence of an organised system where there really existed very little. What existed was a situation rather than a system. This absence of serious organisation, which in effect bespoke both the inertial and the opportunistic character of classical studies, came painfully to the fore when the Classical Association was organised in 1903. The remarkably revealing early reports of this association, which are virtually verbatim accounts of their conversations, display a group of people associated with a body of knowledge and vocation of teaching who suddenly found themselves naked to their enemies. The occasion for the founding of the Classical Association was the debate over abolishing compulsory Greek, the already accomplished sudden removal of Latin as a prerequisite for admission to the military academies, the more general political debate over national efficiency, and what Professor A. G. Ramsay of the Scottish Classical Association termed, 'the mischief that South Kensington, with its miserable technical schemes, has done to education in this country ...'.[8] Teachers and researchers of classical subjects now found it necessary to defend what they did and how they did it. In the words of Ernest Gardner, the historian of ancient art, 'The present time is a critical one for classical studies, because their *prescriptive right* to be recognized as the basis of education is now being challenged on all sides.'[9] Most particularly, the benefits of intellectual rigour and pedagogical discipline that classicists had long ascribed to their subject matter now seemed replicable through instruction in a number of subjects open to students.

What the papers and comments at the early meetings of the Classical Association reveal is not the organisation of classical study but rather serious disorganisation that had made little difference so long as that 'prescriptive right' had remained unchallenged. Indeed, the single subject that took up the

[7] George Eliot, *Middlemarch*, Bk. 1, Ch. 7.
[8] *Classical Association of England & Wales, Proceedings, 1904*, p. 9.
[9] *Classical Association of England & Wales, Proceedings, 1905*, p. 47. (Italics mine, FMT.)

most time and roused the highest passion at the early meetings was the question of the pronunciation of Latin. In 1905 Professor S. H. Butcher observed that the absence of an agreed upon system of Latin pronunciation had been noted as early as the 1872 Head Masters' Conference (itself an organisation formed in 1869 to resist the recommendations of the Taunton Commission), but no action had been taken. Sometimes two different pronunciations were taught in the same school. Boys confronted changes in Latin pronunciation from preparatory school to secondary school and then again in universities. There were differences both among and within Oxford and Cambridge Colleges. Butcher complained that '. . . not even a consistently incorrect system' prevailed anywhere.[10] More uniformity existed in the provincial and Scottish universities. Butcher observed, 'We cannot perhaps look forward to any international *lingua Franca*, but we may hope for uniform pronunciation of Latin in the United Kingdom.'[11] The problem reached the larger English reading public in a dramatic moment in Hilton's *Good-Bye Mr. Chips* (1935), when Chips refuses the demand of the new headmaster to teach boys to say 'Kickero' when for the rest of their lives he knew they would say 'Cicero'.

What had sustained the study of classics in the absence of organisation was its function as a powerful vehicle for training in leadership, most especially at Oxford. Until 1864 at Oxford a compulsory programme in the Literae Humaniores prevailed meaning that all students had to pass examinations in the ancient languages. Thereafter, although students could take degrees in other subjects, Oxford classicists under Jowett's leadership at Balliol transformed the Literae Humaniories into a school for modern leadership. Within this programme late-Victorian classical instruction took place within a frame of reference that furnished the Oxford elite with language, symbols, and examples whereby they discussed, evaluated, and analysed modern political and social issues as well as the requirements for modern domestic and imperial leadership through the parallels drawn with the ancient world. For example, commentary on a Platonic dialogue permitted Jowett to introduce the following meditation on the requirements of modern statesmanship:

> A true statesman is he who brings order out of disorder; who first organizes and then administers the government of his own country; and having made a nation, seeks to reconcile the national interests with those of Europe and of mankind He is not a mere theorist, not yet a dealer in expedients; the whole and the parts grow together in his mind; while the head is conceiving, the hand is executing. Although obliged to descend to the world, he is not of the world. His thoughts are fixed not

[10] *Classical Association of England & Wales, Proceedings, 1905*, p. 7.

[11] *Classical Association of England & Wales, Proceedings, 1905*, p. 9.

> on power or riches or extension of territory, but on an ideal state, in which all the citizens have an equal chance of health and life, and the highest education is within the reach of all, and the moral and intellectual qualities of every individual are freely developed, and the 'idea of good' is the animating principle of the whole. Not the attainment of freedom alone, or of order alone, but how to unite freedom with order is the problem which has to be solved.[12]

Through such injunctions Jowett and other Oxford dons directly employed ancient philosophy as a vehicle for discussing modern questions of politics, ethics, and social policy. Moreover, the classicists could claim there were no stronger minds with which their students could learn to work through those modern problems than the philosophers and historians of the ancient world.

Jowett's programme achieved its goals. As M. C. Curthoys has noted, 'Before 1914 Greats educated more future high court judges than the jurisprudence school, more bishops than the theology school, and more politicians of cabinet rank than the modern history school.'[13] No other subject of study functioned in this fashion in Victorian society. Education in the classics was education for leadership.

The classics were able to function in this manner in the late Victorian universities because at mid-century, working outside any university setting, George Grote had forged a progressive intellectual identity for the study of ancient languages, literature, philosophy, and history.[14] In so doing, he nudged an essentially conservative pedagogical enterprise forward allowing its practitioners to assume the mantle of modern relevance. Despite the generally static structure of classical instruction in schools and universities, Grote introduced dynamic modern ideas into classical scholarship and sustained the classics as a force for modern instruction. Paradoxically, Grote's progressive scholarship and the responses to it made the world safe for many quite humble, backward-looking teachers of language.

Much irony surrounds the impact of George Grote on British and European classical study. He had first pursued a career as a banker and then

[12] Benjamin Jowett, *The Dialogues of Plato, Translated into English with Analyses and Introductions*, 3rd edn., rev. and corr., 5 vols. (Oxford, 1924), vol. 2, pp. 308–9. On the general influence of the Literae Humaniores, see Linda Dowling, *Hellenism and Homosexuality in Victorian Oxford* (Ithaca, 1994), and V. Larson, 'Classics and the Acquisition and Validation of Power in Britain's "Imperial Century" ', *International Journal of the Classical Tradition*, 6 (1999), 185–225.

[13] M. C. Curthoys, 'The Careers of Oxford Men', in M. G. Brock and M. C. Curthoys (eds.), *The History of the University of Oxford, Volume 6: Nineteenth-Century Oxford, Part I* (Oxford, 1997), p. 502. This entire essay bears on the subject as does M. C. Curthoys, 'The Examination System', and John H. Jones, 'Balliol: From Obscurity to Pre-eminence', ibid., pp. 339–74, 174–82. For contemporary developments at Cambridge, consult Stray, *Classics Transformed*, pp. 140–66.

[14] *The Greek Heritage in Victorian England* (New Haven, 1981), *passim*, 'The Homeric Question', in Ian Morris and Barry Powell (eds.), *A New Companion to Homer* (Leiden, 1997), pp. 123–45.

entered the reformed Parliament as one of the Benthamite philosophical radicals. He was also associated with the founding and oversight of the Utilitarian inspired University College London. But Grote from the late 1820s onward was determined to change the mind of the conservative British governing elite. He clearly understood that recasting the existing conservative interpretation of the ancient world as then taught in the universities could transform the minds and thinking of that elite.

Grote single-handedly transformed the study of ancient Greece in the English-speaking world. Deeply versed in German scholarship as well as both British and French philosophy, Grote made himself the Victorian master of ancient Greek history and philosophy. Between 1846 and 1856 he published his monumental twelve-volume *History of Greece*. His three-volume *Plato, and the Other Companions of Socrates* appeared in 1865. In these seminal studies he framed Greek cultural, religious, literary, and philosophical history around utilitarian rationalism, critical philology, democratic politics, and Auguste Comte's three-stage theory of human intellectual development. Grote used Comte's philosophy to interpret ancient Greek myth as illustrating a particular moment of human intellectual development rather than as recording any events that had actually occurred. Grote brought the German discussion of the Homeric question before the English reading public and made his own highly original contribution to that debate. His narration of Athenian history powerfully defended ancient democratic politics, blaming its defects on the sinister influences of Athenian aristocrats and ancient superstition. He presented Socrates and later Plato as epitomising a critical rationalist philosophy that appeared as an ancient prototype of the eighteenth-century enlightenment.

In this manner Grote's voluminous studies represented a frontal assault that reshaped the British understanding of the ancient world through the application of modern methods of philology and historical criticism, rationalist philosophy, and radical political thought. Grote had intended his volumes to take the interpretation of Greece out of the hands of conservative political writers and in that he brilliantly succeeded. Because there was so little classical scholarship being carried out in the universities, anyone teaching about ancient Greece had to use Grote. Consequently, within the inertially stolid world of classical studies Greece became the location for intellectual advance influenced by Continental thought. This situation was not inherent in anything Greek, but rather because progressive or intellectually and politically radical ideas and methods could become attached to the study of Greece.

Grote's radical interpretation of Greek religion, literature, politics and philosophy eventually called forth a response from inside the universities, but only a quarter century after the first volume of his *History of Greece* had appeared. Grote's radical rationalistic approach to ancient Greece stirred Benjamin Jowett to produce in his translations and commentaries on the dialogues of Plato an alternative vision of ancient Greece based on modern German idealist philosophy. In this manner the study of the ancient world provided the venue for the ongoing battle between the two dominant philosophic outlooks of the nineteenth century.

In 1871 Jowett published *Dialogues of Plato, Translated into English with Analyses and Introductions*, which with revisions became the Plato of the English-speaking world long into the twentieth century.[15] Hegelian idealist philosophy permeated his commentary, as did a lightly disguised liberal Christianity presented in ancient Greek guise. Whereas Grote had presented a critical rationalist Socrates and Plato, Jowett presented them as ancient idealists. Whereas Grote had presented them as prefiguring the European enlightenment and Utilitarianism, in Jowett's pages they opposed naked rationalism and utilitarian politics. For Jowett they sought knowledge and religion that went beyond the world of the senses. Moreover, Jowett presented Plato as working through the very difficult problems arising from pursuing the life of the mind in a radically democratic polity. Most importantly Jowett's Plato championed an ethic of personal duty. Jowett's commentaries responded directly to Grote and implicitly recognised that Grote had made ancient Greece a powerful device for debating a host of modern issues in politics, philosophy, ethics, and religion.

Despite the wide training that students received in Latin, there was no similar parallel modernising development in Roman studies until the turn of the century.[16] Even then it was a pale shadow to the dominance of Greece. During the nineteenth century there had been a major split between Hellenists and Latinists who had remained largely indifferent to each other's fields. Almost alone Thomas Arnold made serious contributions to each field, writing Roman history and producing a critical, annotated edition of Thucydides. On one level, the straightforward matter of specialisation may account for the split. On another, ancient Greece and ancient Rome were very

[15] Turner, *Greek Heritage*, pp. 414–46; *Contesting Cultural Authority: Essays in Victorian Intellectual Life* (Cambridge, 1993), pp. 322–61.

[16] Frank M. Turner, 'Why the Greeks and Not the Romans in Victorian Britain?', in G. W. Clarke (ed.), *Rediscovering Hellenism: The Hellenic Inheritance and the English Imagination* (Cambridge, 1989), pp. 61–82, and Turner, *Contesting Cultural Authority*, pp. 231–61. For treatments that see greater Roman influences than the present author see, Catharine Edwards, *Roman Presences: Receptions of Rome in European Culture, 1789–1945* (Cambridge, 1999) and Norman Vance, *The Victorians and Ancient Rome* (Oxford, 1997); Stray, *Classics Transformed*, pp. 271–97.

different cultures with very different histories. To the extent that scholars of ancient Greece and ancient Rome actually appealed to modern Victorian constituencies, those constituencies were different. The study of ancient Greece permitted an encoded discussion of mythology, biblical composition through the Homeric question, democracy, aesthetics, and philosophy each of which particularly invited devising parallels with modern ideas and ideologies. Although the study of Rome could address issues of empire and issues of modern Caesarist leadership, Victorian Latin scholars and teachers could never address contemporary issues with the panache and certainty of their Hellenist counterparts. During the Victorian age, there were very few serious examples of Roman history in English. The studies of the Roman poets concentrated primarily on their aesthetic and stylistic qualities. Generally speaking, the study of things Roman, though carried out in the Victorian age, at best modestly interfaced with the larger social, political, or intellectual forces of the day.

Matters changed somewhat for Roman studies at the turn of the century. Then the drive for domestic political order and national efficiency and the rise of a substantial body of antidemocratic social imperial thought attached itself to things Roman. By 1900 Latinists believed they could pull ahead of the classical pack. Compulsory Greek rather than Latin had become the symbolic issue in dispute among proponents of different kinds of education. The study of Latin with its reading of Caesar and the study of Roman imperial history appeared directly relevant at the moment when the expansion of empire and the debacles of the Boer War had brought national efficiency to the fore.

This opportunistic rush of Latinists to make the most of the situation appeared in 1904 during the very first meeting of the Classical Association. At that meeting J. W. MacKail delivered an address 'On the Place of Greek and Latin in Human Life.' Although, as previously noted, he had assured all classicists of their ongoing influence, he was anything but evenhanded in his championing of Rome over Greece. He explained that

> ... scientific research emphasizes what is sufficiently obvious on a general view, that Greece and Rome represent two civilizations which, though they over lap and intermingle, though enwound and engrafted one on the other, have a different parentage, a distinct essence, and a separate product.[17]

Consequently, he thought,

> It is not undesirable, when this Association is being inaugurated, to emphasize the difference between the two spheres which classical studies include, and to realise

[17] *Classical Association of England & Wales, Proceedings, 1904*, p. 11.

> fully that they represent forces in the education and control of life which are complementary, or even opposed to one another ... The distinction, no less than the likeness, between the two spheres of classical study is of importance not only towards clear thought, but towards the pressing and practical question of the place which each holds separately and which both hold jointly in education, in culture, in our whole view and handling of human life.[18]

He then asserted,

> The place of Rome, of the Latin temper and civilization, the Latin achievement in the conquest of life, is definite and assured. It represents all the constructive and conservative forces which make life into an organic structure ... The return to Rome need never be made, because we have never quitted her. Rome we know ... Greece is in contrast something which we are so far from knowing that we hardly have a name for it.[19]

Roman history and literature would prosper during the twentieth century more fully than during the nineteenth, but it still never achieved quite the standing of Greece.

While Edwardian Hellenists and Latinists quarrelled over who would dominate the future teaching of classics, another development occurred within the university setting. Certain university classicists began to associate themselves with the research ideal, which in the past had been more vigorously championed by scientists, economists, and historians.[20] These professionalising classicists recognised that whatever the standing of classics within the society at large, the study of ancient languages, philosophy, culture, and history could hold its place in changing universities only if the pursuit of the classics came to imitate other subjects as engines for the creation of new knowledge.

The most conspicuous feature of the Victorian geography of classical research, as demonstrated by the role of Grote, had been the general absence of university researchers until the last thirty years or so of the century. This general absence of university research, of course, generally differentiates British Victorian classical scholarship from that of Germany, a fact that becomes all the more evident when one walks through open library stacks of nineteenth-century classical books and journals. The Victorian teaching of classical languages and occasionally of other classical subjects resided in the schools and universities, but they were not the home of research or broad writing in the classics. As listed in the first volume of the *Journal of Hellenic*

[18] *Classical Association of England & Wales, Proceedings, 1904*, p. 12.
[19] *Classical Association of England & Wales, Proceedings, 1904*, p. 14.
[20] Stray, *Classics Transformed*, pp. 202–35.

Studies of 1880 only 22 of the founding 112 members of the Society for the Promotion of Hellenic Studies were directly associated with universities. The location of research in classical studies during the first two-thirds of the century was more often than not the study of the independent scholar, most importantly George Grote and Anthony Trollope, the outstanding Victorian biographer of Cicero, or of clergy within the Church, such as Connop Thirlwall and Charles Merivale, the Roman historian, or of persons working in the British Museum, such as Charles Newton, or of Walter Leaf, the foremost late Victorian commentator on Homer who, like Grote, was a banker. These observations, which could be considerably expanded, simply manifest the more familiar fact that on the whole Victorian universities did not embrace the research ideal, which constitutes another factor leading to the largely decentralised and disorganised situation of the classics.

It is important to recognise why the turn of university classical studies to the research ideal could really commence only very late in the century. Previously, there had existed within British universities very real inhibitions to such research, inhibitions that had not arisen from lethargy among the classicists themselves. Until quite late in the century the two major English universities remained overwhelmingly clerical and, of course, Protestant in character. It was not easy for a classical scholar to advocate advanced Continental theories and methods of critical history and philology when so many of the people around him were convinced that those theories would undercut Christianity. For example, there had existed much apprehension from the time of F. A. Wolf's late eighteenth-century theory of Homeric composition that the study of the classics according to modern German methods would lead to destructive, rationalist criticism of Christian Scripture. Thomas Arnold had forecast this situation. E. B. Pusey, Regius Professor of Hebrew at Oxford, once directly made that assertion in the middle of the century. Jowett encountered personal persecution relating to his salary as Professor of Greek because of his biblical studies. Much later James Frazer indicated as much and refrained from certain topics in his publications. Other examples could be cited.

Beyond the parallels between the higher criticism of the Bible and philological studies of secular classical texts, the anthropological study of ancient religion such as that of Lewis Farnell and Frazer was almost bound to clash with the privileged status accorded sacred history. The advanced, critical study of the classics in Victorian Britain had in point of fact to reside in the cultural interstices not occupied by religion and theology. The universities until the very close of the century could not provide such a venue. It is inconceivable, for example, that Grote could have set forth his views of Greek mythology and Homeric composition in the Oxbridge setting.

The late nineteenth- and early twentieth-century professionalisation of British university classical studies was not the inevitable result of the march of knowledge, but rather the path that certain classicists had to tread in order to maintain their position in the increasingly research oriented university world. Embracing the research ideal particularly in regard to philological and textual criticism served two purposes. Within the university classicists could appear to be research scholars; outside the universities they could appear to possess the scientific rigor of competing subjects of study. This research orientation could lead to a good deal of abusive language from one generation of classicists to another. In 1922 A. E. Housman wrote,

> Textual criticism, like most other sciences, is an aristocratic affair, not communicable to all men, nor to most men. Not to be a textual critic is no reproach to anyone unless he pretends to be what he is not. To *be* a textual critic requires aptitude for thinking and willingness to think; and though it also requires other things, those things are supplements and cannot be substitutes. Knowledge is good; method is good, but one thing beyond all others is necessary; and that is to have a head, not a pumpkin, on your shoulders, and brains, not pudding, in your head.[21]

Such sardonic criticism directed against Victorian predecessors was to demonstrate that the new professionals were prepared to be citizens of a new kind of university that looked to the Continent for its model. Their assaults on their Victorian predecessors replicated the mid-Victorian criticism of clerical natural theologians by professionalising scientists.

It is most useful *not* to view the history of Victorian classical study as that of amateurism moving toward professionalism. Rather, the professionalisation of the classics should be seen as one of several strategies employed to sustain university classical studies. What carried the subject in universities, and most particularly in Oxford, was the interfacing of classical studies with public life and morality. It was that conscious interface dating to the days of Jowett that sustained the Greats at Oxford to the point that in 1960 the programme enjoyed the highest enrollment in its history. Throughout the twentieth century the debate continued among classicists themselves whether they were to be rigidly narrow professional scholars of the Germanic mode or teachers of a large Hellenic worldview. In a sense, the two university groups mutually supported each other with the textual scholars bringing scientific rigour to the classics and the Hellenists assuring enrollments.

[21] A. E. Housman, 'Application of Thought to Textual Criticism', in *The Classical Papers of A. E. Housman*, ed. J. Diggle and F. R. D. Goodyear, 3 vols. (Cambridge, 1972), vol. 3, p. 1069.

CHAPTER EIGHT

The Evolution and Dissemination of Historical Knowledge

MICHAEL BENTLEY

Two words in my title have a Victorian resonance and both require some care. The dangers of 'evolution' will not be lost on a Victorian audience. It calls up a sense of a lower form giving way to a higher, of primitive beginnings becoming complex in some Spencerian progression from homogeneity to heterogeneity. It allows the mind to fall into a comfortable location of the Victorian past marked by teleology. That memorable question of Seeley's asking about the general goal or drift of British history[1] might easily become the organising mantra for history as a whole, leaving behind it all the characteristics of triumphalism and progress against which Herbert Butterfield railed so successfully in 1931.[2] But intended here is rather a sense of struggle without prefigured conclusion. Victorian history evolved in its self-consciousness, its teaching and its audience in fits and starts — now producing a moment of excitement and extension, now lapsing into complacency and quietude. The subject that inflamed Carlyle[3] and Macaulay[4] in the 1830s had become the despair of many young Turks in the 1890s. Where

[1] See in particular his chapter on 'Tendency in English History' in *The Expansion of England* (1883, 1971 edn., Chicago), pp. 7–18. Cf. *The Growth of British Policy: An Historical Essay* (2 vols., Cambridge, 1895). Sir John Seeley (1834–95), Regius Professor of Modern History, Cambridge, 1869–95. See also his best-selling *Ecce Homo* (London, 1865), discussed below on p. 194, and *The Life and Times of Stein* (London, 1878). It should be noted that all biographical notes in this chapter mention only major posts and publications.

[2] Herbert Butterfield, *The Whig Interpretation of History* (London, 1931)

[3] Thomas Carlyle (1795–1881). Rebarbative Scot who lived at Cheyne Row, Chelsea, from 1834. Prolific author with inimitable prose. *Sartor Resartus* (London, 1831); *The French Revolution*, 3 vols. (London, 1837); *Chartism* (London, 1839); *Past and Present* (London, 1843); *Oliver Cromwell's Letters and Speeches* (London, 1845); *History of Friedrich II of Prussia called Frederick the Great*, 6 vols. (London, 1858–65), etc.

[4] Thomas Babington Macaulay, 1st Baron (1800–59). Reviewer for the *Edinburgh Review*; parliamentary and ministerial career. Began *History of England* in 1839. Published in 5 vols., 1848–59.

historians of professionalism might want to speak of advance, those considering intellectual content or status of the discipline might want to speak instead of regression into wooden formulae. Where a historian in the 1930s could portray the nineteenth century as a movement towards modernisation and sophistication, a post-millennial and post-structural contributor could reasonably ask whether a more complicated story remains to be told than a grand narrative of professional entrenchment or a professorial will-to-power.[5] Both moods will appear in what follows but the choice of 'evolution' as a term of blind friction will persist in a story more resembling the collapse and supersession of paradigms envisaged by Kuhn[6] than the smooth journey on a temporal barge implied by Seeley.

The second term that conspires to confuse as much as inform is one that Victorians would have found transparent and whose opacities modern historians often fail to notice. Only the constraints of usage and elegance, after all, should prevent us from speaking about 'knowledges' in the plural. Several concerns lie behind this conviction. First, it seems important to recall that what Victorians meant by historical knowledge had its own unwritten and unacknowledged limits. There was more to *not* being knowledge than lying beyond the ken of the Master of Balliol;[7] and that intellectual space requires our attention whether or not it gained theirs. So many concerns now deemed fundamental to the historian — issues relating to the nature of historical understanding and the place of certain cultural ingredients in that understanding — would have struck Bishop Stubbs[8] or Edward Augustus Freeman[9] as

[5] It will be evident from what follows that I share neither Peter Slee's narrative of professionalisation nor Reba Soffer's cogent, but in my view misguided, argument about the instrumentalisation of historical knowledge by an aspirant elite seeking to make claims on behalf of a 'new' discipline. See Peter R. H. Slee, *Learning and a Liberal Education: The Study of Modern History in the Universities of Oxford, Cambridge and Manchester, 1800–1914* (Manchester, 1986) and Reba Soffer, *Discipline and Power: The University, History, and the Making of an English Elite* (Stanford, 1994). These sources should be consulted for changes in curriculum, however, and for the impact of university reform in the wake of successive Royal Commissions — an aspect of the subject that I shall not stress here.

[6] Thomas Kuhn, *The Structure of Scientific Revolutions* (Chicago, 1962).

[7] The cliché about Benjamin Jowett has many renditions of a type beginning:

> I am the Master of this College
> And what I don't know isn't knowledge.

Benjamin Jowett (1817–93), Master of Balliol, 1870–93, Regius Professor of Greek from 1855. Translations of Plato, Aristotle and Thucydides.

[8] William Stubbs (1825–1901), Regius Chair, Oxford, 1866–84; bishop of Chester, 1884–8; bishop of Oxford, 1888–1901. *Constitutional History of England*, 3 vols. (London, 1866); *Select Charters* (1866); vast output of editorial work.

[9] Edward Augustus Freeman (1823–92), succeeded Stubbs in the Regius Chair at Oxford. *History of the Norman Conquest*, 6 vols. (London, 1867–79); *History of Sicily*, 4 vols. (London, 1891–4).

trivial or immoral. So many questions that appear on our examination papers would have seemed pointless, diffuse, tediously philosophical or just too hard to the examiners of the mid-Victorian universities. Contrast the situation with the status of Victorian mathematics within a culture in which most men (for we are largely speaking of men) continued advanced study of the subject beyond school. Lord Robert Cecil was perhaps alone in finding malicious amusement in the examination for a clerkship in the Education Department that presented applicants with a question requiring them to approximate to the cube root of 31 by means of the binomial theorem.[10] But the question implies a context of some sophistication. An examination paper in history looked very different and often called for simple descriptions of known events. Here, too, a particular 'knowledge' lies embedded, one that would lead Acton[11] to see his mission, famously, as rescuing historical knowledge from its then current function in burdening the memory and making of it an illumination of the soul. Knowledges, understood as paradigms of what was and what was not to count as worth knowing, changed over our eighty year period and that evolution complicates the assessment of Victorian achievement.

Those knowledges also had a range of provenance and legitimacy. Historians working in established centres of history represented by the modern university readily succumb to an image of nineteenth-century historians operating in the same framework and from similar suppositions about what history is for. Yet in so far as that image has any relation to reality at all, it dates only from the very end of the period and throws light on only one sector of historical writing and thinking. Macaulay and Carlyle did not burden themselves with university posts and even if they had it would not have disturbed in any radical way the sense of the subject they had formed in their very different *milieux*. Macaulay spoke as a voice of official culture; Carlyle spoke in order to subvert it; neither had the ambitions of C. H. Firth[12] or F. W. Maitland[13] to speak for university scholarship. Neither felt dissuaded

[10] See Michael Bentley, *Lord Salisbury's World: Conservative Environments in late-Victorian Politics* (Cambridge, 2001), p. 172.

[11] John Emerich Edward Dalberg, 1st Baron Acton (1834–1902). Roman Catholic historian and thinker. Succeeded Seeley in Cambridge Regius Chair. First editor of the *Cambridge Modern History*.

[12] Charles Harding Firth (1857–1936), Regius Chair at Oxford, 1904–25. Edited Cromwell's letters and Macaulay's *History*. *Cromwell's Army* (London, 1902); *The Last Years of the Protectorate, 1656–8*, 2 vols. (London, 1909).

[13] Frederic William Maitland (1850–1906), Downing Professor of the Laws of England, Cambridge, 1888–1906. Formidable intelligence married to a majestic literary style. F. Pollock and F. W. Maitland, *The History of English Law before the time of Edward I* (London, 1895); *Domesday Book and Beyond* (London, 1897); *The Constitutional History of England*, ed. H. A. L. Fisher (Cambridge, 1909).

thereby from writing important theoretical papers about the nature of historical knowledge and understanding[14] — papers which stressed the need for historians to write the narratives which their counter-Enlightenment conception of a changing audience prescribed. While they immersed themselves in the French Revolution and the History of England, Chartist working men persisted in their conviction that the Norman Yoke had destroyed Saxon liberties and their faith that universal suffrage, which had flourished, they believed, before 1066, would soon become re-established.[15] While Maitland and Firth made their calls for an austere understanding of research that would turn historians into *Wissenschaftler*, working men and women gathered around the young D. H. Lawrence at Eastwood to learn about socialist images of the past, reading their Morris and their Carpenter and the range of literature that Jonathan Rose has recently brought to our attention.[16] It is easy to see what the first regime in these coupled contrasts would have said to the second: only *our* knowledge is knowledge; yours is at best mythology, at worst simple error, the product of a lack of education. It seems important that we, a century later, do not go down the same road without reflection and dismiss as illegitimate the thought-worlds of a million obscure Judes out of a preference for the productions of a dozen Christminsters.

There were, indeed, very few of them. If we stand astride the Great Reform Act and look about us, then beyond Oxford and Cambridge lie the new colleges in London—the original University (now University College) of 1826, its self-conscious, Christian other in King's College (1829) and George Birkbeck's Mechanics' Institution of 1824 which few imagined would later grow into 'the Birkbeck College'. Only the new creation of Van Mildert in Durham suggested the presence of a provincial dimension unless (patronisingly and erroneously) one ignores the ancient universities of Scotland (St Andrews, Edinburgh, Glasgow and the two Aberdeen colleges), and of course Trinity College, Dublin. History's profile was low in each of them before the 1870s: more pressing matters in the classical languages, the felt need to continue with mathematics, and the enhanced dignity of natural science and medicine displaced

[14] In particular see Macaulay's essay 'History' (1828) and Carlyle's 'On History' (1830), both of which are excerpted conveniently in Fritz Stern (ed.), *The Varieties of History: From Voltaire to the Present* (London, 1957), pp. 72–89 and 90–101.

[15] Christopher Hill, 'The Norman Yoke' in *Puritanism and Revolution: Studies in Interpretation of the English Revolution of the Seventeenth Century* (London, 1958), pp. 50–122.

[16] Jonathan Rose, *The Intellectual Life of the British Working Classes* (New Haven, 2001); Michael Bentley, 'Lawrence's Political Thought: some English contexts, 1906–19', in Christopher Heywood (ed.), *D. H. Lawrence: New Studies* (Basingstoke, 1987), pp. 59–83.

training in a dangerous subject.[17] Reversing the bias of undergraduates known to all teachers of history, early Victorians found history *too* relevant to constitute a comfortable site for the acquisition of dispassionate knowledge. For many, historical knowledge could not be allowed dispassion in any case for it underpinned Christian knowledge. Remember the violence of intellectual and ecclesiastical reaction to the founding of 'the godless college in Gower Street', as Thomas Arnold called it,[18] with its Benthamite and secular statement about the point of a university and therefore of knowledge itself. The poet William Mackworth Praed drew blood from its images:

> Ye Dons and ye Doctors, ye Provosts and Proctors
> Who are paid to monopolize knowledge,
> Come, make opposition, by vote and petition
> To the radical infidel College.[19]

Responding to such gibes by establishing King's College did not make the issue go away and the intertwining of sect and historical certainty wove its way through the century. Which side of Elizabeth Reid should we see first? The visionary whose Ladies' College in Bedford Square held so much of the future in it in 1849? Or the wife of a Leicester man stained with the University of Edinburgh, a woman whose Enlightenment Unitarianism rivalled that of her confidante Harriet Martineau?[20] Which side of Charles Kingsley[21] and John Robert Seeley first catches the eye? Certainly not the part that sat in the Regius Chair of Modern History in Cambridge but rather the Christianity that made prime ministers see a safe pair of hands. Or recall the doomed and slightly farcical attempt of Gladstone's first government to create a national university for Ireland that would explicitly have included history among the subjects forbidden to its teachers.[22]

[17] 'Till the other day [history] was regarded by her elder sisters, by Mathematics and Philosophy and the languages of Greece and Rome with the patronizing but somewhat distant air which is natural to senior and sole possession.' G. W. Prothero, *Why Should We Study History?* (Edinburgh, 1894), p. 3.
[18] Arnold to W. Empson, 28 Nov. 1837, in A. P. Stanley, *The Life and Correspondence of Thomas Arnold*, 2 vols. (London, 1844), vol. 2, p. 97. Thomas Arnold (1795–1842), headmaster of Rugby school, 1828–42; Regius Professor of History at Oxford for a few months before his death. *History of Rome*, 3 vols. (London, 1838–43).
[19] 'Discourse delivered by a College Tutor at a Supper Party, July 1, 1825', quoted in H. Hale Bellot, *University College London, 1826–1926* (London, 1929), p. 71.
[20] See Margaret J. Tuke, *A History of Bedford College for Women, 1849–1937* (London, 1939), pp. 1–17.
[21] Charles Kingsley (1819–75). Regius Chair at Cambridge, 1860–9. Canon of Chester, 1869–73, and of Westminster, 1873–5. *Alton Locke* (1850); *Westward Ho!* (1855); *The Water Babies* (1863), etc.
[22] For the 'gagging clauses' and the fate of the bill in Parliament, see J. P. Parry, *Democracy and Religion: Gladstone and the Liberal Party, 1867–75* (Cambridge, 1986), pp. 353–65.

But of course this winding vine of religion wrapped itself around more than history. Frank Turner taught intellectual historians long ago to abandon hopes of simplicity when entering the conversation of religion and science,[23] and we can find spirituality in the most positivistic remarks of contemporaries about the function of historical knowledge, just as eminent Christians are detected welcoming and baptising infants whom logic might have urged them to drown. It suffices here merely to remark on that complication and recall that knowledge was not a matter of Royal Commission and expanding access. Historical knowledge formed a forum in which hegemonic claims jostled with the challenges of an industrialising and modernising society and became the arena for forms of negotiation. Those great civic university colleges of the 1880s and 1890s with their Gothic windows and italianate towers make statements that go far beyond red brick and mortar. They are themselves part of a Victorian intellectual compromise between innovation and tradition. We see it, in the case of history, by thinking inevitably of change over time in the provisions made for the serious study of history as a single-focused subject in the universities of England before 1870 and elsewhere in the British Isles. But often it appears in sharper focus when the lens is also trained elsewhere. Many of the points requiring stress about the British case cannot be made effectively within a purely national frame of reference. This is especially the case when we turn to the fundamental insight that the situation of mid-Victorian history in both its teaching and its research-base reflected the peculiarity of its casual origins and its comparatively distant relation to the state. In glancing sideways at a European clerisy dominated by burgeoning nationalism and the implications of state formation, it seems clear that we have reached one among many facets of the story that cannot be told by he and she who only England know.

The development of a sophisticated and organised historical scholarship in Britain vastly post-dated the consolidation of the British state. In Germany, Italy, Russia and to a degree in the United States these processes ran in tandem. In certain parts of the world—one thinks of Scandinavia—the coming of history pre-dated at least the more mature elements of state formation. France behaved eccentrically in having both a mature state and a new one grafted onto it by the Revolution and Napoleonic imperatives. To the extent that these notions hold good they point to a singularity in the British experience that needs some acknowledgement. It comes down to this: the historiography

[23] See in particular his essays on 'The Religious and the Secular in Victorian Britain' and 'The Conflict between Science and Religion', in Turner, *Contesting Cultural Authority: Essays in Victorian Intellectual Life* (Cambridge, 1993), pp. 3–37 and 171–200.

practised in Britain before 1870 was neither kick-started by state initiatives nor dominated by a style of nationalism intended to help make the state come into being. Like the French, British historians operated in a post-Enlightenment intellectual structure in which the history of the present (or at least of modernity) seemed more pressing, at least before mid-century, than a concern with medieval origins of the state. Hallam[24] wrote about the constitution, certainly; Macaulay participated in it to the extent of holding, like Gibbon before him, political office. Carlyle hated the state, the constitution, political office, the universities and most historians. None reflected the world of the University of Berlin, founded in a moment of national renewal in 1810 under the impress of Humboldt and Stein, or that of Bonn in 1818 which so inspired Thomas Campbell in his dreams for a University of London. Both these institutions conspired in conjuring a German past that could legitimate the foundation of a longed-for, *völkisch* state. Italian historiography, apart from its Catholic mission to promote a Roman *Weltgeschichte,* became inseparable from the aspiration for *Risorgimento.* In the United States, as Peter Novick has shown,[25] the commitment to an historical culture of objectivity both reflected and interacted with a prior commitment to America itself—its society and its institutions—as the way, the truth and the life. Every schoolboy knows that Victorian British history, too, shrieked its own national story; England was, as the great textbook later announced, top nation.[26] But it was a nationalism resting on past and present supremacies, one held to reside not in government or state and only epiphenomenally in political institutions. It was manifest not in collective scaffolding but rather as the sum of individual virtues, a temporally distilled civilisation and character. When Henry Thomas Buckle began in the 1850s his *History of English Civilization*[27] with an unusual avowal not to talk about courts and governments, he said more than he knew about the historiography of his day and more than Ranke preferred to know because, for all the latter's acute observation that institutional England amounted to church and hustings, his stress lay always on constitutional and parliamentary elements in the English past.[28]

[24] Henry Hallam (1777–1859). Legal and administrative career. Best known for his *Constitutional History of England* (London, 1827).

[25] Peter Novick, *That Noble Dream: The 'Objectivity Question' and the American Historical Profession* (Cambridge, 1988), pp. 6–7, 61–85.

[26] W. C. Sellar and R. J. Yeatman, *1066 and All That* (London, 1930).

[27] H. T. Buckle, *History of Civilization in England*, 2 vols. (London, 1857–8). Buckle (1821–62) was the son of a wealthy shipowner who devoted his life to reading and self-education.

[28] This aspect of Ranke's thinking is well-illustrated in Leonard Krieger, *Ranke: The Meaning of History* (Chicago, 1977), pp. 278–84.

Yet the institutional Prussia served by Ranke and his colleagues appropriated historians as *Beamte* and provided the framework within which a *soi-disant* 'scientific' historical knowledge could flourish. It nurtured *Quellenkritik*; it invigorated and later exported the doctoral thesis. It established a university structure which housed not tutors but professors of history: eight of them in Berlin by the 1870s, another eight in Leipzig. American universities soon felt the weight of that Germanism and with the equal weight of private money developed a system that professionalised at remarkable speed and sprouted graduate schools of considerable distinction in the later years of the century, especially for historians at Johns Hopkins and Columbia where talented students now turned for their doctoral work rather than Berlin or Heidelberg or Jena.[29] Even the French, whose higher-education potential had almost collapsed in the face of Napoleon's destruction of the university system, revived with the foundation of the republic and Ferry's reforms that soon filled university chairs with able historians.[30] State-sponsored educational initiatives, underpinned by countries undergoing, revolution, invasion, consolidation and their first industrial revolution, lent a pace and urgency to the acquisition of historical knowledge that left Britain an apparent backwater and Oxford the home of causes not yet lost because not yet seriously challenged. Exclusions from the privilege of education made their mark, to be sure: the Royal Commissions on the ancient universities testified to that; the beginning of a national school system after 1870 argued something similar; the coming of women into some areas of the system spoke likewise. There is a familiar narrative that needs no rehearsal here. But the fact of British, a fortiori English, peculiarity remains in who made the history, who consumed it and who wanted something different before the moment after 1870 when thinking historians shared a European and American impulsion toward change.

History in early Victorian Britain was written by amateurs— gentlemen and ladies who mostly had no connection at all with a university. Those who did tended not to take their connection over-seriously, giving lectures that swept across vast tracts of predominantly British history in a small number of performances designed to convey drama rather than knowledge. One who dissented—Robert Vaughan at University College London, in the second half

[29] Novick, *Noble Dream*, pp. 47–60. Cf. Michael Bentley, *Modern Historiography: An Introduction* (London, 1999), pp. 93–102.

[30] William R. Keylor, *Academy and Community: The Foundation of the French Historical Profession* (Cambridge, MA, 1975), esp. pp. 55–74. The Parisian complex of academic institutions mounted over 50 courses in history by 1883.

of the 1830s[31]—argued the need for 'a sound habit of criticism in regard to historical testimony', 'a wise discrimination as to the value of historical facts' and 'a refusal to cull out of [the past] a series of its pictures.'[32] He got his audience down to six within five years and resigned. Teachers who survived these challenges needed to draw from their men the 'manly tears' reported among Kingsley's audience[33] rather than a taste for analysis. Those beyond the university who wished to call themselves historians required a private income, a professional salary or a very busy pen. Of these a few were women—the redoubtable Mrs Trimmer and Mrs Markham left early traces in history books for children still used in the Victorian period[34]—but their number seems to have been small and their target the very young. In his brilliant analysis of the situation in France during the 1860s and 1870s, Charles-Olivier Carbonell found that only about 2% of the total number of works on history published in that period came from female authors;[35] and that figure is unlikely to have been significantly greater in Britain granted the difficulty faced by women in acquiring an historical education in the first half of our period. The men who wrote, moreover, often did so in maturity rather than in youth because of the exigencies of creating a livelihood or following a parallel profession. Carlyle's strenuous heroics as a young man need no recollection; but the desperate early years of William Stubbs or Mandell Creighton[36] exhibit as much heroism if less strain. A country without lectureships, without *Privatdozenten*, without the salaries that might make history a professional possibility for young men with little wealth in their background, left little opportunity for youth. Albert Pollard[37] wrote from his

[31] Robert Vaughan (1795–1868). Congregationalist minister. Professor of History, University College London, 1834–43; President of the Lancashire Independent College, Manchester, 1843–6. *Memorials of the Stuart Dynasty*, 2 vols. (London, 1831); *The History of England* (London, 1840); *Revolutions in English History*, 3 vols. (London, 1859–63).

[32] Quoted in Hale Bellot, *University College London*, p. 117.

[33] *Charles Kingsley: His Letters and Memories of his Life, Edited by his Wife*, 2 vols. (London, 1879), vol. 2, 118. Manliness was also an historical subject: J. B. Lightfoot discovered it in Henry III and Simon de Montfort (*Historical Essays* (London, 1874), pp. 103, 113) and Herbert Paul found it in Stubbs himself— 'simple, manly, straightforward'. See his *Stray Leaves* (London, 1906), p. 198.

[34] Sarah Trimmer, *General Outline of Antient History* (London, ?1795); Elizabeth Penrose (Mrs Markham), *A History of France, with Conversations at the end of each Chapter*, 2 vols. (London, 1828).

[35] C-O. Carbonell, *Histoire et historiens: une mutation idéologique des historiens français: 1865–1885* (Toulouse, 1976), p. 177.

[36] Mandell Creighton (1843–1901), first Dixie Professor of Ecclesiastical History, Cambridge, 1884–91; bishop of Peterborough, 1891–7; bishop of London, 1897–1901. *A History of the Papacy during the period of the Reformation*, 5 vols. (London, 1892–4); *A History of the Papacy from the Great Schism to the Sack of Rome*, 6 vols. (London, 1897).

[37] Albert Pollard (1869–1948), Professor of Constitutional History, University of London, 1903–31. *Henry VIII* (London, 1902); *Factors in Modern History* (London, 1907); *The History of England* (London, 1912); *The Evolution of Parliament* (London, 1920).

university chair in London as late as 1910 that 'Gibbon could not have written his *Decline and Fall of the Roman Empire* nor Macaulay his *History of England* if they had not possessed independent means; and the first requisite for an historian in England is neither skill nor industry, neither knowledge of documents nor a faculty for turning them into literature, but a command of financial resources independent of those which can be derived from the writing of history.'[38] His opinion clashes sharply with descriptions of conditions in Germany, France and America.

The German situation remained unique in its class basis and the age structure of the profession. Wolfgang Weber's researches at the beginning of the 1980s demonstrated a persistent family continuity in the German historical professoriate after mid-century—the fathers of professors tended to be professors or *Beamte*—and, then as now, the age at which a full chair might be gained reflected the long apprenticeship and an average gap of ten years between *Habilitation* and appointment.[39] But the presence of a professional structure never the less contrasted obviously with the British case. Similarly, that 'revanche de la jeunesse' that Carbonell locates in France in the 1860s and 1870s lacked its crucial precondition in Britain. 'Une vocation les appelle, parfois à l'origine d'un métier.'[40] Britain had no *métier*. The rise, again, of the American farm-boy from the mid-West or the small-town prodigy from an unglamorous home had not made itself felt in Carlisle and Knaresborough; yet look where it would lead as the economic expansion of the United States took hold.

> Before 1914 the professionalization of history had served as a dramatically successful ladder of personal social and economic mobility for dozens of small-town boys of lower-middle class backgrounds. In the rapidly-expanding university world of prewar America, it was not unusual for a bright young man to become a full professor within a few years of receiving the doctorate, and to achieve national eminence before he was out of his thirties. Salaries, for the most successful, compared favourably with those of many other professionals. In the more difficult to measure area of status, the college professor was a figure of consequence in the local community.[41]

No wonder Felix Gilbert, writing against this background, doubted Peter Slee's contention that a teaching *profession* had arrived in Oxford by the 1860s.[42]

[38] See his *Factors in Modern History* (London, 1907), p. 267.

[39] Wolfgang Weber, *Priester der Klio: Historisch-sozialwissenschaftliche Studien zur Herkunft und Karriere deutcher Historiker und zur Geschichte der Geschichtswissenschaft 1800–1970* (Frankfurt am Main, 1984), pp. 71–7.

[40] Carbonell, *Histoire et historiens*, pp. 116, 170.

[41] Novick, *Noble Dream*, 169.

[42] For Slee's views on Gilbert, see Peter Slee, *Learning and a Liberal Education*, p. 100. Reba Soffer also sees the 1860s and 1870s as a significant threshold in this development: *Discipline and Power*, pp. 1–6, 11–12, 54–6.

One way of thinking about such contentions lies in re-thinking the place in communicating historical knowledge of one of the most imaginative Victorian experiments in advancing sophisticated scholarship in the humanities: the foundation and uneven career of Owens College, Manchester. Coming into being in the year of the Great Exhibition, the new college promised civic pride and cotton money. But there was no money for a history professor until 1853 and then the appointee, Christie,[43] who had graduated from Oxford six months before, not only taught all the chronology but maintained three chairs simultaneously (History, Political Economy and Law) in so far as it were possible for him to maintain anything at all while continuing his Law practice. By 1862–3 he had built up the history class to twenty-six, all the same, on his course in the history of Britain from the Roman invasion to 1688, his textbook Hume's *History of England*, his fee £2.12*s.* 6*d.*[44] He was better than his stand-in predecessor, Professor Greenwood, one of whose unforgettable examination questions ran: 'Enumerate, without any detail, the chief battles fought during the [English Civil] war, stating in each case with which side the victory lay.'[45] On the other hand he was less distinguished than two highly significant successors, Adolphus Ward[46] and Stanley Jevons.[47] The development of a distinguished professoriate certainly helped the cause of historical knowledge in Manchester, therefore; but a notice board in 1875 still carried an ominous advertisement for one of its history courses: 'The class will be catechetical.'[48] From Owens College to the University of Manchester there turned out to lay a long and frustrating road via the strange experiment of the Victoria University. But even with that achieved, Thomas Frederick Tout[49] saw all too

[43] Richard Copley Christie (1830–1901). Joint legatee of Sir Joseph Whitworth and benefactor of Owens College. Monograph on *Etienne Dolet: The Martyr of the Renaissance* (London, 1880).

[44] T. F. Tout, 'Schools of History', *The Collected Papers of Thomas Frederick Tout*, 3 vols. (Manchester, 1932–4), vol. 1, pp. 93–109 at 95.

[45] Tout, 'Schools of History', ibid., pp. 60–89 at 63.

[46] Adolphus Ward (1837–1924), Professor of History and English Literature, Owens College, 1866–90; Principal, 1890–7; Master of Peterhouse, Cambridge, 1900–24. Edited *Cambridge Modern History* after Acton's death in 1902, made substantial contributions to it and to the *Cambridge History of English Literature*. His period was the eighteenth century.

[47] Stanley Jevons (1835–82). Professor of Logic, Political Economy and Philosophy, Owens College, 1866–76; Professor of Political Economy, University College London, 1876–80. Publications in fields of monetary theory, science and logic.

[48] Tout, 'Schools of History', p. 71. According to Lionel Gossman, no less a professor than Jacob Burckhardt also preferred this method when teaching at Basel: a warning against europhilia. See Gossman, *Basel in the Age of Burckhardt: A Study in Unseasonable Ideas* (Chicago, 2000).

[49] Thomas Frederick Tout (1855–1929), Professor of Modern History, St David's College, Lampeter, 1881–90; Professor of History, Manchester, 1890–1925. Demanding and significant scholar of medieval administration. *The Place of Edward II in English History* (Oxford, 1914); *Chapters in the Administrative History of Medieval England*, 6 vols. (London, 1920–33).

clearly that the juvenile success of Christie could not be replicated even in the vastly improved circumstances of 1910. '[I]t is useless to train the men,' he said, 'unless you have modest careers to offer them. We shall always be behind France and Germany, if we are behind them in finding posts for our own historical scholars.'[50]

With sources and societies, as with the scholars to enjoy them, comparison proved painful. Where was the British *École des chartes*, where its *Monumenta*? One clear answer appeared in Vivian Galbraith's seminal account of the British public records, published in 1934. The British parallel, he said, could be seen in the Rolls series, modelled self-consciously on Pertz's *Monumenta Germaniae Historica* and turning for the first time to the systematic publication of medieval sources.[51] The similarities evaporate, however, if one thinks not about the form of the series but its function. Pertz and his collaborators wished to make a Germany by finding a truly German past evoked by an *Urvolk*. The Rolls series consummated a trend of antiquarian researches reaching back into the seventeenth and eighteenth centuries and were driven more by a sense of national honour than nationalist imperatives. Another candidate for progress appeared in the Camden Society of 1838, but that seems even more British in its origins and spirit, rather like the Surtees Society.[52] The Camden grew out of the brains of a restricted number of notables, each with an entry in the *Dictionary of National Biography*, though it acknowledged the state at least in so far as the imminent Public Record Office Act, which laid the foundations for a Public Record Office, ran concurrently with it.[53] The society flourished briefly but then

[50] Tout, 'The School of History', 83. It even crossed Maitland's mind to wonder whether there was point in stimulating any young scholar who lacked 'independent means': F. W. Maitland to A. F. Pollard, 16 May 1903, Pollard MSS 860 box 47.

[51] V. H. Galbraith, *An Introduction to the Use of the Public Records* (London, 1934), pp. 71–2. The Rolls series, more properly *Rerum Britannicum Medii Aevi Scriptores*, began to appear, at the instigation of the Master of the Rolls, in 1858.

[52] The Surtees Society began in 1834 with the object of printing documents concerning 'the intellectual, the moral, the religious, and social condition' of those northern counties deemed to have constituted 'the Ancient Kingdom of Northumbria'. See the brief 'Remarks' in the first volume on *Reginaldi Monachi Dunelmensis* and the history of the society by A. Hamilton Thompson, *The Surtees Society, 1834–1934*, both in *Publications of the Surtees Society*, vols. I (London, 1835), xi and 150 (Durham, 1939), pp. 2–4.

[53] Charles Johnson, 'The Camden Society', *Transactions of the Royal Historical Society*, 4th ser., xxii (1940), partially reprinted in R. A. Humphreys, *The Royal Historical Society, 1868–1968* (London, 1969), pp. 52–67 at 52–3. Cf. F. J. Levy, 'The Founding of the Camden Society', *Victorian Studies*, 7 (1963–4), 295–305. The notables included John Bruce, author of numerous monographs and editions in seventeenth-century history, Joseph Hunter of Yorkshire fame and Sir Frederick Madden of the British Museum.

suffered the fate of most publishing endeavours in becoming a shoe-string enterprise. It allowed itself to become absorbed in the Royal Historical Society in 1897 when the society became a series. Meanwhile the establishment of the new Public Record Office that opened in Chancery Lane in 1858,[54] and the Royal Historical Society itself, founded a decade later, suggested something about changing public views of history though quite what they suggested seems unclear. Looking back on the history of the RHS from his presidential chair after the First World War, Tout said that '[i]t came into existence because, more than a generation ago, historians began to believe that history was a definite branch of knowledge to be studied by itself for its own sake'; [55] but little in the amateur origins of the society and little in Tout's own opinions before the First World War corroborate that. Until the election of Acton, Maitland, Creighton and Cunningham[56] in the 1880s[57] the society better reflected the atmosphere of most mid-Victorian gatherings of gentlemen than it implied the formation of a professionalising cell. And by then the entire predicament of history, for such it had become, appeared far more manifest, not least because European predominance had finally given rise to concern. Long before the meeting at Wiesbaden in 1899 that helped stimulate the foundation of the British Academy, Europe finally came home to British historians.

So many streams fed into this current that even a sketch-map of them presents problems of representation. By no mean all of them began in Europe. Stubbs's famous class of 1874 had gone out into the world, apprised of Ranke, familiar with forensic method, and including one in R. L. Poole[58] who would establish British diplomatic on an entirely new level of expertise. Acton's own arrival in the Cambridge Regius Chair in 1895 brought a European inheritance directly to the heart of academic history in Britain. The *English Historical Review* which he and Creighton had done much to

[54] See Elizabeth M. Hallam, 'Nine Centuries of Keeping the Public Records' in G. Martin and P. Spufforth (eds.), *Records of the Nation: the Public Record Office, 1838–1988* (Woodbridge, 1990), pp. 23–42, esp. 38–9.

[55] Tout's presidential address, 'International Co-operation in History', 10 Feb. 1927, in *Collected Papers*, vol. 1, pp. 110–23 at 112.

[56] William Cunningham (1849–1919). Ordained 1873; chaplain, Trinity College, Cambridge, 1880–91; archdeacon of Ely, 1907; Tooke Professor of Economy and Statistics, King's College, London, 1891–7. Pioneer of economic history: *The Growth of English History and Commerce* (Cambridge, 1882); *Politics and Economics* (London, 1885); *An Essay on Western Civilization in its Economic Aspects*, 2 vols. (Cambridge, 1898).

[57] Humphreys, *Royal Historical Society*, p. 20.

[58] Reginald Lane Poole (1857–1939), Lecturer, then Reader, in Diplomatic, University of Oxford, 1896–1927. Edited the *English Historical Review*, 1901–20. *A History of the Huguenots* (London, 1880); *The Exchequer in the Twelfth Century* (Oxford, 1912); *Chronicles and Annals* (London, 1926).

stimulate in 1886 placed an English journal at last beside the magisterial *Historische Zeitschrift* of 1859 and the *Revue historique* of 1876, though Acton's inaugural essay on the German School showed how far there was to go and in which direction.[59] But it is surely the structural aspects of explaining change that claim attention before the personal: an economy that had lost its way after 1873, a cultural malaise in the wake of the European exhibitions that made the Great British version of 1851 now seem a dinosaur and *Made in Germany* a threatening mantra; the call for technological universities on the German model and the response, bursting with civic pride and civic cash, in cities from Manchester, Leeds and Liverpool, to Sheffield, Birmingham and Newcastle.[60] Few of these had departments of history in their early days but they taught it alongside other humanities subjects and employed the brighter products of the Modern History schools in Oxford and Cambridge (themselves a recent development) who were not successful in gaining fellowships. Peter Slee tells us that over 100 men a year were graduating with honours in history from Oxford in the first half of the 1890s and about a quarter of that number in Cambridge:[61] no derisory cohort for the core of a teaching elite. Against this, however, we should set the London experience of Albert Pollard who reflected in some depression on the failure to attract candidates to the new BA in History after 1896 and the solitary First produced between 1896 and 1901. His depression deepened when he tried to set up a memorial chair in history after the death of Creighton in 1901 only to give up after raising a mere £300.[62]

The long Victorian period helps iron out some of these setbacks and false starts, especially if one distends posterity to the end of the First World War and the attempts to found Institutes of Historical Research in London and Manchester (one successful, one not) in 1921. Seen in that perspective, the period after 1880 reveals a marked acceleration in the organisation of historical expertise, the acquisition of European approaches to historical method, the consolidation of a professional academy in 1902, the extension of the

[59] Lord Acton, 'German Schools of History', *EHR*, vol. 1 (1886), 7–42. 'My object has been to show neither their infirmity nor their strength, but the ways in which they break new ground and add to the notion and to the work of history.' (42).

[60] For general treatments of this issue, see Michael Sanderson, *The Universities and British Industry, 1850–1970* (London, 1972) and Sanderson (ed.), *The Universities in the Nineteenth Century* (London, 1975). For the spectacular contribution of one industrialist to the establishment of a civic university (Birmingham), see Peter J. Marsh, *Joseph Chamberlain: Entrepreneur in Politics* (New Haven, 1994), pp. 460–2.

[61] Slee, *Learning and a Liberal Education*, p. 125.

[62] *Factors in Modern History*, p. 263.

academy towards a more general public in the Historical Association of 1906 and in emerging volumes of the Cambridge Modern History under the guidance of Adolphus Ward and others. The universities may not have yet 'focus[ed] knowledge' in the style sought by Pollard[63] but they had come a long way in deciding what a sophisticated historical knowledge ought to be about.

Common sense suggests that historical knowledge is drawn from and dependent upon historical sources. This banal thought never the less has more force in its negative than its positive aspects: it rightly contends that historians cannot operate without sources of some kind but offers no guidance about how they locate them or what they do with them. It misleads especially when it implies that sources lie around libraries as a 'given' range of material from which the historian need only make a selection in order to prove a point. More discriminating ways of presenting the problem have to acknowledge the senses in which historians *create* their sources by asking intelligent questions about the past and then deciding what they would need to know in order to answer them. Sometimes new sources become available because scientific developments make possible what had not been possible before: carbon-dating of materials or computer analyses of statistical arrays too complex for manual manipulation supply cases of this kind. But very often in historiography we see new material coming into play as a result of someone asking a new question or offering a fresh insight. What had previously been a mere artefact—a laundry list, a farmer's last will and testament, a report of a public ritual or celebration—undergoes transformation and becomes evidence for an historical assertion. The knife used to carve last Sunday's joint of meat may be the same knife described as *Exhibit A* in a murder trial three months hence. It will not have changed its knife-ness but instead of lying in a drawer unremarked it will be called into a new status by people wishing to make a case about a particular historical event. Historians, like lawyers, lend status to dead artefacts by making them relevant to cases or, in their language, to historical arguments that they are considering. In this way a dead thing becomes live and what we think of as historical knowledge may expand through that process to include facts that previous generations may have thought irrelevant to their interests or simply nor worth knowing. The crucial point is that what counts as historical knowledge within a given culture is not determined by the past itself, presenting itself as a story waiting to be read, but rather by those who are entrusted with modulating that past for particular audiences. Neither propaganda nor falsehood need follow from what is normally, outside

[63] Ibid., p. 287.

totalitarian regimes, a process of great subtlety; but its presence is what makes historiography as a form of enquiry both difficult and necessary.

Theoretical exordia soon weary the reader but the foregoing is important if one is to see the ways in which bland statements of 'fact' in Victorian historical knowledge may conceal interesting contentions, usually implied, about what ought to be known and what could safely be left in oblivion. Take, for example, historical textbooks: numbingly dull compilations of facts and dates which Victorian schoolchildren had to learn by heart in those 'catechetical' classes that we have seen flourishing even in the universities. Frances Lawrence explains in her analysis of these Victorian volumes that 'the structure of textbooks is a function of learning theories',[64] that is, all such compendia rest on an implicit view of what there is to be learned, how it shall be learned, and what will count as knowledge. Once this is grasped, then the Victorian history textbook makes compelling sense.

> If it is believed, as was the case, that the mind is a storehouse, then stocking it is clearly the business of education ... Simple repetition, drills, complicated strategies such as dates painted on ceilings, nonsense rhymes, etc. were necessary and respectable rote-learning methods. The whole range of dates which late Victorian and Edwardian children learned—dates of kings and queens, genealogical tables, battles and wars, capes and bays, model drawings, moral tales, arithmetical tables and the like were seen as necessary storage material ... It was generally held that the stockpiling was best achieved by adding the general to the particular, the complicated to the simple, the abstract to the concrete; in other words the data to be stored were seen to have certain optimal positions in the layers of knowledge. The effective study of history depended therefore on an accurate chronology, a definite ordering of facts, beginning at the beginning and moving forward in time.[65]

These assumptions could reinforce a view of historical method such as that described by Charles Harding Firth in his Oxford inaugural lecture of 1904. First, he said, comes the collection of facts: this is a task 'purely scientific' in nature, 'like the process by which the man of science gathers and weighs the results of his experiments and observations'. Then and only then comes the artistic side of the enterprise:

> When he has discovered the truth the second part of the historian's task begins. He has to state the truth as it appears to him. He has to combine his facts, and to construct something out of them, either a description, or a story, or a demonstration. All his facts are equally true, but all are not equally important ... By this process of selection and arrangement he endeavours to reproduce the effect which the whole

[64] Frances Lawrence, 'Textbooks', in William Lamont (ed.), *The Realities of Teaching History: Beginnings* (London, 1972), pp. 110–43 at 114.
[65] Ibid.

> of the evidence has produced upon his mind. As we say familiarly, 'he puts his ideas upon paper', that is he strives to embody in some material form a conception of the past which is floating in his head.[66]

These assumptions and methods did not in themselves over-determine the output of historians but they could exercise a pervasive effect on the historical mind, especially if applied to the subject areas that became traditional within historiography 'when a cold-blooded utilitarianism,' as Herbert Butterfield later lamented, 'put its damp hand upon the nineteenth century . . .'.[67] The concentration on, as it were, 'atomic' truth-claims militated against more 'molecular' assertions that might encompass structures and processes that could not readily be reduced to the fine 'powder' required by approved historical method.[68] As the century proceeded, moreover, the grip of such assumptions increased and contentions that might have seemed acceptable to Hallam or Macaulay looked unscientific and tendentious to Gardiner[69] or Firth in the later years of Victorian England. None the less we can see certain pervasive tendencies within the period as a whole about what needed to be taught and learned. In this age of self-conscious democratisation, the theme of liberation, emancipation, the plotting of freedom's narrative against oppression and tyranny, is never far away from the concerns of English historians. Acton's unwritten masterpiece embodying that narrative may be seen in one sense as the tip of an invisible iceberg, in another as counter-thematic in wanting to approach a vast trajectory rather than describe a small section of it. But then Acton was as much German or Italian as English and had no fear of Rankian

[66] C. H. Firth, *A Plea for the Historical Teaching of History* (Oxford, 1904), pp. 7–8. Cf. the view of the German theologian Adolf von Harnack, announced at about the same time: '[History] does not of course encompass the deepest knowledge, and it makes no value judgments. None the less, it is a possession of the highest value — a collection of historically attested facts.' Quoted in Ulrich Muhlack, 'Universal History and National History', in Benedikt Stuchkey and Peter Wende (eds.), *British and German History, 1750–1950: Traditions, Perspectives and Transfers* (Oxford, 2000), pp. 34–5.

[67] 'There is a foreign book . . .', 'Early Writing', p. 7, Butterfield miscellany. (This small collection of fragments is in the care of the author and currently closed to research.)

[68] For historical evidence as powder, see Charles Langlois and Charles Seignobos, *Introduction to Historical Method* (London, 1898). 'Historical construction has . . . to be performed with an incoherent mass of minute facts, with detail-knowledge reduced as it were to powder.' (214). F. York Powell, introducing the English edition agreed that '[i]t will be a positive gain to have the road cleared of rubbish, that has hindered the advance of knowledge. History must be worked at in a scientific spirit, as biology or chemistry is worked at.' (vii).

[69] Samuel Rawson Gardiner (1829–1902), Professor of Modern History, King's College London, 1877–85; Joint editor of *EHR*, 1891–1901; director Camden Society, 1869–97. *History of England from the Accession of James I to the Outbreak of the English Civil War, 1627–42*, 10 vols. (London, 1873–4); *History of the Civil War 1642–49*, 3 vols. (London, 1886–91); *History of the Commonwealth and Protectorate 1649–60*, 3 vols. (London, 1894–1903).

scale. More typical within the English fraternity appeared to be a vast narrative, to be sure, but concentrated on a smaller period and fastening on a particular theme: the Norman conquest, Magna Carta, the reign of Henry VIII, the seventeenth-century constitution, the English Civil War, the apotheosis of whiggery in the eighteenth century. John Burrow has given us a majestic account of how these themes had their own history, each reflecting the thought-world of a particular slice of nineteenth-century experience, from the urgency of 1688 for the generation of Hallam, through the discovery of a teutonic heritage and the building of a new picture of medieval England after mid-century, to the eruption of a Tudor fascination in the age of empire.[70] Victorian historians joined hands to celebrate the genius of the English as a race and their constitution as a magical embodiment of all that was best and most permanent in the national heritage.

But this 'knowledge' ran into friction with the method by which, increasingly, it sought to be validated and that friction retarded the possibility of romantic summaries covering centuries or millennia in the style of a universal history. Hume's continuators in English history preserved an eighteenth-century tradition through the 1820s—the decade of William Cobbett's parliamentary history since the Norman Conquest and Lingard's Catholic vision of English history from the Romans to the Glorious Revolution.[71] Later versions faltered in face of the need to demonstrate deeper knowledge of events and a denser narrative texture. Even the most famous and determined narrator, Thomas Babington Macaulay, found it impossible to carry his *History of England, from the Accession of James II* (5 vols., 1849–65) any further than the end of the seventeenth century, let alone anywhere close to the reign of George IV where he had originally intended to terminate the account.[72] Thereafter, histories of England, written in the grand manner and across many centuries, petered out until after the turn of the century, apart from Stubbs's *Constitutional History* which prosecuted its particular theme

[70] John Burrow, *A Liberal Descent: Victorian Historians and the English Past* (Cambridge, 1981). Burrow tells his story through a consideration of Macaulay, Stubbs, Freeman and Froude but the contentions of the study run far wider and provide a picture of English historiography as a whole between 1830 and 1890.

[71] Robert Scott [James Robins], *History of England*, 4 vols. (London, 1824); William Jones, *History of England*, 3 vols. (London, 1825); William Cobbett (ed.), *Cobbett's Parliamentary History of England … 1066 to … 1803*, 36 vols. (London, 1806–20); John Lingard, *A History of England from Invasion by the Romans to the Revolution in 1688*, 8 vols. (London, 1819–30).

[72] 'In 1838 he thought he might end it in 1830. By 1841 he thought he might end with the death of Anne in 1714. In the end, he barely reached the close of William III's reign.' William Thomas, *The Quarrel of Macaulay and Croker: Politics and History in the Age of Reform* (Oxford, 2000), p. 249.

and prompted treatments of more modern periods from this angle.[73] Only at the more popular level of John Richard Green's *Short History of the English People* did the ambition to sweep through the chronology persist.[74] Regnal years still formed the *termini* of most studies and it became rare to find historical knowledge projected into coverage of much more than a century.[75] Contemporaries remained all but oblivious of these patterns which only the perspective provided by distance would help reveal; in their eyes their century offered an accretion of facts about the past on which future generations would build. And to some degree they were right to believe this: only in 2002 did a self-conscious attempt to replace Gardiner's narrative of the pre-civil-war years appear[76] and all medievalists continue to pay their respects to Stubbs, Maitland and Round.[77] What nineteenth-century writers could not foresee was how much their knowledge would come to seem specific responses to particular questions that often left in shadow much that the twentieth century wanted to know.

First, the concentration on issues raised by constitutional convention and law in British history and the more legalistic side of international relations in

[73] William Stubbs, *The Constitutional History of England,* 3 vols. (London, 1866); Sir Thomas Erskine May, *The Constitutional History of England since the Accession of George III*, 2 vols. (London, 1861–3); Rudolf Gneist, *Englische Verfassungsgeschichte* (Berlin, 1882). Events in British politics after 1880 put particular stress on an historiographical treatment of the House of Lords. 'People have got right views about most other parts of the constitution,' Mandell Creighton wrote in 1884, 'but they are rather befogged about the House of Lords.' (Creighton to Edward Freeman, 22 Aug. 1884, Freeman MSS FAI/7/119.) Cf. L. O. Pike, *A Constitutional History of the House of Lords* (London, 1894).

[74] J. R. Green (1837–83). Ecclesiastical career; librarian at Lambeth Palace. *A Short History of the English People* (1874); *History of the English People*, 4 vols. (London, 1877–80). Cf. J. F. Smith and William Howitt, *John Cassell's Illustrated History of England*, 8 vols. (London, 1856–64).

[75] Examples of the more condensed style are Thomas Smart Hughes, *The History of England from the Accession of George III, 1760, to the Accession of Queen Victoria, 1837*, 5 vols. (London, 1834–6); P. H. Stanhope, Viscount Mahon, *History of England from the Peace of Utrecht to the Peace of Versailles, 1713–83*, 7 vols. (London, 1836–54); James Anthony Froude, *A History of England from the Fall of Wolsey to the Defeat of the Spanish Armada*, 12 vols. (London, 1856–70); W. E. H. Lecky, *A History of England in the Eighteenth Century*, 8 vols. (London, 1878–90); Spencer Walpole, *A History of England from the Conclusion of the Great War in 1815*, 5 vols. (London, 1878–86); S. R. Gardiner, *History of England from the Accession of James I to the Outbreak of the Civil War, 1603–42*, 10 vols. (London, 1883–4). Perhaps the most celebrated study of a single reign was the *History of Britain from the Accession to the Decease of George III*, 7 vols. (London, 1840–45) by John Adolphus.

[76] See Austin Woolrych, *Britain in Revolution 1625–1660* (Oxford, 2002).

[77] John Horace Round (1854–1928). Infirm, isolated and combative medievalist who lived on a private income in Brighton and Essex. *Feudal England* (London, 1895); *The King's Sergeants and Officers of State* (London, 1911). Creighton, editing *EHR*, was nettled into thinking him 'really rather cracked' (Creighton to Freeman, 20 Nov. 1889, Freeman MSS FA1/7/127a) but there is a more sympathetic reading in a recent biography, W. Raymond Powell, *John Horace Round: Historian and Gentleman of Essex* (Chelmsford, 2001).

European studies starved out the possibility of a serious school of social history. Freeman's cliché describing history as past politics had its inevitable result in Trevelyan's cliché describing social history as history with the politics left out; and neither produced a rounded view of the subject. Second, the preferencing of event over process rarely allowed economic knowledge to intrude into the historical conspectus, at least until the 1880s when the German example led to pioneering work by the elder Arnold Toynbee, William Cunningham and the young J. H. Clapham[78] in the Edwardian period. Third, the persistence of a confessional element in Victorian historiography hampered the production of that value-free knowledge on which historians so frequently dwelled.[79] But, fourthly, it is also relevant to ask whether the low status granted to the idea of 'research' and the equally low expectations of undergraduate education did not fatally undermine the commitment to 'knowledge' as Victorian historians increasingly wanted to define it. Two *ideas* of historical knowledge had collided with one another by 1880. One of them stressed the global nature of what one had to know and dwelled on what nowadays we might call 'coverage'; the other wanted to emphasise the detail and sophistication of what was known, together with the sources on which such knowledge was conceived to rest. The former argued the need for a generalist education gleaned from textbooks, the latter a familiarity with primary sources (or 'authorities' as the nineteenth century still saw them) and a grounding in research method. Making these competing claims compatible foxed the twentieth century as much as the nineteenth, but the very confusion has helped engender in a more self-conscious intelligentsia certain reticences about the status of historical knowledge itself. The Victorians knew no such reticence: historical work was supposed to produce consensual, accretional, reliable knowledge about the past and those studying it had to be tested on their grasp of nothing less. But the more they tested it, the more it seemed elusive—a result that caused some critical minds great pain. Firth's agony at Oxford is too well-known to rehearse again, especially when he remarked so openly on it in his inaugural lecture, which Oxford tutors made him apologise for having delivered, with its apparent attack on the entire Oxford system of education. 'Whenever any one seeks to alter the Modern History School,'

[78] Sir John Clapham (1873–1946), Professor of Economic History, Cambridge, 1928–38 and the premier economic historian of his generation. *The Woollen and Worsted Industries* (1907); *The Economic Development of France and Germany, 1815–1914* (Cambridge, 1921); *An Economic History of Modern Britain*, 3 vols. (Cambridge, 1926–38).

[79] This large subject cannot be developed here but I have written about it elsewhere: see Michael Bentley, 'Victorian Historians and the Larger Hope', in Bentley (ed.), *Public and Private Doctrine: Essays in British History Presented to Maurice Cowling* (Cambridge, 1993), pp. 127–48.

he said, 'in order to make it a better training for historians, he is met by the objection that it is not meant to give a professional, but a general training. Yet, at the same time, this training is regarded and accepted by all colleges as an adequate professional training. It is legal tender everywhere in Oxford ...'[80]

This frustration existed further east. Twenty years before Firth's *cri de coeur*, Mandell Creighton already felt a similar unease over the Cambridge History Tripos which only *pretended* to impart the historical knowledge that it claimed for itself.

> It seems to me that no one reading for the exam[inatio]n ever looks at an original authority. The English History and the Constitutional History are both very general. Stubbs' Charters seem almost unknown. What the papers 3.4.5. come to I do not know.[81] But I think that they are general talk à la Seeley. The Ancient History period is a mere delusion: it is a scrap of Greek or Roman History read in a textbook.

He clinched his argument in this letter to Freeman by citing not only his own view but that of a current Cambridge undergraduate, conveyed in a recent letter. The tripos, according to the student, 'is entirely fragmentary & leads to no real knowledge. The abstract subjects are too large. The Historical subjects are dotted about over a large space, & the intervals are not covered. We skim a few textbooks. The examn. gives no encouragement to sound reading on any one of the subjects.'[82] Indeed, despite all the 'advances' in historical knowledge published since 1870, there is little evidence that such material reached undergraduates in Cambridge. Pressed to explain what students taking the Constitutional History paper actually *read* in 1911 Clapham pointed out cheerfully that the men of King's were still reading Hallam and Bagehot as well as more recent bits from Anson, Prothero and Dicey.[83]

[80] C. H. Firth, *Plea for the Historical Teaching of History*, p. 28.

[81] The papers covered political philosophy, political economy and economic history, and international law.

[82] Creighton to Freeman, 8 Mar. 1885, Freeman MSS FAI/7/122. This opinion sits comfortably with Soffer's judgement that 'the student did not investigate the topic but instead mastered an existing, already organized body of knowledge in the form of broad surveys and prepared "outlines"'. *Discipline and Power*, p. 160.

[83] J. H. Clapham to Oscar Browning, 7 Jul. n.y. [1911], Browning MSS i/C: Clapham. Sir William Anson was best known among historians for his *Law and Custom of the Constitution*, 2 vols. (London, 1886) and Albert Venn Dicey for his *Lectures Introductory to the Study of the Law of the Constitution* (1885). Sir George Prothero (1848–1922), Lecturer in History at Cambridge, 1876–94 and Professor of History in the University of Edinburgh, 1894–9, was a generalist who wrote on Simon de Montfort as well as his special period in the seventeenth century. He also wrote the *Nelson's School History of Great Britain and Ireland* (London, 1908).

Undergraduates made up one important element of the Victorian audience for historical knowledge but there were many others and they demand comment. There is room here only for a coda but the problems in providing a commentary on the Victorian audience run far beyond considerations of space. We know very little, as yet, about the penetration of historical writing into a wider readership, despite the pioneering work of Jonathan Rose and others,[84] not least because the *function* of that audience within the culture lacks clear conceptualisation. Size undoubtedly matters. But the provision of more and more sales figures will not supply an account of whether the buyers of books read them, what they did with their reading and what classes of people participated. Winding back the assumptions of a hundred years later can obscure ways, moreover, in which not only did the audience behave differently from a current one soaked in 'media', but also ways in which the aspirations of historians about their audience could run counter to those normal today. We assume that authors want to reach the widest possible audience but Victorian writers, obsessed by the tension between brains and numbers, could become *anxious* in the face of a broadened appeal. Consider a great Victorian 'success', a study of the historical Christ, *Ecce Homo*, written by John Robert Seeley and published anonymously by Macmillan in 1865. Alexander Macmillan's reports to the author tell their own story:

13 February 1866:	'we have sold about 300 in London'
21 February 1866:	'we have not quite 500 copies left of the second edition. Your share of the spoil of edition 2 will be £175'
20 April 1866:	'The fourth edition is actually printed, and we have just subscribed it to the trade and sold over *1200* copies which I confess surprised even me.'
18 March 1867:	'We are at press with our second edition of 3000 in the cheap form. The first is quite sold.'[85]

One might expect Seeley to have been pleased. But when he planned his next book for the same publisher his tone registered more caution than pleasure:

> Of course one would not like the book to be a failure, but beyond that I do not really much care. The success of Ecce Homo was rather alarming than otherwise.

[84] Rose, *Intellectual Life of the British Working Classes*, can be supplemented by studies of readership and print in general, such as Laurel Blake, *Print in Transition, 1850–1900: Studies in Media and Book History* (London, 2001) and by publishers' individual histories, most recently David Finkelstein, *The House of Blackwood: Author–Publisher Relations in the Victorian Era* (London, 2002) and Elizabeth James, *Macmillan: A Publishing Tradition from 1843* (London, 2002). There remains a long way to go.

[85] All from Seeley MSS 903/3A/1, University of London Library.

> If I knew any way in which I could prevent all weak or rash heads from reading me, I would certainly adopt it. It is this feeling which leads me to delay so much, I mean the feeling that however much good I may hope to do I cannot fail also to do harm.[86]

Attitudes of this kind form part of an authorial tendency within an intelligentsia preoccupied by the danger of ideas in destabilising a democratising and secularising nation. We have to recognise at the outset that historians did not necessarily *wish* their work to be disseminated to a wider public unprepared for its message.

Most of them need not have worried. With the exceptions of Macaulay's *History*, whose first volumes led to the besieging of Longmans in Paternoster Row in 1848,[87] J. R. Green's *Short History of the English People* (1874) and Acton's posthumously published lectures, historians, especially those in the developing university system, seem unlikely to have reached a wide public with their books before 1880 unless they wrote school textbooks. Against *Ecce Homo* we can readily place Freeman's study of Federalism which Macmillan reported in 1863 having sold 'very little over 100 copies.'[88] True, Alexander Macmillan jumped at Freeman's idea of writing a history of the Norman conquest, providing that he would write it 'in a clear, popular style'.[89] But when part of it began to reach him, he bridled at once at the way that a self-conscious academic mind approached what ought to be a good story. 'A man does not go through the kitchen with his cook,' he complained, 'or through the dissecting room with his physician. He wants his dinner cooked & his pill or draft in their complete form without the din of pestle or the splatter of the spit.'[90] Historians had their own view of the audience and it found little fit, as ever, with what publishers wanted. Money pressed from both sides: tradesmen needed to sell, authors need to earn but often with little idea of the spartan economics involved. Benjamin Thorpe, from a more gentle generation, grew depressed when his translation of Lappenberg

[86] Seeley to Macmillan, 7 Jul. 1872, Macmillan MSS, BL Add. MS 55074 f.8. Cf. Adolphus Ward's concern over the 'difference between keeping in view the necessity of *instructing* that inoffensive animal the general reader, and appealing to his tastes, which are frequently the offspring of his ignorance'. Ward to Freeman, 10 April 1877, Freeman MSS FA1/7/791a, John Rylands Library.

[87] See J. H. Plumb, 'Thomas Babington Macaulay', *University of Toronto Quarterly*, 26 (1956), 17–31.

[88] Macmillan to Freeman, 3 Mar. 1863, Freeman MSS FA1/7/493.

[89] Macmillan to Freeman, 5 Dec. 1865: 'A History of the Norman Conquest written in a clear, popular style would undoubtedly be a book I would willingly undertake the publication of, at my own risk, dividing with you the profits.' Freeman MSS FA1/7/497.

[90] Macmillan to Freeman, 18 Feb. 1867, Freeman MSS FA1/7/500.

on Norman kingship[91] sold hardly at all, for example, and became 'completely tired of losing not only [his] labour, but [his] pecuniary means'. He threw aside his intended translation of 'Pauli's "History" in something bordering on disgust'.[92] Perhaps, as one historian conjectures, the explosion of interest in the historical novel in the wake of Sir Walter Scott, Harrison Ainsworth, Charles Reade and others, raised the required standard of style and readability;[93] perhaps history became more saleable at the same time that it became harder for professional academic historians to write it in the form demanded. Turning to textbooks for the growing university curriculum and to books for schools preparing students for that curriculum better suited the talents of those traditionally trained in formal education.

The years after the Crimean War, on the other hand, inaugurated the heyday of the serious magazine—*Macmillan's* (1859), *Cornhill* (1860), the *Fortnightly Review* (1865) and *Contemporary Review* (1866)—to set beside the staples of *Fraser's, Blackwood's*, the *Edinburgh* and the *Quarterly*. Some of these outlets offered more money than an historian might make for writing a complete book. Seeley certainly thought so and became a regular contributor to *Macmillan's* and elsewhere, partly on that ground.[94] Articles and reviews certainly reached an audience in gentlemen's clubs and among a small but influential subscription-list. For the inner-circle of the historical community, meanwhile, pressure built from the 1860s for a specialist journal on the lines of the *Historische Zeitschrift*. When it finally appeared in 1886, even its greatest supporters did not believe that it would command a wide readership. Its editor reflected on the problems in 1890:

> I cannot say that the H[istorical] R[eview] increases quickly in circulation. It is read by those interested in history, and is well-known abroad: but it goes to Libraries rather than to private buyers: the student is proverbially impecunious; & the public is so flooded with magazines that one which has neither novels nor politics nor

[91] J. M. Lappenberg, *A History of England under the Norman Kings* (trans. Thorpe) (London, 1857). Benjamin Thorpe (1782–1870) learned his linguistic skills under Rask at Copenhagen and became a somewhat literal translator and editor. His own major statement was *Ancient Laws and Institutes of England* (London, 1840).

[92] Thorpe to Freeman, 28 Dec. 1858, Freeman MSS FA1/7/761. Thorpe probably had in mind the *Geschichte von England*, 10 vols. (Hamburg, 1834–53) produced collaboratively by J. M. Lappenberg, R. Pauli and M. Brosch. He had translated in 1853 Pauli's *König Aelfred und seine Stelle in der Geschichte Englands* (Berlin, 1851).

[93] Peter Clark, 'Henry Hallam Reconsidered', *Quarterly Review*, 305 (1967), 410–19 at 418.

[94] Seeley to Delegates of Oxford University Press, 5 Dec. 1889, Seeley MSS 903/1A/2, for the financial incentive. On the depth of his commitment, note his report that he has 'got the papers on Schiller & Goethe (the last I think will attract notice) which you can have for March & April. The paper on Peace is not half-finished yet. I had thought of offering it to the Contemporary . . .' Seeley to Macmillan, 2 Jan. n.y. [?1895–6], Macmillan MSS BL Add. MS 55074 f.52.

> social improvement schemes among its interests is not considered suitable for the drawing room table.[95]

He identified a situation that would not change significantly during the period of professionalisation. Judging from reports sent to the editors by Longman after the First World War, it appears that sales of *EHR* hovered between just 650 and 800 copies during the 1920s.[96]

Victorian historians had organised themselves, in short, to a level of specialisation from which it would prove difficult to reach out to a general audience. The British Academy institutionalised that level of expertise and excellence. The Historical Association began a long (and losing) battle to modulate it. Andrew Lang noticed the tension between these objectives in the year of the Historical Association's foundation in 1906. Thinking back to the controversy between Freeman and Froude[97] he meditated on the impossibility of 'satisfy[ing] both the public (as far as there is now a public for history) and the scientific historical professors and professionals. The public, what there is of it, wants a smooth narrative of past events, told in a pleasant, positive spirit, as if the historian had been present at the battles, Parliaments, sieges, burnings, sermons, and in the cabinets of kings, and the boudoirs of queens, beautiful and wicked, or good and unlucky.'[98] It was unlucky for history itself to be caught within the web of this impossibility. Only in the 1930s, and then to a small degree, did a rival style of historiography gain any momentum. For the foreseeable future in Edwardian England, those who, like Tout and Pollard, wanted a more urgent and communicable history discovered how hard it would be to break the mould of Victorian knowledge and ignorance. When Pollard tried, as the First World War veered toward its end, to persuade Longman toward a new history of England, he found them ready enough; but they reminded him that it would not do 'to go too far in the way of reform: it is only possible to carry [school]masters and examiners a certain distance from the paths they know so well'.[99] Victorian historians beat those paths and around them an entire, sometimes closed, world had been made. Not one but two world wars would have to pass before new realities could erase those paths and permit the treading of fresh ground.

[95] Mandell Creighton to Freeman, 26 Aug. 1890, Freeman MSS FA1/7/128.

[96] See correspondence between C. J. Longman and G. N. Clark in Clark MSS 159, Bodleian Library.

[97] James Anthony Froude (1818–94). Private scholar made notorious by *Nemesis of Faith* (1849) but who occupied the Regius Chair of Modern History at Oxford for the last ten years of his life. Published extensively and controversially on Carlyle whose literary executor he was. Imperial sympathies lurk in *Oceana, or England and her Colonies* (London, 1886) and Protestant ones in his major narrative *History of England from the Fall of Wolsey to the Defeat of the Spanish Armada*, 12 vols. (London, 1856–70).

[98] Andrew Lang, 'Freeman versus Froude', *Cornhill Magazine*, NS 20 (1906), 251–63 at 251.

[99] Longman to Pollard, 16 Jul. 1918, Pollard MSS 860 box 47.

CHAPTER NINE

Specialisation and Social Utility: Disciplining English Studies

JOSEPHINE M. GUY

Most discussions today about the social organisation of knowledge would probably start by considering the expanding role of the internet, and the ways in which electronic publishing challenges traditional mechanisms of intellectual authority and the role of the university as arbiter of intellectual probity. Such concerns, moreover, may seem far removed from the production of knowledge in the late nineteenth century—a time, after all, when it was the typewriter (rather than computer) which was the latest innovation. Nonetheless it is worth noting that much of the impetus behind the use of information technology in universities has derived from a need to accommodate increasing student numbers following a dramatic (and continuing) expansion of the higher education sector, particularly in the United Kingdom. Alongside this expansion there have been fundamental reform of syllabuses and restructuring of faculty; these in turn have led to a blurring of traditional disciplinary boundaries, and, in some cases, to the mapping out of new areas of study. It is precisely here, as Amanda Anderson and Joseph Valente have recently argued, that we can appreciate the relevance of nineteenth-century discussions about the organisation of knowledge to those debates taking place today. 'What has often been lacking in our current disciplinary debates', they suggest, 'is a longer perspective that would enable us to understand better their historical conditions and developments.'[1] This statement has particular force in relation to English studies, a discipline whose status has been contested more or less continuously since its inception in the late nineteenth century, and whose disciplinary boundaries are still the focus of considerable dispute.

[1] Amanda Anderson and Joseph Valente (eds.), *Disciplinarity at the Fin de Siècle* (Princeton and Oxford, 2002), p. 1.

Mapping the connections between nineteenth-century and modern debates about the discipline of English is complicated by the fact that the history of the discipline is itself a contested issue. One reason for this state of affairs is that such histories have often been explicitly used to endorse particular views about how the modern discipline should be shaped. In this respect, the value of appealing to that 'longer perspective' enjoined by Anderson and Valente has long been recognised among polemicists in English departments, although sometimes in a manner in which history becomes a crude form of doxography—a rewriting of the past in terms which fit current political agendas. The most extreme (and influential) example of this practice was a sequence of histories of the discipline written during the 1980s.[2] In his contribution to this volume, Lawrence Goldman hints at a tendency among historians of social science to reconstruct a somewhat idealised past, one in which their discipline was characterised by a coherence and rigour which it lacks today. In the case of English, however, historians in the 1980s took a rather different path, explaining their discipline's history in a way which pointed to a need, in their view, to effect a radical break with what had gone before. That is to say, the early history of the discipline was described in terms of a process of ideological control and crude cultural engineering, in which a narrowly constructed canon of literary works, authorised by the prestige of the university, was used to socialise students into an equally narrow set of nationalist values. In this line of argument, the academic discipline of English was seen as inseparable from the rise in the late nineteenth century of a (now discredited) English nationalism. It followed that the discipline in the 1980s needed to be fundamentally reconceived in order to appeal to a wider and more politically diverse set of interests. That reconception in turn centred on a redefinition of the practice of literary criticism. Far from playing a formative role in defining the canon, critical analysis was now envisaged as a process which contested it; and it did so by revealing the ideological interests held to underlie attributions of literary identity and literary value. In Terry Eagleton's populist formulation, the modern discipline of English was viewed as a kind of metadiscipline whose goal was nothing less than 'human emancipation'.[3] In short, this new (post) modern, politically aware

[2] See, for example, Peter Widdowson (ed.), *Re-Reading English* (London, 1982); Terry Eagleton, *Literary Theory: An Introduction* (Oxford, 1983); and Brian Doyle, *English and Englishness* (London, 1989). These histories were more explicitly political than earlier studies, such as Sheldon Rothblatt's *The Revolution of the Dons* (London, 1968) and *Tradition and Change in English Liberal Education* (London, 1976).

[3] Eagleton, *Literary Theory*, p. 211. It is worth noting that this rewriting of the history of the discipline coincided with, and was in part prompted by, the introduction into literature departments of a

English studies, as detailed by critics such as Eagleton, required for its definition an old, illiberal, and oppressive past.

These histories, now themselves some twenty years old, were popular at the time, despite a number of limitations, not least of which was a tendency to be highly selective, to the point of misrepresentation, in their use of contemporary evidence.[4] More generally, they suffered from a habit of treating English in isolation from other disciplines of knowledge—a strategy which was itself born from an assumption that English was unique among disciplines. Its special understanding of the relationship between language, power, and representation was thought to afford English the status, as I have noted, of a metadiscipline which was able to critique all other disciplines of knowledge. This somewhat over-blown claim (one, it is worth noting, which was not widely recognised by those other disciplines assumed to be subordinate to, or lacking the political awareness of English[5]) in turn led to a mischaracterisation of the reasons why the discipline of English was initially dominated by philology rather than the study of literary works (a point to which I shall return). Such accounts also tended to conflate what may be called exogenous and endogenous explanations for discipline development—or rather, they tended to see only exogenous forces at work. More recent studies have gone a long way towards correcting these problems, and in the process have, unsurprisingly, given a rather different view of the formation of English as a discipline.

It is now more common to understand the development of the discipline of English in terms of wider changes in the social organisation of knowledge which took place in the late decades of the nineteenth century, particularly the twin processes of professionalisation and specialisation.[6] Of particular significance in relation to English is the requirement that professional knowledge be socially useful and at the same time difficult or specialist to the extent that the 'ordinary'

---

variety of new critical practices which today are generally referred to as 'modern critical theory'. They included, in Eagleton's case, the application of Marxist theory to literary works. These theoretical paradigms are themselves contested by some scholars, and there is now a large body of work devoted to discussing the role and value of critical theory in English studies.

[4] These limitations were first pointed out by myself and Ian Small in a series of essays written in the late 1980s and early 1990s which in turn formed the basis of *Politics and Value in English Studies* (Cambridge, 1993).

[5] One of the more amusing examples of the response by other disciplines of knowledge to the claims made by theorists in English studies is recorded in Alan Sokal and Jean Bricmont, *Literary Impostures* (London, 1998). Sokal and Bricmont are both physicists.

[6] These processes have been described in detail both by sociologists and by historians of intellectual culture. An accessible overview of them can be found in T. W. Heyck's *The Transformation of Intellectual Life in Victorian England* (London, 1982), the central argument of which is summarised by Carol Atherton. A more detailed discussion of this body of evidence is given in Guy and Small, *Politics and Value in English Studies*, pp. 51–6.

citizen will not be in a position to acquire it. It is worth emphasising at this stage that a framework which places English in relation to general criteria for disciplinary knowledge by no means represents a complete or sufficient understanding of its history. There are several other factors which need to be attended to. These include the role played by local institutional politics and practices as well as particular individuals. Contrary to the implication of some earlier histories, there is no firm evidence in the late nineteenth century of an official government or state conception of 'English', nor indeed of any centralised plan to implement it nationwide in the university curriculum (although this is not to deny a connection between the institutionalised study of English, the construction of cultural identity, and nationhood). As Carol Atherton argues in the chapter which follows, the implementation of English in university curricula was far from a coherent or unified process. On the contrary, the precise timing of the appearance of English in degree programmes, together with the foundation of the first full professorships in English, differed markedly from institution to institution, and often depended on pragmatic factors, such as the quality and availability of the prospective applicants for chairs. Her attention to previously neglected evidence, such as examination papers and memoranda surrounding chair appointments—that is, to practice rather than simply to rhetoric—reveals the process of discipline formation to be a fractious and muddled affair.

Another important and often overlooked dimension of the development of English as a discipline concerns the role played by different countries and nationalities. Generalisations about the rise of English studies in the late nineteenth century have often elided differences between higher education in England and Scotland,[7] and, more especially, between England and the USA. John Guillory, for example, has written about the 'Anglo-American' university, an abstraction which makes little sense to the British reader, and which understates the different ways in which British and American universities were (and are) established, regulated and funded.[8] A case has also been made by Gauri

[7] An important exception here is the work of Robert Crawford in *Devolving English Literature* (Oxford, 1994) and Crawford (ed.), *The Scottish Invention of English Literature* (Cambridge, 1998).

[8] Guillory, for example, has recently described the institutional position of English in the 1890s as one in which 'four different disciplinary practices (philology, literary history, belles lettres, composition) came to cohabit under the roof of one department'—a description which may hold true for America, but which is inapplicable to England were there was little literary criticism until the 1920s (and only then at Cambridge University), and no 'composition' (this last practice is still relatively rare in English universities). See J. Guillory, 'Literary study and the modern system of disciplines', in Anderson and Valente (eds.), *Disciplinarity at the Fin de Siècle*, pp. 19–43. The historical relationship between endowments, state grants, state regulation, and the intellectual independence of universities (in issues such as the design of curricula, appointments, and maintenance of academic standards) is complex, and differs between countries and between institutions within countries.

Viswanathan for the formative role of colonial India in the creation of the discipline of English. Viswanathan has further observed that the task of integrating these various domestic and international narratives—which have, after all, only recently been recognised—has yet to be undertaken.[9] Finally, it is also necessary to acknowledge that the processes which constitute professionalisation and specialisation are themselves complex and open to a variety of interpretations and evaluations.[10] These caveats aside, it is nevertheless the case that attention to the twin demands of social utility and specialisation are a helpful starting point in understanding the formation of the discipline of English, for they go some way towards explaining some initially puzzling elements about its early history.

The main puzzle concerns the fact that compared to several other humanities disciplines English gained its status as a discrete discipline of knowledge relatively late. It is not until the 1880s that there was sustained agitation for an autonomous discipline of English, and even when the subject was institutionalised in universities in the 1890s and 1900s, for several years it remained parasitic upon other disciplines for its skills and methods. As Carol Atherton shows, a study of early syllabuses, reading lists, and examination papers reveals that for much of the late nineteenth century and well into the early decades of the twentieth, university English looked a lot more like a branch of history or of classics than a discipline in its own right. Frank Turner's observations about the status of classics in the nineteenth century are relevant here: the fact that many proponents for a new discipline of English (particularly one centred on literary studies) looked so insistently to the study of classical culture for methodological rigour is testimony to the relative security which that area of knowledge enjoyed.[11] (And of course it may also

[9] See Gauri Viswanathan, *Masks of Conquest: Literary Study and British Rule in India* (New York, 1989) and 'Subjecting English and the question of representation', in Anderson and Valente (eds.), *Disciplinarity at the Fin de Siècle*, pp. 177–95.

[10] There is a very considerable body of sociological research examining the ways in which professional knowledge is defined, authorised, and policed. Moreover, and as one might expect, it encompasses a wide spectrum of opinion ranging from Foucauldian theorists who see professional knowledge as inseparable from questions of power and control, and functionalists who tend to view the specialisation of knowledge as a precondition of modernity. Moreover, there are also theorists who straddle both positions: while they acknowledge the necessity for specialisation and professionalisation, they nevertheless have anxieties about the specific ways in which particular professions are regulated and the ways in which the knowledge they produce is used. It is unfortunately beyond the remit of this chapter to enter into these complex debates. That said, it is worth noting that the general impetus towards specialisation and professionalisation in the late nineteenth century, and the role of these processes in explaining which particular bodies of knowledge came to be seen as disciplines, is not in itself contested.

[11] One of the most vociferous polemicists for the interdependence of literary studies and classics was John Churton Collins; his contribution to the founding of the discipline is discussed in detail by Anthony Kearney in *The Louse on the Locks of Literature* (Edinburgh, 1986), and more briefly by Carol Atherton in the chapter which follows.

be due to the fact that most aspiring professors of English would themselves have received an education in classics, hence their assumption that it presented an appropriate model of professional practice in the humanities.) At any rate, the transition from what one early twentieth-century commentator despairingly called 'home reading' to a subject-area considered sufficiently complex and sophisticated to be studied within a university by professionals—this was by no means a straightforward or self-evident process.[12] And it is precisely this sense of belatedness and insecurity which is the most striking feature of the founding of English in the late nineteenth century, and which is the one most difficult to reconcile with the proposition that its inception as a discipline was politically driven and centrally controlled.

As I have hinted, a common explanation for the late introduction of English into university degree programmes is made in terms of the rise, at that time (that is, the 1880s) of English nationalism. In this view, the institutionalisation of English is seen to be part of a larger project of cultural renewal, in its turn prompted by an alleged crisis in imperialism and anxieties about cultural degeneration. Simply put, this argument holds that the moral qualities of literary works permitted literary study to be seen as an important repository of national values. This sort of argument, which attends to exogenous factors in discipline development, is problematic for two reasons. It ignores the fact that the main source of hostility towards English actually came from within universities themselves—that is, from those very conservative elites whose values are typically identified with English nationalism. It also neglects to mention that the modern discipline of English encompasses three quite different practices—text-editing, literary history and literary criticism—and that attitudes towards the professionalisation of these practices in the late nineteenth century were by no means uniform.[13] In brief, it was relatively unproblematic to accommodate text-editing and literary history to the new criteria of professionalisation, for both could in principle (if not always in practice) draw explicitly on methodologies and skills developed in other professionalised humanities disciplines such as history.[14] Paradoxically,

[12] The comment occurs during an address by F. W. Moorman, Professor of English Language at the University of Leeds, to the English Association in 1914; see the *Proceedings of the English Association*, no. 22 (Feb. 1914), 11.

[13] The study of modern English language did not become part of the discipline of English studies until much later in the twentieth century, and even then departments of linguistics were often established quite separately from departments of English literature on the grounds that the former subject belonged to the sciences rather than humanities.

[14] This is not to imply that in the late nineteenth century there was necessarily any uniformity in the practices of literary history and text-editing—far from it. At this time there were plenty of examples of histories, some even written by academics, such as Edmund Gosse's *From Shakespeare to Pope*

though, the very fact that such practices could be aligned with those of another discipline tended to weaken their claims to disciplinary autonomy. In other words, it was not the historiographical skills of literary historians, nor the bibliographical credentials of text-editors, that was at issue so much as the particular nature of their object of study: to make a strong case for an autonomous discipline of English it was necessary to establish the 'specialness' of literature, and so the uniqueness of what constituted the knowledge and skills required to identify a given text as a *literary* work. These were tasks which lay within the purview of literary critics, rather than text-editors or historians (both of whom tended to work with given definitions of literary value and identity).

Literary works had of course been read in universities for many years prior to the founding of English as an autonomous discipline. Indeed literature was read, studied, and written about in a variety of educational contexts throughout the nineteenth century. Significantly, English literature was a key component in the idea of a liberal education promoted by cultural critics such as Matthew Arnold in the 1860s and which was being implemented from the second half of the century onwards in a variety of civic colleges; likewise lectures on literary subjects were popular on the metropolitan and regional lecture circuits.[15] Despite the obvious cultural value attached to literary study, however, the first professors of English were philologists, and it was philology (which in late nineteenth-century Britain referred to the study of the history of the language, and of culture via language, rather than of literature) which was initially seen as the body of knowledge which would define the new discipline. This circumstance significantly complicates the role played by civic colleges in the founding of English as a discipline, because the 'English' which was taught in those institutions, and in extension lectures, was emphatically not considered to be a form of study worthy of professionalisation. Why was this? If the study of literature had been acknowledged as an important component of a general education, and if literary works had the

(Cambridge, 1885), which did not even attempt to meet the new standards of scholarly rigour. For a discussion of the role of scholarship in literary history in the late nineteenth century, see Ian Small, *Conditions for Criticism: Authority, Knowledge, and Literature in the Late Nineteenth Century* (Oxford, 1991), pp. 57–63.

[15] In the late nineteenth century there were several kinds of public lectures, and literary topics figured in all of them: there was the widespread system of extension lecturing, organised by the universities; there were also numerous professional lecture circuits, run by agents, and used by aspiring writers chiefly as a means of making money and placing their name before the public; finally, there were lectures organised by various philanthropic societies which were designed to bring learning to those who did not have access to traditional educational institutions.

potential to make a direct contribution towards defining a national identity through the process of canon-formation, then why was literary study explicitly rejected as a model for the new discipline?

The principal reason why philologists, rather than literary critics, occupied nearly all the new academic posts was because they were best able to meet the twin criteria of specialisation and social utility which, by the late decades of the century, had come to define and authorise professional knowledge as a whole. Philologists could lay claim to a discrete and specialist body of knowledge—one based on empirical research—as well as a set of specialist practices, and they could also argue that by teaching linguistic competence and the history of language and culture, the knowledge they produced was socially useful. It has been noted that in the nineteenth century British academics from a variety of disciplines tended to look to Continental models of disciplinary practice and authority; this is certainly true of philology which drew extensively from German scholarship. By contrast, those who wanted the study of literature to be the central activity of the new discipline were unable to argue convincingly that the reading of literary works required specialist skills or specialist knowledge. John Morley, an enthusiastic advocate for the academic study of literature, noted ruefully that when compared to the sciences, the desire for a literary education could all too easily be seen as savouring 'a little of self-indulgence, and sentimentality, and other objectionable qualities'.[16] Ironically the very grounds which had been used by figures such as Matthew Arnold to define the social importance of literature as a part of a liberal education—the idea that reading literary works could inculcate moral values in readers and thus socialise them into the values of their culture—disabled the parallel professional demand for specialisation. The paradox was that if the moral knowledge allegedly embodied in literary works was so complex that it could only be understood by specialists, then literature itself forfeited any claim it had to be socially useful.

Nineteenth-century critics could have argued that they acted as mediators of this moral knowledge, and that their specialist expertise lay not in their moral acuity but in their superior understanding of literary devices or literary language. Their role would therefore be to show how literary works embodied such knowledge. And the function of the professional literary critic would be to 'de-code' literary works—to teach the public how to read so that all might have access to the moral insights which literary works offered. This kind of argument had been made by philosophers such as John Stuart Mill as early

[16] John Morley, 'On the Study of Literature', in *Studies in Literature* (London, 1891), p. 199.

as the 1830s. However, many other critics had taken a directly opposite tack, suggesting that if a particular work required such decoding then it could not properly be called literature in the first instance. So novels or poems which were judged to be difficult or obscure were routinely condemned, and their authors were exhorted to learn how to write, as Arnold put it, 'with clearness of arrangement, rigour of development, [and] simplicity of style'.[17] In 1876, Benjamin Jowett, deploring the obscurities to be found in 'modern poets', commented that 'the use of language ought in every generation to become clearer and clearer'.[18] In the late decades of the nineteenth century a number of literary societies were set up in order to explicate for a popular audience the work of writers thought difficult but morally instructive. Many, however, were ridiculed for their amateurishness, and this disparagement almost certainly mitigated against such activity being seen as a potentially professional practice which should be located in a university. A case in point was the work of the often lampooned Browning Society. Founded in 1881 to explicate the work of the poet Robert Browning (who had been criticised for obscurity throughout his career), the society was popularly seen as a haven for old maids and clergymen, and has been described by one modern historian as 'the most satirized institution in England'.[19] Of course not all nineteenth-century literary societies were objects of ridicule. Organisations such as the 'Early English Text Society' founded in 1864 by Frederick Furnivall, were much more respectable and respected institutions. Significantly, however, Furnivall was also a member of the Philological Society, and such authority that he (and his amateur colleagues) enjoyed can almost certainly be attributed to the fact that their editorial treatment of literature—their attempt, that is, to build up a scholarly archive of literary works—explicitly mimicked the practices of other newly professionalised humanities disciplines, such as history. They were not, that is, setting themselves up as professional *literary* critics.

In general terms, in the late nineteenth century it proved extraordinarily difficult for aspiring professors of English literature to define literary study in terms which required for it a specialist set of practices which could be taught and examined. We can begin to appreciate the difficulties involved by returning for a moment to Matthew Arnold—that writer who may seem to have

[17] This prescription for linguistic clarity was often repeated by Arnold, and is elaborated most clearly in the preface to the first edition of *Poems* (London, 1853) which was later reprinted in *Irish Essays and Others* (London, 1882).

[18] Benjamin Jowett, *The Republic of Plato* (Oxford, 1876), p. 1.

[19] See William S. Peterson, *Interrogating the Oracle: A History of the London Browning Society* (Athens, Ohio, 1969), p. 173.

made the best case for professionalising English by attributing such social importance to reading literature. Ironically, though, it turns out that his definition of criticism, as a practice which was informed by what he termed 'the best that is thought and known in the world', was actually a problematic one for professionalisation, because it could be applied to any area of knowledge, to politics, religion, or what he sometimes called 'affairs'. Arnold's 'critical faculty', defined as 'the free play of the mind upon all subjects', had no special force as a methodology for studying literature; and this in turn implied that the study of literature itself did not require any particular, let alone unique, sort of skills. Even more ironically, Arnold had been sceptical about the possibility that contemporary critics, in England at least, were even capable of engaging in the rigorously disinterested practice he had in mind, commenting disparagingly that there 'was little original sympathy in the practical English nature' for 'real criticism'.[20] Here it is worth emphasising that Arnold's conception of the critic's role was never as a simple explicator or interpreter of texts (literary or otherwise); quite the opposite. His ambition to revalue criticism as a first- rather than second-order practice required him to separate the role of the critic from that of the creative writer. In this respect, he defined the critic's role in a manner more akin to what we might today term the intellectual—someone who, through the disinterested play of his mind upon all forms of cultural production, provided the raw materials (those 'best ideas') for creative writers to work with. Arnold took it as axiomatic that it was then the responsibility of the novelist or poet to ensure that they represented those ideas in forms which were both accessible and entertaining to a general readership.

Although Arnold had stressed the social value of reading literary works, and the cultural importance of criticism, his arguments were of little use for those who wanted to define a professional practice of literary criticism. Correspondence between Arnold and John Churton Collins, who (as Carol Atherton explains) was one of the principal campaigners for an autonomous discipline of English, reveals that Arnold had no sympathy for such a project. While he supported the idea that the study of literary works ought to form a part of the *Literae Humaniores* examination—'I have no difficulty in saying that I should like to see standard English Authors joined to the standard Authors of Greek and Latin literature'—he was very much against the idea of what he termed a 'new' or 'separate' school for modern literature or modern languages. He rather favoured the revival of 'the old examination in

[20] Arnold, 'The Function of Criticism at the Present Time', in *The Complete Works of Matthew Arnold, Vol III. Lectures and Essays in Criticism* (Michigan, 1962), pp. 284, 268.

honours, with philosophy, history and belles lettres all included in it'. Arnold wished literature to be understood not as a new specialism, but in terms of what he referred to as the 'large sense of the word', by which he meant the literature of 'Greece and Rome'. A further, and more revealing reason for his opposition to Churton Collins's project was that Arnold had 'no confidence in those who at the Universities regulate studies, degrees and honours. To regulate these matters great experience of the world, steadiness, simplicity, breadth of view are desirable.' Arnold went on: 'I do not see how those who actually regulate them can well have these qualifications.' It is clear here that Arnold's whole conception of criticism—of intellectual activity, even—was quite at odds with the processes of professionalisation and specialisation that had come to dominate universities; as he warned Churton Collins, 'I fear ... that while you are seeking an object altogether good—the completing of the old and great degree in Arts—you may obtain something which will not only not be that, but will be a positive hindrance to it.'[21]

By the late 1870s, however, Arnold's concept of cultural criticism had begun to be superseded by an alternative definition of a critical practice, one which was understood in terms of an appreciation of the aesthetic rather than moral values of literary works, and for which personal integrity and uniqueness of temperament were seen as the essential qualities of a literary–critical sensibility. In the hands of the most important advocate for this programme, the Oxford don, Walter Pater, literary study did finally come to be defined as a properly specialist activity, one accessible to what he termed in his 1889 essay 'Style', 'the select few'.[22] However, Pater's specialised few should not be confused with the specialist activities housed within universities. By defining his 'select few' as, in his words, 'men of a finer thread' who were in possession of a 'special kind of temperament', Pater effectively restricted the appreciation of literature to a tiny elite, but it was one whose critical authority resided in a quality—that notion of temperament or personality—which was innate and therefore by definition unteachable. Pater had attended to the role of scholarship in literary appreciation, talking of his own practice as that of a 'scholar writing for the scholarly'; but he defined

[21] Cecil Y. Lang (ed.), *The Letters of Matthew Arnold. Vol. VI. 1885–1888* (Charlottesville and Virginia, 2002), pp. 213 and 245–6. Interestingly, in this same correspondence, dated Oct. and Dec. 1886, Arnold also confessed to his lack of political influence and indeed interest in the whole matter: 'to do these things one needs position and power, and I, in spite of what you kindly say, have neither:—have no longer even the wish to have either' (213). Arnold's arduous work as Inspector of Schools, a post which he was soon to resign, seems to have wearied him of educational debates.

[22] Walter Pater, 'Style', *Fortnightly Review* (Dec. 1888), 728–43.

scholarship in terms of a particular kind of attitude—that of serious contemplation, or what he referred to as '*mind* in style'—rather than in relation to specific skills or knowledge.[23] In short, Pater's notion of specialness ran counter to the very processes of specialisation which, at that time, had come to define professional knowledge—the use of formal academic language, and the requirement for evidence to be corroborated and verified by agreed procedures and standards.[24]

For most of his life Pater earned his living by working in a university (Oxford) where he taught classics, yet many of his publications were on literary and artistic subjects. They included a novel, a collection of short stories, and some volumes of critical essays. Pater self-consciously dissociated his activity as a critic from his work as an academic. He was always willing to concede that literary works were widely read by the general public, and he was apparently untroubled by the fact that such reading occurred without the intervening guidance of an academic or professional. In Pater's view, many people might read a work such as Shakespeare's *Measure for Measure*; but only a 'select few' could possibly appreciate it *as art*. In other words, Pater's concept of aesthetic criticism was self-consciously exclusionary, and as such ran exactly counter to the demand that professional knowledge be socially useful. Pater, that is, was no more willing than Arnold to concede a secondary role to the critic—as an interpreter or explicator of texts for others. The only person Pater's critic answered to was, logically speaking, him or herself. Pater's notion of aesthetic criticism was thus designed not to mediate literary knowledge to the mass, but to preserve it for a cultural elite. Moreover, that elite was defined quite differently from the professionals who were in the process of dominating universities. This circumstance is an important reminder that in the late nineteenth century intellectual authority had not been totally collapsed into professionalism. Pater's publications had relatively

[23] Pater, 'Style', 731–5. Pater's scepticism about the possibility of an objective or abstract account of literariness in fact extended to all forms of knowledge: 'To the modern spirit', he argued, 'nothing is, or can be rightly known, except relatively and under conditions.' He went on to explain that 'truth' did not mean the 'truth of eternal outlines ascertained once for all, but a world of fine gradations and subtly linked conditions, shifting intricately as we ourselves change—and bids us, by a constant clearing of the organs of observation and perfecting of analysis, to make what we can of these'. ('Coleridge' in *Appreciations* (1889; London, 1910), pp. 66–8.) Here Pater acknowledged the scientific demand that authoritative knowledge be based on observable and verifiable facts, but then proceeded to undermine the epistemological basis of empiricism by suggesting that the complexity of man as a 'physical organism' subject to constant change made such certainties impossible.

[24] Pater's attitude towards the new mechanisms of intellectual authority which had come to define professional knowledge has been discussed in detail by Ian Small in *Conditions for Criticism*, pp. 91–111.

buoyant sales,[25] and the cultural authority which he enjoyed as a critic was largely unrelated to his university post. At the same time, though, Pater's explicit separation of his criticism from his academic work forces us to recognise the extent to which professionalisation had come to dominate university practices. Pater's university career was largely unsuccessful, and this failure was not unrelated to the institutional disapproval of his critical writing, particularly by Benjamin Jowett, the Master of Balliol College, Professor of Greek and one of the most powerful figures at Oxford.[26]

There is one further factor to attend to in trying to explain why the study of literary works did not become the basis of the new discipline of English in the late nineteenth century. The 1880s and 1890s were decades which saw a significant growth of leisure-time, especially for the working and lower-middle classes. And the industry which above all others catered to these newly empowered groups was publishing, especially the publishing of literature. As James Raven explains in his contribution to this volume, the transformation in printing capacity in the 1870s and the increasingly energetic capitalisation of the industry to meet growing consumer demand, led to a dramatic increase in numbers and kinds of books, particularly cheap reprints of popular fiction. At this time, then, there certainly appears to have been a demand for information about what to read, and how to read it critically. Cheap papers such as the *Pall Mall Gazette*, for example, carried contributions on topics such as 'The Hundred Best Books' as well as brief lists of 'What Not to Read'. There is evidence, too, of considerable anxiety about a decline in taste due to the quality of the fiction which the general public was reading. In 1883, the *Nineteenth Century* reproduced a Memorandum by Sir Henry Taylor addressed to the Government concerning a proposal to set up what was termed an 'Academy of Literature'. The need for such an institution was set out somewhat baldly:

> The increase of wealth and the extension of education have been adverse in more ways than one to studious reading and sound learning. They have produced what

[25] Sales figures for Pater's works are provided by Robert Seiler in *The Book Beautiful: Walter Pater and the House of Macmillan* (London, 1999). *Appreciations*, Pater's volume of literary criticism, had an initial print-run of 1,000 copies; a second edition of 1,500 copies was brought out just a month later; third and fourth editions and an *Edition de Luxe* appeared in 1895, 1901 and 1900 respectively; there were also several reprints of these editions usually in runs of between 500 and 1000.

[26] The institutional difficulties experienced by Pater at Oxford, and the blocking of his career by Jowett, are hinted at by Richard Ellmann in *Oscar Wilde* (London, 1987) and described in detail by Billie Andrew Inman in 'Estrangement and Connection: Walter Pater, Benjamin Jowett, and William M. Hardinge', in Laurel Brake and Ian Small (eds.), *Pater in the 1990s* (Greensboro, NC, 1991), pp. 1–20.

> may be not unfitly called a reading populace—a multitude of readers, who, standing in point of taste and information midway between the learned and the illiterate classes, constitute the great body of customers for books.[27]

Taylor went on to claim that these new sorts of readers were 'debasing the material of literature'; and he was particularly critical of the role played by popular journalism in enfranchising such taste by pandering to its purchasing power. Surprisingly, the date of the original Memorandum turns out to have been February 1835; as Taylor explains, it had been drafted originally at the instigation of the poet, Robert Southey, and at the time had been given favourable consideration by Sir Robert Peel, only to fall by the wayside when Peel's ministry collapsed. In reprinting the Memorandum nearly fifty years later, the *Nineteenth Century* implied that the situation, far from improving, had in fact grown considerably worse, with the continued enlargement both of the reading public and of the popular press. There are numerous articles in the monthlies and quarterlies in the 1880s which testify to a similar anxiety—that an increasing readership had led to a decline in literary standards which in turn had brought about a weakening of the critic's authority. For example, in 1882, the *Fortnightly Review* published an essay by the best-selling author, Grant Allen, entitled pessimistically, 'The Decay of Criticism'. Allen was actually responding to an alleged crisis in criticism in France as documented in a recent number of the *Revue des deux mondes*. However, his piece made frequent comparisons with the situation in England, which he saw as little better. He singled out the pernicious influence of popular journalism, arguing in a manner which echoed Taylor's words first uttered half a century earlier, that 'current criticism' was of 'a very empirical and hasty character', and that it was 'absurdly inadequate for anything like real criticism!' Allen despaired at what he termed 'the depths of human inanity that are poured daily out of the British printing-press', and of the complicity of the general reading public in the 'decadence of newspaper criticism' that had resulted from the overwhelming numbers of books that were published. 'Who can seriously sit down to examine critically the mass of trash that is turned out daily in London alone?' he mused. 'And when the reviewer

[27] Sir Henry Taylor, 'An Academy of Literature for Great Britain', *Nineteenth Century*, 14 (Nov. 1883), 782. It is worth pointing out that the term 'literature' of the title was understood by Taylor in the wider sense invoked by Arnold—that is, to mean 'letters' or 'writing'. On the other hand, the detailed proposals for the institution, modelled in part on the *Académie Française*, revealed that it was to consist of four separate divisions, one of which broadly corresponds to the study of literature understood in the narrower sense more common today: 'one for physical and mathematical science, a second for moral and political, a third for general literature, and a fourth for classical and antiquarian learning' (786).

comes unexpectedly across a genuine pearl, who is going to listen to the voice of one crying in the wilderness of anonymity, and proclaiming that he, the anonymous one, had at last discovered a real live author?'[28]

The disquieting similarity between the polemic of Taylor and Allen, separated initially by nearly fifty years, should have been a bracing lesson for the aspiring professional critic in the 1880s. It was an uncomfortable reminder that the general reading public, though apparently lacking in refinement and literary taste, had been remarkably impervious to a serious critical education. If Taylor's original Memorandum had identified (somewhat prematurely, perhaps) an urgent need for professional critics to mould the taste of the general reader, then Allen's piece spoke eloquently of the general reader's consistent disregard for such advice: 'The public does not want criticism', he complained, 'because it does not want literature.'[29] It has often been assumed that the proliferation of readers and books in the late nineteenth century would have automatically opened up a space where the professional academic critic could flourish. At no other time, it might seem, was there a more pressing need for the critic both as judge and as explicator of literary works. In such an argument, the failure to establish literary study at the centre of the new discipline of English is understood primarily as a failure of the would-be professionals to make their argument—that is, the failure of campaigners such as John Churton Collins to define a critical practice which adequately met current criteria of professional knowledge. But this is almost certainly only half the story. It is worth reiterating here that Allen's gloom over current standards of critical writing was not accompanied by a call for a new kind of *academic* critic to resolve the crisis; in fact he saw the specialisation then 'rampant' at Oxford to be a source of 'menace'.[30] His argument was rather about two different sorts of journalism: the hack reviewing to be found in the popular penny papers (which he deplored), and the marginalisation of a more serious, belletrist kind of criticism which had traditionally appeared in the expensive monthlies and quarterlies. By the late nineteenth century such periodicals were occupying an increasingly precarious position in a literary market place which had become much more diversified and

[28] Grant Allen, 'The Decay of Criticism', *Fortnightly Review*, 31 NS (March 1882), 347–9.

[29] Ibid., 349.

[30] Ibid., 350. Allen went on to identify the movement towards specialisation with German scholarship, complaining that 'Englishmen' were 'a little over-anxious to covert ourselves forthwith into the image of the fashionable Teutonic monographist'. He further suggested, in terms very reminiscent of Arnold, that 'all embracing generalisations of the world', 'a broad philosophic temperament', and 'a certain kindred noble expansiveness ... wholly alien to the microscopic pettiness of modern specialism' were 'our own English traits' (351).

competitive. And this in turn suggested that the audience for the kind of serious criticism which Allen envisaged was waning in significance (if not in actual numbers), a circumstance which in turn hints that even if universities had produced a new academic profession of critics, if they had indeed succeeded in defining a codifiable and teachable set of literary critical skills, the general reading public might still have been uninterested in what they had to offer. Another way of putting this is to say that the concept of social utility is defined not simply by producers of specialist knowledge but also by its users, and in the late nineteenth century it was not at all clear who the users of literary critical-knowledge were or could have been.[31]

The fact that in the late nineteenth century the activity of reading, especially of fiction, was increasingly associated with leisure worked strongly against the authority of the professional or academic critic, as Allen himself somewhat bitterly recognised.[32] The general reader might appreciate a list of the year's best books, or a quick plot summary of the latest novel—that is, precisely the sort of information provided by the popular reviewer of the *Pall Mall Gazette* (and by the Sunday supplements today). But why would the same reader want (or need) to be told 'how to read'; on what grounds would they prefer the opinions of an academic critic to their own? Oscar Wilde, for a long time a reviewer for the *Pall Mall Gazette*, caught this paradox perfectly in his 1895 play *The Importance of Being Earnest* when one character comments to another: 'Literary Criticism is not your forte dear fellow. Don't try it. You should leave that to people who haven't been at a University.' We can see this simply as a joke, inspired in part by the sour grapes of an Oxford graduate who failed to gain a college fellowship. But jokes only work at this level if they resonate culturally. Wilde tapped into exactly that sentiment which ensured that in the late nineteenth century the new English departments, and

[31] It is important to acknowledge that the general reader is not the only possible user of the literary knowledge provided by academic critics—teachers in primary and secondary education are also beneficiaries, as are those in a variety of other professions, including the civil service, which require generalised skills in literacy and analytical thinking. However, the fact that training in a variety of humanities disciplines (such as history and philosophy, for example) is seen to provide similar sorts of skills is clearly of no help in establishing a particular case for the academic study of literature. The relationship between the needs of the general public and the kinds of literary knowledge produced by departments of English has often been overlooked, particularly in the last two decades.

[32] It is worth noting in passing that the sort of literature which seems to best lend itself to critical explication—poetry—was apparently in decline in the late nineteenth century in that numerous writers testify to the difficulty in finding publishers for new volumes of poetry, and publishers themselves comment on the fact such books were no longer profitable because their readership was so small. The conundrum here was that those readers who appreciated difficult or complex works of literature had little need for critics to interpret them, while those who required such explication were unlikely to be attracted to such works in the first instance.

their new degree programmes, were dominated by the work of philologists and textual editors: it was only their work which could claim to be both specialist and to serve larger social purposes. No one, it seemed, but a small elite either needed or wanted the services of professional literary critics. Seen from this perspective, Pater's effective privatisation of literary criticism, his attempt to remove it from both the new processes of professionalism as well as the increasing commodification of culture as epitomised in the growth of newspaper reviewing, is entirely understandable.[33]

I suggested earlier that interest in the history of English as a discipline has generally been prompted by the relevance it has for the way the discipline is conceived today. I want briefly to return to this issue. Regardless of how we view the processes of professionalisation and specialisation, their impact on universities, and on the way knowledge produced in universities is authorised and valued, is undeniable. Currently there is a crisis in academic publishing in the area of literary studies so much so that many publishing houses (including many university presses) are scaling down their commitment to the literary monograph because the sales of these works are steadily declining. Today, as in the late nineteenth century, there is strong evidence of a cultural demand for literature itself (sales of fiction, including 'the classics', remain strong) and an audience for writing about literature, especially literary biography. Nonetheless there is not much of an audience for the writing about literature produced by universities, much of which has become so specialised and arcane in its terminology, that even members of the profession do not read each other's work. In 1882 Allen observed:

> There are still critics—ay, and good ones too. But they cannot stem the tide of public taste: they find themselves slowly stranded and isolated on their own little critical islets. Their authority is only recognised within a small sphere of picked intellects, and does not affect the general current of the popular mind. They have reputations, but they have not influence. Some, addressing themselves to the narrow circle of experts, appear but rarely in print.[34]

Allen, who was paraphrasing his French source here, thought this too harsh an account of the state of criticism in England—too harsh in 1882, but not, perhaps, too harsh in 2002. It would be pernicious to name a particular academic literary monograph, yet there are any number of recent publications

[33] I have described Pater's reaction to the growth of a consumerist attitude towards reading in 'Aesthetics, Economics and Commodity Culture: Theorizing Value in Late Nineteenth-Century Britain', *English Literature in Transition*, 42 (1999), 143–71. The general relationship between the processes of professionalisation and the development of consumer culture in the late nineteenth century has yet to be adequately explored.

[34] Allen, 'The Decay of Criticism', 340.

which answer to Allen's description. The acute problem for English studies (certainly for literary studies) is that today, as in the 1880s, the largest potential group of users of the knowledge which the profession produces—the general reader—has no good reason to accept or prefer the professional's interpretation of a literary work, or the professional's views about which literary works are most valuable. The general reader will almost certainly not be persuaded that reading literature is as difficult as some academic critics claim. So while an academic monograph on Charles Dickens might have sales of 500, annual world sales of his actual works are well over a million. Certain late nineteenth-century commentators on English—and I include here both the philologists and critics such as Pater—recognised this circumstance very well. Both groups (albeit for very different reasons) understood that reading literature, although a valuable experience for an individual, was not an activity which could easily sustain systematic enquiry, and this meant that there was no body of information which might be authorised as 'literary knowledge', and thus widely accepted as a pre-requisite for an appropriate literary understanding.

Modern academics have continued to struggle with this conundrum, and attempts to define the value of literary study continue to fall foul of the criteria for professional knowledge. Some academics take up where their colleagues in the 1980s left off—they continue to make large claims for their subject, seeing it as a kind of meta-discipline in which a specialist object of study virtually disappears. Others make interpretation increasingly difficult by grounding it in ever more detailed historical knowledge, or justifying it by an over-elaborate theoretical apparatus. The first tactic, by defining criticism as a form of general political understanding, satisfies the criterion of social utility but forfeits specialisation; the second assigns priority to specialisation to such an extent that the knowledge produced no longer has much use for the general reader. Rarely do the extremes meet. Ironically contemporary academics, such as Harold Bloom, John Sutherland and David Lodge, who did (and still do) write for the general public are often derided by their professional colleagues. Today, as in the nineteenth century, some of the most influential writing about literature continues to take place outside of, in spite of, and sometimes in opposition to, professional practices in universities. The review columns of Sunday newspapers, together with television and radio programmes, and the popularity of informal reading groups, are probably more influential in shaping public taste than collections of academic essays. This is a healthy reminder that in the twenty-first century (as in the late nineteenth) professional critics still have to compete for authority with non-professional groups.

Whether this circumstance is viewed positively or negatively depends a great deal on the significance which we give to the knowledge which certain professions produce, and also on the way we view their claims to authority. In the 1980s it was a perception that their authority was in crisis that led certain modern academics in English studies to take such a interest in their discipline's history. A commonplace of that history, as I have suggested, was to see a conservatism in the narrow way in which the first professors of English conceived of their new discipline. However, the assumption in the nineteenth century that philology and textual criticism would provide the most sound basis for professionalisation may have been more far-sighted than some modern commentators are prepared to acknowledge. The one area of research in English studies which has remained fairly secure over the past hundred years, in the sense that it constitutes both a specialist body of knowledge and practices underpinned by a sophisticated theoretical apparatus, *and* that it is also of use to the general reader, is textual scholarship. The production of reliable, scholarly editions, which often provide the basis for popular paper-back texts, is considered to be both academically and generally useful—scholarly editions, that is, provide the conditions for *all* critical practices, for the amateur, professional, or 'home reader'. Moreover, of all the activities which take place in modern departments of English, it is the one practice which would be most easily recognised and valued by our nineteenth-century predecessors.

CHAPTER TEN

The Organisation of Literary Knowledge: The Study of English in the Late Nineteenth Century

CAROL ATHERTON

The last two decades have witnessed a number of concerns about the existence of a 'crisis in English studies',[1] a sense that traditional assumptions about the nature and purpose of the study of English literature are being eroded by a version of the discipline that is much more fragmentary and uncertain. This model of disciplinary development has a tendency to see this 'crisis' as a new phenomenon, brought about by such factors as the rise of literary theory, the expansion of the literary canon, and a concomitant questioning of both the central subject matter of English and the manner in which this body of knowledge is studied and evaluated. Yet behind this model there is also a notion that there was a time when the discipline of English Literature was secure: that there was, at some point, a stable and commonly held set of beliefs about what the discipline should involve, and what it intended to achieve. This survey of the arguments surrounding the early years of English in English universities intends to demonstrate that such stability is hard to find, and will argue that for the first few decades of its existence, the discipline was riven by suspicion and dissent. These conflicts suggest that the perceived 'crisis' within contemporary English studies may have its roots in a much older set of debates.

In the previous chapter, Josephine Guy outlined the tendency of historians of English studies to interpret the discipline's history in the light of contemporary political concerns. Such interpretations frequently predicate themselves on the belief that the subject grew from a solid, unified set of foundations whose underlying assumptions must now be treated with

[1] This notion has been discussed by Chris Baldick, *The Social Mission of English Criticism, 1848–1932* (Oxford, 1987), pp. 1–2; by Terry Eagleton, 'The Enemy Within', *NATE News* (Summer 1991), 5; and by Gary Day, in *Textual Practice*, 6 (1992), 513–19, among others.

suspicion. For Chris Baldick, the 'rewriting' of the discipline of English that began in the early 1980s was part of an attempt to deconstruct the 'lazy' ideologies on which attitudes to English are based—in particular, 'the assumption that the existing institutions and values of society are natural and eternal rather than artificial and temporary'.[2] Terry Eagleton, in his hugely influential *Literary Theory: An Introduction* (1983), describes the study of literature as an 'ideological enterprise' that would 'rehearse the masses in the habits of pluralistic thought and feeling', being 'admirably well-fitted to carry through the ideological task which religion left off'.[3] More recently, Peter Widdowson has described the teaching of literature as 'an ideologically-driven initiative to "humanise" and "civilise" potentially disruptive elements in a developing class-stratified society'.[4] Such interpretations have created a paradigmatic history of the 'rise of English studies' as a process driven by social rather than intellectual ends, in which the emerging discipline was seen, unproblematically, as 'uniquely suited to a mission of national cultivation'.[5]

It is true that the emergence of English as an academic subject in the nineteenth century was accompanied by a particular brand of humanist rhetoric, and that such rhetoric is highly amenable to political interpretations. In 1826, the Reverend Hugh James Rose, one of the founders of King's College in London, stated that the study of literature could 'correct the taste … strengthen the judgement … [and] instruct us in the wisdom of men better than ourselves'. Later in the century, John Churton Collins, who led a campaign on behalf of English at the University of Oxford, claimed that the study of literature might contribute 'to the formation of sound conclusions on social and political questions; to right feeling and right thinking in all that appertains to morality and religion; to refinement in judgment, taste, and sentiment, to all, in short, which constitutes in the proper sense of the term the education of the British citizen'.[6] Such rhetoric has become central to an interpretation of English as what is often termed 'the poor man's Classics',[7] a subject that was at once both accessible and elevating, designed to promote harmony between social groups, deference to one's superiors, and a belief in the greatness of the British Empire. Yet in emphasising the social function of literary

[2] Baldick, *Social Mission*, p. 2.
[3] Terry Eagleton, *Literary Theory: An Introduction* (Oxford, 1983), pp. 25–6.
[4] Peter Widdowson, *Literature* (London, 1999), p. 42.
[5] Brian Doyle, *English and Englishness* (London, 1989), pp. 11–12.
[6] John Churton Collins, 'The Universities in Contact with the People', *Nineteenth Century*, 26 (1889), pp. 582–3.
[7] This term has been used by Baldick (*The Social Mission of English Criticism*, p. 62), and Eagleton (*Literary Theory*, p. 27).

study, and in drawing their evidence from those institutions (such as the Working Men's Colleges and university extension movement) where the claims made for English reached their greatest intensity, such interpretations fail to pay attention to the highly complex arguments that surrounded the subject's entry into the universities. These arguments often took the form of a resistance to the notion that English should achieve disciplinary status, with this resistance undermining claims that this status was secured by the discipline's importance as a means of ideological control. This resistance focused on the subject's perceived lack of academic validity, and on the belief that it was concerned with judgements rather than knowledge, making it difficult to teach and assess. Its supporters therefore had to demonstrate that it was possible to formulate an appropriate academic methodology for English—to set down what the study of English literature was to involve, the kinds of knowledge it was to produce and why these were to be considered valuable.

The desire to codify the study of literature for academic purposes was part of the set of changes in nineteenth-century intellectual life that are usually seen in terms of the related processes of professionalisation and specialisation. T. W. Heyck, in *The Transformation of Intellectual Life in Victorian England* (1982), has traced the way in which these processes led to the gradual disappearance of the early Victorian 'man of letters' or 'sage', a figure who made a living by writing on a range of topics—from history, politics and religion to literature, philosophy and natural science—for a broad and general audience. Such men were replaced, over the course of the century, by professional academics who wrote for specialist audiences—in other words, their professional peer-group—and were governed by professional codes, structures and methodologies. This situation was made possible by changing perceptions of knowledge itself, including how this knowledge was to be accumulated and used, and what purpose it was to serve. As academia became a profession, the knowledge that fell within this professional domain had to be regulated and defined. In the sciences, which expanded rapidly in the nineteenth century, this regulation and definition included a number of factors: ideas about progression through specialisation (the sciences were fast becoming so wide-ranging that generalisation was impractical); precise methods of research; a belief that the accumulation of knowledge should not be limited by the demands of the market; and a concomitant desire to pursue knowledge for its own sake. Beliefs about the theory and practice of scientific research, particularly practical ideas about research methodology and the importance of precision and impartiality, subsequently came to act as a paradigm for other areas of intellectual activity that were seeking academic status. History, for instance, became institutionalised—and professionalised—along scientific lines, gaining new methodological approaches that emphasised an investigation of original sources, the avoidance of bias and the use of externally verifiable evidence, as opposed to the earlier, narrative-driven history of writers such as Macaulay.[8]

The advantage of Heyck's model of disciplinary development over the political models of academic history cited at the beginning of this chapter is that it allows for a greater focus on the institutional processes that governed the early development of the academic discipline of English. One aim of this chapter is to demonstrate how the early degree courses in English literature at a number of English universities were characterised by attempts to make the subject fulfil the disciplinary criteria that Heyck outlines: namely, that it should be rigorous, teachable and objective. Nevertheless, this process was by no means straightforward. As Josephine Guy noted in the previous chapter, Matthew Arnold's notion of criticism was of a generalist faculty that was by no means confined to practitioners of an academic discipline. Meanwhile, E. A. Freeman, Regius Professor of History at the University of Oxford, believed that the appreciation of literature lay outside the ambit of the university altogether: 'facts may be taught, but surely the delicacies and elegances of literature cannot be driven into any man: he must learn to appreciate them for himself'.[9] Freeman also doubted whether literature itself was suitable as subject matter for an academic discipline, opining that literary study was 'all very well in its own way, perhaps amusing, perhaps even instructive, but ... not quite of that solid character which we were used to look for in any branch of a University course'.[10] The study of literature could all too easily descend into 'chatter about Shelley',[11] a mere recreation, whereas Freeman was keen to draw attention to the need for rigour and objectivity: 'As subjects for examination we must have subjects in which it is possible to examine.'[12]

English at Oxford

Freeman's comments about literary study formed part of a series of debates that surrounded the teaching of English literature at Oxford. For many years,

[8] See T. W. Heyck, *The Transformation of Intellectual Life in Victorian England* (London & Canberra, 1982); and Philippa Levine, *The Amateur and the Professional: Antiquarians, Historians and Archaeologists in Victorian England, 1838–1886* (Cambridge, 1986).
[9] E. A. Freeman, quoted in D. J. Palmer, *The Rise of English Studies* (Oxford, 1965), p. 99.
[10] Ibid., p. 98.
[11] Ibid., p. 96.
[12] Ibid., p. 99.

Oxford had included the study of early English literature in the syllabus for its Honour School of Medieval and Modern Languages. However, this course was philological in nature, concentrating on the comparative and historical study of language and drawing on the objective, schematic principles being established in Germanic scholarship. The first sign of a shift in favour of literature came in the inauguration of the Merton Professorship of English Language and Literature in 1885. University statutes declared that the new professor would be required to 'lecture and give instruction on the history and criticism of English Language and Literature, and on the works of approved English authors'—a pronouncement that appeared to signal a diversion from philology into literary criticism.[13] Perhaps predictably, the philologists reacted with scorn. The phonetician Henry Sweet, whose *Anglo-Saxon Primer* (first published in 1882) is still a staple text for students of Old English, claimed that the appointment of a 'literary' man would 'add to the social attractions of Oxford, and pose as a kind of high priest of literary refinement and general culture, but will be otherwise sterile, neither adding to knowledge himself nor training others to do so'.[14] Sweet's claims were refuted by the author and scholar Andrew Lang, who argued that the 'literary' man 'should, perhaps, not be regarded as a mere trifler'.[15] However, it is perhaps a mark of the strength of the counter-arguments that the first appointment to the Merton Professorship, Arthur Sampson Napier, was a philologist. Oxford's first tentative acknowledgement of literary study appeared to have been withdrawn.

An unsuccessful candidate for the Merton Professorship, and one of the most vehement campaigners on behalf of the study of English literature, was John Churton Collins, a Balliol classics graduate who worked as an extension lecturer and tutor for the Civil Service examinations. In the 1880s and 1890s Collins mounted a number of attacks on the refusal of Oxford and Cambridge to teach English literature as a separate subject, including a series of very public broadsides in the press and a questionnaire circulated in 1886 to eminent figures such as the archbishop of Canterbury, leading headmasters and politicians and distinguished writers and scientists. Collins's main argument was that the enormous popularity of English literature on the extension lecture circuits made it essential for Oxford and Cambridge to include it in their syllabuses, in order to secure the education of generations of future teachers. He was also opposed to the dryness of philology, and was therefore keen to

[13] Oxford University *Statutes*, quoted in Palmer, *Rise of English Studies*, p. 79.
[14] Henry Sweet, *Academy,* 27 (9 May 1885), 331.
[15] Andrew Lang, *Academy*, 27 (20 June 1885), 439.

formulate a model for the study of literature that avoided the sterility of a fact-laden curriculum. Collins's own educational background led him to turn to Classics to provide this model, advancing a view of literature as inextricable from the 'sentiment, ethic and thought' of a particular society.[16] His claims for the subject were grandiose: it was to be 'as susceptible of serious, methodical, and profitable treatment as history itself',[17] yet also able to act as an 'instrument of culture',[18] capable of exercising an influence 'on taste, on tone, on sentiment, on opinion, on character'.[19]

Yet while this duality of purpose was central to Collins's vision of literary study, it also served to weaken it. Collins was ambitious in his plans for English but ultimately unable to convert his ideals into a practical programme of study that would justify English Literature's claim to disciplinary status. For if English was intended to justify its existence by taking up a central role in a broad social project, it could not be a specialist academic discipline: the very qualities that made it so important were precisely those that also made it unteachable. Knowledge about the facts pertaining to literature could be examined, but the influence of literature upon one's character and morality could not. Significantly, while Oxford did eventually gain a degree course in English in 1894, this course was dominated by the philological study of Old and Middle English, and gave only grudging space to the study of post-Chaucerian literature. In fact, the statutes pertaining to the English School's foundation recommended that students should show a knowledge of Classics and History to support their study of literature—a clear sign that English was still viewed with suspicion. This was later joined by the regulation that the School would only admit candidates who had already passed the First Public Examination of another Honour School.[20] Clearly, Oxford was not yet ready to accept that the study of English Literature could be an independent academic discipline. For the time being, it would have to lean on other subjects to lend it the intellectual authority it needed.

The new universities: London and Manchester

Collins's campaign, and the debate about the Merton Professorship, mean that Oxford is frequently given a central role in disciplinary histories of English.

[16] John Churton Collins, 'Can English Literature be Taught?', *Nineteenth Century*, 22 (1887), 651.
[17] Ibid., 657.
[18] John Churton Collins, 'English Literature at the Universities', *Quarterly Review,* 163 (1886), 313.
[19] Collins, 'The Universities in Contact with the People', 583.
[20] Palmer, *Rise of English Studies*, pp. 111–12.

However, these controversies—with the conflicting views of literary study they embodied, and the hostilities they aroused—often mask the fact that many of the new university colleges had already been teaching English Literature for several decades before Oxford finally gained its Honour School of English Language and Literature in 1894. Both King's College in London (founded 1829) and Owens College in Manchester (founded 1851) had included English Literature amongst their courses from the very beginning, as part of a general Bachelor of Arts programme in which students would follow courses in five or six different subjects. The University of London BA, taken by students at King's and Nottingham, offered English as an option alongside Latin, Greek, Mathematics, Logic, History, Political Economy and various modern languages, with students having to offer four subjects at Intermediate and Pass levels.[21] English could also be studied on its own for Honours, which involved a further year's study after completion of the Pass course. The University of Manchester BA allowed for a little more specialisation, with students being allowed to opt for courses that were broadly historical, classical, philosophical or literary and linguistic in character, but within these groups students still had to follow a relatively broad curriculum, with the latter course covering English Language, English Literature, Ancient and Modern History, Latin, French, German and Mathematics.[22]

Nevertheless, the version of English these colleges actually taught was clearly influenced by the need to codify the subject and bring it into line with other professionalised disciplines, rather than allowing it to exist at the idealistic level implied by its designation as 'poor man's Classics'. The model of the subject they established consisted of a number of clearly defined periods of literary history, with each year of study typically consisting of one of these periods and a number of canonical authors. The knowledge students were expected to acquire was factual rather than critical, with an emphasis being placed on the historical and social contexts of canonical authors. At Manchester in 1882, students were asked to give an account of 'the impressions which might have been made upon Chaucer by the general aspect of national affairs in the time of his early manhood'.[23] In the same year, the London examinations asked students to quote some of Shakespeare's allusions to current events.[24] There were also frequent questions on Shakespeare's historical accuracy, and on the relevance of particular historical characters

[21] *The Calendar of King's College, London* (1903–4), pp. 84–5.
[22] *Victoria University Calendar* (1881–2), pp. 30–1.
[23] *Victoria University Calendar* (1882–3), p. cxxiv.
[24] *The Calendar of King's College, London* (1882–3), p. 636.

and events to his work. Some questions made use of the growing field of text-editing, which had helped historians to generate a reliable corpus of sources and address questions of the authenticity of historical evidence. The University of London examinations asked about methods of dating Shakespeare's plays, and about the textual history of *Richard III*.[25] Other questions focused on the analysis of metre and the definition of various technical terms. And both examining bodies asked some questions that were a straightforward test of memory, with students being asked to put a list of texts in chronological order, or simply to quote as much as they could of particular works. A question at Manchester in 1882 asked students to give an outline of any one of the *Canterbury Tales*, while the London examinations of 1881 asked students to summarise and quote part of Coleridge's 'Christabel'.[26]

To look at these examinations today is to be confronted with a very different kind of subject from the contemporary discipline of English Literature. What these examinations tested was not literary criticism, but literary knowledge. Moreover, this was a factual brand of knowledge that seemed to invite 'cramming'. While some questions did seem to require a more critical approach, these were often framed in a way that left little room for debate: questions such as 'Show exactly why Pope fails comparatively as a writer of prose' and 'Describe the true genius of Spenser',[27] suggest that students were not meant to form judgements of their own, but to repeat the judgements they had learned in lectures or through their reading. The use of the essay as a vehicle for discussion was rare: often what students were expected to write was not an essay at all, but a summary or a list. Rubrics do not always specify how many questions students had to answer, but it is clear that in some three-hour papers it was between five and seven questions out of around fourteen. A common instruction was to 'write notes' on a given topic, and it seems that the ability to condense one's knowledge was at a premium, with students being assessed on their factual accuracy rather than their capacity to argue a case.

The nature of the early professors of English may help to explain this factual bias. Many of them were non-specialists who taught a range of subjects, often in unrelated disciplines. This situation seems to have been the result

[25] *The Calendar of King's College, London* (1880–1), p. 647; *The Calendar of King's College, London* (1883–4), p. 630.

[26] *Victoria University Calendar* (1882–3), p. cxxiv; *The Calendar of King's College, London* (1881–2), p. 644.

[27] *The Calendar of King's College, London* (1900–1), p. lxxvi; *The Calendar of King's College, London* (1887–8), p. 664.

of a shortage of suitable staff rather than the result of a conscious policy of generalisation. In its early years, King's linked English Literature with Modern History under a joint professorship, but this post was not filled until four years after its inauguration, with its duties being carried out by the professors of Mathematics and Classical Literature in the meantime. The post was also empty between 1855 and 1865. A similar arrangement took place at Manchester, where Adolphus Ward was Professor of English Literature and History from 1866. In his history of the development of the English Faculty at Cambridge, E. M. W. Tillyard describes Ward as one of the 'patriarchs in the history of English studies'. Nevertheless, Tillyard also acknowledged that Ward was a historian first and foremost, and that his writing on literature took the form of literary history rather than criticism.[28] Ward's own preference is indicated by the fact that while he resigned from the literary element of his post in 1889, he did not relinquish History until eight years later.

There are signs that such arrangements fulfilled the mutual needs of both institutions and individuals. As a typical professorship involved between three and five hours' teaching each week, it would certainly have been possible for one person to teach a number of subjects, and such an arrangement would have enabled some people to make a full-time living from university teaching, albeit in a wide range of subject areas. Alan Bacon has suggested that the need to save money was a factor in the linking of English and History at King's,[29] and the system of joint professorships would have been an obvious solution to the problem of staff shortages. Nevertheless, it is difficult to imagine any contemporary professorship encompassing such a diverse range of subjects. Neither was there a clear career structure for aspiring academics: when the Professorship of English Literature and Modern History at King's College was advertised in November 1853, the only qualifications stipulated were membership of the Church of England and a degree from Oxford or Cambridge.[30] Indeed, specialist knowledge may have been a positive handicap. The successful candidate, the philologist George Webbe Dasent, was warned by the college authorities that the furtherance of his academic interests did not form part of his professorial role, and that the pursuit of knowledge should be directed to 'the glory of God' rather than to the furtherance of one's own professional aims. Dasent's resignation, less than two years later,

[28] E. M. W. Tillyard, *The Muse Unchained: An Intimate Account of the Revolution in English Studies at Cambridge* (London, 1958), pp. 24–5.

[29] Bacon, 'English Literature Becomes a University Subject', p. 603.

[30] Minutes of Special Committee Meetings, King's College, London (King's College Archive, KA/CS/M2), p. 18.

appears to have been motivated by his frustration at the restrictions that such warnings imposed on him.[31]

However, as time went on, and as the generalists reached retirement, both courses and academic posts became more specialised. At King's, English and History had gained separate professorships by 1880, with John Wesley Hales being appointed Professor of English Language and Literature in 1877 and succeeded by Israel Gollancz in 1903. C. H. Herford replaced Adolphus Ward as Professor of English Language and Literature at Manchester. This new generation of professors had a different set of duties and a different kind of role: they were, increasingly, the heads of larger departments (Gollancz and Herford led departments of eight and five respectively) and managers who were expected to carry out administration and supervise teaching and research. They oversaw the appointment of staff to fill specific roles—the department at King's had a Professor in English Bibliography and a Lecturer in English Philology as well as a number of general posts—and their research and publications became an increasingly important way of demonstrating an institution's academic strength, as well as evidence of a growing sophistication in intellectual activity.

Nevertheless, it may be significant that the work carried out by this new generation of professors was, for the most part, confined to literary histories and editions of texts. Israel Gollancz, for instance, was a translator and editor of medieval literature: C. H. Herford edited the First Quarto of *Hamlet* and a number of Shakespeare's other plays. To say that these early professors were professional *critics* would be misleading. They undoubtedly made an important contribution to the emerging discipline of English literature: their literary histories defined the discipline's subject-matter, while their editorial work (often part of series aimed at the growing student market) provided undergraduates with cheap and reliable copies of canonical works. However, what students were supposed to do with this raw material was still uncertain. The study of literature was not coterminous with literary criticism, an activity that makes up the vast majority of undergraduate courses in English Literature today. Neither was the canon used as a vehicle for moral and political aims, as has so often been claimed. Instead, it was used to make available certain kinds of factual knowledge, from the straightforward recall of quotations to the more sophisticated awareness of philology, bibliography and literary history tested in questions set by the boards at both Manchester

[31] Minutes of Special Committee Meetings, King's College, London (King's College Archive, KA/CS/M2), pp. 24–5, 70. The Minutes record that a special committee had been formed to investigate the circumstances surrounding Dasent's resignation, but contain no further references to this.

and London. It is almost as if such knowledge embodied not the 'cultural capital' that English is commonly held to represent,[32] but a kind of 'intellectual capital' that gave English a status equal to that of other disciplines: a value that was concerned with difficulty, with mastering a particular subject area, and therefore with the emerging structures of modern academia.

The resistance to scholarship

The universities' attempts to define literary knowledge in terms of a particular set of scholarly activities did not meet with universal approval. These attempts took place within a society in which the knowledge to which the amateur could lay claim was gradually being eroded, leading to what Stefan Collini has described as 'a heightened sense that a wide range of intellectual, scientific, and literary topics were starting to become the preserve of people ... whose authority was more than personal, deriving ultimately from the socially endorsed authority of the institutions of the "higher learning"'.[33] They also aimed to professionalise a subject that had long been associated with these amateur forms of knowledge. E. A. Freeman's distaste for 'chatter about Shelley' was only one example of this link: as late as 1910, a Dr Mayo of the University of Cambridge would complain that 'before [students] left the nursery they were taught the use of their mother tongue; and by and bye they acquired the knowledge of the combination of letters, and that was called reading ... With that knowledge they obtained in the nursery, nothing stood between them and the acquirement of a knowledge of current English literature.'[34] Yet just as the supporters of academic English had been faced with the knowledge that English would need to relinquish its claims to a wider sphere of influence in order to become a specialist activity, this move towards greater specialisation was being resisted by a number of writers who were keen to preserve the subject's less tangible qualities. Even after literary criticism became a part of institutional syllabuses, its place there was questioned by a number of writers, both inside and outside the universities, who felt that its benefits could not be reduced to a regulated process of scholarship and research. Stanley Leathes, whose reshaping of the Civil Service examinations

[32] The concept of 'cultural capital', borrowed from Pierre Bourdieu, has been discussed at length by John Guillory in *Cultural Capital: The Problem of Literary Canon Formation* (Chicago and London, 1993).

[33] Stefan Collini, *English Pasts: Essays in History and Culture* (Oxford, 1999), p. 308.

[34] Quoted in *Cambridge University Reporter* (13 Dec. 1910), p. 406.

in English in the early twentieth century earned him considerable influence over the founders of Cambridge's English Tripos, felt that 'there is danger in submitting the delicate flowers of English literature to the methods of the lecture room, the schedules and tests of the examination room. If in any conditions English literature is being spontaneously studied, it is best to leave those conditions alone.'[35]

Leathes's elevation of 'amateur' values over those of the 'professional' rested on a belief that the kinds of knowledge possessed by the amateur were more genuine than those gained through academic study, which was seen as stifling literature's humanising power. Other critics shared these feelings, and expressed them in a series of meditations on the value of a scientific approach to literary criticism. In an article published in the *Quarterly Review* in 1886, John Churton Collins attacked Edmund Gosse for his failure to adhere to standards of scholarly accuracy in his historical survey *From Shakespeare to Pope*, including a lengthy enumeration of errors of chronology, the misidentification of various authors and the designation of certain prose works as poems. For Collins, such errors were 'not mere slips of the pen', but the result of ignorance, a sign of the disregard in which literary study was held by both Oxford and Cambridge. Nevertheless, while Collins was convinced that the study of literature was 'worthy of minute, of patient, of systematic study', he was also cautious about taking such an approach to extremes, railing against the 'repulsive' annotation of 'some historical allusion ... some problem in antiquities, or ... wholly superfluous parallel passages'.[36] Ironically, Collins's scepticism about the validity of a scholarly approach was shared by Gosse himself, who used the extended metaphor of a chemical reaction to show the unsuitability of quasi-scientific forms of criticism:

> Within the last quarter of a century, systems by which to test the authenticity and the chronology of the plays have been produced with great confidence, metrical formulas which are to act as reagents and to identify the component parts of a given passage with scientific exactitude. Of these 'verse-texts' and 'pause-texts' no account can here be given. That the results of their employment have been curious and valuable shall not be denied; but there is already manifest in the gravest criticism a reaction against excess of confidence in them. At one time it was supposed that the 'end-stopt' criterium, for instance, might be dropped, like a chemical substance, on the page of Shakespeare, and would there immediately and finally determine minute quantities of Peele or Kyd, that a fragment of Fletcher would turn purple under it, or a greenish tinge betray a layer of Rowley. It is not thus that poetry

[35] Stanley Leathes, *The Teaching of English at the Universities* (English Association pamphlet no. 26, Oct. 1913), p. 9.
[36] Collins, 'English Literature at the Universities', 300, 313–14.

> is composed; and this ultra-scientific theory showed a grotesque ignorance of the human pliability of art.[37]

For Gosse, the special nature of art meant that science was too gross and unsophisticated a method to be applied to its study, blurring the more subtle knowledge that could be gained through a sensitive exploration of the literary text. Meanwhile, W. P. Ker, who was Professor of Literature at Cardiff from 1883 to 1889 and subsequently Quain Professor at University College London, articulated his own belief in the special status of literature through his feeling that the literary critic should maintain 'a certain dignity' that was not commensurate with a move towards a more scientific methodology. A concern for the minutiae of scholarly conventions was seen by Ker as a distasteful intrusion:

> Books of Science are often very ugly. They have a trick of scattering symbols over their pages. Our philosophers, who ought to know better, have caught this ugly trick. Locke, Berkeley and Hume had more self-respect than to patch themselves with algebra—like Mr. W. S. Jevons and Mr. F. H. Bradley and others. Modern psychologists again will consort with medical students and bring away nasty things out of the dissecting rooms. The older generation had many friends in the faculty of medicine, but they were treated like men of the world; there was no prurient curiosity about the *arcana* of the profession.[38]

Ker even complained about the systems of referencing—'the classification, the naming, the scientific apparatus'—that had 'spoilt' Alexander Bain's 'Emotional Qualities of Style', claiming rather haughtily that 'No work can stand high as literature that allows itself to jumble up large type and small type on the same page. The Germans do it, but we know what the Germans are.'[39]

These reactions against scientific methodology should not, however, be taken as signs of a wholesale move towards a reactionary bellettrism. If the professional authority represented by literary scholarship was viewed as unfavourable, it at least made critics aware of a need to defend and define their own methods, often in the form of a search for some kind of accommodation with the demands of objective accuracy. George Saintsbury's mistrust of 'the merely dilettante and "tasting" critic' hinted at a desire for a more rigorous form of critical practice which acknowledged the value of the new scholarship in enabling the critic to 'hunt the fugitive by a closer trail than

[37] Edmund Gosse, *A Short History of Modern English Literature* (London, 1897; repr., 1925), p. 106.
[38] W. P. Ker, *On Modern Literature: Lectures and Addresses*, ed. Terence Spencer and James Sutherland (Oxford, 1955), p. 182.
[39] Ibid., pp. 183–4.

usual through the chambers of her flight'.[40] Saintsbury regretted that philology had 'claim[ed] the term "scholarship" exclusively for itself', as this led to an opposition between philology and literary study that left the latter to a 'looser æsthetics', and to those who 'consider themselves entitled to neglect scholarship in any proper sense with a similarly scornful indifference'. While he felt that literature could 'never be scientific', what he sought was a return to a form of critical enquiry which drew on the 'sufficiently minute' yet 'still clung to the literary side proper', retaining a sense of the perceived 'specialness' that set literature apart from other fields of knowledge.[41]

Nevertheless, even literary scholarship was excluded from the remit of the British Academy when it was founded in 1902. According to Henry Butcher, an early President of the Academy, literature was a subjective topic, whose 'tests' were 'impalpable compared with those of eminent discovery in science'. Literature did not belong within a society concerned with the organisation of knowledge, since it represented a 'genius' which 'cannot be organized'.[42] This emphasis on scientific criteria of truth meant that when literature was given a place within the Academy, it was in the form of literary history and textual scholarship rather than critical or creative endeavour: by 1910, Butcher was able to state that 'although Literature on its artistic . . . side is outside the scope of the Academy, Literature on its scientific side is as certainly within its province'.[43]

Later in the twentieth century, Sir Arthur Quiller-Couch—the King Edward VII Professor of English Literature at Cambridge—would act as a figurehead for a very different kind of English degree to those inaugurated at Oxford and the civic colleges. Quiller-Couch aimed to 'train [students] in understanding, rather than test them in memorised information':[44] the English Tripos at Cambridge, which began in 1917, would eschew the safe academic qualities of complexity and historicity in favour of questions that would, by 1920, encompass the contemporary novel, the poetry of the First World War and the dramatic possibilities of film. Yet this was not without a struggle. Arguments at Cambridge about the inauguration of the King Edward VII professorship replicated those at Oxford, a quarter of a century earlier. Again, the academic validity of English was questioned, and again, the Chair's first

[40] George Saintsbury, *A History of Nineteenth-Century Literature* (London, 1896; repr., 1906), pp. 445, 461.

[41] Ibid., pp. 478–80.

[42] Henry Butcher, Presidential Address to the British Academy, delivered 27 Oct. 1909, *Proceedings of the British Academy*, 4 (London, 1909–10), p. 23.

[43] Ibid., pp. 14–15.

[44] Sir Arthur Quiller-Couch, 'On Reading for the English Tripos', in *Studies in Literature: Third Series* (Cambridge, 1927; repr., 1948), p. 149.

incumbent was a philologist. Furthermore, the dynamism of the early English Tripos was, in some respects, short-lived. The foundation of an independent English Faculty at Cambridge in 1926, and the subsequent centralisation of teaching and administration, led to what Francis Mulhern has described as a dilution of the '"creative" sources' of the English School,[45] and what, for F. R. Leavis, was a sign of the encroachment of 'technologico-Benthamite' forces on academic life.[46] Nevertheless, it was at Cambridge that I. A. Richards delivered his famous lectures on 'Practical Criticism', the method of close reading and textual analysis which was arguably the first important attempt to describe literary criticism in scientific terms. And it was at Cambridge that Leavis himself would formulate his vision of the ideal university as a 'creative centre of civilisation',[47] a place in which the study of English literature would foster 'a scrupulously sensitive yet enterprising use of intelligence'[48] that would, in turn, contribute to the Arnoldian task of promoting the values of a humane culture.

The history of English Literature's rise to disciplinary status is, then, one which is marked by tension and debate, rather than adhering to the simplistic paradigms offered by the story of English as 'poor man's Classics', or by the teleological narrative of professionalisation. While it would be naïve to suggest that political concerns were wholly absent from the institutional development of English Literature, it would be equally naïve to allow questions of politics to overshadow the highly complex arguments that arose from this institutionalisation. In order for English to gain its place in the universities, it had to set aside its claims to a wider social significance in favour of an emphasis on the more specialised forms of knowledge represented by philology, literary history and text-editing. Yet in turn, this specialisation led to an implicit devaluing of other ways of understanding and writing about literature: a movement that was vigorously resisted by a range of critics and writers.

This tension between differing conceptions of literary knowledge is still ongoing. Martin Amis has recently alluded to the 'historical vulnerability' of literary study, remarking that its contested status is due to the fact that 'it has never seemed difficult enough ... Interacting with literature is easy. Anyone can join in.'[49] In schools, the recent reform of English Literature at A-level

[45] Francis Mulhern, *The Moment of 'Scrutiny'* (London, 1979; repr., 1981), p. 29.
[46] F. R. Leavis, *English Literature in Our Time and the University* (Cambridge, 1969), pp. 23–4.
[47] Ibid., p. 3.
[48] F. R. Leavis, *Education and the University: A Sketch for an 'English School'* (London, 1943), pp. 58–9.
[49] Martin Amis, *The War Against Cliché: Essays and Reviews, 1971–2000* (London, 2001), pp. xiii–xiv.

has been marked by continuing debates about the amount of specialist knowledge that should be expected from students preparing for university entrance:[50] the reform's initial goal of closing the gap between school and university has been undermined by complaints about the perceived elitism of a curriculum whose emphasis of historical contexts and critical debates has been seen as devaluing a more 'personal and creative engagement'[51] between text and reader. For Stefan Collini, many of the controversies that have faced literary studies can be understood in terms of 'the unresolved, and perhaps unresolvable, tension between, on the one hand, being simply one specialized activity alongside other specialisms ... and, on the other hand, still carrying the burden of being a kind of residual cultural space within which general existential and ethical questions can be addressed'.[52] Clearly, the study of literature is expected to be many things to many people: this struggle for ownership means that its nature and purpose are still contested, and still indistinct.

[50] The debates surrounding the new A-level are discussed in Chapter Six of my 2003 Ph.D. thesis, 'Defining Literary Criticism: Scholarship, Authority and the Possession of Literary Knowledge, 1880–2002' (University of Nottingham). This chapter is based, in part, on my paper 'The Literary: Theory, Education, and Academic Knowledge', delivered at the 'Post-Theory: Politics, Economics and Culture' conference at De Montfort University on 7 Sept. 2001, and on my article 'The new English A-level: contexts, criticism and the nature of literary knowledge', *The Use of English*, 54 (2003), 97–109.

[51] Mike Craddock, 'Idealism, Theory, Practice and the New 'A' Levels', *The Use of English,* 52 (2001), 107–11, 108.

[52] Collini, *English Pasts*, p. 313.

CHAPTER ELEVEN

'Old Studies and New': The Organisation of Knowledge in University Curriculum

JOHN R. GIBBINS

> Desmond went up to Cambridge in October 1894. University life suited him from the first: everything about it—the pursuit of friendship and self discovery; the social life, with its endless talk at a high intellectual level, light as well as serious; the public debates, the papers read to undergraduate clubs, the leisurely reading parties—were congenial. The lack of structure in an undergraduate's life agreed with him.[1]

Influence and power in the history of intellectual ideas is generally understood in terms of the generation of great authors, ideas, theories, texts and movements. Intellectual biography most commonly mirrors this understanding, taking us through a sumptuous life of youthful influences, catalytic friendships and associations, social and cultural networks and clubs, sexual and political awakenings. In many ways both exemplify the kind of vanity we experience at the theatre. We sit and enter a world of meaning, plot and message, forgetting that the experience is made possible only through a myriad of structural and organisational forms and processes. The autobiographies and biographies of the wider MacCarthy circle, of Trevelyan, Forster, Moore, Fry and even Lowes Dickinson and Browning, confirm that the genre depicts intellectual life in a particular way: great theories and thinkers are generated from the less organised social and cultural milieu rather than as the result of curriculum, syllabus, set books, lectures, and examinations, delivered by more formal processes and procedures, albeit within a setting of congeniality. In an effort to get behind the formal and the organised, perhaps we have lost sight of the structure that organises intellectual life, and even underpins everyday intellectual experience.

[1] Hugh and Mirabel Cecil, *Clever Hearts: Desmond and Mary MacCarthy* (London, 1991), p. 35.

Yet a closer reading of late Victorian intellectual lives and ideas, can reveal the underlying structures, principles and forms that make up the canon of texts, the regimes of learning, the architectures of knowledge, the means of teaching that fashioned the minds and lives of the few and the many. Undergraduate memoirs testify to the challenge that set books and reading posed, the terror that missing a high place or being 'plucked' in examinations held with candidates, the boredom or exhilaration that were experienced attending lectures and tutorials, the daily bout of 'cram' in the library and 'grind' to keep body and mind tuned for assessment. Again, university archives, histories, letters and memoirs testify to the proportion of time a don spent at Syndics, Subject and Department Boards devising and managing the curriculum before his time and energies are accounted for preparation, tuition, lecturing, question setting, marking and overseeing quality. The papers of 'Dons as Scholars', as they are termed by Annan—men such as Maitland, Whewell, Grote, Mayor, and Sedgwick—have curriculum matters heavily represented.[2] Even the concerns of elite groups, such as the 'Apostles', featured 'recasting of the university courses of study' as a priority.[3] The national and regional newspapers, such as *The Times* and the *Cambridge Chronicle,* published Tripos results as if they were lottery numbers, and the university *Calendars* and occasional *Handbooks*, until the turn of the century, published past successes and failures at examinations, as both testimony to their students, their families, to themselves and as evidence of completion of a mission to the State and their patrons. In short, curriculum was more central to the organising of academic and intellectual life in Britain in the nineteenth century than is usually given credit. It is rare for us to focus upon the organisations of knowledge, such as Academies, Libraries, Laboratories, and Museums, let alone to concentrate attention upon, syllabus, examinations and curriculum, as do Winstanley, Collini, Winch and Burrow and Stray and Smith.[4] Yet curricula embodied precisely what those endowed with legitimacy agreed constituted knowledge and the correct form for its reproduction. In addition it may be argued that as organisers of knowledge, curriculum impacted on more lives than did its competitors for transmission of knowledge in the nineteenth century, namely the churches, novelists,

[2] Noel Annan, *The Dons: Mentors, Eccentrics and Genius*, (London, 1999), pp. 79–97.

[3] William Lubenow, *The Cambridge Apostles, 1820–1914* (Cambridge, 1998), p. 341.

[4] Stefan Collini, Donald Winch and John Burrows, *That Noble Science: A Study in Nineteenth-Century Intellectual History* (Cambridge, 1983); John Smith and Christopher Stray (eds.), *Teaching and Learning in Nineteenth-Century Cambridge* (Cambridge, 2001), exemplify the new rigour and approaches in the field, though the genre began with David Winstanley, *Early Victorian Cambridge* (Cambridge, 1940); David Winstanley, *Later Victorian Cambridge* (Cambridge, 1945).

sages, journalists and even the popular cultural forms of cartoon and music hall. By the end of the century, the popular sages responded to the growing division in authority and power between literary gentlemen and the university specialised dons, by incorporating themselves within the universities via curriculum.

Knowledge, Curriculum and Authority

In the 1970s, the American Academy of Arts and Sciences, instituted a study into the 'Organisation of Knowledge in Modern America'.[5] Edward Shils, the American sociologist, described and analysed the reasons for the success of universities in America in terms of a widespread public 'drift toward the appreciation of knowledge'.[6] His major insight was that it was universities which had gained the monopoly on knowledge production and transmission in America.

> The universities were vouchsafed the vocation because they appeared to be the best imaginable instrument for the performance of the dual cognitive function. They could not only produce more knowledge, more reliably and more continuously than any other learned organisation, but they could transmit it, thus making provision for the persistence of that progress. No other arrangement of intellectual activities could approximate their success in this regard.[7]

The 'drift' to university centralisation of knowledge production and transmission had only commenced in America in the 1870s, but the process and its success had been signalled earlier in Germany, Scotland and England. By 1880, the universities in Britain had established an autonomy and hegemony over knowledge that was to remain very much intact for seven decades. Even then, only an organisation as powerful as the State could mount a challenge to this university hegemony.

Shils's analysis, however, begs the questions of how the universities produced and transmitted knowledge so successfully, why they beat off competition from churches, publishers with encyclopaedias, academicians, humanising sages such as Mill, Grote, Arnold, Carlyle, and Ruskin, novelists and journalists such as Dickens? Several competitive answers to our question

[5] Alexandra Olson and John Voss (eds.), *The Organisation of Knowledge in Modern America, 1860–1922* (Baltimore and London, 1979), pp. 46–7.

[6] Edward Shils, 'The Order of Learning in the United States: The Ascendancy of the University', in Olsen and Voss (eds.), *Organisation of Knowledge*, p. 46.

[7] Ibid., pp. 46–7.

will be explored elsewhere in this collection, namely, that the dons became more professional (Endersby); that disciplines were becoming more specialised and technical (Goldman); better classified (Endersby); more sectarian and competitive (Cohen); more diversified (Goldman); that specialism was finding a rapprochement with the new book buying publics (Guy, McKitterick); or with public life (Turner, Lubenow); that discipline groups were becoming more national (Turner), or international (Beard and Stray); that national scholars were becoming better networked in clubs and societies (Lubenow), or in prestigious national centres of excellence; that the whole university system was expanding into the provinces, undermining rival local producers (Alberti). Only Carol Atherton takes seriously the proposition that the organisation and production of syllabus, curriculum design and reproduction via organised teaching, were the primary source of the expanding authority, prestige and power of knowledge in our period.

The answer to be explored here is that the success of the universities and of scholars in transmitting knowledge was due to two factors: the inherited authority that curriculum gave within and without the university, and the growing organisation of curriculum that developed and extended over the century. Most of the power to control the structure and shape of knowledge in the late nineteenth century lay in the universities' control of the syllabus that then impacted upon the wider curriculum of professions, colleges, and schools in Britain and the Empire. Subsidiary questions then arise. Why, within the universities, were the 'dons'—university lecturers and researchers—more powerful than the university, administrators, and colleges; and why, compared with outsiders, were they replacing the amateur intellectuals, sages and literary gentlemen, as the agents of knowledge and cultural production and reproduction? The answer to be explored is that the dons and academics, who constituted the 'Academy', had the organisational and positional advantage that lay in being an 'owner of knowledge', able to design, construct and, above all, to reproduce knowledge for elite and mass audiences, through syllabus and curriculum. Managing what the dons owned did not give the administrators authority. Producing ideas that could not be owned, validated, formally taught, examined and tested, put sages at a great disadvantage. To be 'great' or a 'classic' meant it had to be placed in a coveted syllabus.

How then, did the possession and organisation of knowledge confer power on the university? Tapper and Salter identified the outline of an answer in 1992: 'Because they are, and have always been, the institutions at the top of the educational hierarchy, universities make the ultimate decisions on how knowledge should be organised, and what status should be attached to different knowledge areas.'[8] Any other rival source of knowledge had to seek the validation, accreditation and legitimation of their canon from the universities via their curriculum. 'Likewise, any significant change in the content of or boundary of a knowledge area has to be sanctioned by the universities, if it is to carry lasting weight.' Universities were granted these supreme powers and, to the middle of the twentieth century, were trusted to exercise them. So it was that they had the power to confer legitimacy on the claims of outsiders to have knowledge, such as wealth owners, corporate managers, politicians, and media moguls. Tapper and Salter concede other factors help explain how producing knowledge granted tangible power: the universities persuaded the professions to contract to them the granting of professional status; they persuaded other elites to allow them to 'make authoritative statements about values'.[9] In sum, what accounts for the power of the universities is that they were trusted by all ranks and tiers of society, to organise, produce, reproduce and apply knowledge.[10]

What is a curriculum? What are the properties that give it this productive power? What is its modern history? Curriculum derives from *currere*, to run, often referring to a racecourse. In this metaphor we have intimations of a test of intellectual skills resting on endurance and ability to surmount obstacles over an extended period of time. It was this usage that attracted Leslie Stephen in his satirical *Sketches from Cambridge, by a Don.*[11] Students are likened to fancied horses or rowers, prepared in college stables to complete in curriculum and examination races, under the watchful eye of private or college trainers. The analogy does not hold completely, but enough for critics of the 'gold fever' built into the 'pernicious' competitive system in the late century.[12] Curriculum was however, more organised, professional, and regulated than horse and boat racing. University curricula between 1830 and 1880 involved at least the following formal elements, however differently related and prioritised: a period of study, usually involving residence in a town or college; membership of the university and often, though not necessarily, a college with a fee and regulations attached; adoption into a course of study, a degree or tripos, with varying levels and gradations; attendance at some prescribed teaching and learning, and other procedural events, such as lectures,

[8] Ted Tapper and Brian Salter, *Oxford, Cambridge and the Changing Idea of the Universities: The Challenge to Donnish Domination* (Buckingham, 1992), p. 4.

[9] Ibid., pp. 5–6.

[10] Ibid., pp. 113–16.

[11] Leslie Stephen, *Sketches from Cambridge, by a Don* (London, 1865).

[12] Michael G. Brock and Mark C. Curthoys (eds.) *The History of the University of Oxford: Vol. VI, Nineteenth-Century Oxford, Part 1* (Oxford, 1997), pp. 367–9.

tutorials and dinners; examination at stages on set books or problems; conformity to often complicated and localised procedures and practices. Informal elements were appended, such as imbibing and conforming to the cultural norms and values of a group; reciprocating in a variety of networks; and deferring to local authorities, leaders and champions.[13]

A syllabus is a more detailed and planned outline of the ground to be covered in the course. It details the jumps and the rules of racing. Overlapping in definition and content curriculum and syllabus organise knowledge from opposite ends. The syllabus details are more like the detailed plan of reading, researching, learning, practising and testing of skills that are laid down in course guides. The curriculum is the general map of the area to be covered, setting out the general aims of the course, its rationale, learning objectives and methods, its rules and administrative structure. Curriculum also embraces the beliefs, values, and priorities, like Whig or 'liberal education' values, that are not planned, but are delivered through the course, in what Snyder terms *The Hidden Curriculum.*[14] Together syllabus and curriculum are a composite course of studies, learning experiences and assessments of competence, set for students leading to a qualification that has recognised and transferable value. Ranges of qualifications could be expanded, added to and modified—as they were during the nineteenth century—in an effort to remain competitive.

Comparisons of the value of each institution's qualifications were subjective and hotly contested, with Royal Commission Reports providing some sort of national benchmarking as the century progressed. Few curricula were independent of the universities, and those such as medical, legal, the Indian and Civil Service examinations, were gradually incorporated into the university system. External colleges and the working men's and women's education system were closely attached, both formally and informally, to the universities. Indeed, in London, their examination schemes became one and the same by the early twentieth century. Rothblatt noted accurately that 'the absence of any de facto university direction over the organisation of secondary education allowed a considerable amount of education independence in the determination of programmes of study' in the early nineteenth century. However, as the century passed the universities extended authority over secondary schools, teacher training, and professional training, by imposing their organisation.[15]

[13] John R. Gibbins, 'Designing Curricula: The Moral Sciences in Cambridge, Oxford, Edinburgh, London and Dublin', *Conference on Teaching and Learning in Nineteenth-Century Cambridge*, Cambridge, Trinity College, 2001 (forthcoming in *History of Universities*).

[14] Benson R. Snyder, *The Hidden Curriculum* (New York, 1971).

[15] Sheldon Rothblatt, *Tradition and Change in English Liberal Education: An Essay in History and Culture* (London, 1976), p. 75.

But Rothblatt only briefly makes the important point that perhaps curriculum organisation itself had a major impact upon the direction of knowledge and education in the late nineteenth century.[16]

Curricula within disciplines could be, and were, organised around differing logics, foci and problems, and the tensions between the options created the fault lines of many contemporary debates. The syllabus could focus on one or more of the following concerns. (1) What was the subject matter itself: what periods, subjects, and events are included; what topics are to be prioritised? For example, should only one or all civilisations be studied, and should modern languages be allowed for honours students? (2) Issues of scholarship within the discipline arise from the need to investigate and teach the subject matter. For example, should we focus on primary or secondary sources, single or comparative studies, and consideration of reliability. (3) Another concern was research or gaining new knowledge in the discipline: researching, investigating, applying new theories and methods. (4) New techniques, technologies or skills in learning or problem solving in an area arose, such as the application of new catalogues, computing systems, microscopes, text books, examinations, or new learning and teaching theories. (5) Finally, the need for interdisciplinary study and the relationship between subjects raised questions, for example over the overlapping claims of disciplines to explain an event or process.

Despite pressures from the world beyond the quadrangle, the organising principles inside the universities in the nineteenth century moved from the first logic (the discipline as subject matter) towards the fifth (relating disciplines) to the third (how to research while developing discipline theory and methods). The shifting balance between these foci is part of the history of curriculum development in the Victorian period, and reveals a growing divide between professional academics and professions, on one side, and the users of knowledge, 'sages' and public officials, on the other. The development amongst academics of respect for the development of subject-specific and specialist epistemologies and methods to research them, grew over the century, in contrast to the demands of public commissioners and inspectors that curriculum should focus more closely on the subject matter and the techniques for learning about them, a debate that will be visited below when we examine the efforts of John Grote, Mark Pattison, Matthew Arnold and Thomas Huxley.[17] In this context we may say that the challenge to the dominance of liberal education and the classics in the late nineteenth century

[16] Ibid., p. 194.

[17] Ibid., pp. 174–7.

was less a challenge from new groups and subjects, and more about this division within curriculum pedagogy. Mill, Huxley and George Grote were not wholly opposed to classics and liberal education; they were more focused on issues of what else to study, how to study, and what to do with the knowledge.

The guardians of any curriculum or syllabus, any structure of knowledge, in a university needed to solve at least three problems, 'First there is the problem of the organization of the disciplines: how many there are; what they are; and how they are related to one another. Second, there is the problem of the substantive conceptual structures used by each discipline. Third, there is the problem of syntax of each discipline: what its canons of evidence and proof are and how well they can be applied.'[18] Solving these problems was a major concern, and much of it was to do with classification and the development of classificatory systems: creating and denoting classes, placing them into systems, then arranging items in them became a feverish activity of scholars. Disciplines that we now know in the arts and social sciences, were forming in the nineteenth century from the classics like offshoots of old stars, and denoting became unavoidable. Sociology, psychology, philosophy, politics, economics, history, anthropology, geography, languages, literature, philology and education, became mature or *sui generis* disciplines in this period. Conceptualisation, creating the language and vocabulary of each discipline then called forth attention. Alfred Marshall, for all his contributions, should be remembered not least for the construction of the modern discourse of economics. The definitive articles on the new disciplines in the *Encyclopaedia Britannica*, illustrated by James Ward's on psychology, marked the achievements of scholars to date. But solving the third problem of syntax and methods was to prove the most taxing, and remained incomplete in 1900. George Eliot may have effectively lampooned the donnish preoccupation of Mark Pattison's high concerns for theory and method in *Middlemarch,* but these very concerns were novel, and marked the emergence of the research and learning pedagogy that has dominated the later university profession.[19] That very few new disciplines, discipline discourses and discipline methodologies have emerged since 1900 in the arts, humanities and social sciences, is a testament to the rigour and creativity of the two generations of scholars that pioneered the organisation of knowledge in Britain from 1830. These scholars designed and constructed the architecture of knowledge that their successors have modified, repaired and developed, but left essentially as conceived.

[18] G. W. Ford and L. Pugno (eds.), *The Structure of Knowledge and the Curriculum* (Chicago, 1964), pp. 14–15.

[19] John Sparrow, *Mark Pattison and the Idea of a University* (Cambridge, 1967), pp. 1–30, 31, 42–7.

Another interesting question concerns the source of the five curriculum logics, problem areas and foci detailed above. Pressure for change could come from a number of directions. First, the discipline, subject matter and curriculum itself, for example the need to teach a new topic such as modern literature. Second, problems particular to discipline producers and teachers, that is problems of pedagogy and professional standing. Third, problems expressed by consumers of the discipline, that is students, parents, and employers. Fourth, problems expressed by external interests aiming to use curriculum to solve extraneous problems, such as pressures on universities from the state to help administer the Empire, to close the knowledge gap on international competitors, or to help restructure British industry. While in our period the latter two sources of pressure on the curriculum were growing, before 1880 we could argue that the first two sources of influence were predominant.

A curriculum has to be delivered, and teaching is a part of the organisation of the curriculum. To accommodate the new central logic of curriculum, teaching changed in two ways. First, the centralised professorial system began to replace the hastily developed mid-century specialist college tutorial system, being cheaper to provide, and easier to monitor and assess. Universities knew what students were getting if one professor did the production and transmission; comparative standing could be established in the chairs created and the appointments made to them. Secondly, the professor and subordinate tutors now changed role. From curriculum gods, professors become subordinate to their discipline and subject, its purveyors not its author.[20] Becoming a subject specialist, who knew how to research his field and knew the latest research findings, was a characteristic development of the period from 1860 to 1900, and was pioneered by Pattison at Oxford. At Cambridge John Grote made new knowledge real in the work of his new moral science tutors, including Henry Sidgwick, Alfred Marshall, John Venn, Joseph Mayor and John Seeley, who met professionally as members of the Grote Society and Club.[21] How could individuals, sages or external movements, compete with this organised and combined mass of knowledge production? The answer is that they could not, and hence the search for substitute organisational forms, of which the Club, like the *Athenaeum* and the new Academies and Societies became the most effective. But with only journals,

[20] Ibid, p. 178.

[21] Sheldon Rothblatt, *Revolution of the Dons* (London, 1969), p. 139; Alfred Marshall, Minutes of Grote Society Meetings, 1866–1867, Trinity College Library, Add. MS 104 65; J. R. Mozely, Letter to Joseph Mayor about John Grote, 1904, ibid., Add. MS. 104 66); Simon J. Cook, 'The Place of Reforming Cambridge in Alfred Marshall's Construction of an Economic Organon, 1861–1890,' Ph.D. thesis, University of Cambridge, 2001.

proceedings, and public lectures at their disposal, how could they reproduce their knowledge and expand their authority? Unable to find an effective answer, the metropolitan universities grew to be regional supernovas.

Within the universities the transfers of power over curriculum were complex, contested and divergent.[22] However, when comparing the early and later parts of the century, the major line of development was the gradual, and often faltering, transfer of control from the colleges to the university.[23] This is associated with the rise of the 'new Don', the professional rather than clergyman don, that began in the 1850s in Cambridge, picked up pace in mid century as the Royal Commissions spread good practice, and took firmer shape after the 1877 Royal Commission.[24] Engel correctly notes that the colleges were not left behind but kept power by accommodating the shift, by professionalising their statutes, offering prizes, appointing specialist discipline tutors and altering the tenures of tutor and fellows. But control did shift as tuition moved to specialist departments and faculties, as syllabus design moved to central syndicates, and as curriculum management moved to boards of studies.

This shift has been examined and well explained for Cambridge, Oxford, Dublin, London, and Edinburgh.[25] A comparative analysis of the five universities in terms of curriculum for the moral sciences reveals interesting results.[26] The story is complex, with universities influencing one another, but many of

[22] John R. Gibbins, 'Constructing Knowledge in Mid-Victorian Cambridge: The Moral Science Tripos, 1850–1870', in John Smith and Christopher Stray (eds.), *Teaching and Learning in Nineteenth-Century Cambridge* (Cambridge, 2001), pp. 61–88. Anon, 'Cambridge University Reform', *The British Quarterly Review*, 32, July 1860, 204–30.

[23] A. J. Engel, *From Clergyman to Don: The Rise of the Academic Profession in Nineteenth Century Oxford* (Oxford, 1983) p. 285.

[24] Ibid., pp. 257–80.

[25] Ibid., Winstanley, *Early Victorian Cambridge*; *Later Victorian Cambridge*; D. B. Horn, *Short History of the University of Edinburgh, 1556–1889* (Edinburgh, 1967); Rothblatt, *Revolution of the Dons;* Gordon Huelin, *Kings College, London, 1828–1978* (London, 1978); Martha Garland, *Cambridge Before Darwin: The Ideal of a Liberal Education, 1800–1860* (Cambridge, 1980); R. B. McDowell and D. A. Webb, *Trinity College Dublin, 1592–1952, An Academic History* (Cambridge, 1982); F. M. L. Thompson (ed.), *The University of London and the World of Learning, 1836–1986*, (London, 1990); Christopher N. L. Brooke, *A History of the University of Cambridge, Volume IV, 1870–1990* (Cambridge, 1993); Michael G. Brock and Mark C. Curthoys (eds.), *The History of the University of Oxford: Vol. VI, Nineteenth-Century Oxford, Part 1* (Oxford, 1997); Peter Searby, *A History of the University of Cambridge, Volume III, 1750–1870* (Cambridge, 1997).

[26] John R. Gibbins, 'Designing Curricula: The Moral Sciences in Cambridge, Oxford, Edinburgh, London and Dublin', *Conference on Teaching and Learning in Nineteenth-Century Cambridge*, Cambridge, 2001 (forthcoming in *History of Universities*). There is useful comparative coverage in T. W. Heyck, *The Transformation of Intellectual Life in Victorian England* (London, 1982); Peter Slee, *Learning and Liberal Education: The Study of Modern History in the Universities of Oxford, Cambridge and Manchester, 1800–1914* (Manchester, 1986); Reba Soffer, *Discipline and Power: The University, History and the Making of an English Elite, 1870–1930* (Stanford, 1994).

the newest innovations after 1830 were developed first at Cambridge, travelled quickly to Oxford and more slowly to London, Dublin and Edinburgh. This is seen most clearly in the innovation of specialist subject tutors being appointed in colleges; the appointment of university-level boards of studies and examiners; provision of written rather than oral examination; appointment of examiners external to the university; provision of central and departmental libraries to enhance college provision. These innovations are now understood as milestones in the development of the modern university and of modern disciplines, and indeed it was these debates that have occasioned fundamental research in the area of curriculum. What we need to do now is look at the same events within a different narrative. Perhaps what made universities become so authoritative was their monopoly on knowledge production gained through their right to set curriculum. Perhaps the professionalisation of disciplines was made possible because the new curriculum agencies, of syndics, boards and commissions, gave subject specialists a platform on which to perform, and prizes to pursue. Perhaps curriculum can be pictured as the driving force behind the development of the new disciplines and the universities. Perhaps we can place curriculum and syllabus closer to the centre of power in our explanation of university history, rather than on the periphery?

Sedgwick and Mill: Discourses on the Studies of the University of Cambridge

In a passing comment, Anthony Quinton made reference to a phenomenon of great importance in understanding the development of Victorian ideas in general and the massive rivalry between the forces of 'intuitionism' and 'empiricism' denoted by John Stuart Mill. The comment refers to the *amateur* status of philosophers aligned to the empiricist, utilitarian, positivist and materialist causes. Referring to contemporary twentieth-century historians and philosophers he wrote:

> Under pressure they would describe the course of philosophy between Hume and Russell in roughly the following terms: first of all there is Mill carrying on in a more or less eighteenth-century fashion, besides him spring up a whole lot of amateur philosophers like Spencer, of materialistic tendencies and intoxicated by the doctrine of evolution, at which point the defenders of religion and public order pull themselves together and input a quantity of surplus metaphysical material from Germany, whose rich obscurity soon puts an end to the complacency of secular rationalism.[27]

[27] Anthony Quinton, 'Victorian Philosophy', in *Thought and Thinker* (London, 1982), p. 182.

Outside the universities, Bentham, Mill and George Grote in the 1830s sought to construct a new intellectual current that they hoped would replace that of the sinister interests, namely the monarch, the church, the aristocracy, and their source of legitimation, the universities. Inside the universities, business was very much as usual; reforms were underway but the sons of the aristocracy still came up to read for a 'pass' degree, the professions gained elementary training, traditional knowledge was transmitted to traditional elites. But in 1833, the young and ambitious Adam Sedgwick of Trinity College published his *A Discourse on the Studies of the University of Cambridge,* and drew attention to the course of studies provided there.[28] Going through many editions, and growing in size many times, it became a kind of early handbook for prospective students. Its genesis began as the 1833 Annual Commemoration Lecture at Trinity College, Cambridge designed to explore, elaborate and celebrate the form and content of studies on 'the classical, metaphysical and moral studies of the university'.[29]

In the 1833 'Lecture' that spawned the *Discourse,* the logic Sedgwick enunciated was essentially and thoroughly theocentric. We should remember the genre expectation of such Commemoration Lectures, but Sedgwick exceeded even the demands of the convention. The studies at the university he advocated should be expected to recognise, and be compatible with the glories of God's creation and to detect the inner workings of divine 'overruling intelligence' and providence, from its 'outer emanations'. Three branches of study are identified: the study of laws, natural and divine, focusing on the 'harvest' that Newton had sowed in the college; the study of ancient literatures; and the 'study of ourselves, considered as individuals and as social beings'.[30] For thirty pages of the original lecture Sedgwick impatiently squares natural theology and natural sciences, using his favourite discipline of geology as exemplar, before passing on to the classics. Ancient languages allow us access, he argues, 'to the magazines of thought—we find way through the vast storehouse wherein are piled the intellectual treasures of a nation, as soon as we have capacity to understand their value, and strength to turn them to good account'.[31] So whereas the study of science and mathematics is driven by knowing the mind of God, and hence being able to help

[28] Adam Sedgwick, 'A Discourse on the Studies of the University of Cambridge', The Annual Commemoration Lecture, Delivered in the Chapel, Trinity College, Cambridge, 1833 in *A Discourse on the Studies of the University of Cambridge*, 5th edn. (Cambridge, 1850), pp. 1–94.

[29] Ibid., p. x.

[30] Ibid., pp. 10–11.

[31] Ibid., pp. 33–4.

realise his providential scheme, the study of classics is driven by human concerns, gaining knowledge, wisdom and judgement 'to kindle delightful emotions—to gratify the imagination and taste—but also to instruct the understanding'.[32]

Philosophy and ethics, exemplified in Socrates, Plato and Aristotle, and also history, are treated here as sub-species of classics, though they are viewed as *sui generis* in a later part of his lecture. Under philosophy Sedgwick defends narrowness and he produces cases for the study of Locke and Paley that depend upon their compatibility with natural theology.[33] But another theme re-emerges in the fifth edition's 'Preface to the First Edition', namely that the books chosen for the examination in philosophy must reflect the theocentric and positivist rivalry, the foundational debates between rationalism and empiricism on knowledge, and intuitionalism versus utilitarianism in ethics. The books and figures of Descartes and Clarke are advanced against Locke and Hobbes; and in ethics Bishop Butler's *Sermons* are opposed to Paley's *Moral Philosophy*.[34] The syllabus for politics is drafted without reference to books, being centred upon defending established institutional and legal arrangements upon intuitional revelations confirmed by historical analysis.[35] A previous century of enlightened reformers and radicals are despatched swiftly as 'Moral fanatics', bent on 'moral perfection' but led by men 'sunk in infidelity'.[36] The theme of sensualism versus sacred learning completed this survey 'over your course of studies'.[37]

But there are many significant refinements, advances in scholarship and discipline developments in the next decades of later editions of the *Discourses*, mostly in the extended 'Preface to the Fifth Edition', the 'Appendix' and 'Notes'.[38] These were occasioned by critical responses from inside and outside the university, which forced Sedgwick into more ideocentric and sociocentric veins.[39] Rigorous description and analysis, textual critique, methodological and factual disputes are brought to bear. The change is understandable, for what had started as a Commemorative gloss on a conservative syllabus and institutions had brought ignominy to both the author

[32] Ibid., p. 38.
[33] Ibid., p. 45.
[34] Ibid., pp. xi–56–82.
[35] Ibid., pp. 82–9.
[36] Ibid., p. 88.
[37] Ibid., p. 89.
[38] Ibid., pp. ix–ccccxlii; pp. 95–322.
[39] For this distinction see Paul L. Dressel, 'Curriculum and Instruction in Higher Education', in *The Encyclopedia of Education Research*, vol. i, 5th edn. (London, 1982), p. 401.

and the university. No critic had hit harder and more effectively than John Stuart Mill, who in the *London Review* of April 1835 launched his broadside, *Professor Sedgwick's Discourse on the Studies of the University of Cambridge.*[40] What is interesting here is the reference to the intellectual, ideological and sociological phenomenon of the age, the mirroring of the major philosophical division between intuitionism and empiricism in the battle between the universities and the amateur literary gentlemen of the age. Further elaboration of the conflict and its development can only be sketched, but we can start to picture the conflicts of curriculum in the 1830s in similar terms.

That the Victorian universities were to some considerable extent reactionary bastions of social privilege and church dogma is undoubtedly true, though Martha Garland and Sheldon Rothblatt have done well to correct former exaggeration. John Stuart Mill and other external critics of the universities added the more dubious rider that the universities were also intellectually sterile, a belief that probably explains James Mill's decision not to send John to Trinity College, Cambridge in 1823.[41] With his father and Jeremy Bentham, John Mill tied the universities with the churches as vehicles of the 'sinister interests'. According to Mill, university statutes and endowments ensured not academic freedom as was claimed by their custodians but academic immobility. 'All beyond this, is to make the dead, judges of the exigencies of the living, to erect, not merely the ends, but the means, not merely the speculative opinions, but the practical expedients of a gone by age, into an irrevocable law for the present.'[42]

In his critique of *Professor Sedgwick's Discourses on the Studies of the University of Cambridge,* Mill adds that because of the security given them by ancient status and aristocratic endowments the universities and colleges had become homes for complacent and self-perpetuating elites. Intellectual 'degeneracy' was the result of this complacency, and so, with obvious reference to the *Discourse,* he concluded, 'while they are thus eulogizing their own efforts, and the results of their efforts; philosophy — not any particular school of philosophy, but philosophy altogether — speculation of any comprehensive kind, and upon any deep or extensive subject—has been falling more and more into distastefulness and disrepute among the educated class of England'.[43] The shocking conclusion was that the universities could not be

[40] John S. Mill, 'Professor Sedgwick's Discourse on the Studies of the University of Cambridge', in *Dissertations and Discussions*, vol. 1, 2nd edn. (London, 1867), pp. 95–159.

[41] Alexander Bain, *J. S. Mill: A Criticism with Personal Recollections* (London, 1902), p. 28.

[42] John Stuart Mill, 'Corporation and Church Endowment', in *Dissertations and Discussions*, vol. 1, 2nd edn. (London, 1867), p. 5.

[43] Ibid., pp. 98–9; also see pp. 175, 192–200.

trusted to produce and reproduce knowledge, they could not be allowed a monopoly on 'the education by which great minds are formed'.[44] The consequences of the decline Mill saw as worrying for politicians, civil servants and patriot as well as parent and employer:

> In the intellectual pursuits which form great minds, this country was formerly pre-eminent. England once stood at the head of European philosophy. Where stands she now? Consult the general opinion of Europe. The celebrity of England, in the present day, rests on her docks, her canals, her railroads. In intellect she is distinguished only for a kind of sober good sense, free from extravagance, but also void of lofty aspiration; and for doing all those things which are best done where man most resembles a machine with the precision of a machine.[45]

Few people outside the universities took exception to these general indictments, though John Morell's histories tell a very different story and David Masson wrote in 1866 that 'Even at the time when Mr Mill wrote these words I cannot but think they described matters as somewhat worse than they really were.'[46]

On syllabus and curriculum Mill was not as detailed or devastating as he was on unpicking the ideological glue that held together the intellectual arguments of Sedgwick's *Discourse*. Responding to Sedgwick's tripartite organisation of the syllabus, Mill complained: 'How many errors in expression and classification in one short passage!' He defended the point with ample evidence and sound logical inference.[47] The paucity of all branches of the curriculum were cruelly and expertly exposed. 'Of the true reasons, and there are most substantial and cogent ones, for assigning to classical studies a high place in general education, we find not a word in Mr Sedgwick's tract.'[48] Where the battle became utterly unequal was over metaphysics and ethics. Mill was by now a uniquely well-read, well-trained, experienced professional philosopher, engaging a widely read don, a well-trained geologist with little experience of debating or writing philosophy, and it shows. The defects of intuitional ethical argument are attacked from an equally implausible utilitarian standpoint, but in a manner that speaks of the gap in professionalism

[44] Ibid., p. 95.
[45] Ibid., p. 96.
[46] David Masson, *Recent British Philosophy: A Review with Criticisms,* 3rd edn. (London and Cambridge, 1877), p. 3; John D. Morell, *An Historical and Critical View of the Speculative Philosophy of Europe in the Nineteenth Century,* 2 vols. (London, 1846); John D. Morell, *On the Philosophical Tendencies of the Age; Being Four Lectures Delivered at Edinburgh and Glasgow* (London, 1848).
[47] Mill, 'Corporation and Church Endowment', pp. 101–5.
[48] Mill, 'Corporation and Church Endowment', p. 110.

between Mill, the metropolitan intellectual and sage, and his rival the university don.

Mill sought to repeat the victory over Cambridge studies again in 1852 with his challenge to the new Cambridge champion, in his *Dr. Whewell on Moral Philosophy* (1852).[49] This followed a review of Whewell's views on Cambridge curriculum of 1848 by another Philosophical Radical, the Scotsman Alexander Bain, who in the *Westminister and Foreign Quarterly* described its tutorial system as 'lax and inefficient to the highest degree', advising that in the teaching of ethics, Professor Jardine and the Glasgow lecturers 'might furnish some surprises for Cambridgemen if these would condescend to read them'.[50] Whewell was a reforming don of the new order, catalyst in the production of the next generation of professional scholars. The battle was now more even and the result still debated. Whewell's points against Mill, empiricism, positivism, materialism, and utilitarianism have entered the canon of philosophical discourse on a par with Mill's.[51] Similarly the long debate over the correct interpretation of the lessons of Bacon and Newton for the logic of scientific discovery raised important questions.[52] Whewell established the Moral Science Tripos with a clearly defined, defensible and organised syllabus in 1851. He initiated the process that reformed the examination, tutoring and lecturing systems that organised the curriculum, as well as helping reform the statutes of colleges and the university. His efforts at building intellectual capacity bore fruit by 1860 when the Tripos was more radically revised by John Grote, and Whewell's three books on curriculum amount to a substantial contribution to nineteenth-century developments.[53]

[49] John Stuart Mill, 'Dr Whewell on Moral Philosophy', in *Dissertations and Discussion*, ii, pp. 450–509.

[50] Alexander Bain, 'Review of "Of a Liberal Education in General with Reference to the Leading Studies of the University of Cambridge" by William Whewell', *Westminster and Foreign Quarterly Review*, July 1848, 20–3; William Whewell, *Of a Liberal Education in General* (London, 1845).

[51] Evaluations can be found in Rothblatt, *Revolution*, pp. 101–5; Alan Ryan, *J. S. Mill* (London, 1974), pp. 95–124; William Thomas, *Mill* (Oxford, 1985), pp. 61–3; Menachem Fisch, *William Whewell: Philosopher of Science* (Oxford, 1991), pp. 141, 147, 151, 155, 159; Menachem Fisch and Simon Schaffer (eds.), *William Whewell: A Composite Portrait* (Oxford, 1991), pp. 311–44, 346–9, 352–7.

[52] Ronald Fletcher, *John Stuart Mill: A Logical Critique of Sociology* (London, 1971), pp. 27–9; 54–7; Cook, 'The Place of Reforming Cambridge', pp. 66–73.

[53] William Whewell, *On the Principles of English University Education* (Cambridge, 1837); William Whewell, *Of a Liberal Education in General* (London, 1845); William Whewell, *Of a Liberal Education in General: The Revised Statutes of 1851–2*, 2nd. edn. (London, 1850); Perry Williams, 'Passing the Torch: William Whewell's Philosophy and the Principles of English University Education', in Fisch and Schaffer (eds.), *Whewell*, pp. 117–48; David Palfrey, 'The Moral and Science Tripos at Cambridge University, 1848–1860', Ph.D. thesis, University of Cambridge, 2002.

Old Studies and New, Mark Pattison and John Grote, 1855–1856

Meanwhile Mill's efforts in terms of knowledge building, transfer, and organisation in this period can be seen as less successful. His critique of Sedgwick was less a critique of Cambridge curriculum and more a vehicle for the Philosophical Radicals to attack their rationalist and intuitionalist opponents. Mill rarely suggested alternative texts, avoided discussion of teaching, assessment schemes and syllabus. This characterises the bulk of his writings on education though we do have glimpses of what he considered to be a good course of reading in his *Autobiography* (1873), and in a detailed list of reading proposed to Florence May in 1868.[54] Indeed this may be a pattern exhibited in the works of other Victorian sages who sought to influence higher education and culture from outside the universities. And there may be one central reason, for these writers did not have the everyday engagement with teaching and learning in an institutional setting; they did not have to organise their knowledge in a form that was to be tested, evaluated and certified for public as well as private usage and exchange. These 'Sages' or 'Prophets', had little to say on teaching and learning, syllabus and curriculum.[55]

John W. Parker, the publisher, commissioned essays from leading university scholars from Oxford and Cambridge, publishing three volumes before abandoning the project. In the Cambridge volume for 1856, John Grote addressed the key issue of what the curriculum was and how it should develop, and how it should balance 'Old Studies and New'.[56] In the Oxford volume for 1855 Mark Pattison, addressed wider issues of university reform, introducing an agenda that lead to his book on 'Academical Organization'. His essay was flanked by contributions from other major participants in debates on the Oxford curriculum: J. A. Froude on teaching English history; H. Smith on 'The Plurality of Worlds'; W. Thompson on 'Crime and its Excuses'; and the most original essay by T. C. Saunders on 'Hegel's Philosophy of Right'.[57] In retrospect, the essays by Grote and Pattison were significant contributions to the changing role of the university in knowledge production. Both ask and answer several core questions: what is education,

[54] John S. Mill, *Autobiography* (London, 1924); 'Letter to Florence May', *Mill's Collected Works, XVI, Letters, 1849–1873* (Toronto, 1972), pp. 1472–5.

[55] George Watson, *The English Ideology: Studies in the Languages of Victorian Politics* (London, 1973); Peter Keating (ed.) *The Victorian Prophets: A Reader from Carlyle to Wells* (London, 1981).

[56] John Grote, 'Old Studies and New', in *Cambridge Essays 1856* (London, 1856), pp. 74–114.

[57] Mark Pattison, 'Oxford Studies', in *Oxford Essays 1855* (London, 1855), pp. 251–310.

within a school and a university context? What means will deliver these ambitions? What justifications are there for classical education amongst new studies? Should the classical and mathematical syllabus be supplemented with new and specialist studies such as philosophy, philology, history and economics? Should university education seek to prepare students for professional or vocational life? Pattison sought to address an additional and parochial question, how his own university and the colleges could reform to widen their appeal and cement a position of authority in society? Both provided detail as well as rumination, prescription as well as critique, evaluation as well as description.

In line with his belief that words gain their meaning from contexts and usages, John Grote refused to produce an essentialist answer to his first question on the nature of education, preferring the idealist edict that education is to prepare young people for what they can become, offering self-realisation.[58] On the means to this ideal he was elusive, referring back to the need to relate old and new studies in different ways for different goals. His justification of studying classical texts was novel and instructive, for while acceding to the authority of the received wisdom embodied in tradition, he stressed the value inherent in studying any language, whether classical or modern. The value of studying languages was their capacity to convey meaning, to make accessible cultures and their knowledge. He put this clearly in a later essay on 'Thought versus Learning', where he argued that more can be learned from conversation and the study of words than from reading books, because a language contains the entire stock of the knowledge of a society, and conversation allows its exploration.[59] Grote invited his readers to take modern languages more seriously, anticipating the growth of English, French and German studies later in the century. Anxious to protect the idea that an education is about thought and meaning rather than learning and form, he set out an agenda to tame the ambitions of philology to replace classical and philosophical studies. Comparative philology may offer many prospects, but it cannot provide the lessons, the learning and the guidance provided by the classics.

Faced as the universities were with the demand to make their studies vocationally and professionally relevant, Grote rehearsed an argument that remained effective for another century. The best way for an education to be professionally relevant was to teach students how to converse, how to argue,

[58] On John Grote see John R. Gibbins, 'John Grote and Modern Cambridge Philosophy', *Philosophy,* 73 (1998), 453–77.

[59] John Grote, 'Thought versus Learning', *Good Words*, 12 (1871), 818–23; Grote, 'Old Studies and New', pp. 93, 96–7.

to think and write. The object of study was less important than the approach, the organisation, and effort at meaning and understanding. Indeed, to study objects as such, to study practical and professional activities immediately and directly, would handicap the key task of inducing and facilitating intellectual engagement. The nascent study of history within the new Historical Tripos could be strangled at birth if it were to be made the servant of political expediency as anticipated by Mill and Sedgwick.[60] Similarly, he argued that the physical sciences should be encouraged to develop their own language, methods and courses, independently and free from interference from the old studies, with the caveat that they should know and keep their place in the organisation of knowledge.[61] The worlds and languages of disciplines such as history, science, philology, psychology and philosophy were to be kept apart. A university, Grote claimed, 'ought to be a place of great variety of study'. Universities should be reserved for those with 'intellectual interest and desire for knowledge' who would come to have their mind 'called out', their knowledge treated as a 'blessing'. If the pursuit of knowledge in itself were embraced by universities, then the likely by-product would be 'happiness and usefulness'.[62]

Grafting the best of the new onto the strong mature trunk of old studies was John Grote's programme for reform of the curriculum.[63] The guiding principles of selection in curriculum should be those that allow a person to think more clearly, to pay more attention to what passes before them, so that the individuals could understand themselves and others by understanding what they say. The key methods of delivery to be encouraged were talking and conversing clearly, reading great literature, imagining and understanding. The methods to be avoided were cramming books, seeking to impose uniformity when variety was better, and attempting to impose universal methods, theory and language onto disciplines that flourish only when their particular language, methods, rules and theory are respected.[64]

Pattison would have approved of Grote's position and of the strategy of conservative adaptation towards liberal goals of spreading and refining knowledge for the benefits of all. However, his stress in *Oxford Studies* of 1855 was less on subjects and books, and more on reform of institutions, procedures and curriculum. Writing immediately after the trauma of the

[60] Ibid., pp. 109–13.
[61] Ibid., p. 96.
[62] Ibid., pp. 105–8.
[63] Ibid., p. 107.
[64] Ibid., pp. 113–14.

Royal Commission and the Oxford Reform Act, Pattison took stock of the new challenge to the university and to the dons. For the dons, the aim must be to gain the freedom to 'review their own views, to realise the connexion of those bodies with the nation and to draw from careful, and continued study of the national problem, more enlarged conceptions of the new duties, the powers, and the glorious opportunities opening to us'.[65] The essential task of a scholar was to focus on the 'central and proper object of human knowledge'.[66] Maintaining a liberal education remained an object, but his focus was more idealist, an elaboration and development of methods that would allow the Idea of mankind to be achieved through the realisation of the intellectual potential of students and dons.[67] With such a purpose, it is not surprising that Pattison, like John Grote, held that philosophy would be the key to all disciplinary developments. Philosophy of knowledge would allow each unique discipline to be classified, to ground itself and its knowledge claims, free from extraneous political and utilitarian demands.[68]

So long as disciplines were well grounded in epistemology and well taught, Pattison assumed products of value to society would follow: the growth of knowledge, development of private and public judgement and mental cultivation.[69] This grounding required the inculcation of several intellectual qualities or curriculum virtues, namely 'a breadth of cultivation, a scientific formulation of mind, a concert of the intellectual faculties'.[70] The intellectual virtues curriculum delivery would cultivate were, 'clear-sightedness, sagacity, philosophical reach in mind'. Curriculum utility, which was defined in terms of success in the development of human faculties was, like happiness to Aristotle, an end not found or pursued directly. Useful knowledge and the practical and professional application sought by utilitarians, was best pursued by the cultivation of a philosophical approach to knowledge. Development of a 'comprehensive intellect' is emblematic of this generation of university dons, from Whewell and Jowett, to Sidgwick and Green.

More complex detail on the delivery curriculum was proffered by Pattison, especially advice on the merits and organisation of examinations: the need to ensure 'comparability' of examination classes in specialist and general subjects; the requirement that examiners are as well read and versed in new methods as the students; the necessity that tests are of understanding

[65] Pattison, 'Oxford Studies', p. 251.
[66] Ibid., p. 253.
[67] Ibid., pp. 267–8.
[68] Ibid., pp. 269–70.
[69] Ibid., p. 272.
[70] Ibid., p. 285.

and not just of comprehension or cramming; the desirability of showing some progression in learning, moving from skills to comprehension of books, to understanding and application of methods over three, or perhaps, four years.[71] The shift to written examinations, as Christopher Stray has shown, begins with the influence of Newtonianism in the eighteenth century, reinforced by the growing respect for individual ability and distrust of socio-cultural assessment; the difficulty of orally testing in some disciplines such as mathematics, as well as student numbers and local political issues.[72] But Whewell, Shairp, and Pattison saw the shift in terms of factors designed to improve the credibility and authority of the curriculum. 'Public examination' with published 'Written Papers', a 'Board of Examiners' and 'External Examiners' denoted opposition to patronage and prejudice, and concern for individual ownership, professional rigour, 'testability', evidence-based accreditation and objectivity through comparability, fairness and equity.[73] Whewell prevaricated until 1852 and the University of Edinburgh delayed until even later, but by the 1860s written examinations became the primary teaching and learning tool in Oxbridge with new applications of termly examinations, terminal examinations, scholarship and prize examinations, internal college examinations to check on progress, and importantly, examinations for fellowships. The universities were obliged to recognise this system as the price to be paid by them or rather their students for external recognition of their legitimacy to design and deliver the national and professional agenda for knowledge. That this fitted the liberal market economic prioritisation of individualism, competition and survival of the fittest, only cemented the confidence expressed in examinations. Extra examinations for prizes and scholarships were now entered by the richest and the most able in search of honours and status, rather than by the poor and lowly in search of subsistence allowances. Regulation of the adjudicators became a hot issue as the career significance of achieving prizes and scholarships grew.

Showing real insight into the need for a coherent learning experience for students, Pattison promoted the use of a course in the history of ethics and

[71] Ibid., pp. 289–301.

[72] Christopher Stray, 'The Shift from Oral to Written Examination: Cambridge and Oxford, 1700–1900', *Assessment in Education*, 8 (2002), 33–50.

[73] M. C. Curthoys, 'The Examination System', in Brock and Curthoys (eds.), *History of the University of Oxford*, pp. 339–74; Gibbins, 'Designing Curricula: The Moral Sciences in Cambridge, Oxford, Edinburgh, London and Dublin', *Conference on Teaching and Learning in Nineteenth-Century Cambridge,* Cambridge, Trinity College, 2001 (forthcoming in *History of Universities*), 13–14, John Campbell Shairp, *The Wants of the Scottish Universities and some of the Remedies* (Edinburgh, 1856); pp. 35–48, William Whewell, *Of a Liberal Education in General: The Revised Statutes of 1851–2*, 2nd edn. (London, 1852), pp. 13–56.

philosophy as central to the general and new specialist degrees.[74] Philosophy should be the core subject in all disciplines including specialist science curriculum, and the much vaunted claims for philology, the universal science of all languages, as its required replacement, were rejected as pretentious.[75] Always, it should be the quality of intellect, not its scope, extent or capacity for retrieval, that should be valued and tested through the curriculum.[76]

The Universities, Sages and Curriculum

There was nothing like the Royal Commissions on the universities for the popular writers, journalists, sages and prophets of the age, who could do little but cheer or wring their hands as the results of the profound changes in university organisations took shape. John Grote's elder brother George and other radicals identified the deficits that accompanied exclusion from academic institutions. The early founding of Literary and Philosophical Societies, museums, municipal art galleries and Working Men's Educational Associations were only a prelude to the founding of colleges, later to be incorporated into universities. George Grote worked hard to establish the new London University, incorporating not only colleges, schools, academies and a professional library, but also a different culture, environment and students.[77] Later the old universities were to learn to accommodate to the new universities, following their ever improving and impressive results. However, accommodations were made to the Oxbridge model and in many ways the new metropolitan universities moved closer to the Oxbridge model through the century, than vice versa. Central features of the process of accommodation included the maintenance of college systems and powers; a shift of tuition and teaching from college to central departments; the centralisation of university administration and finance; the professionalisation and empowerment of lecturers and professors; the movement from examining books to subjects and discipline-relevant theory and methods; bringing external examiners onto boards of studies; and above all blending the best of old studies, such as the classics, philosophy and mathematics with the most exciting of the new, such as history, law, psychology, anthropology, philology,

[74] Pattison, 'Oxford Studies', pp. 295–7.
[75] Ibid., p. 298.
[76] Ibid., p. 309.
[77] Thompson (ed.), *The University of London*; Martin L. Clarke, *George Grote: A Biography* (London, 1962).

politics and economics. The arts however, remained relatively unreformed and hence comparatively backward in mid century, the BA being modernised late in the century.[78]

Under the influence of George Grote, London also sought to benefit from the expertise that was emerging from the Oxbridge cohorts of the 1850s and 1860s. The list of Oxbridge lecturers who gravitated to London as lecturers, examiners, professors and administrators was extensive. Once the university in London was established, George Grote, philosophical radical, atheist and MP not only remained a Senate member for several decades, but became an influential vice-chancellor. He equipped the library with the best of the old and the new, brought in new talent to fill new buildings, laboratories and lecture theatres. While we may detect continuity with the older Grote in the insistence on non-clerical appointments to chairs, with radicals and utilitarians such as Alexander Bain taking influential posts, he also held ideas on university reform and curriculum that were closer to his brother John at Cambridge by the end of the 1860s. Mill's appreciation of Oxbridge mellowed in older age while he became more jaundiced about institutions such as London University and the new crop of professional academies. In 1865 he wrote, 'The whole career of that Institution is a melancholy proof of the rarity of any desire in the middle classes for London to be given the benefit of a good education to their sons.'[79] 'Academies whether for literature or science generally prefer inoffensive mediocrities to men of original genius.' He feared that 'Such bodies, having only a collective responsibility, are often even more addicted to abusing their patronage than single functionaries, the members are apt to job for one another and vote for each others protégés.'[80]

The struggle Thomas Huxley had through his life to inform university scientific knowledge via curriculum, moving from sage to don, illustrates the case that without the authority that curriculum endows, the reproduction of knowledge cannot be guaranteed. The earliest journal entries of Thomas Huxley describe the reading and study that he set for himself in 1841 and which became the basis for his future career.[81] It was not, however, a curriculum. His consumption of curriculum was disjointed, including a period at Sydenham College and Charing Cross Hospital studying medicine, gaining

[78] Thompson (ed.), *The University of London*, pp. 61–9.

[79] John Stuart Mill, 'Letter to Prof. John E Cairnes', 16 Nov. 1865, *Later Letters, Mill's Collected Works,* XVII (Toronto, 1972), pp. 1663–4.

[80] John Stuart Mill, 'Letter to Sir Ray Lankester', *Later Letters, Mill's Collected Works, XVII* (Toronto, 1972), p. 1937.

[81] Thomas Henry Huxley, 'Early Journal', in Leonard Huxley, *Life and Letters of Thomas Henry Huxley*, 3 vols. (London, 1903), i, 16–20.

a MB of London University in 1845. Despite all his efforts at research, his great success with numerous publications, a role in university administration and reform, and a short experience of university examining in London, he did not shape or manage a course of study for students until late in life. Like Mill, Carlyle and Arnold, he was a prophet without a church institution to reproduce and implant the knowledge he produced until he found various organisational locations. Having such an institutional and organisational disadvantage in his early career, he adopted the more public, but in authoritative terms, less effective means and modes of delivering and reproducing his ideas: public lectures, pamphlets and books, and membership of organisations to rival the university, namely the British Association, the Royal Society, the Zoological Society, various literary clubs, Royal Commissions and numerous other public bodies.

Huxley remained anxious all his life about the organisation and transmission of knowledge, and this drew him back regularly to issues around curriculum. He refused a university post in London on financial grounds, arguing that 'a man who chooses a life of science chooses not a life of poverty, but so far as I can see, a life of *nothing,* and the art of living upon nothing at all has yet to be discovered'.[82] He sought, unsuccessfully, better paid university posts in Toronto, Aberdeen, and King's College London from 1851 to 1853.[83] Eventually, he obtained lectureships at the Royal Institution and the Royal College of Surgeons where he was able to construct a syllabus and develop a new form of laboratory-led teaching, culminating in the Chair in Natural History at the School of Mines at the University of London that he held for thirty-one years.[84] It was from this centre that his influence radiated. But he was never convinced that the life of a professional don suited him and his mission. On the rumour that he was to be offered the Mastership of University College, Oxford in 1881, he wrote that 'when I came to the matter closely there were many disadvantages. I do not think I am cut out to be a Don there nor your mother for a Donness—we have had thirty years of freedom in London, and are too old to be put in harness.'[85]

In 1892, the chance arose, as a leading member of the Senate, to impact on the future of teaching and learning within London University when the whole issue of university reform re-emerged. The core question was whether to incorporate the numerous colleges and institutions and to make

[82] Huxley, 'Early Journal', i, 100.
[83] Ibid., 112–115.
[84] Thompson (ed.), *The University of London*, pp. 116–17.
[85] Huxley, *Life and Letters*, ii, 307.

the university a teaching and not solely an examining body.[86] His policy was clear though his success in implementation was limited. London University should incorporate all the colleges, widen the curriculum, centralise teaching, and professionalise the roles of lecturers and professors.[87] The job of the lecturer is to 'train pioneers', to 'teach him what is already known, and train him in the methods of knowing more'.[88] He remained, like George Grote, concerned to keep education away from 'parsons' and to oppose the 'obsession' with liberal education.[89] But in an advisory letter to a parent on the education of his son in 1892, Huxley revealed an accommodation with the old academic order: 'A very good scientific education is to be had at both Oxford and Cambridge, especially at Cambridge', though 'putting him through the Latin and Greek mill will be indispensable.'[90]

Matthew Arnold adopted different strategies to maximise the reproductive potential of his ideas. This amounted to bouts of independence and unconstrained writing, opting in and out of fellowships and chairs at Oxford, advising on the founding of the University of London, various posts overseeing School Inspection and, finally researching the role and effectiveness of Continental higher education systems. He is remembered by most commentators for his prophetic and sage-like utterances, exemplified by *Culture and Anarchy* of 1869, but his role in curriculum design for schools and the universities was significant and he never lost the influence and authority that his roles in teaching and learning bestowed. Hugh Kingsmill wrote in 1928 that 'Arnold ceased to be Professor of Poetry in Oxford in 1867. No longer hampered by an official position, and having through his official position acquired a certain reputation and authority, he considered the moment right for adventure. So forth he sallied, mounted on Zeit-Geist, a hobby horse, his right hand gently twirling Charm, a lance without a point, and on his head, reminder that he was, after all, a don of Oxford, not of La Mancha, the mortar-board of Persuasion.'[91] Mill sallied forth in a different direction, celebrating university studies in his Inaugural Address to the University of St Andrews in 1867.[92]

86 Huxley, *Life and Letters*, iii, 225–40.
87 Ibid., 231.
88 Ibid.
89 Ibid., 233.
90 Ibid., 242.
91 Hugh Kingsmill, *Matthew Arnold* (London, 1928), p. 234.
92 John Stuart Mill, 'Inaugural Address Delivered to the University of St Andrews' (1867), *Essays on Equality, Law and Education, Mill's Collected Works,* xxi (Toronto, 1972), pp. 217–57.

Dons and Sages: Fault Lines in the Organisation of Knowledge since late Nineteenth-Century Britain

If universities were gaining ascendancy in the production and reproduction of knowledge in late nineteenth-century Britain, then several new questions begin to emerge. What fault lines appeared within the universities over who was to author the new knowledge? Who were to be the knowledge guardians in the universities, and how were they to prove competent guardianship? How did those outside the universities who were losing status respond to the new situation? How were they to organise themselves in the face of the organisational advantages that a university site bestowed? Who were the university's new competitors, who was to challenge and then take possession of such a prize? How did the role of sage, opinion leader, shaman, guru, literati and expert emerge and develop? How were competitors to imbricate, shape and control the production and management of curriculum? Was the 'Decline of Donnish Dominion' intended, or rather one of the unplanned consequences of other policies and processes?[93]

Halsey claims that while still influential, the contemporary university 'has a monopoly of nothing'.[94] He sees this decline resulting not just from the emergence of even newer disciplines, but from a change from an old to a new set of 'arrangements for making, storing, and retrieving intellectual products'. Refusing to accept the popular line of argument that seeks to trace a shift in the debate on the 'idea' of the university associated with Newman and Mill, Halsey argues instead that the debate was 'not so much about the quintessential idea of a university as about the relations between the shape and purpose of intellectual activity'.[95] In the old way, 'men of knowledge' reigned as trusted producers of knowledge, but gradually they were replaced by a 'people of new knowledge' located in industry, the civil service departments and multi-national corporations such as Microsoft. The modern struggle, as he saw it, was over 'what is to be sought and taught', and 'who should learn', hence shaping social structure by 'controlling access to highly valued cultural elements, differentiating the capacity of individuals to enter a hierarchy of labour markets, and therefore being intrinsically inegalitarian institutions'.

[93] Albert H. Halsey, *Decline of Donnish Dominion: The British Academic Profession in the Twentieth Century* (Oxford, 1992). For another diagnosis see Sheldon Rothblatt, *The Modern University and its Discontents: The Fate of Newman's Legacies in Britain and America* (Cambridge, 1997).

[94] Halsey, *Decline of Donnish Dominion*, p. 17.

[95] Ibid., p. 18.

But others diagnose the decline of the university in other more radical terms, involving 'the end of knowledge' itself. Not only has the university come to the end of its tenure on knowledge construction and design, but faith in knowledge and its foundations has declined in an age where almost anyone can claim to be an author of, and owner of knowledge, and where irony rules.[96] How, then, did and can the universities and the academy respond to this apparent loss of authority between 1900 and 1990? Can we identify some of the lines of struggle in the late nineteenth century at the dawn of the British Academy? What was the new knowledge that challenged that of the universities, and who were its organisers, producers and owners?

[96] On these debates see several special issues of the journal edited by Steve Fuller, *Social Epistemology: Journal of Knowledge, Culture and Policy*, esp. 14, 4 (2000); 15, 1 (2001); G. Delanty, 'The idea of the university in the global era', *Social Epistemology,* 12, 3–25 (2002); and M. Jacob and T. Hellstrom (eds.), *The Future of Knowledge Production in the Academy* (Buckingham, 2000); John R. Gibbins, 'Political Philosophy without Foundations and Anti-Foundational Politics', in Dave Morland and Mark Cowling (eds.), *Political Issues for the Twenty-First Century* (Aldershot, 2004), pp. 13–45.

CHAPTER TWELVE

The Promotion and Constraints of Knowledge: The Changing Structure of Publishing in Victorian Britain

JAMES RAVEN

The role of publishers and booksellers in organising knowledge by initiating, managing and promoting literature was forcibly interpreted by two troubled critics, one writing shortly before and the other close to the end of the reign of Victoria:

> You know not what a rapacious, dishonest set these booksellers are ... those fellows hate us. The reason I take to be, that contrary to other trades, in which the master gets all the credit, (a jeweler or silversmith for instance) and the journeyman, who really does the fine work, is in the background,—in *our* work the world gives all the credit to us, whom *they* consider as *their* journeymen, and therefore they do hate us, and cheat us, and oppress us, and would wring the blood of us out, to put another sixpence in their mechanic pouches! (Charles Lamb, 1833)[1]

> [John Murray II] did as much as any of his contemporaries to swell that movement in his profession towards complete individual liberty, which had been growing almost from the foundation of the Stationers' Company. Had his life been prolonged, he would have witnessed the disappearance in the trade of many institutions which he reverenced and always sought to develop. ... The old association of booksellers, with its accompaniment of trade-books, dwindled with the growth of the spirit of competition and the greater facility of communication, so that the co-operation between the booksellers of London and Edinburgh was no more than a memory.... Speculation [for retail booksellers to buy on special terms] has now almost ceased in consequence of the enormous number of books published. The country

[1] Charles Lamb to Bernard Barton, cited in Frank Arthur Mumby, *Publishing and Bookselling* (London, 1930), pp. 276–7.

> booksellers—a class in which Murray was always deeply interested—are dying out. Profits on books being cut down to a minimum, these tradesmen find it almost impossible to live by the sale of books alone. … Cheap bookselling, the characteristic of the age, has been promoted by the removal of the tax on paper. This cheapness … has been accompanied by a distinct deterioration in the taste and industry of the general reader. The multiplication of Reviews, Magazines, manuals, and abstracts, has impaired the love of, and perhaps the capacity for study, research, and scholarship on which the general quality of literature must depend. (Samuel Smiles, 1891)[2]

One of the constants of publishing was the particular personality of the publisher; Lamb-like condemnations can be countered by Smilesian encomiums to 'lettered bookmen', even though these are depicted as a declining troupe. More fundamentally, however, as even Smiles had to admit, Victorian publishing was dominated (as publishing had been since at least the late seventeenth century) by questions of capitalisation, centralised production and control, technological constraints (and breakthroughs), and the efficiency of distribution networks.[3] Within this structure, mass popular publishing responded to growing consumer demand, advanced by the continued expansion of part-issues, periodicals and newspapers, circulating libraries, public libraries, and in late Victorian Britain, by new demand for educational literature and schoolbooks.[4] The transformation in printing capacity, beginning in the 1820s and quickening again in the 1870s, was the unlocking key. In the previous century technological advance had been a limited force in British book trades development, restricted to typefounding and design, and to a lesser extent to paper manufacture and experiments with intaglio techniques and the rolling press, but the introduction of steam-driven printing presses from 1814 (to replace manual presses) shattered the principal technological constraint of three-and-a-half centuries.[5]

[2] Samuel Smiles, *A Publisher and his Friends: Memoir and Correspondence of the Late John Murray*, 2 vols. (London, 1891), 2: 516–17.

[3] John Feather, *A History of British Publishing* (London, 1988), pp. 129–79; Aled Jones, *Powers of the Press: Newspapers, Power and the Public in Nineteenth-Century England* (Aldershot, 1996), pp. 1–28; John Sutherland 'The Institutionalisation of the British Book Trade to the 1890s', in Robin Myers and Michael Harris (eds.), *Development of the English Book Trade, 1700–1899* (Oxford, 1981), pp. 95–105; vol. 6 [1830–1914] of *The Cambridge History of the Book*, ed. Simon Eliot and David McKitterick, is in progress.

[4] Simon Eliot, *Some Patterns and Trends in British Publishing, 1800–1919: Occasional Papers of the Bibliographical Society*, 8, 1994; Jones, *Powers of the Press*, pp. 98–139, 180–203; Simon Eliot, '"To You in Your Vast Business": Some Features of the Quantitative History of Macmillan, 1843–91', in Elizabeth James (ed.), *Macmillan: A Publishing Tradition* (London, 2002), pp. 11–51.

[5] Philip Gaskell, *A New Introduction to Bibliography* (Oxford, 1972), pp. 251–83, 289–96. Cf. Michael Twyman, *Lithography, 1800–1850* (Oxford, 1970).

Nevertheless, it is important to understand that there *had* been a late eighteenth-century commercial revolution and it was upon that basis that the Victorian literary infrastructure and book trade system advanced. The take-off in publication totals from the 1740s onwards reflected the expansion of distribution networks and increased institutional demand. New productivity was based on financial and organisational innovation, but very much within a trading structure dominated by the cartels of large, powerful bookseller–publishers investing in copyrights under legal copyright protection (as they conveniently interpreted it). The changing mechanics of distribution were a pivotal feature of this publishing history, and control, by both local and national government and their agents both a restraint and a stimulus.[6]

In outline, by the early nineteenth century (and especially after the challenges to the cartels in the 1770s) a freer, more competitive and expanding market, together with more efficient technologies and distributive systems, all provided enterprising publishers with unprecedented opportunities.[7] New industrial processes and the use of cheaper raw materials (notably including new papermaking processes) hugely improved the return on invested capital and lowered unit costs. Between 1846 and 1916 the volume of publication quadrupled while the average price of literature was halved.[8] The expansion of printing and publishing was further enabled by the greater capitalisation of the industry during the later eighteenth and then, more energetically, in the mid and later nineteenth century. It is clear that book trades profits and monies reinvested in publishing in Britain from the mid-eighteenth to the late nineteenth century resulted not only from greater diversification of trading practices, but from the deepening of money markets and of the financial infrastructure available. In particular, readier circulation and more flexible use of assets were ensured by new means of accessing capital and limiting risk. Inflows of capital from increased mercantile activity backed the expanding London money market (with freer availability of monies to trading partners by the readier discounting of bills of exchange), enabling credit to go further and extending credit chains.[9]

[6] James Raven, 'The Book Trades', in Isabel Rivers (ed.), *Books and Their Readers in Eighteenth-Century England: New Essays* (London and New York, 2001), pp. 1–34; James Raven, *The Commercialization of the Book: Booksellers and the Commodification of Literature in Britain, 1450–1900* (Cambridge, 2005).

[7] James Raven, 'British Publishing and Bookselling: Constraints and Developments', in Jean-Yves Mollier and Jean Michon (eds.), *Les mutations du livre et des l'éditions dans le monde du XVIIIe siècle à l'an 2000* (Quebec, 2001).

[8] Alexis Weedon, *Victorian Publishing: The Economics of Book Production for a Mass Market, 1836–1916* (Aldershot and Burlington, VT, 2003), p. 158.

[9] Raven, 'British Publishing and Bookselling'; I am grateful to Nigel Hall and Peter Martland for allowing me access to their research in advance of publication.

In such ways the broader changes in the economic structure of publishing supported the advance of printed knowledge. From their fragile and limited beginnings in the late seventeenth century, through to their mature development in the imperial decades of the late nineteenth century, banking and insurance services reduced publishers' and booksellers' risk on stock, buildings, shipping and other transportation (although fire insurance remained the most valued safeguard). Credit and insurance availability lowered book trades transaction costs, even though such development was not even. Until at least the early nineteenth century (and even to some degree in Victorian Britain) banking operations remained based primarily on the relative respectability and credit reputation of the operators.

Those in the book trades who had benefited most from new financial mechanisms and opportunities were well-resourced printer–publishers and bookseller–publishers such as Strahan, Cadell, Robinson, and the Rivingtons, the Murrays and the Longmans, spanning the late eighteenth to the final third of the nineteenth century. The new book trade leviathans of the nineteenth century notably included Murray and his son John III, John Blackwood, Richard Bentley, Smith, Elder and Company, Thomas Norton Longman III and Thomas Longman IV and Charles and Francis Rivington and their successors. All were able to demonstrate the respect and trust of a far-flung commercial elite.[10] By the mid-Victorian years the beneficiaries of such weighting were prominent houses like Macmillan, able to broaden their market appeal to become general trade publishers and dominate the British publishing industry by a variant form of the cartelisation practised by earlier leading booksellers. The Macmillan book was never categorised by one genre, and in this at least the firm contrasted with specialist leading publishers like Cassell, Collins, and Chambers, and also with publishers and promoters of popular fiction and periodicals for the working classes like Edward Lloyd, George Stiff, T. B. Smithies, and George W. M. Reynolds.[11] Murray and then, even more successfully, Routledge furthered their business by reprint series, building again upon earlier foundations, although Murray also

[10] F. A. Mumby, *Publishing and Bookselling* (London, 1930), chs. 12 and 13; Asa Briggs, *A History of the House of Longman* (London, 2005), Royal A. Gettman, *A Victorian Publisher: A Study of the Bentley Papers* (Cambridge, 1960).

[11] Virginia Berridge, 'Popular Sunday Papers and Mid-Victorian Society' and Peter Roger Mountjoy, 'The Working-Class Press and Working-Class Conservatism', in George Boyce, *et al.* (eds.), *Newspaper History from the Seventeenth Century to the Present Day* (London and Beverly Hills, CA, 1978), pp. 246–80; Jones, *Powers of the Press*, ch. 5; Eliot, 'To You in Your Vast Business', and Bill Bell, 'From Parnassus to Grub Street: Matthew Arnold and the House of Macmillan', in James (ed.), *Macmillan*, pp. 11–51 and 52–69; Simon Nowell-Smith, *The House of Cassell, 1848–1958* (London, 1958).

followed a path of broadening appeal.[12] What is quite clear, however (and embodied in the different relationships between prominent authors and prominent publishers), is that all of this still left the early Victorian publishing house working largely in the image of its publisher, a firm centred on the businessman and his particular tastes.[13]

The profile of the firm founded by Alexander and Daniel Macmillan in 1843 graphically charts the changes.[14] The first Macmillan bestseller in 1855, Charles Kingsley's *Westward Ho!*, was followed by Thomas Hughes's *Tom Brown's School Days* (1857), Palgrave's *Golden Treasury* (1861), *Alice's Adventures in Wonderland* (1865), and the first edition of *Nature* (1869). In 1869 the Macmillan New York office opened, and six years later the firm published its first textbooks for Indian schools. In 1878 the firm issued the first of four volumes of Grove's *Dictionary of Music and Musicians*, and in 1886 launched *The Colonial Library* series.[15] Four years later Macmillan published the first book with an agreed net price, Alfred Marshall's *Principles of Economics*. In 1895, a year before the death of Alexander Macmillan, the firm appointed its first Australian representative, and six years later in 1901 a branch was opened in Bombay. As Macmillan's experience demonstrated, colonial trade comprised a crucial division of the British book market, with Australia the leading destination for British book exports from 1889 to 1953. Between 1889 and 1901 Melbourne received more colonial editions than any other port of the empire.[16]

One result, therefore, of nineteenth-century publishing profiles that had developed from an original basis of personal reputation, was the widening of differences between the book traders. The humblest operators struggled to cope with credit and risk conveyance, while the grandest publishers invested more diversely in property, annuities, and a broader range of commercial and banking activities including investments overseas and in the colonial trades. No publisher, however, could escape one other result of this development—that credit broking, insurance services, and economic

[12] F. A. Mumby, *The House of Routledge, 1834–1934* (London, 1934).

[13] For contemporary accounts see Charles Knight, *Passages of a Working Life*, 3 vols. (London, 1864–5); Henry Curwen, *A History of Booksellers, the Old and the New* (London, 1874).

[14] See James (ed.), *Macmillan*, esp. Eliot, 'To You in Your Vast Business'; Thomas Hughes, *Memoir of Daniel Macmillan* (London, 1882).

[15] Elizabeth James, 'Introduction', in James (ed.), *Macmillan*, p. 2.

[16] Richard Nile and David Walker, 'The "Paternoster Row Machine" and the Australian Book Trade, 1890–1945', in Martyn Lyons and John Arnold (eds.), *A History of the Book in Australia, 1891–1945: A National Culture in a Colonised Market* (St Lucia, Queensland, 2001), pp. 3–18 (pp. 10–11); Weedon, *Victorian Publishing*, pp. 38–45, 157; Simon Nowell-Smith, *International Copyright and the Publisher in the Reign of Queen Victoria* (Oxford, 1968), pp. 85–105.

confidence were made even more sensitive to external commercial pressures. In one way or another, the charts of book trades output and bankruptcies register the crisis years of the Revolutionary wars of the 1790s and the ensuing Napoleonic shortages, the 1826 crash, the 1839–42 trade depression, the transatlantic slump of 1860–4, and the agricultural depression of the 1870s. It is in this context that we must understand the emphasis in book trade histories, noted as 'distinctively British,' of uneven developmental surges—of growth in the 1840s and early 1850s, then an apparent plateau in the years from about 1858 to 1872, then acceleration from the late 1870s until the outbreak of the First World War, and finally, sharp recovery from 1919.[17]

The transformation of the trade and the range of printed literature in the first half of the nineteenth century was led by the so-called 'list' publishers including Blackwoods, Longmans, Murray, and Bentley, in which tens of thousands of copies of an edition were published.[18] Recent assessment of change in the relative prices of books during the eighteenth century suggests that by the very early nineteenth century the book was more and not less a luxury item than it had been a hundred years earlier.[19] Such estimates (despite the many difficulties in calculating any 'average' price) magnify further the steep rise in publication tallies from the 1820s and the lowering of publication costs, certain transaction costs, and the reduction in market prices, even before the alterations in stamp duties at mid-century. The production of very cheap books in large quantities and in slighter formats replaced the earlier economic necessity of publishing small editions, often in cumbersome multi-volumes, at very high prices. Even so, high status novels and other luxury publications continued in expensive multi-volume forms until the mid 1890s. At the same time, as Alexis Weedon has demonstrated, publishers widened their market by offering variously priced editions, appealing to a range of incomes, and encompassing notably increased demand for educational texts, travel books and science literature.[20]

Early Victorian publishing, however, continued to operate under broader legislative constraints—constraints which across most of Continental Europe erected political and legal barriers to the social extension of knowledge and education. In Britain, devolution of economic and policing functions by the

[17] James J. Barnes, 'Depression and Innovation in the British and American Book Trade, 1819–1939', in Kenneth E. Carpenter (ed.), *Books and Society in History* (New York and London, 1983), pp. 231–48; Eliot, *Patterns and Trends in British Publishing*.

[18] Feather, *History of British Publishing*, ch. 12.

[19] James Raven, 'The Book as a Commodity', in Michael Suarez and Michael Turner (eds.), *History of the Book in Britain*, vol. 5 (Cambridge, 2005).

[20] Weedon, *Victorian Publishing*, pp. 1, 90–3, 127–39.

state remained a crucial feature of book trade development. Before the great changes of the mid nineteenth century, two of the most distinctive features of British book trade structure were the devolved policing of the trade and the regulation of copyright.[21] Parliament and the courts continued to intervene in the modern British book trade, and their actions (and attempted actions) affected both the exercise of residual powers by the Stationers' Company and the development of cartels for the protection of copyrights, reinforced by (increasingly challenged) legislation. Just as significantly, the Company created the 'English Stock', distributing dividends to its members from the publication of almanacs, the mainstay of cheap publishing even by the early Victorian years.[22] In addition to controlling apprenticeship and entry, the Company offered welfare and guardianship, but it was also very rarely a force for innovation, its loss of power increasingly apparent during the nineteenth century.[23]

Government exercised more direct intervention in the book market by attempts to derive fiscal advantage from increased book and newspaper publication.[24] In London, where the manufacture of paper had moved largely to the home counties and then to the midland and northern cities, a complex system of paper warehousing and distribution had developed. After the first Act to impose an excise tax on home-produced paper in 1711 (and then the infamous Stamp Act of 1712), some 26 further acts were passed in the next 150 years. Subsequently, until 1855, the only legal source of supply for newspaper stamped paper was the warehouse of the Commissioners of Stamps in Lincoln's Inn, to where unsold papers also had to be returned in order to claim a rebate. As protest mounted against the curbing of cheaper print, the war-chests of successive governments, from the War of the Spanish Succession through to the Crimea, were assisted by book trade revenues.[25]

[21] Mark Rose, *Authors and Owners: The Invention of Copyright* (Cambridge, MA, and London, 1993); Raven, 'The Book Trades'.

[22] R. K. Webb, *The British Working-Class Reader: Literacy and Social Tension, 1790–1848* (London, 1955).

[23] Cyprian Blagden, *The Stationers' Company: A History, 1403–1959* (London, 1960); Robin Myers and Michael Harris (eds.), *The Stationers' Company and the Book Trade, 1550–1900* (Winchester and New Castle, DE, 1997); Michael Henry, 'The Nineteenth-Century Printing Apprenticeship: Elements of Change', in Robin Myers and Michael Harris (eds.), *Aspects of Printing from 1600* (Oxford, 1987), pp. 90–113.

[24] Michael Harris, 'The Structure, Ownership, and Control of the Press, 1620–1780', in Boyce, *et al.* (eds.), *Newspaper History*, pp. 82–97; and Ivon Asquith, 'The Structure, Ownership, and Control of the Press, 1780–1855', in Boyce, *et al.* (eds.), *Newspaper History*, pp. 98–116.

[25] C. Dobson Collet, *History of the Taxes on Knowledge* (London, 1899); Frederick Seaton Siebert, *Freedom of the Press in England, 1476–1776: The Rise and Decline of Government Controls* (Urbana, Ill., 1952), pp. 308–22.

Campaigns to protect and extend copyright and to abolish the stamp tax both became, therefore, central to Victorian argument about freedoms of the press and the literary marketplace. A crucial difference existed between the two lobbies, however. Those seeking to reform copyright legislation aimed to improve the lot of authors; campaigners against duties on paper and newspapers aimed to cheapen literature (and were often hostile to promoters of new copyright legislation).[26]

In many respects the results of mid-nineteenth-century copyright legislation were more far-reaching than those of the eighteenth century, despite the furore over the legal decisions concerning copyright in 1768 and 1774.[27] After five years' debate, the Copyright Act of 1842 offered legislative protection of copyright for the life of the author plus either seven years or 42 years from the date of publication, whichever was the greater. The 1842 Act replaced an 1814 Act (itself following a period of stagnation since the climactic events of 1774) with its term of 28 years or the term of the author's life if this was longer. To a limited extent, authors did benefit from the greater legislative control. Originally sponsored by Lamb's friend, Thomas Noon Talfourd, MP, the 1842 Act assured certain protection to the families of the most successful authors. Among these were now a highly select few able to name impressive prices with publishers. In many ways the 1842 debate was more important than the result, given the relative modesty of the actual change. Even the clause protecting the imperial trade, forbidding colonial reprinting of books copyrighted in Britain, could not be effectively policed. In the longer perspective, it has been argued that the 1842 Act proved more important for offering foundations for the later 1911 Act and even for the Acts of 1956 and 1988.[28]

The other great mid-Victorian copyright battle concerned foreign reprints of British books, with the first International Copyright Act passed in 1838 to invite reciprocal foreign copyright agreements.[29] The 1842 domestic Act did extend to the colonies and the 1838 Act seems to have been successful in Europe. In addition, the Tauchnitz agreement, following the 1842 Act, although effectively excluding British publishers from the European market, did protect home interests, and, more significantly, offered authors and publishers assistance in confronting the much more difficult American market.

[26] Joel H. Weiner, *The War of the Unstamped: The Movement to Repeal the British Newspaper Tax, 1830–1836* (Ithaca, NY, 1969).

[27] See Rose, *Authors and Owners*; Raven, 'Book Trades'.

[28] Catherine Seville, *Literary Copyright Reform in Early Victorian England* (Cambridge, 1999), pp. 210–18.

[29] Nowell-Smith, *House of Cassell*, p. 13.

A British-American governmental agreement was signed in 1853, but remained unratified by the United States Senate, and unauthorised reprinting of British books continued in America until an 1891 Act of Congress (and even that offered only limited arrangements).[30] In a few respects at least (and quite besides the notorious American reprint battles fought by Dickens and his publishers), the threat of American piracies encouraged new investment by London publishers. Most notable, perhaps, was Longman's determined promotion of Macaulay's one-volume collected *Essays*, the subject of separate American publishing ventures.[31]

Underpinning the copyright campaign was recognition of the cultural worth of literature and a rejection of its appreciation simply as a commodity. Parliament considered no fewer than eleven versions of copyright Bills in the five years before 1842 when the final Act embodied a compromise sponsored by Macaulay (who by then had become heartily dispirited by it all). Talfourd, barrister, Member of Parliament, contributor to the *London Magazine* and the *New Monthly*, led the campaign for justice for authors. In doing so, he drew on a glorious if gloriously ineffective history in defence of authors' rights going back at least to Trusler's Society of Authors in the 1760s and continuing through the establishment of the Royal Literary Fund in the closing years of the eighteenth century. The Literary Fund flourished in the mid Victorian years, and was hailed by Talfourd and his supporters as a valiant challenger to the unwitting revolution instigated by the Copyright Act of Anne, depriving authors of their rightful rewards for the increase of knowledge and instruction.[32]

By contrast, many of those who campaigned in support of cheap literature and for the reduction and then abolition of the taxation on knowledge positioned author's rights against the extension of knowledge.[33] The SPCK and the SDUK (Society for the Diffusion of Useful Knowledge, founded in 1827) were certainly not on the side of the Talfourd and Macaulay campaigns to give authors and their families greater rewards for their writing.[34] Radicals campaigned against new copyright legislation, demonising it, in Catherine Seville's words, as 'an intolerable fetter on the diffusion of knowledge'.[35]

[30] James J. Barnes, *Authors, Publishers and Politicians: The Quest for an Anglo-American Copyright Agreement, 1815–54* (London, 1974), pp. 241–62.

[31] James J. Barnes, *Free Trade in Books: A Study of the London Book Trade since 1800* (Oxford, 1964), pp. 83, 120.

[32] The campaign is fully detailed in Seville, *Literary Copyright*.

[33] William H. Wickwar, *The Struggle for the Freedom of the Press, 1819–1832* (London, 1928).

[34] Seville, *Literary Copyright*, p. 21.

[35] Seville, *Literary Copyright*, p. 8.

Brougham's 50,000 edition of *Practical Observations for the Education of the People*, known as the 'gospel of the alphabet' and a best-seller as Queen Victoria ascended the throne, typified pamphleteering supporting the extension of cheaper literature and opposing alteration in the copyright laws. Advertisement tax was reduced to 1*s.* 6*d.* in 1834 (and abolished altogether in 1853), with more general campaigning intensifying after radicals triumphantly forced the reduction of the 1819 4*d.* stamp duty to 1*d.* in 1836. Stamp duty on newspapers was finally removed in 1855, although the one remaining 'tax on knowledge', that levied on paper, was not abolished until 1861.[36] The unstamped newspapers that appeared during the struggle to repeal the Stamp Duty proved, according to the bookseller Charles Knight, the 'desire amongst the mass of the people for the species of knowledge which a newspaper supplies'.[37]

Following the 1855 Act the prices of newspapers, periodicals and a huge range of cheap magazines fell dramatically, encouraging the formation of dozens of new magazine publishing companies.[38] New freedoms, however, also brought new reactions. Legislative and judicial responses to the abolition of paper duties and the advance of cheap publishing and its distribution networks most notably included the 1857 Obscene Publications Act and an 1868 ruling that the 'test of obscenity is whether the tendency of the matter charged is to deprave and corrupt'. A further commercial battle concerned the advocacy of free trade in bibles, led by the politician and publisher for the SPUK, Charles Knight.[39] In the years after publication of his successful *Pictorial Bible* in 1836, Knight campaigned not only for reform of the stoutly defended typographical and design conventions of bible printing, but for a market-led uprising against the 'bibliopolist' patent-holders of the university presses and the Queen's Printer. The success of this crusade during the 1850s (when the privileged presses also dared not alter their prices in response) preceded a further campaign, led by the Bible Society, to improve the overseas dispatch of cheap bibles.[40]

[36] Weiner, *War of the Unstamped*; Jones, *Powers of the Press*, pp. 21–3; Kevin Gilmartin, *Print Politics: The Press and Radical Opposition in Early Nineteenth-Century England* (Cambridge, 1996), ch. 2.

[37] Charles Knight, *The Newspaper Stamp and the Duty on Paper*, cited in Jones, *Powers of the Press*, p. 21.

[38] Scott Bennet, *Cheapening of Books*; Webb, *British Working-Class Reader*.

[39] Knight, *Passages of a Working Life*; Alice A. Clowes, *Charles Knight: A Sketch* (London, 1892).

[40] Leslie Howsam, *Cheap Bibles; Nineteenth-Century Publishing and the British and Foreign Bible Society* (Cambridge, 1991), pp. 190–202; cf. Louis Billington, 'The Religious Periodical and Newspaper Press, 1770–1870', in Michael Harris and Alan Lee (eds.), *Press in English Society from the Seventeenth to the Nineteenth Centuries* (Rutherford, 1986), pp. 113–32.

In all these market contests price remained a crucial consideration. At the beginning of the nineteenth century popular reprint series had been issued by all types of bookseller, from the confident newcomer acting on his own, to the more established Stationers' Company or other livery company member, in all likelihood sharing publication with others and shadowing earlier, more exclusive collaborative practice. The weakening of the share book system also increased the risk for all and rewards resulted from many gambles in book trades expansion. As a consequence, a material feature of the system for publishing and marketing books, was the involved relationship between booksellers, both financing bookseller–publishers and their retailing, usually bookseller, agents. Cooperation in some form was essential to most operations. The increased number of book trade bankruptcies in the nineteenth century, most spectacularly heralded by the 1826 book trade crash, was testimony to the new adventuring.[41]

Few authors were beneficiaries of the fresh economic opportunities in the book trade.[42] Before the early nineteenth century, very few writers in Britain and certainly very few first-time writers could avoid outright copyright sale, full self-financing (and thus acting as publisher themselves), or deals in which the author bore liability for all losses. Commission agreements whereby the bookseller put up the capital for printing an edition on the understanding that the author would bear any loss, seem to have been very rare. Great literary lions (most notably Pope and Robertson in the eighteenth century; Scott in the early nineteenth) had always provided the exception—and the model for an army of disappointed but imitative scribblers (and the hacks employed by publishers as translators and compilers).[43] The burgeoning mass market bestowed on literary grandees a wealth and earning power that created new tensions with their publishers. Scott had been able to negotiate separate and half-profit agreements on each of his editions. Dickens's convoluted merry-go-round of publishers certainly involved him in early financial difficulties but by mid-career he was very much in the driving seat (with a profit of some £10,000 for Dombey and Son in 1846–8). In 1836 Disraeli's receipt of £2,100 from Longmans for the copyright of all ten volumes of his novels was a

[41] John Sutherland, 'The British Book Trade and the Crash of 1826', *The Library*, 6th ser., 9 (1987), 148–61.

[42] Nigel Cross, *The Common Writer: Life in Nineteenth-Century Grub Street* (London, 1985).

[43] Jan Fergus and Janice Farrar Thaddeus, 'Women, Publishers, and Money, 1790–1820', *Studies in Eighteenth-Century Culture*, 17 (1988), 191–207; Peter Garside, 'The English Novel in the Romantic Era: Consolidation and Dispersal', in Peter Garside, James Raven, and Rainer Schöwerling (eds.), *The English Novel, 1770–1829: A Bibliographical Survey of Prose Fiction Published in the British Isles*, 2 vols. (Oxford, 2000), 2: 15–103.

direct, agreed transaction, but twenty years later, Macaulay gained £20,000 'on account' of profits for the third and fourth volumes of his *History*.[44]

Even so, the fortune-making of the few did nothing to improve the general lot of writers. By the end of the nineteenth century royalty agreements were the aim of most authors and their agents, but all too often the author was regarded as a mere supplier of goods to the industry. Most booksellers appear to have interpreted commissions as between $7\frac{1}{2}$ and 10 per cent of the wholesale price, although few agreements have survived. A turning point came with the Net Book Agreement, proposed first by Frederick Macmillan in 1890, which, because it fixed retail prices, provided a basis upon which royalties could be paid.[45] It also led directly to the enlargement of the London Booksellers Society (from 1895 the Associated Booksellers of Great Britain and Ireland) promoting the idea of net books, and to the formation of the Publishers Association.[46]

In fact, the Net Book Agreement was driven more by concern about the onward selling of books. In the 1850s Carlyle and Dickens energetically defended the notion of a 'free trade in books', but the resulting abandonment of the retail price maintenance attempted from 1829, led to underselling and disorder. The general agreement between a group of major publishers and booksellers under the 1829 Bookselling Regulations, did lead to the formation of a Booksellers' Association, but was stretched to breaking point in the 1840s and finally destroyed with the dissolution of the Association in 1852. As a result, most readers in mid-Victorian England could expect a discount on the cover price of a book, but the division between publishers and retail booksellers greatly increased and the ever larger editions of cheap books risked on the market forced tighter and tighter profit margins from the booksellers.[47]

In a period of unrestricted competition many booksellers were forced increasingly to work in concert to combat variable trade and retail pricing. The 1890 Agreement offered a solution for both parties, assuring the onward-selling bookseller a basic profit, but making it impossible for him to sell the book for under the fixed, net price. When booksellers met in January 1895 to found the Booksellers' Association of Great Britain and Ireland they immediately sought to persuade publishers to adopt systematically the 'net' price—fixed retail prices from which there could be no discount. Finally

[44] John Sutherland, *Victorian Novelists and their Publishers* (London, 1976), pp. 137–8.

[45] Sir Frederick Macmillan, *The Net Book Agreement, 1899, and the Book War, 1906–1908* (Glasgow, 1924), pp. 1–30.

[46] Nile and Walker, 'Paternoster Row Machine', pp. 7–9, 86.

[47] Macmillan, *Net Book Agreement*, pp. 1–10; Weedon, *Victorian Publishing*, pp. 57–8.

signed in 1900, the net price agreement protected booksellers working to a guaranteed margin and enabled the British book industry to become much more efficient. Bookshops were better stocked, while the pre-eminence of the publisher was enhanced by authors' increasing desire to be identified with a major publishing house. In 1905 *The Times* launched and then failed to maintain a challenge to the agreement by attempting to establish a low-price book borrowing club (a challenge implicit in the circulating library efforts of Smith's and Mudie's for twenty years[48]). *The Times*'s defeat confirmed that Macmillan had founded the effective marketing system of the modern British book trade.[49]

The principal beneficiaries of all these changes remained publishers and the rising profession of literary agents rather than all but the most prominent and successful of authors. Despite the successes of Talfourd and his copyright campaigners, the economic lot of most writers was not a happy one; their plight was all the more pitiful when set against the history of the Victorian book trade with its late-century capital flows and big-firm market development. The risks of high capital expenditure and storage made it unwise to print large editions, but there were clear exceptions. The monster editions of popular titles reprinted over and over again included school books (especially the Board School textbooks after 1870), hymn books and the cheap morality periodicals of Cassell, Knight and the Chambers brothers.[50] From new sites in London (with Piccadilly a new focus for the trade, in addition to Paternoster Row and Fleet Street), many publishers also found success in new types of publication with mass appeal. As early as 1836, for example, John Murray III launched his extraordinarily successful series of travel guides (from whose profits he launched the *Origin of Species* and *Lavengro*).

The bringing of new money into the trades and its more versatile deployment, is also the more striking given how broader resource limitations had continued to constrain business expansion and technological advances. Across all trades most fixed capital had been invested in ways that produced only indirect gain. The publishing sector was especially handicapped by the requirement to have so much capital tied up in a particular item of production (an edition) before any part of this could be sold to realise returns. The book trades further suffered from the relatively inefficient deployment of resources

[48] Eliot, 'Bookselling by the Backdoor', pp. 162–3.

[49] James (ed.), *Macmillan*; Macmillan, *Net Book Agreement*, pp. 31–77.

[50] See Alan Rauch, *'Useful Knowledge': the Victorians, Morality and the March of Intellect* (Durham, NC, and London, 2001); Nowell-Smith, *House of Cassell*; Webb, *British Working-Class Reader*.

that economists now term path dependency, that is, the continuation of particular (but in theory not inflexible) working practices because of cultural inertia and a resistance to change. The transformation of the British book trades in the nineteenth century can be found here: the breaking of an earlier economic regime that allowed only low productivity rates, with particularly high labour-intensity.

The fundamental enabler of this revolution in production volume was the invention of mechanised printing and mechanised paper-making, even if this was no overnight process. Although Koenig's steam press allowed the printing of 1,000 impressions each hour, the new machine was not speedily adopted. What *The Times* called 'the greatest improvement connected with printing since the discovery of the art itself' was not used for many other such publications until the 1820s. Even by the beginning of Victoria's reign the difference between town and country remained. In 1838 Jeremiah Garnett's new machinery for the *Manchester Guardian* printed 1,500 impressions an hour, and yet most country newspaper printing continued on Stanhope iron presses. The printer of the *Salisbury Journal*, for example, did not introduce steam power until 1852.[51] Mechanised papermaking first became commercially viable in 1807, but throughout the century one of the most common complaints of the local stationer concerned the shortage of inexpensive paper.[52] Even so, by 1825 half of all paper in England was manufactured by machine, with total output increasing thirty-fold between 1820 and 1900.[53]

After the technology, the market. Beyond the unit-cost questions of available capital, labour and technological capabilities, the pricing of books and other print in Victorian Britain was based on the evaluation of the market. Expansion in retailing and allied services (as well as the amount and length of credit offered) derived from the changing commercial potential of the audience, while prices of books had often been inflated, not discounted, in order to attract purchasers.[54] Elite patronage of specialist literature had also been nurtured by subscription collection and by publishers directing their output to specific regions or professional clients. Further direct retailing centred on the active second-hand market and the sales of smaller productions, notably the thousands of almanacks, pamphlets and chapbooks peddled by chapmen and general traders.[55]

[51] Gaskell, *New Introduction to Bibliography*, pp. 251–8.

[52] Gaskell, *New Introduction to Bibliography*, pp. 214–21.

[53] Weedon, *Victorian Publishing*, p. 64.

[54] Explored further in Raven, 'Book as a Commodity'.

[55] Robin Myers and Michael Harris (eds.), *Serials and their Readers, 1620–1914* (Winchester and New Castle, DE, 1993).

Although it was clearly increased custom from the propertied classes that was responsible from the mid eighteenth century for remodelling the retailing of books,[56] the Victorian publishing industry was propelled by cheap popular literature and notably by reprint series such as John Murray's *Family Library*, first issued in 1829. Later, prominent examples included George Routledge's *Railway Library* of more than 1,000 titles that commenced in 1848, the year of W. H. Smith's first station bookstall.[57] The extension of cheap print supported the development of a new working-class market, quite distinct by the mid nineteenth century from the older chapbook and ballad readership of the previous two centuries.[58] The boom in production led by belles lettres, magazines, novels and practical books from the final quarter of the eighteenth century was followed by the steam-driven surge of the 1830s, and then by the bibliographical equivalent of the 'age of equipoise' of the 1850s, much with a sense of mission to bring knowledge to the working classes (and then to the less fortunate abroad, with the extraordinary development of the colonial and overseas market). Provincial sales outlets were extended and London booksellers launched unprecedented numbers of titles with no advanced assured custom. For the majority of metropolitan booksellers, the sales of open market publications became the basis for survival.[59]

Regional variation did distinguish this market, and although interest in the expanding provincial custom was important (crucially so in terms of the great new cities of the midlands and the north by the mid nineteenth century), the London market remained pivotal. London dominated the economy and, more importantly, grew disproportionately faster during the eighteenth and early nineteenth centuries, its population fed by immigration from the regions. Here was a market close to the centres of production, with fewer distribution problems and with a particularly affluent leading-edge. The structural concentration of the trade in London determined advances in the stimulation of demand and the attempt to confound a general recognition (not only confined to the book trades) that if the market was limited, profit margins could never be high. Ultimately, however, it was the reduction in printing, typesetting and paper costs that enabled new economies of scale and the satisfaction by publishers of new levels of demand.[60]

56 Raven, 'Book Trades'.

57 Mumby, *House of Routledge*; Charles Wilson, *First with the News: The History of W. H. Smith, 1792–1972* (London, 1985), pp. 88–179.

58 Webb, *British Working-Class Reader*; James Routledge, *Chapters in the History of Popular Progress Chiefly in Relation to the Freedom of the Press and Trial by Jury* (London, 1876).

59 Alan J. Lee, *The Origins of the Popular Press in England, 1855–1914* (London, 1976); Lee Erickson, *The Economy of Literary Form: English Literature and the Industrialization of Publishing, 1800–1850* (Baltimore and London, 1996), pp. 170–90.

60 Weedon, *Victorian Publishing*, pp. 158–61.

The radial distribution network outwards from London marked British book trade organisation (as the dominance of a metropole did in so many other European states), but certain competitive advantages maintained by the British trade during the eighteenth and early nineteenth centuries were eroded by the close of Victoria's reign. By the early nineteenth century some 90 per cent of all titles were still published in the capital and the mushrooming numbers of provincial booksellers served not as publishers of new titles but mostly as book distribution agents and sometimes as newspaper printers (the newspapers themselves acting as advertising platforms for the London publishers).[61] In turn, however, some London wholesale houses, such as Simpkin and Co., developed reciprocal arrangements and acted as London agents for provincial books. The centrality of London (and Edinburgh) publishing did not change but with the advance of new transport systems and increasing book and magazine publication in Manchester, Glasgow, Liverpool, Newcastle, Leeds and other cities, the position of London in both distribution and publishing was affected for the first time since the Restoration Licensing Laws, and, arguably, since the invention of printing. The centre of publishing remained London but Blacks and William Blackwood and Sons of Edinburgh and Blackie and Collins of Glasgow, among others, established major firms (and ones with branch outlets in London).[62]

Further pricing decisions and the advance of a wholesaling discount system depended upon distribution and transport developments. Given the necessity of selling as quickly as possible the whole edition in which so much was usually invested, the efficiency and cost of distribution remained critical. During the eighteenth century the cost of newspaper distribution had been lowered by the activity of groups with Post Office franking privileges, and many booksellers adopted the public postal service to assist with newsprint distribution. Even so, for a century the fastest, most direct means of sending stock to provincial retailers and customers had been by the common London carriers. Books and magazines left on the coaches departing from Ludgate and the Poultry to travel to distant parts. The great coaching inns acted in some respects as the models for the great Victorian train stations from mid-century, located on each side of London and serving their own distinct routes.[63]

[61] Eliot, *Patterns and Trends in British Publishing*.

[62] Mumby, *Publishing and Bookselling*, pp. 311–14; Feather, *History of British Publishing*, p. 122; Weedon, *Victorian Publishing*, pp. 34–8, 173–4; David Finkelstein, *The House of Blackwood: Author–Publisher Relations in the Victorian Era* (University Park, PA, 2002).

[63] James Raven, 'St Paul's Precinct and the Book Trade to 1800', in Derek Keene, Arthur Burns and Andrew Saint (eds.), *St Paul's Cathedral: The Cathedral Church of London, 604–2004* (London, 2004), pp. 430–8.

The provincial dispatch of printed instruction and entertainment advanced erratically, however. Even though, following the turnpike mania of the third quarter of the eighteenth century, some 20,000 miles of road were maintained by trusts by the end of the 1830s, heavy traffic on the London roads and the failure of metropolitan trusts to effect repairs lead to furious complaints. A correspondent to *The Times* had even demanded regional management of the London turnpikes to curb the proliferation of disruptive tolls every few miles.[64] Economic historians have similarly supposed the state of the roads by the early Victorian years to be limits to growth; trains were the major break-through.

In the enlargement of the readership for print, the advancing railway system proved critical. The railway book edition, W. H. Smith's bookstalls, and the railway circulating libraries, effectively mapped the extension of the tracks. Although we can speak of a national market for cheap print from an early date, with various means of transport employed (including some coastal shipping), it was not until the railways that the British mass produced book, newspaper and print market really advanced. Railway extension (after the inaugural lines of the early 1830s) was in fact slow before 1850, although great cities like Manchester were soon served. Thereafter, the railway age boosted all levels of distribution, developing for books and journals what amounted to a new stage of opportunity in book and print production, marketing, distribution and reception. Railways created new markets as well as supplying existing ones; Smith's bookstalls supplied both those travelling regularly to work and long-distance passengers, and popularised reading in trains (much easier than in horse-drawn coaches).[65]

As the market base of book production changed, the industry responded swiftly, publishing specialist works to appeal to new professional interests as well as to new fashions in entertainment and instruction. Advance in the market for educational books further challenged the role of the university presses, while the expansion of series of titles, often named 'library series' and usually aimed at 'aspirational' readerships, counted among the greatest successes of late-Victorian general publishing. The 1835–62 volume of *The English Catalogue* listed 165 series compared with 883 series listed in the 1890–7 volume.[66] Research in the relative costings of educational books has only recently been developed, but the strength and depth of the market (in which

[64] William Albert, *The Turnpike Road System in England, 1663–1840* (Cambridge, 1972). *Times* letter, cit., p. 65.

[65] Wilson, *First with the News*.

[66] Leslie Howsam, 'Sustained Literary Ventures: The Series in Victorian Book Publishing', *Publishing History*, 31 (1992), 5–26.

history came to account for well over a tenth of annual trade output) can be gauged not only by the success of Macmillan's almost constant reprinting of J. R. Green's *Short History of the English People* (1874) but also by Longman's commitment to *The English Historical Review* (from 1886). Leslie Howsam's further comparison of *The English Historical Review* and Freemantle's *Historical Course for Schools* (published by Macmillan) also suggests that boundaries between popular and professional literature, between commercial publications and the journals of learned societies were not clear-cut.[67]

Contemporary estimates of profitability for such publications were usually based on assumptions of full sale of each print run, an accounting procedure that at least confirms the continuing reliance on the reprinting of modestly sized editions in order to minimise risk. Indeed, tighter profit margins in an increasingly competitive market, with publishers having to sell a greater proportion of an edition to cover costs, accentuated the need for more accurate forecasting of demand and the printing of low-risk quantities. In addition, however, as Alexis Weedon comments, 'longer print runs were used to cash in on the economies of faster and larger powered-presses when demand was strong'.[68] The new reprinting regime was marked by the changing size of average print runs, based on the reduced unit cost of the book, where, in the changing economics of book manufacturing, the average cost of paper used in book printing halved between 1865 and 1885 and fell further still before 1900.[69] Recent research suggests that the size of the average print run doubled between 1836 and 1916, with an average print run of 500 copies in the 1830s, 750 in the 1840s, and 1,000 between 1860 and 1920. The mean edition size of titles issued by George Bell and Sons, estimated as 1,210 during the 1860s, rose to 2,089 during the first decade of the twentieth century. To demonstrate this another way, well under a tenth of the titles published by Bell and Sons in the 1860s boasted print runs in excess of 2,000 copies, but by 1900–10 such print runs comprised more than a fifth of the firm's total output.[70]

The surging demand for educational books was never homogenous but it did broaden, as prestige titles led a multitude of cheap, small format books for elementary schools and service overseas. Comparisons between new titles

[67] Leslie Howsam, 'Academic Discipline or Literary Genre? The Establishment of Boundaries in Historical Writing', in Regina Gagnier and Angelique Richardson (eds.), *Victorian Literature and Culture,* special issue, 2004, pp. 413–33.

[68] Weedon, *Victorian Publishing*, p. 61.

[69] Ibid., p. 67.

[70] Ibid., pp. 28, 49.

published between 1830 and 1870 suggest a certain alteration in the popularity of different subject categories, but this disguises greater fluctuations in edition sizes. The relative decline in geography and history titles after a boom in publication in the 1830s and 1840s was paralleled by a fall in science titles that recovered only by the 1890s. According to print-run statistics, however, science and language books maintained higher than average production levels, particularly compared with modest print runs for titles in literature. The literary market also depended upon greater 'churn', requiring fresh titles to maintain its strength.[71]

As publishers sold more books but received less per volume, market building was sustained by a transformation in distribution systems and greater competitiveness in foreign markets. Other domestic supporting agencies ranged from commercial libraries (and most notably Charles Edward Mudie's from 1842)[72] and subscription book-clubs to private and town debating and literary societies, advancing working-men's clubs (founded either by or for working men) and the solemn recommendations of the periodical reviews and magazines.[73] The novel also continued to sustain many leading publishers, its production also heightening differences between literary categories. It has generally been claimed that the publication of the infamous three-decker novel supported the circulating libraries;[74] more certainly, railway stalls were supplied by cheap fiction in single volumes, part-issues, and so-called 'library series'. The immensity of production runs for the most successful titles needs special emphasis. In an industry of unprecedented publishing capacity, Chapman and Hall alone published and sold more than half a million volumes of Dickens in the last three years of the author's life.[75]

The extension of knowledge further depended upon the availability of the means of knowing what was published and from where books might be bought or acquired. Already by the mid eighteenth century, advertising had served as the financial mainstay for most newspapers published, and in long-running newspapers from both the country towns and the capitals, an increasing proportion of the total space was devoted to advertising. The advertising role of newspapers retained its importance—as James Secord's study of the

[71] Weedon, *Victorian Publishing*, ch. 4, esp. fig. 4.1 and tables 4.2 and 4.3.

[72] Guinevere L. Greist, *Mudie's Circulating Library and the Victorian Novel* (Newton Abbot, 1970).

[73] Simon Eliot, 'Bookselling by the Backdoor: Circulating Libraries, Booksellers and Book Clubs, 1876–1966', in Robin Myers and Michael Harris (eds.), *A Genius for Letters: Booksellers and Bookselling from the Sixteenth to the Twentieth Century* (Winchester and New Castle, DE, 1995), pp. 145–66.

[74] Work in progress by Simon Eliot analyses fiction in Mudie catalogues from 1857 and questions the dependency on the three-decker.

[75] Arthur Waugh, *A Hundred Years of Publishing: Being the Story of Chapman and Hall Ltd* (London, 1930); Sutherland, *Victorian Novelists*, pp. 41–2.

publishing sensation of the *Vestiges* clearly shows.[76] In addition to the *Publishers' Circular*, *The Bookseller*, and other trade records, some publishing firms also revived retrospective cataloguing. Most spectacular of the published backlists was Macmillan's immense 1891 *Bibliographical Catalogue, 1843–1889*.[77] Above all, the British bookselling enterprise continued to be buttressed by newspaper publication. In the provinces commercial advertising and newspaper circuits effectively maintained the solvency of the leading book distributors for the great London and, later, Edinburgh, wholesalers.

Long-running newspapers were more an exception than the norm, but by the first decade of the nineteenth century about forty newspapers and periodicals began publication each year. The widespread adoption and further modification of the mechanised press in the 1830s hugely increased production volume. Further opportunities were created by the mechanisation of paper manufacture. By 1850 ten times more newspapers were published than in 1750, and nearly three times more than in 1830. In 1832 an extraordinary 250 new newspaper and periodical titles were launched. The country town newspaper in particular almost always had to succeed against powerful obstacles including distribution and production difficulties, metropolitan and regional competition, local vested interests, and, before their reduction and abolition, the stamp taxes. Circulation and sales were very variable. In 1821, 267 different newspapers and periodicals were published in England and Wales; by 1851 this total reached 563.[78] During the same period the structure of ownership and financing fundamentally changed; a large number of London firms, subcontracting printing, design and other functions, replaced many of the one-man print-shops. The real price of newspapers and print fell markedly in the 1840s and then again, still more sharply, from the 1860s. Thereafter the newspaper market (and periodical printing) confidently advanced on the basis of the new lower middle-class and working-class market, sustained by new and cheaper raw materials for paper manufacture. By 1907 newspaper production accounted for 28 per cent of the total net value of all British publications.[79]

Nevertheless, business development was not without costs and high risks, while new production and distribution methods were not uniform across the

[76] James A. Secord, *Victorian Sensation: The Extraordinary Publication, Reception, and Secret Authorship of* Vestiges of the Natural History of Creation (Chicago and London, 2000), pp. 125–38.

[77] James (ed.), *Macmillan*.

[78] Harris, 'Structure, Ownership, and Control of the Press', pp. 86–93; cf. G. A. Cranfield, *The Development of the Provincial Newspaper, 1700–1760* (Oxford, 1962), and R. M. Wiles, *Freshest Advices: Early Provincial Newspapers in England* (Columbus, Ohio, 1965).

[79] Eliot, *Patterns and Trends in British Publishing*, p. 105; cf. Stephen Koss, *The Rise and Fall of the Political Press in Britain* (London, 1990).

country. Bankruptcies, especially in the 1820s, and again in the 1880s, were common; a very large proportion of new magazine and newspaper titles ceased publication within a few years of their launch. More subtle changes are often just as significant—such as the timing of the publishing period. By the 1840s the publishing peaks of October to November and February to April were eroded by the primacy of the Christmas weeks, a period even more clearly dominant in the publishing year during the final two decades of Victoria's reign.[80]

By the final decades of the nineteenth century the breaking of more technological constraints again forced the pace. The second great transformation of the book trades in this century was led by new technical processes: stereotyping, gradually increasing from the late 1820s, rotary printing from 1870s, hot-metal typesetting from the late 1880s, and the use of lithographic and photographic techniques at the very end of the century.[81] This final phase, further advanced by the introduction of electricity, brought major changes in working practices but also new literary systems, new professional agents and associations (representing authors, publishers and booksellers), and the mass circulation of daily newspapers. It helped the growth of a new royalty system and refined United States and world-wide copyright systems. In 1841 some 50,000 men and women were employed in the paper, printing, book and stationery trades; by 1871 the total was some 125,000; by 1901 some 323,000; and by 1921 some 314,000. The proportion of women employed in the trades trebled over the same period, from 12 per cent in 1841 to 39 per cent in 1921.[82]

During the nineteenth century the greatly expanding number of titles and hugely increased volume of print (as well as its increasing secularisation and specialisation) clearly resulted in more extensive distribution and a wider readership. Given the doubts about the extent that increased book production in the century before Victoria indicated a greatly increased number of book readers (given that demand from institutions and from those already acquiring books was the more obvious than that from working men and women), the extension of cheap print and also newspaper circulation from the 1840s represents the most pointed evidence for expanded literacy and of a broader audience for print. At the same time, new publications catered for increasing numbers of special interest groups—not just the followers of influential

[80] Greist, *Mudie's Circulating Library*; Eliot, 'Bookselling by the Backdoor', pp. 146–8; Weedon, *Victorian Publishing*, pp. 143–55; see also, however, n. 74 above, and Simon Eliot, 'The Three-Decker Novel and its First Cheap Reprint, 1862–94', *The Library*, 6th ser., 7 (1985), 38–53.

[81] Weedon, *Victorian Publishing*, pp. 61.

[82] Eliot, *Patterns and Trends in British Publishing*, pp. 93–6, 104–5; Philip Unwin, *The Printing Unwins, 1826–1926* (London, 1976).

radical agitators, but other political or religious works intended for the professional classes. These changes also brought revisions to the physical appearance of books, print and newspapers, enabled by advances in font design and engraving and other typographical techniques. Newly efficient distribution systems, the circumvention of restrictive practices and the employment of labour in the publishing industry on an entirely new scale underpinned the revolution in the dissemination of print.[83]

What of the changed literary role of the publisher? In assessing the full spectrum of publication, we should not be led by numbers alone. Small markets and particular clients were important and supported the regeneration of small firms at the end of the century. Substance, quality and subject matter are, quite evidently, principal considerations against the sheer quantity of publication or distribution numbers. The revival in the success of new small firms was marked by the 1890s, exactly when the new large limited companies dominated the book trade.

The success of the minnows is important in three respects. First, credit and success in the pre-Victorian trade were usually predicated upon respectability; smaller or arriviste firms had difficulty in expanding or even maintaining their market position if their reputation were sullied. By the end of the century, however, more institutionalised forms of credit raising and insurance based risk limitation allowed more new niche-market firms to flourish. Second, the success of small firms increased the range of publications for both entertainment and instruction and regenerated the quality market. The new firms of the 1880s and 1890s included Elkin Mathews, John Lane, J. M. Dent and Grant Richards.[84] Select editions far surpassed the poorly designed, cheaply printed books of Bentley, Longmans and the rest (with bindings described by one modern critic as 'hopelessly Victorian in their clutter and bizarre decorative affects'[85]). The third significant feature of the new firms is that they tested the sort of 'knowledge' allowed under the 1857 Obscene Publication Act and its later clarifications. The late-century renaissance in small publishing firms included a regeneration of radical and morally controversial literature, notably undertaken by Leonard Smithers. A generation after the disreputable publications of John Camden Hotten, Smithers circulated pornographic books with Harry Sidney Nichols, a young

[83] Russi J. Taraporevala, *Competition and its Control in the British Book Trade, 1850–1939* (Bombay, 1969).

[84] Henry R. Dent (ed.), *The House of Dent, 1888–1938* (London, 1938); John Ryder, *The Bodley Head, 1857–1957* (London, 1970).

[85] James G. Nelson, *Publisher to the Decadents: Leonard Smithers in the Careers of Beardsley, Wilde, Dowson* (University Park, PA, 2000), p. 2.

Sheffield printer, from the late 1880s, challenging the bookselling establishment. A former Sheffield solicitor inspired by Burton's *The Thousand Nights and One*, Smithers published Beardsley, Wilde, Dowson and the other Decadents.[86] With great rectitude, Mudie assured patrons of his circulating libraries that 'novels of objectionable character or inferior ability are almost invariably excluded'.[87]

The market forces that allowed specialist publishers to proliferate, also contributed to more thorough-going change to the book trade establishment. Through the 1880s and 1890s the management structure of many of the leading firms (in common with those of many other industries) fundamentally changed, with existing partnerships (unlimited private companies under personal or family ownership) converted to limited liability or joint stock companies. In most cases, the aim was to recapitalise the firm, bringing in new men and new money, but also to transfer assets (and with this the mortgaging of the future of the business) in such a way as to retain control within the family (given the composition of the continuing boards of directors, and given the various types of share ownership). Such a course, effectively minimising risk and maximising profits, was taken (among others) by Chapman and Hall in 1880, Cassell and Co. in 1883, Routledge in 1889, Kegan Paul, Trench and Trubner in 1889, Sweet and Maxwell in 1889, Newnes in 1891, and Macmillan in 1895.[88] The establishment of the new companies infused them with fresh capital, but in many cases also seems to have been designed as an exercise in asset stripping. Re-establishment also invited cross-ownership of companies, allowing, for example, distribution, retail and paper-making firms to take shares in the major publishing firms they served. In turn, various major printing and paper wholesaling firms were themselves converted to limited liability companies, including John Dickinson in 1886 and H. Spicer in 1888.

Although the difference between public and private limited companies was still developing, certain of the new companies were traded on the open market (although many remained as privately traded). The recapitalisation offered a major challenge to the enduring connection between the ownership of the publishing firm and the direction of its published output. For the most successful of the lettered bookmen–publishers knowledge and profits had hardly been unrelated, but now a wider ownership in the firm diluted the original individual or family direction of literary affairs. Shareholders and the

86 Nelson, *Publisher to the Decadents*.

87 Sutherland, *Victorian Novelists*, p. 26, cited in Leslie Howsam, *Kegan Paul, A Victorian Imprint: Publishers, Books and Cultural History* (London and Toronto, 1998), p. 9.

88 Waugh, *Hundred Years of Publishing*; Nowell-Smith, *House of Cassell*; Mumby, *House of Routledge*; Howsam, *Kegan Paul*.

board (who were in some cases identical) now assumed broader responsibilities; and profits and knowledge were more closely entangled. Already by the 1870s the relative dominance of the Bible and Prayer Book in publishing annals had greatly diminished and, at least according to the *Publishers' Circular*, 'literature' outpaced 'religion' in production quantities. According to other estimates 'literature' accounted for a third of all titles published between 1890 and 1910.[89]

In summary, the freedoms of Lamb's rapacious bookseller and Smiles's heroic publisher, developing publication lists according to their own instincts, were effectively curtailed by the end of the nineteenth century. Leading publishers of the high Victorian years had pursued new freedoms and new skills, before the disposal of assets at the end of the period and the establishment of the boards of the joint-stock companies (varying, of course, in terms of family control and input, between firms). The 1860s and 1870s appear in this light to be a golden age of effective publishing house management by one individual reflecting his (almost entirely *his*) particular political, religious or literary tastes. One of many exemplars was Charles Kegan Paul, who, in the words of his obituarist, 'was still the hope of authors. He was their fellow clubman; he had excellent taste; he had a pen of his own.'[90] As a result, the history of many of the different Victorian imprints is one of personally managed firms, introducing readers to writers but also fundamentally shaping the nature of that contact.[91] In this respect, Smiles rather than Lamb was able to eulogise a world already passing, an industry in which publishers and booksellers, in Leslie Howsam's words, left 'the imprint of their taste and judgment on the culture in which they lived'.[92]

[89] Eliot, *Patterns and Trends in British Publishing*; cf. Howsam, *Cheap Bibles*.

[90] [Wilfrid Meynell], 'Charles Kegan Paul. By One who Knew Him', *The Academy and Literature* (26 July 1902), cited in Howsam, *Kegan Paul*, p. 83.

[91] Howsam, *Kegan Paul*, p. 190.

[92] Howsam, *Kegan Paul*, p. 3.

CHAPTER THIRTEEN
Libraries, Knowledge and Public Identity

DAVID MCKITTERICK

Insofar as it is possible to suggest a single event that marks the conjunction of libraries, knowledge and public identity in Britain, that is the founding of the British Museum in 1753, by an Act of Parliament that made explicit the primary importance of three libraries: of Sir Hans Sloane, Lord Harley and Sir Robert Cotton.[1] Both Sloane's wishes for his collections, and the many discussions that surrounded the destinations of private libraries in the preceding century, were couched in terms of national and public interest and, often, national and public loss. Prior to 1753, the first Licensing Act of 1662[2] had taken under its wing the provision that copies of all new books published in Britain were to be presented to the Royal Library and to the universities of Oxford and Cambridge. This part of the Act was repeated in 1709 with the so-called Copyright Act of Queen Anne, which also gave privileges of copyright deposit to six other libraries, including five in Scotland.[3]

Vital though all of these pieces of legislation were, it was only in the reign of Queen Victoria, and more particularly in the second half of the nineteenth century, that a mixture of parliamentary government, local activism, literary confidence and professional appeal fused to create in libraries what we may call a sense of identity in public knowledge—an identity not merely

[1] David McKitterick, 'Wantonness and use: ambitions for research libraries in early eighteenth-century England', in R. G. W. Anderson *et al.* (eds.), *Enlightening the British: Knowledge, Discovery and the Museum in the Eighteenth Century* (London, 2003), pp. 37–47.

[2] 14 Car. II c.33, *An Act for Preventing the Frequent Abuses in Printing Seditious Treasonable and Unlicensed Bookes and Pamphlets and for Regulating of Printing and Printing Presses.*

[3] The standard history is R. C. Barrington Partridge, *The History of Legal Deposit of Books Throughout the British Empire* (London, 1938). But now see also, for example, J. C. T. Oates and David McKitterick, *Cambridge University Library: a History*, 2 vols. (Cambridge, 1986); for the British Museum Library, see P. R. Harris, *A History of the British Museum Library, 1753–1973* (London, 1998).

encompassed in the political, social and economic constraints and goads of Acts of Parliament (though they played a large part), but also by a debate that was formed and charged by local opinion across many branches of society.

When in 1877 John Winter Jones, Director and Principal Librarian of the British Museum, presented his opening address at the first national conference of librarians in Britain, he looked back to 1835, the first year of a Royal Commission on the British Museum that had also heard much about foreign libraries. For him, the occasion had marked the beginning of *Bibliothekswissenschaft* in Britain.[4] It also became widely acknowledged as the beginning of what became known as the Public Library movement, epitomised in the Public Libraries Act of 1850 and, as it was taken up often with anguished slowness across the country, the subject for self-congratulation, castigation, opposition, folly and debate for the rest of the century and beyond.

The Library Association, much beset in the closing years of the century with dissent as well as with often justifiable accusations of lack of leadership, issued the first number of its official journal, the *Library Association Record*, in January 1899.[5] Thus the reign of Queen Victoria very nearly coincided with the identification of libraries as a national and public issue and with the establishment of librarianship as an identifiable profession, cohering through a professional journal. Questions of how libraries across the country were to be used, funded, governed and organised moved from being local issues to ones that were debated nationally, while the place of the national library itself, the British Museum, was re-examined in the context of provisions for an interested population that could no longer be identified by London alone.

This last issue was summed up by William Axon, the Honorary Secretary of the Manchester Literary Club, in 1877:

> The final utility of a national library is that, to the utmost degree possible, it shall help the advancement of people to whom it belongs. As a matter of fact the British Museum library is used almost exclusively by those resident in London. Doubtless there are many adventurous spirits who, coming from the northern wilds, make occasional inroads. But, speaking broadly, the British Museum in a direct sense is

[4] Edward B. Nicholson and Henry R. Tedder (ed.), *Transactions and Proceedings of the Conference of Librarians held in London, October, 1877* (London, 1878), p. 1.

[5] The official history is W. A. Munford, *A History of the Library Association, 1877–1977* (London, 1976). See also the biography of J. Y. W. MacAlister, first editor of *The Library*: Shane Godbolt and W. A. Munford, *The Incomparable Mac* (London, 1983).

> an instrument of metropolitan and not of provincial culture. Only in a secondary sense is it an instrument of national culture rightly so called.[6]

Axon reminded his audience that Lord Grenville had recently remarked that London was not an excrescence on the nation; equally, said Axon, the provinces were not excrescences on national life. 'London alone is not the nation.' Truism as it was, and quite apart from Manchester's manufacturing and commercial strength, the timing was apt. The Manchester Art-Treasures exhibition of 1857, the first of its kind, and cast on the grandest scale, had demonstrated both the riches of private collections and the weaknesses of provision for the National Gallery in London.[7]

The public library, supported mainly by public money rather than by private endowment or subscriptions, was a Victorian invention. It was born of the Public Libraries Act of 1850, and by the end of the century had developed criteria of selection, methods of presentation, physical organisation and organisation of readers that were broadly similar across the country. By then, library committees and librarians having been overcome in their reluctance to admit people of unpredictable classes and habits to the publicly owned stocks of books, readers were also able to go to open shelves to select books for themselves, rather than have to order them through the intermediaries of catalogues and librarians. Because of the distinctiveness of public libraries in this period, and because the arguments surrounding their development engage public and private values concerning the organisation of knowledge in several spheres, they deserve particular attention.

They were not, of course, the only kinds of libraries available to the public. In 1849, in a very incomplete survey, some 164 parochial libraries were identified, many of them established by the Associates of Dr Bray in the early eighteenth century. While the majority of these had been founded for the express use of clergy, others were more widely accessible; but stocks were generally out of date, and there was little endowment money for their upkeep.[8] In Scotland there were a further seventeen, in similar

[6] William E. A. Axon, 'The British Museum in its relation to provincial culture', in Nicholson and Tedder (eds.), *Transactions*, pp. 29–32, at pp. 30–1. For wider issues in the relationships between the centre and localities, see K. Theodore Hoppen, *The Mid-Victorian Generation, 1846–1886* (Oxford, 1998), pp. 104–8, with further references.

[7] Ulrich Finke, 'The Art-Treasures Exhibition', in John H. G. Archer (ed.), *Art and architecture in Victorian Manchester* (Manchester, 1985), pp. 102–26.

[8] *Report from the Select Committee on Public Libraries*, 2 vols. (London, 1849–50), *Minutes*, pp. 306–9; J. W. Hudson, *The History of Adult Education, in Which is Comprised a Full and Complete History of the Mechanics' and Literary Institutions ... of Great Britain, Ireland, America*... (London, 1851); Mabel Tylecote, *The Mechanics' Institutes of Lancashire and Yorkshire Before 1851* (Manchester, 1957), p. 258.

circumstances.[9] In cathedral cities, some of the cathedral libraries were available to the public. As a way of meeting more contemporary needs, mechanics' and literary institutes and similar bodies, dependent on private subscriptions, were founded and designed partly as a means of obtaining wide ranges of books and other reading matter. By 1849 there were almost ninety such institutes in Yorkshire alone, and in the country as a whole they numbered about seven hundred. A new breed of university colleges founded in the last decades of the century brought fresh libraries in further places. Nationally funded libraries included not just those in receipt of books deposited under copyright legislation, but also those in the new national museums. Across the country, there were clubs and professional bodies, many of them with their own libraries and some that developed apace over the second half of the century, as the trade in books and periodicals grew both nationally and internationally.[10]

The Parliamentary committee that sat under the chairmanship of William Ewart[11] from March to July 1849 and then again in March and June 1850 resulted in legislation that in 1850 permitted local authorities, after a popular vote, to establish libraries funded by local ratepayers. In that similar provision had been made for local museums just five years before, in the Museums Act of 1845, museums, the study of the past, of manufacture and of the natural world, came before libraries.[12]

The Ewart committee began with a comparative question, the same that had partly inspired Thomas Carlyle and others in the foundation of the London Library in 1841.[13] For all Britain's wealth, it lagged behind foreign countries in its provision of libraries. The opening witness in 1849 was Edward Edwards, assistant in the Department of Printed Books in the British Museum and as author of various publications on libraries and their history a name not unfamiliar to those interested in the subject.[14] He had known Ewart

[9] *Report from the Select Committee on Public Libraries*, *Minutes*, pp. 221–6, 304–5.

[10] There is no adequate general history of libraries in nineteenth-century Britain. For some details, see for example B. C. Bloomfield (ed.), *A Directory of Rare Book and Special Collections in the United Kingdom and the Republic of Ireland*, 2nd edn. (London, 1997), and the series of surveys edited by Denis F. Keeling, *British Library History: Bibliography, 1962–1968* (London, 1972) and following.

[11] W. A. Munford, *William Ewart, M.P., 1798–1869: Portrait of a Radical* (London, 1960).

[12] The close relationship between legislation for museums and for libraries, and similar issues in their funding, organisation and aspirations, are clear in Thomas Greenwood, *Museums and Art Galleries* (London, 1888). Greenwood had also published a study of *Free Public Libraries* in 1886, which reached its fourth edition in 1891.

[13] W. D. Christie, *An Explanation of the Scheme of the London Library, in a Letter to the Earl of Clarendon* (London, 1841).

[14] Thomas Greenwood, *Edward Edwards, the Chief Pioneer of Municipal Public Libraries* (London, 1902); W. A. Munford, *Edward Edwards, 1812–1886: Portrait of a Librarian* (London, 1963).

since the 1830s. After the personal questions as to identity and qualifications were completed, Ewart put the first question: 'Have you turned your attention to a comparison of the number and extent of the libraries accessible to the public in the principal states of Europe?'[15]

It was one almost certainly agreed beforehand, and it set the stage for most of the proceedings that followed. Britain not only had no public library system. Even those libraries that it did possess provided a very much lower level of support, in terms of books per head of population, than almost any other country worthy of comparison. Ewart's committee was to be no merely domestic enquiry. It set itself an international agenda. Edwards was followed in the witness stand by François Guizot, former Prime Minister of France. Again Ewart's questions were leading ones. 'Do you attribute good results to the literature and character of the people of France from the power of free access to such libraries?'—'Yes, very good results.' The same question was put to the Belgian Ambassador, with a similar response.[16] Henry Stevens, bringing experience of libraries at Yale, and knowledge of several of the main libraries on the European Continent,[17] was examined on American libraries—of colleges, of states (especially New York) and the Library of Congress. In the course of his evidence he explained that John Jacob Astor had died in 1848, leaving provision for a public library in the city of New York; that a library to be known as the Smithsonian Institution was about to be established at Washington; that New Orleans had recently established a public library; and that in 1847 Boston had voted to establish one likewise.[18] When published, and thanks in part to Edwards, who was indefatigable in his collaboration with Ewart, the Report was supported by statistics on 330 libraries in Continental Europe, and by further statistics of books per head of population in the cities containing major libraries: the figure for Britain was considerably less than half that for France.[19] Long answers to

[15] *Report from the Select Committee on Public Libraries*, *Minutes*, para. 6.

[16] Ibid., *Minutes*, paras. 467, 583. Van der Weyer, the Belgian Ambassador, was well-known for his interest in printing: in 1851 he was made chairman of the judges at the Great Exhibition for the section on paper, printing and bookbinding. For France, see Dominique Varry, *Histoire des Bibliothèques Françaises. Les Bibliothèques de la Révolution et du XIXe siècle, 1789–1914* (Paris, 1991).

[17] Wyman W. Parker, *Henry Stevens of Vermont: an American Book Dealer in London, 1845–1886* (Amsterdam, 1963).

[18] Charles C. Jewett, *Notices of Public Libraries in the United States of America* (Washington, DC, 1851); H. M. Lyndenberg, *History of the New York Public Library, Astor, Lenox and Tilden Foundations* (New York, 1923); Phyllis Dain, *The New York Public Library: a History of its Founding and Early Years* (New York, 1972); G. B. Goode (ed.), *The Smithsonian Institution, 1846–1896: the History of its First Half Century* (Washington, DC, 1897); Walter Muir Whitehill, *Boston Public Library: a Centennial History* (Cambridge, Mass., 1956).

[19] *Report from the Select Committee on Public Libraries*, Appendix, p. 275.

questionnaires on finances, book-stocks and reader management sent out to libraries in Prussia, France, Austria, Switzerland, Tuscany, Belgium, Russia and other parts of Europe were all reprinted, in their original languages, in a final appendix running to almost 300 pages. Hand-coloured maps were included showing the locations of major libraries in Paris, Vienna, Berlin, Dresden, Munich, Copenhagen, Rome and Florence, and a further map showed the relative density of books per head of population from Portugal to Russia (both depicted as slightly better in this respect than Britain or Holland). With the help of Palmerston, further details of foreign libraries, including Brazil and Peru, were added in a supplementary report of 1851.

All this was further supported by a comprehensive list of publicly accessible libraries known to exist at this time in Britain, from the smallest of the Bray libraries attached to parish churches, to the many literary and mechanics' institutes, as well as the more obvious libraries in London. The burden of the report was a comparative one, but it made plain by its arguments that it was also one aiming at social, educational and material improvement on a national scale, in the national interest.

On public libraries abroad, the Ewart report took up the evidence of Guizot and the Belgian Ambassdor:

> It can scarcely be doubted that their existence has been fraught with advantage to the literature and to the general character of the countries in which they have been founded.[20]

Moving into a different key, and addressing the question of how libraries might profitably be introduced into rural areas as well as towns, the portion of the report dealing with village libraries suggested that they could be stocked with cast-offs from the 'larger subscribers' (thus developing ideas advanced by J. J. Smith, of Gonville and Caius College, Cambridge).[21] The future well-being of the agricultural population depending on such libraries, their foundation could be encouraged and materially helped by landed proprietors and local clergy.

> By such means the frivolous or unprincipled books which now circulate among our rural population, may be replaced by sound, healthy, and genuinely English literature. The people may be taught many lessons which concern their material (as well as their moral and religious) welfare. The cleanliness and ventilation of their

[20] *Report from the Select Committee on Public Libraries*, p. iii.

[21] In 1849 Smith gave up his fellowship at his college, where he had shown considerable interest in antiquarian and bibliographical matters. He married and became Vicar of Loddon, a small market town of about 1,200 inhabitants ten miles south-east of Norwich. His views on the need for libraries in agricultural communities were developed chiefly from his experience there.

> dwellings, habits of providence, of temperance, a taste for something better than mere animal enjoyment, may be instilled into them through the instrumentality of well-chosen books.[22]

They could also offer useful information on emigration.[23] But, even while looking yet again overseas, the report returned to the theme that was to become one of the most powerful of all in the library movement in the second half of the century: the importance of access to English literature, of its force as a national determinant, and, by extension, of its definition by the compilation of bibliographical works of reference. Nationhood, language, literature and bibliography became fused in questions concerning the potentials of libraries and the tasks of those employed in them.

Against this general background, questions and implications of public knowledge and identity in the specific context of libraries may be set out. I now turn to these, beginning with legislation.

The Public Libraries Act of 1850, known also as the Ewart Act after William Ewart, its progenitor and chairman of the committee on whose work it was founded, gave power to local authorities to levy rates with which to support a local library.[24] It was only patchily taken up not just for several years, but even for several decades. Modified and extended in 1855 principally so as to double the legal rate to one penny, this remained in force until 1892. Norwich was the first to adopt the 1850 Act, and in 1853 it was adopted by Blackburn, Cambridge, Ipswich and Sheffield—a group of towns sufficiently disparate to suggest that the principles were probably the right ones. Edward Edwards introduced his conclusion to a history of libraries in 1859 with a remark that

> recent experience in the History of Libraries, whether it be British, American, or Foreign, points, alike and unmistakeably, to the conclusion that for the Libraries of the Future we must mainly look to the local action of Towns; but to that, only in constant combination with national furtherance, and with national supervision.[25]

However, in the early 1870s it was still rejected by Newcastle on Tyne, Worcester, Aberdeen and Bath.[26] In London, the same years saw refusals by

[22] Ibid., p. xi.

[23] Many government and public institutions in India and the colonies were active in ensuring that their publications reached the major public libraries in the latter part of the century.

[24] Thomas Kelly, *Early Public Libraries: a History of Public Libraries in Great Britain before 1850* (London, 1966), remains the best short guide to its subject. For the history of public libraries since the mid-century, see (representing very different viewpoints) Thomas Kelly, *History of Public Libraries in Great Britain, 1845–1965* (London, 1973), and Alistair Black, *A New History of the English Public Library: Social and Intellectual Contexts, 1850–1914* (London, 1996).

[25] Edward Edwards, *Memoirs of Libraries, Including a Handbook of Library Economy* (London, 1859), p. 557.

[26] Details from John J. Ogle, *The Free Library: its History and Present Condition* (London, 1897).

Islington, St Pancras and Kensington. The refusals, like the acceptances, were from very disparate localities. Nonetheless, the Public Libraries movement had an inexorable effect on redefining the shape of the nation. For the first time, the foundation of libraries was made dependent both on national legislation and on what were in effect nationally proposed rates of tax, even if that tax was not accepted or exacted universally.

Though each decision had to be taken locally, the grounds of argument were remarkably similar: that public libraries would encourage education; that they would reduce crime; that they would keep the working classes out of public houses.[27] These were matters of national, not only local, interest.

No attempt was made to legislate for the kinds of books to be made available in these libraries, and the debates that ensued over the following decades centred on a number of issues, some moral, some literary and some more straightforwardly financial. Whatever the nature of their concerns, the tendency was centrifugal, assuming a national canon of literature that served as a comparator for further activities.

When in 1877 the American bookseller Henry Stevens addressed the infant Library Association, he was unequivocal. Based for most of his time in London, where he dealt in new American books and dealt even more extensively in old European books for export to the United States, Stevens was in the best possible position to make informed judgements about British libraries. He accordingly based his remarks on experience in searching out old books from British libraries. 'A nation's books are her vouchers. Her libraries are her muniments.'[28] It followed that it was the responsibility, as well as the interest, of librarians to ensure that they were organised in such a way, with appropriate guides, that the national literature could be recovered.

If we look at the stock of miscellaneous libraries before the Public Libraries Act—those of circulating libraries, private clubs, learned societies, cathedrals, colleges—we find little coherence beyond the most obvious. Parish libraries, dating from the late sixteenth century onwards, were well known for housing quantities of theology far beyond the capacity or interest of the vast majority of such readers as they had. By definition, commercial circulating libraries had to stock what was most wanted, fiction most notoriously but also an assortment of other recent literature. The emphasis was on novelty. It is only with the growth of interest in public libraries in the

[27] Ibid., pp. 20–1.

[28] Henry Stevens, 'Photo-bibliography; or, a central bibliographical clearing-house', in Nicholson and Tedder (ed.), *Transactions*, pp. 70–81, at pp. 70–1. For Stevens's activities as an international trader, see for example McKitterick, *Cambridge University Library: a History. The Eighteenth and Nineteenth Centuries*, pp. 634–46.

modern sense that there emerged a general and national debate as to what should be included as a general stock.

There were other influences that meant that it is difficult to speak coherently of issues in national librarianship before the 1850s. Cathedral libraries were not only parts of independent bodies, and intended primarily for deans and chapters, but they also, as a result, developed in very different ways depending on the activeness and interests of those most closely involved.[29] For lay readerships, the larger towns had several competing circulating or commercial subscription libraries. By the mid-1830s, Pigot's *Directory* listed fourteen such businesses in Birmingham.[30] In Manchester, many years later, one author recalled that there were seven public libraries in 1829, from Chetham's to the Portico (opened in 1806) to the Law Library and the Mechanics' Institution.[31] Commercial libraries, large and small, thrived or failed in a world of social and financial rivalry. In Norwich, home of one of the oldest public libraries in the country, with a history dating from 1608, there were five subscription libraries (one specifically for medicine) and thirteen circulating libraries in 1845.[32] The Norfolk and Norwich Literary Institution was founded in 1822. In the 1840s it had about 260 subscribers and shareholders, compared with over twice that of its rival, the older Public Library (which, despite its name, and despite its including the ancient City Library, was a private subscription library). The two libraries issued printed catalogues within five years of each other in 1842 and 1847. Though there was some overlap in membership, in such worlds division was more important than cohesion. For many of its critics, the Public Libraries Act was unacceptable exactly because it sought to achieve a measure of cohesion, by requiring a local vote on the issue before such a library could be founded, by public taxation rather than private subscription, and by free entry regardless of wealth or occupation.

In 1849, the Ewart report on public libraries was frank: 'It may be safely inferred that British literature (as compared with that of foreign nations) has suffered from the want of Public Libraries, for more than a century.'[33] Edwards, as always, was clear: Shakespeare and the standard authors of

[29] Beriah Botfield, *Notes on the Cathedral Libraries of England* (London, 1849) was chiefly concerned with the more notable early books in the collections, but he included some comments on more recent publications.

[30] *Pigot & Co.'s National Commercial Directory* (London, 1835).

[31] J. T. Slugg, *Reminiscences of Manchester Fifty Years Ago* (Manchester, 1881), p. 273.

[32] William White, *History, Gazetteer, and Directory of Norfolk* (Sheffield, 1845), p. 198. See also G. A. Stephens, *Three Centuries of a City Library* (Norwich, 1917).

[33] *Report from the Select Committee on Public Libraries*, p. iii.

British literature were requirements in all public libraries. He was less practical on which editions should be collected, since he had a residual hankering for the scholarly where the pressure from the ratepayers who were paying for such libraries was (not surprisingly) more towards books that could be used more widely.

> Vigilance, conjoined with patience, is nowhere more certain of its reward than amongst the second-hand bookshops, even in these days of keen competition. Just as the Alchemist of old in his vain search after the grand elixir, stumbled on many a precious secret by the way, so the Bookworm who sets out in good earnest, on the hunt after a series of Shakespearian quartos, will hardly fail to have his quest rewarded by some choice treasures, however ill he may fare with his chief quarry.[34]

Gifts of rare books were to be encouraged, Glasgow, Birmingham and Manchester all forming major collections intended partly as balances to London. At Wigan likewise, thanks to the presence of the bibliophile Earls of Crawford as well as a large endowment and a librarian anxious to spend it on early books, it was also found desirable to build up a major reference collection for the use of the nearby population.[35] Cardiff, the first Welsh authority to adopt the Public Library Act, was initially slower to build up its collections. With a library focused on English authors, it found itself outmanoeuvred when in 1896 a committee was established to found a national library in Aberystwyth, where the Welsh language was stronger.[36]

Local loyalties and self-dependence nonetheless expected support from London. One of the first departments of government to see the point of distributing its publications to the country's libraries was the Record Commission. Other publications (such as catalogues of the collections in the British Museum) were treated in the same way, the circulation list including the great public schools and the cathedral libraries. By the mid-century, the patterns and demands of library provision could no longer justify such a privileged circulation list, and arguments switched to how far such schemes might be extended to the new public libraries—and if so, since not all libraries served equally large populations, to which.

[34] Edwards, *Memoirs of Libraries*, pp. 631–2.

[35] Henry Tennyson Folkard, *Wigan Free Public Library: Its Rise and Progress: a List of Some of Its Treasures* ... (Wigan, 1901). From 1978 onwards, the library disposed to the trade and to the British Library about 50,000 older books.

[36] Philip Henry Jones, 'Welsh public libraries to 1914', in Philip Henry Jones and Eiluned Rees (ed.), *A Nation and Its Books; a History of the Book in Wales* (Aberystwyth, 1998), pp. 277–86; Gwyn Walters, 'The National Library of Wales, the art of the book, and Welsh bibliography', ibid., pp. 388–98. The National Library of Wales was opened in 1909.

Manchester, for example, had by the late 1850s succeeded in obtaining the publications from the Board of Trade, the Poor Law Board, the Registrar General and the Colonial Office, documents that had been printed at public expense. The East India Company had also been cooperative. But other departments had been less forthcoming.[37] Edwards saw matters from one point of view. On the other, the cost of government printing was rising, and had somehow to be checked: by the 1880s, volumes of the *Calendar of State Papers* were just one series being sold at a low fixed price, regardless of production costs.[38]

Parliamentary blue books, the building blocks of Victorian administration, were by no means universally regarded as having especial value. In their omnivorous attention to detail they were even something of a national joke. There were moves in the mid-century at least to reduce the number of volumes of minutes and evidence that were printed: they could, it was suggested, be simply preserved at Westminster, while only the reports were printed. But there was another, more enlightened side, that emerged when it was discovered that the comparable experiences even of neighbouring towns could remain unknown to local populations. The Tufnell committee on Parliamentary papers in 1853 was inclined to be generous, recommending that wherever free public libraries were established:

> Your Committee recommend that, upon application from the managing body, the Parliamentary Papers should thereupon be sent to them, free of all charge, immediately upon publication.[39]

Meanwhile, libraries suffered from broken runs of publications from the old Record Commissions.[40] By the Patent Law Amendment Act of 1852 copies of patents could be placed in such public libraries and museums as the Commissioners of Patents thought fit. In fact, nothing was done in the first years of the new Patent Office, until 1855.[41] Once the energetic Bennet Woodcroft was appointed in charge of the department in 1864, many more efforts were made to ensure the national distribution of patent literature: the Patent Office Library itself was opened in 1855. By the mid-1870s,

[37] Ibid., p. 607.

[38] Hugh Barty-King, *Her Majesty's Stationery Office: The Story of the First 200 Years, 1786 1986* (London, 1986), pp. 25–6; *First Report of the Controller of Her Majesty's Stationery Office* (London, 1881), p. 531.

[39] *Report from the Select Committee on Parliamentary Papers* (London, 1853), p. v, quoted in Edwards, *Memoirs of Libraries*, pp. 613–14.

[40] For some of the background, see John D. Carswell, *The Public Record Office, 1838–1958* (London, 1991).

[41] 15 & 16 Vic. c. 83. Edwards, *Memoirs of Libraries*, pp. 615, 618–19.

the number of patents held in Birmingham Public Library was about 5 per cent of the entire library.

Again, Edwards was to the fore, urging:

> Effective measures with respect to the free circulation and diffusion, under proper regulation, of all Public records, State papers, Chronicles, Calendars, Indexes, Parliamentary Papers, Public Books, Maps, or Charts of all kinds, as are or shall be printed at the public charge. This free circulation (to permanent and thoroughly accessible Libraries) should be regarded as the primary object of the production of such Records and books, and should aim at ensuring their presence in all Libraries wherein they are likely to be of public utility, and thus transform what has too often been a matter of false economy and petty intrigue, into a systematic and potent means for the encouragement of literary and scientific effort, and for the wider diffusion of that enlightened interest in public affairs which is the sheet-anchor of a well-governed community.[42]

Constantly, there were comparisons to be made with overseas. In particular, America seemed to offer much where the British government failed. Edwards pointed out in 1859 that, poorly printed though they were, congressional and state documents were widely, almost over-generously, available. 'In respect of their systematic use of the creation of public opinion and for the furtherance of education, the American practice is greatly in advance of ours.'[43] No less than 500 sets of congressional papers were reserved to be bound up for distribution to public libraries, historical societies and colleges. This was enshrined in a law dating from as far back as 1814.

When we turn from institutions to individuals, to their training and eventually their professional organisation, we find similar themes, where standards for the management of knowledge are discoverable partly through comparisons, both national and international.

The first modern manual of librarianship in Britain is generally said to be the second volume of Edward Edwards's *Memoirs of Libraries*, published in 1859. Among much else, he argued for a change in employment practice: 'Librarianship, like schoolkeeping, has, in England, too frequently been made a respectable sort of "refuge for the Destitute".'[44]

The American Library Association was founded in 1876, the year of the Bureau of Education report on American libraries—the fullest of its kind for

[42] Edwards, *Memoirs of Libraries*, p. 563.

[43] Ibid., pp. 620–1. See also R. W. Kerr, *History of the Government Printing Office, With a Brief Record of the Public Printing for a Century, 1789–1881* (Washington, DC, 1881).

[44] Ibid., p. 1064. See especially the *Second Report of the Civil Service Inquiry Commission* (London, 1875); Robert Harrison, 'The salaries of librarians', in Henry R. Tedder and Ernest C. Thomas (eds.), *Transactions and Proceedings of the First Annual Meeting of the Library Association of the United Kingdom held at Oxford, October 1, 2, 3, 1878* (London, 1879), pp. 90–5.

any country in the nineteenth century. Britain followed with the Library Association in 1877.[45] But professional training came slowly. The first library school in America, at Columbia College, was opened under the administration of Dewey in 1887.[46] In London, a summer school for librarians was inaugurated in 1893, but the professional examinations of the Library Association at the end of the century attracted few candidates, and by 1900 only two people had gained a full certificate: one reason advanced was a widespread belief that the examinations were too difficult.[47] There was no library school until 1919 at University College London, which perforce became the national arbiter of library education.

For so book-based an occupation, it was a surprisingly long time before professional manuals and periodicals were commonplace. The first of Edwards's two volumes was concerned with the history of libraries in much of Europe as well as in Britain. The latter part of the second consisted of a systematic discussion of issues of library management, including catalogues, buildings, fittings, heating, organisation and regulation. This remained the *locus classicus* for several decades, and it was not until 1897 that John Ogle, Librarian of Bootle, produced a study of *The Free Library* for a series of books edited by Richard Garnett that also included works on library architecture and administration and on book prices.

Periodical literature, here as in other professional circles during the second half of the century, was both crucial and defining. For its first few years the Library Association had no journal: far and away its most important publications were the reports of the annual meetings. For everyday affairs, the British library profession meanwhile depended on the *Library Journal*, founded by the infant American Library Association in 1886 and published in America initially by Frederick Leypoldt and then by R. R. Bowker, the dominant figures in American bibliographical publishing circles. It remained the only serious professional journal available to British librarians until 1899. The *Monthly Notes* of the Library Association began in January 1880, but they were little more than the briefest reports of papers offered at local meetings, with a sprinkling of news items. Melvil Dewey, by contrast, Secretary of the American Library Association, was endlessly inventive.

For the professionals, the work of Dewey from Columbia College in New York was almost required reading. In 1886 he launched *Library Notes*,

[45] Munford, *History of the Library Association, 1877–1977.*

[46] *School of Library Economy at Columbia College, 1887–1889: Documents for a History* (New York, 1937).

[47] Thomas Greenwood, *Greenwood's Library Year Book* (London, 1897), pp. 57–8; Henry D. Roberts, 'The educational work of the Library Association', *British Library Year Book, 1900–1901*, pp. 57–60.

published also in London by Trübner and in Leipzig by Stechert. Its primary audience was in American public libraries, in particular what he termed 'apathetic libraries, which still so largely outnumber those imbued with the modern library spirit'. By this time, the *Library Journal* was in difficulties. Its original appeal to both sides of the Atlantic had been overtaken by events, and the American Library Association was uppermost in its attentions—as it was in those of Dewey. Insofar as there had been an experiment in international cooperation, it had been a relatively short one.

Nonetheless, by the end of the century the shelf of library periodicals was considerable. In a world where the amateur and the professional were never to be easily distinguished, few of them were addressed solely to librarians. Instead, editors and publishers sought their readership in a mixture of the professional and the ordinary informed reading public. In 1889, Swann Sonnenschein launched *The Periodical Press Index*, aiming gradually to increase coverage of American, colonial and Continental periodicals. *The Library* (1889), The *Library Review* (1891), *The Book Lover* (1898) presented a range of interests at prices and sizes designed to catch all possible parts of the market: Hutchinson published both the *Library Review* and *The Book Lover*. In the wake of the Chace Act (1891), Edward Arnold issued *Arnold's Literary List of American and French Books* (from 1891), designed to address literature of a kind otherwise not provided for. Some of these were more commercial than bibliothecarial. In 1892, for example, Sweet and Maxwell launched *The Law Library*, with the principal aim of extending the sale of law books.

While the Library Association continued its skirmishes within the profession, the Library Supply Company issued the first number of the *Library World* in 1898, the sub-title *A medium of intercommunication for librarians* speaking all too clearly of the failures of a profession which, ironically, was dedicated to improving communication. The new journal was not shy of attacking the Council of the Library Association, and in the following year the first number of the official *Library Association Record* was published, edited by Henry Guppy, Librarian of Sion College, who later in the year was appointed to the new John Rylands Library in Manchester.

All these, by tackling questions and topics of common import, encouraged a sense not just of self-identity in which the person working in the smallest town could see some relationship to colleagues in the largest conurbations, but also how knowledge was to be presented, shared and promulgated. The scale was different, but the issues were surprisingly often common to every kind of library.

The personalities and the disputes within the profession would be of little relevance here save that they once more drew attention to issues that were on the one hand almost domestic—to claim them as national would, in many instances, be to grant them too much dignity—and on the other hand international. National questions were defined, as they had been in 1836, in 1849 and in 1877 by foreign comparisons and reports. In its first year, besides reports—sometimes of about 500 words—from libraries round Britain, the *Record* included details from America, France, Germany, Italy, Greece, South Africa, Australia and Japan. The ostensible purpose was simply one of information. In fact, as each report brought news either of a fresh idea or of improvements in service, or of benefactions, each also tended inevitably to be measured against the experiences of readers, most of whom were firmly based in British libraries. There was a clear educative motive for Britain and its place in the world that underlay the apparently simple provision of news.

The public identity of libraries was not just in their collections. It lay also in how such collections were shared and interpreted. As repositories of history as well as of current knowledge, their principles of selection and presentation in turn denoted national and local aspirations linked, by a scale of values that may be broadly defined as social, to a sense of the past. Library exhibitions offered one obvious means of such participation and definition.

The anniversaries of what were for many Victorians the two dominant figures of English literature, Shakespeare and Caxton, fell within fourteen years of each other, in 1864 and 1877. In 1864, Stratford-on-Avon claimed to be at the centre of the celebrations, and in the town hall there was a large exhibition of paintings and drawings.[48] The Shakespeare Memorial Library was not established until 1877. In that year, the Caxton exhibition, embracing books, pictures and equipment for printing, type-casting and paper-making, both from Britain and from overseas, celebrated a man widely recognised as one of England's national heroes. This, too, was organised not by libraries, or by professional historians, but at the instance of a printer, William Blades, author of a biography of Caxton that has only been replaced within the last thirty years.[49] What we may call the canon of literary achievement was only to some extent established by the choice in 1869–70 of books and manuscripts for the permanent exhibition in the British Museum. The catalogue

[48] *Catalogue of Pictures & Drawings Exhibited in the Town Hall, Stratford-on-Avon* (London, 1864). The tercentenary became a cause for jealousy when celebrations in Stratford clashed with those in London.

[49] Caxton's establishment of his press in Westminster was much later discovered to have been in 1476, and it may well have been at the end of 1475. For the 1877 celebrations see George Bullen (ed.), *Caxton Celebration, 1877: Catalogue of the Loan Collection of Antiquities, Curiosities and Appliances Connected with the Art of Printing* (London, 1877). Blades's own copy of the exhibition catalogue, extended to eight volumes with documents relating to the exhibition and other celebrations, as well as with examples of early printing, is in the British Library.

devoted to the printed books gave priority to the history of printing, but placed Shakespeare in odd company, sandwiched between what was described as the first book printed by Europeans in China (Macao, 1590) and the Madrid edition of *Don Quixote* (1605). Printing in Canton intervened between *Paradise Lost* and *Robinson Crusoe*. In the manuscripts, Castiglione and Voltaire stood between Bacon and Waller, while in the separate exhibition of autographs the first group was devoted to figures in the Continental Reformation. It was several years before the exhibitions were changed.[50] While there were many other, more temporary, library exhibitions around the country, some with their own catalogues and frequently of high quality, these local affairs, often initiatives by local private collectors, could not have the same defining potential as that in the British Museum.

In other words, while libraries strove to collect old books as well as new, and to ensure that they held the major works of English literature, the most prominent occasions either were not necessarily the result of library leadership, or (as in the case of the British Museum) presented an incoherent picture that did not accord with the many summary handbooks of English literature that appeared in the wake of the 1870 Education Act.

For librarians and the country as a whole, the most obvious collaboration lay in the potential for union catalogues and national bibliography. This was a topic of the greatest interest to the early Library Association, though in fact some of the best ideas came from outside that body. First was the question of sharing information on cataloguing and on the whereabouts of books. In 1849, Carlyle offered his opinion to the British Museum Commission that the Museum's catalogue should be printed and made as widely available as possible. In the year before the Public Libraries Act, he linked what he called 'real study' in English provincial libraries to such supply:

> The object of such distribution of the catalogue is to encourage that. If there is not going to be any real study in England, there is, of course, little use in distributing catalogues,—there is little use in keeping up the library [of the British Museum] at all. But I hope the time is coming when there will be a public library in every county; when no Englishman will be born who will not have a chance of getting books out of the public libraries. I am sorry to believe that we, of this country, are worse supplied with books than almost any other people in the civilized world.

[50] The printed catalogue of the exhibition of printed books and manuscripts in 1880 was identical. Harris, *History of the British Museum Library*, p. 319, records that it was reorganised in 1886. The first temporary exhibition devoted to a single author and for which a special catalogue was prepared seems to have been that for Luther, in 1883. For autographs, see *A guide to the autograph letters, manuscripts, original charters ... exhibited ... in the Department of Manuscripts* (London, 1869).

> I have seen it stated that in the island of Iceland a man has a better chance of getting books out of the public resources than we have.[51]

Until the all but universal introduction of the card and sheaf catalogue at the end of the century, many libraries printed and reprinted their catalogues.[52] Libraries in turn elsewhere were exhorted to collect these catalogues.[53] But, as Richard Garnett and many others realised, a union catalogue was only to be achieved by a combination of collaboration and individual dedication. Garnett found an analogy in James Murray and the team of collaborators he assembled for the *New English Dictionary*. The Philological Society could achieve nothing by itself; Murray, by dint of personal dedication, accomplished what even a committed body could not.[54] In 1849, apparently thinking independently, both William Cooley (Secretary of the Hakluyt Society) and Charles C. Jewett (Librarian of Boston Public Library in America) put forward schemes for making catalogue records available nationally by proposing that they should be set in type, and stereo plates made which could be selected and used as required.[55] By such means not only could a universal catalogue be created; it would also be possible for librarians to catalogue even books that they had not yet seen—a feature commented on with some sarcasm by Edwards.[56] Others were less scathing, and at the end of the century this system—still untried after almost fifty years—could be referred to as 'most masterly', with 'boundless' applications in bibliography.[57]

Britain was by no means the only country to hanker after a union catalogue. In France, Ferdinand Bonnange, Archiviste du Ministère de l'Agriculture et du Commerce, proposed a new method of providing security

[51] *Report of the Commissioners Appointed to Inquire into the British Museum* (London, 1850), *Evidence*, paras 4386, 4388.

[52] For reflections by the Librarian of Chelsea Public Libraries on changing needs and practices, see J. Henry Quinn, 'Developments in library cataloguing', in Thomas Greenwood (ed.), *British Library Year Book* (London, 1900–1), pp. 37–45, at pp. 44–5.

[53] See for example Edwards, *Memoirs of Libraries*, p. 563. Thomas Greenwood, advocate of public libraries, built up a large collection of library literature which he gave to Manchester Public Library in 1904.

[54] Richard Garnett, 'Address to the Library Association' (Aberdeen, 1893), repr. in his *Essays in Librarianship and Bibliography* (London, 1899), pp. 1–31, at pp. 20–1. For Murray, see K. M. Elisabeth Murray, *Caught in the Web of Words: James A. H. Murray and the Oxford English Dictionary* (New Haven, 1977).

[55] Cooley proposed this in his evidence to the British Museum Commission, 1849, Evidence, paras 4727–39. See also Joseph A. Borome, *Charles Coffin Jewett* (Boston, 1972), pp. 43–63, 178.

[56] Edwards, *Memoirs of Libraries*, pp. 864–8. But see also *The Athenaeum*, 11 May 1850, pp. 501–2.

[57] Frank Campbell, *The Theory of National and International Bibliography* (London, 1896), p. 249. In 1901 the Library of Congress began its programme of selling catalogue cards. The principle was widely taken up elsewhere in Anglo-American librarianship in the twentieth century, with the distribution of all kinds of prepared catalogue cards, and became a basis for computer-based schemes.

in card catalogues for the purpose: it seems to have been one of the earliest occasions on which such catalogues were introduced into the discussions of professional librarianship.[58] Henry Stevens, ever resourceful, put forward proposals that were far ahead of their time. His 'photograms' (combining photographs of the book with bibliographical details) were to be printed up and sold to libraries as required: they would be provided also with subject classifications. On this, the librarian could then write local press-marks and other additions in manuscript suited to the particular copy or library.[59]

The first attempt at a national bibliography of books published in England had been by a London bookseller, Andrew Maunsell, in 1595. For the following three centuries, libraries (and book-buyers and scholars generally) relied on a succession of trade publications.[60] By 1838 these were for current, new, books, principally the *London Catalogue*, with a history dating from the eighteenth century, and the new fortnightly *Publishers' Circular*, founded in 1837. Neither was comprehensive, and as the number of publications grew, and centres of production outside London became ever more active, so they became increasingly unreliable. By the end of the century, information was being published both by the *Bookseller* and by the *Publishers' Circular*, the latter cumulated in the annual *English Catalogue*. But the numbers of books received on copyright deposit in the British Museum were not comprehensive either. It was the most obvious of all gaps in the national bibliographical armoury. In 1896, Frank Campbell, a member of the Museum's staff, quoted Seeley on the question of such a record, 'incomparably the greatest question which we can discuss'.[61] Campbell was adamant: if a record of the national literature were to be compiled, it must be done in the national library, and arrangements for deposit must be improved. The whole would, in his scheme, be the responsibility of a National Bureau for the Record of National Literature.

Campbell was a man of much invention, and he worked hard to promote his ideas, but he eschewed continuous prose, preferring instead a staccato

[58] Ferdinand Bonnange, *Le Bilan de l'Esprit Humain; Projet d'un Catalogue Universel des Productions Intellectuelles* (Paris, 1874).

[59] See n. 28 above. Stevens had first put forward the idea in 1872: see Parker, *Henry Stevens of Vermont*, pp. 295–6, 324, 327–8. He later published the proposals in pamphlet form: *Photo-bibliography or a Word on Printed Card Catalogues of Old, Rare, Beautiful and Costly Books and How to Make Them on a Cooperative System* (London, 1878).

[60] A. Growoll and Wilberforce Eames, *Three Centuries of English Booktrade Bibliography* (London, 1903).

[61] Campbell, *Theory of National and International Bibliography*, p. 188. For the disparity between copyright deposit and the actual numbers of new titles published, see Simon Eliot, *Some Patterns and Trends in British Publishing, 1800–1919* (London, 1994).

delivery of short sections under headings in bold type, emphasising his search for organisation in his work by setting it out under numbered heads. His writings therefore sat uncomfortably beside those of men such as Garnett or Greenwood. What might be termed his modernist terminology did not help his cause. The British Museum Library, his place of employment, was 'the best Bibliographical Observatory in the world' (p. ix). More seriously, he was liable to dictate, or to seem to do so. Thus, authors were not to combine two subjects within the same volume, because this would cause trouble to librarians who might not have the patience or time to ensure adequate cross-referencing (pp. 3–4). Titles of books were to describe the contents—again, so that librarians could construct subject indexes without needing to look further (pp. 18–19). These were not arguments to win friends outside his profession. The Library Bureau, which published his *Theory of National and International Bibliography* in 1896, was the brainchild of Melvil Dewey, a man of much more flexible ideas, able to accept human frailties.

This was, however, only one aspect of the problem: of current literature. There remained also that of the older literature. Here, even more, is to be seen the fusion of library interest with national identity. To those wishing in the mid-century to discover details of what had been published in the British Isles before about 1700, the most convenient reference manual to hand was William Thomas Lowndes's *Bibliographer's Manual.* First issued by William Pickering in 1834, it was enlarged and republished in 1857–64 by Henry George Bohn, publisher of several well-known cheap series of editions of literature and history, and as a second-hand bookseller responsible for easily the fattest catalogue to be issued thus far from such a source: it ran, in 1841, to about 2,000 pages. In 1864 the stereotype plates for Lowndes were purchased by Bell and Daldy, who reprinted them repeatedly until the plates were finally melted down in 1914.[62] In other words, here as in the bibliographical control of periodical literature, and of current publications, libraries and their users were dependent on commercial investment.

In 1850, reflecting on the British Museum, Charles Wentworth Dilke proposed in *The Athenaeum* that there should be a retrospective catalogue of English literature.[63] His idea was taken up in similar terms by Cornelius Walford, also no librarian but a respected statistician and insurance expert as well as book collector on a substantial scale, whose brother owned

[62] William Cole, 'Do you know your Lowndes? A bibliographical essay on William Thomas Lowndes and incidentally on Robert Watt and Henry G. Bohn', *Papers of the Bibliographical Society of America* 1 (1939), pp. 1–22, repr. in Donald C. Dickinson, *George Watson Cole* (Great Bibliographers Series) (Metuchen, NJ, 1990), pp. 212–31.

[63] *The Athenaeum*, 11 May 1850, pp. 499–502.

a second-hand bookshop in the Strand. At the first national meeting of librarians in 1877 the proposal was placed high on the list of priorities. Meanwhile, the Society of Arts had taken an interest in the idea,[64] and Sir Henry Cole organised the printing of a specimen in 1875. Even the Prince of Wales became involved, enquiring into the likely cost of producing such a catalogue down to 1600. Opinion was divided as to whether the catalogue should be in alphabetical order of author, by subject, or by date. It was divided, too, on the *terminus ad quem*: 1550, 1558, 1600, 1603 or 1640, but the principle was clear. In the words of the report to the Oxford meeting of the Library Association (its first annual conference), such a catalogue

> should comprehend all books printed in English either in the United Kingdom or abroad, including Pamphlets, Broadsides, Newspapers, Periodicals, together with Translations of Foreign Works, but not editions in foreign languages even with brief English notes.[65]

It should also be brought down to the most recent date possible.

The notion of studying early English books down to 1640 was one based on historical events. In 1641, Star Chamber was abolished, and with it (however temporarily as it proved) direct government control of printing and publication. It was clear to many that a national bibliography would have to be based on a catalogue of the British Museum's own collection. This was part of the reason for the venom that surrounded so much of the debate about the printing of its entire *General catalogue*: the failure in 1841 after just one volume, the arguments (many of them rehearsed before Parliamentary enquiries) on the merits of longer or shorter entries, the re-commencement of printing the catalogue in 1881, and the realisation long before this was finished that the whole would immediately have to be faced again.[66] Outside the Museum, there was plenty of support for a national retrospective bibliography. In 1877, Walford recognised that such a catalogue would have to be a collaborative venture among many libraries, and he even proposed what became a familiar feature of such catalogues: that contributing libraries should be clearly identified by brief sigla in the catalogue itself.[67] Discussions on the matter collapsed into argument. When fifteen years later W. A. Copinger addressed

[64] *Journal of the Society of Arts*, 25 Jan., 15 and 22 Feb., 23 and 30 Aug., 6 Sept. 1878.

[65] 'Preliminary report of the Committee on a general catalogue of English literature', in Tedder and Thomas (ed.), *Transactions and Proceedings of the First Annual Meeting of the Library Association, 1878* (London, 1879), pp. 8–10.

[66] A. H. Chaplin, *GK: 150 Years of the General Catalogue of Printed Books in the British Museum* (London, 1987).

[67] Cornelius Walford, 'A new general catalogue of English literature', in Nicholson and Tedder (ed.), *Transactions and Proceedings, 1877*, pp. 101–3.

the infant Bibliographical Society the matter was still unresolved, in an environment where 'English' was the usual adjective—taking no notice of other languages in the British Isles—and where most, but not all, wished to restrict any lists to publications in these islands.[68]

The catalogue of English books down to 1640 in the British Museum was the work of George Bullen, Keeper of Printed Books. It was published in three volumes in 1884, and proved to be the basis of all subsequent work, including the current on-line *English Short-title Catalogue* of books published down to 1800. Bullen organised his entries alphabetically by author or, for anonymous work, following the increasingly familiar rules for cataloguing books in the British Museum. The other principal collections in the country were in the university libraries at Oxford and Cambridge. At Cambridge, the traditions of Henry Bradshaw in the study of fifteenth-century printing lived on under his successor but one, Francis Jenkinson, who engaged Charles Sayle to compile a catalogue of English books down to 1640 in the University Library.[69] It was anticipated (correctly) that this would supplement the Museum catalogue at many points. Even more importantly, it was planned that it would be organised not alphabetically by author, but by printers and by places of printing, so enabling the study of the history and bibliography of printing in the British Isles to be examined according to the same principles laid down by Bradshaw and others for incunabula. It would in some measure offer both a complement and alternative to Bullen. Sayle's catalogue was finally published in 1900–7. No such catalogue was ever published for the Bodleian. Other, smaller, libraries, were to follow, thus building up by local enterprise and labour the foundations of Pollard and Redgrave's *Short-title Catalogue of English Books to 1640* itself in 1926.[70]

Work specifically on early English printing ceased for the present with 1640. The whole had been driven by a mixture of national enthusiasm and (in that it also included books in English published overseas, including recusant presses and—just—the first press in British North America) a fusion of geographical with linguistic boundaries. Importantly, libraries had taken on this task of national self-fashioning as their own, a proper use of public money,

[68] W. A. Copinger, 'Inaugural address', *Trans. Bibliographical Soc.*, 1 (London, 1893), pp. 29–43, at pp. 35–8; see also Henry B. Wheatley, 'The present condition of English bibliography, and suggestions for the future', ibid., pp. 61–74.

[69] J. C. T. Oates, 'Charles Edward Sayle', *Trans. Cambridge Bibliographical Soc.,* 8 (Cambridge, 1982), pp. 236–69.

[70] *The Bibliographical Society, 1892–1942: Studies in Retrospect* (London, 1945); Julian Roberts, 'The Bibliographical Society as a band of pioneers', in Robin Myers and Michael Harris (ed.), *Pioneers in Bibliography* (London, 1988), pp. 86–99.

time and staff. The national libraries were not just for collecting. Like public libraries, with their appeal to all classes (one based on the fact that they were rate-supported, but in fact having many overtones of means to social stability), they also found a political purpose.

Periodical literature was much more evasive. W. F. Poole's *Index*, first published in 1848, and revised in 1853, was begun when he was a student at Yale University.[71] By 1877, while the fledgling American Library Association sought to place its revision and enlargement on a formal footing, many libraries had their own manuscript continuations.[72] The scope and number of periodicals to be indexed had grown to 182, divided roughly equally between Britain and North America.

For the selection of modern books, librarians showed some reluctance to engage in activities that might seem too akin to the book trade. While lists of popular books were published in the printed catalogues of public libraries that achieved circulation far beyond their localities, and the catalogue of the London Library, conveniently encompassing a large collection of books within the confines of a single, if bulky, volume, became a familiar work of reference as a general list up and down the country, the task of publishing lists of recommended books remained chiefly one for the trade. The list of 25,000 *Best Books* published by Swann Sonnenschein in 1887, and still being enlarged in 1935, became the most familiar of all bibliographical handbooks in the public library, out-doing its smaller rivals.[73]

The end of the century saw libraries with many questions, many projects half-done, and a gradually better defined relationship between the national libraries (by the 1890s these included the National Art Library in the Victoria and Albert Museum[74]) and public libraries. But while national issues had been identified, the library world as a whole was by no means a unity. Long-standing suspicions remained between the older subscription libraries and the public libraries. Dozens of towns were still without public libraries because there was no local agreement on funding. The County Councils Act of 1888 offered one way in which the public library movement might be advanced. Even in towns which possessed public libraries there was wide divergence of opinion and practice. Not all knowledge was appropriate to be provided from public funds. In Aston Manor (Middlesbrough) and in some other towns,

[71] W. L. Williamson, *William Frederick Poole and the Modern Library Movement* (New York, 1963).

[72] Nicholson and Tedder (ed.), *Transactions and Proceedings of the Conference of Librarians, 1877*, p. 163.

[73] Its most serious commercial competitor was E. B. Sargant and B. Whishaw, *Guide-book to Books* (London, 1891), which listed only about 6,000 titles.

[74] W. H. J. Weale, *The History and Cataloguing of the National Art Library* (London, 1898).

the librarians blacked out the racing results in newspapers lest undesirable people should be tempted into the newspaper reading rooms.[75] Some library authorities opened on Sundays, and some did not—almost identical arguments being used both for and against this practice.

Most of the above has been about books, new or old. But these were only one part of libraries. For many people, newspapers were of much greater interest and daily importance. The invention of machine-made paper, and its eventual linking to web-fed rotary printing presses, were the technical prerequisites for the extraordinary increase in newspaper publication and readership in the second half of the nineteenth century as prices came down in the wake of tax abolition, cheaper materials and increasing advertising revenue. For the newly literate, newspapers were sometimes of greater appeal than books, a fact well recognised by public library authorities. In subscription libraries, a range of newspapers provided, like books, what was not available at home. By 1883, there were 75 daily morning newspapers in the British Isles, including eleven each in Scotland and Ireland, and 97 evening papers. Of 2,172 newspaper titles in all, well over half had been founded since 1861.[76]

At the end of the nineteenth century, the Liverpool Athenaeum, founded in 1798, claimed to have been one of the first institutions, if not the first, to combine a library and a newspaper room.[77] Half a century later, when public libraries were being founded, provision of newspapers was commonplace. Yet few spaces in public libraries caused more unease than the newspaper room. More than any other part, it embodied the social and educational ambitions of the public library as the natural resort for news in preference to the public house. The debates preceding the 1850 Act also discovered a range of opinion, partly anxiety that the rural parts of boroughs would be supporting libraries—and newspaper reading—disproportionately to the use that they could make of them. Sir Alexander Cockburn, Attorney-General, took a wider view: that nothing was so attractive as political knowledge, and that if newspapers were shut out from libraries this would merely send people back to public houses.[78]

[75] *Greenwood's Library Yearbook* (London, 1897), p. 4. For further examples of this practice, see W. A. Munford, *Penny Rate: Aspects of British Public Library History, 1850–1950* (London, 1951), pp. 107–8. See also Tony Mason, 'Sporting news, 1860–1914', in Michael Harris and Alan Lee (ed.), *The Press in English Society from the Seventeenth to the Nineteenth Centuries* (Cranbury, NJ, 1986), pp. 168–86. When in 1914 the *Daily Herald* stopped offering racing tips, circulation fell noticeably.

[76] *May's British & Irish Press Guide 1883*, p. 20.

[77] George T. Shaw and W. Forshaw Wilson, *History of the Athenaeum, Liverpool, 1798–1898* (Liverpool, 1898), p. 34.

[78] Ogle, *The Free Library: its History and Present Condition*, p. 25.

But which newspapers were available? 'Beware, unless your funds are very ample, of introducing denominational papers', wrote one standard authority on the subject.[79] While the new public libraries undoubtedly made much more reading matter available to the general population than ever hitherto, it remains that so far too little has been recovered from contemporary sources about what was offered, and where. The Mitchell Library in Glasgow, founded not on a local rate but on the bequest of a local manufacturer, did not hesitate to buy religious papers—nonconformist, Anglican or Roman Catholic.[80] One danger in writing newspaper history is that social and geographical relationships, in distribution patterns, are by no means always easily defined, and this is particularly true of libraries.[81] The choice of newspapers could be affected by distance, cost and, most importantly, politics. Immigrants needed newspapers in their own languages, either imported or published locally, while other kinds of readers demanded foreign newspapers for commercial, political or literary purposes: in the 1890s, the Liverpool Athenaeum took six foreign papers, besides fifteen dailies from London. Rail and sea transport made communication quicker, and extended choice. In that choice lay, consciously or no, not just questions of money or the appropriateness of particular kinds of knowledge, but also social and political identity and the means for its modification.

With newspapers and magazines came pictures. In a period that saw a revolution in the ways that these were reproduced, from the escalation of commercial wood-engravings, the development of steel-engraving and the introduction of colour lithography, to the application of photography even in the cheapest printing by the 1890s, libraries had to come to terms with what could easily be presented as inferior to hard-won literacy. While publishers—of newspapers and of books—exploited the complementarity of image and text as means of providing knowledge or entertainment, to some of those charged with the management and development of libraries the printed image remained questionable. It was easily defended, as Francis Barrett, Librarian of the Mitchell Library, demonstrated to those of his fellow Glaswegians who in the early 1890s objected to *Punch*, *The Graphic*, and *The Illustrated London News*:

> The fact remains that many people get a much more vivid conception of an incident or a scene from an engraving than from a page of letterpress, however graphic; and this education through the eye is often at once direct and effective.[82]

[79] J. D. Mullins, *Free Libraries and Newsrooms* (London, 1869), p. 7. The same point was made ten years later in the third edition, 1879.
[80] *Report of the Mitchell Library, Glasgow, 1874–1879* (Glasgow, 1880), pp. 30–2.
[81] Brown, *Victorian News and Newspapers* (Oxford, 1985), ch. 2.
[82] Mitchell Library, *Eleventh General Report… 1889–1891* (Glasgow, 1892), p. 13.

The connection between libraries, knowledge and nation-building in much of what is presented above will be self-evident. But as a reminder that this is no modern hypothesis, we may end with two of the most influential writers on libraries of the whole reign. Edwards (1859) concluded with reflections on the importance of local libraries' ensuring that they built up and maintained collections relating to the locality:

> Its promoters should start with the conviction that books have as truly their right work to do in strengthening and deepening our patriotism ... preventing a just national pride from sinking into mere senile vanity.[83]

However, in everything so far, one name is obviously missing. I have left it until the end because it is on the one hand so familiar and on the other so associated (however wrongly) with just one institution. By contrast, I have referred repeatedly to Edwards, who served under him and whose dismissal from the British Museum he ultimately engineered. In 1849, when asked by a Parliamentary committee on the acquisitions policies of the British Museum Library, Panizzi enunciated what has become more recently almost a catch phrase, one that he had coined thirteen years previously: 'this emphatically British library'. It is worth pausing to consider what he meant. Most importantly, he was thinking only of book acquisitions, 'most particularly to British works, and to works relating to the British Empire'. Besides these, he advocated the collecting of what he termed 'the old and rare, as well as the critical editions of ancient classics', and the standard works of foreign literature. 'The public have, moreover, a right to find in their national library heavy, as well as expensive foreign works, such as literary journals, transactions of societies, large collections, historical or otherwise, complete series of newspapers, and collections of laws, and their best interpreters.'[84]

Panizzi's early life as a lawyer in pre-unification Italy coloured some of his views, as now he thought naturally in terms of a British national library. Not for nothing was he the friend of Gladstone, that most nation-conscious of Prime Ministers, and of Cavour and Garibaldi. Panizzi's commitment to Italian reunification is one measure of the way in which he pursued his ends. But he had a more limited view of how this should be reflected in libraries than did Edwards, his difficult (and more consistently radical in library matters) member of staff. Panizzi's view was a limited one. It is not even clear

[83] Edwards, *Memoirs of Libraries*, p. 1065.

[84] *Report of the Commissioners Appointed to Inquire into the British Museum* (London, 1850), *Evidence*, para. 8975. On Panizzi, see especially Edward Miller, *Prince of Librarians: the Life and Times of Antonio Panizzi of the British Museum* (London, 1967). Harris, *History of the British Museum Library* offers a wider view of this period at the Museum.

from his formula for purchases that he appreciated the relationship between British and foreign interests, and in how they needed to be served by foreign purchases designed to inform what had become world-wide imperialism. He had little wish to alarm his Parliamentary hearers, and the acquisition policies were in fact more ambitious in this respect than he was prepared to argue. He showed less wish, here or in most daily routines, to suggest how the Museum might also be a national centre for other library activities. That was left partly to the public libraries, partly to a small group of other institutional librarians (including E. B. Nicholson in the Bodleian, H. R. Tedder of the Athenaeum Club, and B. R. Wheatley of the Royal Medical and Chirurgical Society) and partly to his successors in the Museum.

The first President of the Library Association was John Winter Jones, of the British Museum.[85] Much of the profession's early rhetoric pays obeisance to the largest copyright libraries: the Museum (headed by Richard Garnett, who served as President in 1892–3, and who spoke regularly at meetings), Cambridge University Library (headed by Henry Bradshaw until his death in 1886) and the Bodleian (headed by H. O. Coxe until 1881 and then by the much more active and forward-looking Nicholson until 1912). Though there were proud exceptions, the librarians of the largest local authorities tended to look to these older and larger libraries for leadership. But if in this respect the new professional body echoed past attitudes in the country's bibliographical hierarchy, in others there were not only new voices, but also new perspectives. The authority given under the public libraries legislation for local authorities to levy a penny rate specifically for the development and upkeep of local libraries meant that all decisions respecting such libraries were subject to notions of public identity. Knowledge was not simply something that could be obtained from books. It was subject to public management. At a personal level, the point could hardly have been made in a more fundamental way, since it affected personal income. Nonetheless, and whatever the intentions, legislation alone could not provide sufficient definitions. This was as true of public and local libraries as it was of national ones. It was made clear in the slow taking up by local authorities of the 1850 Act over the following decades, and in the disparate nature of what was agreed locally as distinct from nationally. Knowledge and public identity lay also in the interaction between different parts of the library world and, decisively, in variety.

[85] Garnett's obituary of his former colleague is reprinted in Garnett, *Essays*, pp. 304–24.

CHAPTER FOURTEEN

Measuring the World: Exploration, Empire and the Reform of the Royal Geographical Society, *c.*1874–93

MAX JONES

Not so long ago, the history of geography in Victorian Britain was a straightforward tale of professional progress, of pioneering scientists battling against amateurs and adventurers to establish the credentials of their academic discipline. 'Beside the solid hunks of British manhood who came home and thrilled audiences with accounts of perilous journeys over Arctic or Antarctic ice-caps', wrote T. W. Freeman of the period around 1900, 'the struggling academics of the time could hardly expect to become glamorous public heroes, even if they desired to do so. But they were laying effective foundations in British geography for the later extension of research and teaching.'[1] Yet, even as Freeman's words were written, a revolution was underway. First, in 1977, Brian Hudson published an influential article arguing that the study of geography in the final quarter of the nineteenth century was 'vigorously promoted ... largely, if not mainly, to serve the interests of imperialism in its various aspects including territorial acquisition, economic exploitation, militarism and the practice of class and race domination'.[2] The following year, Edward Said's *Orientalism* inspired a generation of scholars to reconsider the influence of empire on European culture, identifying geography as the imperial science par excellence.[3]

[1] T. W. Freeman, *History of Modern British Geography* (London, 1980), p. 69.
[2] B. Hudson, 'The new geography and the new imperialism, 1870–1918', *Antipode*, 9, 2 (1977), 12.
[3] E. Said, *Orientalism* (New York, 1978).

The last twenty years have witnessed a plethora of investigations into the linkages between geography, exploration and empire.[4] A new history of geography has emerged, distinguished both by its critical perspective, and by its attempt to situate the geographical enterprise in a broader historical context.[5] Some of this work has fallen victim to 'the determinist fix' diagnosed by Gareth Stedman Jones, substituting a new grand narrative of imperial expansion for the old text-book chronicle of professionalisation.[6] But penetrating studies by David Livingstone and Felix Driver have mapped the myriad impulses which shaped the geographical enterprise in the nineteenth century, putting empire in its place.[7] Driver has highlighted the diverse 'cultures of exploration' which circulated through the nineteenth century, as geographical information and ideas were recycled through government departments, scientific societies, philanthropic groups, sociological investigations, legal proceedings, exhibitions, novels, newspapers and periodicals.

The following essay intervenes in these debates by focusing on the quasi-official headquarters of Victorian exploration, the Royal Geographical Society (RGS). The essay describes the transformation of the RGS after the burial of the missionary explorer Dr Livingstone in 1874, a transformation which has been neglected in the existing scholarship. The officers of the RGS initiated a comprehensive series of reforms, which both promoted the accurate measurement of the world as the central aim of exploration, and overhauled the channels through which the information generated by expeditions was distributed and archived. The study exposes how a single institution influenced the manifold ways in which a particular form of knowledge was organised, and offers insights into the influence of empire in the critical decades when the academic structures of Victorian Britain began to coalesce into a recognisably modern form.

[4] See, among many, R. A. Stafford, *Scientist of Empire: Sir Roderick Murchison, Scientific Exploration and Victorian Imperialism* (Cambridge, 1989); A. Godlewska and N. Smith (eds.), *Geography and Empire* (Oxford, 1994); M. Bell, R. Butlin and M. Heffernan (eds.), *Geography and Imperialism, 1820–1940* (Manchester, 1995); S. Ryan, *The Cartographic Eye: How Explorers Saw Australia* (Cambridge, 1996); R. Phillips, *Mapping Men and Empire: a Geography of Adventure* (London, 1997); J. R. Ryan, *Picturing Empire: Photography and the Visualisation of the British Empire* (London, 1997).

[5] Much recent research has investigated the place of the geographical enterprise within the Enlightenment. See F. Driver, 'Review article: Geography, Enlightenment, and improvement', *Historical Journal*, 45 (2002), 229–33.

[6] G. Stedman Jones, 'The determinist fix: some obstacles to the further development of the linguistic approach to history in the 1990s', *History Workshop Journal*, 42 (1996), 19–35.

[7] D. N. Livingstone, *The Geographical Tradition: Episodes in the History of a Contested Enterprise* (Oxford, 1992); F. Driver, *Geography Militant: Cultures of Exploration and Empire* (Oxford, 2001). D. R. Stoddart, *On Geography and its History* (Oxford, 1986), also offers valuable insights, although it does not engage directly with the issues raised by Said.

I

The RGS grew out of the Raleigh Travellers' Club, a dining society founded in 1827. At a meeting of the Club on 24 May 1830, John Barrow, Second Secretary to the Admiralty, submitted two memoranda for consideration. The first declared 'a Society was needed whose sole object should be the promotion and diffusion of that most important and entertaining branch of knowledge—geography'. This 'department of science' was of 'the first importance to mankind in general, and paramount to the welfare of a maritime nation like Great Britain, with its numerous and extensive foreign possessions'. A geographical society could gather the vast store of geographical information dispersed throughout Britain and afford 'a copious source of rational amusement' to its members.

The second memorandum set out six specific objectives for the proposed society: '1. To collect, register and digest, and to print . . . such new, interesting and useful facts and discoveries as the Society may have in its possession, and may from time to time acquire'; '2. To accumulate gradually a library of the best books on geography', and a collection of maps, so that the prospective traveller may be 'aware, previously to his setting out, of what has been already done, and what is still wanting, in the countries he may intend to visit'; '3. To secure specimens of such instruments' which might be useful for a traveller; '4. To prepare brief instructions for such as are setting out' noting the most important areas to visit, phenomena to be observed and 'the researches most essential to make'. The society also hoped in the future to be able to offer 'pecuniary assistance to such travellers as may require it, in order to facilitate the attainment of some particular object of research'; '5. To correspond with similar Societies' and individuals interested in geography 'in different parts of the world' and in 'various remote settlements of the Empire'; and, finally, '6. To open a communication with all those philosophical and literary societies with which Geography is connected'.[8] Both memoranda were adopted by acclamation. At a later date the first bye-law affirmed that the society was founded for the 'Advancement of Geographical Science'.[9]

A range of commercial, imperial and scientific interests found expression in the new society. The assortment of aristocrats, government officials, naval and military men involved in the Raleigh Club, indicated the worldliness of the geographical enterprise, a public pursuit with practical applications.

[8] Report of meeting of Raleigh Travellers' Club, 24 May 1830, 'The Raleigh Club, 1827–54', Additional papers 115, Royal Geographical Society, London (RGS).

[9] J. S. Keltie, 'Thirty years' work of the Royal Geographical Society', *Geographical Journal*, 49 (1917), 361.

From its inception, the new geographical society was a hybrid institution: gentlemen's club, geographical archive, publishing house, forum for scientific debate and sponsor of exploration. This hybrid character would influence the emergence of geography as an academic discipline.

The new society secured its own accommodation in 1839, leasing a suite of rooms at 3 Waterloo Place, London, although meetings continued to be held in the hall of the Horticultural Society. Extravagant sponsorship of expeditions in these early years almost brought disaster, however, and the society ran up deficits in 1836, 1837, 1839, 1840, 1844 and 1849. Membership remained relatively stagnant, with 758 fellows in 1839 and 793 in 1851.[10] But the society recovered in the 1850s, receiving an annual grant of £500 from the Treasury from 1854, to support its collection of books and maps, and a Royal Charter in 1859.[11] The growth of the RGS after the financial crises of the 1840s emerged from the conjunction of three factors: the move to larger premises at 15 Whitehall Place, London, in 1854; the astute stewardship of Sir Roderick Murchison (RGS President, 1843–5, 1851–3, 1856–9 and 1862–71); and the growth of public interest in African exploration.

From the mid-nineteenth century a series of expeditions, including the crossing of the Australian deserts, the search for a North-West passage and the mystery surrounding the fate of Sir John Franklin, raised the profile of exploration in Britain.[12] This interest was fuelled by the expansion of print media, which found ideal copy for its growing readership in the adventure stories and exotic locations of explorers.[13] The RGS benefited most from the wave of popular enthusiasm for African exploration, and Dr Livingstone in particular. Livingstone received a tumultuous welcome when he returned to Britain in December 1856 after his first expedition. The RGS President, Sir Roderick Murchison, interrupted his Christmas holiday with the Prime Minister, Lord Palmerston, to return to England to promote Livingstone's achievements. Murchison cultivated Livingstone's reputation, associating the RGS with his achievements in order to attract subscriptions.[14] A reception

[10] Rawson W. Rawson, 'Tabular view of the history and finances of the Royal Geographical Society from the commencement in 1830 to the close of the year 1892', Additional papers 26a, RGS.

[11] The award of the grant was secured through the efforts of Lord Ellesmere (RGS President, 1853–5), and Murchison. See H. R. Mill, *The Record of the Royal Geographical Society, 1830–1930* (London, 1930), pp. 65–7.

[12] See Mill, *Record*, chs. 1–5 and C. R. Markham, *The Fifty Years' Work of the Royal Geographical Society* (London, 1880), for RGS involvement in exploration between 1830 and 1874.

[13] B. Riffenburgh, *The Myth of the Explorer: the Press, Sensationalism and Geographical Discovery* (Oxford, 1994). See also R. G. David, *The Arctic in the British Imagination, 1818–1914* (Manchester, 2000), ch. 4.

[14] R. Bridges, 'The sponsorship and financing of Livingstone's last journey', *African Historical Studies*, 1 (1968), 84.

for Livingstone was organised at the society's headquarters, forestalling the London Missionary Society, which, with an overdraft of £13,000, was also anxious to exploit Livingstone's popularity.[15] With his connections in Westminster and Whitehall, Murchison proved Livingstone's most influential patron, establishing contact with the Foreign Secretary, Lord Clarendon, which resulted in Livingstone's appointment as leader of a government-sponsored expedition up the River Zambezi in 1858.[16]

Murchison's calculated investment in the quest for the sources of the Nile paid ample dividends. The fellowship of the RGS increased steadily from 1,022 in 1854 to over 2,000 in 1861 and passed 3,000 for the first time in 1872.[17] In 1876 the RGS hired St James's Hall in an effort to accommodate all those who wished to hear Lieutenant Verney Cameron's account of the expedition he had commanded to relieve Livingstone. Yet even this venue, with room for 2,000, proved too small, and many angry fellows, who regarded attendance at such events as the prime benefit of fellowship, were locked out of the meeting.[18] This expansion consolidated the society's finances and by 1870 funded capital amounted to £19,250. With the expiration of the lease at Whitehall Place, the RGS purchased the freehold of 1 Savile Row for £14,527. An additional £18,250 were spent on alterations to the house during the 1870s, an indication of the strength brought by annual receipts of £3,000–£5,000 in membership fees alone.[19]

Two aspects of this expansion are significant. First, the RGS was reliant on the subscriptions of fellows. With a turnover of over £17,000 in 1874, the government grant of £500 was a token gesture.[20] Interest in African exploration swelled the society's coffers, but new members were in continual demand. The society's prosperity, then, was built on the ability of expeditions to resonate outside the confines of Savile Row. The prominence accorded to pioneering expeditions, however, has tended to obscure other initiatives: the maintenance of a library and map room, the publication of a journal and the promotion of geographical education. In part, the RGS simply did not have the resources to finance large-scale expeditions. Opening the new session in 1877, the diplomat Rutherford Alcock, who served as President

[15] T. Jeal, *Livingstone* (New York, 1985), pp. 164–5.

[16] T. Jeal, 'David Livingstone: a brief biographical account', in J. M. MacKenzie (ed.), *David Livingstone and the Victorian Encounter with Africa* (London, 1996), pp. 40–1.

[17] Rawson, 'Tabular view', records the fellowship of the society increasing every year from 793 fellows in 1851, 2,093 fellows in 1861, 3,132 fellows in 1872 and 4,068 fellows in 1879.

[18] Mill, *Record*, p. 118. Protests led to the limitation of the privilege of each fellow to invite guests to the society's meetings.

[19] Markham, *Fifty Years' Work*, pp. 113–15

[20] Rawson, 'Tabular view': in 1874 receipts totalled £9,296, while expenditure totalled £7,876.

from 1876 to 1878, declared 'It is so much and so absolutely a question of money, that the Exploration Committee have not hitherto felt justified in entering upon any serious undertaking or new expedition for exploratory purposes.'[21] At a meeting of subscribers to the special African Exploration Fund established in 1878, it was explained that 'the Society cannot compete with governments or even with Missionary Societies in explorations on a large scale having neither the powers of the first, or the pecuniary resources of the second'.[22] Expedition expenses were notoriously difficult to control and the financial crises of the 1840s had demonstrated the dangers of uncapped expenditure. But, although direct sponsorship was too expensive, the society's officers found other ways to influence the conduct of explorers.

II

Two years after Livingstone's spectacular funeral at Westminster Abbey in April 1874, Rutherford Alcock explained that the

> progress of science and exact knowledge in every direction creates new exigencies. Distinction to the future explorer can only be secured therefore by a certain scientific training. It can no longer be won by mere descriptive power . . . [this] must now be accompanied by instrumental observations of an order sufficiently high to place numerically before Geographers all the characteristics of the explored region.[23]

The RGS would have to adjust to the end of the age of pioneer explorers signalled by Livingstone's death. The society's officers responded after 1874 in two ways: first, by training the next generation of explorers; and, secondly, by promoting new educational initiatives.

The RGS had paid little attention to education until the 1860s, when the young explorer and father of eugenics, Francis Galton, began to campaign for the more active promotion of geography in schools. In 1874 the council made its first approach to the vice-chancellors of Oxford and Cambridge, 'urging the claims of Geographical science to due recognition in any future distribution of Academical Revenues'.[24] A reply was delayed until the report of the royal commission appointed to investigate the universities' finances.

[21] R. Alcock, 'Opening address', *Proceedings of the Royal Geographical Society*, 22 (1877–8), 24.
[22] Quoted in T. W. Freeman, 'The Royal Geographical Society and the development of geography', in E. H. Brown (ed.), *Geography: Yesterday and Tomorrow* (Oxford, 1980), 9.
[23] R. Alcock, 'Opening address', *Proc. RGS*, 21 (1876–7), 23.
[24] 'Geographical professorships at Oxford and Cambridge', *Proc. RGS*, NS 1 (1879), 261.

In the interim, the council resolved in June 1876 to set aside up to £500 each year for 'the promotion of special scientific branches of geography', and created a separate scientific purposes committee to administer the sum.[25] The committee's first initiative was the assignment of three of each session's evening meetings for a lecture by a geographical expert. The series ran for three years and produced important papers by Archibald Geikie and John Ball, among others.[26] However, the lectures were abandoned in 1879 as they attracted few fellows, in marked contrast to the clamour for tickets which greeted the announcement of papers at St James's Hall by Cameron in 1876 and H. M. Stanley in 1878.

After this uncertain start, the transformation of the RGS gathered pace on 26 May 1879, when the scientific purposes committee was asked to prepare a 'Memorandum on a plan for training travellers to make useful scientific observations'.[27] The committee prepared a detailed report which was presented to the council on 9 June. The report observed that every year 'wanderers, in various professions and engaged upon diverse avocations, spread themselves over every quarter of the globe. Yet, for want of necessary training, they travel and return without any or with few results that can be utilised for geographical knowledge'. The report proposed the RGS 'assist in providing this preliminary training' to 'promote the increase of valuable observations for geographical purposes in all parts of the world'. Nine categories of traveller were cited who would benefit from such training: officers in the army and navy; clerks employed in merchants' houses; planters and settlers; engineers; missionaries; colonial officials; collectors; and 'sportsmen and ordinary travellers, who visit little-known regions for their own amusement'.[28]

The committee suggested the instruction 'should at present be limited to surveying and mapping, including the fixing of positions by astronomical observations'.[29] Such training in the use of the sextant, artificial horizon and prismatic compass,

> is absolutely essential for every traveller who wishes to bring back useful work. It is the groundwork of the acquirements which he ought to possess.

[25] Francis Galton produced a circular, 'Promotion of scientific branches of geography', to publicise the society's decision, inserted in Scientific purposes committee minutes, 3 Jan. 1878, RGS.

[26] A. Geikie, 'Geographical evolution', *Proc. RGS*, NS 1 (1879), 422–44; J. Ball, 'On the origin of the flora of the European Alps', *Proc. RGS*, NS 1 (1879), 564–89.

[27] Council minutes, 26 May 1879, RGS.

[28] Council minutes, 9 June 1879, RGS.

[29] Scientific purposes committee minutes, 16 June 1879, RGS. Markham noted that Coles's course involved 'the use of the transit-theodolite, ordinary 5-inch theodolite, sextant and artificial horizon, hyposometrical apparatus, manner of plotting a traverse-survey by means of the prismatic compass, and map construction', Markham, *Fifty Years' Work*, p. 108.

> A traveller in unknown or little-known regions should be an instructed observer. It is not necessary that he should be a botanist, a zoologist, or a geologist, but he must know how to make and record observations which will be useful as regards those sciences.[30]

The costs of the instruction were to be met in part by the trainee and in part by the RGS.[31] John Coles, map curator since 1877, was appointed as 'Instructor in Practical Astronomy and Surveying to the R. G. S.' at the beginning of 1881.[32]

The RGS invested in the new scheme. An observatory was built on the roof at Savile Row, at a cost of £152.[33] In 1884, as envisaged in the original memorandum, the range of courses on offer was broadened to include instruction in photography, botany, zoology and geology. However, all prospective travellers had first to complete Coles's surveying course.[34] Indeed, completion of the course became an essential prerequisite for RGS support. Mr Arnott's request for assistance for an expedition to Central Africa was declined in 1886 'on the ground that the council have not sufficient information of the applicant's capacity for using the instruments applied for'.[35] The Reverend H. Lansdell's request regarding a journey to Chinese Turkistan was rejected on similar grounds, even though he had already secured passports, guides, scientific equipment and £1,000.[36]

The introduction of Coles's course was complemented by two additional reforms: the formation of a new instruments committee to supervise the lending of equipment to explorers, and the publication of a revised edition of the society's *Hints to Travellers*. The first *Hints to Travellers*, published in 1854, comprised a thirty-one-page collection of articles designed to answer questions which were frequently addressed to the RGS.[37] A range of institutions including the Hydrographic Office and the British Association published guidelines on field observation in the mid-nineteenth century. Francis Galton wrote eight pages on equipment and outfit, which he hoped

[30] Council minutes, 9 June 1879, RGS.

[31] Scientific purposes committee minutes, 16 June 1879, RGS.

[32] Scientific purposes committee minutes, 27 Jan. 1881, RGS.

[33] Council report 1880, 'Council reports, 1830–96' (bound pamphlet), Publications Collection, RGS library.

[34] Scientific purposes committee minutes, 17 March 1884, RGS. Council report 1888, records the delivery of 26 lessons in botany, 20 in photography and 19 in geology.

[35] Council minutes, 22 Feb. 1886, RGS.

[36] Council minutes, 13 Feb. 1888, RGS.

[37] R. Fitzroy and H. Raper (eds.), *Hints to Travellers* (1st edn., London, 1854).

would be 'of infinite service to young travellers'.[38] Subsequent editions appeared in 1865, 1871 and 1878.[39]

But, in the 1880s, *Hints to Travellers* was transformed from an assortment of miscellaneous articles, into a systematic and comprehensive 'How to' manual for the prospective explorer. In 1881 a new *Hints to Travellers* committee and an editorial subcommittee were established to oversee the publication of a fifth edition, to complement John Coles's new surveying course. *Hints to Travellers* was substantially revised and the edition published in 1883 trebled in length to almost 300 pages. The editors explained in a preface that 'the Council have been anxious to increase the usefulness of the volume, and to make it meet the in some ways higher requirements of a new generation of young travellers, many of whom receive scientific instruction in the society's office before leaving England'. While noting the 'first object' of the book was to offer advice to 'the intelligent explorer who, in the hope of obtaining from his travels valuable geographical results, has been at some pains to acquaint himself with the use of instruments', they also hoped to advise those who had not undertaken any formal instruction, by showing how 'at a trifling expense of well-directed energy, they may add to the daily interest of their travels, and bring home results valuable to science'.[40]

The section titled 'Surveying and Astronomical Observations', prepared by Coles, was described as 'the principal portion of the work'.[41] It consisted of an extensive 188-page account of the latest surveying equipment and techniques, from advice on how 'to find the Distance of an inaccessible object with a Measuring Line', to 'Finding the Error of a Compass by the Sun's Azimuth'. The section concluded with fifty pages of mathematical tables, for use in the computations which had been described. The rest of the volume included sections on meteorology, geology, natural history, anthropology, photography, outfit and medical advice.

The ruler inscribed on the front-cover indicated the centrality of accurate measurement to *Hints to Travellers*. The sixth edition, published in 1889, introduced a new section on 'Industry and Commerce'.[42] But the 'Hints on Surveying

[38] F. Galton, 'Letter addressed by F. Galton, Esq., to the Secretary', Fitzroy and Raper, *Hints*, p. 18.
[39] G. Back, R. Collinson and F. Galton (eds.), *Hints to Travellers* (2nd edn., London, 1865); G. Back, R. Collinson and F. Galton (eds.), *Hints to Travellers* (3rd edn., London, 1871); F. Galton (ed.), *Hints to Travellers* (4th edn., London, 1878).
[40] D. W. Freshfield, H. H. Godwen-Austen and J. K. Laughton (eds.), *Hints to Travellers* (5th edn., London, 1883), p. iv.
[41] Ibid.
[42] D. W. Freshfield and W. J. L. Wharton (eds.), *Hints to Travellers* (6th edn., London, 1889), pp. 411–19.

and Astronomical Observations' remained the principal portion of the work, taking up 225 of 420 pages in 1889,[43] and 237 of 497 pages in the seventh edition of 1893.[44] Finally, in 1901, the RGS published *Hints to Travellers* in two volumes, with the first volume of 425 pages devoted solely to surveying.[45]

Detailed instructions, though, were of little use if the explorer did not have access to the latest equipment. In conjunction with the publication of the fifth edition of *Hints* in 1883, a separate instruments committee was established with 'control over the purchase and testing of instruments, and the granting of loans of instruments to travellers'.[46] The RGS's loan of instruments to explorers increased steadily after the establishment of the committee, with 15 expeditions supplied in the 1860s, 27 in the 1870s, 61 in the 1880s and 106 in the 1890s.[47] Between 1877 and 1900, the RGS supplied instruments to 186 expeditions, ranging all over the world, from Captain A. H. Markham's voyage to the Arctic in 1879 to the Reverend Weston's trip to Japan in 1893, and from A. P. Maudslay's expedition to Guatemala in 1888 to W. M. Conway's exploration of the Himalayas in 1892.

The introduction of a course in surveying, the revision of *Hints to Travellers* and the establishment of a separate instruments committee, firmly promoted the production of an accurate survey as the central aim of exploration. The departure of Joseph Thomson's East African Expedition was delayed for a month in 1883, so that Thomson could receive additional tuition from Coles.[48] Thomson received detailed instructions, which stated that the

> objects of the expedition are to ascertain if a practicable direct route for European travellers exists through the Masai country from ports on the East African coast to the Victoria Nyanza, and to examine Mount Kenia; to gather data for constructing as complete a map as possible in a preliminary survey, and to make all practicable observations on the meteorology, geology, natural history and ethnology of the region traversed.[49]

[43] Freshfield and Wharton, *Hints* (1889), pp. 70–294.

[44] D. W. Freshfield and W. J. L. Wharton (eds.), *Hints to Travellers* (7th edn., London, 1893), pp. 83–320.

[45] J. Coles (ed.), *Hints to Travellers vol. I: Surveying and Practical Astronomy* (8th edn., London, 1901).

[46] Council minutes, 11 June 1883, RGS. In 1885 Coles was given the power to grant instruments at his own discretion, with the concession of Mr Bates and any member of the instruments committee, if the traveller was leaving before the start of the society's annual session (Instruments committee minutes, 25 Nov. 1885, RGS).

[47] Instruments Lent to Travellers, vol. 1, Administrative Records, RGS. This volume lists the name of the explorer, date of withdrawal, and destination of the expedition, but not the instruments borrowed.

[48] Expedition committee minutes, 16 Nov. 1882, RGS.

[49] 'Instructions to Mr Thomson', inserted in Expedition committee minutes, 8 Dec. 1882, RGS.

When Sir Joseph Hooker informed the council that the British Association had granted £500 to send a naturalist as far as Mount Kilimanjaro with Thomson, he was politely informed that the

> Expedition has for its main object the exploration of a line of route through the unexplored country between Kilimanjaro and Victoria Nyanza, and that its time and resources will be fully occupied in that work. It will not therefore be able to give material aid to the Botanical Expedition. Mr. Thomson will however be happy to have the companionship of Dr. Aitchison and his party as far as Kilimanjaro, and render him such assistance as circumstances may permit.

An offer of £400 towards the cost of the expedition from the Church Missionary Society was also rejected, as the attached 'conditions' were 'inconvenient' and the council desired to be 'unfettered, with regard to the route their expedition shall take'.[50] The rejection of these offers, which would have covered around a third of the expedition's total cost, indicate the primacy attached to surveying.

The society's annual awards further reinforced the message. From the 1870s pioneering journeys were explicitly rejected as grounds for an award if they were not accompanied by a detailed survey. Lieutenant Cameron, Major Serpa Pinto and Fridtjof Nansen, for example, all received the society's prestigious gold medal for making detailed observations of the topography of a previously unknown region in hostile conditions.[51]

Markham spelt out this manifesto for mapping at a meeting of the Geographical Section of the British Association in 1879.

> Our first work as geographers is to measure all parts of earth and sea, to ascertain the relative positions of all places upon the surface of the globe, and to delineate the varied features of that surface …
>
> Accurate maps are the basis of all inquiry conducted on scientific principles. Without them a geological survey is impossible; nor can botany, zoology, or ethnology be viewed in their broader aspects, unless considerations of locality, altitude, and latitude are kept in view.[52]

Markham repeated this geographical agenda in 1897: 'The first work of geographers is to answer the question "Where is it?" '[53]

[50] Expedition committee minutes, 27 Oct. 1882, RGS.

[51] 'Presentation of the Royal and other awards', *Proc. RGS*, 20 (1875–6), 368–9; 'Presentation of the Royal medals', *Proc. RGS*, NS 3 (1881), 432; 'Presentation of the Royal medals', *Proc. RGS*, NS 13 (1891), 493. For further discussion see M. H. Jones, 'The Royal Geographical Society and The commemoration of Captain Scott's last Antarctic expedition', unpublished Ph.D. thesis, Cambridge University, 2000, ch. 1, part b.

[52] 'Proceedings of the Geographical Section of the British Association, Sheffield meeting, 1879', *Proc. RGS*, NS 1 (1879), 602–3.

[53] C. R. Markham, 'The field of geography', *Geographical Journal*, 11 (1898), 2.

III

In 1891 the RGS President, the Sir Montstuart Elphinstone Grant Duff, divided the 'duties' of the RGS into 'two great classes, the acquisition and the diffusion of knowledge'.[54] The emphasis on the accurate measurement of the world was reinforced by a series of reforms which increased the efficiency of the RGS as an archive of geographical information. The library expanded steadily after the move to Savile Row, from 15,687 books and pamphlets in 1874, to 32,399 in 1896.[55] An assistant librarian was appointed for the first time in 1875 to ease the increased workload. Donations were regularly received from foreign administrations, scientific societies, private collectors and a number of government departments, including the foreign, colonial, war and India offices, and the Admiralty. E. C. Rye (RGS Librarian, 1874–85) declared the society 'most especially indebted to the various Departments of Her Majesty's Government for invaluable and continued support'.[56]

Clements Markham produced the first alphabetical catalogue of the library's holdings in 1865, with a supplementary volume prepared by Mr Evans of the British Museum in 1871,[57] but the arrangement of books was made 'satisfactory for the first time' only after Rye's appointment three years later.[58] Under his supervision, 1,250 copies of a second supplementary catalogue of 380 pages were printed in 1881 and distributed to fellows free of charge on application.[59] A list of librarian's duties was drawn up for the first time after John Scott Keltie succeeded Rye in 1885.[60] Keltie prepared a third supplementary catalogue in 1890. Rather than issue this catalogue separately, the council decided to compile a single volume, arranged alphabetically, to include acquisitions up to 1893.[61] This volume was eventually published in 1895 and its 834 pages covered the 50,000 titles in the society's collection.[62] H. R. Mill (RGS Librarian, 1892–1902) also introduced a complete list of additions to the library in the *Geographical Journal*

[54] M. E. Grant Duff, 'The annual address on the progress of geography', *Proc. RGS*, NS 13 (1891), 382.
[55] Figures calculated from 'Council reports, 1830–96'.
[56] Markham, *Fifty years' work*, pp. 102–3.
[57] Mill, *Record*, pp. 238–9.
[58] Ibid., pp. 105–6.
[59] Library and map committee minutes, 22 June 1881 and 25 Jan. 1882, RGS.
[60] Council minutes, 23 March 1885, RGS, record the decision of the finance committee on 2 March 1885 'that written rules should be prepared defining the duties of the Librarian'. 'Duties of the Librarian' inserted in Library and map committee minutes, 29 April 1885, RGS.
[61] C. R. Markham, 'Address to the Royal Geographical Society', *Geographical Journal*, 4 (1894), 2.
[62] Mill, *Record*, p. 238.

(see below), with the monthly entries pasted onto cards and classified to form a subject catalogue.[63] Mill recalled how 'the days were over when the library of the R. G. S. was a comfortable study in which the librarian was free to read all day. The work at Savile Row had been extended and speeded up.'[64]

A similar pattern of reform characterised the development of the map room, which had been sponsored by central government from 1854, when Aberdeen's coalition ministry was persuaded to provide an annual grant of £500 for the provision of an apartment 'in which the society's valuable collection of maps may be rendered available for general reference'.[65] The map room was also closely tied to government. From 1854 the society published an annual report on the progress of Admiralty surveys and in 1867 the Admiralty agreed to supply the RGS with all its hydrographic charts as they were published.[66] In 1868 the War Office, India Office and Ordnance Survey undertook to do the same, and, later, maps were donated by the Air Ministry and the map section of the United States army.[67]

The appointment of Coles as map curator initiated a new era, marked by the erection of a sign above the map room door in 1878.[68] The society's map collection almost trebled between 1874 and 1896, from around 23,000 to over 62,000 sheets.[69] E. A. Reeves was appointed as the first assistant to the map curator at the end of 1881, to help Coles cope with his increasing workload.[70] Ten new map cases were ordered in 1887 to house the new acquisitions, at a cost of nearly £100.[71] Coles compiled a catalogue of map room holdings in 1880, and in 1884 was instructed to organise the society's collection of diagrams for the first time.[72] In response to requests from Douglas Freshfield, 1884 also saw the establishment of a collection of photographs.[73]

63 H. R. Mill, *An Autobiography* (London, 1951), p. 95. A subject catalogue had been prepared by Godfrey Evans in 1871, but by 1894 covered less than half of the books in the library, C. R. Markham, 'Address to the Royal Geographical Society', *Geographical Journal*, 4 (1894), 3.

64 Mill, *Record*, p. 142.

65 Quoted in I. Cameron, *To the Farthest Ends of the Earth: the History of the Royal Geographical Society* (London, 1980), p. 207.

66 Markham, *Fifty Years' Work*, p. 99.

67 Cameron, *To the Farthest Ends of the Earth,* p. 207.

68 Finance committee minutes, 4 Feb. 1878, RGS.

69 Council reports, 1874–96 list acquisitions to the map room. However, reports do not include the total number of sheets held. I have used 35,000 sheets held in 1880 (Keltie, 'Thirty years' work', 358) as a base figure.

70 Council minutes, 28 Nov. 1881, RGS.

71 Council minutes, 31 Jan. 1887, RGS.

72 Coles was instructed to mark 'those which are obsolete or otherwise require renewal: marking the superficial dimensions and scale of each, and the limiting degrees of latitude and longitude', Library and map committee minutes, 19 Nov. 1884, RGS.

73 Mill, *Record*, pp. 239–40.

The RGS not only collected maps, it also produced them. The move to Savile Row facilitated the appointment in 1873 of the society's first map draughtsman, W. J. Turner, to prepare maps on the premises under the supervision of the curator. The duties of the map draughtsman were first written down in 1881, when Henry Scharbau replaced Turner. Scharbau's overtime fees soared as RGS involvement in map production increased sharply. In 1885 the system of overtime payments was abolished, Scharbau's salary was raised and Mr Milne, who had been working on a temporary basis, was appointed assistant map draughtsman, on condition that both men agreed in writing 'to prepare, in good time, the maps and diagrams required by the Secretary for the Society's Meetings and Publications without further remuneration'.[74] A separate 'Map Drawing Account' was established in 1886, consisting almost entirely of Milne and Scharbau's salaries, and the cost of materials.[75]

Scharbau and Milne were kept busy. At the end of 1885 the library and map committee proposed the preparation of small maps of relevant regions for distribution at evening meetings[76] and, in 1888, the expedition committee ruled that 'maps of the regions in which the explorations recommended to them are proposed to be made should be placed before them'.[77] Some councillors expressed concern at delays in the preparation of maps.[78] However, internal enquiries concluded the work undertaken was highly intensive, involving such time-consuming operations as the interweaving of new lines of survey of varying accuracy into existing maps.[79] Before 1873 the society did not employ a permanent map draughtsman. By 1893 technological improvements, and the commitment of the RGS to a vision of scientific exploration centred around surveying, strained the capabilities of two full-time professionals.

The principal forum for the display of geographical information was the RGS's monthly periodical. The initial *Journal of the Royal Geographical Society* was almost entirely confined to the publication of papers read at evening meetings. From 1855 a separate *Proceedings* was published, containing additional information of geographical interest.[80] Dissatisfied with the society's publications as 'imperfect, dull and over-formal', Clements

[74] Library and map committee minutes, 21 Jan. 1885, RGS.
[75] RGS ledgers vol. 1: 1877–86, RGS marks the first appearance of the 'Map Drawing Account'.
[76] Library and map committee special meeting minutes, 2 Dec. 1885, RGS.
[77] Expedition committee minutes, 27 April 1888, RGS.
[78] Finance committee minutes, 5 Nov. 1887, and Library and map committee minutes, 21 June 1888, RGS.
[79] Mill, *Record*, p. 240.
[80] Keltie, 'Thirty years' work', 371.

Markham began to edit his own journal entitled *Ocean Highways—the Geographical Record*.[81] By September 1878 the renamed *Geographical Magazine* had attained a circulation of 1,200 copies a month. Supported by these sales, Markham submitted a memorandum to the RGS council proposing to replace the existing *Proceedings* and *Journal* with a single publication based on the *Geographical Magazine*.[82] Markham intended to make the new publication 'the leading authority in the world on all subjects relating to geography'.[83] Each edition would contain a list of all geographical works published, with reviews of the more important, news about expeditions and matters of geographical interest, and a comprehensive index. In the interval between sessions, the new publication would report the Presidential addresses and the papers read at the Geographical Section of the British Association. And each issue would contain at least one map.[84]

The council adopted Markham's recommendations and the publications committee resolved to discontinue the *Journal* with its fiftieth edition as it had been 'superseded' by the 'improved' *Proceedings* 'as a permanent and additional record of the work of the society'.[85] As a concession to those who objected to the inclusion of illustrations as undignified, the title of *Proceedings of the Royal Geographical Society and the Monthly Record of Geography* was adopted, with no suggestion of that scandalous word 'magazine'. In the annual

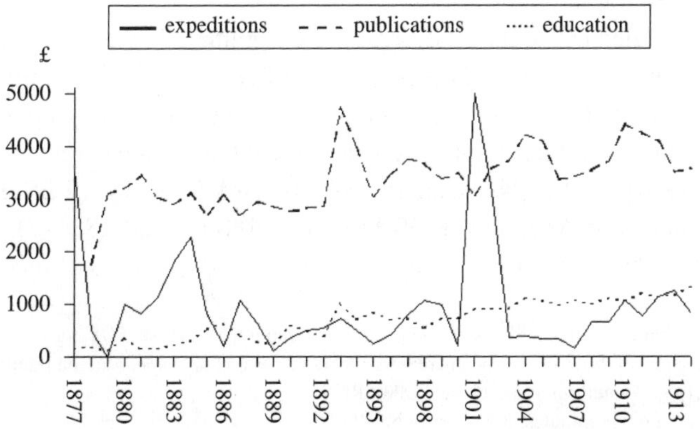

Figure 1. RGS Annual Expenditure on Expeditions, Publications and Education, 1877–1914.
Source: RGS ledgers vol. 1, 1877–86; vol. 2, 1887–95; vol. 3, 1896–1905; vol. 4, 1906–14, RGS.

[81] Mill, *Record*, p. 242.
[82] Memo inserted in Council minutes, 7 Nov. 1888, RGS.
[83] Markham, *Fifty Years' Work*, p. 98.
[84] Memo inserted in Council minutes, 7 Nov. 1878, RGS.
[85] Publications committee minutes, 6 May 1881, RGS.

address on the progress of geography in 1879, the new *Proceedings* was described as 'a vast improvement', although given the speaker was Markham himself this judgement was hardly surprising.[86] Between 1878 and 1914, the monthly journal remained the largest single item of expenditure, with the sole exception of the grants to Captain Scott's first Antarctic expedition (Fig. 1 and Table 1).[87] A separate *Proceedings* account was opened to administer the increased expenditure.[88] The increase was partly offset, as Markham had hoped, by extra revenue from advertising and from sales to non-fellows.

In 1893 the new series of the *Proceedings* was replaced by the *Geographical Journal*. Keltie and H. R. Mill consolidated the improvements made in 1879: the 'Monthly Record' of geographical notes was arranged more systematically; the bibliography was expanded to include all articles of geographical interest from the many journals received by the RGS; and a complete list of additions to the library was included.[89] The success of the new *Geographical Journal* was indicated by the increase in the number of pages devoted to advertising from four to an average of twenty-two per number.[90] The new series of the *Proceedings* and the *Geographical Journal* were the cornerstones of the edifice of geographical knowledge constructed by the RGS in the late nineteenth century. When awarding grants, the society always secured the right to publish the expedition's results[91] and a system of ten-year indexes was introduced, to enhance the utility of the publication as a source of geographical information.[92]

The final element of the RGS's reform programme in the last quarter of the nineteenth century concerned the promotion of geographical education.[93] In the 1880s a number of fellows committed to the promotion of geography teaching in Britain gained influence on the council, including Douglas Freshfield (RGS Joint Secretary, 1881–94), General Sir Richard Strachey (RGS President, 1887–9) and Lord Aberdare (RGS President, 1880–5 and 1886–7). After the cessation of Francis Galton's medals scheme in 1884, a series of meetings was

[86] C. R. Markham, 'Annual address on the progress of geography', *Proc. RGS*, NS 1 (1879), 366.

[87] The new series of the *Proceedings* increased the Society's annual expenditure on publications from £763 to £2,193, Council minutes, 12 Jan. 1880, RGS.

[88] Finance committee minutes, 3 March 1879, RGS.

[89] Mill, *Autobiography*, p. 95.

[90] C. R. Markham. 'Address to the Royal Geographical Society', *Geographical Journal*, 4 (1894), 4.

[91] For example, the instructions issued to James Last and Joseph Thomson, set down that *all* products of the expedition, diaries, maps, photographs etc., were the property of the society, 'Instructions to Mr. Thomson' inserted in Expedition committee minutes, 8 Dec. 1882, 'Instructions to Mr. Last' inserted in Expedition committee minutes, 18 June 1885, RGS.

[92] Mill, *Record*, p. 243.

[93] See A. D. Grady, 'The role of geographical societies in Britain from 1900 to 1914', unpublished Ph.D. thesis, University of London, 1972, especially chs. 2–4.

Table 1. RGS Grants of over £500 to Expeditions, 1830–1914

	Years	Total RGS Grant	Total Grant as % age of RGS Receipts
Robert Hermann Schomburgk's expedition to Guiana	1834–9	£976	8.5
James Alexander's expedition to South Africa	1836–8	£580	12.0
William Ainsworth's expedition to Kurdistan	1838–41	£1,854	20.7
David Livingstone's last expedition to Africa	1865	£500	10.3
George W. Hayward's expedition to East Turkistan	1869–70	£600	4.0
Livingstone relief expedition to Africa	1872–4	£2,891	11.7
Verney Lovett Cameron's expedition to East Africa*	1873–7	£2,996	6.9
A. Keith Johnston's expedition to Africa	1877–80	£2,000	5.8
The relief expedition to the Arctic for the *Eira*	1882	£1,000 (repaid by expedition)	10.8
Joseph Thomson's expedition to East Africa	1882–4	£3,595	13.0
J. T. Last's expedition to East Africa	1885–7	£989	2.8
The Emin Pasha relief fund	1887	£1,000	12.1
William Conway's expedition to the Korakorum mountain range	1891–3	£600	1.9
Robert Scott's *Discovery* expedition to the Antarctic	1901–2	£8,000	25.5
C. E. Fagan's expedition to New Guinea	1909–12	£1,500	1.7
Robert Scott's *Terra Nova* expedition to the Antarctic	1910	£500	1.5
Douglas Mawson's *Aurora* expedition to the Antarctic	1912–13	£600	1.4
Ernest Shackleton's *Endurance* expedition to the Antarctic	1914	£500	3.2

Sources (1830–77): C. R. Markham, *The Fifty Years' Work of the Royal Geographical Society* (London, 1880), pp. 150–1, for grants to expeditions, and Rawson W. Rawson, 'Tabular view of the history and finances of the Royal Geographical Society from the commencement in 1830 to the close of the year 1892', Add. papers 26a, RGS, for total receipts.
Sources (1878–1914): RGS ledgers vol. 1: 1877–86, vol. 2: 1887–95, vol. 3: 1896–1905 & vol. 4: 1906–14, RGS.
* Cameron's expedition is an exceptional case. Cameron ran up substantial bills with foreign traders during his expedition, which were charged to the RGS. Markham, *Fifty Years' Work*, p. 151 estimates that the total cost of the expedition eventually came to £11,101 13*s*. 3*d*. £3,000 of this sum was paid for by a special parliamentary grant. For the purposes of this study, however, I have counted only the four specific grants voted to the expedition by the RGS Council: £484 in 1873, £500 in 1875, £1,000 in 1876 and £1,012 in 1877 = total £2,996.

held to discuss ways in which the RGS could promote geographical education in Britain.[94] The scientific purposes committee submitted two proposals which were adopted by the council. First, courses in geology, botany, zoology and photography were added to the surveying course.[95] Secondly, John Scott

[94] Scientific purposes committee minutes, 8 Feb. 1884, 15 Feb. 1884 and 17 March 1884, RGS.
[95] Council minutes, 24 March 1884, RGS. A proposal for the Society to fund a lecturer to deliver occasional educational courses was postponed until after the receipt of the Inspector's report. A number of fellows and councillors felt that the financing of an independent lecturer was beyond the scope of the Society.

Keltie was appointed as the RGS's 'Inspector of Geographical Education', to investigate the teaching of geography in Britain and abroad.[96]

Keltie's report, published in 1885, was highly critical of the standard of British geography teaching compared with France and Germany in particular, and has long been regarded as a key moment in the development of geography as an academic discipline in Britain.[97] The RGS financed an 'Exhibition of Appliances in Geographical Education' in London, with an accompanying series of lectures, to promote Keltie's report. This exhibition of the latest apparatus which Keltie had collected on his travels was a great success and was staged by a number of other institutions, including the newly formed Scottish and Manchester Geographical Societies, before being presented to the Teachers' Guild of Great Britain.[98]

The geographical education committee, established to oversee the exhibition, submitted a number of additional proposals to stimulate the teaching of geography in Britain. The council adopted some of these proposals, offering prizes in geography to students at teacher training colleges and supporting the appointment of a lecturer in geography for the Oxford University extension course.[99] Most importantly, the council resolved to present detailed proposals for the establishment of a lecturer or reader in geography to the vice-chancellors of Oxford and Cambridge.[100] Before the end of 1887, Halford Mackinder had been appointed Reader in Geography at Oxford and agreement had been reached for a lectureship at Cambridge.[101] The RGS agreed to share the costs of the appointments with the universities and also funded scholarships to encourage undergraduates to take geography courses.

[96] Council minutes, 23 June 1884, RGS.

[97] O. J. R. Howarth, 'The centenary of section E (geography) in the British Association', *Scottish Geographical Magazine*, 67 (1951), 157.

[98] Mill, *Record*, pp. 248–9.

[99] The prosposals were considered on 12 April 1886, Council minutes, 12 April 1896, RGS. The 'Geographical Report' committee suggested: (1) the appointment of a geography lecturer at £200 a year to lecture throughout the country, and, if possible, deliver courses at Oxford and Cambridge; (2) the award of an annual prize to the best geographical essay on a specified subject at Oxford and Cambridge; (3) the support of the geographical lectures of the university extension course; (4) the award of a medal to the best student in physical geography in the first part of the natural sciences tripos at Cambridge, and a similar medal at Oxford; (5) the award of prizes to students at the teacher-training colleges; (6) the distribution of copies of the *Proceedings* to public school libraries; (7) the establishment of contacts between geographical lecturers and headmasters; (8) the circulation of the society's collection of geographical appliances around schools and local centres; (9) the provision of more space for the review of text-books in the *Proceedings*.

[100] Council minutes, 28 June 1886, RGS. Letters were addressed to the vice-chancellors at Oxford on 9 July 1886 and at Cambridge on 9 Dec. 1886, D. I. Scargill, 'The RGS and the foundations of geography at Oxford', *Geographical Journal*, 142 (1976), 443.

[101] Stoddart, *On Geography*, p. 88.

The RGS donated £4,583 to Oxford and Cambridge between 1887 and 1900, compared with £8,104 spent on the sponsorship of expeditions.[102] H. R. Mill calculated that the RGS contributed £7,500 to support geography at Cambridge between 1883 and 1923, and £11,000 to support geography at Oxford between 1887 and 1924.[103] This support was essential to the establishment of geography as an independent subject at both universities.

IV

In 1859 Roderick Murchison felt compelled to justify the selection of Francis Galton's paper on 'Sun signals for the use of travellers' to entertain a meeting of RGS fellows. 'Doubtless many of those who were then assembled may be more gratified by descriptions of foreign travel;' explained Murchsion, 'but the Society could not be too thankful to those who, from time to time, refer back to the elements of the science and bring to its notice the consideration of instruments of real value to the explorer.'[104] Twenty years later the colonial administrator Sir Henry Barkly chastised the Reverend Chauncy Maples for neglecting survey work on his recent African expedition. Barkly counselled that missionaries 'might help the cause of scientific geography still more if they were able to take those astronomical and hypsometrical observations which were necessary for fixing the position of places with certainty'.[105]

The systematic reform of so many aspects of the activities of the RGS after Livingstone's burial in 1874 has been neglected in the existing scholarship. The fellowship did not, of course, suddenly subscribe to a single vision of the geographical enterprise. The RGS remained, in Felix Driver's words, 'an arena, a site where competing visions of geographical knowledge were debated and institutionalized'.[106] Once the results of expeditions sponsored by the RGS left the confines of Savile Row, the diverse cultures of exploration through which they circulated amplified different notes, as racial undertones surfaced in Charles Booth's surveys of East End London, and heroic deeds filled the columns of the popular press. But the accurate measurement of the world offered a broad, flexible mission, encompassing a wide range of geographical practitioners.

[102] RGS ledgers, vol. 2: 1887–95 & vol. 3: 1896–1905, RGS.

[103] Mill, *Record*, p. 251. Scargill, 'The RGS and Oxford', 458 repeats these figures, while Stoddart, *On Geography*, p. 124 claims £7,250 was given to Cambridge over 35 years.

[104] F. Galton, 'Sun signals for the use of travellers (hand heliostat)', *Proc. RGS*, 4 (1859–60), 18.

[105] C. Maples, 'Masai and the Rovuma district in East Africa', *Proc. RGS*, NS 2 (1880), 353.

[106] Driver, *Geography militant*, p. 65.

Why did this transformation occur? Brian Hudson's assertion that the imperatives of the new imperialism drove the emergence of the new geography in the final quarter of the nineteenth century still commands attention. Travellers' tales were of little use to those seeking to exploit the empire. The RGS provided maps for the British representatives at the Berlin West Africa Conference in 1884, traditionally portrayed as the beginning of the 'scramble for Africa'.[107] At the request of the Secretary of State for India the following year, the society reprinted 100 copies of a map of Khorassan from the September number of the *Proceedings*, for the revenue and statistics department of the India Office.[108] The new course in surveying specifically targeted colonial officials. When Coles asked for a raise he justified his request with reference not to the fellowship, but to the service he provided the Foreign Office, War Office, Colonial Office, and Admiralty.[109] In 1892 the President, Grant Duff, reported that forty-eight 'servants of the Government, soldiers, sailors, and others, of whom twenty-one were employed on special service and boundary commissions' had recently been trained by Coles.[110] E. A. Reeves later estimated that 1,700 people took the six to twelve week RGS surveying course between 1902 and 1933, including 890 sent from the Colonial Office.[111] The RGS was enmeshed in the expanding network of British imperial administration.

Yet, the establishment of a *causal* link between the new imperialism and the transformation of the RGS is problematic. The requirements of a maritime empire had shaped the society from its foundation in 1830, and it is difficult to identify any specific change which triggered the reforms of the 1870s. Both the vocal opposition to Queen Victoria's installation as Empress of India in 1877, and the success of Gladstone's attacks on Beaconsfieldism, demonstrate that imperial topics remained hotly contested throughout the decade; the increasing prominence of imperial themes within British popular culture was much more a phenomenon of the 1880s.[112] References to empire

[107] Council minutes, 24 Nov. 1884, RGS.

[108] Council minutes, 14 Nov. 1881, RGS.

[109] Council minutes, 23 Feb. 1885, RGS.

[110] M. E. Grant Duff, 'The annual address on the progress of geography', *Proc. RGS*, NS 14 (1892), 359. In 1898 Markham noted that among Coles's pupils over the past year had been 'twenty-six civilians, twenty-four officers of the army and navy, four in the colonial service, four civil engineers, and two missionaries', C. R. Markham, 'Anniversary address, 1898', *Geographical Journal*, 12 (1898), 9.

[111] E. A. Reeves, *The Recollections of a Geographer* (London, 1933), 87–90. Colonial officials who took the course were exempted from taking further examinations for their survey departments abroad. After Coles's resignation through ill-health, Reeves was appointed map curator in 1901, scientific instructor in 1902, and head of the map drawing department in 1904.

[112] R. Koebner and H. D. Schmidt, *Imperialism: the Story and Significance of a Political Word, 1840–1960* (Cambridge, 1964). The party political allegiances of RGS officers deserve further

certainly grew more frequent in the pronouncements of the society's officers in this period. But behind this grandiose rhetoric, the promotion of the accurate measurement of the world and new educational initiatives arguably diluted the imperial utility of the work of the RGS. Indeed, the formation of provincial geographical societies in Manchester, Tyneside, Liverpool, Southampton and Hull after 1885, stemmed from the belief that the RGS was neglecting the commercial applications of geography.[113]

Rather, the transformation of the RGS resulted from the operation of four further forces within a particular institutional setting, in which the new imperialism acted as catalyst rather than cause. First, the scientific revolution unleashed by the publication of Darwin's *Origin of Species* in 1859. Secondly, the global rise of ideas of bureaucratic government and expertise. Thirdly, the expansion of the British education system. And finally, the challenge posed by the inexorable extension of the map of the world, and consequent realisation that, in the dramatic phrase of Alexander the Great, there would soon be 'no more worlds to conquer'.[114]

The initial trigger for reform was more mundane: the deaths of Roderick Murchison in 1871 and David Livingstone in 1873. Both Francis Galton and William Gladstone had foreseen the end of the age of pioneering exploration in the 1860s.[115] But the deaths of Murchison and Livingstone, the men most responsible for the society's expansion, forced a fundamental re-evaluation of RGS activities. The society's *raison d'être* once the blank spaces on the map of the world had been filled in, remained a consistent preoccupation of RGS officers up to 1914 and beyond.[116]

Clements Markham led those who sought to train the surveyors who would follow in the footsteps of the pioneers. As Archibald Geikie predicted in a lecture in 1879, the work of future explorers would 'need to make up in the variety, amount, and value of its detail, what it lacks in the freshness of

attention. In the 1870s and 1880s leading Liberals such as Lord Aberdare appear to have played a more prominent role than Conservative politicians.

113 J. M. MacKenzie, 'The provincial geographical societies in Britain, 1884–1914', in Bell, *Geography and Imperialism*, pp. 93–124.

114 M. E. Grant Duff, 'The annual address on the progress of geography', *Proc. RGS*, NS 12 (1890), 383. Also see Gladstone quoted in R. A. Stafford, 'Scientific exploration and empire', in A. N. Porter (ed.), *The Oxford History of the British Empire. Vol. III: The Nineteenth Century* (Oxford, 1999), p. 300 and Marquis of Lorne, 'The annual address on the progress of geography', *Proc. RGS*, NS 8 (1886), 436.

115 Galton quoted in Cameron, *To the farthest ends*, p. 200 and Gladstone quoted in Stafford, 'Scientific exploration', 300.

116 See, among many, M. E. Grant Duff, 'The annual address on the progress of geography', *Proc. RGS*, NS 12 (1890), 383 and G. N. Curzon, 'Address to the Royal Geographical Society', *Geographical Journal*, 42 (1913), 1.

first glimpses into new lands'.[117] But Freshfield, Strachey and Aberdare went further than Markham, proposing a more fundamental reorientation from exploration to education, from the field to the study. Markham strongly objected to some of their proposals, particularly when they involved expenditure which the RGS did not control. And so, only eight years after masterminding the establishment of John Coles's surveying course and the new series of the society's *Proceedings,* he resigned from his post as Honorary Secretary.

The organisation of the earth sciences in Britain might have taken a different form, had the RGS council, with Freshfield's encouragement, not proposed to admit women as fellows in August 1892, eager to attract their subscriptions, and prompted by the establishment of a London branch of the Scottish Geographical Society, whose Edinburgh headquarters had admitted women since its foundation in 1884.[118] A bitter dispute developed, in which a coterie of retired admirals and naval officers, led by a young Conservative MP, George Curzon, outmanoeuvred Freshfield and the council, and succeeded in blocking the election of any further women fellows. The chief proponents of educational initiatives disassociated themselves from the RGS in the wake of the dispute, and Clements Markham returned as President.[119] In his twelve year term from 1893 to 1905, Markham refocused the society's energies on exploration and the Antarctic, his personal obsession, in particular. But, crucially, investment in geography at Oxford and Cambridge continued. Different institutional contexts conditioned the emergence of geography at both universities, but the financial support of the RGS was critical in sustaining a geographical presence in the face of both institutional intransigence and disciplinary rivalry with geology in particular. The paradox, identified by David Stoddart, was that 'British geography emerged as a scientific discipline without the benefit of aid from strictly scientific men'.[120]

The paradox dissolves when we move beyond simple oppositions between exploration and education and attempt instead to view the full spectrum of geographical visions projected within the RGS, a spectrum complicated by

[117] Geikie, 'Geographical evolution', 423–4.

[118] For accounts of this dispute see Mill, *Record,* pp. 107–12; A. Blunt, *Travel, Gender, and Imperialism: Mary Kingsley and West Africa* (London, 1994); M. Bell and C. McEwan, 'The admission of women Fellows to the Royal Geographical Society 1892–1914; the controversy and the outcome', *Geographical Journal*, 162 (1996), 295–312; and M. H. Jones, *The Last Great Quest: Captain Scott's Antarctic Sacrifice* (Oxford, 2003), pp. 51–8.

[119] A new biography of Clements Markham to replace his cousin A. H. Markham's, *The Life of Sir Clements R. Markham* (London, 1917) is urgently required. The call of Stoddart, *On Geography*, p. 76, for a re-examination of Geikie's and Freshfield's roles also remains unanswered.

[120] Stoddart, *On Geography*, p. 67.

personal animosities which do not map easily onto ideological positions. Clements Markham himself, in conciliatory mood after assuming the presidency in 1893, declared that 'the work of explorers is co-ordinated and rendered useful in many ways by geographical students, whose valuable labours desire equal attention and encouragement'.[121] Two years later he proposed 'a scheme of geographical education under the immediate auspices of the Society', which would involve

> personal instruction in all the branches of our science, attendance at lectures, examinations, and the granting of certificates and diplomas. We alone have the needful apparatus for conducting such a course of instruction; we alone have the library, and the collection of maps and instruments, and the knowledge of what is required, and in no way can our splendid collections be put to better use.[122]

Even Markham, then, supported some educational initiatives. But he envisaged students and explorers working in tandem under the control of the RGS. Markham's vision was reflected in the society's ledgers, which classified the grants to Oxford and Cambridge in the same category as expenditure on Coles's surveying course, under the headings 'scientific purposes account' from 1887 to 1894, and 'education account' from 1896 to 1905.[123]

The first Reader in Geography at Oxford, Halford Mackinder, worked with Markham when developing a plan for a new Institute of Geography 'in London, as an imperial centre, an institution working in harmony with the Royal Geographical Society, and more or less controlled by it, which should have two sides to its work: on the one side, research, on the other, higher teaching'.[124] Markham announced in May 1897 that the 'Council has now resolved to give a large measure of support, out of the society's funds, to a London School of Geography, if such an institution should be successfully established under Mr. Mackinder's auspices'.[125] The council pledged to commit £1,000 annually to the new school. Concern about the financial commitment involved eventually forced a reversion to an earlier proposal to establish a School of Geography at Oxford.[126] But the collaboration of Mackinder, the first professional geographer, and Markham, the arch amateur, in the scheme for a London School of Geography indicates the need to move beyond simple oppositional models, which set amateurs against professionals.

[121] C. R. Markham, 'The present standpoint of geography', *Geographical Journal*, 2 (1893), 500.

[122] C. R. Markham, 'Address to the Royal Geographical Society', *Geographical Journal*, 6 (1895), 5.

[123] RGS ledgers, vol. 2: 1887–95 & vol. 3: 1896–1905, RGS.

[124] Mackinder quoted in L. M. Cantor, 'The Royal Geographical Society and the projected London Institute of geography, 1892–99', *Geographical Journal*, 128 (1962), 33.

[125] C. R. Markham, 'Anniversary address, 1897', *Geographical Journal*, 9 (1897), 603.

[126] Cantor, 'The projected London Institute', 34.

This analysis of a pivotal and neglected period in the history of the RGS offers insights into the organisation of knowledge in Victorian Britain. First, the reforms narrated here expose how the RGS exerted a profound influence over the production and distribution of geographical information, emphasising how institutions furnished the particular stages upon which discursive negotiations were enacted.[127] The distinctive character of the RGS, both private society and government archive, suggests that further study of the peculiar ways in which the British state supported science would prove fruitful. Secondly, the history of the RGS warns against accounts of historical change which rely on a monolithic imperial dynamic. The experiences of empire shaped geography and exploration in Britain, but the transformation of the RGS after 1874 was driven more by western science's voracious, undifferentiated appetite for space, than the strategic, military and commercial needs of the new imperialism.[128] The two forces were intimately related, but they were not identical. If the distinction is collapsed, the society's preoccupation with Antarctica in the twenty years before 1914 becomes unintelligible. Finally, the reform of the RGS in the twilight of the age of pioneering exploration, emphasises the public and practical character of geography and exploration.[129] The forms of knowledge generated by expeditions engaged military officers and government officials, provincial businessmen and professional scientists, romantics, evangelicals and pragmatists. This public engagement, mediated through the RGS, continues to shape the geographical enterprise in Britain.

[127] Compare the RGS, for example, with the Royal Botanical Gardens at Kew described in R. Drayton, *Nature's Government: Science, Imperial Britain, and the 'Improvement' of the World* (New Haven and London, 2000).

[128] For the growing literature on maps as instruments of power, see M. H. Edney, *Mapping an Empire. The Geographical Construction of British India, 1765–1843* (Chicago and London, 1997) and P. Joyce, *The Rule of Freedom: Liberalism and the Modern City* (London, 2003).

[129] For a discussion of the 'sternly practical' pursuit of geography in an imperial age see Livingstone, *Geographical Tradition*, ch. 7.

CHAPTER FIFTEEN

Civic Cultures and Civic Colleges in Victorian England*

SAMUEL J. M. M. ALBERTI

This volume is concerned with the development of distinct bodies of knowledge in Victorian Britain. To understand these disciplines (as they were to become) we need to engage with their institutional structures and contexts as well as their internal developments, not only within the 'golden triangle' of London, Oxford, and Cambridge, but also across the country. Accordingly, this chapter focuses on the emergence of those institutions that are recognised as the predecessors of the present-day redbrick universities, as a contribution to a wider account of the changes in higher education in Victorian England. These 'civic colleges' played a vital role in the emergence of autonomous professional groups associated with a raft of new disciplines between 1860 and the Great War.[1] The homogeneity of twenty-first-century provincial universities should not obscure their distinct and locally contingent origins: the formation of this novel mode of higher education in provincial England was an uneven endeavour involving a wide variety of individuals and institutions. Late-Victorian university-style colleges were *not* merely smaller and more primitive versions of their present selves; rather, they fulfilled different functions and met different needs, occupying distinct and often tenuous places in the complex web of civic culture.

Historians have commonly explained the origins of the civic universities in broad-brush social and economic terms. My first and major object in this

* I am grateful to John Pickstone, Keith Vernon, Alison Kraft, Jo Alberti, Chandak Sengoopta, and Fay Bound for their helpful comments and criticisms. Writing this chapter was made possible by the support of the Wellcome Trust.

[1] Konrad H. Jarausch (ed.), *The Transformation of Higher Learning, 1860–1930: Expansion, Diversification, Social Opening, and Professionalization in England, Germany, Russia, and the United States* (Stuttgart, 1982); Detlef K. Müller, Fritz Ringer, and Brian Simon (eds.), *The Rise of the Modern Educational System: Structural Change and Social Reproduction, 1870–1920* (Cambridge, 1987).

chapter is to survey these explanations as a series of four related issues: (a) industrial 'declinism'—that is, the fear of the decline of British science and technology relative to that of Continental Europe; (b) the development of the professions, especially medicine; (c) changes within schooling, for children and adults; and finally (d) university extension and the heterogeneous campaign for liberal education. To talk only about nebulous national movements, however, is to ignore specific developments in individual locales. As Rothblatt argues, the expansion of higher education in England bore a close relationship to the changes within urban culture.[2] Accordingly, for each of these listed themes I illustrate the national trend with its local institutional manifestations, including mechanics' institutes, medical schools, and university extension associations. Civic culture was formalised in this diverse range of middle-class institutions, and the construction of academic communities in the provinces was heavily dependent upon their form and interrelations.

In my penultimate section I turn to an aspect of the development of provincial universities that has regularly been overlooked in histories of higher education: the role played by local learned societies and other cultural institutions, particularly literary and philosophical societies. Like these voluntary associations, civic colleges were manifestations of the efforts of the provincial middle classes to express their cultural maturity, drawing on and yet independent of London, Cambridge, and Oxford. The establishment and early growth of the provincial English universities can be better understood when viewed in these local institutional contexts.

Mid-nineteenth-century England had only four universities, with fewer students per capita than any other major European power.[3] The ancient universities offered expensive classical or mathematical education to sons of the gentry and upper professionals in oligarchic Anglican institutions, which made the Scottish universities more feasible for many students.[4] Although

[2] Sheldon Rothblatt, 'The diversification of higher education in England', in Jarausch (ed.), *The Transformation of Higher Learning*, pp. 131–48; Keith Vernon, 'Universities and urban identity in England, *c*.1870–1910', unpublished paper given at the Urban History Group Meeting, Glasgow, March 2001, cited by kind permission of the author.

[3] Arthur Engel, 'The English universities and professional education', in Jarausch (ed.), *The Transformation of Higher Learning*, pp. 293–305; Sheldon Rothblatt, *The Modern University and its Discontents: the Fate of Newman's Legacies in Britain and America* (Cambridge, 1997); Negley Harte, *The University of London, 1836–1986: an Illustrated History* (London, 1986); F. M. L. Thompson (ed.), *The University of London and the World of Learning, 1836–1986* (London, 1990); Charles E. Whiting, *The University of Durham, 1832–1932* (London, 1932).

[4] The distinctiveness of the Scottish Universities has been discussed at length: see for example Jennifer J. Carter and Donald J. Withrington (eds.), *Scottish Universities: Distinctiveness and Diversity* (Edinburgh, 1992).

Oxford and Cambridge changed considerably in the second half of the century, especially in their disciplinary diversification, reform was tempered by stout conservatism. The University of Durham, meanwhile, founded in 1832, was predominately theological, and was struggling by the late 1850s (as a Royal Commission found in 1862). The University of London had been established as an examining body in 1836, initially serving University College (established in 1826) and King's College (1829). In the 1860s, dozens of colleges across Britain and the Empire were affiliated to London, which was also open to external candidates. By this time, almost every region in Britain's sphere of influence—whether Ireland, India or Australia — had university colleges; only the English provinces did not.[5]

This, then, was the national arena that Owens College, Manchester, entered in 1851. Its first decades were troubled, and it was only in the late 1870s that it began to thrive. This new-found success was in part responsible for inspiring, within the space of a single generation, similar institutions in a further eight towns, giving rise to six independent universities by 1909 (Fig. 1).[6] These were

[5] See for example W. J. Gardner, *Colonial Cap and Gown: Studies in the mid-Victorian Universities of Australasia* (Christchurch, 1979).

[6] W. H. G. Armytage, *Civic Universities: Aspects of a British Tradition* (London, 1955); David R. Jones, *The Origins of Civic Universities: Manchester, Leeds and Liverpool* (London, 1988); Michael Sanderson, *The Universities and British Industry, 1850–1970* (London, 1972); id., *The Universities in the Nineteenth Century* (London, 1975); id., *Education and Economic Decline in Britain, 1870 to the 1990s* (Cambridge, 1999); H. Silver and S. J. Teague, *The History of British Universities, 1800–1969 Excluding Oxford and Cambridge: a Bibliography* (London, 1970); W. B. Stephens, *Education in Britain, 1750–1914* (London, 1998); Keith Vernon, 'Civic colleges and the idea of the university', in Martin Hewitt, (ed.), *Scholarship in Victorian Britain* (Leeds, 1998), pp. 42–52; id., *Universities and the State in England, 1850–1939* (London, forthcoming). On Birmingham, see: Asa Briggs, *History of Birmingham, Volume 2—Borough and City: 1865–1938* (London, 1952); John Thackray Bunce, *Josiah Mason: a Biography* (London, 1890); Diane Drummond, '"The Power of our Provincial Cities" and "The Opportunities for the Highest Culture": the call for a University of Birmingham and university scholarship in late-Victorian England', in Hewitt (ed.), *Scholarship in Victorian Britain*, pp. 53–65; A. M. D. Hughes, *The University of Birmingham: a Short History* (Birmingham, 1950); Eric Ives, Diane Drummond, and Leonard Schwarz, *The First Civic University: Birmingham 1880–1980* (Birmingham, 2000); Oliver Lodge, 'Early history of the University and its parent institutions', in J. H. Muirhead (ed.), *Birmingham Institutions: Lectures Given at the University* (Birmingham, 1911), pp. 61–84; Eric W. Vincent and Percival Hinton, *The University of Birmingham: its History and Significance* (Birmingham, 1947). On Bristol: Don Carleton, *A University for Bristol: an Informal History in Text and Pictures* (Bristol, 1984); Basil Cottle and J. W. Sherborne, *The Life of a University* (rev. edn., Bristol, 1959); Helen E. Meller, *Leisure and the Changing City, 1870–1914* (London, 1976). On Leeds: E. J. Brown, *The Private Donor in the History of the University* (Leeds, 1953); P. H. J. H. Gosden and Arthur J. Taylor (eds.), *Studies in the History of a University, 1874–1974: to Commemorate the Centenary of the University of Leeds* (Leeds, 1975); A. N. Shimmin, *The University of Leeds: the First Half-Century* (Cambridge, 1954). On Liverpool: Thomas Kelly, *For Advancement of Learning: the University of Liverpool, 1881–1981* (Liverpool University Press, 1981); University of Liverpool, *University of Liverpool, 1882–1907: Brief Record*

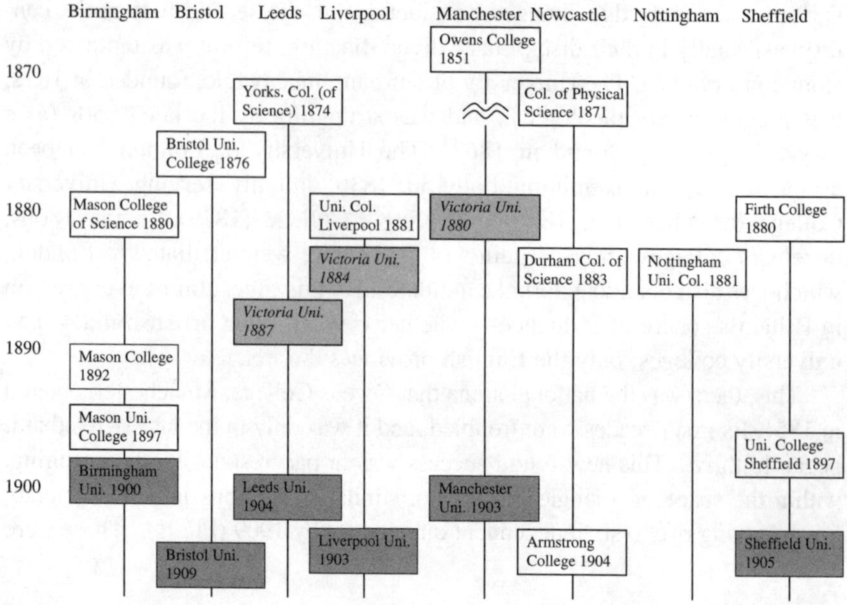

Figure 1. Civic Colleges in Victorian England.

the 'civic colleges': large, secular, educational establishments in major provincial towns offering varied curricula at a range of levels. They charged little for their courses, enrolling a broad, non-residential clientele with entrance examinations only for the young (if at all). Most had their roots in local liberal traditions, and all except Bristol were in the highly populated North and Midlands. There, local mercantile-industrial wealth supplied the colleges with much of their endowment funds. Fortunes were bestowed by cotton merchant

of Work and Progress (Liverpool, 1907). On Manchester: H. B. Charlton, *Portrait of a University, 1851–1951: to Commemorate the Centenary of Manchester University* (Manchester, 1951); Edward Fiddes, *Chapters in the History of Owens College and of Manchester University, 1851–1914* (Manchester, 1937); Robert H. Kargon, *Science in Victorian Manchester: Enterprise and Expertise* (Manchester, 1977); Colin Lees and Alex Robertson, 'Early students and the "University of the Busy": the Quay Street years of Owens College, 1851–1870', *Bulletin of the John Rylands University Library of Manchester*, 79 (1997), 161–94; Joseph Thompson, *The Owens College: its Foundation and Growth* (Manchester, 1886). On Newcastle: E. M. Bettenson, *The University of Newcastle upon Tyne: a Historical Introduction, 1834–1971* (Newcastle, 1971); Arthur G. Lane, *The History of Armstrong College* (Newcastle-upon-Tyne, 1907); Whiting, *The University of Durham.* On Nottingham: Edith M. Becket, *The University College of Nottingham* (Nottingham, 1928); Alfred C. Wood, *A History of the University College, Nottingham, 1881–1948* (Oxford, 1953). On Sheffield: Maureen Boylan and Gillian Riley, *The University of Sheffield: an Illustrated History* (Sheffield, 1981); Arthur W. Chapman, *The Story of a Modern University: a History of the University of Sheffield* (London, 1955).

John Owens, pen manufacturer Josiah Mason, cutler Mark Firth. Later came monies from drug baron Jesse Boot, and more modest but nonetheless significant sums from countless Baineses, Frys, and Rathbones.[7] Liverpool had no single benefactor (and accordingly a non-eponymous college), but its establishment and early success was nonetheless dependent upon the Victorian culture of philanthropy, receiving extensive backing from a range of good citizens. Claims that the emergence of a system of higher education in Victorian England was dependent entirely on local industrialists' largesse, however, should be treated with caution. Even the largest of endowments was quickly eaten up by spiralling building costs, leaving the young colleges in precarious financial straits. They depended on income generated by leftover endowments (if any), a trickle of student fees, and repeated calls to the town's citizenry for more cash.

Although most colleges were run as independent trusts, they nevertheless benefited from the support and collaboration of local government. Corporation members often sat on their council; some colleges were given land, housed within municipal buildings or adjoined them; and in Manchester the local authority macadamised nearby streets to reduce noise.[8] Nottingham's support of its university college was unusual—it was sustained by a town rate from its inception in 1881 and effectively run by 13 aldermen—and was only really echoed in Bristol and Liverpool, neither of which had large single benefactions. Others would not enjoy this level of support until later in the century, as part of the 'municipalisation' of civic culture, when towns took up more civic amenities.[9] This did not, however, prevent corporations boasting the presence of a university college in their quest to gain the status of 'city'.[10]

For most of the nineteenth century, central government support of higher education was minimal and unsystematic. Whitehall had responsibility for the Scottish and Irish universities, but not their provincial English counterparts. Although Owens had a state subsidy to run the Victoria University as a degree-awarding institution, only in 1889 did a delegation from the civics approach Lord Salisbury's government as a united lobby to appeal for more

[7] From Owens, £100,000; from Firth, £20,000; from Mason (in total) £200,000; and from Boot (in the 1920s) £170,000.

[8] Jones, *The Origins of Civic Universities*. See also Sophie Forgan and Graeme J. N. Gooday, 'Constructing South Kensington: the buildings and politics of T. H. Huxley's working environments', *British Journal for the History of Science*, 29 (1996), 435–68.

[9] Meller, *Leisure and the Changing City*; Kate Hill, 'Municipal museums in the North-West, 1850–1914: reproduction and cultural activity in Liverpool and Preston' (Ph.D. thesis, Lancaster University, 1996).

[10] Liverpool became a city in 1880 (by purchasing a Bishopric); Birmingham in 1889; Leeds in 1893; Sheffield in 1893. Derek Fraser (ed.), *Municipal Reform and the Industrial City* (Leicester, 1982).

systematic funding across the country. Championed by a group of provincial Liberal MPs including A. J. Mundella and Henry Roscoe (previously Professor of Chemistry at Owens College), the deputation secured an annual grant of £15,000 in total.[11] Local authorities supplemented this support with funds raised by the 1889 Technical Instruction Act, which benefited some civics and/or the technical schools closely associated with them. The following year they were also able to channel some of the 'Whiskey Money'—the Local Taxation [Customs and Excise] Act—towards technical education. In Nottingham, for example, 80 per cent of the monies raised by the two Acts went to the University College.

State and municipal subsidies did more for the prestige of the civics than for their coffers (£15,000 was equivalent to the state subsidy of Zurich Polytechnic alone). More financially significant were changes in student enrolments. Their early students had opted mostly for part-time, evening courses, and only a small minority sat University of London degrees, or went up to Oxbridge through the various schemes that allowed them to bypass early years of degree courses. Slowly, the civics attracted more students, who increasingly undertook (more expensive) full-time day courses and degrees.[12] The proportion of very young and mature students decreased, and the student body settled into the 18–24 age range.

Civic colleges were further strengthened by a series of amalgamations in the last years of the century. Those medical and technical schools that had hitherto remained independent although closely associated (as discussed below) were formally absorbed by the civics. In Sheffield, for example, the Medical School, Firth College and the Technical School combined to form a university college (which epithet implied a broad syllabus). Sheffield's primary aim in this merger was to gain admission to the tricuspid Victoria

[11] Keith Vernon, 'Calling the tune: British universities and the state, 1880–1914', *History of Education*, 30 (2001), 251–71. In the 'grant in aid for university colleges' the Treasury awarded monies to Kings College London; University College London; Owens College, Manchester; Mason College, Birmingham; Firth College, Sheffield; the Yorkshire College in Leeds; University College Bristol; University College Liverpool; University College Nottingham; Durham College of Science in Newcastle; and University College Dundee. Of the original delegation, only the Hartley Institution in Southampton was refused, and largely as a result did not become a university college until 1902—see A. Temple Patterson, *The University of Southampton: a Centenary History of the Evolution and Development of the University of Southampton, 1862–1962* (Southampton, 1962). The grant was raised to £25,000 in 1897.

[12] Lowe shows that as a fraction of total population, students rose from only 0.04% in 1881 to 0.054% in 1901. Roy Lowe, 'The expansion of higher education in England', in Jarausch (ed.), *The Transformation of Higher Learning*, pp. 37–56. See also Lees and Robertson 'Early students'; Keith Vernon, 'Civic colleges'.

University formed by Owens College, University College Liverpool, and the Yorkshire College in Leeds in the 1880s (Fig. 1). In this federal arrangement—also mooted in the Midlands and later implemented in Wales—the Victoria was not merely an examining board like the University of London, but was controlled (however inconveniently) by its constituent members, and its courses and examinations were determined by its teachers.[13] The Victoria explicitly constituted the first step in the campaigns for university status independent of London. A powerful motive for these late-century mergers, then, was the prospect of independent charters, and the benefits—not least financial—of gaining their own degree-awarding powers. To this end civics moved away from non-degree courses and broadened their curricula. They realised their goals in the 'charter rush' of the Edwardian era: Birmingham was awarded university status in 1900, followed closely by Manchester, Liverpool, Leeds, Sheffield, and Bristol (Fig. 1).

The cause most regularly cited for the success and synchronicity of the civics is the impact of industrial change, local and national. This is most often expressed by historians of science and technology, drawing especially on sources such as the reports of the Royal Commission on Scientific Instruction, 1870–5 (the 'Devonshire Commission').[14] Two aspects are of interest here: the demand for skills and the fear of foreign development. Britain's high industrial phase in the mid to late nineteenth century involved the growth of existing industries (shipbuilding, mining) and the development of new fields more closely related to the sciences (chemicals, engineering), which all demanded a more highly skilled labour force.[15] College donors, often major employers, wanted workers trained in the requisite scientific and technical fields. Accordingly the civics included applied sciences in their curricula from the outset—metallurgy in Sheffield and textiles in Leeds, and later brewing in

[13] The University of Wales was founded in 1893 by Royal Charter, comprising University College of Wales in Aberystwyth (founded in 1872), University College of South Wales and Monmouthshire, Cardiff (1883), and University College of North Wales, Bangor (1884). T. I. Ellis, *The Development of Higher Education in Wales* (Wrexham, 1935); David Emrys Evans, *The University of Wales: a Historical Sketch* (Cardiff, 1953); J. Gwynn Williams, *A History of the University of Wales, Volume 2: 1893–1939* (Cardiff, 1997).

[14] Michael Argles, *South Kensington to Robbins: an Account of English Technical and Scientific Education Since 1851* (London, 1964); Donald S. L. Cardwell, *The Organisation of Science in England* (London, 1957); G. W. Roderick and M. D. Stephens, *Scientific and Technical Education in Nineteenth-Century England: a Symposium* (Newton Abbot, 1972); Sanderson, *The Universities and British Industry*.

[15] Robert Fox and Anna Guagnini (eds.), *Education, Technology and Industrial Performance in Europe, 1850–1939* (Cambridge, 1993); eid., *Laboratories, Workshops, and Sites: Concepts and Practices of Research in Industrial Europe, 1800–1914* (Berkeley, 1999).

Birmingham and naval engineering in Liverpool and Newcastle. 'Without Education', wrote Thomas Nussey, a prominent Leeds merchant, 'we cannot expect to have skilled workmen of the highest class.'[16] In this respect the colleges differed according to regional industries, offering *local* knowledge.

Coupled with this positive response to industrial change, however, was the paranoia associated with the decline of British industrial might compared with that of Europe and America. Central to this fear was the Paris Exhibition of 1867, at which British industrialists felt themselves overshadowed by foreign competitors.[17] Historians have often been seduced by the exhibition as the deciding factor in the birth of the civics, possibly because so many colleges were founded within the following ten or fifteen years—conveniently the gestation period of a large civic institution. Moreover, the exhibition was staged at the beginning of an economic boom (1868–73) that provided means for founding the colleges; followed by a decade of depression, which provided motive. Recently, however, historians of technology have criticised the narrative of decline, demonstrating that the British fears were largely unjustified.[18] Contemporaries may well have used the Paris Exhibition to exploit paranoia, but any attempts to do so for the sake of the civics at their genesis largely had limited success. At the local level, aside from bequests from individuals at the outset, industries *en masse* were initially reluctant to finance the colleges. Leeds industrialists, for example, did not respond as generously as the Yorkshire College Council had hoped. Ultimately the Clothworkers' Company of London funded the textile department, as part of their efforts to establish a system of technical textile training based on a Continental model. Even some German firms contributed, and yet Yorkshire companies were reluctant.[19] Some towns fared even worse: in Southampton, the great shipping barons—largely non-resident and feeling no great attachment to the town—were not forthcoming in endowing a university college. Elsewhere, mercantile rather than industrial interests were more important, especially in

[16] Cited in Shimmin, *The University of Leeds*, p. 11.

[17] See for example the appendices to the Royal Commission on Scientific Instruction and the Advancement of Science, *First, Supplementary, and Second Reports, with Minutes of Evidence and Appendices* (London, 1872).

[18] David Edgerton, *Science, Technology and the British Industrial 'Decline', 1870–1970* (Cambridge, 1996); Graeme J. N. Gooday, 'Lies, damned lies and declinism: Lyon Playfair, the Paris 1867 exhibition and the contested rhetorics of scientific education and industrial performance', in Ian Inkster (ed.), *The Golden Age: Essays in British Social and Economic History, 1850–1870* (Aldershot, 2000), pp. 105–20; Steven J. Nicholas, 'Technical education and the decline of Britain', in Ian Inkster (ed.), *The Steam Intellect Societies: Essays on Culture, Education and Industry circa 1820–1914* (Nottingham, 1985), pp. 80–93; Sanderson, *Education and Economic Decline*.

[19] Cardwell, *The Organisation of Science*.

the trading centres—for example in the support given University College Bristol by the Merchant Venturers.[20]

The demand for technical education, however, did contribute significantly to the continuing success of the technical schools that initially existed alongside (or later within) many of the civic colleges. In Sheffield, for example, industrialists including Henry Stephenson and Frederick Mappin contributed to the associated technical school established in 1886 rather than Firth College per se. Such schools were part of a raft of educational schemes that grew out of the mechanics' institutes that had been founded in the early century by the civic elite in order to educate the masses. Here they serve as the first of a series of local institutions whose complex and variable institutional pedigrees played important roles in the history of the civics, whether in the background of civic educational enterprises, or more directly.[21]

The failure of mechanics' institutes to attract working-class men to their scientific lectures is well documented, and many historians consequently abandon them after the 1850s, ignoring their massive expansion in the later Victorian period.[22] This growth was largely due to a prolonged influx of lower middle-class attendees at the institutes' classes, including many teachers and clerks. Their syllabuses diversified and they merged with various other establishments, forming polytechnic institutes, technical colleges, or more expansive entities such as the Leeds Institute of Science, Art, and Literature.[23] Many of the classes sponsored by the Department of Science and Art were held within their walls, and they also played host to schemes such

[20] Although the presence of the Merchant Venturers' Technical College may have hindered the growth of the University College. Vernon, 'Universities and Urban Identity'.

[21] Fowler and Wyke have traced the descendants of Manchester Mechanics' Institution, established in 1824, to the current Manchester Metropolitan University, showing the manifold connections and relationships with other higher education institutions in the town, including the other universities. Alan Fowler and Terry J. Wyke, *Many Arts, Many Skills: the Origins of the Manchester Metropolitan University* (Manchester, 1993).

[22] Ian Inkster, 'Science and the mechanics' institutes, 1820–1850: the case of Sheffield', *Annals of Science*, 32 (1975), 451–74; id., 'The social context of an educational movement: a revisionist approach to the English mechanics' institutes, 1820–1850', *Oxford Review of Education*, 2 (1976), 277–307; id. (ed.), *The Steam Intellect Societies*; Ian Inkster and Jack Morrell (eds.), *Metropolis and Province: Science in British Culture, 1780–1850* (London, 1983); Steven Shapin and Barry Barnes, 'Science, nature and control: interpreting mechanics' institutes', *Social Studies of Science*, 7 (1977), 31–74; Mabel Phythian Tylecote, *The Mechanics' Institutes of Lancashire and Yorkshire Before 1851* (Manchester, 1957). For the later century, see John P. Hemming, 'The mechanics' institute movement in the textile districts of Lancashire and Yorkshire in the second half of the nineteenth century' (Ph.D. thesis, University of Leeds, 1974); John Laurent, 'Science, society and politics in late nineteenth-century England: a further look at mechanics' institutes', *Social Studies of Science*, 14 (1984), 585–619.

[23] Leeds Institute of Science, Art and Literature, *A Historical Sketch of One Hundred Years' Work (1824–1923)* (Leeds, 1923).

as the Gilchrist lectures and City and Guilds courses. They spawned or housed schools of science, of art and design, and of music (for example at the massive Birmingham and Midland Institute), which often supplied the new civics with students, especially for their evening classes.[24] The institutes also provided many staff, and sometimes shared space with the young colleges. Otherwise, as in the case of Queen's College Liverpool (a school of science set up by the Mechanics' Institute), institutes were superseded by colleges—presumably transferring their potential student catchment. At the century's end, municipalities had largely assumed control of schools of art, science, and technology, and those that had not been absorbed by the civic college were run by the town in tandem with them.

By the turn of the century, civic colleges were also being provided with better-prepared students by the expanding secondary school system. This 'pressure from below' has been credited with having an enormous impact upon the growth of higher education in England: especially grammar schools, which commonly sent representatives to college councils, and fed them students. At the outset, however, the lack of adequate secondary education had hindered the colleges' grander aspirations to advanced instruction, and during their early years they found it necessary to provide a more fundamental education than they had intended. But as the new secondary system emerged, schools assumed this role and provided the civics with an increasing proportion of their students, as the Bryce Commission reported in 1895.[25] The expansion of elementary education also provided the civic colleges with a new string to their bow in the day training colleges for teachers opened in the 1890s, usually in close conjunction with the local university college, so prompting a massive increase in enrolment. From 1897 to 1905 the day training college at Sheffield, for example, provided the university college with nearly half of its student body.

Also providing the civics with students was a range of institutions and organisations devoted to adult education. Church institutes, athenaeums, and voluntary educational bodies such as the Yorkshire Board of Education and the Liverpool Council for Education all sought to provide the urban populace with some level of instruction in a variety of subjects; as did the adult school movement that had emerged from bible-reading classes in the early century. Particularly important among these institutions were the people's colleges (such as that founded in Sheffield in 1842), and countless

[24] Arthur Godlee, 'The Birmingham and Midland Institute', in Muirhead (ed.), *Birmingham Institutions*, pp. 315–62.

[25] James Bryce, *Report of the Royal Commission on Secondary Education* (London, 1895).

working men's colleges. Owens College absorbed the Manchester Working Man's College in 1861, for example, thus doubling the size of its evening classes. The relationships between these adult education providers and the new civic colleges varied, but in general they continued to supply basic education while their role in providing more advanced teaching was adopted by the colleges. Although the People's College, Sheffield closed shortly after Firth College started up, there were nonetheless over 1,600 adult schools nationwide in 1911.[26] Important too were the dissenting academies: although many had not survived long into the nineteenth century, their alumni were to be found at the forefront of the campaigns for new universities.

A major factor in the expansion of adult education was the women's education movement. A loose alliance of groups emerged, campaigning for admittance to institutions of higher education, lobbying the colleges for access and facilities.[27] Notable among these many individuals and local groups were the Clifton Association for the Higher Education of Women and the Reverend John Percival (later instrumental in setting up Somerville College, Oxford); and Anne Jemima Clough, Josephine Butler, and the North of England Council for Promoting the Higher Education of Women. The University of London had admitted women for degrees in 1878; Owens opened classes to women from 1883; others admitted both sexes (in principle) from the outset. Nevertheless, provision was sadly lacking, and women's attendance was only really significant after the opening of day training colleges for teachers in the 1890s.

Concomitant with and closely linked to the campaign for Victorian women's admittance to education was a similar movement to gain admittance to the professions. The further institutionalisation of the old professions, the consolidation of professional communities in many new areas, and the emergence of the professional middle classes generally, all had roles in the shaping of English higher education broadly and the civic colleges in particular.[28]

[26] Mrs George Cadbury, 'Adult schools', in Muirhead (ed.), *Birmingham Institutions*, pp. 199–232.

[27] Carol Dyhouse, *No Distinction of Sex? Women in British Universities, 1870–1939* (London, 1995); Simon Morgan, 'Middle-class women, civic virtue and identity: Leeds and the West Riding of Yorkshire, *c.*1830–*c.*1860' (Ph.D. thesis, University of York, 2000); R. D. Pope and M. G. Verbeke, 'Ladies' educational organisations in England, 1865–1885', *Paedagogica Historica*, 16 (1976), 336–61; A. B. Robertson, 'Manchester, Owens College and the higher education of women: "a large hole for the cat and a small one for the kitten"', *Bulletin of the John Rylands University Library of Manchester*, 77 (1995), 201–20; Mabel Phythian Tylecote, *The Education of Women at Manchester University, 1883–1933* (Manchester, 1941).

[28] A. M. Carr-Saunders and P. A. Wilson, *The Professions* (Oxford, 1933); Engel, 'The English universities'; Harold Perkin, *Origins of Modern English Society* (London, 1969); id., *The Rise of Professional Society: England Since 1880* (London, 1989); W. J. Reader, *Professional Men: the Rise of the Professional Classes in Nineteenth-Century England* (London, 1966).

Of the old professions, medicine played the most significant role. Medical training had been increasingly formalised over the course of the century by such legislation as the Apothecaries Act of 1815 and the 1858 regulation of admission to the medical register. Medical schools were established across the provinces in the 1820s and 1830s—larger towns had more than one school, and competition between them was often intense.[29] They were important precedents for the civics, and their staff provided influential lobbyists and instructors for the new colleges. In Birmingham, for example, a Midlands university was first proposed by Edward Johnstone, President of the School of Medicine and Surgery.

The civics, once established, in turn supplied the medical schools with basic science instruction.[30] Such courses were vital after the General Medical Council decreed that medical training should be laboratory-based in 1866, and from 1877 the University of London demanded laboratory training in chemistry and physics for its MB. The medical authorities wanted a new professional training to replace the traditional role of apprenticeship; henceforth instruction was to include a firm grounding in basic sciences, which the civics were glad to offer. The relationship was reciprocal: while early life science departments at the civics offered the medical schools essential teaching, they used space and facilities offered by the schools and benefited from a steady flow of students (however rowdy). Furthermore, as indicated above, many of these schools merged with the civics in the late century during the campaign for independent university status. The Royal Manchester School of Medicine was an early example, amalgamating with Owens in 1872–3. Other towns followed suit over the next three decades: Liverpool in 1881; Leeds in 1884; Birmingham (Queen's College) in 1892; Bristol in 1893; and Sheffield in 1897.

Other professional areas did not have as much impact as the medical establishment on the early years of the civic colleges. Although the introduction of

[29] In Manchester, the first recognised medical school was established in 1817; in Birmingham in 1825; Sheffield in 1828; Leeds in 1831; Newcastle in 1832; Bristol in 1833; and in Liverpool in 1834.

[30] Stephen T. Anning and W. Kenneth J. Walls, *A History of the Leeds School of Medicine* (Leeds, 1982); Stella Butler, 'A transformation in training: the formation of university medical faculties in Manchester, Leeds, and Liverpool, 1870–84', *Medical History*, 30 (1986), 115–32; G. Grey Turner and W. D. Arnison, *The Newcastle upon Tyne School of Medicine, 1834–1934* (Newcastle upon Tyne, 1934); Alison Kraft and Samuel J. M. M. Alberti, '"Equal though different": laboratories, museums and the institutional development of biology in the late-Victorian industrial North', *Studies in History and Philosophy of Biological and Biomedical Sciences*, 34 (2003), 203–36; William Smith Porter, *The Medical School in Sheffield, 1828–1928* (Sheffield, 1928); Steve Sturdy, 'The political economy of scientific medicine: science, education and the transformation of medical practice in Sheffield, 1890–1922', *Medical History*, 36 (1992), 125–59.

competitive examinations for the civil service (in 1853 for India and 1870 at home) has been heralded as a major landmark in the development of British higher education, it is unclear how much it affected the colleges. There is no direct evidence that large numbers of students attended for this purpose. There were theological colleges in many towns providing higher education beyond religious studies for their students, but they do not appear to have significantly helped (or hindered) the young civics.

Vocational training for the professions sat uneasily alongside another major justification for university-level instruction in the nineteenth century—the provision of a liberal education.[31] Lyon Playfair argued that the goal of a civic college should be ‘to increase the science and intelligence of the community, and not to teach industries which they know a great deal better than the professors’.[32] Rather than supplying only technical training, they sought to emulate the German university ideal of *Wissenschaft*: pure knowledge for its own sake. Metropolitan players, including John Stuart Mill and T. H. Huxley, advocated a comprehensive ideal of a broad university education for the colleges. A honed, flexible mind, stretched by grappling with abstract concepts, was an end in itself. In seeking to provide such instruction, the civics distinguished themselves from the technical colleges, and attracted ever more middle-class audiences. A general education was at once social preparation for the budding bourgeoisie, and a social emollient.

According to the Firth College principal Viriamu Jones, although ‘the advantages of technical education in a town like Sheffield cannot be overestimated’, there was no denying that ‘enlightened interest in some branch of literature, philosophy or science is the very best way of spending the leisure time of a busy life’.[33] Others contended that liberal education was important not only for leisure, but for a professional or business career. The colleges accordingly expanded beyond an explicitly technical education from the outset or soon after, developing syllabuses that included literature and non-industrial arts and sciences. Even the Yorkshire College and Mason College, perhaps the most technically minded of the civics in the early years, soon relented and included other subjects in abundance (and both dropped ‘science’ from their titles). The improving middle classes wanted a liberal

[31] John Henry Newman, *The Idea of a University* (ed.) Frank Turner (New Haven, 1996); Sheldon Rothblatt, *Tradition and Change in English Liberal Education: an Essay in History and Culture* (London, 1976); id., ‘The diversification of higher education’; Martha McMackin Garland, *Cambridge before Darwin: the Ideal of a Liberal Education, 1800–1860* (Cambridge, 1980).

[32] Cited in Arthur J. Taylor, ‘County college and civic university: an introductory essay’, in Gosden and Taylor (eds.), *Studies in the History of a University*, pp. 1–42, at p. 4.

[33] Cited in Chapman, *The Story of a Modern University*, pp. 33, 34.

education for their sons, strong in modern languages, English literature, history, and pure science. Most colleges began by teaching at least maths, chemistry, and physics, but those who lacked modern languages, English and natural history at the outset very soon included them. English literature was especially popular (although as Guy points out in this volume, not necessarily as part of a programme of liberal education).

Even at these early stages, the civics' governing bodies asserted—correctly—that such curricular diversification would increase their chances of gaining charters. Although in seeking to become independent degree-awarding institutions, they were in part striving to challenge the ancient universities, there was nonetheless a strong element of Oxbridge emulation in their motivation to provide liberal education. At Firth College's inception, Mark Firth intended that it 'be forever used and employed [...] for such purposes of higher education, and especially for the teaching and cultivation of any branches of learning taught or cultivated in the English Universities'.[34] University representatives sat on the council, and in 1886 Firth became an affiliated college of Oxford and Cambridge. In Bristol, John Percival sought to establish close ties between the new university college and the universities, in collaboration with the Master of Balliol, the classical scholar Benjamin Jowett.[35] The ancient universities provided many staff for the civics, especially in the arts: in Nottingham, for example, three of the four original professors were Cambridge men. Both Oxford and Cambridge continued to provide powerful models of curricula and approach in the twentieth century.[36]

Perhaps the strongest link to the ancients was the university extension scheme in its various forms. Initiated between 1867 and 1873, the extension lectures were the brainchild of James Stuart, Professor of Mechanics at Trinity College, Cambridge, in the wake of university reform and the repeal of the Test Acts.[37] Stuart and other reformers established these broad-syllabus lecture schemes in order to spread university-style liberal education in the industrial provinces. Mostly delivered by Oxbridge Dons imported for the occasion, they were popular among middle-class audiences. University extension was particularly important in Bristol and in Sheffield; the success of the lectures at the latter convinced Firth of the feasibility of a college of higher education. In Reading and Exeter, the roles played by the university extension

[34] Cited in the Firth College Sheffield, *Calendar* (1891–2), p. 14.

[35] John Percival, *The Connnection of the Universities and the Great Towns* (London, 1873).

[36] Sarah V. Barnes, 'England's civic universities and the triumph of the Oxbridge ideal', *History of Education Quarterly*, 36 (1996), 271–305.

[37] Edwin Welch, *The Peripatetic University: Cambridge Local Lectures, 1873–1973* (Cambridge, 1973); Lawrence Goldman, *Dons and Workers: Oxford and Adult Education Since 1850* (Oxford, 1995).

colleges set up in 1892 and 1893 were similar to those played by the civics in other towns.[38] It seems that Matthew Arnold's dream had come true: 'We must plant faculties in eight or ten principal seats of population, and let the students follow the lectures there from their own homes . . . It would be everything for the great seats of population to be thus made intellectual centres as well as mere places of business.'[39]

Although the extension scheme could be viewed as the result of active Oxbridge educationalists coming to the aid of the docile provincials, the scheme would have floundered at the outset had it not been for the support of local societies supplying space, funds, and audience. Like the Gilchrist lectures and other schemes, extension lectures were held across the country at mechanics' institutes, philosophical societies, and by a wave of university extension societies and associations for the promotion of higher education. The Nottingham Mechanics' Institute, rebuilt after their building was destroyed by fire in 1867, housed the first university extension course. Henry Sidgwick, who taught it, reckoned the extension movement 'would have remained an idea, but for the action taken by Nottingham'.[40] The popularity of the lectures reinforced the organising committee's commitment to founding the university college three years later.

Although their example was undoubtedly important, the English universities were clearly not the only institutions worth emulating. Delegations were sent out around the country and to Europe for architectural, curricular, and enrolment advice. In 1898, the Birmingham syndics even sent a delegation to the USA and Canada. But the civics' favourite was closer to home: the Scottish model of university teacher in particular, Rothblatt argues, was far more important than that of the Oxbridge Don.[41] Furthermore, University College London's role is often overlooked, as is the extent to which the civic colleges built on each other. Owens, as the oldest, was particularly important in this respect, and the Manchester emphasis on a broad curriculum and middle-class clientele resounded across England. Civic pride, interprovincial rivalry, and basic pragmatism meant that the civics competed amongst themselves more than with Oxbridge or the Continent.

The breadth of the education the civics provided was further bolstered by the thriving cultural and non-technical educational environment in which the colleges grew up. Campaigns to provide liberal education were as much about

[38] William MacBride Childs, *Making a University: an Account of the University Movement at Reading* (London, 1933); Robert Newton, *Victorian Exeter, 1837–1914* (Leicester, 1968).
[39] Matthew Arnold, *Schools and Universities on the Continent* (London, 1868), p. 276.
[40] Cited in Armytage, *Civic Universities*, p. 226.
[41] Rothblatt, 'The diversification of higher education'.

the independent cultural assertions of the new mercantile and industrial middle classes as they were about mimicking the collegiate ideal.

The cultural institution that was perhaps most important to a young college was the local literary and philosophical society. Founded in almost every provincial town in the period 1780–1830, 'lit and phils' were part of the culture of the voluntary association that was fundamental to the emergence of the new urban provincial middle classes.[42] Building upon the tradition of the itinerant lecturer, the activities of these groups spanned many aspects of civic culture. By avoiding the volatile topics of religion and politics, such voluntary associations bound together with civic pride a dynamic but fragmented stratum of society.[43] Historians of higher education have too often ignored the role of philosophical and other local learned societies in the founding and support of the young colleges, and yet these organisations had as profound an impact on college growth and curricula as medical schools and industrial lobbying, which are more commonly identified. It was within their walls that the first calls for a local university were often made. As early as 1826, for

[42] Samuel J. M. M. Alberti, 'Natural history and the philosophical societies of late Victorian Yorkshire', *Archives of Natural History*, 30 (2003), 342–58; Paul Elliott, 'The origins of the "creative class": provincial urban society, scientific culture and socio-political marginality in Britain in the eighteenth and nineteenth centuries', *Social History*, 28 (2003), 361–87; Ian Inkster, 'The public lecture as an instrument of science education for adults — the case of Great Britain, *c.*1750–1850', *Paedagogica Historica*, 20 (1980), 80–107; Inkster and Morrell (eds.), *Metropolis and Province*; E. Kitson Clark, *The History of 100 Years of Life of the Leeds Philosophical and Literary Society* (Leeds, 1924); Philip D. Lowe, 'Locals and cosmopolitans: a model for the social organisation of science in the nineteenth century' (M.Phil., University of Sussex, 1978); Chris E. Makepeace, *Science and Technology in Manchester: Two Hundred Years of the Lit. and Phil.* (Manchester, 1984); R. J. Morris, *Class, Sect and Party: the Making of the British Middle Class, Leeds 1820–1850* (Manchester, 1990); id., 'Clubs, societies and associations', in F. M. L. Thompson (ed.), *The Cambridge Social History of Britain 1750–1950. Volume 3: Social Agencies and Institutions* (Cambridge, 1990), pp. 395–443; William Smith Porter, *Sheffield Literary and Philosophical Society: a Centenary Retrospect, 1822–1922* (Sheffield, 1922); G. W. Roderick and M. D. Stephens, 'The role of nineteenth-century provincial literary and philosophical societies in fostering adult education', *Journal of Educational Administration and History*, 5 (1973), 28–33; Arnold Thackray, 'Natural knowledge in cultural context: the Manchester model', *American Historical Review*, 79 (1974), 672–709; Robert Spence Watson, *The History of the Literary and Philosophical Society, Newcastle-upon-Tyne (1793–1896)* (London, 1897).

[43] On the emergence of the middle classes, see Leonore Davidoff and Catherine Hall, *Family Fortunes: Men and Women of the English Middle Class, 1780–1850* (London, 1987); Simon Gunn, *The Public Culture of the Victorian Middle Class: Ritual and Authority in the English Industrial City, 1840–1914* (Manchester, 2000); K. Theodore Hoppen, *The mid-Victorian Generation, 1846–1886* (Oxford, 1998); Alan Kidd and David Nicholls (eds.), *Gender, Civic Culture and Consumerism: Middle-Class Identity in Britain, 1800–1940* (Manchester, 1999); Dror Wahrman, *Imagining the Middle Class: the Political Representation of Class in Britain, c.1780–1840* (Cambridge, 1995); Janet Wolff and John Seed (eds.), *The Culture of Capital: Art, Power and the Nineteenth-Century Middle Class* (Manchester, 1988).

example, the Leeds flax merchant and MP John Marshall, then President of the Philosophical and Literary Society, began to lobby for a university for Yorkshire.[44] Early subscription campaigns were commonly initiated by individual or group donations from lit and phils in this way. Learned societies were then instrumental in fostering the colleges in their infancy, providing premises, use of libraries, and other facilities. Many faculty members were part-time at the college and found other employment at the lit and phil. Those who did not need extra work participated as members and as lecturers in the society's programmes or as part of the extramural activities of the colleges, and some married into the cultural elite who ran the societies. There was often considerable overlap between the two institutions' ruling bodies: the physician John Deakin Heaton, for example, a prominent member of the Leeds Philosophical, was the first Chairman of the Yorkshire College Council, which, like other civics, later included society representatives *ex officio*.[45] Lit and phils, by definition eclectic, were at the forefront of the move to expand college syllabuses to include arts and pure sciences.

A relatively small group of civic grandees were bound to be involved in most worthy cultural and educational activities in the town: the *éminences grises* of middle-class civic culture, they sat on college councils and contributed to calls for pubic support, collectively, and individually.[46] These same self-appointed *cognoscenti* also supported related ventures throughout the century, many of which began as spin-offs of the lit and phils—halls of science, athenaeums, societies for the promotion or diffusion of knowledge, church educational institutes, and YMCAs. Increasingly, learned associations with broad remits were joined by a plethora of groups dedicated to a specific area of knowledge, as evidenced by the astounding growth of the corresponding societies of the British Association in the 1870s.[47] These were also crucial to the early functions of the civic colleges: natural history clubs, for example, provided both students and staff for early biology departments.[48]

[44] Shimmin, *The University of Leeds*.

[45] T. W. Reid (ed.), *A Memoir of John Deakin Heaton, M.D., of Leeds* (London, 1883).

[46] As demonstrated so effectively for Bristol by Meller, *Leisure and the Changing City*.

[47] O. J. R. Howarth, *The British Association for the Advancement of Science: a Retrospect, 1831–1931* (London, 1931); Roy MacLeod, J. R. Friday, and C. Gregor, *The Corresponding Societies of the British Association for the Advancement of Science, 1883–1929: a Survey of Historical Records, Archives and Publications* (London, 1975); Roy MacLeod and Peter Collins (eds.), *The Parliament of Science: the British Association for the Advancement of Science* (Northwood, 1981). The association had instituted a subcommittee on local scientific societies a decade earlier.

[48] Samuel J. M. M. Alberti, 'Amateurs and professionals in one county: biology and natural history in late Victorian Yorkshire', *Journal of the History of Biology*, 34 (2001), 115–47.

In each urban context, particular local factors and active individuals favoured different aspects of this spectrum of civic activity, and the strongest support for the colleges came from different directions. In Manchester, the statistical society played an important role in the early life of Owens College. A proposed university was mooted at a society meeting in 1836; half of the Trustees of Owens's will were committee members; and the society encouraged the study of economics at the college.[49] In Liverpool, the Royal Institution (for the promotion of science, literature, and arts, where a young Italian refugee, Antonio Panizzi, taught for a spell) was crucial in the early growth of the university college, alongside the Royal Infirmary Medical School and the university extension scheme.[50] The individual architectural histories of the colleges also tell of their local institutional contexts, and how rarely their organisers had the luxury of choice. University College Liverpool was first housed in a disused lunatic asylum; Bristol University College started its life in the old Deaf and Dumb Institute; and Newcastle's College of Science took rooms where it could, including the Literary and Philosophical Society's hall and the coal trade buildings. The colleges, once ensconced in their own halls and laboratories, returned the favour, and many civic groups held their evening meetings in their rooms.

The new colleges required not only funding, staff, and space. They needed the material culture upon which Victorian education depended: books and journals, and museum space and specimens. Some societies offered the colleges use of their libraries (both books and rooms); others found themselves struggling in the late century and were relieved to find a good home for their collections permanently. Thus the Manchester Medical Society deposited its library with Owens College; Bristol University College inherited the tomes of the Medico-Chirurgical Society and University College Liverpool's collection was expanded considerably by the donations from both the Literary and Philosophical Society and the Royal Institution.

Museum specimens were as important as printed matter to many departments, especially in the sciences and in fine art.[51] And so the Arundel Society

[49] Thomas Ashton, *Economic and Social Investigations in Manchester, 1833–1933: a Centenary History of the Manchester Statistical Society* (London, 1934); David Elesh, 'The Manchester Statistical Society', *Journal of the History of the Behavioural Sciences*, 8 (1972), 280–301. Jones lists six other voluntary associations whose members, individually, and collectively, contributed to the establishment of Owens College. Jones, *The Origins of Civic Universities*.

[50] Kelly, *For Advancement of Learning*; Henry A. Ormerod, *The Liverpool Royal Institution: a Record and a Retrospect* (Liverpool, 1953).

[51] On the importance of museums to the new universities, whether within or beside them, see Sophie Forgan, 'The architecture of display: museums, universities and objects in nineteenth-century Britain', *History of Science*, 32 (1994), 139–62; id., 'Museum and university: spaces for learning and the shape of disciplines', in Hewitt (ed.), *Scholarship in Victorian Britain*, pp. 66–77.

lent University College Liverpool lithographs and the Manchester Natural History Society dissolved and gave its sizeable collections to Owens College. Museum buildings were also important sources of teaching and research space, as in Leeds, where the collections in the philosophical hall were rearranged for the use of Yorkshire College students, and Louis C. Miall was both professor at the college and curator of the museum for twenty years.[52] In Nottingham, the university college was opened as part of the same municipal complex as the natural history museum. Senior figures within civic college governing bodies, unsurprisingly, were also important in the governance of museums and libraries. The antiquary and architect Sir James Picton, for example, sat on the University College Liverpool Committee, and chaired the town's library, museum and arts committee. College, library, and museum operated in physical and administrative juxtaposition in the late nineteenth century.

The civic colleges, it is clear, emerged from a complex web of civic intellectual, educational, and cultural associations that constituted middle-class public life. Although metropolitan and Oxbridge heavyweights from Charles Dickens to Mark Pattison lamented the intellectual philistinism of the provincial middle-classes, the colleges' growth depended on these thriving cultural milieux.[53] Developing good relations with existing groups was essential for their survival, and such links were oiled by exchanges in money, staff, students, accommodation, material culture, and especially by interlocking directorates.

Emphasising the role of existing middle-class institutional culture in the genesis of the civic colleges is not to deny altogether the importance of the economic growth of the 1860s and 1870s. We should remember, however, that this was also a period of great expansion in voluntary associations in provincial towns, a late-century cultural regeneration that saw older groups grow larger and stronger, and a host of new societies join the fray. This carried on through the late century, when on Merseyside the city fathers sought to re-light the 'Liverpool Renaissance' of a century before, and in Birmingham civic culture thrived under Joseph Chamberlain's mayoralty. In this atmosphere, the colleges outgrew their institutional antecedents, absorbing them or

[52] Samuel J. M. M. Alberti, 'The Bengal tiger in context: the Leeds Museum in the nineteenth century', *Leeds Museums and Galleries Review*, 4 (2001–2), pp. 13–6; R. A. Baker and R. A. Bayliss, 'Louis Compton Miall, F.R.S.: scientist and educator, 1842–1921', *Notes and Records of the Royal Society of London,* 37 (1982), 201–34.

[53] Charles Dickens, *The Mudfog Papers, etc.* (London, 1880); Roy Lowe, 'Structural change in English higher education, 1870–1920', in Müller, Ringer, Simon (eds.), *The Rise of the Modern Educational System*, pp. 163–78.

assuming their role in urban life. The colleges, like many societies, institutes, museums, and libraries, were shaped by civic pride—they were but the latest phase in a series of parallel projects designed, as Anderson writes, 'to assert the cultural maturity of the great Victorian cities'.[54] They staged conversaziones, open days and exhibitions as visible manifestations of civic pride, and it was this pride that induced many local philanthropists to donate on such a grand scale.[55] Their towering Gothic and Italianate edifices proclaimed their prominence within their town, and their town's standing within the nation.[56] The middle-class elite displayed themselves through named wings and buildings, and adorned college chambers with their likenesses—busts of local dignitaries stared sombrely down at the students and visitors. The idealised notions of citizenship with which the middle classes were imbued included not only the rational benefits of applied science and technology but also the cultivation offered by the arts and pure sciences. The colleges were at once expressions of these desires and a means for their reproduction, and they played key roles in the consolidation of provincial middle-class identity and cultural authority.

The expansion of higher education in Victorian England, then, depended not only on the demand for technical instruction, the growth of secondary education, the formalisation of professional training, and provincial emulation of Oxbridge; also of key importance in shaping the early institutional history of the redbrick universities was the urban elite's involvement in widespread cultural activities. They did not spring fully formed in an urban vacuum, but rather were carefully cultivated by a range of existing educational institutions, from mechanics' institutes to medical schools. Only with the support of dynamic networks of cultural associations could such endeavours succeed, and by exploring them we better understand the institutional organisation of knowledge in Victorian England.

[54] R. D. Anderson, *Universities and elites in Britain since 1800* (Cambridge, 1992), pp. 31–2.

[55] Samuel J. M. M. Alberti, 'Conversaziones and the experience of science in Victorian England', *Journal of Victorian Culture*, 8 (2003), 208–30.

[56] Kate Hill, '"Thoroughly Embued with the Spirit of Ancient Greece": symbolism and space in Victorian civic culture', in Kidd and Nicholls (eds.), *Gender, Civic Culture and Consumerism*, pp. 99–111.

CHAPTER SIXTEEN

Intimacy, Imagination and the Inner Dialectics of Knowledge Communities: The Synthetic Society, 1896–1908

W. C. LUBENOW

> And what you have called world, that shall be created only by you: your reason, your image, your will, your love shall thus be realized. And verily, for your own bliss, you lovers of knowledge. (Nietzsche)[1]

In 1938 Toscanini said, 'I've never taken part in Societies, either political or artistic. I've always been a loner. I've always believed that only *an individual* can be a gentleman.'[2] Well, Toscanini might have been a gentleman but he could never be a British gentleman. It is a common jibe that when two Britons meet, they form a club. E. M. Forster famously said, 'only connect'. From the sixteenth century associational behaviour has performed all sorts of political, social, and cultural functions.[3] In the nineteenth century, now separated from birth and military fantasies and now attached to the professions and university learning, respectability, what it meant to be a gentleman—loyalty, trust, social integration, belonging—was attached to a dense network of formal and informal associations.

These served the valuable function of easing young men into the metropolitan world from the isolation of provincial life. In addressing St George's Club, a club for Catholic professional men, Cardinal Manning said it gave them 'the opportunity of forming the acquaintance and cultivating the

[1] Walter Kaufmann (ed.), *The Portable Nietzsche* (New York, 1954), p. 198.

[2] Quoted in Michael Kimmelman, 'Music, Maestro, Please!' *New York Review of Books*, (7 Nov. 2002), 20, 22.

[3] Peter Clark, *British Clubs and Societies, 1580–1800: The Origins of an Associational World* (Oxford, 2000).

friendship of those who, being already in the careers of life, may be able to assist' others.[4] Some were political, represented by clubs with partisan association: the Carlton, the Reform, Brooks's. Some were parliamentary, as for example Grillions. Some were fashionable, such as White's. (One writer described White's as the club 'frequented by the rich, the rakish, the well-born, and the merely ambitious'.[5]) And there were college and university clubs. The club habit was formed early in life, as the history of Pop at Eton shows. One nineteenth-century writer traced club life to 'the earliest off-shoots of Man's habitually gregarious social inclination'. Naturally, he found this impulse in the 'polished Athenians' who had in addition to 'their general *symposia*, friendly meetings, where every one sent his own portion of the feast, bore a proportionate part of the expense, or gave a pledge at a fixed price'.[6] Some clubs were knowledge communities. Of these, some were old organisations which transformed themselves, such as the Royal Society.[7] The Athenaeum reconstituted itself, becoming very much less aristocratic and very much more professional in its social composition.[8] Other societies were freshly formed, such as the Social Science Association.[9]

Some smaller knowledge communities formed themselves at the interstices of university and metropolitan life. The Committee for the Revision of the Bible was founded in 1870. The Metaphysical Society was founded in 1869 for the rapprochement of scientific and religious ideas. The Eranus Society was founded in 1872. The Society for Psychical Research was founded in 1882 to promote the investigation of a spiritual existence. Each, in different ways, explored issues at the edge of accepted conceptual intellectual categories.

B. F. Westcott, J. B. Lightfoot, and F. J. A. Hort founded the Eranus Society but its purposes were not primarily theological. Indeed, as Henry Sidgwick put it, '[i]ts fundamental idea was to include students in different lines and afford them the regular opportunity for a somewhat more serious and methodical interchange of ideas than ordinary social gatherings allow'.[10]

[4] Cardinal Manning's speech to St George's Club, 17 Dec. 1884, Arundel Castle Archives, fifteenth Duke of Norfolk MSS., C. 718.

[5] Kenneth Rose, *Elusive Rothschild: The Life of Victor, Third Baron* (London, 2003), p. 116.

[6] John Timbs, *Club and Club Life in London* (London, 1872), p. 1.

[7] Marie Boas Hall, *All Scientists Now: The Royal Society in the Nineteenth Century* (Cambridge, 1984), pp. 92–142.

[8] J. Mordaunt Crook, 'Locked Out of Paradise: Blackballing at the Athenaeum, 1824–1935', in *Armchair Athenians: Essays from Athenaeum Life* (London, 2001), pp. 26–9.

[9] Lawrence Goldman, *Science, Reform, and Politics in Victorian Britain* (Cambridge, 2002).

[10] Henry Sidgwick to Lord Acton, 29 Oct. 1895, Acton Papers, Cambridge University Library, Add. MS. 8119 (5) 595.

Founded at one of those tipping points in university life when academic disciplines as they might be known in the twentieth century were coming into existence, it provided occasions for threshing out different lines of inquiry in the new 'special studies'.[11] At one meeting, Westcott offered the thought that he would be prepared to award a degree to a person who was able to ask twelve good questions. Westcott was careful and precise in his approach to intellectual questions, yet he avoided 'formulas, because truth seemed to be too great to be contained in them'. Westcott read one of the earliest papers to the society on theories of knowledge.[12] Hort, with his wide-ranging intellectual interests, read a paper on Lyell's theories of geological uniformitarianism. In 1877 Arthur Balfour read a paper on 'Contradiction in the Automatic Theory of Knowledge'.[13] In his 'Notes on Archival Research, 1864–1868', which he read to the society in 1895, Lord Acton concluded, in turning from books to archives 'we exchange doubt for certainty, and become our own masters. We explore a new heaven and a new earth, and at each step forward, the world moves with us.'[14] Henry Sidgwick, Clerk Maxwell, and Coutts Trotter were among the society's early members.[15] George Darwin, F. W. Maitland, Donald Macalister, Vincent Stanton, Henry Jackson, and James Ward were among its members at the end of the century when Acton became a member.[16]

Societies of scientists are of particular interest. The X-Club met from 1864 to 1892.[17] It was a dining club to advance the members' scientific ideas against the views of more conservative scientists, theologians, and politicians. Its purpose was to provide support and encouragement for each other professionally. John Tyndall was a member. So were Huxley, Spencer, Hooker, and John Lubbock. It had no rules except to have none. Its purposes were serious but Spencer remembered the liveliness of their meetings and in 1866, for example, they assigned nicknames to each other: the Xquiste Lubbock, the Xperienced Hooker, the Xalted Huxley, the Xcentric Tyndall. They dined together on the

[11] Arthur Fenton Hort, *The Life and Letters of Fenton John Anthony Hort* (London, 1896), vol. II, pp. 184–5.

[12] Arthur Westcott, *The Life and Letters of Brooke Foss Westcott, D.D., D.C.L., Sometime Bishop of Durham* (London, 1903), vol. I, pp. 384–6.

[13] Hort, *The Life and Letters of Fenton John Anthony Hort*, vol. II, p. 184.

[14] Printed in Damian McElrath, *Lord Acton: The Decisive Decade, 1864–1874* (Louvain, 1970), pp. 121–140, quote at p. 140.

[15] Hort, *The Life and Letters of Fenton John Anthony Hort*, vol. II, p. 184.

[16] Sidgwick to Acton, 29 Oct. 1895, Acton Papers, Cambridge University Library, Add. MS. 8119 (5) 595.

[17] For what follows see, J. Vernon Jensen, 'The X-Club: Fraternity of Victorian Scientists', *British Journal for the History of Science*, 5 (17) (1970), 63–72 and, for a more extensive treatment, Roy MacLeod, 'The X-Club: A Social Network of Science in Late-Victorian England', *Notes and Records of the Royal Society of London* (Dec. 1970), 305–22; Ruth Barton, ' "An Influential Set of Chaps": The X-Club and Royal Society Politics, 1864–85', *British Journal for the History of Science*, 23 (1990), 53–81.

first Thursday of the month, first at St George's Hotel, Albemarle Street, and later at Almond's Hotel, Clifford Street, and later yet at the Athenaeum. The Club dined together two hundred-forty times, and an average of seven members gathered together. Though they achieved eminence and rose to positions of power in the Royal Society, they felt on the edge of things and their gatherings provided professional and emotional solidarity.

Such societies were held together by various forms of fear. They were marked by conceptual uncertainty and professional anxiety. Through the threshing out of ideas they sought mutual reassurance and intellectual confirmation. An emotional matter as much as a cerebral concern, such societies relied on their intimate associations to produce professional integrity. Knowledge communities occupied a space between university learning and civil society. Their sociological edges were often soft. Their conceptual edges were soft as well. They helped produce some of the intangible features of social capital: an intellectual infrastructure (albeit often ephemeral), social networks, transparency, trust, and mutual monitoring.[18] Social capital, therefore, was important for policy-making in the public sphere,[19] and knowledge communities assisted in its creation in the indeterminate interstices of informal and tacit social and mental behaviour.

Knowledge communities were also engines of change. The changes they promoted were driven less by ideology, philosophy, or programme than they were by the yearning for completeness through the reorganisation of symbolic worlds. They investigated and tested the truth (or truths) of opinion. The knowledge they sought exposed conditional, hypothetical, and discursive mental and emotional worlds. So, intimacy and imagination conspired together to produce feelings of trust, loyalty, integrity, and belonging. The creation, confirmation, and dissemination of knowledge had therefore more than intellectual, social, and political significance. It had emotional significance as well. I wish to follow these processes more fully by examining one knowledge community—the Synthetic Society—in more detail.

On 24 January 1896[20] Arthur Balfour,[21] Edward Talbot, who would become the bishop of Rochester, Charles Gore who would become the

[18] For a discussion of these features for economic development, see Ben Fine, 'The Developmental State is Dead — Long Live Social Capital?' *Development and Change*, 30 (1) (Jan. 1999).

[19] Martin J. Daunton, *Trusting Leviathan: The Politics of Taxation in Britain, 1799–1914* (Cambridge, 2001), pp. 10 ff.

[20] The following paragraphs on the founding, the Rules, and the membership of the Synthetic Society are based upon *Papers Read Before the Synthetic Society, 1896–1908*, presented to the members by A. J. Balfour, Aug. 1909 (London, 1909), pp. v–viii.

[21] For a complete account of Arthur Balfour's ideas and his part in the Synthetic Society we shall have to await the new biography of him by Professor R. J. Q. Adams.

bishop of Birmingham, and Wilfrid Ward met for a dinner at the Junior Carlton Club and agreed to the name of a new society. They drew up a list of potential members. On 28 February they held a preliminary meeting at the Westminster Palace Hotel when Wilfrid Ward read a paper describing the purposes of the society. This was attended, in addition to the founders, by newly recruited members such as James Bryce, R. B. Haldane, R. H. Hutton, Gerald Balfour, and George Wyndham. The first regular meeting of the Synthetic Society took place on 25 March when Arthur Balfour read a paper.

The Rules of the Synthetic Society called for its members to dine together on the last Friday of the months of January, February, March, April, and May. Members were permitted to invite two guests to the dinner and meeting, but their names had to be approved by the chairman two weeks in advance. Following dinner a paper, previously printed and circulated, was to be presented in not more than thirty minutes. Each member was then to be allowed seven minutes to make formal remarks. After all had a chance to make criticisms, the speaker was to reply. Then, 'at his discretion', the chairman would allow informal discussion of the question at issue. The election of new members required unanimity. The chairman was to be elected annually. Bishop Talbot, Sir Alfred Lyall, Henry Sidgwick, R. B. Haldane, Sir Oliver Lodge, and Arthur Balfour were chairmen.

The forms of knowledge the Synthetic Society was established to expose had soft conceptual edges. They fell between, or outside, the existing categories and methods of learning. Such concepts were unbounded, fitting definitions uncertainly, uneasily, and nervously.[22] They had to do with the nature of religious belief. They were not so much theological as psychological in character. The society's foundation was provoked by the publication of Arthur Balfour's *Foundations of Belief* (1895). Wilfrid Ward reviewed it in the *Quarterly Review* and his article called forth a correspondence which led to the meeting of Balfour, Ward, Talbot, and Gore at the Junior Carlton Club. That is, the formation of the society took place not in the universities with the new curriculums which were emerging at the end of the nineteenth century, nor in the pages of the established literary publications, but in a new society established for a special, experimental purpose.

[22] Timothy Williamson, *Vagueness* (London and New York, 1994); *Identity and Discrimination* (Oxford, 1990); R. M. Sainsbury, *Concepts without Boundaries* (London, 1991); Gregory L. Murphy, *The Big Book of Concepts* (Cambridge, MA, and London, 2002) but cf. Jerry Fodor, 'Is it a Bird: Problems with Old and New Approaches to the Theory of Concepts', *Times Literary Supplement*, 17 Jan. 2003, pp. 3–4; Robert Gregg, *Inside Out, Outside In: Essays in Comparative History* (London, 2000).

The Rules of the Synthetic Society specified that its objects were 'to consider existing Agnostic tendencies, and to contribute toward a working philosophy of religious belief'. A point should be made about this. The members were to seek a 'working knowledge'. They were not to seek finalities or certainties. They were not to seek dogmas or doctrines. The knowledge they sought was to confirm soft conceptual edges, not firm ones. The Rules went on to specify that as controversies arose in the society's discussions members were to remember that their aim was 'mutual understanding' for the purpose 'of the maintenance of the beliefs they held in common'. And this is another point to stress. Their objective was to expose various views and to seek in them not only mutual understanding but to identify which of those concepts they held in common. When James Bryce wrote to Lord Acton to ask him to join, he said that the Synthetic Society 'is intended to presuppose only' that some common theological connections can be found and 'the desire to reach them'.[23] As Wilfrid Ward pointed out in the first paper read to the society, a hundred years of 'destructive criticism' had 'impaired the effectiveness' of existing religious systems. The first principles of traditional Christianity had been exposed as legitimate objects of doubt and criticism. What was needed was a 'much fuller philosophical consideration and elaboration than they had yet received alike as to premises and as to proofs'.[24]

Members expressed the conceptual uncertainties and ambiguities with which they struggled in a number of ways. Some were optimistic and some were pessimistic. Henry Sidgwick hesitated when he was asked to join the Synthetic Society, because of 'the tendency of an exciting evening to produce a wakeful night'.[25] Lord Hugh Cecil thought it unlikely that the society would solve the great questions it was posing but 'it is surely a centre of intellectual interest—and also a witness to metaphysics in the same sort of sense as the Church is to be a witness to the Truth!'[26] Father Tyrrell wondered whether the society should merely 'labour together for the defence of as much religion as can be based on bare theism' or whether it 'should strive to find out how much more' members shared in common. To strive for more than 'bare theism' might provoke intense controversies and would, he concluded,

[23] James Bryce to Lord Acton, [the stamp on the envelope was ripped off taking with it the day and the month of the letter with it, but 1896], Acton Papers, Cambridge University Library, Add. MS. 8119 (1) B 245.

[24] Wilfrid Ward, 'Synthetic Society', *Papers Read Before the Synthetic Society, 1896–1908*, p. 1.

[25] [A.S. and E.M.S.] *Henry Sidgwick: A Memoir* (London, 1906), p. 556.

[26] Maisie Ward, *The Wilfrid Wards and the Transition, II: Insurrection Versus Resurrection* (London, 1937), p. 143.

'require more generosity and intellectual self denial than can be expected of any mixed assembly'.[27]

Haldane was highly pessimistic about the work of the society. The evenings were agreeable and 'it is always pleasant to meet with the clergy', but 'for serious purposes the time has just been thrown away'. 'Half of those present do not understand what the other half are talking about' and 'the discussions on speculative subjects are deplorably bad'. The majority had not read the *Treatise on Human Nature* or the *Critique of Pure Reason* and, as a consequence are 'not furnished even with the elements of knowledge that is wanted'. Ward attempted to answer Haldane's charges, but Sidgwick thought that Ward's remarks about 'stiff metaphysics' and his pedantry 'might be taken by Haldane as personal'.[28] The ambiguity and emotional character of the Synthetic Society is revealed in a letter about Haldane from Sidgwick to Arthur Balfour:

> I agree broadly with you about Haldane, except that I do not, I fear, grasp his position sufficiently to judge precisely how far your attack hit.
>
> I thought it was a *fundamental* doctrine of Hegel's logic that what is logically prior is—being more abstract—*less* real that what is logically posterior. Yet H's argument seems based on the opposite assumption.
>
> The Neo-Hegelian epistemology is a Proteus that eludes my grasp: it is always appearing in a new form.
>
> I also agree with much of Rashdall, whose turn of mind suits mine—only I am more realistic & commonsensical as regards the physical world than he, or perhaps you, I mean than you would be if forced to dogmatize.[29]

If Haldane thought other members of the Synthetic Society were philosophically deficient, Balfour and Ward found his Hegelian diatribes pretty incomprehensible. As Balfour put it, 'I confess I have derived a certain amount of amusement from Haldane talking what is to most of his hearers absolutely unintelligible gibberish, with an expression of serene self-confidence which would benefit a conversation about the weather'.[30] If they were going to be synthetic, the society was prepared to welcome all sorts of opinion, and Balfour thought Haldane would be an excellent chairman when he was

[27] Ward, *The Wilfrid Wards and the Transition, I: The Nineteenth Century* (London, 1934), pp. 373–4.

[28] Ward, *The Wilfrid Wards and the Transition, I: The Nineteenth Century*, p. 371.

[29] Henry Sidgwick [writing from Newnham College] to Arthur Balfour, 9 April 1897, Balfour Papers, British Library, Add. MS. 48932, ff. 89–90.

[30] Balfour to Wilfrid Ward, 28 May 1896, quoted in John David Foot, 'The Philosophical and Religious Thought of Arthur James Balfour (1848–1930)', *Journal of British Studies*, 19 (Spring 1980), p. 137.

elected in 1903. The mental economy of the Synthetic Society was marked by a high level of ambiguity, uncertainty, and emotional contingency.

If the conceptual edges at which the Synthetic Society laboured were soft and indeterminate, so also were its sociological edges. It was distinctly un-aristocratic. To be sure, Lord Hugh Cecil was a member. So, too, was Lord Rayleigh, who as a countryman was true to his obligations to his estates. But Rayleigh's claim to status rested more on his intellectual attainments as Cavendish Professor at Cambridge than on his birth and pedigree. Haldane was elevated to the peerage, but in recognition of his statesmanship and his contributions to the law and philosophy. Friedrich von Hügel held a foreign title. If members of the Synthetic Society were aristocrats, they were intellectual aristocrats whose social role was derived from university learning and service in the professions.[31] There is a sort of family nexus in the membership of the Synthetic Society: Arthur Balfour and his brother Gerald, and their brothers-in-law Henry Sidgwick and Lord Rayleigh. Oxford was represented there: Rashdall, Bryce, and Dicey; rather more heavily, Cambridge: Rayleigh, F. W. Myers. In fact there was a heavy sprinkling of Cambridge Apostles: Gerald Balfour, Alfred Lyttelton, Bernard Holland, Richard Jebb, Henry Sidgwick, James Ward, Warre Cornish, MacTaggart, Lowes Dickinson.

Their religious diversity is rather more important that their social diversity. Among the Anglicans there was considerable doctrinal and pietistic variation. Talbot and Gore wrote in *Lux Mundi*. Canon Scott Holland was a socialist high churchman. Hugh Cecil was a high churchman in the tradition of Laud and was opposed to the views of *Lux Mundi* and Christian socialism. As Henry Sidgwick wrote to Wilfrid Ward, 'we have no pure-blooded Protestants'.[32] Father Waggett was a Cowley father who wore his cassock to Synthetic Society meetings. Then there were the Roman Catholics: W. J. Williams, Father Robert Clarke, Wilfrid Ward, and the Modernists von Hügel and George Tyrrell.[33] And then there were those whose religious views were especially indeterminate. Bernard Holland was an agnostic as a young man,[34] but he followed his mother to Rome and tried to write a biography of the fifteenth Duke of Norfolk.[35]

[31] William C. Lubenow, 'Making Words Flesh: Changing Roles of University Learning and the Professions in Nineteenth Century England', *Minerva*, 40 (3) (2002), 217–34.

[32] Quoted in Maisie Ward, *The Wilfrid Wards and the Transition, I: The Nineteenth Century*, p. 356.

[33] Nicholas Sagorsky, *'On God's Side': A Life of George Tyrrell* (Oxford, 1990), pp. 69–70, 90, 101, 175, 190.

[34] Clive Dewey, *The Passing of Barchester: A Real Life Version of Trollope* (London and Rio Grande: Hambledon Press, 1991), pp. 122–3.

[35] Gwendolen Norfolk to Bernard Holland, 9 Sep. 1919, Lord Edmund Talbot to Bernard Holland, 21 Nov. 1920, Winefride Freeman to Francis Steer, 25 May 1972, Arundel Castle Archives, G4/138, 120, 84.

Lowes Dickinson's religious views, emotional and pantheistic, and extremely difficult to pin down, were distinctly unchristian. Wilfrid Ward's daughter claimed that McTaggart's polytheistic agnosticism 'had no acceptance in the Society beyond his brain'.[36]

These were not young men, early in their careers, seeking to carve out youthful identities. They were established men, rooted in other communities, some of which were other knowledge communities. The groups to which they belonged were interlocking and overlapped. Dennis Palmu has pointed out the way in which F. J. A. Hort, for example, was a member of the committee to revise the Bible, an Apostle, and a member of Eranus. Henry Alford was a member of the committee to revise the Bible, an Apostle, and a member of the Metaphysical Society.[37] The same point might be made about members of the Synthetic Society. Its members had multiple intellectual and social connections and these relations magnified their importance and the significance of the Synthetic Society. Knowledge communities with such interlocking memberships, a feature of their social indeterminacy, exercised an influence larger than their numbers.

The Synthetic Society's world was highly contingent at every point in its history: whether Arthur Balfour should publish his book on religious belief, whether Ward would review it, whether his review would lead to a correspondence between them, whether they would dine together at the Junior Carlton Club, whether the members elected would be the members elected, whether at their meetings members would write the papers they wrote and whether they would respond in the way they would respond—all this was uncertain and unpredictable. In fact, it might be said that the Synthetic Society was designed to create an indeterminate social environment in which mental contingency and ambiguity would be psychologically safe.

The Rules of the Synthetic Society were designed to negotiate its contingent conceptual and social edges. The matter of elections, of membership, of attendance, of the character of papers and the manner in which they were to be discussed were elastic yet controlled, open yet closed. They sought like in difference and difference in like. Rules are about processes, not structures or results. Processes are not random; they are guided by such regulations. But the regulations of the Synthetic Society were ironic. Wilfrid Ward articulated these ironies in the first words of the first paper he gave to the society on 28 February 1896.

36 Ward, *The Wilfrid Wards and the Transition, I: The Nineteenth Century*, p. 358.

37 I am grateful to Dennis B. Palmu for providing me with this information.

> The thought of forming the Synthetic Society first occurred to a few persons differing from each other in theological opinion, and yet equally desirous of union in the effort to find a philosophical basis for religious belief.[38]

The desire for union among people 'differing from each other' to obtain a 'basis for religious belief' contains impulses which run at odds with each other yet at the same time seek convergence. The rules of the Synthetic Society limited, but also liberated. Rules create constraints, but they also liberate specific sorts of impulses. The society's procedures made certain kinds of agreements more possible than others.[39] They permitted actions of a particular kind. These rules were devices for mental and emotional negotiation. They were transactionist: they were inventions to permit invention.

In ending, it may be possible to cast the discussion in the largest possible terms. The Synthetic Society was not some sort of flight from the action of the material world. It represented a point of purchase from which ideas about the material world could be negotiated. During its years of activity the Balfours, Bryce, Haldane, and Wyndham were all in government. When the society was founded Arthur Balfour was preparing to succeed Lord Salisbury (for Bob was his uncle, after all) as leader of the Tory party and as prime minister. As he wrote to Wilfrid Ward while preparing his first paper, 'I will do my best about the paper, though more unlucky circumstances under which to ask a philosopher to compose a philosophical paper I cannot imagine, as I can hardly get through my day-to-day tasks, which are by no means philosophical.'[40] The first meeting of the society occurred on the evening of the Speaker's *levée* and Balfour, Haldane, and Bryce were in their Privy Council uniforms. Henry Scott Holland remarked, 'And you ought to have seen Haldane making a speech about Hegel in a Court suit of black velvet.'[41] Such knowledge communities as the Synthetic Society operated on the frontiers of action and thought, the margins of the material and mental worlds, seeking metaphors where they could find them in order to reconcile their different understandings about the way the world wagged.

The intimacy of the Synthetic Society served to contest knowledge about religious belief. As Bishop Gore put it, the purpose of the society was to seek agreement 'with regard to those matters which underlie our life—the great principles of philosophy and religion'.[42] What people believe is central to what they

[38] Wilfrid Ward, 'Synthetic Society', *Papers Read Before the Synthetic Society, 1896–1908*, p. 1.

[39] William M. Reddy, 'The Logic of Action, Indeterminacy, Emotion, and Historical Narrative', *History and Theory*, 40 (Dec. 2001), 31.

[40] Balfour to Wilfred Ward, 5 March 1896, quoted in Root, 'The Philsophical and Religious Thought of Arthur James Balfour (1848–1903)', p. 134.

[41] Stephen Paget (ed.), *Henry Scott Holland: Memoir and Letters* (London, 1921), p. 273.

[42] Quoted in [A.S. and E.M.S.], *Henry Sidgwick: A Memoir*, p. 556.

are. Therefore, the Synthetic Society exposed knowledge about religious belief but, in so doing, it exposed knowledge about the self. Tyrrell said: '... think the educative value of mutual understanding with a view of better self-understanding is simply enormous'.[43] The reality principle is not located in some mystical region of interiority; it is social and material. The self appears in action: in the actions of forming the Synthetic Society, in crafting its rules, in the choices involved in the election of members and chairmen, in the struggle over ideas and for understanding, in the social forms and concrete expressions of the material world. The self is not essentialist, or fixed; it is a matter of reason and choice.[44] The authority and the ethics of the self come not from nature or from the other world but in the dialectical relations between people, between intimacy and imagination in the social relations of such places as knowledge communities.

The imagination at work in the Synthetic Society and other knowledge communities was philosophical and speculative. It was concerned with examining the underlying assumptions and premises of belief. It was concerned, as Wittgenstein might put it, with what cannot be 'said' but can be 'shown'. It might not be defined, but it could be evoked.[45] It was a concern with meaning and value. Wilfrid Ward, in describing Sidgwick's qualities of mind and spirit, gave an intimation of the imaginative qualities necessary in knowledge communities like the Synthetic Society: a sympathy which goes deeper, a passion for truth, the capacity in discussing mental questions which gives it 'an almost religious earnestness', a minute, persistent dissecting process which goes beyond the logic of the question.[46] Such questions as the Synthetic Society took up, those at the margins of scholarly disciplines, on the metes and bounds of intellectual life, could not be left to specialists, to 'philosophers'. Though he worked hard during his whole career to bolster the professional character of university dons, for Sidgwick the moral judgements of specialists had to be 'aided, checked, and controlled by the moral judgement of persons with less philosophy but more special experience'.[47]

Henry Sidgwick made a big impression on the Synthetic Society, as he did on all the societies to which he belonged. When he died, the society almost died with him.[48] After he was diagnosed with the cancer that would

[43] Ward, *The Wilfrid Wards and the Transition, I: The Nineteenth Century*, pp. 372–3.

[44] Amartya Sen, 'East and West: The Reach of Reason', *New York Review of Books* (20 July 2000), p. 37, and *Reason Before Identity: The Romanes Lecture for 1998* (Oxford, 1999).

[45] W. C. Lubenow, 'Religion in the University', *Minerva*, 42 (2004), 269–83.

[46] Ward, *The Wilfrid Wards and the Transition, I: The Nineteenth Century*, pp. 344–5.

[47] Quoted in Stefan Collini, '"My Roles and Duties": Henry Sidgwick as Philosopher, Professor and Public Moralist', in Ross Harrison (ed.), *Henry Sidgwick* (Oxford, 2001), p. 26.

[48] Ward, *The Wilfrid Wards and the Transition, I: The Nineteenth Century*, p. 379.

kill him, Sidgwick presided over a meeting of the Synthetic Society on 25 May 1900 at which Arthur Balfour read a paper on prayer. Balfour talked of 'the instinct which impels men to appeal to a loving Ruler of the Universe'. He spoke of the difficulties of people like Sidgwick to reconcile the idea of prayer with 'their general view of the laws by which the universe is governed'.[49] Frederick Myers described Sidgwick's reaction: '[T]hus it came about that my friend's last utterance—not public indeed, but spoken intimately to a small company of like minded men—was an appeal for pure spirituality in all human supplication—a gentle summons to desire only such things as cannot pass away.'[50] This all points to the emotional features of knowledge formation and organisation.[51]

Knowledge communities are marked by conflicting and contradictory impulses. Some, the Eranus Society and the Synthetic Society for example, with loose rules and no fixed meeting places, are rather like cults. They destabilise the knowledge with which they deal. Others, the Royal Society and the British Academy for example, with their handsome buildings, Royal Charters, archives, proceedings, and necrologies, are fetishes.[52] They stabilise the knowledge with which they deal. But impulses toward destabilisation and stabilisation are not necessarily mutually exclusive. They are not opposing binaries on some institutional continuum. The former are transformational; the latter may be transactional, but as those who have studied tipping points, phase transitions, and *sattelzeits* show, transformations often occur within a pattern of transactions.[53] As a comparison of the membership of the Synthetic Society and the list of the founding fellows of the British Academy shows, the same individuals were often driven by both impulses. Henry Sidgwick, having died, could not become a Fellow of the British Academy, but he was instrumental in the Academy's creation.[54] Arthur Balfour, James Bryce, A. V. Dicey, Sir Richard Jebb, and James Ward were members of the Synthetic Society who were also founding fellows of the

[49] *Papers Read Before the Synthetic Society, 1896–1908*, pp. 331–2.

[50] Quoted in [A.S. and E.M.S.], *Henry Sidgwick: A Memoir*, p. 588.

[51] William M. Reddy, *The Navigation of Feeling: A Framework for the History of Emotions* (Cambridge, 2001).

[52] Though he may not approve of or agree with the use I make of it, I owe the distinction between cults and fetishes to Dr Richard Drayton of Corpus Christi College, Cambridge.

[53] I have not the space, nor is this the place for a full discussion of these ideas but I shall examine them more completely in a paper 'The Royal Society, the British Academy, and the Invention of "Two Cultures"', and in part three, on knowledge communities, of my book *Making Words Flesh: Authority, Society, and Deliberative Liberalism in Modern Britain, 1815–1914* (both forthcoming).

[54] Henry Sidgwick to Arthur Balfour, 26 Nov. 1899 and 20 Dec. 1899, Balfour Papers, British Library, Add. MS. 48932, ff. 106–7, 108.

British Academy.[55] Arthur Balfour regarded the Synthetic Society as ephemeral. He proposed to wind it up when Henry Sidgwick died in 1900, while, as he put it, the society 'is yet in full strength, and before the inevitable period of senile decay sets in'. He went on: 'we might bring our work to a dignified, if somewhat premature conclusion; and in a few years when, as it must inevitably happen, new schools of thought rise to prominence, hope to see its work revived by a successor'.[56] James Ward looked forward to the more fetishising features the British Academy might provide. 'Possibly', he said, 'the projected new Academy, if the project is achieved, may afford a better opportunity for philosophic discussions. The Synthetic at any rate seemed to me too much of an "*omnium gatherum*".'[57]

So, finally, knowledge is located in human relations. Knowledge communities have these characteristics: they operate with soft conceptual and social edges. They have these functions: through intimacy and imagination they create the processes for negotiating and contesting knowledge about value and meaning. They produce these results: since they construct, they separate the social from the natural; through construction they persuade. Therefore, knowledge communities are at once liberal and modern.

Now where is the rigour here, the discipline? Some might wish to write off knowledge communities of this sort as intellectually soft and socially amateurish. I think that would be wrong. The questions they raised cannot be fitted into the conceptual boxes we have constructed in twentieth-century academic disciplines, nor into the methodologies they have spawned. Because their questions were at the conceptual edges of knowledge they devised different social processes to deal with them. And these were people of action, with strong commitments to the public world, to politics and what is political. Their rigour and their discipline have to be judged against different and more interesting standards. In these knowledge communities, through intimacy and imagination, the distinction between what is professional and amateur, what is disciplinary and not, collapses in on itself. These were people of competence. Not completely creatures of the state or of the universities, from Baltimore to Berlin, in what was after all a transatlantic phenomenon, they devised knowledge communities to deal with issues which did not easily fit the emerging disciplinary or professional

[55] *Proceedings of the British Academy, 1903–1904* (London, 1904), pp. x–xi.

[56] Arthur Balfour to [Wilfrid Ward] (copy), 23 Oct. 1900, Balfour Papers, British Library, Add. MS. 49853, ff. 241–2.

[57] James Ward to Arthur Balfour, 6 Jan. 1902, Balfour Papers, British Library, Add. MS. 49854, f. 147.

niches.[58] A knowledge of knowledge communities opens a way to consider the ironies of ambiguity and points to dynamic and dialogical conceptions of understanding, complicated and complicating processes which liberate both the self and whatever is not the self and which reveal the complex social relations of those regions between the state and the university.[59] Discussing the soft conceptual and sociological edges of knowledge communities like the Synthetic Society is a way of speaking precisely about ambiguity.

[58] Daniel T. Rodgers, *Atlantic Crossings: Social Politics in a Progressive Age* (Cambridge, MA, and London, 1998), pp. 25–7; for the Austrian marginal utility school and the German historical school of economists, see Thomas L. Haskell, *Objectivity Is Not Neutrality: Explanatory Schemes in History* (Baltimore and London, 1998), pp. 91–2; for the relationship between Oliver Wendell Holmes and Sir Frederick Pollock, see Louis Menand, *The Metaphysical Club: A Story of Ideas in America* (New York, 2001), pp. 62, 68, 77, 217, 345, 436–7, and Mark DeWolfe Howe (ed.), *Holmes–Pollock Letters: The Correspondence of Mr. Justice Holmes, Jr., and Sir Frederick Pollock, 1874–1932* (Cambridge, MA, 1941), 2 vols.

[59] See Lorenzo C. Simpson, *The Unfinished Project: Towards a Postmodern Humanism* (London, 2002) and Lois McNay, 'A New Humanity', *Times Literary Supplement*, 27 Dec. 2002, p. 25.

CHAPTER SEVENTEEN

The Academy Abroad: The Nineteenth-Century Origin of the British School at Athens

MARY BEARD AND CHRISTOPHER STRAY

In March 1882, *The Times* offered its readers a thundering attack on a new development in classical studies: 'We sincerely hope,' the article opened,

> that the ardent but mistaken Hellenists who are trying to establish a ... school of classical studies in Athens will take counsel of their good sense before it is too late and abandon the project. Greek is a good thing, no doubt, whether taken plain from the grammar or in history, archaeology, or literature. But as President Barnard has very sensibly pointed out, it is wholly unnecessary to go clear to Athens to get it. 'It certainly seems to me,' says this experienced educator, 'that if only classical knowledge is to be acquired, students can be instructed fully as well in this country as in Athens.' We are glad to have this utterance of a cool-headed and conservative college President to temper and check the unthinking enthusiasm of the younger Fellows, like Mr F. J. Peyster, Prof. Goodwin, Dr Potter and Prof. White, before our colleagues are fully committed to the foolish undertaking. The intentions of these young gentlemen cannot be questioned, of course. They were doubtless inspired by a sincere zeal for the cause of sounder classical education. But their scheme of a ... school for the study of the language and literature of Greece on the very spot where that language and literature reached their highest development is manifestly absurd.

These words did not appear in *The Times* of London, but in *The New York Times*:[1] President Barnard was the famous late-nineteenth century President of Columbia University; Peyster, Goodwin and the rest were members of the US (classical) establishment.[2] Nor is the thunder quite so simple as it seems.

[1] 31 March, 1882, quoted in L. E. Lord, *A History of the American School of Classical Studies at Athens, 1882–1942: an Intercollegiate Project* (Cambridge, MA, 1947), pp. 8–10.

[2] All four were members of the founding committee of the American School of Classical Studies at Athens: Frederick de Peyster was a New York lawyer; William Watson Goodwin, Eliot Professor of Greek Literature at Harvard; Henry C. Potter a Bishop of the Episcopalian Church; John Williams White, Professor of Greek at Harvard.

This is, in fact, a journalistic parody of the arguments of President Barnard, who—like some others in 1882—was none too keen in devoting part of his university budget to the establishment of an American outpost in Athens; and it is a parody that becomes increasingly obvious and ludicrous as it goes on.

> Is not American Greek good enough for Americans? If the time has come when an American boy can no longer sit on a wooden bench in New Haven, Cambridge or Amherst, and ... analyze the metres of a chorus of Sophocles with the same profound unintelligibility and painstaking misunderstanding that have characterized the class-room work of our colleges for the past century, then Greek is no longer a fit study for the youth of this Republic ... It is not to the Orient we must go for our Greek, but to the free and boundless West. Go to Chicago, not to Athens, for your Professors of Greek, gentlemen![3]

As an American parody, this article prompts reflections and questions that underlie much of this paper: the contestations that inevitably surround such radical educational innovations as the foundation of 'schools of classical studies' abroad; the different, or similar, perspectives that you find in different national initiatives (the British supporters of 'schools abroad', predictably enough, waved the banner of the example of the United States, without allowing a chink of the American dissent to show through); and how we can now read the rhetoric of such Victorian debates about 'the organisation of knowledge', couched as they are in the jargon-loaded, ironising and 'much-more-foreign-than-we-think' idiom of nineteenth-century intellectuals.

We approach those larger questions through an, apparently, more parochial story: the foundation and early history of the British School at Athens, launched in 1883, the first of a small group of British academic institutes abroad—including the Rome School founded in 1899, and later in more distant locations such as Baghdad (1932), Ankara (1948), Tehran (1961) and Amman (1978).[4] We are able to draw on previously unpublished documents concerning the origins of the Athens School to expose some of the hard work, the behind-the-scenes manoeuvres and lobbying, the late-Victorian patronage and string-pulling usually hidden under the brief triumphalist narrative of an institution's

[3] The reference to the analysis of metre is probably a jibe at J. H. H. Schmidt, whose theories of Greek metre were adopted by White of Harvard, as well as by Richard Jebb in Britain. Despite the attack here, Barnard was not an out-and-out conservative: he was, for example, a supporter of women's university education (hence Barnard College).

[4] There are published histories of both the Athens and Rome Schools: G. A. Macmillan, 'A Short History of the British School at Athens, 1886–1911', *ABSA*, XVII (1910–1911), ix–xxxviii; H. Waterhouse, *The British School at Athens: the First Hundred Years* (BSA Supplementary Vol. 19; London, 1986); A. Wallace-Hadrill, *The British School at Rome: One Hundred Years* (London, 2001); T. P. Wiseman, *A Short History of the British School at Rome* (London, 1990). For the American School of Classical Studies at Athens, see Lord, *A History of the American School*.

'foundation'. At the same time we try to show how the story of such foreign institutes intersects with many of the key issues in the rethinking of Classics (and what was to count as 'Classics') in the late Victorian period, when the subject was being—both radically and conservatively —redesigned to produce something like the disciplinary structure we have today. These issues involve: the role of so-called 'archaeology' within the study of 'Classics', and how that 'archaeology' was to be defined and bounded; the relationship between the study of Classics and the modern lands of Greece and Italy, particularly in the light of growing 'middle-class' tourism and its infrastructures. As Jane Harrison's star pupil, Jessie Crum, was to write in her diary after a visit to the Acropolis in Athens on 27 March 1901: 'the whole of Cambridge seemed assembled'—and proceeded to list sixteen of the Cambridge Faculty also on the Rock that very morning.[5] This was a degree of integration of Greece itself into academic horizons that would have been inconceivable fifty years earlier, though it has other implications too, of course, to which we shall return.

The British School at Athens continues to exist and to thrive, with a whole series of its own powerful and self-fashioning mythologies, which makes exploring its history both more interesting and more difficult. Anyone who has spent any time in any of the British Schools abroad will appreciate that their functions, their disciplinary priorities and their role within the foreign communities in which they are situated, are deeply contested; that controversies about whom, and what, these institutions are for have become integral to their contemporary definition, character and image. Part of the point of this paper is to suggest that such disputes were integral to these institutions from their very foundation; they are not, in other words, an indication that the late twentieth century somehow 'lost the message'. Or to put that the other way round: scratch the surface of this paper and you will find that we are suggesting that most of the definitional arguments within late Victorian Classics—whether in the case of the foreign schools or more generally—are ones that we still (must) debate; there are very few nineteenth-century controversies about the subject's intellectual organisation and its territorial and disciplinary boundaries that we have resolved or dispatched.[6]

[5] The diary is now on deposit in Cambridge University Library; see, for its background, C. Stray, 'Digs and Degrees: Jessie Crum's tour of Greece, Easter 1901', *Classics Ireland*, II (1995), 121–31.

[6] This point is emphasised in M. Beard, 'The Invention (and Re-invention) of "Group D": an archaeology of the Classical Tripos, 1879–1984' in C. Stray (ed.), *Classics in Nineteenth and Twentieth Century Cambridge: Curriculum, Culture and Community* (Cambridge Philological Society, Supplementary vol., 24, 1999), pp. 95–134 and M. Beard, 'Learning to Pick the Easy Plums: the invention of ancient history in nineteeth-century Classics', in J. Smith and C. Stray (eds.), *Teaching and Learning in Nineteenth-Century Cambridge* (History of the University of Cambridge, Texts and Studies 4, Woodbridge, 2001), 89–106.

The first glimmer of an idea about establishing a classical school in Athens is usually attributed to Richard Jebb, who wrote a letter to *The Times* in September 1878, followed up by an article in the *Contemporary Review*, urging just such a foundation.[7] Jebb was then Professor of Greek at Glasgow, but with his eye firmly fixed (so everyone assumed) on the Regius Chair of Greek in Cambridge—and his finger remained, despite six months a year residence in Scotland, in most Cambridge pies. He was duly elected to the Regius chair when B. H. Kennedy at last died in 1889, and became a Member of Parliament for the university in 1891, devoting a good deal of effort to being influential.[8] Certainly he was, as we shall see, a mover and shaker in getting the Schools off the ground. But he was not the first to 'go public' with a proposal. For in July 1878 William Wolfe Capes—a much less pushy Oxford classical don, antiquarian and historian (immortalised in the guise of St Barnabas in the stained glass windows of St Mary the Virgin, Bramshott, where he was for a time rector)—had already published an article in *Fraser's Magazine*, describing in detail the structure and the academic achievements of the École Française at Athens (founded in 1846) and at Rome (founded in 1873).[9] His article ended with an appeal for a similar initiative in England:

> It is not creditable to English scholarship that these materials of history [the material remains in Greece and Italy] should be so little known among us, and that the studies of our Universities should have drawn so scantily from these abundant sources. Large chapters of the history of the social life in Greece and Rome are being entirely re-written, as new evidence is coming to hand from various sides, but the original data to be found in the inscriptions and the coins are seldom referred to in our text books, and are quite unknown for the most to our students, as indeed to many of their teachers. An institution like the École Française at Athens and at Rome might be of signal use in this respect.

He proceeded to outline a scheme for diverting various slices of Oxbridge fellowship money and endowments towards this purpose, while reassuring his

[7] *The Times,* 18 Sept., 1878, 11 under the title 'Archaeology in Athens and Rome'; *Contemporary Review*, XXXIII (1878), 776–91; and see below, p. 382.

[8] On Jebb's career, see C. Jebb, *Life and Letters of Sir R. C. Jebb* (Cambridge, 1907). Two chapters on Jebb and his work are included in C. Stray (ed.), *The Owl of Minerva: the Cambridge Praelections of 1906* (Cambridge Philological Society, Supplementary Vol., 2004 forthcoming).

[9] *Fraser's Magazine*, CIII (1878), 103–12. Capes was more productive and energetic than this summary suggests (his bibliography includes an edition of Livy Books XXI and XXII (London, 1883), a history of the English Church in the fourteenth and fifteenth centuries (London, 1900) and numerous editions of ecclesiastical archives); he was also a great traveller, who is said once to have walked from Oxford to Rome and back. His allusions to 'large chapters of the history of the social life in Greece and Rome ... being entirely re-written' may be a reference to (e.g.) J. P. Mahaffy's *Social Life in Greece* (London, 1874) and *Rambles and Studies in Greece* (London, 1876).

readers that it really could all be done on the cheap: 'No costly buildings or appliances would be required; the materials for study exist already in abundance in the museums, galleries of art, and ancient monuments: the classical lands would be libraries of reference themselves, and the *genius loci* would do more to stimulate research than any professorial lectures.'

However half-baked this scheme was, Jebb saw his opening. His first business-like letter to *The Times* rehearsed the archaeological achievements of the French and German Schools in Athens (the German arrangements went back to the old Prussian 'Institute of Archaeological Correspondence' in Rome, the 'Corrispondenza'—but had been reorganised with parallel Athenian and Roman branches in 1874), and suggested the establishment of an English equivalent. He seems, predictably enough, to have thought carefully about how exactly to phrase this appeal—or so the various drafts preserved in the archive of King's College London suggest. One, apparently written while in Athens, tried out a much more high-pitched, political appeal: 'I stood yesterday on the acropolis of Athens, as the setting sun lit up the mountains and the sea; there at my feet were the waters where the tide of Asiatic barbarism was rolled back for two thousand years ...'; and he went on to lament the likelihood of a new Oriental threat to Greek freedom.[10]

The follow-up article in the *Contemporary Review* laid out more details of a possible scheme. Jebb again summarised the organisation of the French and German schools, their library provision, accommodation, staffing and management structure; he contrasted the rather dirigiste programme of the French School (with a clear syllabus laid down for each of the students) with the more laid back (and cheaper) German version—which 'leaves the adult student more at liberty to follow his own bent'. Not surprisingly, he concluded that the German version was more appropriate and feasible—given only the use (as Capes had suggested) of some Oxbridge fellowship money which could send some suitable Oxbridge graduates to classical lands; all that was needed besides was an English guiding committee and a Director or some kind of secretariat on the spot in Athens and Rome to advise the students. A house and a library could come later, if necessary.[11]

Nothing happened. But some years later Jebb was to make a further intervention, in the *Fortnightly Review* for May 1883. He had been in touch with Thomas Escott, the *Fortnightly*'s editor, since the previous August, when Escott had asked Jebb to write for his magazine. His first article, 'A tour in the Troad', appeared in April 1883, closely followed by what was now a

[10] R. C. Jebb papers, King's College London archives, with *The Times*, 18 Sept. 1878, 11.

[11] *Contemporary Review*, XXXIII (1878), 776–91.

narrower proposal than before for a British classical initiative abroad: an appeal for a British Institute in Athens alone.[12] The arguments were similar to those deployed earlier ('a classical training cannot be better supplemented than by travel and study in Hellenic or Hellenised lands') though now the example of the American School (founded in 1882, despite the lack of enthusiasm from President Barnard) could be added to the French and Germans. Jebb felt able to be even more explicit about the School's aims and objectives: it was to 'promote archaeological science by the exploration of sites, by the collection of inscriptions and in every other branch of kindred research'; in addition, it was to act 'as a centre for British travellers who wished to supplement their classical studies by an intelligent survey of the classical lands'.

Crucially, at this point Jebb addressed the issue of funding head-on. In a dazzling display of competence ('speaking not without knowledge of house-hunting at Athens') he costed out the whole project—which was now to include a house for the Director (whether rented or built) and a library. In short, what was needed was an endowment of £18,900 (almost exactly, and not coincidentally, what the Americans had calculated they needed in 1881). The key section in his article, however, was the final one. Here he addressed not so much the raw cost, but where the money was to come from. 'No assistance whatever can be expected from Government. It is well to look this fact in the face at once, since attempts to blink it could only end in disappointment.' It would have to be private endowment.

Jebb's spin brilliantly wove together some high Victorian wit ('When Joshua Barnes was bringing out his edition of Homer, he extorted the consent of Mrs Barnes to the investment of her fortune in that work by representing the Iliad as the composition of King Solomon') with what we would now call the sociology of private finance initiatives, plus some deft comparison between the euergetism of ancient culture itself and nineteenth-century benefaction. He took the example of the richest Athenian of them all, Herodes Atticus, a millionaire of the second century AD. Herodes, he said, was a great benefactor—'but the distinction of his munificence was versatility not originality'. There were plenty of his equivalents in late nineteenth-century Britain.

> The British Herodes Atticus is the very rich man who restores a cathedral at his own cost, who provides a picture gallery for the dwellers at Bethnal Green, who presents a public park to the toilers of some grimy town, who heads the subscription list whenever some calamity of exceptional magnitude appeals to the comprehensive

[12] 'A Plea for a British Institute at Athens', *Fortnightly Review*, NS XXXIII (May, 1883), 705–14. The now separate story of the foundation of the British School at Rome is taken up by Wiseman, *A Short History* and Wallace-Hadrill, *The British School.*

> charities of the Mansion House ... Of such men happily this country has not a few. What we seem to lack is... rather a more original and inventive instinct of munificence.

Namely the kind of benefactor who would chance his arm to found a British School at Athens, a 'Victorian Maecenas'.

How that money was, in fact, raised throws vivid light on the mechanisms of patronage for academic projects in Victorian England. Unpublished letters preserved in the British School give a rare glimpse of Jebb's abilities (and difficulties) in manipulating his powerful contacts towards his own academic goals. It becomes clear from these that, since the appearance of his article in the *Contemporary Review*, he had been taking soundings among friends, and actual and potential allies. Several of them had poured cold water both on the prospect of raising £20,000, and on his hopes of securing support from the Treasury. His friend Sidney Colvin wrote to him on 6 December 1882:[13]

> On the preliminary question whether £20,000, or any similar sum, could be raised by subscription, I confess I have much misgiving. I do not know the history of the fund for the Celtic chair: but should imagine that zeal for philology, or archaeology contributed but a small proportion of the sum, and that zeal for the honour of a quasi-national cause was the powerful instrument of extraction. Could we hope for any equally potent motive in England for things Hellenic? That you and Newton are hopeful is very encouraging. But personally I do not see how to rely on anything but instructed millionaires.

A few months later another friend, Frederick Pollock, commented in similar vein on a set of proposals Jebb had drawn up:[14]

> I agree generally with your paper of suggestions: the only hope that strikes me as rash is that which you express in the last paragraph but one. I don't think the Treasury is likely to be moved in that direction for a long time yet—especially as there is a great deal still to be done for the proper care and housing of our own national collections.

In his own response, William Gladstone, then prime minister, significantly made no mention of state funding, focusing instead on the ancient universities:[15]

> The only point on which I am tempted to remark is the relation of the scheme to the Government and to the Universities. The great endowments existing in England

[13] This letter and the other quoted here were sent to the British School at Athens' London office in 1935 by Jebb's nephew, also Richard Jebb. They are now in the School's archive in Athens and are quoted by permission of the Committee of Management. The 'Newton' referred to here is Charles Newton of the British Museum (see below, p. 379). The reference to the Celtic chair is probably to the Edinburgh Chair (est. 1882), rather than the Oxford Chair established at Jesus College in 1876. A campaign for the Edinburgh chair led by J. S. Blackie had by April 1882 collected £14,000.

[14] 2 Feb. 1883.

[15] 6 Feb. 1883.

> create a broad difference between our case, and that of France or Germany. This you have frankly recognized in contemplating public subscription as your main resource. But I should have thought that more might be expected, than your paper contemplates, from the official action, so to call it, of the Universities, in respect both of authority, and of funds.

Jebb's main problem, apart from the size of the fund and the difficulty of working out where to get the money from, was that the Hellenic Society council, the obvious organising group for a campaign, was divided on the issue and rather lukewarm about his own proposal. Jebb himself, typically, sensed conspiracy. His suspects were the Oxford classicist A. H. Sayce and J. P. Mahaffy of Dublin, whose savage review of a book Jebb had published in 1876 had led to a bitter exchange of pamphlets.[16] George Macmillan, whose firm published both Mahaffy and Jebb, was stuck in the middle; and since he was a friend of Mahaffy (their tour of Greece in 1877 had in fact led to the foundation of the Hellenic Society), Jebb was for some time suspicious of Macmillan too.

Yet Macmillan had a fruitful—and what was to turn out to be a winning— suggestion:[17]

> Your plan of action too seems to me to be the right one. But I cannot, with all my zeal, feel hopeful about raising such a sum as £20,000—unless the Prince of Wales will take it under his wing, like the Royal College of Music. I wonder if the fraternal bond between the Princess and King George could not in some way be brought to bear.

Jebb was able to pursue this suggestion through his link with Thomas Escott. On 3 April, Jebb sent the text for his article in the *Fortnightly* to Escott, and urged him to show it to Lord Carnarvon, the Prince's private secretary, before publication. On the 29th Jebb was advising Escott on the best way to handle a meeting with the Prince of Wales and his younger brother Prince Leopold. He stressed that it was vital to establish 'whether their sympathy was likely to be warm and active, or whether, on the other hand, it did not rise above the temperature of ordinary courtesy'.[18]

[16] The offending book was Jebb's *The Attic Orators* (London, 1876). Mahaffy reviewed it in *The Academy* IX (1876 [1 April]), 314–16; Jebb responded with a pamphlet, *The Attic Orators from Antiphon to Isaeus: Some Remarks on an Article by the Rev. Prof. J. P. Mahaffy in The Academy of April 1, 1876* (London, 1876). Mahaffy replied with *The Attic Orators from Antiphon to Isaeus: Reply to the Remarks of R. C. Jebb Esq., M.A. on a Review in The Academy* (London, 1876), and Jebb replied again in *The Attic Orators from Antiphon to Isaeus: A Rejoinder to Prof. Mahaffy's Reply* (London, 1876).

[17] 22 Feb. 1883. The Princess of Wales was the sister of King George I of the Hellenes, previously Prince Christian of Schleswig-Holstein.

[18] R. C. Jebb to T. H. Escott, 29 April 1883 (Escott papers). British Library, Add. MS 58783, f.11. The other Jebb/Escott letters referred to belong to the same sequence (Aug. 1882–May 1884).

It turned out to be warm enough. The royal connection was successfully established, and a meeting arranged at HRH's official residence, Marlborough House, for 25 June. About eighty notables assembled, including Mr Gladstone, Lord Salisbury and Lord Rosebery. The doubters on the Hellenic Society's council had by now jumped aboard the royal bandwagon, and Jebb gained advice from them on future action, especially from Charles Newton, whose position as Keeper of Greek and Roman Antiquities at the British Museum made him a crucial figure. A management committee was formed and within two years sufficient money had been raised to build a Director's house on land donated by the Greek government; and by 1886 the school even had a Director installed, the architectural historian F. C. Penrose, together with a handful of students.[19]

Beyond the day-to-day domestic and institutional history of the Athens School in its early years—the turn-over of directors, the more or less successful, or awkward, students, the internal squabbles typical of almost any expatriate institution, the usual incentives to spend more money than was available—a few themes, of success, failure, and innovation, stand out.

First, again, finance. Within ten years of its foundation, after an appeal to the Treasury signed by an impressively motley crew of clerics, politicians and academics, the British School at Athens received a government grant of (initially) £500 per annum. And in the same year (1895), with the Prince of Wales being induced to weigh in once more on the School's behalf, a further appeal for funds was made, which elicited amongst other new income an annual grant from the University of Cambridge of £100. The School continued to harp on about its poverty, and in particular its relative poverty when compared with its equivalent institutions in Athens. But the fact is that by the end of the century, and only fifteen years from its experimental creation, this outpost in Athens must count as a reasonably well-subsidised institution of British research and higher education, in receipt of a substantial public grant. True, British classicists constantly trailed the £1,400 annual income of the American School; though it is not clear, when the different capital costs and the added expense of distance for the Americans are taken into account, that the British were substantially worse off.[20]

Second, gender. Within all the predictable constraints, the School was a mixed institution from its inception. One version of the School's history tells this as a story of exclusion: women were not originally allowed to participate in excavations run by the School, nor (once a hostel had been built

[19] Waterhouse, *The British School*, 7–9.
[20] Macmillan, 'A Short History', xii–xiii.

for students at the school in 1895) could they reside there. On the other hand, women were admitted as students almost from the beginning (in 1890, Eugenie Sellers, later as Mrs Arthur Strong (widow) to be Assistant Director of the Rome School, became the first female student, and many followed). Sellers's letters from Greece at that time show her operating with considerable freedom in the archaeological world of Athens. In creating an academic institution outside the British (and especially Oxbridge) context, even when they anticipated the students being drawn 'from the two Universities', the founders of the School did not narrowly replicate the gender rules and distinctions that applied at home.[21]

Third, excavation. From the beginning of the twentieth century, after the dramatic intervention of Arthur Evans at Knossos, the British School at Athens was associated with flagship excavation of prehistoric Greece (and has been ever since). The first fifteen years of the School's activity is a quite different story. Despite the lure of the major sites dug by the French and Germans (the Germans had got hold of Olympia, the French of Delphi), there was not enough money for anything on a grand scale, until the government grant kicked in. Instead they put what resources they had into surveying (well) Byzantine churches[22] and into excavating (badly) the Boeotian town of Megalopolis, and particularly its theatre. Driving this excavation were the then controversial questions about the technical details of ancient stagecraft and theatrical design, particularly the layout and form of the classical Greek stage. Similar concerns lay behind one of the first excavations by the American school in Athens, at the theatre of Thorikos—not to mention the many late nineteenth-century attempts in England to re-enact 'original Greek drama' on the London, or Oxbridge, stage. Although we might now easily assume that literary concerns alone gave the impulse to this revival of performances of Greek tragedy in the original language, archaeology and accurate archaeological reconstruction were as significant in the minds of most directors, producers and actors.[23]

[21] For Sellers's activities in Athens, see M. Beard, *The Invention of Jane Harrison* (Cambridge, MA, 2000), pp. 68–70; on women's involvement in the School more generally, D. W. J. Gill, '"The Passion of Hazard": women at the British School at Athens before the First World War', *ABSA*, XCVII (2002), 491–510.

[22] The earliest Byzantine projects and their funding are described in Macmillan, 'A Short History', x, xvi, xxiv–xxv.

[23] See, for example, P. E. Easterling, 'The Early Years of the Cambridge Greek Play, 1882–1912', in Stray (ed.), *Classics in Nineteenth- and Twentieth-Century Cambridge*, pp. 27–47, esp. pp. 31–32. She notes the involvement of Charles Waldstein, see below n. 26, in the earliest Cambridge productions. John Todhunter's production of *Helena in Troas*, in London 1886, was particularly notable for its attempt to reconstruct ancient stage design.

The excavation at Megalopolis was, frankly, a disaster—on any standard of archaeology, nineteenth-, twentieth- or twenty-first century; and their work was devastatingly criticised by the German archaeological doyen in Athens, Wilhelm Dörpfeld. Miss Sellers was in a way lucky to be excluded from participating. For her letters make it clear that she was well aware that Dörpfeld had seen through the British muddle and archaeological misinterpretation: although the excavators had convinced themselves that their discoveries supported the view that classical Greek actors performed on a raised stage, with the chorus below, Dörpfeld saw that the remains which had been uncovered suggested exactly the reverse (namely that the classical chorus and actors performed on the same level).[24] In the lustre of Evans and other notable successes of the early twentieth century, the official mythology of the School has conveniently forgotten these first campaigns of excavation; but it was a very rocky start.

Fourth, internationalism. The School's official documentation constantly marks a rivalrous distance between the British School and the other foreign academies in Athens. Even when the American School (which though established earlier found a permanent site slightly later than the British) began to be built right next door, the British politely rejected American overtures about sharing a library and lecture hall. The only thing they have ever agreed to share is a tennis court.[25] But underneath and around such formal demarcation, there was a considerable amount of academic contact between the different schools—and sometimes indeed an overlap of personnel. The notorious Charles Waldstein, the first Lecturer and Reader in Classical Archaeology at Cambridge, was between 1888 and 1892 simultaneously Director of the American School in Athens.[26] The British School at Athens provided one of the main late nineteenth-century contexts for British classicists to meet their European and American counterparts.

So far we have discussed the problems of launching the British School at Athens largely in terms of funding, benefaction and patronage. These are certainly important considerations (and Jebb's clever piece on the nature of British and ancient munificence is as insightful as it is witty). But there are

[24] The Megalopolis controversy (and the role of Sellers) is summarised in Beard, *Jane Harrison*, pp. 66–70. The flavour of the sometimes ill-tempered muddle is conveyed by W. Dörpfeld, E. A. Gardner, W. Loring, joint statement in *CR*, 5 (1891), 284–5; E. A. Gardner *et al.*, *Excavations at Megalopolis, 1890–1891*, *JHS*, Suppl. 1 (1892), esp. 69–91; W. Loring, 'The Theatre at Megalopolis', *JHS*, 13 (1892–3), 356–8.

[25] These negotiations are described (from the American side) by Lord, *A History of the American School*, pp. 30–2.

[26] For a brief resumé of Waldstein's career, see Beard, 'An archaeology of the Classical Tripos', pp. 117–22 with the hilarious caricature in E. F. Benson, *As We Were: a Victorian Peep Show* (London and New York, 1930), pp. 139–42.

other issues at stake, which relate to the intellectual rather than the economic background against which the Athens School was conceived. Some of these were raised in the parody of President Barnard and his ventriloquised claim that it would be better to go to Chicago than to Athens if you wanted to learn Greek. In this final section we shall look at the intellectual context out of which the British School at Athens was founded and developed, at its impact on Classics and classical archaeology in Britain and at some wider debates about the nature of foreign study and archaeological work 'in the field' in which the School was inevitably implicated. In discussing the classical controversies in Britain through the period of the School's foundation, we have drawn primarily on material from Jebb's own University of Cambridge, though similar conflicts were at that point being fought in many British classical institutions.

Jebb's first plea for English Schools abroad in *The Times* and *Contemporary Review* in 1878 was timely and loaded. For his starting point—namely that *archaeology* was an integral and important part of Classics—was at that precise moment the cause of bitter dispute. As is well known, through much of the 1860s and 1870s, in Cambridge and elsewhere, the boundaries of Classics as a discipline were being even more aggressively redefined than ever. The standard way of seeing this process is as a battle between traditionalists on the one hand (the advocates of 'pure scholarship' who wanted the Classics to consist in little more than translation, from Latin and Greek to English and, *par excellence*, from English into Latin and Greek) and reformers on the other, those who urged the inclusion within the discipline of a much wider range of classical subjects—ancient philosophy, literary studies, history, law and archaeology. That polarisation in many ways oversimplifies the conflict, bypassing some of the most radical proposals on all sides (the inclusion, for example, of compulsory Sanskrit as a third classical language next to Latin and Greek) and ignoring the closely connected and equally pressing issue of how Classics was to define its position in relation to the range of new disciplines that were themselves at that moment being devised (it was, for example, possible for both so-called 'conservatives' and 'radicals' to think that the best disciplinary home for ancient philosophy was with Moral Sciences, not Classics).[27]

It was the role of archaeology within Classics, particularly at Cambridge, that provoked the most opposition, some of it not unlike the parody in the *New York Times* that we quoted as an introduction. The old guard, notably the

[27] An overview of these changes and debates is provided by C. Stray, *Classics Transformed: schools, universities, and society in England, 1830–1960* (Oxford, 1998), pp. 117–66, and Beard, 'An archaeology of the Classical Tripos'.

(quite appalling, if not self-parodying) sixth-form master at Charterhouse, T. E. Page, was totally opposed to seeing Classics formally embrace a subject that was not founded on what had long been dubbed 'the best' classical authors, or on the linguistic training that went hand-in-hand with the study of the 'best authors'. They might tolerate an examination in ancient philosophy on the grounds that it was strongly focused on the text of Plato, but they viciously ridiculed an examination 'in which distinction may be obtained for a knowledge of chorography and topography, of Italian dialects and the *Corpus Inscriptionum*'. Even some of the more open-minded wondered whether archaeology would not be better served by travelling scholarships than an examination in the Tripos.[28]

A compromise was reached in 1879, whereby 'pure scholarship' continued to reign supreme in Part I and all the other delights of Classics, from Plato to pots were found a home in a new optional Part II. Archaeology was firmly put on the Cambridge Classical map, comprising one whole 'section' out of five in Part II. It is hard not to see Jebb's plea for archaeological schools abroad as, in part, a clever and well-placed intervention in that particular dispute. The foundation of a British School of Archaeology in Athens by a clutch of leading Classicists was a powerful argument for the inclusion of archaeology within the discipline; while at the same time the teaching of the new subject at Cambridge and Oxford would create further demand (and a ready-made clientèle) for such foreign schools.

But there is more to it than that. It is not just a question of whether archaeology was to be incorporated within Classics, but what kind of archaeology, and what difference the British School at Athens was to make to the definition of archaeological study in the last decades of the nineteenth century. Or, to put it in more general terms, what difference did the existence of an academic institution abroad, on Greek soil, make to disciplinary disputes at home? The background to this is extremely complicated, more so than there is space fully to discuss here. We should not forget, for example, that Jebb himself in the late 1870s was deeply embroiled in the long running arguments over Schliemann's discoveries, suggesting that Schliemann had misidentified what he had found at Hissarlik and Mycenae, that it was not 'Homeric' and much of it not even prehistoric.[29]

[28] *The Times*, 19 March 1879, 5; 24 March, 1879, 11. For a (somewhat) more favourable view of Page than that offered here, see Stray, *Classics Transformed*, pp. 147–8; and more favourable still, W. J. N. Rudd, *T. E. Page, Schoolmaster Extraordinary* (Bristol, 1981).

[29] For the British controversies over Schliemann (which included vigorous support from the likes of Gladstone and Mahaffy, as well as opposition from Jebb and his friends), see W. M. Calder III and J. Cobet (eds.), *Heinrich Schliemann nach hundert Jahren* (Frankfurt, 1990), articles by D. A. Traill and J. Vaio; D. Traill, *Schliemann of Troy: Treasure and Deceit* (London, 1995), pp. 216–50. The level of insults tossed about in the argument can be judged from Jebb's review article in the *Fortnightly Review*, NS XXXV (April, 1884), 433–52.

Something of this decidedly ill-tempered campaign underlay his archaeological 'enthusiasm' at this point. But—however we second guess Jebb's motives—the crucial fact is that classical 'archaeology' as it was defined in the new Classical Tripos in 1879 was significantly different from the discipline as we define it today and significantly different from its more specialised European equivalents. It included, alongside the study of architecture, sculpture, artefacts, coins and inscriptions, the much wider interdisciplinary repertoire of comparative religion and mythology, social history and 'antiquities' in the broadest sense. It aspired to be what we would call a 'cultural history' of the classical world, and students in the early days of the classical archaeology examination at Cambridge were asked questions on the organisation of slave labour, human sacrifice and ancient dice-playing as well as the more predictable topics of sculptural style and the development of the Athenian Acropolis.[30]

The narrowing of 'archaeology' to something like 'our' subject took place relatively quickly through the 1880s and 1890s and into the early years of the twentieth century. If the foundation of the British School at Athens had originally played a part in the launch of classical archaeology in its broadest sense, then its operations over the first decades of its history—and particularly the international connections with 'European' archaeology which it fostered—almost certainly had some part to play in the changing definition. Miss Sellers found Athens a place where she came face to face with German archaeological scholarship, in the shape of Wilhelm Dörpfeld; Charles Waldstein, who was for several years based in Athens as well as Cambridge, had a foot in a number of European intellectual camps; and when Jessie Crum met 'the whole of Cambridge' crawling over the Acropolis in March 1901 (many of them based at the School), it was already an academic world that was prizing archaeological objects, stones and excavation above theories of myth or ancient Greek gambling. It is hard to resist the conclusion that the British archaeological base in Athens acted as an entry port for an increasingly European, if not German, definition of what archaeology was to become.[31]

The issues are, however, still more complicated than this, and there are other key questions about how such foreign schools related to the broader picture of the organisation of classical knowledge in the late nineteenth century:

[30] Beard, 'An archaeology of the Classical Tripos' quotes these and a further selection of early questions in Archaeology.

[31] Crum also gives a flavour of the social life between the various foreign Schools in Athens, including a meeting between Jane Harrison and the prominent German art historian Adolf Furtwängler (who loathed each other); they were playfully reintroduced by Dörpfeld over tea at the German Institute. See Stray, 'Digs and Degrees', 126–7.

what difference did it make when the institutional frameworks were established for confronting material culture *in situ* rather than in the library? How did the Academy, in all senses of the word, incorporate Greece? How did archaeology define, or re-define, Greece for itself and its own purposes? Many factors are relevant here, not least the increasing incorporation of Greece into the relatively familiar world of middle-class travel. So, for example, each new edition of Murray's *Handbook to Greece* through the nineteenth century clearly documents the growing infrastructure of elite and sub-elite tourism in Athens especially. They document more, and more European, hotels, more convenient travel arrangements, and—notwithstanding such nasty incidents as the Dilessi murders, when a party of tourists were captured by 'brigands' near Marathon and some eventually killed (1870)—an increasingly secure environment.[32] It is this increasing opportunity for autopsy, combined with the academic facilities of the new British School, that helped write 'fieldwork' and first-hand acquaintance of antiquities into the classical archaeological agenda at home.

Yet there is a sting in the tail. *Autopsy* was certainly built into the growth and definition of British classical archaeology. But a simple model of a gradually increasing emphasis on what we would call 'field-visits' still underestimates the complexities of the ideas of place and context in nineteenth-century archaeology. It tends to occlude further questions that lay at the heart of some of classical archaeology's dilemmas: where was the raw material for classical archaeology to be found? Was it essentially an Oxbridge desk job as Frazer had made anthropology (the author of the *Golden Bough* was, after all, heralded by British newspapers at the end of his career as the man who had spent all his life working on 'savages' but had never met one)?[33]

One side of these debates continued to stress the spirit of adventure and exotic exploration that was a part of all 'hands-on' archaeology. But on the other side an enormous amount of cultural energy went into domesticating Athens and its archaeological environment. We tend now to joke about the British School at Athens being an 'Oxbridge by the sea'; but that is, of course, exactly what some of its founders and early users had in mind—a tool of

[32] The first edition of the *Handbook* was published in 1840 (London) only a few years after the end of the devastating war of Independence; by the seventh edition in 1900 Greece could be presented as an altogether more domestic environment. For the Dilessi murders, see R. J. H. Jenkins, *The Dilessi Murders* (London, 1961).

[33] 'He is fond of saying he has never met a savage in his life' (according to a syndicated article published on 15 April 1936 in, among other newspapers, the *Northern Daily Mail*, *West Lancashire Evening Gazette*, *Yorkshire Evening News*, *South Wales Evening Post*). Frazer's desk-bound (and classicising) construction of the 'Other' and its popular appeal for the British press in the early twentieth century is one theme of M. Beard, 'Frazer, Leach and Virgil: the popularity (and unpopularity) of the *Golden Bough*', *CSSH*, 34.2 (1992), 203–24.

British study, and on British terms, abroad. And along with that went a variety of radical claims that saw the archaeological material of Greece not as an aspect of potentially dangerous foreign territory, but as principally a part of the scholar's resources. Witness, for example, Wolfe Capes's confidence that a library was not needed in any school abroad because the classical lands themselves were 'libraries'; and even the radical Frederic Harrison (no relation of Jane) writing an article in 1890 in the *Nineteenth Century* which advocated the return to Athens of the Elgin marbles, used the argument that Athens was now 'a central archaeological school' and so, as it were, needed some of her specimens back.[34] Jessie Crum's perceptive comments that Athens had effectively become an outpost of Cambridge, was an echo of the remarks of J. E. Sandys on his visit to Delphi in the 1880s; he took care to note the presence (or absence) of friends' names in the visitors' book, as if to define the site by the British academics who had visited it.[35]

This could take an even more extreme turn. For others made a pitch at re-presenting Athens and its environs as if part of their well known British landscape. Mahaffy, for example, saw his own Irish 'Rock of Cashel' in the Acropolis and Virginia Woolf (a little later, in 1906) could only think of the Cornish cliffs.[36] But the political domestication of the Acropolis rock went even further than that. A letter to *The Times* in September 1886 complained about the tipping of the spoil from the excavations of the Acropolis surface down over the side of the rock. It was more than just a mess—it risked, as the writer explained—obliterating the distinctive profile of the north-east corner. For 'it may interest some of your readers to know that the NE angle of the rock, as seen from the roof of Dr Schliemann's house ... presents a capital profile likeness of Mr Gladstone, which may be obliterated by the casting of rubbish over the walls ...'[37] The corner of the Acropolis, in other words, could be so British that it embodied the natural likeness of the British prime minister.

Of course, in some sense all travel—academic and archaeological as much as 'popular'—is caught in the dilemma between domesticating and parading the 'otherness' of the foreign country. But it was particularly loaded in the case of archaeological exploration of Greece, when there were equally strident claims for the raw material of Greek archaeology being and belonging on British soil. It was, after all, one of the most significant legacies of

[34] 'Give Back the Elgin Marbles', *Nineteenth Century*, XXVIII (Dec., 1890), 980–7. He also stressed the international character of Athenian scholarship, thanks to the presence of the foreign institutes.
[35] J. E. Sandys, *An Easter Vacation in Greece* (London, 1887), p. 78.
[36] J. P. Mahaffy, *Rambles and Studies,* pp. 101–2 (page. ref. from 5th edn., 1907); V. Woolf, *A Passionate Apprentice: the Early Journals, 1897–1909* (ed. M. A. Leaska) (London, 1990), p. 321.
[37] *The Times*, 14 Sept. 1886, 7.

the Elgin Marbles (and of the splitting of the Parthenon sculpture between Athens and London) that the location of Greek archaeological inheritance should be a matter of dispute. But throughout the nineteenth century, as more and more travellers visited Greece itself, Hellas arrived more and more emphatically in London, Oxford and Cambridge. In fact, the galleries of plaster casts at both the ancient universities and that assembled for the Great Exhibition of 1851, provided what was called (on the scientific model) 'laboratories for the archaeologists'—as if all the work could really be done in the library and the home lab.[38] They were seen by many as a better educational tool for an archaeologist than the original works themselves, partly because they brought together material that time, chance (and Lord Elgin) had inconveniently separated.

This cultural oxymoron reached absurd limits in 1902, when a gardener at a country house at Essex was trying to sort out a rather ramshackle rock garden. His spade hit a larger than expected piece of masonry, which he dug out of the ground. It was a piece of relief sculpture which was soon identified as being a not insignificant fragment of the Parthenon frieze, which is now in the British Museum.[39] The mystery of how it fetched up there has only ever been half solved. But it was a curious and unexpected affirmation of the embeddedness of Greek archaeology, and its raw materials, in Britain and its soil. It was in this deeply ambivalent cultural context that the foundation of an outpost of Oxbridge in Athens belonged.

[38] The analogy is made directly by both Charles Newton and (in a letter read to the gathering) A. Michaelis at the opening of the new collection of casts in Cambridge in 1884; the speeches are recorded in the *Cambridge University Reporter*, 25 June 1885, 964–79.

[39] Part of slab N XXXVI; the find was reported in *The Times,* 19 Nov. 1902, 11. The house (Colne Park) was once owned by the son of the antiquarian, Thomas Astle. The best guess is that the piece was originally part of a collection formed in Athens by James Stuart, the partner of Nicholas Revett.

CHAPTER EIGHTEEN

The Strange Late Birth of the British Academy

RICHARD DRAYTON

I

When in 1900 the International Association of Academies held its first meeting in Paris, the United Kingdom was not represented in any discipline in the humanities.[1] For there was no public body then deemed competent to speak for British historical, philosophical, or philological studies. On the European Continent, learned academies had united literary men and sometimes women, and bestowed marks of distinction and salaries on them, for hundreds of years. Why did Britain, at the Victorian climax of its prosperity and power, lack a similar national institution?

That Britain lacked an academy can only be blamed partly on the Victorians. Its real cause lay in the balance of private to public interests in its intellectual life, over the longer term. We may find some clue to the problem in Sir Joseph Banks's explanation in 1789 of the facts which distinguished the Royal Society from Continental academies:

> They are associations of learned men called together by their respective monarchs ... We are a set of Free Englishmen [these two words capitalized in the manuscript] elected by each other and supported at our own expense without accepting any pension or other emolument.[2]

Banks was less than candid about the appetite of 'Free Englishmen', including himself, for places and pensions, and less than fair about the ways in which the Crown personal, and the English state, had patronised learning.

[1] 'A Brief Account of the Foundation of the Academy', *Proceedings of the British Academy*, 1 (1903–4), pp. vii–ix.

[2] Banks to Windischgrätz, 2 June [undated], *Archives of the Royal Botanic Gardens, Kew*: Banks Correspondence, III (1), 3.

But he accurately described what we might call the 'Country' ideology of the intellect: that idea that English learning, like English liberty, depended, and ought to depend on the independence of property. This idea paid homage to the unusually privatised character of English intellectual life as it had emerged in the seventeenth and eighteenth centuries. That dependence of scholarship, like charity, on the Church or the enthusiasm of the volunteer, was the reality underlying the assumption that learning might be left to gentlemen amateurs. Its enduring and pernicious consequence was the British state's underinvestment in research of all kinds. Victorian intellectuals and the political classes, as they agreed to inhabit this Augustan ideology, share responsibility for the fact that it took until 1902 for the British Academy to be born.

The Academy's receipt of a royal charter in 1902 did not mean a shift in government attitudes: the Treasury during the next two decades persistently resisted assigning even a small grant, perhaps the value of a dreadnought's anchor, for humane learning. It was not until 1924, long after the Royal Society began to receive public funds, that the Treasury agreed to make a modest annual grant of £2,000 to the Academy.[3] This grant was clawed back twice in the next decades, and only after the Second World War was it increased. Might one fairly identify a tradition of philistinism in the culture of government in this country? What is clear is that excellence in the humanities has rarely been prized by the British state as among the highest expressions of national achievement. War and money-making, and more recently sport, television, and popular music, have been the preferred targets of public honours and resources. The story of the strange late birth of the British Academy is a parable of time present as much as of the Victorian past.

II

The modern institution of the Academy emerged out of Italian humanism.[4] The Porticus Antonianus of Naples in 1443, the Accademia Pomponiana of

[3] For the unflattering history of the British government's treatment of the British Academy during its first decades see F. G. Kenyon, *The British Academy: The First Fifty Years* (London, 1952), pp. 15, 29–31.

[4] For the life of the early academies see J. D. Reuss, *Repertorium Commentationum a Societatibus Litterariis Editarum, Secundum Disciplinarum Ordinem* (16 vols., Göttingen, 1801–21); and W. Eamon, *Science and the Secrets of Nature: Books of Secrets in Medieval and Early Modern Culture* (Princeton, 1996).

Rome in 1460, the Accademia Platonica of Florence in 1462, the Accademia Fiorentina of 1540, to name only some of the most famous, all fostered belles-lettres and civic culture. All predated the foundation in 1560 of the first specifically scientific academy: the Academia dei segreti of Naples. Academies were integrated into the culture of Renaissance courts, with the Florentine academy beginning literally in the chambers of the Medici, and incarnating that union of secular power and universal learning prized by neoplatonists. It was on the example of such courts that Francis Bacon formed that vision of the alliance of science and monarchical power framed in the *Advancement of Learning* and the *New Atlantis*. But it was in France rather than England, as Julian Martin has argued, that Bacon's vision was realised with the foundation of the Académie Française in 1635, the Petite Académie of 1663 (which became the Académie des Inscriptions et Belles-Lettres in the next century) and the Académie des Sciences of 1666.[5]

In 1619, in the twilight years of James I's reign, several gentlemen in Buckingham's circle had proposed an 'Academ Roial' for the encouragement of history and literature.[6] The petitioners, from the outset, feared that nothing would result, that the 'maidenliness and inaudacitie of our island's genius which is reputed cold to sodein singularities is alone enough to quash this affair in the embrion'.[7] But a lack of virtue was not the problem—a strange charge, in any event, given the role of women in patronising academies in sixteenth-century Italy and France. The matter was presented to Parliament in 1621, and James I had encouraged his son to support 'such publicke work'. But the Crown was poor, and the political classes unwilling to tax themselves, and Charles I, on his accession, unenthusiastic. It seems clear that Archbishop Laud, who came closest to being England's Richelieu, could have created an 'Académie Anglaise' but preferred not to do so. Perhaps he did not wish to create an independent centre of intellectual authority which might challenge the Church and its grip on the colleges of Oxford and Cambridge.

What is certain is that it was in 1645, when Laud lost his head, that meetings began in London which culminated in the 'Invisible College for the promoting of Physico-Mathematical Experimental Learning', which in 1663, with the sealing of its second charter became the 'Royal Society for the Improvement of Natural Knowledge'.[8] There was no equivalent voluntary movement towards a national society for humane studies in the late seventeenth

[5] J. Martin, *Francis Bacon, the State, and the Reform of Natural Philosophy* (Cambridge, 1992).

[6] E. M. Portal, 'The Academ Roial of King James I', *Proceedings of the British Academy,* 8 (1915–16), pp. 189–208.

[7] *Harleian Mss. 6103,* quoted in Portal, 'The Academ Roial', p. 192.

[8] M. Ornstein, *The Role of Scientific Societies in the Seventeenth Century* (London, 1963).

century—in a period in which provincial academies were regularly constituted in France, the Italian peninsula, and the German cities and states. Perhaps the Royal Society aimed to evade, and bishops and the Crown to restrain, the controversial dangers of debates about religion, history and politics.

Across the British Isles, however, there was significant voluntary organisation in the humanities. Associational activity, ranging from circles of friends to local clubs, sustained the study of antiquities, local history, and ancient and modern literature. This came to an institutional climax in the early eighteenth-century, with the rise of a variety of national and provincial clubs and societies. In London, from 1707, in the year of the act of union, the Society of Antiquaries undertook to recover the national past. In the countryside, the Spalding Gentleman's Society of 1710 and the Peterborough Gentleman's Society of 1730 stood as low-budget equivalents to France's provincial academies. All these located intellect and culture relative to the idea of the 'gentleman', that amalgam of Castiglione's courtier and of Locke's industrious and rational landowner, the 'virtuoso' who might combine breeding, manners, and curiosity with propertied independence.[9] Private enthusiasm about learning of all kinds, located in coffee houses and drinking clubs rather than in academies private or public—that world in which Roy Porter was our unequalled companion—provided the economic basis for Banks's ideal English literary intellectual. Men like Addison, Steele, Defoe, Pope, and Swift, or such Victorian descendants as the Mills, Carlyle, Ruskin and Arnold, could live by writing for money; they did not have to depend on pensions or subsidies.

This was just as well, given the lack of public support for intellectuals in England. On the European Continent, princes and their ministers continued in the late seventeenth and early eighteenth century to initiate academies which united study of the arts and sciences, as in Slovenia in the 1690s, the Berlin Academy and the Royal Academy of Belles Lettres of Barcelona in 1700, the Royal Spanish Academy in 1713, and the Portuguese Academy of History in 1720. The only significant English extension of this current came in the early years of the Hanoverians, when George I and II and Caroline imported the cultural habits of the German courts. They sponsored the re-founding of the Society of Antiquaries in 1717, established regius chairs in history and

[9] W. E. Houghton, 'The English Virtuoso in the Seventeenth Century?', *Journal of the History of Ideas*, 3 (1942), 51–73, 190–219; L. Klein, *Shaftesbury and the Culture of Politeness: Moral Discourse and Cultural Politics in Early Eighteenth-Century England* (Cambridge, 1994); P. Carter, *Men and the Emergence of Polite Society: Britain, 1660–1800* (Harlow, 2000).

lectureships in modern languages at Oxford and Cambridge, and cultivated contemporary intellectuals. The problem was, however, that these cultural initiatives were, for many contemporaries, linked with the political interests of the Court, with the coercive and anti-Jacobite politics of Walpole and the Whigs, with private peculation and public corruption.

III

It was in this political context that the 'Country' ideology of the intellect took its mature form. Those who opposed the concentration of power in the Hanoverian court constituted the ideal of the intellectual, unsupported by public money and thus independent, free to be guided by his conscience. Jonathan Swift in 1711 had urged the imitation of the French Academy in his proposal 'for correcting, Improving, and Ascertaining the English tongue'. But a few years later, when in opposition, he penned the most vicious satire on court intellectuals: Swift shows us Gulliver in the Academy of Lagado, meeting a ragged man, ten years into his project for the extraction of sunlight from cucumbers, who entreats Gulliver to

> give him something as an encouragement to ingenuity ... I made him a small present, for my Lord had furnished me with money on purpose, because he knew their practice of begging from all who go to see them.[10]

In the background to the joke, we may find an implicit argument about the connection between a humiliating dependency and fruitlessness: in a world where experimenters with cucumbers, or literary men, had to live through selling their product, Swift seems to argue, ten years would not so easily be wasted. The scholar who was not a placeman would be more practical and useful, as well as being more free in thought and free in citizenship. Swift represents to us that suspicion, which has endured in this nation's culture, that scholars as placemen would end up counting angels on the heads of pins, examining their navels, or attempting to turn faeces into food.[11]

The Country ideology of the intellect prized the practical, celebrating agriculture and the arts over abstract speculation, and honouring that clear style which would make scholarship open to all gentlemen. It was (and perhaps still is) instinctively suspicious of complexity, being quick to jeer at it as pedantry, and distrusting work comprehensible only to initiates. Dependence

[10] J. Swift, *Gulliver's Travels* (London, 1967), pp. 223–4.
[11] R. Porter, *Enlightenment: Britain and the Making of the Modern World* (London, 2000), p. 33.

on private means, or the acclaim and money of fellow citizens, kept the intellect healthy. This virtuous circuit between liberty, property, and intellectual creativity, is explicitly celebrated by David Hume where he argued, in his essay on 'The Rise and Progress of the Arts and the Sciences', that free governments were 'the only proper nursery for the arts and the sciences'.[12] Academies, linked to the life of European courts, were easily opposed to the vitality of literature, arts, and sciences sustained by the independent curiosity of 'Free Englishmen'.

By the middle of the eighteenth century, this idea of the intellectual, among other 'Country' values, became culturally ascendant. Those who, in any event, would have prized the idea of the gentleman scholar over that of the academician, could point proudly at England's magnificent scientific and literary achievements as achievements of voluntary intellectual life. And this patriotic narcissism had the help of French intellectuals, and in particular of Voltaire, who, in their attacks on the Bourbons, had opposed England's political liberty, religious tolerance, and intellectual vitality, to the repressive world of absolutist government and its dependence on the Court. The English happily reimported this image of themselves: 'By accepting England's myth of itself', Nicholas Henshall argues, 'the *philosophes* made it immortal'.[13] Erasmus Darwin found it easy to celebrate Britannia as the 'potent Queen of ideas on whom fair art and meek Religion smiles'.[14] Banks's description of the character of the Royal Society was representative of a common belief that the English model worked best.

This myth of the freeborn English intellectual happily ignored the places in Cambridge and at the Mint which had allowed Newton philosophical leisure, the funnelled cash and government jobs which accompanied Augustan journalistic and literary enterprise, the pensions and sinecures which supported Samuel Johnson and Horace Walpole. It ignored the desperation of intellectuals without independent means: 'There mark what ills the scholar's life assail', Johnson complained in *The Vanity of Human Wishes* (II, ll. 159–60), 'Toil, envy, want, the Patron, and the jail'. It ignored, too, the ways in which the English state had, in various periods, imitated European example, and included learning within an expanded scope of government activity. In the 1780s, for example, in the wake of the American defeat, Continental policy was discreetly imported into many spheres of British

[12] D. Hume, *Essays: Moral, Political, and Literary* (Indianapolis, 1987), p. 119.

[13] N. Henshall, *The Myth of Absolutism: Change and Continuity in Early Modern European Monarchy* (London, 1992), p. 206.

[14] Erasmus Darwin, *The Botanic Garden* (London, 1789–91), Pt. II, l. 421.

domestic and imperial administration.[15] Ironically, Banks himself helped to shape a significant expansion of public expenditure on research, aimed principally at science and technology, and especially in alliance with the needs of the army, navy, the East India Company, and colonies, but also including antiquities, anthropology, and Oriental studies. During the wars with revolutionary France and Napoleon, there was a significant growth in the size and efficiency of the state, and with it the emergence of a number of new salaried positions for geographers, botanists, mathematicians, engineers, physicians, linguists, and political economists.

At the beginning of the nineteenth century, many 'Free Englishmen' wanted an even more substantial public commitment to education and scholarship, and a less gentlemanly approach. It was clear that Continental dirigism had generated, as in France, the most remarkable scientific flowering. *Ancien régime* academies, revolutionary museums, and Napoleonic institutes were spaces in which poor men could earn their living while practising their literary or scientific gifts. But it was not simply a question that the economic threshold for cultural participation was set too high, its intellectual level was set too low. Against the 'country' notion of a universe of cultivated gentlemen, there was an emerging appreciation for the need and value of intellectual specialisation. Adam Smith in *The Wealth of Nations* had argued that the principle of the division of labour applied to intellectual work: 'In opulent or commercial society, to think or reason comes to be, like every other form of employment, a particular business, which is carried on by a very few people.'[16] The importance of such a community of intellectuals to the nation was celebrated in Coleridge's vision of a 'Clerisy' which would 'secure and improve that civilization, without which the nation could be neither permanent nor progressive'.[17]

Yet Coleridge and others continued to assign privileged roles to the old elites in the Church and the universities. For the classics, theology, history, these old refuges and the literary marketplace provided acceptable options. It would take a generation for intellectuals in the humanities, such as the younger Arnold, to give a more militant cast to Coleridge's argument. But men of science, largely shut out of the universities, the discontented of the intellectual old regime, responded more immediately. During Banks's long reign over the Royal Society, mathematicians and astronomers began to assert their identity as professionals, and to their right to be rewarded for their

[15] As a guide to which see R. Drayton, *Nature's Government* (London and New Haven, 2000), chap. 4.

[16] Quoted in Porter, *Enlightenment*, p. 477.

[17] S. Coleridge, 'On the Constitution of Church and State', *Aids to Reflection* (London, 1825).

expertise, and to receive public support. But the scientists, as they came to call themselves after 1833, like scholars in the humanities some generations later, found themselves in collision with politicians and civil servants who, for their own reasons, favoured the idea that scholarship should fund itself.

How did this Country ideology of the intellect establish itself in the political culture of Britain? The essential mediating current was that anti-Court and anti-Crown political movement which emerged in the 1780s as the call for 'economical reform'.[18] The Georgian attack on the Crown's expenditure, became the post-Waterloo demand for 'retrenchment' and cheap government, relative to which the demands of scholars for funding for their research looked like special pleading.[19] If learning was the expression of the will and pleasure of the individual, and the origin of a kind of property, why should the public subsidise it? The ideal of the gentleman scholar, with its identification of both the liberty of individual conscience and voluntary activity, was a thread with which both Liberals and Conservatives might build their nests. Like so many other elements of 'Country' values, it was woven into the fabric of nineteenth-century politics.

After the Napoleonic Wars, both financial and ideological pressures drove an attack on the growth of government. By 1816, Liverpool aimed at abolishing every office which could not be defended as essential to the public service.[20] Over the next thirteen years, Frederick Robinson and Henry Goulburn applied stringent economies to every area of government expenditure. For different but convergent reasons, Liberal Tories such as Peel and Goulbourn, Whigs such as Melbourne, and Radicals such as Joseph Hume and Richard Cobden, were instinctively uneasy with the idea of the public purse funding the private enthusiasms of gentlemen. As Peel joked with Haddington in 1842, one should not hastily conclude that 'everything which a man of science recommends must be advantageous to the public interest'.[21] A Treasury Minute of 1844 underlined the essential principle: government could only support literary and scientific institutions if as many private sources as possible were drawn upon, and if their utility, and economy of management, were transparent.[22] Goulburn in 1845 deprecated 'extravagant

[18] P. Harling, *The Waning of 'Old Corruption': The Politics of Economical Reform in Britain, 1779–1846* (Oxford, 1996).

[19] For the importance of 'cheap government' in nineteenth-century Britain see M. Daunton, *Trusting Leviathan: The Politics of Taxation in Britain, 1799–1914* (Cambridge, 2001).

[20] Liverpool to Palmerston, 30 Dec. 1816, British Library Add. MS. 38264, f. 72.

[21] Peel to Haddington, [1842], British Library Add. MS. 40456, f. 98.

[22] See 'Treasury Minute' and Treasury to Board of Woods and Forests, 2 July and 4 July 1844, *Kew*: [Kewensia] *Royal Gardens Kew. Reports & Documents, 1784–1884*.

expenditure especially when concerned with the encouragement of fine arts and the improvement of the people'.[23] By the middle of the century, Goulbourn's protégé, William Gladstone, would make 'retrenchment' into a mass-political cause.[24] The needs of democracy and fiscal morality converged in that Treasury tradition of 'cheese paring' which was shared by all political parties by the end of the century, and relative to which spending on the unessential was anathema.[25] The enduring dilemma of scholarship in the humanities was that its usefulness was not as obvious as science and technology, and that, linked with the special interests of a minority, it would always appear to rank beneath the more democratic needs for education, health, transport or prisons.

IV

This order survived so long as intellectuals failed to make their claim to a better deal. It was the Victorian scientists, not its men of letters, who came to demand a new dispensation. In the 1830s and 1840s, around Herschel and Babbage, then a generation later in the 1850s, 1860s, and 1870s around figures such as Huxley, Lockyear, and Tyndall, they demanded public recognition of their achievements and contribution, and funding for research.[26] They reminded the political classes of what France in the first half of the nineteenth century, and Germany at its end, were doing for the sciences, and demanded equivalent English research museums, botanic gardens, and laboratories. Those who later sought public support for the humanities would similarly appeal to the example of state funding in Europe for universities, museums, and such research institutes as the Ecoles Françaises of Rome and Athens, as Mary Beard shows.

But the campaigning men of science also took as their target the relatively privileged place of the humanities in the education system in general, and the universities in particular: the natural and human sciences were now competitors.

[23] Goulburn to Peel, [] June 1845, British Library Add. MS. 40576, f. 44.

[24] E. Biagini, *Liberty, Retrenchment, and Reform: Popular Liberalism in the Age of Gladstone, 1860–1880* (Cambridge 1992).

[25] P. R. Ghosh, 'Disraelian Conservatism. A Financial Approach', *English Historical Review*, 99 (1984).

[26] R. MacLeod, 'The X-Club: A Social Network of Science in Late Victorian England', *Notes and Records of the Royal Society of London*, 24 (1970), 305–22, and 'The Support of Victorian Science: The Endowment of Research Movement in Great Britain, 1868–1900', *Minerva*, 9 (1971), 197–230; R. MacLeod, ed., *Government and Expertise: Specialists, Administrators and Professionals, 1860–1919* (Cambridge, 1988); F. M. Turner, 'Public Science in Britain, 1880–1919', *Isis*, 71, (1980), 589–608.

And classicists and clerics, who had some stake in the prevailing arrangements made the error of firing back. B. H. Kennedy, headmaster of Shrewsbury and author of the famous *Latin Primer*, commented to the Clarendon Commission that he opposed any significant introduction of the natural sciences because they did not 'furnish a basis for education'.[27] Benjamin Jowett, Master of Balliol College at Oxford, similarly declared to the Devonshire Commission that he thought that 'A cabinet which consisted of persons who only knew Latin and Greek would probably be a better cabinet [than one] consisting entirely of chemists.'[28] Even if Oxford and Cambridge created honours schools in science as acts of defensive modernisation in the 1850s, the clerics, classicists, and mathematicians largely excluded scientists from many fellowships. There was bad blood between the two, and this would be significant in later discussions.

The gentlemanly community of the men of letters never got around to an uprising. They did rail against mammonism or the cash nexus or barbarians and philistines, just as their Augustan ancestors had rhymed against commercial society. But selling their books to a wide public, or cosseted in the ancient universities, complacent in their cultural centrality, hesitant to see themselves as professionals, they lacked that energising sense of being part of an excluded intellectual *Tiers état* which propelled scientific figures such as Huxley.

Yet literary intellectuals, even as they fitted comfortably into the armchairs of the Athenaeum, did yearn for something more.[29] In the last decades of the nineteenth century we see the picking up of new currents. Matthew Arnold in June 1864 delivered a lecture at Oxford on 'The Influence of Academies on National Spirit and Literature'. This was a direct paean to the Academie Française as an instrument for preserving national genius and style. But in that praise song Arnold wrapped a Coleridgian assertion of the role of the intelligentsia in providing spiritual leadership, that claim that humane learning should guide a nation to its 'best self' which he made a key motif of *Culture and Anarchy* (1867–8). Travelling as a school inspector through Germany and France, Arnold had watched with fascination the energy with which the state promoted both research and education. Henry Sidgwick, was equally impressed, and responded to his scientific colleagues' demands for the endowment of research with a call for equal support for work

[27] P.P. 1862 (89) XXIII, f. 289.

[28] Jowett in response to Sir J. Kay Shuttleworth, Bart., 10 Dec. 1870. *Royal Commission of Scientific Instruction and the Advancement of Science. Minutes of Evidence*, 1 (1872), 255.

[29] S. Collini, *Public Moralists: Political Thought and Intellectual Life in Britain, 1850–1930* (Oxford, 1991).

in 'other studies and departments of thought'.[30] But there seems to have been no clear convergence, at this stage, between Arnold's vision of an Academy and Sidgwick's wish for more support for research in the humanities.

But in November 1899 the Council of the Royal Society prodded the literary gentlemen into action. It sent a letter to prominent scholars suggesting the formation of some body to represent Britain in disciplines other than the natural sciences.[31] By December a meeting of the scholars gave its support for a suggestion from Sidgwick himself that the Royal Society be asked either to reinvent itself, so that it might give room to literary and humane sciences in a special section, or support the foundation of a separate body. For over a year the Royal Society deliberated, but concluded in June of 1901 that it could neither include the literary sciences within it, nor initiate the establishing of a British academy. It was thus the scientists who provided both stimulus and constraint for the mobilisation of humane knowledge in the British Academy, refusing to follow the example of the Berlin Academy (whose bicentenary had been the occasion for the international convention of learned societies) and to welcome all branches of intellectual enterprise within one temple. The split in the 'two cultures' was, to this extent, the fault of the scientists, but their behaviour was merely payback for the neglect and hostility which the classics and theology had shown to the sciences in an earlier period.

V

The British Academy founded in 1902 had no budget, no meeting place or office, the younger and infinitely poorer cousin of its European equivalents. It is interesting to note that its main achievements in its first decade were exclusively in Oriental Studies. The India Office, in which the traditions of Enlightened despotism remained fortunately entrenched, was the only arm of the British administration which undertook to finance a branch of British Academy research, in this case work on an Encyclopaedia of Islam, an edition of the Mahabharata, and a Pali dictionary.[32] But these projects depended on the intellectual manpower of German and Austrian universities and research institutes, and when the First World War arrived they collapsed. The War also gave the Treasury an excuse to withdraw the grant it promised in

[30] Collini, *Public Moralists*, p. 200.

[31] This and below from 'A Brief Account of the Foundation of the Academy'.

[32] Kenyon, *The British Academy*, p. 17.

1913 of £400 for a series of records of British Economic and Social History. In the end, it was private endowments for lectures and research funds which gave the Academy the means to become visible. Only in the 1920s would Balfour and Haldane secure from the Treasury a regular budget for the Academy. Four centuries after France, and three after Prussia, the British nation claimed the humanities as its own.

Research in historical, literary, philological, and philosophical scholarship have never been a priority for government spending in this country. But their status and value, in the eyes of politicians and civil servants, have declined in the last two decades. In the common view of Thatcherites and New Labour, the humanities are neither 'wealth creators' nor are they sufficiently 'democratic'. A new breed of academic has, at the same time, agreed to pander to the idea that the purpose of universities is to produce knowledge or workers of economic use. Whichever major party is in power they would prefer to buy 'smart bombs' than to endow that research in the humanities which would allow Britain to punch above its weight in the world of ideas. Private money has, in part, filled the gap. Without the Leverhulme, the Wolfson, the Wellcome, and now the Rausing foundations, and the private endowments of Oxford and Cambridge, humanities research in Britain would be in general crisis, and even more of the best scholars would be looking for berths abroad. But the predicament of the humanities is that there is little hope that the rich in the United Kingdom are ready to take any more of the slack. Around the country, vast sums have been ploughed into 'Development Offices' with only modest results: one of the legacies of the welfare state seems to be the assumption that support for obscure kinds of research should come from the government. There is no equivalent here to that tradition of private giving which in the United States has generated that remarkable diaspora of libraries and institutes rich enough to pay researchers to come to them.

Scholars in the humanities in the United Kingdom should begin, perhaps, to examine their history and situation. They might do worse than to examine how their Victorian predecessors failed, unlike the professional scientists of the nineteenth century, to fight for their interests. Even today, we have no humanities counterpart to 'Save British Science', which has flourished for some decades. Perhaps it is time for the British Academy to be less a club of Immortals, an intellectual appendix to the Athenaeum and the Reform, and more of a campaigning body which takes up the challenge of persuading the nation of the value and the necessity of our work and expertise?

Index

Note: page numbers in italics refer to illustrations; page numbers in bold refer to tables